CW00417503

ROUTLEDGE HANDBOOK OF THERAVĀDA BUDDHISM

Among one of the older subfields in Buddhist Studies, the study of Theravāda Buddhism is undergoing a revival by contemporary scholars who are revising long-held conventional views of the tradition while undertaking new approaches and engaging new subject matter. The term Theravāda has been refined, and research has expanded beyond the analysis of canonical texts to examine contemporary cultural forms, social movements linked with meditation practices, material culture, and vernacular language texts. The *Routledge Handbook of Theravāda Buddhism* illustrates the growth and new directions of scholarship in the study of Theravāda Buddhism and is structured in four parts:

- Ideas/Ideals
- Practices/Persons
- Texts/Teachings
- Images/Imaginations

Owing largely to the continued vitality of Theravāda Buddhist communities in countries like Sri Lanka, Myanmar, Thailand, Cambodia, and Laos, as well as in diaspora communities across the globe, traditions associated with what is commonly (and fairly recently) called Theravāda attract considerable attention from scholars and practitioners around the world. An in-depth guide to the distinctive features of Theravāda, the *Handbook* will be an invaluable resource for providing structure and guidance for scholars and students of Asian religion, Buddhism, and, in particular, Theravāda Buddhism.

Stephen C. Berkwitz is Professor and Head of the Department of Religious Studies, Missouri State University, USA. His research is focused on the literature and cultural history of Sri Lankan Buddhism. He has published *South Asian Buddhism: A Survey* (Routledge 2009) and is the editor of the *Routledge Critical Studies in Buddhism* series.

Ashley Thompson is Hiram W. Woodward Chair in Southeast Asian Art at SOAS, University of London, UK. She is a specialist in Southeast Asian Cultural Histories, with particular expertise on premodern Cambodian arts. Her most recent monograph is *Engendering the Buddhist State: Territory, Sovereignty and Sexual Difference in the Inventions of Angkor* (Routledge 2016).

ROUTLEDGE HANDBOOK OF THERAVĀDA BUDDHISM

Edited by Stephen C. Berkwitz and Ashley Thompson

Routledge
Taylor & Francis Group
LONDON AND NEW YORK

Cover image: @ Getty Images

First published 2022
by Routledge
4 Park Square, Milton Park, Abingdon, Oxon OX14 4RN

and by Routledge
605 Third Avenue, New York, NY 10158

Routledge is an imprint of the Taylor & Francis Group, an informa business

British Library Cataloguing-in-Publication Data
A catalogue record for this book is available from the British Library

Library of Congress Cataloging-in-Publication Data
A catalog record has been requested for this book

ISBN: 978-1-138-49393-3 (hbk)
ISBN: 978-1-032-18672-6 (pbk)
ISBN: 978-1-351-02666-6 (ebk)

DOI: 10.4324/9781351026666

Typeset in Bembo
by SPi Technologies India Pvt Ltd (Straive)

CONTENTS

List of illustrations — *viii*
List of contributors — *x*
Acknowledgments — *xiv*
List of abbreviations — *xvi*
Technical notes — *xviii*
Theravāda Civilizations Project — *xix*

Introduction — 1
Stephen C. Berkwitz and Ashley Thompson

PART I
Ideas/Ideals — **13**

1 "Theravāda": sectarianism and diversity in Mahāvihāra historiography — 15
Sven Bretfeld

2 Pāli: its place in the Theravāda Buddhist tradition — 43
Alastair Gornall

3 Circulations: linked spaces and divergent temporalities in the Pāli world — 58
Anne M. Blackburn

4 Statecraft: from Buddhist kingship to modern states — 70
Patrice Ladwig

5 Reform: ideas and events in modern Theravāda reformism — 83
Anne R. Hansen and Anthony Lovenheim Irwin

6 Tradition: nuns and "Theravāda" in Sri Lanka 99
Nirmala S. Salgado

Part II
Practices/Persons **113**

7 Merit: ritual giving and its cultural mediations 115
Juliane Schober

8 Meditation: techniques and processes of transformation 127
Pyi Phyo Kyaw and Kate Crosby

9 Repetition: Pāli iterations of ritual commitment, commentarial refrain, and assiduous practice 140
Christoph Emmrich

10 Filial piety: shades of difference across Theravādin traditions 156
Grégory Kourilsky

11 Laity: status, role, and practice in Theravāda 170
Asanga Tilakaratne

12 Discipline: beyond the Vinaya 182
Thomas Borchert

13 Funerals: changing funerary practices 194
Katherine A. Bowie

Part III
Texts/Teachings **207**

14 Canons: authoritative texts of the Theravaṃsa 209
Peter Skilling

15 Abhidhamma: Theravāda thought in relation to Sarvāstivāda thought 227
Rupert Gethin

16 Vaṃsa: history and lineage in the Theravāda 243
Stephen C. Berkwitz

17 Merit: Ten ways of making merit in Theravāda exegetical literature and contemporary Sri Lanka 257
Rita Langer

18 Bilingualism: Theravāda bitexts across South and Southeast Asia 271
Trent Walker

Part IV
Images/Imaginations **285**

19 Visual narratives: Buddha life stories in the "medieval Theravāda" of Southeast Asia 287
Samerchai Poolsuwan

20 Icons: standing out from the narrative in Theravādin art 305
Ashley Thompson

21 Affect: notes from contemporary Southeast Asian visual culture 327
Chairat Polmuk

22 Deities: supernatural forces in Theravāda Buddhist religious cultures 343
John Clifford Holt

23 Mons: creating a narrative of the origins of Theravāda 355
Patrick McCormick

Index *367*

ILLUSTRATIONS

Figures

1.1 Nikāya genealogy of the *Dīpavaṃsa*, representing the "insider view" of the text 26
4.1 Devotees in front of That Luang *stūpa*, Vientiane, Laos 80
14.1 Stone bar inscribed with Pāli texts, sixth–seventh century, Nakhon Chaisi, Central Thailand 219
14.2 Estampage of seventh–eighth-century Angkor Borei Pāli inscription, National Museum of Cambodia 222
18.1 Pāli-Siamese manuscript in interphrasal format, *Fonds d'édition des manuscrits du Cambodge (FEMC) C.77.VII* 275
18.2 Pāli-Siamese manuscript in interlinear format, FEMC D.11.VII 275
19.1 Mural painting representing the Buddha's meditation during the second and third weeks after the enlightenment, eleventh century, Pātho-htā-mya temple, Pagan, Burma 291
19.2 Mural painting representing the "Eight Major Events" of the Buddha, twelfth century, Loka-hteik-pan temple, Pagan, Burma 294
19.3 Symbolic arrangement of cult images and the murals representing "Majjhimadesa," centered at Bodhgaya, modeled after Pagan temple 664 295
19.4 Mural paintings, Pagan temple 539, thirteenth century: Twin Miracle at Sāvatthi (left) vis-à-vis Second Week Meditation at Animisa Cetiya (right) 295
19.5 Mural painting, Rātchaburana temple crypt, Ayutthaya, Thailand, fifteenth century: Buddha footprint on the summit of Sri Lanka's Sumana Mountain 298
19.6 Mural Painting, Pagan temple 585, thirteenth century: King Aśoka in a previous existence as a child donating a handful of dust for alms to Buddha Gotama 300
19.7 Mural painting, temple 69, Sale, Burma, thirteenth century: Gotama in his remote existences, probably based on the *Sotaṭṭhakīmahānidāna* account 301
20.1 Seventh–eighth-century Buddha statue inscribed with the "dharma relic" on its upper back plus rubbing of the inscription. Found in Tambol Lum Din, Muang District, Ratchaburi, held in Wat Mahathat, Ratchaburi, Thailand. 307

20.2 Spread of a late eighteenth–early nineteenth-century leporello manuscript held in Wat Khao Yi San, Samut Songkhram Province, Thailand 309
20.3 Wat Si Chum, Sukhothai, Thailand: *mondop* preceded by pillared *vihāra* terrace plus one of the one hundred engraved stone *jātaka* plaques from the staired passageway inside the *mondop* wall 315
20.4 Angkor Wat, Siem Reap, Cambodia: temple seen from the west; panel from sixteenth-century reliefs on the eastern section of the northern third-level gallery enclosure; one of the four Buddhas sculpted into sandstone blocks filling in the central sanctuary's doorways 320
21.1 Screenshots *from Phantoms of Nabua* by Apichatpong Weerasethakul, 2009: projection of light from Buddhist reliquaries 331
21.2 Screenshots from *Fireworks (Archives)* Apichatpong Weerasethakul, 2014: the Buddhist *memento mori* as a site of endurance and impermanence 334
21.3 Screenshot from *The Missing Picture* by Rithy Panh, 2013: clay sculpting and sensory memory 335
21.4 Screenshot from *The Missing Picture* by Rithy Panh, 2013: the unending burial 337

Tables

15.1 The dharma lists of the Theravāda and Sarvāstivāda Abhidharma compared 233
18.1 Examples of grammatical annotation particles 276

CONTRIBUTORS

Stephen C. Berkwitz is Professor of Religious Studies at Missouri State University (USA). He has a PhD in Religious Studies from the University of California, Santa Barbara. His research focuses on Sinhala literature and Buddhist culture in Sri Lanka from the medieval up to the contemporary periods. He has published books and articles on Buddhist historiography, poetry, kingship, colonialism, and modern Buddhism.

Anne M. Blackburn is Professor of South Asia Studies and Buddhist Studies in the Department of Asian Studies at Cornell University (USA). Blackburn holds a PhD from the University of Chicago. Anne Blackburn studies Buddhism in South and Southeast Asia at the intersection of literary studies, intellectual history, trade, and political economy, with a particular interest in circulations involving locations now known as Sri Lanka, India, Burma, and Thailand.

Katherine A. Bowie is a Vilas Distinguished Achievement Professor in the Department of Anthropology at the University of Wisconsin–Madison (USA). She received her PhD in Anthropology from the University of Chicago. She served as president of the Association of Asian Studies in 2017–2018. With fieldwork experience in Thailand covering over four decades, her research interests include historical anthropology, village politics, nation-state formation, gender, and Theravāda Buddhism.

Thomas Borchert is Professor of Religion at the University of Vermont (USA). He has a PhD in History of Religions from the University of Chicago. His research focuses on Buddhism and secularity, monastic education, and Buddhism, nationalism, and ethnicity within contemporary Theravāda communities. He is the author of *Educating Monks: Minority Buddhism in Southwest China* (University of Hawai'i Press 2017), and the editor of *Theravada Buddhism in Colonial Contexts* (Routledge 2018).

Sven Bretfeld is Professor of Religious Studies at NTNU Trondheim (Norway). He has studied Indology, Tibetology and Religious Studies in Marburg and Göttingen (Germany) and holds a Dr. phil. (PhD) in these disciplines from the University of Göttingen. His research focuses on Buddhism in India, Tibet, and Sri Lanka. He has published books and articles on Pāli and Sinhala philology, Buddhist historiography in Sri Lanka and Tibet, and Buddhist literature and sociology in medieval and modern periods.

Kate Crosby is Professor of Buddhist Studies at King's College, London (UK). She was educated at the universities of Oxford, Hamburg, and Kelaniya. Her research focuses on Buddhist practice throughout the Theravāda world including pre-reform meditation, and on Pāli and Sanskrit literature. Her books include *Śāntideva's Bodhicaryāvatāra: Buddhist Path to Awakening* (Oxford University Press 1995); *The Mahābhārata: The Dead of Night & the Women* (NYU Press 2009); *Theravada Buddhism: Continuity, Diversity, Identity* (Wiley 2014); and *Esoteric Theravada: The Story of the Forgotten Meditation Tradition of Southeast Asia* (Shambala 2020).

Christoph Emmrich is Associate Professor of Buddhist Studies at the University of Toronto. He has a PhD in classical Indology from Heidelberg University, Germany. His research focuses on Buddhist and Jain rituals, literature, and doctrine in Nepal, Burma, and India between the fifth and the twenty-first century. He has published on time, gender, childhood, ritual manuals, manuscript culture, and literary history.

Rupert Gethin is Professor of Buddhist Studies at the University of Bristol (UK). He has a PhD in Buddhist Studies from the University of Manchester. His research focuses on Indian Buddhist thought in Pāli and Sanskrit Nikāya-Āgama and exegetical literature, especially the Pāli commentaries. He has published books and articles on the theory of Buddhist meditation practice and various other aspects of Buddhist thought.

Alastair Gornall gained his Ph.D. in South Asian Studies from the University of Cambridge in 2013. He is currently Assistant Professor in South and Southeast Asian Studies at the Singapore University of Technology and Design and Research Associate in the School of Language, Cultures, and Linguistics at SOAS, University of London. He is the author of *Rewriting Buddhism: Pali Literature and Monastic Reform in Sri Lanka, 1157–1270* (UCL Press, 2020).

Anne R. Hansen is Professor of Southeast Asian History and Religious Studies in the Department of History at the University of Wisconsin–Madison. She received her PhD in Religious Studies from Harvard University (USA). Her research focuses on the history and development of Theravāda Buddhism in modern Southeast Asia, with recent publications on Buddhist ethics, modern reform movements, Cold War Buddhist history, and Buddhism and colonialism.

John Clifford Holt is Visiting Professor of Theravāda Buddhism at the University of Chicago where he received his Ph.D. in the history of religions, and William Kenan Jr. Professor Emeritus in Religion and Asian Studies at Bowdoin College (Maine, USA). His research and several books have focused on Buddhist monastic jurisprudence, Buddhist ritual cultures, deity veneration, and historical and contemporary relations between Buddhists and Muslims, Hindus, and Christians in Sri Lanka, Myanmar, Laos, and Thailand.

Anthony Lovenheim Irwin is a scholar of Asian religions who thinks, talks, teaches, and writes about the social and ethical resonance of crafting, building, and construction. He has a PhD in Asian languages and cultures from the University of Wisconsin–Madison (USA). Dealing primarily with Buddhism in Thailand, his work focuses on the importance of craftspeople as central figures in the transmission and definition of religious traditions and communities.

Grégory Kourilsky is Associate Professor at the École française d'Extrême-Orient. He received his PhD in religious anthropology and the history of religions at the École pratique des hautes études, Paris. He not only specializes in Thai-Lao Buddhism but also works on Cambodia, Burma, and Southwest China. His research focuses on the ways Buddhist populations in mainland Southeast Asia have maintained their religious and cultural identity despite the intrusion of nonindigenous doctrines, ranging from Indian classical scriptures to modern Western law.

Pyi Phyo Kyaw is Dean of Academic Affairs and Lecturer in Theravāda Studies at Shan State Buddhist University, Taunggyi, Myanmar. She holds a BA in economics and management from Oxford University; an MA in Buddhist Studies from SOAS, University of London, in 2010; and a PhD in Buddhist philosophy from King's College, London. She has undertaken meditation practice within different traditions in Myanmar over the past fifteen years. She specializes in Burmese Buddhism, Abhidhamma, Theravāda meditation, Buddhist business practices, and Buddhist ethics.

Patrice Ladwig studied social anthropology and sociology, and he obtained his PhD from the University of Cambridge. His work focuses on the anthropology of Buddhism (Laos and Thailand), the anthropology of politics, death and funeral cultures, historical anthropology (colonialism and the Cold War), and general social theory. He is currently Senior Research Fellow at the Max Planck Institute for the Study of Religious and Ethnic Diversity (Göttingen, Germany).

Rita Langer is Senior Lecturer in Buddhist Studies at the University of Bristol (UK). Her research focuses on Buddhist ritual and its origin (in South and South East Asia, particularly Sri Lanka) and Buddhist material culture and food. Her approach is interdisciplinary combining textual studies with fieldwork. She has published books and articles on sermons, funeral chanting, and ritual and produced short documentary films on cosmology and food.

Patrick McCormick has been living in Yangon, Burma for the past sixteen years, where he continues his work on the history and languages of the country. He was representative of the École française d'Extrême-Orient and was part of a project on language contact funded by the Swiss National Science Foundation through the University of Zurich. He is currently one of the English-language editors of the *Southeast Asian Studies Journal* of the Center for Southeast Asian Studies at the University of Kyoto.

Chairat Polmuk is Lecturer at the Department of Thai, Chulalongkorn University (Thailand), where he teaches Southeast Asian languages and literature, cultural theory, and media studies. He received a PhD in Asian literature, religion, and culture from Cornell University. His research focuses on affective and intermedial aspects of post–Cold War literature and visual culture. His recent writing has appeared in the *Journal of Letters* and *Southeast of Now: Directions in Contemporary and Modern Art in Asia*. He wrote articles on Apichatpong Weerasethakul and Rithy Panh for Oxford Bibliographies in Cinema and Media Studies.

Samerchai Poolsuwan is Professor of Anthropology at Thammasat University (Thailand) and holds a doctorate degree from the University of Michigan, Ann Arbor. His current research, focusing on the Buddhist iconography in the Theravādin context of Southeast Asia, has yielded a number of publications on the exploration of the Pagan-period and the early–Thai Buddhist murals (e.g., *Artibus Asiae*, 72(2): 377–97 & 76(1): 37–80; *JRAS*, 27(2): 255–94; *Journal of Burma Studies*, 19(1): 145–97; *SUVANNABHUMI*, 6(1): 27–65).

Nirmala S. Salgado is Professor of Religion at Augustana College (USA). She has a PhD in religion from Northwestern University, (Illinois) and an MA from SOAS University of London. Her research focuses on Buddhist nuns, postcolonialism, and contemporary Buddhist practice in Sri Lanka. She is the author of *Buddhist Nuns and Gendered Practice: In Search of the Female Renunciant* (Oxford University Press 2013) and several other publications.

Juliane Schober is Professor of Religious Studies and Director of the Center for Asian Research at Arizona State University (USA). She earned her doctorate in anthropology at the University of Illinois–Urbana. Her research examines Theravāda Buddhist formations and practices in Myanmar and elsewhere in Southeast Asia in colonial and contemporary contexts. She has published books and articles on the intersections of Buddhism and the state, relic veneration, Buddhism and conflict, and lay Buddhist practices.

Peter Skilling is Special Lecturer at Chulalongkorn University, Bangkok (Thailand). Until his retirement in 2017, he was Professor of École française d'Extrême-Orient. He specializes in the literary and material history of Buddhism in South and Southeast Asia. He publishes widely and has been visiting professor at leading universities worldwide. His latest book, *Questioning the Buddha* (Wisdom Books 2021), introduces and translates twenty-five Buddhist sutras.

Ashley Thompson is Hiram W Woodward Chair of Southeast Asian Art at SOAS University of London (UK). Her research focuses on the classical and premodern arts and literature of Southeast Asia, with a particular emphasis on Cambodia. Her most recent book is *Engendering the Buddhist State: Territory, Sovereignty and Sexual Difference in the Inventions of Angkor* (Routledge, Critical Buddhist Studies Series, 2016).

Asanga Tilakaratne (PhD, University of Hawai'i) is emeritus professor of Buddhist Studies and founder head of the Department of Buddhist Studies at the University of Colombo (Sri Lanka). He has published substantially on Buddhist Studies in Sinhala and English. Recently (August 2020), his collected works have been published in eight volumes (03 in Sinhala and 05 in English) in Colombo. Currently Professor Tilakaratne serves as the editor in chief of *Encyclopedia of Buddhism* published by the Government of Sri Lanka.

Trent Walker is the Ho Center for Buddhist Studies Postdoctoral Fellow and a lecturer in Religious Studies at Stanford University (USA). He has a PhD in Buddhist Studies from the University of California, Berkeley, and specializes in ritual, manuscript, and translation cultures from mainland Southeast Asia. Recent publications include articles on Cambodian Dharma songs, Thai Buddhist literary history, and Theravada translation practices in southern Vietnam.

ACKNOWLEDGMENTS

We, as co-editors, would like to acknowledge the generous assistance and encouragement of many others who like us desired to see a substantial reference work published on Theravāda Buddhism. This project originally grew out of our participation in the Theravāda Civilizations Project, which was initiated in 2009 by Juliane Schober and the late Steven Collins with funding from the Henry Luce Foundation's Asia Responsive Grants and Special Initiatives program. Over nearly ten years, we met with up to twenty-one scholars of Theravāda Buddhism in different locations annually to examine and question "Theravāda" in different times and places and from different disciplinary perspectives. The conversations that resulted were always stimulating and convivial, as we were pushed to consider Theravāda beyond our individual prisms, to allow those prisms to themselves be reshaped through the encounters, and to keep an eye, wary or not, on the notions of civilization framing our collective work. In the process, we—co-editors at least and with a lot of help from our friends—came to glimpse the need to apprehend Theravāda as a theoretical object and an analytical category, and to relish the possibilities that perception could afford scholarship. Several of the participants in the Theravāda Civilizations Project have contributed essays to this volume. We would like to express our thanks to all of the Project's participants for helping to advance the field and to develop our thinking.

Charles Hallisey contributed to this *Handbook* in a substantial but less tangible way than those who authored a contribution. He generously read a draft Introduction and challenged us to rethink what we thought we were doing with the volume. We deeply appreciated his comments, which helped us finalize the Introduction, but we hasten to add that the shortcomings therein are our sole responsibility. Others helped recruit contributors, shared encouraging words, and provided helpful feedback on some of the volume's essays. The collaborative work involved in preparing the *Handbook* has expanded our experience of a diverse, exceptionally warm and supportive community of scholars of Theravāda Buddhism.

We also wish to acknowledge the encouragement and guidance of Dorothea Schaefter at Routledge Press, who identified a need for such a *Handbook* and patiently waited for it to take shape. We have received significant help from other people at Routledge, including Alexandra de Brauw and Lily Brown, Saraswathy Narayan, and our production editor Saritha Srinivasan for their skilled assistance in the organization and publication of the volume. We are grateful for the opportunity to work with the excellent staff at Routledge who make publishing a rewarding experience.

Most of the illustrations in this volume have been supplied by the respective contributors. We wish to acknowledge the generosity of the following additional individuals in facilitating the selection and reproduction of images that appear in the *Handbook*: Kim Samnang, Phoeung Dara, Pipad Krajaejun, Udomluck Hoontrakul, Rungroj Bhiromanukul, Prasit Jungsoksomsawat, Thanaphat Limhasanaikul, Anna Prenowitz, Bertrand Porte, Trent Walker, Peter Skilling, and Rithy Panh.

Finally, it feels as although one can measure Time by the time it takes to complete a major book project. We began to conceptualize this volume in the latter part of 2017. We have all experienced the COVID-19 pandemic since, with its disruptions, large or small, to all of our lives. This led not only to some unavoidable delays in completing the work but also to a sort of intensification of commitment to it. The passing of Imali Berkwitz (1970–2018) prior to the pandemic was deeply felt and accompanied the development of the volume. We would like to dedicate the *Handbook* to her memory.

ABBREVIATIONS

Abh-ṭ	*Abhidhānappadīpikā-ṭīkā*
Abhidh-av	*Abhidhammāvatāra*
Abhidh-av-nṭ	*Abhidhammavikāsinī*
Abhidh-k-bh	*Abhidharmakośabhāṣyam*
Abhidh-k-vy	*Abhidharmakośavyākhya*
Abhidh-s	*Abhidhammatthasaṅgaha*
Abhidh-s-mhṭ	*Abhidhammatthavibhāvinī-mahāṭīkā*
Abhidh-s-ṭ	*Abhidhammatthavibhāvinī-ṭīkā*
AN	*Aṅguttara-Nikāya*
Ap	*Apadāna*
As	*Atthasālinī*
B	Burmese
Dhp	*Dhammapada*
Dhs	*Dhammasaṅgaṇī*
Dhs-a	*Dhammasaṅganī-aṭṭhakathā* (= As. *Atthasālinī*)
Dīp	*Dīpavaṃsa*
DN	*Dīgha-Nikāya*
DN-a	*Dīgha-nikāya-aṭṭhakathā* (= Sv. *Sumaṅgalavilāsinī*)
DP	*A Dictionary of Pāli* by Margaret Cone
EB	*Epigraphia Birmanica*
EFEO	École française d'Extrême-Orient
EHS	*Epigraphic and Historical Studies*
EPD	*English–Pali Dictionary*
EZ	*Epigraphia Zeylanica*
FEMC	*Fonds pour Édition des Manuscrits du Cambodge*
It	*Itivuttaka*
It-a	*Itivuttaka-aṭṭhakathā (*= Pd. *Paramatthadīpanī)*
Ja	*Jātaka*
Jinak	*Jinakālamālī*
Kacc	*Kaccāyana and Kaccāyanavutti*

Kh	Khmer
Khp	*Khuddakapāṭha*
KŚekh	*Kāvyaśekhara*
Kv	*Kathāvatthu*
L	Lao
Maṅg-d	*Maṅgalatthadīpanī*
Mil	*Milindapañha*
MN	*Majjhima-Nikāya*
Mogg	*Moggallāna-vyākaraṇa*
Moh	*Mohavicchedanī*
Nikāya-s	Nikāyasaṅgraha
P	Pāli
Paṭis	*Paṭisambhidāmagga*
Paṭis-a	*Saddhammappakāsinī*
Ps	*Papañcasūdanī*
PTS	Pali Text Society
Pv	*Petavatthu*
Pv-a	*Petavatthu-aṭṭhakathā*
Rūp	*Rūpasiddhi*
Saddh	*Saddhammopāyana*
Sinh	Sinhala
Sk	Sanskrit
Sn	*Suttanipāta*
SN	*Saṃyutta-Nikāya*
Sp	*Samantapāsādikā*
Spk	*Sāratthappakāsinī*
Sp-ṭ Be	*Sāratthadīpanī-ṭīkā* (Burmese edition)
Ss	*Sārasaṅgaha*
Subodh	*Subodhālaṅkāra*
Sv	*Sumaṅgalavilāsinī*
Sv-nṭ Be	*Sumaṅgalavilāsinī-navaṭīkā* (Burmese edition)
Sv-ṭ	*Sumaṅgalavilāsinī-ṭīkā*
T	Taishō Shinshu Daizōkyō
Th	Thai
TPMA	*Tipiṭaka pāḷi mranmā abhidhān*
UK	*Upasampadā-Kammavācā* (in context)
Upās	*Upāsakajanālaṅkāra*
Vibh	*Vibhaṅga*
Vibh-a	*Vibhaṅga-aṭṭhakathā* (= *Sammohavinodanī*)
Vin	*Vinayapiṭaka*
Vism	*Visuddhimagga*
Vism-mhṭ	*Visuddhimagga-mahāṭīkā*
Vmv Be	*Vimativinodanī-ṭīkā* (Burmese edition)
Vv	*Vimānavatthu*
Vv-a	*Vimānavatthu-aṭṭhakathā*

TECHNICAL NOTES

For the spelling of South and Southeast Asian proper names and toponyms, we use established phonetic transcriptions when these exist. Likewise, we use established phonetic transcriptions for Sanskrit and Pāli terms commonly used in English—such as the term *Sanskrit*. Otherwise, we generally use the International Alphabet of Sanskrit Transliteration to render Sanskrit and Pāli terminology. Pāli forms are used throughout the volume, with the occasional exception of Sanskrit terms adopted in English usage, such as *dharma* rather than the Pāli *dhamma* when required by context. We have nonetheless allowed some variation in usage from contributor to contributor (e.g. Asoka or Aśoka, Dhamma or Dharma...) in order to respect diverse disciplinary practices and authorial preferences.

South and Southeast Asian vernacular terms are also rendered variously, according to individual author requirements. Some authors oriented more toward oral usage adopt phonetic transcription. Others adopt transliteration systems established for the language in question.

For the most part, references to Pāli texts are to Pali Text Society publications, in which case publication details are not included in the chapter's list of works cited. All Pāli references have been assigned a unique abbreviation by the *Critical Pali Dictionary* (CPD). CPD abbreviations used in individual essays in the *Handbook* are given in the earlier Abbreviations list. In the case of a prose Pāli text, the volume number, if any, is followed by the page number(s). For instance, a reference to *Dīgha-Nikāya*, volume III, page 167, would be shown as DN III 167. In the case of a text in verse, the number of the verse(s) are cited (e.g., Sn 221 for *Suttanipāta*, verse 221).

THERAVĀDA CIVILIZATIONS PROJECT

THERAVADA
BUDDHIST CIVILIZATIONS

The project supports collaborative exchanges among scholars based in the United States, Canada, the United Kingdom, and Southeast Asia with the aim to undertake a thematic study of Theravāda civilizations in South and Southeast Asia.

INTRODUCTION

Stephen C. Berkwitz and Ashley Thompson

Introduction

We are at a moment in time when the appropriateness of the term *Theravāda* for many contexts in which it is regularly used is under fire, when the distortions its very usage has created are being scrutinized. Our moment also affords glimpses into how such distortions and the apprehension of these as such can be integral to the topic at hand—a long-evolving dynamic, discursive, construction always already heterogeneous to "itself." Theravāda Buddhism is not one thing, nor is it an accumulation of different but related things. Nor is it simply nothing. But its ontological status is anything but given. To roughly cite Pāli scholar Charles Hallisey with reference to what the anthropologist James Clifford said about "culture": Theravāda Buddhism is a deeply compromised category that we have not yet learned to do without (cf. Clifford 1988: 10). As such, in this Introduction, we do not attempt to explain or define what Theravāda really is. This *Handbook* provides instead a window into the current state of affairs in the study of Theravāda Buddhism. In providing a wide range of understandings of what comprises Theravāda at a given place and time and how, it also aims to trigger thought on the future of the field.

There is an unresolvable tension between, on one hand, the nominalist dimensions of the issue (how we define what is worthy of consideration when we study Theravāda Buddhism) and, on the other hand, its realist dimensions (the diversity found among the traditions and communities brought together with the name "Theravāda"). In editing this volume, we have struggled to be both nominalist and realist at once and have kept a wary eye on the inevitable inadequacy of the former in relation to the latter. This scholarly context is in some ways analogous to that of Buddhists across history in South and Southeast Asian communities, where vastly different visions and experiences of Theravāda can share the premise that Theravāda has certain features that are discernible and authoritative, worthy of universal recognition, beyond any individual iteration—even if they do not necessarily share in the so-defined same features themselves. In a scholarly distillation of this shared premise, Theravāda can be said to ground itself in a heritage traced to Gotama Buddha and to an interpretation of his legacy shaped by the teachers who created the commentaries on the *Tipiṭaka*, the "Three Baskets" comprising the Pāli canon. What features become worthy of focus against this backdrop is infinitely variable, as are the means by which such focus is articulated. There is no single Theravāda tradition, and no defined canon of salient traits by which any Theravāda worthy of the name can be identified.

DOI: 10.4324/9781351026666-1

There are rather multiple visions about which forms of practice and thought are derived from the Buddha and his earliest disciples. Some forms of Theravāda, moreover, are not wedded to the term itself and may instead define themselves in other ways, for example, through the prisms of national citizenship, ethnolinguistic identity, or particular types of meditation. In such contexts, the primacy of the shared frame can be lesser, indeed wholly subsumed, by other concerns.

The very idea of Theravāda

In this section, we aim to lay out a few basic issues to assist nonspecialists in using this volume. What we say here is developed with greater nuance and precision in the *Handbook*'s individual chapters, which themselves are by and large research-led and, as such, meant also to address advanced students and colleagues in the Buddhist Studies field as well as the other disciplinary fields in which they engage. In current parlance, the Pāli language term *Theravāda* refers to a distinct school of Buddhism with a relatively conservative orientation toward texts, teaching, imagery, and ritual that is predominant in Sri Lanka and the mainland Southeast Asian countries of Burma (Myanmar), Thailand, Laos, and Cambodia. Theravāda Buddhist communities, loosely defined, are also found in Nepal, Bangladesh, India, Vietnam, Yunnan province in southwest China, and in parts of North and South America, Europe, and Africa. Translated variously as the "tradition," "school," "opinion," or "decree" (*vāda*, literally, "the speech") of the Elders (*thera*, as in more senior and knowledgeable monastics), the Theravāda refers in the first instance to a set of texts, teachings, monastic lineages, and associated practices anchored in the Pāli language associated with the Buddha himself and other ancient teachers who were among his followers. The term's association with a large, extant collection of Pāli texts, including a complete *Vinaya* or monastic disciplinary code, means that for the better part of two thousand years some communities of monks (and for some centuries, female renunciants or "nuns") were ordained and taught according to a shared body of Buddhist literature. This canon of Pāli texts possesses significance and authority, partly because the texts are ascribed to the Buddha's own teachings said to have been memorized and written down by his disciples a few centuries after his death.

The use of the Pāli language distinguishes what will become known as the Theravāda from other early schools that coalesced around a Sanskrit canon. The Pāli canon also forms a relatively "closed" canon of texts, compared with other Buddhist schools; this relative closure is an effect of the notion that the teachings should comprise, in the main, those the Buddha preached while he was alive in the world. There is no allowance, in other words, for an expansive canon of texts that were "found" or "revealed" in subsequent centuries by a Buddha who is thought to exist in a heavenly realm and may continue to disseminate teachings by revelation, as in many Mahāyāna forms of the religion. Core to the Theravāda tradition(s) is nonetheless plurivocality. At no place and time, it would seem, has Pāli been used to the exclusion of other languages. Theravāda can, in fact, be characterized by its dizzying array of bilingual forms. Crucially, while the presence of Pāli can be taken, be it retrospectively, to indicate the presence of Theravāda, the opposite does not hold; that is, Theravāda can have a presence in the absence of Pāli language usage per se.

As noted earlier, contemporary scholars have raised serious questions about the salience of the term *Theravāda*. It has been pointed out that the term was of only limited use in Pāli Buddhist texts in the premodern period and that it was not part of the premodern self-conscious identity of Buddhists in South and Southeast Asia (Skilling 2009: 63). In other words, those who considered themselves to be devotees of the Buddha in contexts where Pāli was a language of reference would, generally speaking, not have thought of themselves as belonging to a Theravāda school or community. When the term does appear in premodern Pāli texts—mainly commentarial (*aṭṭhakathā*) or historical (*vaṃsa*) literature, it does so infrequently and usually refers to a tradition of interpretation of the canonical texts developed by Elder Monks (*thera*) who counted themselves within the lineage of the original 500 *arahants* (beings made worthy by their liberation from the fetters of the world) who codified and recorded the Buddha's teachings at a legendary First Council shortly after the Buddha's demise (Gethin 2012: 14, 55). Current consensus among scholarly specialists is that the term *Theravāda* was not the primary label for Buddhists who adhered to Pāli traditions of text and practice before the modern period.

Nevertheless, the idea of Theravāda grew in relevance and currency in the twentieth century. Its usage expanded from a largely monastic tradition of textual interpretation associated with Pāli canonical and commentarial texts into a broad school of practice comprising monastics and laypersons who began to identify themselves with this specific term. This transformation in terminology was helped along by a new discourse that Western monks and scholars promoted as the label for a coherent school of Buddhism found primarily in South and Southeast Asia and that would replace the pejorative "Hīnayāna" (lesser vehicle) label derived from Mahāyāna polemics (Perreira 2012: 460–461). The reification of the construct as a "tradition" on the order of a school or lineage with singularly uninterrupted continuity is itself a modern phenomenon with links rather than roots in an enduring premodern discourse of fidelity to the very words of the Buddha.

While the history of the term as outlined by Perreira and others does point to the relative recentness of the usage of *Theravāda* to designate a type of Buddhism, we are hesitant to label it as a mere anachronism. Pāli and associated vernacular texts commonly speak of *theras* as religious authorities, and there are in any case few efforts in the premodern period to categorize broad Buddhist traditions that could encompass laypersons as well as different orders of monastics, esoteric practices as well as public liturgies, merit-making activities as well as political strategies, women and girls as well as men and boys, or all sorts of artistic representation. This does not, however, mean that the Pāli reference did not both assume and provide a certain coherence among practitioners, lay and monastic. In awaiting the advent of a more perfect approach, and in the hopes that this volume will contribute to its coming, we see "Theravāda" to retain its utility as a category that incorporates a diverse mix of texts, practices, objects, and groups found mainly across South and Southeast Asia, and we note that the term has become commonplace and is regularly invoked by "Theravāda Buddhists" themselves in the modern period (Skilling 2012: xxix–xxx). Searching for a different term from premodern traditions to function in the same sense that the modern *Theravāda* does would, in any case, be a futile exercise itself premised on narrow understandings of language, translation, and scholarship bereft of historicity.

There are several other key terms that help to ground understandings of Theravāda. The Pāli term *sāsana*, often translated as "dispensation," "tradition," and even "religion," figures prominently in the self-definition of what is now frequently called Theravāda Buddhism. Described by Steven Collins (1998: 348) as "an historically instantiated and institutionalized body of knowledge" that was discovered by a Buddha and transmitted by his monastic disciples, the *sāsana* serves as the emic concept that approximates the idea of the Buddhist religion. Understood to consist of the teachings (*dhamma*) and the institutions founded by the Buddha, the *sāsana* is attributed with the authority of its enlightened originator, and it functions as the means by which people in later eras may encounter that which the Buddha allegedly established to assist others in their efforts to reduce suffering, enhance well-being, and ultimately obtain liberation (nirvana). It includes doctrinal teachings, as well as the rules and customs associated with the Buddhist *saṅgha*, or monastic community as elaborated in the *Vinaya*. The *sāsana* is identifiable with the legacy of the Buddha that was taken to have been bestowed directly by him to his followers, and importantly, the *sāsana* is also understood to be subject to historical forces and diminution over time. The Buddhist embrace of impermanence as an irrefutable fact of conditional existence has led the tradition to affirm that even the Buddha's *sāsana* is subject to decay and disappearance. In view of this idea, and despite the widespread acceptance of it, Theravāda Buddhists often work to preserve the *sāsana* in what they nominally hold to be its earliest and most authentic form (Crosby 2014: 9).

One of the primary aspects of the *sāsana* in Theravāda is the Pāli canon, the authoritative collection of texts attributed to the Buddha's very words and preserved in the Pāli language for the express purpose of transmission. Theravāda Buddhists have traditionally held that Pāli was the language spoken by the Buddha, although linguists and scholars generally maintain that as a Middle Indo-Aryan language, Pāli was at best only related to the language in which the Buddha actually spoke. In fact, various historical circumstances led to the preservation in Pāli of the canonical Three Baskets (*Tipiṭaka*) of texts. Divided into categories of monastic rules (*Vinaya*), discursive teachings (*Sutta*), and metaphysical analysis of experience (*Abhidhamma*), the Pāli canon represents the most authoritative version of the Buddha's teachings. Other non-Theravāda Buddhist communities recognize different canonical collections of texts preserved in Sanskrit, Tibetan, or other languages. Learned sectors of the tradition have embraced, and ultimately underpinned, a popular embrace of a historicist and exclusivist idea of canon. Although identified with the Buddha's own words, the collection of texts that is now the canon was circumscribed in the early centuries of the Common Era by a group of Sri Lankan monks who sought to define and legitimate their monastic community against other competitors (Collins 1990: 101–102). This was the community of the Mahāvihāra, which would come to dominate the island of Sri Lanka and subsequently impact Pāli Buddhist practice in Southeast Asia in a substantial manner. The recurrent reference to Sri Lanka as the cradle of Theravāda Buddhism in many Southeast Asian contexts is inseparable from the Mahāvihāra construction as it has been reiterated over time. Nevertheless, different ethnolinguistic communities that recognize Pāli as authoritative will use different vernacular languages (e.g., Sinhala, Burmese, Thai, Lao, and Khmer) while also using Pāli in liturgical and some textual and ritual contexts. Actual relations to Sri Lanka differed significantly in different geo-historical contexts such that Theravāda can be said in many ways to have developed through networks of exchange in multiple locales in parallel rather than through dissemination from a center—be that center located in the Buddha before the Common Era or in Sri Lanka at its start.

There are additional genres of Pāli texts that have been otherwise important for the development of this form of Buddhism. Specifically, the composition of commentarial texts (*aṭṭhakathā*) and sub-commentaries (*ṭīkā*) in the Pāli language has helped establish a textual tradition that was for many centuries almost synonymous with the idea of the "Theravāda" as a body of authoritative opinion or decrees that came down from senior monks (Gethin 2012: 29). In particular, commentaries such as the famed fifth-century scholar-monk Buddhaghosa's *Samantapāsādikā* outline the foundation of a coherent monastic lineage that connects the earliest disciples of the Buddha with later generations of monks in the Mahāvihāra community. Within this particular narrative of origins, it is said that Venerable Mahinda, an Elder Monk who traveled to Sri Lanka in order to transmit the *sāsana* there, had "learnt the complete Tradition of the Elders [*theravādaṃ*] consisting of the works of the Three Piṭakas together with their commentaries handed down at the two Convocations" (Jayawickrama 1986: 46). It is important to note how this account highlights the commentaries along with the canonical texts as comprising the *theravāda*, which in this early, premodern sense refers to the Pāli textual tradition. In this sense, the *aṭṭhakathā* works effectively functioned, in Maria Heim's words, as a continuation of the transmission and unfolding of the Buddha's words from the First Council onwards (Heim 2018: 220).

At the same time, Theravāda's debt to Pāli literature is evidenced in different ways among its various adherents in South and Southeast Asia. While all Theravāda groups subscribe to the Pāli *Tipiṭaka* as an authoritative collection of canonical texts derived from the Buddha's teachings, different communities place different degrees of emphasis on different texts. For instance, *Abhidhamma* texts assume proportionately more importance in formal study in modern Burma than in its mainland neighbors today. Likewise, Burmese Buddhists use the *aṭṭhakathā* commentaries for interpreting the canon more systematically and intensively than their neighbors. Such distinctions were brought into relief in the wake of nineteenth- and twentieth-century religious reforms in Thailand (Crosby 2014: 85). Many Theravāda Buddhists have also composed and utilized handbooks and summaries (sometimes in Pāli) that give shorthand access to the canonical and commentarial literature. Arguably, the most influential and well known of such paracanonical texts is Buddhaghosa's *Visuddhimagga* (Path of Purification), a fifth-century compendium of teachings abstracted from canonical texts on the development of morality (*sīla*), meditation (*samādhi*), and wisdom (*paññā*). The diversity of Theravāda literature is dramatically increased by the long-standing composition of Buddhist texts in literary vernaculars such as Sinhala, Burmese, Shan, Mon, Thai, Lao, and Khmer. Crucially, these works reached diverse audiences within lay and monastic milieux. Ranging from innovative compositions of the Buddha's life story to narrative inventions of the origins and lives of legendary images and relics to monastic ceremonial guides and illustrated meditation manuals, they bear witness to elite scholarly, specialist practitioner, and popular culture evolving in dialogue over time.

In conjunction with written texts, both canonical and noncanonical, Pāli and vernacular, Theravāda has also been defined and transmitted by other forms of material culture across South and Southeast Asia. What we have been calling textual traditions are in fact integral to material culture. These include writing on stone, metal, terracotta, palm leaves, and bark, as well as on paper. In first millennia mainland Southeast Asia, stone inscriptions predominantly bore Pāli liturgical citations, while the second millennia brought a predominance of vernacular and Pāli compositions recording merit-making good works such as the donation of a Buddha image to a temple or more extensive architectural foundations; these were generally associated with eulogies of their (often royal) founders. Such historical records could include accounts of legendary feats of Buddhist figures or socioeconomic organizations centered on temple foundations. Inscriptions from ancient Sri Lanka were also often tied to donative acts, although they increasingly contained eulogistic praise for kings around the turn of the second millennium. The Sri Lankan inscriptions differed from those in Southeast Asia by relying mostly on Sinhala writing, along with a few Sanskrit works, while largely abstaining from the use of Pāli in the island's epigraphy.

Artistic representation of Gotama Buddha, although depicted with stylistic and iconographic variation over space and time, is more or less recognizable to Theravāda Buddhists across the board, serving to convey and embody group cohesion on micro and macro scales in both synchronic and diachronic terms. At the same time, a given Buddha image often carried distinctly local meaning, indiscernible to the uninformed naked eye. The widespread practice in modern Cambodia, for example, of venerating specific Buddha statues not as Buddhas per se but as embodiments of specific male or female historical or legendary figures grew no doubt in relation to ancient Angkorian practices by which the elite were posthumously assimilated with Hindu or Buddhist divinities embodied in statues. Artistic representations of narratives at the core of Theravādin beliefs—the *jātaka* tales illustrating the Buddha's achievement of ethical perfections over past lives, along with the story of Siddhattha Gotama's life and death—provide another, related mode of communication of history, ethics, and ritual practice key to constituting knowledge of Theravāda and experience of Theravādin community. Here, too, vernacular styles, thematic proclivities, strategies of placement and composition, and use of media (stone, wood, brick or stucco sculpture, paint, print) differ significantly over space, time, and given purpose comprise a dynamic, heterogeneous Theravāda. Narrative representations can function in a like manner to the localized Buddha statues noted above, where telltale features—locally styled architecture, the features of a historical king's face, an iconic local temple setting, a landscape, or dress characteristic of home—set the Buddha's life story in the here and now.

Likewise, characteristic architectural forms simultaneously reflect and provide cohesion to the Theravādin community as a whole and to specific communities seen up against others. The funerary monument—a *stūpa*, or a *cetiya* as it has been widely known under its Pāli designations in Southeast Asian usage, and commonly as a *stūpa* or a *dāgäba* in Sri Lanka—is literally and figuratively the most outstanding of these. The singularity of the form, a more or less closed, more or less bulbous symbolic mountain-womb widely understood to comprise an abstract form of the Buddha is never lost in its many iterations over Sri Lankan and mainland Southeast Asian time and space. Yet each and every *stūpa* will have its story of who built it when and for whose relics—the Buddha's and/or others' to be assimilated with those of the Buddha in his abstract form. In some places and times, that abstract form is demonstrably venerated as the Buddha; in others, such veneration is reserved for the statue alone.

Sīmā, or boundary markers are another potent example of dynamic developments of a singular tradition. "One of the prior conditions for the existence and continuance of the Buddhist community is a boundary (*sīmā*) which defines the space within which all members of a single local community have to assemble as a complete Saṅgha … at a place appointed for ecclesiastical acts" (Kieffer-Pülz 1997: 141). Rules regulating *sīmā* were laid out in the *Vinaya*; these were repeatedly subject to review, explanation, modification, and extension over well more than a millennium in the commentarial and sub-commentarial literature. The interpretive process developed also in material terms on the ground. Whereas in Sri Lanka, the *sīmā* are ritually determined boundaries that can be represented by stone markers buried in the ground or designated topographical elements, from the sixth and seventh centuries in areas of mainland Southeast Asia, the *sīmā* became systematically figured in sculpted stones planted to be seen aboveground, over buried markers. Today such usage in Theravādin Southeast Asia is nearly universal and sculpted *sīmā* stones comprise an important element of the region's archaeological, art historical, political, and ethnographic record. Yet *where* exactly they are used and what they can mean differs from one time or one locale to another; in Southeast Asia, such issues have also been the subject of extended textual consideration and regulation, from epigraphic declarations to consecration manuals to court decisions.

In many contexts, Theravāda is best known by its practitioners not by way of authoritative texts but, rather, by way of material culture and associated practices. Acknowledgment of the authority of the text as a general category, as of the Pāli canon broadly conceived, nonetheless irrevocably inflects the forms and meanings of objects-in-practice; and the distinction the present discussion relies on, between text and nontext, does not always maintain insofar as the *dhamma* or teachings is objectified, embodied in objects—books, statues, relics—and venerated as such. Notable also is the fact that artistic styles also traveled by way of Buddhist objects such that something more than "Buddhism" taken to mean doctrinal tenets or the story of the Buddha's life was also exchanged in the adoption here or there of certain forms. In short, this material culture of the *dhamma* is inseparable from the immaterial in myriad ways, such that the knowledge of Theravāda had by Theravādins can pass virtually unnoticed, like perfume in the air. That is, the "practitioners" to whom we refer include people evolving in Theravāda milieu and contributing to them, although not always intentionally so. In these loose Bourdieusian terms, Theravāda names a *habitus*. The material evidence for Theravāda in Southeast Asia indeed attests to a longstanding presence of monastics ordained in the Pāli traditions of the Elder Monks (*theras*) far earlier than many Pāli textual scholars oriented towards Sri Lankan historical and literary phenomena would have imagined. Theravāda became what it is also in areas, people, practices, and things at a great distance from the origins they nonetheless imagined.

Theravāda Civilizations

The idea of this *Handbook* arose out of conversations that took place under the umbrella of the Theravāda Civilizations Project, which originated in 2011 under the direction of Juliane Schober and the late Steven Collins with support from the Luce Foundation. This project enabled the collaborative, interdisciplinary work of a group of scholars to reimagine, refine, and encourage new scholarship on Theravāda Buddhism. The work was developed through conferences, workshops for doctoral and post-doctoral researchers, and the publication of edited collections. Collective publications thus far include *Theravāda Buddhist Encounters with Modernity* (Routledge 2018), and a second volume in press, also with Routledge, on the life of the Buddha. The project also led to the development of the Theravāda Studies Group, which comprises a larger, interdisciplinary group of scholars and is affiliated with the Association for Asian Studies. With contributions from many of the Theravāda Civilizations group members, including we two editors, the present *Handbook* is in many ways another product of the original Luce-funded initiative.

In resonance with the landmark volume *How Theravāda Is Theravāda?* (Skilling 2012), the Theravāda Civilizations group sought to historicize and contextualize what is meant by "Theravāda" by engaging in exchanges explicitly structured to expand disciplinary, period, and area-based knowledge of different iterations of Theravāda. The exchanges were meant at once to enable further accumulation of knowledge within discrete areas of expertise and, in the name of "Theravāda," to break down barriers between the so-defined bodies of knowledge. The latter was consistently the more challenging of our tasks. Marveling at our own incessant production of arrays of shared yet different things—ways of burying the dead, words for "saints," modes of regulating sexuality—came far more easily than considering the import of a lofty word like *civilization*. The latter process involved wrestling with the question of Theravāda's alleged coherence rather than, or in addition to building exchanges on an unacknowledged assumption that it does cohere. We were made periodically aware that the exciting exchanges by which we could cover virtually all geographic and disciplinary grounds flirted with reifying Theravāda as a lineage, school, movement, or some other historical entity and, as such, ran the risk of participating in configurations of power that make authoritative pronouncements on Theravāda's identity and legitimacy. Our collective consciousness of the hegemonic pretensions and violent potentiality of such power structures haunting not only Theravāda but also our endeavors in its regard would likewise periodically rise to the surface.

From this perspective, trying to distinguish whether Theravāda is a singular phenomenon or a diverse set of multiples does not address the more fundamental questions of who can decide what counts for Theravāda and why. Nor does it examine how coherence in tradition and identity is constructed and what makes certain features worthy of study and certain arguments for coherence more compelling than others. Therefore, while scholars may continue to identify new and relatively unexplored features of Theravāda Buddhism that are ripe for study, the challenge of avoiding essentializing pronouncements over what Theravāda is or is not, independently and in place of how practitioners themselves have dealt with these issues, remains salient for us. The challenge lies in recognizing that any meaningful conceptualization of "Theravāda Buddhism" as both a theoretical object and an analytical category must come to terms with the capaciousness, complexity, and even outright contradiction that appears within this historical phenomenon that has proceeded from the human engagement with the idea and reality of the Buddha's awakening and teaching (cf. Ahmed 2016: 6).

In those countries where Pāli and vernacular Buddhist traditions of textuality, ritual, and material culture have predominated for many centuries—for example, Sri Lanka, Burma, Thailand, Laos, and Cambodia—it is possible, we argue still, to speak of Theravāda as civilizational. By this we mean that Theravāda traditions have generated and shaped many different ways that people think and act within a specific cultural setting at the same time that the same people have generated and shaped Theravāda. This mutual, dynamic creation approaches the notion of *habitus* mentioned earlier and is never short of the political, economic, and social frameworks within which the *sāsana* functions. Family and social relationships are, in part, embodied and enacted in accordance with particular Buddhist ideas and practices just as the latter are shaped by specific geo-historical and social circumstances. It is these settings, where Theravāda can be said to be in this way "civilizational," which are the focus of the majority of the chapters. As mentioned earlier, Theravāda is also practiced as a minority tradition in other countries and regions. It is on the largest scale, encompassing specific Theravādin civilizations as well as these other Theravādin groupings, that we speak of "Theravāda civilization."

Organization of the handbook

The *Handbook* is organized around thematic rather than geographical or chronological considerations. We made this editorial choice as a means of emphasizing the nominalist dimensions of our task, that is, of drawing out what we deem to be important features of Theravāda Buddhism that crossnational and period boundaries and other divides such as urban/rural and monastic/lay. Specializations—geographic, period, and/or disciplinary—nonetheless underpin individual contributions and, as such, tend to make the realist dimensions of the collective work felt. We hope that the themes will generate further discussion, including on how this basic editorial choice inflects understandings of Theravāda and on what other key themes we have for one reason or another left out. On this note, we can flag the omission of any chapter singularly devoted to questions of violence in Theravāda Buddhism. While issues of gender and race are addressed within specific contexts, they are not treated as categories in themselves or with sustained consideration of violence in their regard. And we have not included work on Theravāda communities outside of Asia. These themes do however pervade the volume. We have sought to highlight them instead through the index.

We have organized the contributions into four parts under broad headings that serve to group the diverse aspects of Theravāda into related areas of study. Part I, titled "Ideas/Ideals," serves to set the stage with chapters investigating notions used to collectively define what Theravāda is, how it has been organized, and how it has moved through time. Sven Bretfeld's chapter explores the very idea of "Theravāda" by relating this term to a long history of textual efforts to identify the authentic transmission of the Buddha's *sāsana* with the Mahāvihāra monastic lineage in Sri Lanka. By examining several key Pāli and Sinhala premodern texts, Bretfeld's chapter shows how an authoritative Theravāda tradition was fashioned out of a diversity of other Buddhist "sects." Next, Alastair Gornall takes up the subject of "Pāli" as a defining feature of Theravāda. Eschewing the common gesture of attributing its place and power to vague notions of the hegemonic sacred, Gornall proposes a threefold analytical framework for better understanding the complexity of the language's role in constituting what Steven Collins has called the "Pāli imaginaire." Examining how the authority of the language emerges as that performatively constituted by claims and counterclaims in its own regard,

Gornall shows the dynamism of the imaginaire evolving over time. Next, Anne Blackburn's chapter on "Circulations" scrutinizes how Theravāda traditions moved about in what she calls the "Pāli world," or the linked spaces in which Pāli language and texts retained influence. Using the premodern polity of Sukhothai as her case study, Blackburn proposes that we can learn from looking at the transmission of specific elements such as theories of Buddhist sovereignty, styles of Buddhist devotional practice, and cosmological understandings across specific locales as integral to circulatory processes that linked diverse communities. Patrice Ladwig's chapter on "Statecraft" examines key dimensions of traditional conceptions of kingship embraced by Theravāda communities, before moving on to consider these in relation to political practices on the ground in mainland Southeast Asian settings. These systems of political organization and statecraft are ultimately then shown to inform modern forms of governance with concerns for political legitimation and national integration. The chapter on "Reform," co-written by Anne Hansen and Anthony Lovenheim Irwin, looks at how modern Theravāda communities have adopted older themes of purifying and reinvigorating what is deemed to be the authentic Buddhist tradition. Although based on older models, modern reformist movements are shown to have distinctive features. The authors describe mid-twentieth-century movements that might be labeled "decolonizing" before the popularization of the name in epistemological terms, in which monastics and Buddhist politicians embraced local yet cosmopolitan and distinctly non-Western modes of knowledge construction. The last chapter in Part I is Nirmala Salgado's chapter on "Tradition," in which she analyzes the debates over what constitutes "Theravāda" that took place amidst efforts to reestablish the *bhikkhunī* lineage of Buddhist nuns in modern and contemporary Sri Lanka and in dialogue with related initiatives in Thailand and Burma. These debates demonstrate how the practices and lineages that constitute Theravāda traditions are not self-evident but are rather formed through contestation.

Part II, titled "Practices/Persons," aims to highlight different modes of embodiment of Theravāda. That this section is the largest of the volume is indicative of a current scholarly focus on everyday Buddhist life. Juliane Schober's chapter on "Merit" examines social practices of giving in Burma. Her chapter shows that practices of generosity (*dāna*) have relevance not only for understanding Theravāda systems of obtaining rewards for doing good deeds but also occupy an important place in ritual economies, political governance, and institution-building processes. Next, Pyi Phyo Kyaw and Kate Crosby discuss Theravāda practices of "Meditation." After outlining foundational meditation practices and goals of self-transformation as articulated in Pāli texts, the authors home in on techniques elaborated in *Abhidhamma* texts in particular and in pre-reform methods still in active use in multiple Theravāda contexts. Further consideration is given to two living Burmese traditions. Next, Christoph Emmrich offers a theoretical examination of the role of "Repetition" in Theravāda practice. The repetition of select utterances and phrases comprises aspects of performance that aesthetically enable the coming into being of what is said, assist with memorization, facilitate doctrinal explanation in both pedagogical and experiential manners, and determine karmic results. Grégory Kourilsky's chapter on "Filial Piety" explores a paradox at the heart of Theravāda societies: while remarkable value is placed on devotion towards one's parents in explicitly Buddhist terms, the notion of filial piety is not highlighted in the authoritative texts of the Mahāvihāra and indeed appears to run counter to both the central ethic of *karma* and the foundational act of renunciation of family ties performed by the Buddha and monastics in his wake. The chapter on "Laity" by Asanga Tilakaratne debunks categorical distinctions frequently cited in scholarly literature between "nibbanic" and "kammatic" Buddhism when these convey the reductive notion that monastics are singularly oriented to obtaining *nirvana* and the laity to improving their destinies in future lives by performing good works. He begins by recalling how the early Pāli texts describe the roles of Buddhist laypersons chiefly as donors that support the Buddhist *saṅgha*, to then expand upon this traditional trope of the layperson in discussing how in more modern times, the Buddhist laity of Sri Lanka and Burma have become active in meditation, the study of *dhamma* texts, and practices linked with social justice. Next, Thomas Borchert discusses "Discipline" as practiced and negotiated both within and beyond the Pāli *Vinaya*. Focusing on examples from Thailand and Sipsongpannā in southwestern China, Borchert explores how discipline and training are accessed through formal and informal sources in an effort to make monks who behave and look in appropriate ways. The final chapter of this section concerns "Funerals," wherein Katherine Bowie examines how this important Theravāda life-cycle ritual has changed over time in different regions of Thailand. We learn that funerary practices perform diverse cultural work, expressing social divisions and local understandings of death that contribute to an understanding of the complex politico-religious histories of Theravāda lands.

Part III, "Texts/Teachings," is focused on key genres and features of Theravāda texts. Here, too, diversity is forefronted, as we glimpse the extent to which Theravāda is *not* limited to a singular text or to a discrete group of texts. Peter Skilling provides a comprehensive overview of the notion of "Canons" in the lineage of the *theras*, or Elder Monks, who are attributed with authority over the traditions and texts of Theravāda Buddhism. His chapter outlines the different notions, materials, and collections of canonical texts that appear in the Theravāda, emphasizing change over time, with different forms and cultural valences appearing in different settings. Rupert Gethin then analyzes the Theravāda *Abhidhamma*, the third basket of canonical texts which comes to be understood as the ultimate expression of the Buddha's teaching, in relation to the *Abhidhamma* thought associated with the ancient Sarvāstivāda school from northern India. This comparison yields telling similarities and differences found between these two Buddhist versions of systematic thought on physical and mental phenomena. The chapter on "Vaṃsa" by Stephen Berkwitz examines this important genre of historical writing. Focused on recalling the legendary histories of how the Buddha, relics, and the *sāsana*, traveled to Sri Lanka and Southeast Asia, his contribution argues that these texts were instrumental in defining notions of Theravāda and authenticating its lineages of transmission to lands outside of India. Next, in another chapter on "Merit," Rita Langer discusses how certain exegetical texts served to describe how merit is made and to categorize the different actions for making merit. Her focus on the textual sources for understanding merit is complemented by attention to how contemporary Sri Lankan Buddhists understand merit-making practices. The last chapter in Part III deals with the phenomenon of "bilingualism" in Theravāda writing. Trent Walker offers a close analysis of Theravāda "bitexts," works that stitch together portions of Pāli or other Indic prestige language texts and local vernaculars. The chapter details how Theravāda Buddhists have developed critical systems for analyzing, transmitting, and performing texts which are virtually unique in Buddhist worlds.

Part IV, titled "Images/Imaginations," groups together chapters addressing processes—material, ritual, social, and textual—by which diverse Theravāda identities are imagined. Samerchai Poolsuwan discusses "Visual Narratives" in artistic portrayals of the Buddha's life story in the Pagan area of upper Burma. Poolsuwan probes the materials for what they convey of Southeast Asia's "medieval Theravāda," a term he uses to designate a matrix of inter-related local varieties of Pāli-based Buddhism both preceding twelfth-century Sri Lankan reforms and resisting these up until at least the fourteenth century. Next, Ashley Thompson explores the work of "Icons," bolstered as it is by narrative depictions in Theravāda contexts. The chapter points to the pertinence of a series of art-historical debates on emic and etic modes of interpretation for understanding how perceptions of the Buddha as embodying at once a historically conditioned figure and transcendent ideals can be played out on Southeast Asian ground. Next, in a chapter titled "Affect," Chairat Polmuk explores the sensorial experiences that are produced in ritual encounters with relics and in visually mediated forms in contemporary film. Through the lens of affect, Polmuk discusses two films in which relics, *stūpas*, or their cinematic substitutes engender interrogations into traumatic twentieth-century histories of Thailand and Cambodia. John Clifford Holt turns our attention to "Deities" that appear in Theravāda cultures and whose presences, made material or not, structure ritual interactions with the supernatural. Moving from the *devas* of Sri Lanka to the *phi* of Thai-Lao Buddhist cultures to the *neak ta* of Cambodia and the *nats* of Myanmar, Holt describes how these figures participate in Theravāda cosmologies and play important roles in associated social and political organization. Finally, Patrick McCormick examines the "Mons," an ethnolinguistic community whose coherence as such became anchored in imagined origins linked with those of Theravāda itself in mainland Southeast Asia. McCormick focuses on how this imagined foundational association of the Mons and Theravāda developed within British colonial Burma to become the keystone of modern Mon intellectual projects to write and interpret Mon history.

Taken together, the chapters in this *Routledge Handbook of Theravāda Buddhism* provide a detailed picture of Theravāda in different milieu over time and space. As we noted in the opening, they also provide a picture of this particular field of Buddhist Studies today. The ideas, practices, texts, objects, and people associated with Theravāda appear as historically contingent aspects of a tradition that is pluralistic but strives—be it in multifarious ways—toward singularity. Depending on the particular historical, geographical, social, or disciplinary vantage points adopted to view Theravāda, one can arrive at distinctively different interpretations of what Theravāda is. Readers may use the *Handbook* to come to terms with the coherence and contradiction that make up Theravāda Buddhism, exploring further its histories, as well as its use and limits as an analytical category. We hope that the work presented here will inspire new research as well as new research methodologies by which the inadequacy of our nominalist to our realist ambitions might be lessened and which might thus be better equipped to respond to the evolving dynamics of Theravāda and its study.

References

Ahmed, S. 2016. *What is Islam?: The Importance of Being Islamic*. Princeton, NJ: Princeton University Press.

Clifford, J. 1988. *The Predicament of Culture*. Cambridge, MA: Harvard University Press.

Collins, S. 1990. "On the Very Idea of the Pali Canon." *Journal of the Pali Text Society* 15: 89–126.

Collins, S. 1998. *Nirvana and other Buddhist Felicities: Utopias of the Pali Imaginaire*. Cambridge: Cambridge University Press.

Crosby, K. 2014. *Theravāda Buddhism: Continuity, Diversity, and Identity*. Chichester, West Sussex: Wiley Blackwell.

Gethin, R. 2012. "Was Buddhaghosa a Theravādin? Buddhist Identity in the Pali Commentaries and Chronicles." In *How Theravāda is Theravāda? Exploring Buddhist Identities*, eds. P. Skilling, J. Carbine, C. Cicuzza, S. Pakdeekham, 1–63. Chiang Mai: Silkworm Books.

Heim, M. 2018. *Voice of the Buddha: Buddhaghosa on the Immeasurable Words*. New York: Oxford University Press.

Jayawickrama, N.A. 1986. *The Inception of Discipline and the Vinaya Nidāna: Being a Translation and Edition of the Bāhiranidāna of Buddhaghosa's Samantapāsādikā, the Vinaya Commentary*. London: Pali Text Society.

Kieffer-Pülz, P. 1997. "Rules for the *sima* Regulation in the *Vinaya* and its Commentaries and their Application in Thailand." *Journal of the International Association of Buddhist Studies* 20(2): 141–153.

Perreira, T.L. 2012. "Whence Theravāda? The Modern Genealogy of an Ancient Term." In *How Theravāda is Theravāda?*, eds. P. Skilling et al., 443–571. Chiang Mai: Silkworm Books.

Skilling, P. 2009. "Theravāda in History." *Pacific World* 3rd Series, 11 (Fall): 61–93.

Skilling, P. 2012. "Introduction 'Whence Theravāda? The Modern Genealogy of an Ancient Term'." In *How Theravāda is Theravāda?*, eds. P. Skilling et al., xiii–xxxx. Chiang Mai: Silkworm Books.

PART I

Ideas/Ideals

1

THERAVĀDA

Sectarianism and diversity in Mahāvihāra historiography

Sven Bretfeld

Introduction

This chapter investigates how the Buddhist lineages we are accustomed to calling "Theravāda Buddhism" today have participated in historical discourses of institutional identity building and self-positioning against the backdrop of a Buddhist world increasingly characterized by intra-religious diversification and sectarianism.

The Pāli literary tradition has never produced a systematic presentation of Buddhist sects in the style of Vasumitra's *Samayabhedoparacaṇacakra* (second/third centuries?) or Bhavya's *Nikāyabhedavyākhyāna* (sixth centuries) for Sanskrit traditions. The Pāli commentaries indeed, contain plenty of analytical information on individual doctrinal or legal standpoints deemed erroneous or straightforwardly "heretical" by the respective authors. Sometimes such a view is ascribed to an identifiable group. The *Kathāvatthu-Atthakathā* is especially rich in this kind of information. A systematic interpretation of the world of Buddhist sectarianism in total was, however, achieved in a completely different literary form: historical narrative. The *vaṃsa* literature—sometimes called "chronicles" but, better, genealogical literature—does not contain much information on the characteristics of individual sects. But we do learn how the authors of these texts have organized their vision of the Buddhist world as a disintegrated field of intra-religious diversity, how, why, and when they thought the fragmentation of the Buddha's teaching happened; which global and local challenges for the integrity and survival of Buddhism they perceived; and how they defined their own role in this situation. As religious texts with pedagogical and political impact, the *vaṃsas*' ultimate aim is to present role models of good Buddhist behavior (Berkwitz 2004)—in the present context, how they expected that people of authority should act in order to restore the *sāsana* (the Buddhist institution or establishment) and to preserve it for as long as possible.

I will focus the present essay by discussing the two oldest *vaṃsas* that have been preserved—*Dīpavaṃsa* (fourth century) and *Mahāvaṃsa* (fifth century)—and a late fourteenth-century work written in medieval Sinhala—the *Nikāyasaṅgraha*. The latter presents the world of Buddhist sectarianism as a memory of the past, written in a gesture of victory by an author who perceived his own period as a time in which the "true" *sāsana* has prevailed over the heresies of the past.

DOI: 10.4324/9781351026666-3

It is crucial to keep in mind that all three works represent the viewpoint of the Mahāvihāra Nikāya, one of Sri Lanka's ancient Buddhist lineages. Much of their information and conceptual antagonisms have to be interpreted against the background of the sectarian agenda of this lineage. They were not unrivaled, not even within Anurādhapura, the ancient Sri Lankan capital where the Mahāvihāra Nikāya had its original base. Sadly, the alternative perspectives of their local rivals have fallen prey to historical contingency almost completely after the Mahāvihārins prevailed in the early post-Anurādhapura period. Hence, their point of view not only monopolized the cultural memory of the Sri Lankan Buddhists but also shaped the paradigms of Buddhist history-making in Southeast Asia since the thirteenth century when the Sri Lankan Buddhist "neo-orthodoxy" (see the following discussion) started to expand their influence into Burma and Siam. I may add that the antagonistic picture of the Mahāvihāra texts may not necessarily be representative of day-to-day interactions among members of different sects. We have many historical examples for good intersectarian cooperation and exchange, even programmatic curricula for the study of each other's literature. Close friendships between members of different sects may have been as common in historical times as they are today. We should also be cautious with the essentialized qualities and characteristics our sources attribute to different Buddhist lineages—for example, the strict "anti-Mahāyāna" attitude commonly associated with the Mahāvihārins. These may often be idealized images rather than descriptions of social realities.

Sect and *Nikāya*

I use the terms *sect* and *sectarianism* reluctantly. They are increasingly challenged in Religious Studies due to their historical roots in ancient Christian polemics and their underlying pejorative sense in modern use. In Buddhist Studies, the term *sect* is still widely used and has been stripped of much of its Christian heritage. When Buddhist scholars speak of "sects," they usually mean the Sanskrit/Pāli term *nikāya*. The *nikāya* concept is complex and has different connotations in different contexts. But it always defines an institutionalized group identity between the local face-to-face community and the global totality of the "*saṃgha* of the four directions" (*caturdiśasaṃgha*). I prefer the translation "monastic lineage" to "sect" or "school," in order to highlight the genealogical logic implied in the concept and to avoid an overemphasis of a distinguished belief or exegetic system as a defining characteristic. Some points need to be sketched in order to clarify the concept:

- The *nikāya* concept belongs to the field of monasticism. A Buddhist layperson is not a member of any *nikāya*. In this respect, *nikāyas* resemble more the Catholic monastic orders (Franciscan, Dominican, etc.) than Christian denominations or sects (Catholic, Protestant, Jehovah's Witnesses, etc.). Each monk and nun belongs to a *nikāya*. This affiliation is conveyed with the ordination ritual and tied to the *nikāya*-specific version of the *Vinaya* (monastic legal codex) they are ordained into. Unlike the Christian distinction between "the" church (= community of the orthodox) and "a" sect (= community of followers of a heresy), the Buddhist *nikāya* concept is a technical term of monastic collectivization and is per se not tied to polemical contexts.[1]
- A shared *Vinaya* recension (and enactment principles[2]) is constitutive for all members of a *nikāya*. In this respect, a *nikāya* can be interpreted as the virtual community of monks and nuns with ritual and jurisdictional compatibility. Earlier scholarship understood *nikāyas* primarily as dogmatic schools. Some *nikāyas* had their own literary tradition, starting with a specific recension of the *Tripiṭaka*, commentarial material, and so on. However, given

the scarcity of sources, it is unclear to what extent such textual and doctrinal originality was constitutive for the historical *nikāyas*.[3] Moreover, it seems to have been possible for a monk or nun to adopt another *nikāya*'s doctrinal system without abandoning the institutional framework of the *nikāya* in which they were formally ordained (cf. Kieffer-Pülz 2000: 289). A complete formal "conversion" to another *nikāya* required more than a shift of doctrinal orientation. Such a step would demand a full reordination into another *Vinaya* regime, implying that the number of ordination years of the "convert" would be reset to zero—such a relapse of hierarchical rank was surely not chosen often without very good reasons. For the same reason, *nikāyas* are not a characteristic of "Hīnayāna Buddhism," as some scholars suggest by using the term "Nikāya Buddhism" as a replacement for "Hīnayāna" in efforts to eschew usage of the latter for its historically pejorative connotations. The reasons for an individual monastic community to reject or tolerate, accept, or impede "Mahāyānist" or "Tantric" practices have to be sought out among the factors of communal socialization and politics (group pressure, social expectations, internal policies, institutional agendas, etc.) rather than its formal *nikāya* affiliation. As we will see, the Theriya Nikāya—or "Theravāda"—was a strong promoter of Mahāyāna and Tantric texts and practices for many centuries.

- For polemical purposes *vinaya*- and *dharma*-related issues are often conflated. The scholarly sdebate whether *nikāyas* were primarily doctrinal (*dharma*) or legal (*vinaya*) institutions, is fairly obsolete in this context (Bechert 1985, 1993; Walser 2005: 99ff). For the sources discussed in this chapter, *nikāya* schisms are always the result of disrespect for the "true" and "authentic" word of the Buddha. Thus, deviance is a matter of an "evil" (*pāpa*) attitude, not so much of concrete issues and open debates.

It is unclear when and how the *nikāya* concept came into being historically. Scholars have widely accepted the Buddhist view that institutional splits of the *saṃgha* into first two, then several *nikāyas* were the major factor driving the diversification of the early Buddhist movement. It is commonly assumed that this process was well underway by the time of Aśoka (Lamotte 1988: 292, Hirakawa 1990: 105ff., Sasaki 2002, Bechert 2005b: 25.).[4] However, considering the decentralized organization and expansion of the Buddhist movement in its first centuries, I find this archetype-based, linear bifurcation theory implausible. This model is ultimately derived from *nikāya* genealogies that were written at a much later time[5] and that, more likely than not, have projected the sectarian antagonisms of their own period into the remote past. In the following, I suggest a more dynamic relational emergence theory. I assume that religious technologies and contents were not transmitted as fixed sets within well-defined sectarian boundaries within the first four or five centuries of Buddhist history. They rather circulated freely among the more and more widespread Buddhist communities along cross-related paths of short-distance diffusion and long-distance transmission (Neelis 2010). Such a network of confluent, communicating nodes will sooner or later generate "hubs" governing arrays of associated nodes—namely, clusters of monastic communities with close relationships (either through dispersion, local proximity, or intense travel connections), and they will start to condense and to enter a process of tradition building by thematizing the distinctness of their shared religious heritage from others. This process will gradually harden the fluidity of the movement and progressively transform it into a structured landscape of mutually distinguished virtual communities.

As an early step of this process, some geographical hubs seem to have started to self-identify under a toponym by the second or first century BCE. This is, for example, the case for the term *tambapaṇṇika* "(those from) Tambapaṇṇi (= Sri Lanka)," an attribute India-visiting monks from Sri Lanka gave themselves in inscriptions from the first century BCE.[6] Another probable case are the Haimavatas, who seem to have been based somewhere in the Himalaya region originally and to have resettled or founded a colony in Sāñchī by the late second century BCE (Willis 2001). I assume that these early toponyms were not (yet) *nikāya* names conveying the idea of ritual/liturgical exclusivity and institutional autonomy,[7] but they may have connotated a certain degree of distinctness in the sense of a specific local color of Buddhism. A full-fledged *nikāya* identity, in contrast, requires an *institutionalized* comparative self-reflection, demarcating the respective tradition's textual and habitual peculiarities (at minimum its *vinaya* code) *systematically* from others. A *nikāya* is, thus, more than a more or less self-reliant local tradition, even if some like the Tambapaṇṇikas, the Haimavatas, or the Rājagirikas may have started as such. The *nikāya* idea transcends the logic of vernacular tradition building by deterritorializing the identity of the community, turning it—at least potentially—into a mobile and geographically expendable "global player." Most *nikāyas* seem to not have tied their distinctness to a specific geographical origin but to certain characteristics of their religious transmissions and approaches (e.g., Sarvāstivāda, Caityavāda, Sautrāntika, Bahuśrutīya) or to the genealogical affiliation to a certain founding figure (e.g., Kāśyapīya, Dharmaguptaka, Siddhārthaka, Dhammarucika) or to a blend of all this.[8] As far as literary and epigraphical evidence allows for conclusions, the development of *nikāya* identities started not much before the first century CE, when we find the first unambiguous *nikāya* names mentioned in North Indian inscriptions.[9]

The *nikāya* concept, then, seems to be much younger than commonly believed and must be seen not as an outcome of early Buddhist diversification processes but as a product of a later paradigmatic shift of Buddhist self-reflection and interaction. While the Buddhist network had certainly developed diverse approaches to the teaching of the Buddha and varying transmissions of his words virtually right from the beginning, Buddhist authors of the pre-CE period seem to have ignored or de-emphasized such differences (Sujato 2007: 7–12). At a certain point, Buddhist scholars had to acknowledge that the message of the Buddha (*buddhaśāsana*) could no longer plausibly be described as a single entity homogeneously expanding through time and space. It is conceivable that this turning point was less connected to an increase of diversity as such but, rather, to a shift of communication conditions that intensified the perception of diversity across the global Buddhist network and created new discourses stressing difference, incompatibility, and contest.[10] It can be assumed that the availability of tradition-specific *Tripiṭaka* material in written form and the development of pilgrimage sites and metropoles like Bodhgayā, Nāgārjunakoṇḍa, and so on into centers of intra-religious encounter played essential roles in this process. Thus, I assume that most early *nikāyas* emerged not from a series of formal schisms, as tradition has it, but as products of this paradigm shift—that is, when clusters of the Buddhist monastic network and local traditions formulated (or reformulated) their group identities in the new language of the *nikāya* discourse by claiming their ritual and doctrinal uniqueness and autonomy with the new demarcation technologies accompanying concept. Such an emergence theory is, of course, unthinkable from the insider perspective of a Buddhist who believes that Buddhism began as a homogeneous and already complete tradition. Under this assumption, diversity can only be explained as the result of schismatic events, which is what the narratives about the first split between Sthaviras and Mahāsāṃghikas and early *nikāya* genealogists like Vasumitra do.[11] In the following, I argue that the Sri Lankan communities came into contact with the *nikāya* discourse rather late. Probably not before the third century CE, they started to write themselves into an already existing mainland Indian model of *nikāya* diversity that the Mahāvihāravāsins transformed into a self-confident sectarian self-narration in the course of the following century. In this process, older narratives relating the creation of the Buddhist world as the peaceful conquest of a homogeneous *dharma* spreading across the world became overwritten by a diversification account filled with heretics betraying the Buddha's heritage by splitting the unity of the *saṃgha*, textual forgery, and diluting the *dharma* with non-Buddhist ideas.

Theravāda as a Buddhist sect

As I have shown elsewhere, the modern concept "Theravāda Buddhism" is an emergent product of a dialogue triangle involving (a) modern Buddhist answers to the challenges of the global religious field; (b) the historicist agenda, text-centrism, and desire for comparative categories of Religious and Buddhist Studies; and (c) the identity politics of classical Pāli-Buddhist *vaṃsa* and commentary literature (Bretfeld 2012b; Bretfeld 2019). The latter had a direct impact on the formation of the dehistoricized modern concept of "Theravāda" as a conservative, pristine form of Buddhism, usually contrasted with the (likewise problematic) concept of "Mahāyāna Buddhism."

Such essentialist categories mask the historicity of the concepts themselves. The premodern term *theravāda* is a result of Sri Lankan boundary-making activities. To the Indian Buddhist traditions, it was completely unknown,[12] and its significance before the twentieth century was greatly overestimated until recently, even for Sri Lankan and Southeast Asian literature.[13] However, starting with the fourth century CE, the term *theravāda* was coined within a certain stream of Sri Lankan literature production to condense the authenticity claims of a group that believed to protect the true *sāsana* from a world full of "heresies." In other words, "Theravāda" is not a meta-historical entity that predated the inner-Buddhist sectarian debate, but it is a product of this very discourse.

For all we know, the Sri Lankan traditions started to claim a specific sectarian identity rather late, hardly much before the third century CE. The first *nikāya* name that is attested to have been used by them is not Theravāda but Theriya, the Prakrit equivalent to Sanskrit Sthavira or Sthāvirya. Sometime later, from the sixth century onward, Sri Lankan traditions were regularly addressed under this name by Indian, Chinese, and (still later) Tibetan Buddhist authors. Before it appears as a denomination of the Sri Lankan lineage(s), the term *Theriya/Sthavira* already had a history. From around the first or second century CE, the term was known to Indian Buddhists as the name of one of the two groups that allegedly had formed the first two *nikāyas* according to the topos of the initial *nikāya* split. From the fourth century onward, the Sri Lankans claimed to be identical to these "original" Sthaviras. Yet later, when the Indian traditions started to use the term Sthavira for the Sri Lankan lineages, the name seems already to have lost its connotation of originality in mainland India. To complicate matters even more, the related term *theravāda* was coined by fourth-century Sri Lankans, partly as a synonym for this *nikāya* name but investing it with a peculiar idea of "original Buddhism." Here, at the latest, the Indian Buddhist traditions would have stopped to follow the Sri Lankan argument of authenticity.

This is a complex semantic constellation calling for a terminological convention that can be used by scholars to prevent confusions and anachronisms. I use the following nomenclature throughout the rest of this chapter:

STHAVIRA is used for the monastic faction said to have arisen from the assumed first split in the *saṅgha* and as a collective category for the *nikāyas* that are deemed to have emerged from the "original" Sthavira faction.

INDIAN PROTO-THERIYA denotes the historically obscure Indian tradition which transmitted the ordination tradition and the major bulk of canonical material to Sri Lanka. This hypothetical lineage must have used *vinaya* and *abhidhamma* material different from other Sthavira lineages that ultimately developed into the known *Vinaya* and *Abhidhamma Piṭakas* of the so-called Pāli Canon. It is likely that this lineage was already using some form of Pāli.

SRI LANKAN PROTO-THERIYA refers to the Sri Lankan tradition *before* it started to promote itself under a distinct *nikāya* name.

THERIYA (NIKĀYA) represents the Sri Lankan tradition *after* it had started to identify itself as a distinct *nikāya* named Theriya, Theravāda, or Theravaṃsa.

THERIYA SUB-*NIKĀYAS* denote the three sub-lineages into which the Sri Lankan tradition had eventually split between the first century BCE and the fifth century CE. As there is no Pāli word for "sub-*nikāya*," their individual lineage names will be given here as

- Mahāvihāra(-vāsin) Nikāya,
- Abhayagiri(-vāsin) Nikāya (also known as Dharmaruci Nikāya),
- Jetavana(-vāsin) Nikāya (also known as Sāgaliya Nikāya).

THERAVĀDA is not used as a category of analytical meta-language but only as an object-language term to discuss passages of primary literature that explicitly use this word. It is unclear whether the term was a specific word creation of Mahāvihāra authors. As a synonym for Theriya/Sthavira Nikāya it may also have been used as a self-designation by members of the Abhayagiri and Jetavana Nikāyas. That they also used it as a dogmatic concept, like the Mahāvihārins did, is unlikely.

THERAVĀDA BUDDHISM (as a Pāli–English hybrid compound) will be reserved for modern religious contexts. The term was coined in the early twentieth century as a comparative knowledge concept within the then current "world religions" paradigm, investing the term with semantic implications that were foreign to the *nikāya* paradigm (e.g., the understanding of Theravāda Buddhism as a specific Buddhist "creed" constituting religious communities of "believers" and encompassing monastics and lay-people alike).[14]

In this chapter, I follow a "relational" approach to religious history. This means that historical objects are not considered to cause (or suffer) historical changes or continuities as pre-discursive entities. They are rather understood as knowledge concepts that permanently and mutually constitute each other in a discursive field.[15] Collins (1990) has shown some impacts of a relational approach on the "very idea of the Pāli Canon." As one of the practical methodological consequences, we cannot speak of a Theriya lineage or "Theravāda Buddhism" in periods before these concepts were discursively carved out, even if we could be sure that certain constituents of these concepts—like a specific textual transmission, lineage of teacher/pupil succession, or local setting—had a continuity reaching further into the past. It is the specific semantic configuration of the knowledge concept that fashions the reality of the historical actors. We also have to be aware that knowledge concepts are always contested. To give an example, it is a common convention in secondary literature to present the Mahāvihāra lineage as the "orthodox school" of Sri Lanka holding on to the "teachings of the Theravāda," while the "heterodox" Abhayagiri lineage embraced "non-Theravāda" forms of Buddhism. From the perspective of relational analysis, there is a lot wrong with such a statement.[16] Setting aside the historical accuracy of this dualistic image, the question what is "orthodox" and what "heterodox" is a matter of viewpoint; they are not self-evident categories of historical description. Even more important, the statement that the Abhayagiri is *not* a "Theravāda" tradition is a polemical claim of their Mahāvihāra opponents. It is, however, likely that they, too, used this term as a self-designation of their lineage. They surely identified as a subgroup of the Theriya

Nikāya. We can be quite certain about this because of the testimony of the Indian, Chinese, and Tibetan doxographers mentioned earlier. Whether they used the compound Theravāda as a synonym is not clear, but it is likely. Furthermore, they will surely have opposed the notion that being a Theriya/Theravādin *and* being a Mahāyāna adept would mutually exclude each other. As Walters (1997: 107) puts it,

> Thus the Mahāvihāran claim that Theravāda is originally and exclusively a Hīnayāna school was certainly not universally believed in the ancient Buddhist world, nor probably was it believed by much of anyone except by the Mahāvihārans themselves. Even in Sri Lanka, even at the end of the Anurādhapura Period, this claim must have seemed absurd ...

Nāgārjunakoṇḍa: early positioning in a multi-sectarian environment

No inscription found on the island states any *nikāya* identity of the Sri Lankan *saṃgha* as a totality. The first documents in which members of the Sri Lankan Buddhist tradition proclaimed a *nikāya* name are two mid-third-century Prakrit inscriptions found in the South Indian Nāgārjunakoṇḍa.[17] This is at least three centuries after other *nikāyas* of mainland India had developed the custom to refer to their *nikāya* names in monastic inscriptions—a first hint that the Sri Lankan tradition may have been a newcomer to Buddhist sectarianism and wrote themselves into an already established model of Buddhist diversity. It is probably not by chance that this happened in the multi-sectarian context of third- and fourth- century Āndhra, where at least six other *nikāyas* held a steady presence: Mahīśāsakas, Aparaśailas, Pūrvaśailas, Bahuśrutīyas, Rājagirikas, and Siddhārthakas. This environment was obviously expecting that local monastic settlements give a genealogical "home address," defining their position within the *nikāya* model of Buddhist plurality.

The first inscription states the institutional affiliation of the Sri Lankan monastic site as follows:

> [The monastery of] the teachers (belonging to the) Sri Lankan (branch) of the Theriyas who had pleased (i.e. converted to Buddhism) the countries of Kashmir, Gandhāra, Cīna-Cilāta, Tosali, Avaranta, Vaṃsa, Vanavāsi, Yavana, Damila, Palura and Tambapaṇṇidīpa (= Sri Lanka) ...[18]

The second inscription gives a slightly more differentiated version:

> [The monastery of] the teachers (belonging to the) Mahāvihāravāsin (branch) of the Vibhajjavāda (faction among the [?]) Theriyas who had pleased Kashmir, Gandhāra ...[19]

This is the oldest known evidence for Sri Lankans identifying as members of the Theriya Nikāya. At least this term must have been familiar to the other lineages there as the Prākṛti form of the lineage known as Sthavira in Buddhist Sanskrit doxography. As I read the second inscription, it defines a genealogical position in three descending abstraction levels, similar to the structure: tribe, clan, family. The topmost level classifies them as Sthaviras, probably in opposition to the Mahāsāṃghika family of the early *nikāya* models. The term *vibhajjavāda* seems to denote a subgroup of the Sthaviras. Mahāvihāravāsin, in turn, is a subgroup of the Vibhajjavādins. This implies that Mahāvihāravāsin is the concrete *nikāya* name—namely, the lineage based in and named after the Mahāvihāra monastery in the Sri Lankan capital Anurādhapura—while other terms denote larger groups or families of *nikāyas* to which the Mahāvihāravāsins claimed to be affiliated.[20] We will see that this genealogical "home address" is pretty different from the *nikāya* identity that the Sri Lankan *vaṃsa* literature will start to promote about a century later, although the basic elements are already there, including a list of missionized countries which is going to play a major role for the well-known Mahinda legend—that is, the standard origin myth of Sri Lankan Buddhism—of the *vaṃsas*.

The use of *vibhajavāda* in the second inscription is difficult to interpret. It seems to denote something different here than it does in later Pāli historiographical and commentarial literature where *vibhajjavāda* is a doctrinal position shared by all Sthaviras. The present phrase, however, only makes sense if there was a notion that some Sthaviras were considered Vibhajjavādins while others were not. This idea of Vibhajyavāda as a *subgroup* of the Sthaviras is confirmed by at least two early *nikāya* genealogies of the Sanskrit tradition.[21] Cousins's (2001) detailed study on the problem supports Bareau's theory (1955: 169) that this term originally denoted a group of *nikāyas* affiliating to the Sthavira family but decidedly demarcating themselves from some other members of that family—namely, from those *nikāyas* affiliated to the Sarvāstivādins and those commonly labeled with the generic term *Pudgalavāda*. Possibly the term *Vibhajyavāda* originated as something like a group of "others," summarizing those *nikāyas* not profiled as Mahāsāṃghikas, Sarvāstivādins, or Pudgalavādins. According to Cousins, these "Vibhajyavāda *nikāyas*" comprised the Mahīśāsakas, the Dharmaguptakas, the Kāśyapīyas, and the Sri Lankans (Tambapaṇṇikas).[22]

If my interpretation is sound, the Nāgārjunakoṇḍa inscriptions testify to an early phase in which the Sri Lankan tradition orientated itself within the genealogical models of *nikāya* diversification as they had been developed by Indian Buddhists such as Vasumitra and the authors of Bhavya's sources. In this phase, they seem to have positioned themselves in a wider family of *nikāyas* they apparently accepted as equally authentic lineages—among them the Mahīśāsakas with whom the Mahāvihārins of Nāgārjunakoṇḍa were neighbors. This conciliatory idea of belonging to a wider family of "correct" *nikāyas* had changed radically by the time the *Dīpavaṃsa* was written.

A bold claim of exclusive authenticity: Theravāda in the *Dīpavaṃsa* and the *Mahāvaṃsa*

The first *nikāya* genealogy written on Sri Lankan soil was probably the *Dīpavaṃsa*, composed approximately in the fourth century CE, about one century after the Nāgārjunakoṇḍa inscriptions. The *Mahāvaṃsa*, written yet a century later, follows the *Dīpavaṃsa*'s account closely. It adds a perspective of inner–Sri Lankan sectarianism on which the *Dīpavaṃsa* is suspiciously silent. In the present section, I focus on the *Dīpavaṃsa*, mentioning the *Mahāvaṃsa* only when necessary.

It is obvious that the Mahāvihāra tradition had reflected much on *nikāya* genealogies and changed the view on their own sectarian affiliation profoundly since Nāgārjunakoṇḍa. As a result, the *Dīpavaṃsa* and the *Mahāvaṃsa* formulate a full-fledged sectarian statement with an exclusivist attitude that remained seminal for the future literature of the Mahāvihāravāsins. The major milestones were

1 the term *theravāda* appeared;
2 the concept of *vibhajyavāda* as a distinct Sthavira sub-lineage was dropped;
3 the genealogy gives a similarly "full" overview as their Indian counterparts, mentioning twenty-four *nikāyas* in total, and probably conflating Vasumitra's genealogy with something close to Bhavya's second list; and

4 the apparent allegiance with other lineages of the Sthavira branch was replaced by a sole claim to authenticity against all other known *nikāyas*, which were now entirely interpreted as "heretical apostates."

The term *theravāda* is exclusively used in the fifth chapter of the *Dīpavaṃsa*. The chapter starts with the well-known story of the first two rehearsals—that is, the narratives on how the Buddhist text corpus was allegedly created by an assembly of five hundred direct disciples of the Buddha shortly after his death and how, one century later, this collection was "rescued" from being diluted by a group of "wicked Bhikkhus" (*pāpabhikkhū*). The next fifty-five verses (Dīp 5.30–54) relate that endeavors to protect the Buddha's words from alteration were not always successful subsequently. Soon after the Second Rehearsal, the *saṃgha* disintegrated into various discordant lineages, each transmitting its own self-forged version of the *Tripiṭaka*.

It is noteworthy that the story of these rehearsals is narrated two times in the *Dīpavaṃsa*. Chapter 5 is the second version. The first version, located in Chapter 4, knows nothing of the term *theravāda* and does not refer to any permanent splits in the *saṃgha*. The two versions are an example of the well-known fact that the compilers of the *Dīpavaṃsa* conflated two or three different sources, sometimes redoubling or triplicating the same story, when these sources were in disagreement (Frauwallner 1955). As it seems, one of their sources for the two rehearsals was unaware of *nikāya* diversification and sectarian tensions. A confirmation for the existence of such a "*nikāya*-unaware" version of the rehearsals is given in the *Samantapāsādikā*. Like the first version of the *Dīpavaṃsa*, this fifth-century text narrates these stories—the first two rehearsals plus the third—without any mention of *nikāyas* or permanent splits. The terms *theravāda*, *theriya*, and so on are also unknown to the text. This surprising lack of sectarian references was expressed by Gethin (2012: 30) as follows:

> If we only read the *Samantapāsādikā* account we would learn nothing about a split between the Theriyas and Mahāsaṅghikas, nor of any other splits in the ordination lineage of the Saṅgha. The narrative does not even present the crisis that led up to the third council as involving a split in the Saṅgha, let alone indicate which schools might have resulted from that split.

The same could be said for the first account of the *Dīpavaṃsa*. Considering the hypothesis I have formulated in the previous section, the conclusion is obvious: the *Samantapāsādikā* and the first version of the *Dīpavaṃsa* reflect an ancient stock narrative of the two (respectively, three) rehearsals, while the *Dīpavaṃsa*'s second version represents a younger reformulation of this story along the new sectarian paradigm. The source of the *Samantapāsādika* and the *Dīpavaṃsa*'s first version was probably the historical introduction of the lost old-Sinhalese Vinaya commentary *Mahāṭṭhakathā*. The second version was written in a time in which the Sri Lankan traditions had started to reflect upon the fragmentation of the Buddhist world as a menace to the *sāsana*'s survival. It may have been the compilers of the *Dīpavaṃsa* themselves who had reshaped the story into a claim of their own lineage's unique superiority. But if so, it would be strange that they doubled the story at all. It is more likely that the sectarian version was taken from a source slightly older than the *Dīpavaṃsa*—probably from the likewise lost *Sīhaḷaṭṭhakathā-Mahāvaṃsa*.[23] If this interpretation is sound, we have a second indication for the supposition that the Sri Lankan traditions entered the world of *nikāya* diversification as latecomers. Unlike the Nāgārjunakoṇḍa inscriptions, in which they seem to have written themselves into a broader family of *nikāyas*, the fifth chapter of the *Dīpavaṃsa* formulates an exclusive statement of sole authenticity, expressed in the new term *theravāda*.[24]

In order to fashion the term *theravāda* as a trope for an exclusive orthodoxy claim, the *Dīpavaṃsa* conflates two different meanings of the term *vāda*. In Dīp 5.10 *theravāda* denotes a teaching, namely, the teaching (*vāda*) of the five hundred elders (*thera*) who conducted the First Rehearsal one year after the Buddha's death. The implied claim is that there can be nothing in the world of Buddhism that could be more true and authentic than what these personal pupils of the Buddha had compiled from what they had directly heard from the mouth of the master. This claim of authenticity is further emphasized by calling the *theravāda* the "pristine" or "topmost doctrine" (*aggavāda*, Dīp 5.14) and the (textual) "root-corpus" (*mūlasaṃgaha*, Dīp 5.31). In other passages (Dīp 5.16, 45, 49) *theravāda* is used as a lineage name, a succession of teachers from which other *vādas* broke away. The early Pāli *vaṃsas* do not use the term *nikāya*; the word for "sect" in *Dīpavaṃsa* and *Mahāvaṃsa* is *vāda*—a term that is gradually replaced or complemented by the word *nikāya* in later texts.[25] Thus, this second meaning of *theravāda* is pretty much the early Pāli rendering for what is called Sthavira Nikāya in Sanskrit texts.

The *Dīpavaṃsa* deploys a peculiar rhetorical twist in this passage consisting of two logical operations:

1. The already explained fusion of two distinct concepts into a single trope: Theravāda means both a corpus of teachings *and* an institutional succession of persons transmitting this teaching through time and space. With the play on this homonymy, the "original" inventory of Buddhist knowledge was claimed as the exclusive property of a demarcated social group.
2. A peculiar logic of splitting. The *Dīpavaṃsa's nikāya* genealogy is not a hereditary family tree but an "apostasy model." Here the implication is that any *nikāya* bearing a name different from Theravāda is by definition *not* in possession of the "original" doctrine.

The second point has often been misunderstood in Buddhist Studies. Bareau (1955) and other scholars read the relevant passages of the *Dīpavaṃsa* (Dīp 5.30, 54) as a variant of the bipartite pedigree that characterized other early *nikāya* genealogies. In these genealogies of the *première époque*, the *saṃgha* is presented as having split into eighteen *nikāyas* arranged in two *nikāya* families: a Sthavira and a Mahāsāmghika family. Often it is assumed that there was at least some degree of mutual acknowledgment among the members of the same family, whereas the main thrust of antagonism was directed against the members of the other family. In this sense, Gethin argues the main "sectarian" statement of the *Dīpavaṃsa* was: "We are Theriyas, and not Mahāsaṅghikas" (2012: 42). This interpretation completely overlooks the peculiar "insider perspective" of the *Dīpavaṃsa*. The *Dīpavaṃsa* may rely on Vasumitra's or another *première époque nikāya* scheme[26] but reformulates it with an idiosyncratic twist: The compilers did not understand their own lineage, that is, the "Theravāda," as a member—not even the head member—of any *nikāya* family. Even more, neither the *Dīpavaṃsa* nor any other Pāli text has ever stated that the "original" *saṃgha* had *divided into* the eighteen *nikāyas*. They rather understand the logic of division as a sequence of *breakaways*. Hence, for the *Dīpavaṃsa's* insider perspective there is *one* authentic tradition. It was called "Theravāda" right from the outset and before any break happened. This lineage continued "unbroken" ever since its beginning. The other *nikāyas* came up not by breaking the institutional integrity of the lineage, but through individual members turning "apostate," leaving, and starting new lineages.

Hence, the dichotomy of the *Dīpavaṃsa* and all later *vaṃsas* runs *not* between "Theravāda" versus Mahāsaṃghika, but "Theravāda" against all others. This one-against-many antagonism is put in a nutshell by the *Dīpavaṃsa's* famous banyan tree simile:

> There are seventeen breakaway-*vādas* and one unbroken *vāda*, together with the unbroken one they are eighteen altogether. The excellent Theravāda resembles a huge banyan tree. It is the complete *sāsana* of the Jina, with nothing added, nothing removed. The remaining *vādas* are like thorns growing on that tree.[27]

The seventeen "breakaway *vādas*"—or "apostate *vādas*," to use a term familiar to European history adepts—are also collectively labeled *ācariyavādā* in the *Dīpavaṃsa* and later *vaṃsa* literature or *ācāryanikāya* in *Nikāyasaṅgraha* and *Saddharmaratnākara*, "doctrines/lineages of (other) teachers"—a phraseology quite close to the Christian polemical idea of a sect (see the earlier discussion). Among them are eleven non-Mahāsāṃghika groups. For Indian *nikāya* genealogies of the *première époque*, these eleven lineages are members of the Sthavira family. The Pāli *vaṃsas* disagree. For them there is no such thing like a Sthavira family. There is only one Sthavira Nikāya, called "Theravāda" by them. *Nikāyas*, like Mahīśāsaka, Dharmaguptaka, Sarvāstivāda, and so on, are *not* "Theravādins," nor are they in any way superior to the Mahāsāṃghikas. They simply broke away from the "Theravāda" (*pabhinnā theravādato*) a little later. Without exception, all seventeen *ācariyavādas* have

> split the true meaning of the Doctrine and some portions of the Collection; setting aside some portions of difficult passages, they altered them. Forsaking the original rules regarding nouns, genders, composition, and the embellishments of style, they changed all that.[28]

The only true lineage has no *nikāya* name other than "Theravāda." Consequently, neither the Tambapaṇṇikas nor the Mahāvihāravāsins occupy a separate place in the *Dīpavaṃsa*'s or later *nikāya* genealogies (See Figure 1.1). Their compilers/authors identify their own lineage as a mere local emplacement of the original "Theravādins."

In contrast to Bareau's and other scholars' reading, the "sectarian" perspective of the *Dīpavaṃsa* does not see the history of *nikāyas* as falling into two branches (Theravāda and Mahāsāṃghika) but distinguishes only between Theravāda as the "unbroken" *(abhinnavāda)* "original" (*aggavāda*) lineage and seventeen "apostate" breakaway lineages *(bhinnavāda)*, also collectively called "lineages of (other) teachers" (*ācariyavāda*). These breakaway lineages fall into three families. The *Mahāvaṃsa* will later add a fourth family of "apostates," starting with the Abhayagiri. The Mahāvihāra Nikāya never appear in these genealogies because their authors consider it—that is, their own lineage—to never have broken away from the original Theravāda. The six *nikāyas* on the lower margin are considered to have arisen at a later time (*aparo uppannā*). No affiliation is given for them and the reading of the last one seems to be corrupt.

The *Dīpavaṃsa* paints a picture of a Buddhist world in which the prophecy of the "true *dharma*'s decay" (*saddharmavipralopa*) was already widely fulfilled. The remainders of those carrying the "true" *dharma* were surrounded by a multitude of "heretics" promoting only "counterfeit images" thereof (*saddharmapratirūpaka*). This brings us to an important question. Did the compilers and authors of the Pāli *vaṃsa*s accept any community outside of Sri Lanka as legitimate "Theravādins" at all? Or were they presuming that Sri Lanka was meanwhile the only place where "the Theravāda" still existed? This question is not answered, or even raised, by the text itself or any later one. Hence, we can only tentatively assess the probabilities based on indirect evidence.

What would be the *Dīpavaṃsa*'s criteria for the identification of such a group?

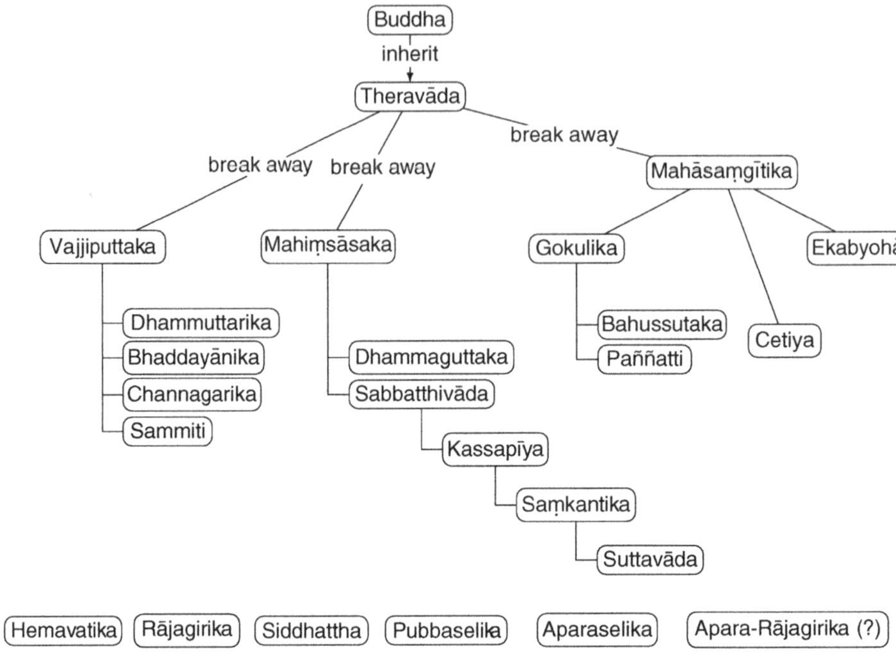

Figure 1.1 ***Nikāya*** genealogy of the ***Dīpavaṃsa***, representing the "insider view" of the text.

1 All twenty-three *ācariyavādas* mentioned in the *Dīpavaṃsa*—seventeen primary plus the six "later" (*aparo upannā*) lineages (Dīp 5.54)—are discarded. This excludes virtually all *nikāyas* known to us from Indian Buddhist literature and epigraphy, including the Mahīśāsakas, Dharmaguptakas, and Kāśyapīyas that Bareau and Cousins allege to have formed a common subgroup with the Sri Lankan lineage. They are as much "apostate lineages" (*bhinnavāda*) as all the others. The same holds true for the Haimavatas, who are regarded as the successors of the "pristine Sthaviras" (*pūrva-Sthavira*) by Vasumitra and two of Bhavya's lists (see the following discussion).

2 The *Dīpavaṃsa* expects a true "Theravāda" community to possess a *Tripiṭaka* exactly identical to the one transmitted by its own lineage. The verse quoted earlier does not explicitly state that this *Tripiṭaka* needs to be in Māgadhī (Pāli), but even if it was in a different dialect, conformity with the Pāli would be expected, down to the rules of grammar and style. This excludes all *Sūtra Piṭaka* parallels—not to speak of *Vinaya* and *Abhidharma* material—ever found on the Indian subcontinent, Central Asia, China, or Tibet. If we take the fluidity and openness of the *Tripiṭaka* idea during the early expansion of Buddhism into account, the chances for the existence of an identical parallel to the Sri Lankan "Pāli Canon" tend toward zero. The only possibility would be that the "Indian Proto-Theriyas" (see earlier discussion) were transmitting an already complete and closed "canon" in the third century BCE and that both, the Proto-Theriya branches of Sri Lanka and India (or elsewhere), had maintained the consistency of that canon until the *Dīpavaṃsa* was written down. Disregarding the unlikeliness of this scenario, such a "Sri Lanka-independent Pāli Canon" was never found or cited in the Buddhist literature of India or elsewhere.[29]

3 For the compilers of the *Dīpavaṃsa* and the authors of later *vaṃsa*s, the Sri Lankan lineage was part of a once widespread group. For them, the "Indian proto-Theriyas," the "Sri Lankan proto-Theriyas," and the Mahāvihārins are all identical to the pristine Sthaviras. The *vaṃsa*s relate the well-known story of how the Sthaviras expanded to the borders of the then known world by an organized missionary effort in the time of Aśoka. They might have at least assumed that "true Theravādins" may still exist in the regions covered by those missionaries. Based on the fact that the *Dīpavaṃsa* still narrates the missionary story, Gethin states that the Sri Lankan Theriyas claimed "not so much to be the authentic Theras, but to be a branch of the authentic Theras" (2012: 47). We need to remark, however, that the compilers/authors of the *vaṃsa*s have been aware that the so-called Aśoka missions are a story about a very remote past. It can hardly have escaped them that the countries mentioned in the narrative as well as the Buddhist heartlands in Northeastern India were "meanwhile" dominated by *nikāya*s they deemed heretical. Likely, their own country, Sri Lanka, was the only exception known to them.

All in all, the chances are low that the Sri Lankan tradition of the fourth century knew about—and even were in contact with—an independent community of "Theravādins" that would have matched the criteria of the *Dīpavaṃsa*. They surely believed that other emplacements of the "pristine Sthaviras" had existed in the remote past, and they might—perhaps—have assumed that descendants of them could still exist somewhere in other borderlands. But the thrust of the *Dīpavaṃsa*'s argument rests definitely not on the idea of a powerful alliance of geographically widespread Ur-Sthaviras, but rather on the heroism of Sri Lanka viewed as a small—and probably the last—resort of "true Buddhism" against the superiority of "apostates," *ācariyavādas*, who promote their "broken" and "adulterated" ways in mainland India nowadays.

Of course, when the *Dīpavaṃsa* was compiled, the Sri Lankan Theriyas were already in the process of gaining territory beyond Sri Lanka. During the following centuries, the three Sri Lankan (sub-)*nikāyas* became one stream of the Buddhist tradition to reckon with in the Buddhist world. They expanded its presence in South and northeastern India and established relationships with Southeast Asia, China, Indonesia, and, for a while, with Tibet. Also, the Indian *nikāya* genealogists no longer ignored them. By the sixth century, the Sri Lankans had secured a position as one of four "major lineages" (*mahānikāya, āryanikāya*) constituting the Buddhist scene of the day. Indian *nikāya* genealogies (Vinītadeva, Yijing, and all schemes of Bareau's *troisième époche*) now collectively call them "the Sthaviras." Sthaviras different from the three Sri Lankan *nikāyas* were unknown to them. Hence, if non–Sri Lanka–derived Sthaviras had ever existed—and I seriously doubt it[30]—they had vanished into thin air by that time.

Buddhist diversity in a retrospective view: the *Nikāyasaṅgraha*

From the sixth century onward, the antithetical models of *nikāya* diversity gradually went out of use in India and gave way to a more conciliatory idea of four equally authentic parallel transmissions of the Buddha's teachings manifested in four "main lineages" (*caturāryanikāya*): Sarvāstivāda, Mahāsāṃghika, Sammatīya, and Sthavira, with the latter collectively denoting the three Sri Lankan lineages. This concept of equally valid parallel transmissions of the Buddhist teaching became the standard approach to history also among later Indian, Chinese, and Tibetan Buddhist authors. In Sri Lanka this model was apparently also shared by many from a certain time onward.[31] Here, it was possibly only Mahāvihārin authors who kept alive the strictly antithetical view, first formulated in *Dīpavaṃsa* and *Mahāvaṃsa* and rewritten in the late colonial period to become one of the basic models of the modern Buddhist organization of diversity.

One of their later works endorsing a rigorous *nikāya* antagonism is the *Nikāyasaṅgraha.*[32] Completed in the late fourteenth century by Jayabāhu Dharmakīrti, this text can be seen as the epitome of the Mahāvihāra tradition's take on Buddhist sectarianism. It presents history as the permanent battle against the "inner enemies" of the *sāsana*, namely, monastic laxity, disunity, and heresy. The work places itself in the tradition of the Pāli *vaṃsas*, so structure and content follow *Mahāvaṃsa, Cūḷavaṃsa*, and *Mahābodhivaṃsa* closely, and they are often cited. The *Nikāyasaṅgraha* was written in Classical Sinhala on the occasion of a *sāsana* purification probably in 1386. The author was the head of the Sri Lankan monastic community (*saṃgharāja* or *mahāsvāmī*) and presided over the purification act.[33]

The text was written after two important historical events that had an influence on its presentation of history:

1 The saṃgha unification of Pārākramabāhu I, which de jure signified the end of *nikāya* diversity within Sri Lanka in the twelfth century. In this time, "neoconservative" forces dominated the clerical hierarchy—now under centralized control by a Saṃgharāja/Mahāsvāmī and a board of monastic representatives (*kāraka-saṃgha*). The new leadership understood the unified *saṃgha* as the continuation of the ancient Mahāvihāra Nikāya, its ordination lineage, and its textual traditions (though the Mahāvihāra monastery proper had been abandoned during the preceding centuries of Sri Lankan/South Indian warfare and though the ordination lineage had to be reintroduced from Southeast Asia). The literary wealth of the Abhayagiri and Jetavana traditions had mostly—if not completely—vanished by the time Jayabāhu Dharmakīrti wrote the *Nikāyasaṅgraha.*[34]
2 The extinction of Buddhism in most parts of mainland India.

Thus, Dharmakīrti was writing in a world in which the "heretical *ācariyavādas*" had vanished, not only in Sri Lanka but also in mainland India, while what he regarded to be the "true" *sāsana*—namely, the "Sthaviravāda" as passed down by the Mahāvihāra lineage—had prevailed. It is unlikely that he knew very much about the flourishing contemporary Buddhist cultures of Tibet and East Asia. His horizon of the Buddhist world must have encompassed an area mainly consisting of Sri Lanka and parts of South India, as well as parts of what were to become Burma and Siam—only a fraction of what constituted the Buddhist world of yore but a world in which the "true" Theriya lineage had finally triumphed over its rivals. Probably Dharmakīrti would have regarded Sri Lanka as the center of this world, the country that preserved the "true" *sāsana* against all dangers for many centuries and caused it to be spread—or revived—in Suvarṇabhūmi (then understood as comprising parts of what were to become Myanmar and Thailand) more recently.

But the danger was not over—considering the Buddhist idea of universal decay, it can never be. As a recent study has shown, the concern for the *saṃgha*'s purity was more acute in post-reform Sri Lanka than ever before (Gornall 2020: 5). Thus, the dominating appeal of the text is the preservation of the *sāsana* for as long as possible, even if against all odds and even if the fight is destined to be ultimately lost. This is the view with which the author looks upon his own time: the "heresies" of old may be gone, but the underlying problems are as vital as ever. Undisciplined monks can populate the *saṃgha* and must be excluded by force. Such *sāsana* purifications (*sāsanavisodhana*)—the removal of "unworthy" monks in a state-enforced monastic act—had already been performed five times after Parākramabāhu unified the *saṃgha*. Dharmakīrti had witnessed two in his own lifetime and acted as a chairman for one of them. The last quarter of the text deals with these purification acts. The earlier three quarters basically show that it was the same form of laxity and disrespectful behavior of monks that caused the historical heresies to arise in the first place.

The distinction between disciplined (*suśīla*) and undisciplined (*duhśīla/pāpa*) monks is the integrative narrative subject from which the *Nikāyasaṅgraha*'s plot, value structure, and message unfold. According to the text, the whole problem started seven days after the Buddha's *parinirvāṇa* when a "bad monk" (*abhadra mahaṇek*) called Subhadra spoke to his fellow brethren who bemoaned the Buddha's death:

> Stop grieving, friends. Stop crying. This chief ascetic, who brought us nothing but trouble by explaining what is good and what is bad, is now dead, and now we are the lords of our own will. Why, then, grieve for something which is cause for joy? From now on we do what we want, and we don't do what we don't want.[35]

On hearing this, the great disciple Mahākāśyapa decided it was necessary to stabilize the teaching of the master by bringing it to a fixed form. Thus, the creation of the Sthaviravāda—as an institutionalized textual entity—was a reaction to upcoming laxity in the *saṃgha* that would have ruined the Buddha's message in the long run. This episode sets the stage for the narrative to unfold. Its major milestones and turning points—the three rehearsals, the *nikāya* schisms, the arrival of the *sāsana* in Sri Lanka, the splits of the Sri Lankan lineages—are well known and need not be repeated here.

In the ideology of the *Nikāyasaṅgraha*, the later emergence of "heretical" *nikāyas* is a logical continuation of Subhadra's destructive "liberalism," namely, his disrespect for the Buddha and his readiness to change the master's teaching for the sake of his own comfort. The first *nikāya* split is directly connected to the "malicious *bhikṣus*" who had been expelled in the context of the Second Rehearsal—the protagonists of the next attempt to water down the principles of the Vinaya. The text states that after being expelled they went to a remote province governed by a ruler who was unable to distinguish *dharma* from non-*dharma*. Hence, free from the coercive control of a competent *dharma*-king, they settled here and composed all kinds of "weird texts nobody had ever heard of before" (*abhūtapūrva vū apūrvapāṭha*) as well as "commentaries in accordance with their own opinions, oblivious to the contradictions to the previous tradition" (*pūrvāparavirōdha no-balā abhiprāyānukūla vū arthakathā*). By this act of "text forgery," they broke away from the Sthaviravāda and formed the Mahāsāṃghika Nikāya.[36]

The rest of the seventeen *ācāryanikāyas* are merely enumerated. No genealogy is given for them and, again, no value distinction between Sthavira-derived and Mahāsāṃghika-derived *nikāyas* is made. In opposition to the *ācāryanikāyas* stands not the "Theravāda" but the Sthāviriya Nikāya. Unlike *Dīpavaṃsa* and *Mahāvaṃsa*, the *Nikāyasaṅgraha* distinguishes clearly between Sthāviriya Nikāya and Sthaviravāda—the former is the "original" lineage of the *saṃgha* and identical to the Mahāvihāra Nikāya, the latter denotes the textual corpus of that lineage. Interestingly the manuscripts always witness several reading variants whenever the term *Sthāviriya* occurs in the text, while they always agree for the term *Sthaviravāda*. This suggests that the former term was rather unfamiliar to the copyists. According to the text, the Pāli *Tripiṭaka* is identical to the Sthaviravāda and contains every single word the Buddha had uttered in the forty-five years between his Awakening and his *parinirvāṇa*.[37] This "sharpened canon formula" excludes the possibility that any authentic Buddha-word can have been transmitted aside the monastic mainstream. In other words, every text attributed to the Buddha but not included in the Pāli *Tripiṭaka* as the author knew it is a "fake-*dharma*" (*saddharmapratibimba*) produced by "evil monks" (*pāpabhikṣu*) or by non-Buddhists disguised as Buddhist monks (*bhikṣupratirūpakatīrthaka*).

For the *Nikāyasaṅgraha*, most such "fake-*dharmas*" were produced by the later *nikāyas* that have originated after the Third Rehearsal. Their story is peculiar. The text follows *Dīpavaṃsa* and *Mahāvaṃsa* insofar as to claim that in the time of Aśoka non-Buddhists (*tīrthaka*) had infiltrated the *saṃgha* and proclaimed their wrong beliefs as the teaching of the Buddha. In the earlier *vaṃsas*, the story is over after these *tīrthakas* had been exposed and expelled. The *Nikāyasaṅgraha* expands their story: they attempted to enter the *saṃgha* again but were rejected by all Sthāviriya communities. However, they were accepted into communities of the other seventeen *nikāyas*. Under their protection, they "reversed and messed up the three *piṭakas*." Finally, they split into nine new *nikāyas*—the six "later *nikāyas*" known from *Dīpavaṃsa* and *Mahāvaṃsa* plus Vaitulya, Andhaka, and Anya-Mahāsāṃghika. Each of these nine *nikāyas* is associated with certain "fake-*dharmas*." The list given by the *Nikāyasaṅgraha* contains well-known proto-Mahāyāna, Mahāyāna and Vajrayāna texts like the *Rāṣṭrapālasūtra*, the *Ratnakūṭa*, the *Sarvatathāgatatattvasaṅgraha*, *Māyājālatantra*, *Guhyasamāja*, *Cakrasaṃvara*, and others. Most interesting in this respect is the list of Tantric texts that is attributed to the Vājiriya or Vajraparvata Nikāya by the *Nikāyasaṅgraha*. This list seems to represent a Sri Lankan version of the "18 Tantras topos" known from Amoghavajra, Jñānamitra and the Tibetan rÑiṅ-ma-pas.[38] This list must go back to the period of strong Tantric Buddhist presence in Sri Lanka (seventh through the ninth centuries, perhaps still later), it was certainly not created by the author of the *Nikāyasaṅgraha*. On the contrary, we can safely assume that Dharmakīrti knew not much more about these texts than their mere titles.

In the context of the antithetical constellation of "true" Buddhism versus heresies, the *Nikāyasaṅgraha*'s image of India is peculiar. After the *sāsana* was brought to Sri Lanka by Mahinda, not much good was coming from Jambudvīpa (India) anymore.[39] Mahinda transformed Sri Lanka into the new home of the "true" Sthaviravāda, carried by the Sthāviriya Nikāya, which, in turn, is embodied in the Mahāvihāra. Jambudvīpa is almost a counter-image. It is a notorious source of "heresies" spilling over to Sri Lanka time and time again. Here they were accepted by the Abhayagiri and Jetavana Nikāyas but fiercely rejected by the Mahāvihāra. It is interesting to note that "heresies" never originated on Sri Lankan soil. Whatever wrong beliefs the Abhayagiri and Jetavana traditions accepted, were always imported from Jambudvīpa. The text even states that King Sena II (ninth century) set up guards all around the Sri Lankan shore to prevent "counterfeit *dharmas*" from entering the country.

The most notorious "heresy" adopted by Abhayagiri and Jetavana was a teaching called Vaitulyavāda. Scholars have generally understood this as some form of Mahāyāna or proto-Mahāyāna.[40] Dharmakīrti sees Vaitulyavāda as an independent Indian *nikāya*. He even speaks of the Vaitulyavādins as a fourth Sri Lankan *nikāya* besides the common three.[41] They transmitted a corpus of texts called *Vaitulyapiṭaka* that, according to the *Nikāyasaṅgraha*, was initially produced by those *tīrthakas* who had infiltrated the *saṃgha* in the time of Aśoka.[42] The *Nikāyasaṅgraha* informs us—accurately or not—that this "heresy" (*adharmavāda*) was suppressed and its books burned in Sri Lanka several times since its first appearance in the third century. But it reappeared again and again. The third arrival in the time of Mahāsena (3rd/4th cent.) is the dramatic nadir of the *Nikāyasaṅgraha* and signifies the blackest hour for the religious heroes of the Mahāvihāra. Due to a conspiracy involving the Abhayagiri monks, the king, and a Vaitulya adept from South India, the faithful monks of the Mahāvihāra were blackmailed into either adopting the Vaitulyavāda or die. Of course, they refused:

> Even if we starve now, if we accept a non-*dharma* as the *dharma*, many people will assume the same and end up in hell. And all will be our fault. Therefore, we will not accept the Vaitulyavāda even if this would mean the end of our lives and chastity.[43]

Instead of dying, the pious monks from several Sthaviravāda-devoted monasteries in and around Anurādhapura abandoned their *vihāras* and fled to the south of the island. In their absence, the Abhayagiri rose to dominance, while the Mahāvihāra monastery was destroyed. The *Mahāvaṃsa* adds that the ruins were looted and taken to enlarge and decorate the Abhayagiri's monastic buildings.[44] This may have been the end of "true" Buddhism in the world. Luckily Mahāvihāra-friendly forces in the palace convinced king Mahāsena to rebuild the monastery and to invite the monks to return. A little later, he endangered the Mahāvihāra's integrity again by trying to build the Jetavana monastery in a spot violating the Mahāvihāra's constitutive boundary (*sīmā*).

This episode is obviously key to the antagonism between Mahāvihāra and Abhayagiri, and I suspect that the interpretation of these two monasteries as the headquarters of two rival *nikāyas* goes back to tensions that gained momentum during Mahāsena's rule.[45] Sadly we know only the Mahāvihāra version of the story, but there are hints suggesting that their version was not unrivaled.[46] It is more than mere speculation to assume that Abhayagirivāsins did not agree with their depiction as the "bogeyman" of Sri Lankan Buddhist history. From indirect evidence, we do at least know that some members of the Abhayagiri and Jetavana launched a counter-accusation, saying that it was the Mahāvihārins, not the Abhayagirivāsins, who corrupted the Vinaya (basically implying that the Mahāvihāra was the actual "apostate" faction).[47]

To my knowledge, scholars have never seriously doubted the historicity of the episode with the Mahāvihāra's temporary abandonment, subsequent destruction, and the attempted ritual disintegration of its compound. However, I think there is good reason to at least consider that we are dealing with a "sectarian" fiction here. From a slab stone inscription found in the Jetavana,[48] we know that the *saṃgha* of Anurādhapura was in turmoil around this time because of the introduction of a "Vayatuḍala book."[49] The inscription is very fragmentary, perhaps intentionally damaged, but it seems to say that the status of the text was disputed across the monasteries of Anurādhapura. There seem to have been advocates as well as opponents in all monasteries of the capital, including Mahāvihāra and Abhayagiri.[50] The king issuing the inscription was clearly in favor of the text in question. He even seems to have ordered (or allowed?) it to be studied and copied in all monasteries.[51] Obviously, the problem was not solved by this verdict, so the status of Vaitulyavāda was still an issue when the *Mahāvaṃsa* was written two centuries later. Strangely, the *Dīpavaṃsa*—probably composed at a time when eyewitnesses of whatever happened under Mahāsena were still alive—remains silent on the whole affair. Therefore, I suspect that the antithetical picture of Mahāvihāra and Abhayagiri as camps of two opposing approaches to Buddhism may have developed gradually—idealized, historically deepened by the account of an early schism and narratively expanded by different versions of the "Mahāvihāra in danger" topos (i.e., its destruction/resurrection and *sīmā* affair) during the intervening period between the composition of *Dīpavaṃsa* and *Mahāvaṃsa*. The extent to which the Mahāvihāra has ever been the decided stronghold of "anti-Vaitulyavāda resistance" has to be reevaluated, once scholars systematically scrutinize the dichotomous image painted by the *Mahāvaṃsa*, the *Nikāyasaṅgraha*, and so on. This picture becomes especially doubtful if we understand "Mahāvihāra" not only as a local monastery of Anurādhapura but also as an island-wide *nikāya* network consisting of hundreds of monastic communities.

The *Nikāyasaṅgraha* reports that the Vaitulyavāda books were again burned after the Mahāvihāra was rebuilt, but these heretics returned for a fourth time in the sixth century.[52] From this time onward, as the text says, the Vaitulyavāda "persisted in this country among the foolish folks" *(bālajanayan kerehi)*. Neither the *Mahāvaṃsa* nor the *Nikāyasaṅgraha* ever specify which text titles the *Vaitulyapiṭaka* concretely contained, and I doubt that Dharmakīrti had more than a vague idea. All he has to say of these texts is based on the meager information earlier Mahāvihāra authors had already given.[53] Interestingly, neither Dharmakīrti nor these earlier sources saw the well-known (proto-)Mahāyāna texts *Rāṣṭrapālaparipṛcchā*, the *Aṅulimālīyasūtra*, and *Ratnakūṭa* as part of the *Vaitulyapiṭaka*; they are assumed to be independent texts. Dharmakīrti even believed them to have been composed by *nikāyas* different from the Vaitulyavādins.[54] We should take this as a reminder for not being overhasty in associating the ancient anti-Vaitulya discourse with what we may understand as "Mahāyāna Buddhism" today. We cannot know for certain which types of texts, ideas, images and practices the fifth- and sixth-century authors of the *Atthakathās* or the *Mahāvaṃsa*—not to speak of much later authors like Dharmakīrti—would have classified as "Vaitulyavāda."

The last big "heresy" that "beset" Sri Lanka was called Vājiriyavāda. According to the *Nikāyasaṅgraha* it was brought to Sri Lanka from Jambudvīpa by a "*tīrthaka* in the guise of a *bhikṣu*" belonging to the Vajraparvata Nikāya" (Nikāya-s chapt. 16). The king of this time was Sena I (early ninth century). The *Nikāyasaṅgraha* calls him "Matvaḷa Sen" ("Mad Sena" or "Sena the Drunkard"). This shows already the text's disregard for this king. He "had not associated with learned people" (*viyatun kerehi no-hasaḷa*) and, therefore, accepted the new "heresy" (*adharma*) "like a grasshopper jumping into fire, taking it for gold" (*ratranä-yi sitā gini vadanā paḷangak'hu seyin*). The text gives little information on the content of the Vājiravāda but describes it as a "secret instruction" (*rahasbaṇa*). The list of text titles attributed to the Vājiriya Nikāya in an earlier chapter (see the previous discussion) makes it obvious that this story reflects the period of Tantric Buddhist activities in Sri Lanka. This suggests a relation of the term *Vājiravāda* to the well-known expression *Vajrayāna*—although we should be similarly cautious as with the Vaitulyavāda = Mahāyāna equation.[55] Interestingly, the *Nikāyasaṅgraha* informs us that the Vājiriyavāda, although it was allegedly suppressed immediately by the following king (Sena II, second half of the ninth century), "persisted secretly among the foolish, unlearned folks (*lāmaka vū ajñānayan*) in this country." The text does not explicitly mention that this "undercover culture" ever vanished, not even in the context of Parākramabāhu's reform.

As an addition to the Vājiravāda chapter, the *Nikāyasaṅgraha* informs us about another "heresy" called the "teaching of the Blue Robe" (*nīlapaṭadarśana*). This teaching never made it to Sri Lanka,[56] but Dharmakīrti seems to have considered it related to the Vājiriyavāda and, therefore, gives us the story of this tradition in India. According to the text, it was created by a member of the Saṃmittīya Nikāya in the time of the Indian king Śrī Harṣa, who ruled in the southern Madhurā (Madurai) and was a contemporary of the Sri Lankan king Kumāradāsa (early sixth century).[57] According to the *Nikāyasaṅgraha* the *Nīlapaṭadarśana* was based on a book proclaiming that the Three Jewels of Buddhism were the whore, booze, and the god of love.[58] In depicting how the Indian king put an end to the group cherishing such an "outrageous book" (*avyavasthitgrantha*), the *Nikāyasaṅgraha* arrives at its peak level of brutality and sarcasm:

> Pretending to be pleased by this teaching, he [the king] sent for the bearers of the *Nīlapaṭadarśana* together with their books. Then he put them into a house together with their books and performed an Agnipūjā.[59]

Dharmakīrti claims that some followers of the group survived this disaster, so that this teaching has "persisted up to now, like pestilence the root of which is unbroken."[60] In this case he definitely means up to his own time, but he is speaking of India, not Sri Lanka.

As already said, the whole trouble produced by the parallelism of different *nikāyas* in Sri Lanka comes to an abrupt end in the 15th year of Parākramabāhu's reign (1165 CE). At least this is so according to the *Nikāyasaṅgraha*, whether the information is historically accurate is a different question.[61] The text says that the king heard about the decline of the *śāsana* due to the *nikāya* splits and because some "evil monks" had accepted non-*dharmas* like the Vaitulyavāda. Supported by the Thera Mahākāśyapa of Udumbagiri, a forest hermitage of the Mahāvihāra Nikāya,

> he sent for several hundred ill-disciplined, evil Bhikṣus of the three *nikāyas* Dharmaruci, Sāgalika and Vaitulyavāda who spoil the unstained Śāsana of the Omniscient One with their wrong practices. He assembled them in a creeper-bower and, standing there through the three watches of the night, he had them all removed from the Śāsana. Having (thus) purified the Śāsana of the Buddha he unified the three *nikāyas*."[62]

To "remove someone from the *Śāsana*" in this context means to exclude them from the *saṃgha*. The king himself is not able to do that. Monks have to perform the required ritual. This is why the causative is used. The king has the duty to prevent the excluded ex-monks—now normal citizens under his jurisdiction—from taking up the robes again.

Interestingly, the Vaitulyavāda is counted as a *nikāya* of its own, separate from Dharmaruci (Abhayagiri) and Sāgalika (Jetavana). Together with the Mahāvihāra, this would be four *nikāyas* in total. In any case, the same sentence speaks of "three *nikāya*" having been unified. This is an example for the many small inconsistencies which abound in the text.

For the *Nikāyasaṅgraha* the era of Buddhist *nikāya* pluralism ends here. For the rest of the text, only the Mahāvihāra tradition has prevailed. Still, supervising and censoring the *saṃgha* is as necessary as ever, with the text calling for regular *sāsana* purifications. We should not romanticize a system installed for the maintenance of the *saṃgha*'s "purity." *Sāsana* purifications are a political instrument of systemic violence, depriving many people of their livelihoods and damaging the social status of the ones expelled from the order as well as their families. These measures are surely not welcomed by everybody and must have confounded large parts of society whenever they were performed. As the acting Saṃgharāja of the island, the author himself held the highest position in this system. As such he needed to be backed by royal force. This is why the *Nikāyasaṅgraha* was written. And this is why it is not addressed to the monks of Sri Lanka but to kings and ministers. To plan and execute a *sāsana* purification the Saṃgharāja needs to convince the state authorities of its appropriateness and necessity:

> Keeping this word in mind, it is proper for noble people with authority, suitable to their time, to make efforts to remove the stains of misconduct, which might have appeared in the Śāsana of the Omniscient in their respective area, to make the Śāsana of the Buddha, which is to persist for 5,000 years, shine in glory and—as the desirable fruit resulting from this act—to attain the fulfillment of everything eligible, namely the future attainment of heaven and liberation.[63]

Conclusion

Reading against the grain of the early *vaṃsa* literature, we have found no traces for the use of sectarian concepts, terminologies or narratives for about five centuries of Sri Lankan Buddhism, neither in the context of local conflicts, nor for the sake of "international" self-promotion. The oldest known evidence for a Sri Lankan *nikāya* identity dates to the third century CE and is connected to a Sri Lankan monastic settlement in the capital of the South Indian Ikṣvāku dynasty. Here they identified as belonging to the lineage family of the Sthaviras, apparently expressing proximity to some and remoteness from other *nikāyas* co-occupying the site. The evidence also indicates that local monastic rivalries in the Sri Lankan capital were meanwhile interpreted as *nikāya* differences. With the compilation of the *Dīpavaṃsa* a new *nikāya* identity was created such that the Sri Lankans no longer claimed proximity to other *nikāyas* of India but highlighted their uniqueness as heirs of the only true and authentic form of Buddhism. A new word was created, *theravāda*, which simultaneously denotes "original" Buddhism and the Sri Lankan lineage. All other *nikāyas* were declared "apostates" who had lost the original heritage of the Buddha. It is not quite clear whether the compilers of the *Dīpavaṃsa* assumed still existing old "Theravāda" communities outside of Sri Lanka, although this is unlikely. Once the imagination of the Buddhist world as a sectarian battle field was established, ancient origin stories, like the accounts of the three rehearsals and the coming of Mahinda, became reformulated as explanations of how Buddhist diversity emerged and how the "correct" Buddhist tradition made it to its Sri Lankan refuge.

The *Mahāvaṃsa* extends the "apostasy" accusation to the traditions of two monasteries of Anurādhapura. The lineages of Abhayagiri and Jetavana were now regarded as "heretics" who had broken with the true "Theravāda," like so many Indian groups before. The Mahāvihāra lineage, to which the author of the *Mahāvaṃsa* belonged, claimed to be the sole representatives of the Sthaviras, or "Theravādins," remaining in Sri Lanka (or on earth?). Their rival lineages' own claim to be legitimate successors of the Sthavira lineage was denied by the *Mahāvaṃsa* and all later Mahāvihāra literature. This denial stood in open contradiction to the Indian and Chinese apperception of the "sectarian" topography of the Buddhist world which, from the sixth century onward, understood Mahāvihāra, Abhayagiri and Jetavana as three equally legitimate representatives of the Sthavira Nikāya. The Abhayagiri's reputation as a "Mahāyāna" and "Tantric" Buddhist center provided no contradiction in this respect. This was only problematic for the Mahāvihārins who claimed to always have "protected" the Pāli-based "original" form of Buddhism from such "heresies."

We should beware of adopting the dualistic projection of Mahāvihāra authors—their "we against the rest"—as a descriptive model for the history of Buddhism, even in Sri Lanka itself. This may obscure more than it explains. The realities of cultural history are often more fluid and complex than the stories projected on them—this is especially the case with insider perspectives of groups narrativizing their own heroism within a world full of enemies. There is clear evidence that the Mahāvihāra's association of the Theriya Nikāya with a certain doctrinal concept—Pāli *Tripiṭaka*-based Śrāvakayāna—was of limited scope before the Polonnaruva period (eleventh century), and perhaps even after. Indian Buddhist scholarship never shared this view. Neither did the Sri Lankan Abhayagiri and Jetavana Nikāyas. Even for the Mahāvihāra Nikāya such a "Pāli/Śrāvakayāna-only approach" may not have been so historically stable and all-encompassing as the historiographers would have us believe.

Furthermore, we should not uncritically imagine the Sri Lankan *nikāyas* of the Anurādhapura period as island-wide organizational and doctrinal unities. Indeed, we have no other information than that the monks of each monastic community on the island were ordained into one of the three Vinaya versions that together constitute the Theriya Nikāya family. Hence, each monastery must have belonged to either the Mahāvihāra, Abhayagiri or Jetavana (sub-)Nikāya. But this does not mean that they all looked upon the respective monastery in the capital as their doctrinal and organizational sovereign. Such a degree of centralization was, at best, achieved in a much later time when the monastic landscape was controlled by a Saṃgharāja. In the Anurādhapura period, the transregional influence of the three *nikāyas* must have been much more limited. The *nikāya* identity of some—perhaps many—monasteries, especially outside of Rājaraṭṭha, may not have been much more to them than a theoretical idea. The fact that they shared the Vinaya infrastructure with one of Anurādhapura's big monasteries may not have affected their autonomy in terms of monastic organization, jurisdiction, economical sustenance—and doctrinal orientation. With this in mind, we should exercise caution in identifying well-known Sri Lankan "Mahāyāna" and "Vajrayāna" sites such as Tiriyaya and Buduruvegala as necessarily Abhayagiri-related. For all we know, they may well have been established, inhabited, and maintained by monks ordained under the Mahāvihāra Vinaya.

The social and historical complexity of the Sri Lankan discourse calls for us to revise our understanding of the Theriya lineage as the carrier of a single, homogeneous *type* or *form* of Buddhism. Special care is demanded in studying the geographically broader scope of the lineage after it had spread into Southeast Asia. As several scholars have indicated—the cultures of the so-called Theravāda countries (Sri Lanka, Myanmar, Thailand, Cambodia, etc.) should not *indiscriminately* be understood as adhering to one and the same Buddhist religion.

Regretfully, the Mahāvihāra's annexation of the term *Theravāda* with its synthetic design as both a *nikāya* name *and* a dogmatic concept, has been reproduced by modern research. The Mahāvihāra historiography's dichotomy of later "heresies" versus an authentic, pristine *sāsana* resonated neatly with the twentieth-century approach to the Buddhist world as subdivided into two basic dogmatic traditions: Mahāyāna and an older, non-Mahāyāna form. In this context the sectarian agenda of Mahāvihāra historiography yielded, perhaps, its strongest effect, when modern scholars and Buddhists established the convention of denoting non-Mahāyāna forms of Buddhism as "Theravāda Buddhism."

Notes

1 The polemical impact of the Christian concept of "sect" is inbuilt into its etymology. It is a common misunderstanding that *sect* was derived from Latin *secare*, "to cut," and meant "section" or "splinter group." The actual etymological root is Latin *sequi*, "to follow," and expressed a disapproval for the act of "dangling after" a heretic teacher. The modern sociological concept of sect, as coined by Ernst Troelsch and Max Weber, is arguably (!) disengaged from its polemical heritage, but still ties a sect to a distinguished belief system as the prime cohesive factor of community building. The logic of the Buddhist *nikāya* concept is different.

2 In practice, different *nikāyas* can be based on the same recension of the Vinaya but deviate in its interpretation or application of the rules. For example, the manner of tying the upper robe around the shoulders (both shoulders covered instead of one) is a characteristic of the Amarapura Nikāya of modern Sri Lanka.

3 The modern *nikāyas* of Sri Lanka and Southeast Asia, for instance, are all based on the same recension of the *Tripiṭaka*.

4 On the different Buddhist traditions on the dating of the first *nikāya* split, see Kieffer-Pülz 2000: 292–293.

5 The earliest extant *nikāya* genealogies like the already mentioned *Samayabhedoparacaṇacakra*, the different accounts compiled in the *Nikāyabhedavyākhyāna*, the *Śāriputra-* and *Mañjuśrīparipṛcchāsūtras*, as well as the *Dīpavaṃsa*, are dated to the first half of the first millennium CE. Bareau (1955) has classified them as the *première époque* of *nikāya* genealogy.

6 See, for example, LL from Bodhgayā (first century BCE).

7 Sujato (2007: 8) has already argued that the term *Haimavata* was still a toponym, not a *nikāya* name, at that time.

8 The Sri Lankan tradition of the third century is a good example for such a blend. The "*nikāya* statement" they left behind in Nāgārjunakoṇḍa is an elaborate taxonomy integrating Kāśyapa as a founding figure (Theriya), Vibhajjavāda as a doctrinal approach and Tambapaṇṇika/Mahāvihāravāsin as local anchors. The Abhayagiri and Jetavana sub-*nikāyas* brought further founding figures (Dhammaruci, Sāgala) into the game (see the following discussion).

9 For a detailed analysis of the *nikāya* concept in Buddhist literature, see Sujato (2007), who has also argued for such a late emergence of the Buddhist *nikāyas*.

10 This does not mean, of course, that *vinaya-* or *dharma*-related conflicts between individual communities were unknown before. The *nikāya* idea just brings such conflicts from a micro- to a meso-sociological level.

11 I agree with Sujato (2007: 9–12) that these accounts are rather origin myths explaining the "sectarian" world of the respective authors than historical memories of actual events.

12 Indeed, we find the Sanskrit equivalent *Sthaviravāda* in older secondary literature on Indian Buddhism. But this term was invented by modern scholars, reading Sri Lankan Pāli terminology into their Sanskrit sources. Skilling (2009: 65) has critically pointed to this momentous terminological inaccuracy of modern Buddhist scholarship. However, Skilling is wrong in calling *Sthaviravāda* a "ghost word." For Indian Sanskrit literature it is. But it often occurs as a "Sinhalized" Sanskritism (or a neologism in lieu of a Sanskrit loanword) for Pāli *theravāda* in the fourteenth- and fifteenth-century Sinhalese works *Nikāyasaṅgraha* and *Saddharmaratnākara*.

13 On the rarity of the term in premodern literature, see Gethin 2012.

14 On the problem of the "belief-centrism" in the Study of Religion see Lopez 1998. See also Bretfeld 2019.

15 On the methodology of some of these approaches—Transnational History, *histoire croisée*, and Global History—and their impacts on Religious and Buddhist Studies see Bretfeld 2012a.

16 Examples can be found abundantly. To give a few examples, Paranavitana (1928: *passim*) qualifies the Mahāvihārins as "orthodox." Also for Holt (1991: 60, 72, 227), the Mahāvihāra and Buddhaghosa represent Sri Lanka's "orthodoxy." Sujato (2007: 101, n. 1) argues for the Mahāvihārins as "the" Theravādins of Sri Lanka. The description of the Abhayagiri tradition as "heterodox Buddhism" is featured in Chandawimala (2013, 2016).

17 On the Nāgārjunakoṇḍa inscriptions, see Vogel 1933, Sircar and Lahiri 1959–1960, and recently Baums et al. 2016.

18 *ācarīyānaṃ Kasmira-Gaṃdhāra-Cīna-Cilāta-Tosali-Avaraṃta-Vaṃga-Vanavāsi-Yavana-Da[mila-Pa]lura-Taṃbaṃṇidīpa-pas[ā]dakānaṃ theriyānaṃ Taṃbapa[ṃ]ṇakānaṃ* (Second Apsidal Temple inscription F, Vogel 1933: 22).

19 *āchariyānaṃ theriyānaṃ vibhajavādānaṃ Kasmira-Gaṃdhāra-Yavana-Vanavāsa-Taṃbapaṃṇidipa-pasādakanaṃ mahāvihāravāsinaṃ* (Footprint slab inscription, Sircar and Lahiri 1959–1960: 250).

20 There is a controversy among scholars as to whether the word *mahāvihāravāsinaṃ* refers to the well-known Sri Lankan sub-*nikāya* of that name or just states that the community in question inhabited some local large monastery (*mahāvihāra*). The latter was the opinion of Sircar and Lahiri (1959–1960: 249). Walters's (1997) and Cousins's (2001) understanding of the word as a reference to the Sri Lankan sub-*nikāya* makes more sense.

21 This is the first and the third list transmitted in the *Tarkajvāla* attributed to Bhavya (cf. Bareau 1955: 17 and 22). Bhavya's second list mentions them too and even separates the Vibhajyavādins completely from the Sthaviras/Mahāsāṃghika dichotomy and declares them a third primordial *nikāya* (Bareau 1955: 23).

22 On Cousins's Vibhajyavādins theory, see also Wynne 2018.

23 That these two historiographic sections of the lost ancient Sinhala commentarial literature (*Sīhaḷaṭṭhakathā*)—and not, as some other scholars believe, a Mahāvihāra and an Abhayagiri recension of the *Sīhaḷaṭṭhakathā*—were the main sources of the *Dīpavaṃsa* was convincingly suggested by Perera 1979. The *Sīhaḷaṭṭhakathā-Mahāvaṃsa* cannot be dated with any certainty. According to Perera (1979: 49–50), it had emancipated itself from the historical introduction of the *Mahāṭṭhakathā* at a certain time and received its final form in the time of Mahāsena (third or fourth century).

24 Also Wynne's recent discussion of Cousins's Vibhajjavāda theory arrives at the conclusion that the Mahāvihāra lineage abandoned their Vibhajjavāda identity around the fourth or fifth century (Wynne 2018: 255). Both authors have, however, not noticed that this process was accompanied by the formation of a new identity that radically denied any family relationship to the extant Indian *nikāyas*—including those (Mahīśāsakas, etc.) with which they may have constituted the Vibhajjavāda group earlier.

25 The *Vaṃsatthappakāsinī*, the commentary on the *Mahāvaṃsa* of an uncertain date, does not know the term *nikāya* either and uses *vāda* as a default. The *Mahābodhivaṃsa* (eleventh century) uses *nikāya* once (Mhbv 96.29) and speaks of *vādas* in other passages. In the *Cūlavaṃsa* (thirteenth) the word *nikāya* occurs frequently, usually to denote the "three *nikāyas*" (*nikāyattaya*) of Sri Lanka (e.g., Culv 41.97, 44.131, 48.73). The *Nikāyasaṅgraha* (fifteenth century) distinguishes the terms *vāda* and *nikāya* rigorously: *vāda* always denotes a teaching, while monastic lineages are called *nikāyas*. The *Sāsanavaṃsa*'s (nineteenth century) default term for "monastic lineage" is *gaṇa* (Sas 13–14), but the adjective *nikāyika* is used for the members of modern Sri Lankan faction usually known as Amarapura Nikāya (Sas 142, 159, 163). On the terms *vāda* and *kula* as equivalents to *nikāya*, see also Gethin 2012: 11.

26 Cousins (2001: 151) states that the *Dīpavaṃsa*'s *nikāya* genealogy "derives ultimately from Vasumitra's treatise." Considering the *nikāya* names known to the *Dīpavaṃsa* but unknown to Vasumitra, I deem it more likely that the *Dīpavaṃsa* used a scheme similar to Bhavya's second list (Bareau 1955: 23), but without adopting its tripartite arrangement.

27 *Sattarasa bhinnavādā eko vādo abhinnako, sabbev' aṭṭhārasa honti 'bhinnavādena te saha. Nigrodho va mahārukkho theravādānam uttamo anūnam anadhikañ c' eva kevalam jinasāsanaṃ, kaṇṭakā viya rukkhamhi nibbattā vādasesakā* (Dīp 5.51–52).

28 *Atthaṃ dhammañ ca bhindiṃsu ekadesañ ca saṃgahaṃ ganṭhiñ ca ekadesamhi chaḍḍetvāna akaṃsu te. Nāmaṃ liṅgaṃ parikkhāram ākappakaraṇāni ca pakatibhāvaṃ vijahetvā tañ ca aññam akaṃsu te.* These two verses, that can be called the *Dīpavaṃsa's* "apostasy formula"—occur two times, once after the Mahāsāṃghikas and their offsprings are enumerated (Dīp 5.43–44) and, again, after the presentation of the Mahiṃsāsakas, Vajjiputtakas and their offsprings (Dīp 5.49–50).

29 The Pāli inscriptions of Śrīkṣetra (Lower Burma) and Dvāravatī (Thailand), dated between the fifth and the eighth centuries, are a possible objection. Their affiliation has been much debated. If they were connected to descendants of an ancient settlement of what we have called the "Indian proto-Theriyas" (e.g., of the Aśoka period or soon after), we may actually have traces of a Sri Lanka–independent parallel transmission of (some version of) the "Pāli Canon." However, I see no good reason to assume such a scenario, even if it may conform to post-Dhammazedi (fifteenth century) origin stories of how Buddhism first arrived in Southeast Asia. As architectural and art-historical evidence suggests, an exchange triangle comprising Āndhra, Sri Lanka, and Southeast Asia was well established from the fourth century onward (cf. Stargardt 1990, Assavavirulhakarn 2010; also Frasch 1998). I deem it therefore likely that the Pāli inscriptions of the Southeast Asian Mon and Pyu cultures go back to these later culture contacts. In other words, together with the Nāgārjunakoṇḍa inscriptions, the earliest of the Southeast Asian Pāli inscriptions seem to witness the beginnings of the Sri Lankan Buddhist tradition(s) "going global"—a process that will gain momentum during the subsequent centuries (see below). It further seems that Buddhaghosa (fifth century) was well aware of these expansive dynamics of the Sri Lankan traditions in his time. It is not unlikely that he had especially "Tambapaṇṇika-related" (and, therefore, Pāli-using) communities like the ones in Āndhra, Kāñcipura, Bodhgayā and—as it seems—Southeast Asia in mind, when he states the reason why he translated the ancient Sinhalese commentaries into Pāli: for the sake of the monks outside the island (*dīpantare bhikkhujanassa*) who cannot understand the language of Sīhaḷadīpa ($Sp_{(J)}$ 1.8).

30 Apart from the fact that there is no epigraphic testimony of a Buddhist group simply calling itself Sthavira, already the early Indian *nikāya* genealogies do not seem to know the Sthaviras "proper" as a (still) living and breathing community. They either identify the Ur-Sthaviras (*pūrva-Sthavira*) with another existing *nikāya*, notably the Haimavatas (Vasumitra, Bhavya I), or they use Sthavira as an umbrella term for (i.e., a common ancestor of) a group of existing *nikāyas* (Bhavya II). Bhavya III is a mix. Was "Sthavira" ever the self-designation of a concrete group or rather *a projected category of historical construction, signifying the assumed original opponent of the Mahāsaṃghikas within early dichotomic models of Buddhist diversification.*

31 A Sanskrit inscription found near the "Twin Ponds" of the Abhayagiri monastery (EZ I 1–9) suggests that the Abhayagirivāsins had adopted the idea of the four main *nikāyas* by the ninth century. They seem to even have hosted members of all four within its compound (Gunawardana 1979: 250–254, but see the objection to this theory in Bechert 1993: 15).

32 I use the title in the stem form instead of the casus rectus, which adds the suffix *-ya* at the end of the title. The widespread spelling *Nikāyasaṅgraha-wa* is morphologically wrong and not attested before Fernando and Gunawardhana 1908 introduced it for no clear reason.

33 I have recently edited and translated the text which is now awaiting publication by the Pali Text Society. As the following refers to a work in print, I have indicated chapters instead of the not yet finalized page and line numbers.

34 Regarding the rich collection of Tantric material the Abhayagiri was famous for between the seventh and ninth century, it is quite obvious that Dharmakīrti had no access to any textual remains but knew of it only through hearsay and older literary references. Also his idea of what a Vaitulya (~Mahāyāna) text may have looked like seems to have been rather vague.

35 *Ävätti śōka no-karava. No-haṅḍava. Yahapata napura kiyā apaṭa vehesa dena mahaṇu maḷa pasu meviṭa apa kämät-tak-ma-ya. Esē heyin somnas vuva manā tanhi kumak piṇisa dormanas va haṅḍavu-da? Metan paṭan apa kämättak karamha. No-kämättak no-karamha-yi kī* (Nikāya-s chapt. 2).

36 Nikāya-s chapt. 5.

37 Nikāya-s chapt. 8.

38 On the topos of the "18 Tantras," see Eastman 1981, Giebel 1995, Gray 2009, Almogi 2014. Many of the titles have been wrongly emended by modern editors of the *Nikāyasaṅgraha*, although the manuscripts partly contain the correct Sanskrit titles of texts known from Tibetan and Chinese translations. The titles seem to have gone through a stage of Pāli transmission before they reached the *Nikāyasaṅgraha*. After the decline of Tantric Buddhism in Sri Lanka, these names seem to have circulated among Mahāvihāra

scholars who probably used them for name-dropping historical examples of "fake-dharmas." A slightly earlier example is a Pāli text called *Sārasaṅgaha* which quotes a shortened version of the same list (Ss 45–46).

39 The only exception mentioned in the text is when Buddhaghosa came to Sri Lanka from Jambudvīpa "to glorify the Pāli-dharma of the *tripiṭaka*" (Nikāya-s chapt. 14) and the Indian Mahāthera Jotipāla who came in the sixth century "to defeat the Vaitulyavāda on the island in debate" (*parājesi vivādena dīpe Vaitulyavādino*, Nikāya-s chapt. 14).

40 For a detailed discussion of this term, see Skilling 2013.

41 Nikāya-s chapt. 19.

42 Nikāya-s chapt. 10.

43 *Api idin sayin vī namut adharmaya "dharmaya ya"-yi gatumō nam bohō denā e-ma gena apāya gata veti. Api häma-da sāparādha vamha. Ebävin apagē jīvitabrahmacariyaṭa antarāya vē namudu Vaitulyavāda no-ganumha-yi* (Nikāya-s chapt. 12).

44 Mhv 37.12–13.

45 I agree with Cousins (2012) that the account of a much earlier nikāya split already in the first century BCE is probably an anachronistic projection of a much later conflict.

46 It is not clear what this rivaling version consisted of or who transmitted it. We know that it existed because the *Mahāvaṃsa-ṭīkā*, commenting on this episode, cites an unknown commentary to the *Dīpavaṃsa* cursing anybody who relates the Mahāsena story "wrongly," that is, differing from how it is told in the *Mahāvaṃsa* (Mhv-ṭ 683). Concretely, there seems to have been a version of the story implying that the *sīmā* of the Mahāvihāra was actually disintegrated or shrunk when the Jetavana monastery was built. See also Walters 1999. On the complex Vinaya jurisdiction this story builds on (and which Geiger has not understood when translating the *Mahāvaṃsa*), see Kieffer-Pülz 1999.

47 Mhv-ṭ 175–176. It is a Mahāvihāra author who reports this story, of course only in order to refute it as a lie (*abhūtavacana*).

48 EZ IV 273–285. For a better reading see Ranawella 2005.

49 The inscription uses the term *Vayatuḍala book* in the singular. Paranavitana (EZ IV 283) even noted the singular of *potahi* but translated it as plural anyway, probably under the influence of the *Nikāyasaṅgraha's* term *Vaitulyapiṭaka*, which suggests a collection of several scriptures.

50 Walters 1997 and Ranawella 2005 have followed Paranavitana (EZ IV 273–285) in reading the *Mahāvaṃsa's* conflict constellation—Mahāvihāra versus Abhayagiri—into the inscription. This is, however, not conclusive from the still legible parts of the text. There are rather indicators suggesting that the pro- and contra-Vayatuḍala groups were not clearly distributed on the map of Anurādhapura's monasteries (see Nikāya-s Introduction).

51 Walters's interpretation goes in this direction (Walters 1997: 113). It seems to be based on the inscription's general tone rather than on a preserved text fragment.

52 Nikāya-s chapt. 14.

53 Dharmakīrti's only addition to the non-Tantric "heretical" texts is their attribution to different *ācārya-nikāyas*. But this is just the mechanical mapping of the *Atthakathās'* text list (see n. 72) with the *Mahāvaṃsa*'s list of *nikāyas* (see Nikāya-s Introduction).

54 The *Raṭṭhapālagajjita* (*Rāṣṭrapālaparipṛcchā*?) and *Aṅgulimālapiṭaka* (*Aṅgulimālīyasūtra*?) are mentioned in Sp IV 742–743 and Spk II 201–202 alongside the *Vetullapiṭaka* and other "inauthentic" texts (*abuddhavacana*).

55 On the controversy around the terms *Vajrayāna*, *Tantrism*, and *Mantraṇaya* in recent scholarship, see, for example, Acri 2016. Pertinent studies show that the Sri Lankans had their own peculiar take on "Esoteric Buddhism," which has not yet been fully explored but contains features differing from north Indian pendants. See, for example, the studies on the Sri Lankan *pāṃsukulika* traditions (Sundberg 2014), the obscure *padhānagharas* (Sundberg 2004), iron Stūpas (Sundberg 2018), *pabbatavihāras* (Powell 2018) and the Tantra list of the *Nikāyasaṅgraha* (Nikaya-s Introduction).

56 Some scholars claim that this teaching arrived in Sri Lanka simultaneously with the Vājiriyavāda (Paranavitana 1928: 39, Bechert 2005a: 63) or in the time of Kumāradāsa, even that it was supported by this king (Deegalle 2004: 57). This is a misreading of the text.

57 The "teaching of the Blue Robe" refers to the Nīlāmbaras or Nilapaṭadarśanin, an antinomian Śaivaist ascetic tradition known from the *Āgamaḍambara* by Bhaṭṭa Jayanta and the *Purāthanprabandhasaṅgraha*. Philological considerations suggest that the *Nikāyasaṅgraha's* chapter goes back to a variant version of the story told in the latter (PPS 19, see Nikāya-s chapt. 17). On this group, see also Sundberg 2014: 179–181 and the literature mentioned there. On their relationship to Buddhism, see Ruegg 1981.

58 Veśyā ratnaṃ surā ratnaṃ ratnaṃ devo manobhavaḥ. Nikāya-s chapt. 17.

59 *Ē darśanayehi pahan ekak'hu men nīlapaṭadharayan hā ovungē patpot hā genvā gena patpot hā samaga ovun pāyeka ätuḷu koṭa agnipūjā kaḷaha* (Nikāya-s chapt. 17). Who would have thought that the titillating sight of burning heretical flesh—so often assigned to medieval Christianity—would have so captured the imagination of Buddhist authors?

60 *Ekala eyin värada giya śēṣaya mul nusun vyādhiyak men mevak perava pävättē-ma-ya.* (Nikāya-s chapt. 17).

61 See, for example, the dispute on the "afterlife" of the Abhayagiri tradition between Gunawardana (1979) and Bechert (1993). Furthermore, the "three *nikāyas*" are still mentioned in the Dambulla inscription by Nissaṅka Malla (1187–1196).

62 *Ikbiti nirmala vū sarvajñaśāsanaya duṣpratipattīn kelesana Dharmaruciya Sāgalikaya Vaitulyavādiya yana nikāyatrayavāsī vū noyek siya gaṇan duḥśīlapāpabhikṣun genvā latāmaṇḍapayehi sannihita karavā tunyam rātriyehi siṭipiyehi siṭa ovun hämadena-ma śāsanāpagata karavā buddhaśāsanaya śuddha koṭa tun nikāya samaga karavā* (Nikāya-s chapt. 19).

63 *Mē pālivacanaya sita tabā tatkālōcita-ājñāpuraḥsarapuruṣōttamayan visin tama tamā avadhiyaṭa sarvajñaśāsanayehi pämiṇi duḥśīlamala paha kirīmen pasvādahasak pavatnā lesa budusasun babuḷuvā eyin janita vū iṣṭavipākayan matu svargamōkṣasampattisaṃkhyātasakalābhimatārthasiddhiyaṭa utsāha situ va yahapati* (Nikāya-s Conclusion).

References

Acri, Andrea. 2016. "Introduction. Esoteric Buddhist Networks along the Maritime Silk Routes, 7th–13th Century AD." In *Esoteric Buddhism in Mediaeval Maritime Asia. Networks of Masters, Texts, Icons*, ed. Andrea Acri, 1–27. Singapore: ISEAS Yusof Ishak Institute.

Almogi, Orna. 2014. "The Eighteen Mahāyoga Tantric Cycles. A Real Canon or the Mere Notion of One." *Revue d'Etudes Tibétaines* 30: 47–110.

Assavavirulhakarn, Prapod. 2010. *The Ascendancy of Theravāda Buddhism in Southeast Asia*. Bangkok: Silkworm Books.

Bareau, André. 1955. *Les sectes bouddhiques du petit véhicule*. Publications de l'École Française d'Extrême-Orient. Saigon: École française d'Extrême-Orient.

Baums, Stefan, et al. 2016. "Early Inscriptions of Āndhradeśa. Results of a Fieldwork in January and February 2016." *Bulletin de l'École française d'Extrême-Orient* 102: 355–398.

Bechert, Heinz. 1985. "Einleitung." In *Zur Schulzugehörigkeit von Werken der Hīnayāna- Literatur. Symposien zur Buddhismusforschung*, III.1, Vol. 1. Abhandlungen der Akademie der Wissenschaften in Göttingen. ed. Heinz Bechert, 20–54. Göttingen: Vandenhoeck & Ruprecht.

Bechert, Heinz. 1993. "The Nikāya-s of Mediaeval Sri Lanka and the Unification of the Saṅgha by Parākramabāhu I." In *Studies on Buddhism in Honour of Professor A. K. Warder*, ed. N.K. Wagle, F. Watanabe, 11–21. Toronto: University of Toronto.

Bechert, Heinz. 2005a. *Eine regionale hochsprachliche Tradition in Südasien. Sanskrit-Literatur bei den buddhistischen Singhalesen*. Veröffentlichungen zu den Sprachen und Kulturen Südasiens, Heft 37. Wien: Verlag der österreichischen Akademie der Wissenschaften.

Bechert, Heinz. 2005b. "Notes on the Formation of Buddhist Sects and the Origins of Mahāyāna." In *Buddhism. Critical Concepts in Religious Studies*, Vol. 2, The Early Buddhist Schools and Doctrinal History; Theravāda Doctrine, ed. Paul Williams, 23–33. London and New York: Routledge.

Berkwitz, Stephen C. 2004. *Buddhist History in the Vernacular. The Power of the Past in Late Medieval Sri Lanka*. Brill's Indological Library, 23. Leiden and Boston: Brill.

Bretfeld, Sven. 2012a. "Dynamiken der Religionsgeschichte. Lokale und translokale Verflechtungen." In *Religionswissenschaft. Ein Studienbuch*, ed. Michael Stausberg, 423–433. Berlin: de Gruyter.

Bretfeld, Sven. 2012b. "Resonant Paradigms in the Study of Religion and the Emergence of Theravāda Buddhism." *Religion* 42 (2): 273–297.

Bretfeld, Sven. 2019. "Theravāda Buddhism." In *Oxford Research Encyclopedia*. Religion. URL: https://oxfordre.com/religion/.

Chandawimala, Rangama. 2013. *Buddhist Heterodoxy of Abhayagiri Sect. A Study of the School of Abhayagiri in Ancient Sri Lanka*. Saarbrücken: Lambert Academic Publishing.

Chandawimala, Rangama. 2016. *Heterodox Buddhism. The School of Abhayagiri*. Colombo: Rangama Chandawimala Thero.

Collins, Steven. 1990. "On the Very Idea of the Pāli Canon." *Journal of the Pali Text Society* 15: 89–126.

Cousins, Lance S. 2001. "On the Vibhajjavādins. The Mahiṃsāsaka, Dhammaguttaka, Kassapiya and Tambapaṇṇiya Branches of the Ancient Theriyas." *Buddhist Studies Review* 18 (2): 131–182.

Cousins, Lance S. 2012. "The Teachings of the Abhayagiri School." In *How Theravāda is Theravāda? Exploring Buddhist Identities*, eds. Peter Skilling et al., 67–127. Chiang Mai: Silkworm Books.

Cūlv. = Dhammakitti. Cūḷavaṃsa. 1925–1927), ed. Wilhelm Geiger. *Cūḷavaṃsa.* 2 vols. London: Pali Text Society.

Deegalle, Mahinda. 1999. "A Search for Mahāyāna in Sri Lanka." *Journal of the International Association of Buddhist Studies* 22: 2.

Deegalle, Mahinda 2004. "Theravāda Pre-understandings in Understanding Mahāyāna." In *Three Mountains and Seven Rivers: Prof. Musashi Tachikawa's Felicitation Volume*, ed. Shoun Hino, 43–64. Delhi: Motilal Banarasidass.

Desző, Csaba. 2004. *Much Ado about Religion. By Bhaṭṭa Jayanta.* The Clay Sanskrit Library. New York: New York University Press and JJC Foundation.

Dīp. = Dīpavaṃsa. 1992. ed. Hermann Oldenberg. *The Dīpavaṃsa. An Ancient Buddhist Historical Record.* Delhi: Williams & Norgate.

Eastman, Kenneth. May 8, 1981. "*The Eighteen Tantras of the Vajraśekhara/Māyājāla*". *Presented to the 26th International Conference of Orientalists in Japan*, Tokyo.

EZ I = Epigraphia Zeylanica. 1904–1912. ed. Don Martino de Zilva Wickremasinghe. *Epigraphia Zeylanica. Being Lithic and Other Inscriptions of Ceylon.* Vol. 2. Archaeological Survey of Ceylon. London: Oxford University Press.

EZ IV = Epigraphica Zeylanica. 1934–1941. ed. Senerat Paranavitana. *Epigraphica Zeylanica. Being Lithic and Other Inscriptions of Ceylon.* Vol. 4. London: Oxford University Press.

Fernando, C.M., Gunawardhana, W.F. 1908. *The Nikāya Saṅgrahawa. Being a History of Buddhism in India and Ceylon.* Colombo: H. C. Cottle.

Frasch, Tilman. 1998 "A Buddhist Network in the Bay of Bengal." In *From the Mediterranean to the South China Sea. Miscellaneous Notes*, ed. Claude Guillot, 69–92. Wiesbaden: Harrassowitz.

Frauwallner, Erich. 1955. "Die ceylonesischen Chroniken und die erste buddhistische Mission nach Hinterindien." In *Actes du IVe Congrès International des Sciences Anthropologiques et Ethnologiques.* Vol. 2, 192–197. Wien: Holzhausen.

Gethin, Rupert. 2012. "Was Buddhaghosa a Theravādin? Buddhist Identity in the Pali Commentaries and Chronicles." In *How Theravāda is Theravāda? Exploring Buddhist Identities*, ed. Peter Skilling et al., 1–66. Chiang Mai: Silkworm Books.

Giebel, Rolf W. 1995. "The Chin-kang-ting ching yü-ch'ieh shi-pa-hui chih-kuei. An Annotated Translation." *Journal of the Naritasan Institute for Buddhist Studies* 18: 107–201.

Gornall, Alastair. 2020. *Rewriting Buddhism. Pali Literature and Monastic Reform in Sri Lanka, 1157–1270.* London: UCL Press.

Gray, David B. 2009. "On the Very Idea of a Tantric Canon. Myth, Politics, and the Formation of the Bka'gyur." *Journal of the International Association of Tibetan Studies* 5: 1–37.

Gunawardana, R.A.L.H. 1979. *Robe and Plough. Monasticism and Economic Interest in Early Medieval Sri Lanka.* Association of Asian Studies, Monographs and Papers, 35. Tucson: University of Arizona Press.

Hirakawa, Akira. 1990. *A History of Indian Buddhism. From Sakyamuni to Early Mahayana.* Asian Studies at Hawaii, 36. Hawaii: University of Hawaii Press.

Holt, John. 1991. *Buddha in the Crown. Avalokiteśvara in the Buddhist Traditions of Sri Lanka.* New York: Oxfort University Press.

Kieffer-Pülz, Petra. 1999. "Ceremonial Boundaries in the Buddhist Monastic Tradition of Sri Lanka." In *Wilhelm Geiger and the Study of the History and Culture of Sri Lanka*, ed. Ulrich Everding and Asanga Tilakaratne, 43–90. Colombo: Goethe Institute, Postgraduate Institute of Pali, and Buddhist Studies.

Kieffer-Pülz, Petra. 2000. "Die buddhistische Gemeinde." In *Der Buddhismus I. Der Indische Buddhismus und seine Verzweigungen*, Religionen der Menschheit, 24.1. ed. Heinz Bechert, 281–402. Stuttgart: Kohlhammer.

Lamotte, Étienne. 1988. *History of Indian Buddhism. From the Origins to the Śaka Era.* Louvain-La-Neuve: Univ. catholique de Louvain. Inst. orientaliste.

LL = Lüders, Heinrich. 1973. *A List of Brāhmī Inscriptions from the Earliest Times to About A. D. 400 With the Exeception of those of Asoka.* Varanasi and Delhi: Indological Book House.

Lopez, Donald S. 1998. "Belief." In *Critical Terms for Religious Studies*, ed. Mark C. Taylor, 21–35. Chicago: University of Chicago Press.

Mhbv: Upatissa. Mahābodhivaṃsa. 2000. ed. S. Arthur Strong. *The Mahābodhivaṃsa.* Oxford: The Pali Text Society.

Mhv-ṭ = Vaṃsatthappakāsinī (Mahāvaṃsa-ṭīkā). 1977. ed. G.P. Malalasekera. *Vaṃsattha-ppakāsinī. Commentary on the Mahāvaṃsa*. 2 vols. Pali Text Society, Text Series, 58. London, Henley, and Boston: The Pali Text Society.

Mhv = Mahānāma. Mahāvaṃsa. 1908. ed. Wilhelm Geiger. *The Mahāvaṃsa*. London: Pali Text Society.

Nattier, Janice J., Prebish, Charles S. 1976. "Mahāsāṃghika Origins. The Beginnings of Buddhist Sectarianism." *History of Religions* 16: 237–272.

Neelis, Jason. 2010. *Early Buddhist Transmission and Trade Networks. Mobility and Exchange Within and Beyond the Northwestern Borderlands of South Asia*, 391. Leiden and New York: Brill.

Nikāya-s = Dharmakīrti, Jayabāhu. Nikāyasaṅgraha. (Forthcoming). ed. Sven Bretfeld. *Nikāyasaṅgraha. A Transmission History of the Śāsana* by Jayabāhu Dēvaraks .ita Dharmakīrti. Critical Edition and English Translation. Oxford: Pali Text Society.

Nikāyabh-vy = Bhāvaviveka. Nikāyabhedavyākhyāna. 2008. ed. and trans. by Malcolm David Eckel. *Bhāvaviveka and his Buddhist Opponents*. Harvard Oriental Series, 70. Cambridge and London: Harvard University Press.

Norman, K.R. 1978. "The Role of Pāli in Early Sinhalese Buddhism." In *Buddhism in Ceylon and Studies on Religious Syncretism in Buddhist Countries*, ed. Heinz Bechert, 28–47. Goottingen: Vandenhoeck & Ruprecht.

Paranavitana, Senerat. 1928. "Mahāyānism in Ceylon." *Ceylon Journal of Science* 2: 35–71.

Perera, Frank. 1979. *The Early Historiography of Ceylon*. Dissertation zur Erlangung des Doktorgrades. Göttingen: Georg-August-Universität Göttingen.

Powell, Kellie Marie. 2018. "Rituals and Ruins. Recovering the History of Vajrayāna Buddhism in Sri Lanka". MA thesis. Berkeley: University of California. https://www.academia.edu/s/ec22581f59/rituals-and-ruins-recovering-the-history-of-vajrayana-buddhism-in-sri-lanka?source=link. online.

PPS = Puratanaprabandhasangraha. 1936. ed. Jinavijaya Muni. *Puratanaprabandhasangraha. A Collection of Many Old Prabandhas Similar and Analogous to the Matter in the Prabandhacintāmaṇi*. Singhi Jaina Series, 2. Calcutta: Adhiṣṭhātā-Siṅghī Jaina Jñānapīṭha.

Ranawella, Sirimal. 2005. "Jētavanārāma Fragmentary Slab Inscription of King Mahāsena (276–303)." In *Sinhala Inscriptions in the Colombo National Museum*, ed. Sirimal Ranawella, 3–5. Spolia Zeylanica: Bulletin of the National Museum of Sri Lanka, 42. Colombo: Department of National Museums.

Ruegg, David Seyfort. 1981. "Deux problèmes d'exégèse et de pratique tantrique selon Dīpaṃkarasrījñāna et le Paiṇḍapātika de Yavadvīpa: Suvarṇadvīpa." In *Tantric and Taoist Studies in Honour of R. A. Stein*, ed. Michael Strickman, 212–226. Bruxelles: Institut belge des hautes études chinoises.

Sās = Sāsanavaṃsa. 1897. ed. Mabel Bode. *Sāsanavaṃsa*. London: Pali Text Society.

Sasaki, Shizuka. 2002. "Methods of Buddhist Sects in the Aśoka Period." In *Buddhist and Indian Studies in Honour of Professor Dr. Sodo Mori*, ed. Publication Committee for Buddhist and Indian Studies in Honour of Professor Dr. Sodo Mori, 311–333. Nagoya: Kokusai Bukkyoto Kyokai.

Silk, Jonathan A. 2002. "What, If Anything, Is Mahāyāna Buddhism. Problems of Definitions and Classifications." *Numen* 49 (4): 355–405.

Sircar, D.C., Lahiri, A.N. 1959–1960. "Footprint Slab Inscription from Nagarjunikonda." *Epigraphia Indica* 33: 247–250.

Skilling, Peter Fall. 2009. "Theravāda in History." *Pacific World: Journal of the Institute of Buddhist Studies*. 3rd ser. 11: 61–93.

Skilling, Peter. 2013. "Vaidalya, Mahāyāna, and Bodhisatva in India. An Essay towards Historical Understanding." In *The Bodhisattva Ideal. Essays on the Emergence of Mahāyāna*, ed. Bhikkhu Nyanatusita, 69–164. Kandy: Buddhist Publication Society.

Skilling, Peter, et al., eds. 2012. *How Theravāda is Theravāda? Exploring Buddhist Identities*. Chiang Mai: Silkworm Books.

Sp = Buddhaghosa. Samantapāsādikā, Vinaya-aṭṭhakathā. 1924–1947. ed. Junjiro Takakusa and M. Nagai. *Samantapāsādikā*. vol. 8. London: Pali Text Society.

Sp(J) = Buddhaghosa. Samantapāsādikā. 1962. ed. Nicholas Abedheera Jayawickrama. *Inception of Discipline and Vinaya-Nidāna. Being a Translation and Edition of the Bāhiranidāna of Buddhaghosa's Samantapāsādikā, the Vinaya Commentary*. Sacred Books of the Buddhists, 21. Bristol: Pali Text Society.

Spk = Buddhaghosa. Sāratthappakāsinī. 1929–1937. ed. Frank Lee Woodward. *Sāratthappakāsinī. Buddhaghosa's Commentary on the Saṭyutta-Nikāya*. 3 vol. London: Pali Text Society.

Ss = Siddhattha. Sārasaṅgaha. 1992. ed. Genjun H. Sasaki. *Sārasaṅgaha*. Oxford: Pali Text Society.

Stargardt, Janice. 1990. *The Ancient Pyu of Burma. Early Pyu Cities in a Man-Made Landscape*, Vol. 1. Cambridge and Singapore: Pacsea.

Sujato, Bhikkhu. 2007. *Sects and Sectarianism. The Origins of Buddhist Schools.* Taiwan: Santipada.
Sundberg, Jeffrey Roger. 2004. "The Wilderness Monks of the Abhayagirivihāra and the Origins of Sino-Javanese Esoteric Buddhism." *Bijdragen tot de Taal-, Land- en Volkenkunde van Nederlandisch-Indië* 160 (1): 95–123.
Sundberg, Jeffrey Roger. 2014. "The Abhayagirivihāra's pāṃśukūlika Monks in Second Lambakaṇṇa Śrī Laṅkā and Śailendra Java. The Fluorescence and Fall of Influential Esoteric Buddhist Adepts." *Pacific World. Journal of the Institute of Buddhist Studies.* 3rd ser. 16: 49–185.
Sundberg, Jeffrey Roger. 2018. "Appreciation of Relics, Stūpas, and Relic Stūpas in Eighth Century Esoteric Buddhism. Taishō Tripiṭaka Texts and Archaeological Residues in Guhyā Laṅkā." Part 2. *The Indian International Journal of Buddhist Studies* 19: 181–458.
Vogel, J.P. 1933. "Prakrit Inscriptions from a Buddhist Site at Nagarjunikonda." *Epigraphia Indica* 20: 1–37.
Walser, Joseph. 2005. *Nāgārjuna in Context. Mahāyāna Buddhism and Early Indian Culture.* New York: Columbia University Press.
Walters, Jonathan S. 1997. "Mahāyāna Theravāda and the Origins of the Mahāvihāra." *The Sri Lanka Journal of the Humanities* 23 (1–2): 100–119.
Walters, Jonathan S. 1999. "Mahāsena at the Mahāvihāra. On the Interpretation and Politics of History in Pre-Colonial Sri Lanka." In *Invoking the Past. The Uses of History in South Asia,* ed. Daud Ali, 322–366. Oxford, New York, and New Delhi: Oxford University Press.
Willis, Michael 2001. "Buddhist Saints in Ancient Vedisa." *Journal of the Royal Asiatic Society* 11 (2): 219–228.
Wynne, Alexander. 2018. "Theriya Networks and the Circulation of the Pāli Canon in South Asia." *Buddhist Studies Review* 35 (1–2): 245–259.

2
PĀLI
Its place in the Theravāda Buddhist tradition

Alastair Gornall

The use of Pāli as a sacred language is often identified as a defining feature of the Theravāda Buddhist tradition. Steven Collins (2017: 17) recently remarked that "if Pāli is present, in any form, then one can, retrospectively and a priori, speak of 'Theravāda Buddhism.'" If this is the case, as I think it is, then the question arises as to how we can define Pāli's presence in the Theravāda tradition in a way that encompasses the diverse array of cultural forms and practices that draw on Pāli and its literature. This chapter offers an analytical framework for thinking about these various aspects of Pāli that goes beyond blanket definitions about the language's sacred status, which often conceal more than they reveal. I offer a threefold typology of Pāli's presence in Theravāda Buddhism: (1) as a language of authoritative tradition, (2) as a language of organization and reform, and (3) as a language of indexical power. While these aspects are interdependent, distinguishing between them offers us analytical flexibility in describing how Pāli defines Theravāda Buddhism in its full diversity.

Authoritative tradition

When encountering the work of the first European Orientalists and philologists in the early nineteenth century, some scholar-monks in Sri Lanka resisted their attempts to describe Pāli alongside Sanskrit and the Prakrits as simply one of South Asia's "classical" languages. George Turnour in the introduction to his 1837 edition and translation of the *Mahāvaṃsa* (*Great History*) noted the monastic opposition to the ideas of philologists and recalled that, in conversation about the relative age of Pāli and Sanskrit, scholar-monks would quote the following Pāli verse "with an air of triumph" at every opportunity (Turnour 1837: xxii–iii):

> sā māgadhī mūlabhāsā narā yāyādikappikā
> brahmāno c' assutālāpā sambuddhā cāpi bhāsare.
>
> (It is Magadhan that is the root language spoken by people of the first eon,
> by Brahmas, by those who have never heard speech, and by the perfectly enlightened.)

We first find this verse quoted in a twelfth-century Pāli grammatical handbook, Buddhappiya's *Rūpasiddhi* (*Construction of Word Forms*, Rūp on Kacc 2013: 52), and throughout the second

DOI: 10.4324/9781351026666-4

millennium variations on it became the go-to definition for scholar-monks seeking to explain the qualities of their sacred language. The verse usefully encapsulates the three main aspects of Pāli's status as a prestigious and authoritative textual language. Pāli is above all the only language buddhas speak; it is the root language of the cosmos spoken by gods, the first men, and those raised without language; and it is also a literary language, the language of Magadha.

The language of Buddhas

Theravāda Buddhist textual history begins with the formation of the *Tipiṭaka*, the three baskets, a collection of the Buddha's discourses as well as those of some of his immediate followers (Skilling, this volume). This Theravāda "canon" is composed entirely in the middle Indic language of Pāli and the earliest commentators on the *Tipiṭaka* were the first to claim that the historical Buddha—and all previous buddhas—only taught in Pāli. It was the Pāli language that primarily distinguished the Theravāda canon from those of others in South Asia, and since they believed that this was the Buddha's language, scholar-monks of the tradition could claim that only they possessed the definitive account of the Buddha's teachings (Collins 1990). In fact, the early commentaries often define the Buddha's Dhamma or doctrine as a whole principally as Pāli scripture (*pariyatti*) or scriptural texts (*pāḷi*, *tanti*; Carter 1976).

And yet, later scholar-monks still debated about *how* Pāli scripture can be identified with the Dhamma. Some argued that it was primarily scripture as a mental language—the Buddha's thoughts rather than words—that defined the Dhamma whereas others claimed that the Dhamma was actually the Pāli sounds of the Buddha's discourses (Sp-ṭ B^{e} i 77; Sv-ṭ i 37–8; Vmv B^{e} i 21; Gornall 2020: 106–10). What was at stake here is the question of whether the authority of Pāli scripture stems primarily from its physical aspect—its literal wording—or from its ideal form as a conceptual object. The eighteenth-century Burmese scholar-monk Ñāṇābhivaṃsa summarises this debate in the following verse (Sv-nṭ B^{e} i 104):

> saddo dhammo desanā ca icc āhu apare garū dhammo paṇṇatti saddo tu desanā vā ti cāpare.

Some teachers say that scriptural wording is both the Dhamma and the teaching. Others say though that the Dhamma is a concept and that scriptural wording is only the teaching.

The root language

The claim about the status of Pāli as the Buddha's only language was accompanied in the early commentaries by the belief that Pāli was the unchanging, root language (*mūlabhāsā*) of the cosmos (Vibh-a 387–8, Vsm XIV 25). It is said that Pāli is spoken throughout the cosmos by animals, ghosts, humans, and gods alike and that it would be the default language of a child brought up without human contact. It is the only language through which one can gain an analytical insight (*paṭisambhidā*) into the Buddha's teachings and, for the adept, its meaning magically manifests "in a thousand ways" upon being heard. Unlike other languages of the world which vary over time, the Pāli language was thought to be fixed and unchanging. Pāli is referred to also as the *sabhāvanirutti* or "essence language" due to its intrinsic and natural connection with the cosmos or, as a later scholar-monk explains, because of its capacity to capture the essence of dhammas, the ultimate entities of reality (Gornall 2020: 56n19). Elsewhere, the Abhidhamma commentaries remark that the Pāli names of some dhammas as well as of other major natural phenomena are said to arise spontaneously in each age (As 390–2, Paṭis-a 306–7;

Collins 1998: 49; Visigalli, forthcoming). From this perspective, Pāli is separated from historical contingency and becomes an exclusive object of soteriological power for those virtuoso scholar-monks who had mastered it.

The language of Magadha

The discourses or Suttas of the Pāli canon rarely reflect on the language of their composition, and it is only in the early commentaries that the language was given a name, "the language of Magadha" or *magadhabhāsā* (e.g., Sp 255; Sp 1214; Vibh-a 387–8; von Hinüber 1994a; Crosby 2004). The formal labeling of the canon's idiom as an independent language, notionally associated with the Buddha's homeland of Magadha, accompanied the decision in Sri Lanka by the fourth- or fifth-century exegete Buddhaghosa to compose Pāli commentaries on the Suttapiṭaka in what he refers to in his opening preamble as the "delightful language" (*manoramaṃ bhāsaṃ*) of the canon (Sv 1; Ps 1; Spk 1, etc.).

Buddhaghosa states that in writing his works he was translating older Sinhala commentaries and explains that these works were themselves translations from a lost Pāli original that was recited at Aśoka's monastic council and brought to Sri Lanka by his son Mahinda. He claims then that by translating these Sinhala works back into Pāli he is restoring the exegetical tradition to its original, pristine state. This early commentarial use of Pāli allowed scholar-monks to bolster their authority by claiming that only they had inherited and recovered the lost exegetical tradition of the early Saṅgha. Some later scholars even refer to Pāli commentaries as the Buddha's "miscellaneous teachings" (*pakiṇṇakadesanā*) in that it was supposedly the Buddha who first established the meaning of his discourses (Sp-ṭ B^e^ i 21; Ss 26).

The preamble to the commentary on the Vinaya introduces another reason for writing in Pāli, namely, that the Sinhala language was not intelligible to all members of the Saṅgha in other lands. The commentator states that he decided to write in Pāli to make his exegetical tradition accessible to this transregional Buddhist community (Sp 1). Scholar-monks writing in later centuries continue to cite Pāli's status as a transregional medium as one of the reasons for composing or translating works into the language. Pāli commentaries then, rather than vernacular exegesis, afforded a frame of reference within which scholar-monks could think of themselves as a transregional monastic circle bound by a common scriptural language.

The cultivation of Pāli into a literary language of exegesis further involved differentiating it from the other literary languages of the region, most notably Sanskrit. While the early commentators occasionally distinguish Pāli usage from Sanskrit (e.g., Sp 1214) it was in the hands of the late medieval grammarians and literary theorists that Pāli's relationship with Sanskrit was fully systematized (Gornall 2020: 63–87; 145–67). These scholar-monks take pains to show that Pāli possessed the same literariness and linguistic capabilities as the other literary languages of classical India but that unlike these languages, it was not dependent on or derived from Sanskrit. It was Pāli's status as a perfect language independent of Sanskrit that led one scholar-monk to refer to it as "pure Magadhan" (*suddha-māgadha*; Subodh 2000: 2) and another twelfth- or thirteenth-century commentator even goes as far as to say that all languages, including Sanskrit, actually derive from Pāli (Moh 1961: 186).

A classical language

This late medieval reflection on Pāli's relationship with Sanskrit and the other literary languages of classical India provided a foundation for the first Western orientalists and philologists to categorize Pāli as one of South Asia's classical languages. Nineteenth-century orientalists compared Pāli with Sanskrit in India and Latin and Greek in Europe and were preoccupied with creating a "natural history" for the language (cf. Ollett 2017, 18–22), in particular by determining Pāli's relative age to Sanskrit. By the late nineteenth century, Western scholars had reached a consensus that Pāli was a "younger sister" of Sanskrit, and this opened the way for later linguists to classify the language more precisely as an amalgamation of various dialects of "Middle Indic" (Oberlies 2019: 9–52). Writing in the preface to the first Pāli dictionary, R. C. Childers (1875: xiii) remarked that "if the proud boast that the Magadhese is the one primeval language fades in the light of comparative philology, Buddhists may console themselves with the thought that the teaching of Gautama confers upon it a greater lustre than it can derive from any fancied antiquity."

The nineteenth-century Sri Lankan monk Vaskaḍuvē Subhūti did not entirely reject the opinions of the orientalists and, in the introduction to his new Pāli grammar, accepts the genealogical model of the philologists but argues rather that Pāli, Sanskrit, and the Prakrits are like "three sons born of the same father who only differ slightly in colour" (Gornall and Gunasena 2018: 6). Subhūti perhaps echoes orientalist rhetoric in arguing at the beginning of his work that as his society had a tradition of grammatical thought it was not uncivilized (*mlecchakama*) or of low intelligence. There was sometimes an elective affinity between the colonial promotion of studying "classical languages" like Pāli and monastic education reforms where scholar-monks sought to revive Pāli studies as a means of protecting Buddhism (Turner 2018). Today, Pāli's status as a classical language can be an important factor in governmental funding for its academic study. Recently in India, for reasons that are opaque, Pāli was stripped of its official status as a classical language, limiting support for research (Singh 2013).

The Pāli imaginaire and the idea of a canon

Steven Collins in *Nirvana and Other Buddhist Felicities* argued that the Theravāda tradition's views about Pāli, as described earlier, gave texts in the language an authority that distinguished them as a unified and privileged body of thought. Collins argued that this world of Pāli literature, which he referred to as the "Pāli imaginaire," has served traditional Southern Asian societies that have supported Theravāda monastic communities as a "cultural system," that is, as their structuring thought and ideology.[1] Collins saw this ideological formation as unified not only by language but also by the imaginaire's stable conceptual coherence, which he argues remained essentially unchanged over much of the Theravāda tradition's premodern history. He thus analytically separated the world of Pāli texts from the sociocultural life of any particular time and place and analyses it as a "cultural system" that has structured the beliefs and practices of Buddhists for millennia (Collins 1998: 72–89; 563–74).

In later works, Collins added some granularity to the necessarily macroscopic theories of *Nirvana and Other Buddhist Felicities* and acknowledged that, while Pāli texts do form an integral part of the Theravāda cultural system, they did not do so in isolation from texts in other languages that the tradition has also treated as authorities (Collins 2017: 17). In fact, the emphasis placed on Pāli's unique sacred status presupposes the existence of other complementary and sometimes competing languages. Texts written in other languages have often formed an important part of the monastic community's authoritative textual tradition. Before Buddhaghosa, Sinhala was the most authoritative exegetical language in Sri Lanka. The Pāli commentators of the first millennium relied on Sanskrit sciences, in particular, grammar, etymology, and lexicography, to write their works. And throughout the second millennium in Sri Lanka and Southeast Asia scholar-monks embraced a wider range of Sanskrit texts, even other Buddhist literature, and began to write independent works in vernacular languages too. From about the sixteenth century, the composition of new Pāli works declined considerably, and modern scholarship has mainly been conducted in vernaculars and sometimes in English.

It is worthwhile rethinking Collins's conception of the Pāli imaginaire in light of the debate that Collins himself began on the idea of a "canon" in Theravāda Buddhism (Collins 1990), for there is a large degree of overlap between textual "canons" and "cultural systems" insofar as both terms encompass an authoritative body of traditional thought. Therein Collins argues that in practice, the *Tipiṭaka* has served more as an authoritative idea and that what we find in Theravāda communities are "ritual canons," which he describes as "the texts, canonical or otherwise, which are in actual use in ritual life in the area concerned" (1990: 104). Anne Blackburn has similarly distinguished between the ideal formal canon, the *Tipiṭaka*, as "the ultimate locus of interpretative authority" and the practical canon, the "units of text actually employed in the practices of collecting manuscripts, copying them, reading them, commenting on them, listening to them, and preaching sermons based upon them that are understood by their users as part of a tipiṭaka-based tradition'" (1999a: 284). These practical canons include parts of the *Tipiṭaka* and its commentaries alongside Pāli, Sanskrit, and vernacular compositions that may or may not relate to texts classified as part of the formal canon.

And yet, as we critically rethink the nature of authoritative textual traditions in Theravāda Buddhism, it is important we do not lose the utility of the analytical dualism inherent in Collins's Pāli imaginaire, which distinguishes between a cultural system, that is, structuring tradition, and sociocultural life. For we should not ascribe canonicity to *every* text found in each locality if the idea of a textual "canon," that is, an authoritative textual tradition, is to continue to have analytical worth. Rather, we should determine which religious texts were authoritative in a particular time and place and which ones were not (or not yet) so that we can be attentive to historical change within local textual traditions and recognize those literary expressions that are actually *responding* to their local canon, whether by expanding, revising, or challenging it. This distinction is important since all texts when they are composed are not part of tradition and are rather engaged in socio-cultural acts of persuasion and argumentation that later may or may not become canonical (cf. Archer 1988: 227–73). Similarly, it should not be taken for granted either that simply because a work is in Pāli that it is still or has ever been authoritative. There are Pāli works, such as the *Peṭaka* and *Sumatāvatāra* (von Hinüber 1996: 206–7), that have not been handed down by the tradition, for instance, and other texts that we might find in local textual traditions may have fallen out of use or exist solely due to the ritual copying of manuscripts rather than their continued relevance to the local thought world.[2]

Organization and reform

Thinking about religious authority as only a potential outcome of writing in Pāli shifts the analytical focus away from seeing Pāli texts as a priori components of an inherited cultural context and rather directs our attention toward Pāli's often neglected sociocultural role as an important language for responding to the Theravāda imaginaire. That is to say, monks wrote new works in Pāli to reshape their textual tradition, to add new ideas, and to stress different points of emphasis. In fact, rather than seeing Pāli texts as inherently authoritative (cf. Collins 1998: 80), we can view all Pāli literature as first responding to tradition before sometimes becoming part of it in a process of cultural development. In this regard, Pāli was as much a language of organization and reform as it was a language of authoritative tradition. In what follows, I distinguish two sides to this activity: (1) a process of "elaboration," in which new texts are developed from within an authoritative tradition, and (2) a process of "encompassment," in which knowledge is brought in from outside of tradition and refigured hierarchically within it.[3]

Elaboration

Theravāda scholar-monks often thought of scriptural texts not as passive objects but rather as things engaged in an ongoing activity. Some grammarians, in particular, liked to explain that scriptural texts were called *pāḷi* as they were "protecting the meaning" (*atthaṃ pāti*; Mogg 7.228; Abh-ṭ on v. 539–40). The idea that scripture's meaning required constant care and attention underpinned the tradition's continuous production of exegetical works. This process of cultural elaboration was carried out mainly in vernacular languages but in Pāli too, and over time, these works introduced confusion and competing ideas, which were also often manifestations of social divisions in the monastic community. At certain points, when frictions in the tradition were perceived to be too much, scholar-monks would initiate a reorganization or reform that involved the composition of Pāli texts that synthesized the various strands of thought or adjudicated between differences. Pāli, in particular, was the language used to reset these cycles of cultural elaboration, although scholar-monks were not always successful and were often themselves competing with rival attempts to reshape the imaginaire.

The most striking examples of this process are the monastic reforms that took place in Sri Lanka between 1157 and 1270, in particular in the aftermath of Parākramabāhu I's reform council of 1165. The 1165 reforms united the Saṅgha in Sri Lanka, which had previously been split into three fraternities, and scholar-monks composed numerous Pāli works to standardize the doctrine and discipline that had become disordered due to the accumulated exegetical activities of the Saṅgha's diverse and rival factions. The reorganization of the imaginaire was not only restricted to systematic thought but also involved the composition of narratives and poems that reworked traditional histories and Buddha biographies in new aesthetic forms (Gornall 2020). One of the leading scholars of the reform, Sāriputta, explained in the opening of his work the need for him to write a new Pāli sub-commentary on the Vinaya as follows:

> I will compose an exposition of the concealed, essential meaning of the Vinaya's commentary that is easy to understand, is complete, and unconfused. Though predecessors explained the hidden meaning, they did not convey that meaning in its entirety to monks in all cases. Among the many glossaries, for instance, some in some places are written in the Sinhala language, which, by nature, is difficult to understand. Someone also wrote a certain glossary mixed with other languages too, even though it was undertaken in the Magadhan language. Precisely there, the burden of unessential learning is often apparent, and confusion is created even when it (the Vinaya commentary) is actually easy to understand. How then can those who live in various regions understand its meaning in its entirety with this kind of incomplete glossary? I will compose an unconfused, complete exegesis by removing the other languages from it and by extracting the essence throughout.
>
> (Gornall 2020: 92)

Sāriputta's opening is typical of the scholarly rhetoric of this era of reform in Sri Lanka. He explains that the proliferation of diverse exegetical thought has led to confusion (*ākula*) about the meaning of the Vinaya. He questions the selective exegesis of his predecessors, the use of vernaculars such as Sinhala that are less precise, and the reliance on other languages and their texts in composing Pāli commentaries. Concerning the latter, it seems Sāriputta had in mind a tenth-century sub-commentary on the Vinaya, the *Vajirabuddhiṭīkā* (*Diamond-Mind Subcommentary*), which sometimes adopts a Sanskritic style and cites a few Sanskrit works in its exegesis, albeit in Pāli translation (Kieffer-Pülz 2013: 57–70; 129–31). Sāriputta claims that by writing in a pure Pāli his commentary above all others is the most complete, clear, and accessible. It is noteworthy that Sāriputta's attempt to reset the cycle of cultural elaboration and redefine his imaginaire was not entirely successful, and soon after, a monk residing in South India, Coḷa Kassapa, composed another Vinaya sub-commentary competing with his work.

Pāli was viewed and used as a language of organization in second-millennium Southeast Asia too, although never to the same programmatic extent as it was in reform-era Sri Lanka. D. C. Lammerts has recently described the rich history of Buddhist law or *dhammasattha* in Burma between the thirteenth and nineteenth centuries. What is interesting is that before the mid-seventeenth century this sphere of authoritative knowledge was likely only written in the vernacular. This changed in 1651/2 when a scholar-monk Taungbhila Sayadaw Tipiṭakālaṅkāra and lay judge Kaingza Manurāja composed a *dhammasattha* work in Pāli verse, the *Manusāra dhammasattha* to "purify" their legal tradition. From then, on scholar-monks occasionally composed works in Pāli specifically because they viewed the language as "precise, durable and efficient" when compared with the vernacular tradition that was regarded as obscure and more susceptible to corruption and degeneration (Lammerts 2018: 90–4).

These interventions in tradition were not always written on palm-leaf texts, and in Southeast Asia, in particular, we find many epigraphs in Pāli. As discussed in the following, Pāli epigraphy in the region for much of the first millennium largely consists of citation inscriptions from the *Tipiṭaka*. From the early second millennium, we find longer, sometimes bilingual, inscriptions, such as the 1479 Kalyāṇī inscription of King Dhammaceti (Frasch 2018; Griffiths and Lammerts 2015; Thompson 2016: 161–8). These lithic works respond to their local imaginaire in several ways. Sometimes Pāli is used in the opening of an inscription as a form of aesthetic power (cf. Pollock 2006) to eulogize the Buddha and royal lineages. Pāli may also have a documentary function and record donations, assert economic rights, or intervene in the monastic discipline. In all these inscriptions, Pāli serves as an authoritative voice that is universal in practice in that it can speak to a cosmopolitan, transregional audience and rhetorically so in that writing in Pāli makes a claim on universal truth and power.

Encompassment

It was not only through cultural elaboration—responding to the imaginaire and working out its internal contestations and contradictions—that Pāli served as a force of cultural change. Throughout history, scholar-monks have continually incorporated new cultural material from outside the tradition too as a result of historical developments in the monastic community's social and political environment. These works in other languages and from other traditions could enter authoritative tradition directly. The rich tradition of Buddhist law in Burma, as we have seen, was largely a vernacular enterprise and, for the most part, sat side by side with Pāli scripture in the local imaginaire. At other times, works and disciplines entering the imaginaire had to be refigured and made more congruous with the previous tradition before they could claim authority. Pāli was an important medium for refiguring and potentially absorbing and lending authority to these new intellectual forms in a process of cultural encompassment.

New knowledge disciplines have long entered into the monastic curriculum through Pāli adaptations. From about the seventh century, scholar-monks first in Sri Lanka and then in Burma became particularly interested in Sanskrit grammar and poetics. While early commentators such as Buddhaghosa had directly used Sanskrit grammars to interpret their scriptures (Pind 1989), scholar-monks now began to compose Pāli grammatical works based on Sanskrit models. Many of these works, such as the *Kaccāyana* and *Moggallāna* grammars, closely followed and translated their Sanskrit sources (Dimitrov 2016: 557–706; Gornall 2020: 63–87; Ruiz-Falqués

2017). This process of rendering Sanskrit philological texts into Pāli often involved a conscious effort to make these works more Buddhist and aligned with the values of the tradition. Sanskrit grammatical examples from Hindu literature, for instance, are swapped for Buddhist versions (Gornall 2013: 89–100). The first work of Pāli poetics produced in Sri Lanka, the *Subodhālaṅkāra* (*Lucid Poetics*), similarly eschews the erotic Sanskrit poetry of its sources and instead replaces it exclusively with devotional verses in praise of the Buddha (Gornall 2020: 145–67). Compare, for instance, the following verse in the *Subodhālaṅkāra* with its Sanskrit source in which a carefully introduced vocative (O Buddha!) turns the description of a lover's face into a verse praising the Buddha's complexion:

> na jātu śaktir indos te mukhena pratigarjitum.kalaṅkino jaḍasyeti pratiṣedhopamaiva sā.
> (*Kāvyādarśa* 2.34)
>
> The frigid, mottled moon does not have the power to ever rival your face. This is a simile through negation.
>
> asamattho mukhen' indu jina te paṭigajjituṃ jaḷo kalaṅkī ti ayaṃ paṭisedhopamā siyā.
> (*Subodhālaṅkāra* 193)
>
> The frigid, mottled moon, O Buddha, is incapable of rivalling your face. This is a simile through negation.

In what is now northern Thailand, Laos, and Burma a process of cultural encompassment took place from the twelfth century onwards in connection specifically with cosmological thought. For the first time in Buddhist history, scholar-monks composed several Pāli manuals dedicated to the topic of cosmology and also astronomy. Some of these Pāli texts have been identified as adaptations and refigurations of Sanskrit cosmological works. The earliest Pāli cosmological work, the twelfth-century *Lokapaññatti* (*Description of the World*), for instance, closely follows the Sanskrit *Lokaprajñāpti* as preserved in its Chinese translation (Denis 1977 I: xix–xxviii). Pāli manuals on the realms of rebirth, such as the *Chagatidīpanī* (*Light on the Six Destinies*) and *Pañcagatidīpanī* (*Light on the Five Destinies*), were similarly composed as close translations and adaptations of works originally in Sanskrit (Mus 1939). Other cosmological works combine material from the Pāli canon and its commentaries with other Sanskrit source material from outside of the tradition. The author of the *Candasuriyagatidīpanī* (*Light on the Movements of the Moon and Sun*), for instance, states he brought together works from the Pāli canon, the commentaries, and other astrological/astronomical texts (*jotisattha*, Sk. *jyotiśāstra*; UPT538.3F, *fol.* 214a).

With a few notable exceptions, it is generally true that in Theravāda Buddhist intellectual history Pāli has served as the main vehicle by which knowledge from the Sanskrit tradition was subsumed and creatively refigured within the imaginaire.[4] In the case of the poetics and grammatical traditions, it is clear that Pāli was viewed as the only language that possessed the same transcendent capacity for literary and linguistic expression as Sanskrit, stemming ultimately from its role as the root language of the cosmos. These works in their openings also often praise the omniscience of the Buddha and, in effect, treat the new knowledge they are translating as something the Buddha already knew.[5] There may be some connection in this regard between describing a "new" aspect of the Buddha's omniscience and the decision to do so in his own language and the language of ultimate truth. This is certainly the case for some of the cosmological material, such as the *Lokapaññatti* and the *Mahākappa-lokasaṇṭhāna-paññatti*

(*Description of the Great Ages and the State of the World*), which present themselves in form and style as Suttas spoken by the Buddha.

The two complementary processes of elaboration and encompassment can be hard to distinguish when it comes to Pāli compendia and literary adaptations due to the diversity of their source material, which may or may not have formed a part of the authoritative tradition prior to composition. In Pāli historiographical or *vaṃsa* literature, we find several works, such as the *Dāṭhāvaṃsa* (*History of the Tooth*), *Hatthavanagallavihāra-vaṃsa* (*History of Hatthavanagalla Monastery*), and *Thūpavaṃsa* (*History of the Relic Shrine*), that rework lost vernacular histories, older Pāli sources and even Sanskrit material (Berkwitz 2004: 83–107; Godakumbura 1956: ix–xvii). The author of the *Dāṭhāvaṃsa*, which was composed for a South Indian prince, states in his opening that he has translated an old Sinhala history into Pāli so that the history could be understood by those from India. The work is composed in an ornate and poetic Pāli modeled on Sanskrit forms deeply associated with political power and court literature. This style of Pāli was perhaps preferred to articulate the monastic community's own brand of aesthetic, devotional politics, particularly to a continental audience (Gornall 2020: 168–89). Many of these Pāli *vaṃsa*s were later treated as the definitive histories of these relics, and the fact they were composed in Pāli must have played a role in the authority they garnered.

Indexical power

In the previous two sections, we have discussed the relationship between Pāli and Theravāda Buddhism exclusively in terms of Pāli as a privileged vehicle of Buddhist thought, whether in transmitting Buddhist intellectual tradition or in responding to and reshaping it. Pāli's role in ordering the ideas of the Theravāda Buddhist imagination was supported by a complex web of cultural associations. We have seen how the use of Pāli has carried with it notions of sacred authority, cosmic truth, literary perfection, political power, social and intellectual order, and universality, for instance. So far, we have only discussed these associations in terms of Pāli's privileged communicative role within the tradition. And yet, in practice, scholar-monks and ritual specialists have often wielded Pāli texts primarily due to their indexical power rather than the information they carried.[6] In such contexts, it is this power of a Pāli expression—the cultural associations manifested by its words and viewed as intrinsic properties of them—that primarily determines its transformational force and not the expression's content.[7]

From rhetoric to magic

The indexical power of a language and its information-carrying function are rarely independent of each other. If we take the Pāli-vernacular bitexts that formed an integral part of Theravāda literary culture from the tenth century onwards (Walker, this volume), for instance, the Pāli text served both literally as the object to be translated and indexically as a bestower of authority to vernacular elaborations that were often exegetically innovative. Note though that this indexical use of Pāli is not derivative of vernacularization or a later development. It has been a constant feature of Pāli textuality and could even be the dominant mode of Pāli usage prior to the development of a scholarly tradition of Pāli composition, as in the case of first-millennium Burma and Thailand. This indexical power can manifest in a variety of ways, whether in the purely rhetorical use of Pāli expressions to assert authority or in a more magical guise in which Pāli forms are treated as having the creative capacity to bring things into existence.

In the case of the tradition of some vernacular commentaries on Pāli texts, such as the *nissaya*, *vohāra*, and *nāmasadda* from Thailand and Laos, for instance, often the vernacular exposition may only invoke the Pāli source text through partial quotations of words and expressions. These Pāli fragments that stand in for the source text may not be entirely meaningful in and of themselves and serve as triggers reminding the audience of the original Pāli text being explicated as well as markers of "reverence, prestige, wisdom, and beauty" (McDaniel 2008: 127). Even vernacular narratives based on Pāli works, such as the fourteenth-century Sinhala *Saddharmālaṅkāraya* and the *Daḷadāpūjāvaliya*, intermittently include parts of the Pāli original work, especially its verse material. Since the sense of the Pāli is often already present and creatively expanded on in the vernacular elaboration (cf. Berkwitz 2004: 121–34), these interjections serve to invoke the prestige, authority, and power of their source and of the Pāli language in general.

This indexical use of Pāli takes on a more magical dimension in the case of benedictory formulas and invocations. Nearly all printed works and manuscripts will at least include a homage to the Buddha in the form of the Pāli formula, *namo tassa bhagavato arahato sammā sambuddhassa*, for instance. Similar practices are reflected in Southeast Asian vernacular inscriptions in which Pāli is used in blessings and other invocations (Frasch 2018). It is common, too, for vernacular commentaries on Pāli texts, especially Sinhala *sannaya* and Burmese *nissaya*, to still begin with a homage to the Buddha, Dhamma, and Saṅgha in Pāli rather than the vernacular. While these formulas may sometimes be informational (providing the name and author of a work, for instance), they primarily serve to generate merit and ward off evil. The fact that they must be in Pāli shows that it is not simply the content of the benediction that provides this merit and protection but rather also the indexical power of the Pāli language. This function is not specific to the role Pāli plays in vernacular works but it is simply that Pāli's ever-present indexical dimension is often clearer to see in such contexts. To different degrees, then, both the rhetorical and magical uses of Pāli share this indexical creativity in that both conjure up something, whether the authority of a source text or a form of protection.

A related magical dimension informs the traditional, ritual use of Pāli citations as devotional objects and as sources of merit. From about the fifth century, for instance, in what is now Burma and Thailand, we find many inscriptions of Pāli texts paralleling those in the *Tipiṭaka* on stone, brick, clay, and even gold plates (Griffiths and Lammerts 2015). These were likely copied and deposited as part of the ritual veneration of the Dhamma. There is evidence from the twelfth- and thirteenth-century Sri Lankan tradition that such objects were treated and enshrined as relics of the historical Buddha (Gornall 2020: 132–7). In these practices, Pāli fragments have a metonymic connection with the Dhamma as a whole—manifesting its meritorious power—and the Dhamma, in turn, serves as a surviving trace of the Buddha's omniscience. This kind of reasoning also underpins the ritual preservation of scripture in which single Pāli texts may be copied to produce merit as a way of caring for and attaining the wisdom of the entire Dhamma (Veidlinger 2007: 164–203).

Performative rituals

There is no clear boundary of separation between the indexical power of Pāli in written language and its performative role in other rituals in the tradition. Whether in monastic legal rites, the recitation of protective texts or *paritta*, or the intonement of Pāli words in meditation, the ritual recitation of Pāli similarly produces transformations based primarily on its indexical power (rather than on its capacity to carry information, which still may persist). It is the case, however, that in many ritual contexts, the very recitation of Pāli may also constitute the performance of a social act (Austin 1962; Tambiah 1973), such as turning someone from a layman into a monk, for instance, whereas this may not always be the case in other instances in which

Pāli is employed for its indexical power, such as in its rhetorical use (although, of course, there are ways of seeing even rhetoric as a form of action; cf. Burke 1966).

The Pāli formulas used in monastic legal rituals are known in the tradition as *kammavācā* (action speech). These formulas enact in their recitation various transformations, such as ordinations and the fixing of monastery boundaries, as long as they are performed in the right ritual environment in the presence of the necessary quorum of monks (Kieffer-Pülz 2000: 360–1). While these formulas are meaningful and may be translated, the monks involved in the rituals make a great effort to ensure the formal accuracy of the Pāli recited (von Hinüber 1994b; Gornall 2014). The incorrect recitation of Pāli formulas, even if the meaning is understood, can invalidate a ritual act. In 1420 some monks of Wat Suandok in Chiang Mai went on pilgrimage to Sri Lanka, and the monks there rejected the validity of their ordination on the basis that their Pāli pronunciation was incorrect (Bizot 1988: 60–1; Premchit and Swearer 1977). Concern for correct Pāli ritual speech led to the production in the wider Lanna region of manuals of Pāli ritual pronunciation. At the end of one manual, monks are warned that an incorrectly pronounced syllable can send them to hell (Bizot 1988: 63–4).

The recitation of Pāli *paritta* texts for protection, merit generation and other worldly benefits, such as warding off illness or ensuring safe childbirth, represents another form of performative ritual (Crosby 2014: 125–9). These protective works meaningfully teach key aspects of the Buddha's doctrine or describe the Buddha's position and power in the wider cosmos (Blackburn 1999b; Shulman 2019), and monks have long studied them as a fundamental part of their education. In practice, however, the ultimate efficacy of *paritta* recitation in its performative role does not depend on whether participants in the ritual understand what is being said. Pāli serves as a language that is intelligible to the gods and spirits that are being propitiated and the recitation of these Pāli texts also indexically manifests the transformative power of the truths that these works were thought to contain (Crosby 2014: 128–9). The recitation of *paritta* and other liturgical texts may also have an affective power since merit is also produced by the feelings of joy (*pīti*, *pasāda*) of those who participate (Cook 2010: 98).

Pāli has an important performative role in traditional meditation practices too. Pāli words can serve as an object of meditation or as a support for concentration. In the forest traditions of Thailand, in particular, it is common also for meditators to recite certain epithets of the Buddha, such as "Buddho" or "Arahaṃ," as the main focus of their practice (Tiyavanich 1997). The Pāli language also plays an integral role in certain meditation traditions developed in Cambodia and Thailand in which Pāli syllables are recited to manifest different aspects of the Dhamma. The meditator uses the cosmogonic power of the Pāli language to construct "the body of the Dhamma" within themselves and to cultivate their own enlightenment (Crosby 2013: 82–4; Bizot and von Hinüber 1994). An understanding of the creative agency of Pāli syllables likely also informs the tradition of Pāli yantras or magical diagrams in which Pāli letters (often from protective formulas or *paritta*) are arranged in images, such as that of the Buddha, usually for protection or to achieve other worldly ends (McDaniel 2011: 77–85).

Conclusion

There are other examples of Pāli usage in the Theravāda tradition that could be described here, and I hope this chapter serves as a starting point for further detailed reflections. I have suggested that Pāli's use in the tradition can be analyzed through three interrelated but distinct modes, namely, as a language of authoritative tradition, organization and reform, and indexical power. These three modes are nearly always interdependent and do not necessarily relate to each other in a form of hierarchy. Theravāda cultures in which one mode of Pāli predominates are not more Theravāda than others. And yet, scholarship on Pāli textual cultures, whether by philologists, historians, or anthropologists, has tended to emphasize one mode or the other as the authentic expression of the Theravāda tradition. Bringing together these different uses of Pāli, which are often dealt with in different disciplinary domains, into a single framework affords us greater analytical flexibility when describing the diverse local forms of Theravāda Buddhism and when thinking critically about how Pāli defines the tradition.

Notes

1 While Collins borrowed the term *imaginaire* from Jacques Le Goff (1988), his analytical model in fact owes much more to the sociology of Margaret Archer (1988).

2 There are, in fact, many more lost Pali works than those listed in von Hinüber 1996, especially philological works (cf. Pind 2012).

3 I use the term *elaboration* here in a similar sense to Archer (1988). On my use of the Dumontian term *encompassment* in this context, cf. Schontal (2018: 194) and Strathern (2019: 77).

4 In Sri Lanka, for instance, we first find a Sinhala adaption of Daṇḍin's *Kāvyādarśa* (*Mirror of Literature*), the *Siyabaslakara* (*Ornaments for Our Own Language*), prior to the creation of the first Pāli manual of poetics, the *Subodhālaṅkāra* (Hallisey 2003).

5 In one passage in the *Saddanīti*, Aggavaṃsa even claims that the Buddha had mastered the literary sciences in previous births but that he had sometimes decided to teach using language that did not conform to these rules (Gornall and Henry 2017: 84).

6 I prefer to use the term *indexical* here rather than symbolic since, unlike a symbol which is purely representational, an index signals the "contextual 'existence' of another entity" and can manifest or present that entity. In the case of pure indexes that have little referential meaning, the thing signaled and manifested can be fairly abstract, such as a powerful value ("truth") or function ("protection"). See Silverstein (1976); also, McDaniel (2011: 103).

7 I have been inspired to think about the transformative function of the Pāli language in this context by Kate Crosby's recent reflections on "transformation" in the Theravāda tradition and the role of meditation as a "technology of transformation" (Crosby 2014: 7–8).

References

Abh-ṭ Be= 1964. *Abhidhānappadīpikāṭīkā*. Chaṭṭhasaṅgāyana edition. Yangon: Buddhasāsanasamiti.

Archer, M.S. 1988. *Culture and Agency: The Place of Culture in Social Theory*. Cambridge: Cambridge University Press.

As = 1979. Müller, E., ed. *The Atthasālinī: Buddhaghosa's Commentary on the Dhammasaṅgaṇi*. 1897. Revised edition, London: Pali Text Society.

Austin, J.L. 1962. *How to Do Things with Words. The William James lectures delivered in Harvard University in 1955*. Oxford: Clarendon Press.

Belvalkar, S.K., ed. and trans. 1924. *Kāvyādarśa of Daṇḍin: Sanskrit Text and English translation*. Poona: Oriental Book-Supplying Agency.

Berkwitz, S.C. 2004. *Buddhist History in the Vernacular: The Power of the Past in Late Medieval Sri Lanka*. Leiden: Brill.

Bizot, F. 1988. *Les traditions de la pabbajjā en Asie du Sud-Est*. Recherches sur le bouddhisme khmer IV. Göttingen: Vandenhoeck und Ruprecht.

Bizot, F. and O. von Hinüber. 1994. *La guirlande de Joyaux*. Textes bouddhiques du Cambodge II. Paris: École française d'Extrême-Orient.

Blackburn, A.M. 1999a. "Looking for the *Vinaya*: Monastic Discipline in the Practical Canons of the Theravāda." *Journal of the International Association of Buddhist Studies* 22 (2): 281–309.

Blackburn, A.M. 1999b. "Magic in the Monastery: Textual Practice and Monastic Identity in Sri Lanka." *History of Religions* 38 (4): 354–372.

Burke, K. 1966. *Language as Symbolic Action: Essays on Life, Literature, and Method*. Berkeley: University of California Press.

Carter, J.R. 1976. "Traditional definitions of the term *dhamma*." *Philosophy East and West* 26 (3): 329–337.

Childers, R.C. 1875. *A Dictionary of the Pali Language*. London: Trübner.

Collins, S. 1990. "On the Very Idea of the Pali Canon." *Journal of the Pali Text Society* 15: 89–126.
Collins, S. 1998. *Nirvana and other Buddhist felicities: Utopias of the Pali imaginaire*. Cambridge: Cambridge University Press.
Collins, S. 2017. "Periodizing Theravāda history. Where to start?." In *Theravāda Buddhist Encounters with Modernity*, eds. J. Schober, S. Collins, 17–27. London: Routledge.
Cook, J. 2010. *Meditation in Modern Buddhism: Renunciation and Change in Thai Monastic Life*. Cambridge: Cambridge University Press.
Crosby, K. 2004. "The Origin of Pāli as a Language Name in Medieval Theravāda Literature." *Journal of the Centre for Buddhist Studies, Sri Lanka* 2: 70–116.
Crosby, K. 2013. *Traditional Theravada Meditation and Its Modern-Era Suppression*. Hong Kong: Buddha Dharma Centre of Hong Kong.
Crosby, K. 2014. *Theravada Buddhism: Continuity, Diversity, and Identity*. Chichester: Wiley-Blackwell.
Denis, E. 1977. *La Lokapaññatti et les idées cosmologiques du bouddhisme ancien*. Vol. 1. Lille; Paris: Atelier Reproduction de thèses, Université de Lille III; Honoré Champion.
Dimitrov, D. 2016. *The Legacy of the Jewel Mind: On the Sanskrit, Pali, and Sinhalese Works by Ratnamati: A Philological Chronicle (Phullalocanavaṃsa)*. Naples: Università degli studi di Napoli "L'Orientale", Dipartimento Asia Africa e Mediterraneo.
Frasch, T. 2018. "Myanmar Epigraphy – Current State and Future Tasks." In *Writing for Eternity: A Survey of Epigraphy in Southeast Asia*, ed. D. Perret, 47–71. Études thématiques 30. Paris: École française d'Extrême-Orient.
Godakumbura, C.E., ed. 1956. *Hatthavanagallavihāravaṃsa*. London: Pali Text Society.
Gornall, A.M. 2013 "Buddhism and Grammar: The Scholarly Cultivation of Pāli in Medieval Laṅkā." PhD thesis, University of Cambridge.
Gornall, A. 2014. "How Many Sounds are in Pāli? Schisms, Identity and Ritual in the Theravāda Saṅgha." *Journal of Indian Philosophy* 42 (5): 511–550.
Gornall, A. 2020. *Rewriting Buddhism: Pali Literature and Monastic Reform in Sri Lanka, 1157–1270*. London: UCL Press.
Gornall, A., Gunasena, A., trans. 2018. "A History of the Pali Grammatical Tradition of South and Southeast Asia by Vaskaḍuvē Subhūti (1876), Part 1." *Journal of the Pali Text Society* 33: 1–53.
Gornall, A., Henry, J. 2017. "Beautifully Moral: Cosmopolitan issues in medieval Pāli literary theory." In *Sri Lanka at the Crossroads of History*, eds. Z. Biedermann, A. Strathern, 77–93. London: UCL Press.
Griffiths, A., Lammerts, D.C. 2015. "Epigraphy: Southeast Asia." In *Brill's Encyclopedia of Buddhism, Volume 1: Literature and Languages*, ed. J. Silk, 988–1009. Leiden: Brill.
Hallisey, C. 2003. "Works and Persons in Sinhala Literary Culture." In *Literary Cultures in History: Reconstructions from South Asia*, ed. S. Pollock, 689–746. Berkeley: University of California Press.
von Hinüber, O. 1994a. "On the History of the Name of the Pāli Language." In *Selected Papers on Pāli Studies*, 76–90. Oxford: Pali Text Society.
von Hinüber, O. 1994b. "Buddhist Law and the Phonetics of Pāli." In *Selected Papers on Pāli Studies*, 198–232. Oxford: Pali Text Society.
von Hinüber, O. 1996. *A Handbook of Pāli Literature*. Berlin: De Gruyter.
Kacc = 2013. Pind, O.H., ed. *Kaccāyana and Kaccāyanavutti*. Bristol: Pali Text Society.
Kieffer-Pülz, P. 2000. "Die buddhistische Gemeinde." In *Der Buddhismus I: Der indische Buddhismus und seine Verzweigungen*, eds. Heinz Bechert et al., 281–402. Stuttgart: W. Kohlhammer.
Kieffer-Pülz, P. 2013. *Verlorene Gaṇṭhipadas zum buddhistischen Ordensrecht. Untersuchungen zu den in der Vajirabuddhiṭīkā zitierten Kommentaren Dhammasiris und Vajirabuddhis*. Teil 1. Veröffentlichungen der Indologischen Kommission 1. Wiesbaden: Harrassowitz.
Lammerts, D.C. 2018. *Buddhist Law in Burma: A History of Dhammasattha Texts and Jurisprudence, 1250–1850*. Honolulu: University of Hawai'i Press.
Le Goff, J. 1988. *The Medieval Imagination*. Translated by Arthur Goldhammer. Chicago: University of Chicago Press.
McDaniel, J.T. 2008. *Gathering Leaves and Lifting Words: Histories of Buddhist Monastic Education in Laos and Thailand*. Seattle: University of Washington Press.
McDaniel, J.T. 2011. *The Lovelorn Ghost and the Magical Monk: Practicing Buddhism in Modern Thailand*. New York: Columbia University Press.
Mogg = 1999. *Moggallānavyākaraṇa*. Chaṭṭhasaṅgāyana CD-Rom Version 3. Dhammagiri, Igatpuri: Vipassana Research Institute.
Moh = 1961. *Mohavicchedanī Abhidhamma-mātikattha-vaṇṇanā by Kassapatthera of Coḷa*, eds. A.P. Buddhadatta, A.K. Warder. London: Pali Text Society.

Mus, P. 1939. *La Lumière sur les Six Voies. Tableau de la transmigration bouddhique d'après des sources sanskrites, pāli, tibétaines et chinoises en majeure partie inédites*. Vol. 1. Paris: Institut d'ethnologie.
Oberlies, T. 2019. *Pāli Grammar: The language of the canonical texts of Theravāda Buddhism*. Vol. 1. Melksham, Wilts: Pali Text Society.
Ollett, A. 2017. *Language of the Snakes: Prakrit, Sanskrit, and the Language Order of Premodern India*. Oakland: University of California Press.
Paṭis-a = 1979. *Saddhammappakāsinī. Commentary on the Paṭisambhidāmagga*. Vol. 1. 1933. Reprinted, ed. C.V. Joshi. London: Pali Text Society.
Pind, O.H. 1989. "Studies in the Pāli Grammarians I: Buddhaghosa's Reference to Grammar and Grammarians." *Journal of the Pali Text Society* 13: 33–82.
Pind, O.H. 2012. "Pali Grammar and Grammarians from Buddhaghosa to Vajirabuddhi: A Survey." *Journal of the Pali Text Society* 31: 57–124.
Pollock, S. 2006. *The Language of the Gods in the World of Men: Sanskrit, Culture, and Power in Premodern India*. Berkeley: University of California Press.
Premchit, S., Swearer, D.K. 1977. "A Translation of Tamnān Mūlasāsanā Wat Pā Daeng: The Chronicle of the Founding of Buddhism of the Wat Pā Daeng Tradition." *Journal of the Siam Society* 65 (2): 73–110.
Ps = 1977. *Papañcasūdanī Majjhimanikāyaṭṭhakathā of Buddhaghosācariya*. Part 1, Suttas 1–10. 1922. Reprint. eds. J.H. Woods, D. Kosambi. London: Pali Text Society.
Ruiz-Falqués, A. 2017. "The Role of Pāli Grammar in Burmese Buddhism." *Journal of Burma Studies* 21 (1): 1–96.
Rūp = 1936. *Maharupasiddhi by Ven. Choliya Buddhapriya Maha Thera, the Head of the Maha Vihara sect in Ceylon, with Sandehavighatani, a Sinhalese paraphrase by an ancient great scholar*, ed. B.K. Dhammaratana. Weligama: Sathmina Press.
Schonthal, B. 2018. "The Tolerations of Theravada Buddhism." In *Tolerations in Comparative Perspective*, ed. V.A. Spencer, 179–196. Lanham: Lexington Books.
Shulman, E. 2019. "The Protective Buddha: On the Cosmological Logic of *Paritta*." *Numen* 66: 207–242.
Silverstein, M. 1976 . "Shifters, Linguistic Categories, and Cultural Description." In *Meaning in Anthropology*, eds. K.H. Basso, H.A. Selby, 11–55. Albuquerque: University of New Mexico Press.
Singh, S. 2013. "Save Pali, ancient classical Indian language of Buddhism in India." *The Buddhist Channel*, April 16 2013: https://www.buddhistchannel.tv/index.php?id=70,11414,0,0,1,0#.X5kdby8RpBw
Skilling, P. 2022. "Canons: Authoritative Texts of the Theravaṃsa." In *The Routledge Handbook of Theravada Buddhism*, eds. S. Berkwitz, A. Thompson, 209–226. London: Routledge.
Sp = 1975–81. *Samantapāsādikā: Buddhaghosa's commentary on the Vinaya Piṭaka*. Vols. 1–7. 1924–47. Reprinted. eds. J. Takakusu, M. Nagai. London: Pali Text Society.
Spk = 1977. *Sārattha-ppakāsinī: Buddhaghosa's commentary on the Saṃyutta-Nikāya*. Vol. 1, On Sagāthā-vagga. 1929. Reprint, ed. F.L. Woodward. London: Pali Text Society.
Sp-ṭ Bᵉ = 1960. *Sāratthadīpanī-ṭīkā*. Vol. 1. Chaṭṭhasaṅgāyana edition. Yangon: Buddhasāsanasamiti.
Ss = 1992 *Sārasaṅgaha*, ed. G.H. Sasaki. Oxford: Pali Text Society.
Strathern, A. 2019. *Unearthly Powers: Religions and Political Change in World History*. Cambridge: Cambridge University Press.
Subodh = 2000. *Subodhālaṅkāra. Porāṇa-ṭīkā (Mahāsāmi-ṭīkā) by Saṅgharakkhita Mahāsāmi, Abhinava-ṭīkā (Nissaya) (anonymous)*, ed. P.S. Jaini. Oxford: Pali Text Society.
Sv = 1968. *The Sumaṅgala-Vilāsinī, Buddhaghosa's Commentary on the Dīgha-Nikāya*. Part 1. 1886. Reprint. eds. T.W. Rhys Davids, J.E. Carpenter. London: Pali Text Society.
Sv-nṭ Bᵉ = 1961. *Sādhuvilāsinī, Sumaṅgalavilāsinī-navaṭīkā, Sīlakkhandhavagga-abhinavaṭīkā*. Vol. 1. Chaṭṭhasaṅgāyana edition. Yangon: Buddhasāsanasamiti.
Sv-ṭ = 1970 *Dīghanikāy-aṭṭhakathāṭīkā Līnatthavaṇṇanā*. Vol. 1. ed. L. De Silva. London: Pali Text Society.
Tambiah, S.J. 1973. "Form and Meaning of Magical Acts: A Point of View." In *Modes of Thought: Essays on thinking in Western and non-Western societies*, eds. R. Horton, R. Finnegan, 199–229. London: Faber and Faber.
Thompson, A. 2016. *Engendering the Buddhist State: Territory, Sovereignty and Sexual Difference in the Inventions of Angkor*. London: Routledge.
Tiyavanich, K. 1997. *Forest Recollections: Wandering Monks in Twentieth-Century Thailand*. Honolulu: University of Hawai'i Press.
Turner, A. 2018. "Pali Scholarship "in Its Truest Sense" in Burma: The Multiple Trajectories in Colonial Deployments of Religion." *Journal of Asian Studies* 77.1: 123–138.

Turnour, G. 1837. *The Mahāvanso in Roman Characters, with the Translation Subjoined; And an Introductory Essay on Pali Buddhistical Literature.* Vol. 1. Ceylon: Cotta Church Mission Press.

UPT538.3F = (n.d.) *Candasuriyagatidīpanī* manuscript from U Po Thi Library, Myanmar, digitized by the Myanmar Manuscript Digital Library and hosted by the University of Toronto (https://mmdl.utoronto.ca).

Veidlinger, D.M. 2007. *Spreading the Dhamma: Writing, Orality, and Textual Transmission in Buddhist Northern Thailand.* Honolulu: University of Hawai'i Press.

Vibh-a = 1980. *Sammoha-vinodanī Abhidhamma-Piṭake Vibhaṅgaṭṭhakathā.* 1923. ed. A.P. Buddhadatta. London: Pali Text Society.

Visigalli, P. (Forthcoming) "The classification of nouns (*nāma*) in Buddhaghosa and Pāli scholastic literature." *Bulletin of the School of Oriental and African Studies.*

Vmv B^e = 1960. *Vimativinodanī-ṭīkā.* Vol. 1. Chaṭṭhasaṅgāyana edition. Yangon: Buddhasāsanasamiti.

Vsm = 1950. *Visuddhimagga of Buddhaghosācariya.* Revised by Dharmananda Kosambi. ed. H.C. Warren. Harvard Oriental Series 41. Cambridge, Massachusetts: Harvard University Press.

Walker, T. 2022. "Bilingualism: Theravāda Bitexts across South and Southeast Asia'." In *The Routledge Handbook of Theravada Buddhism*, eds. S. Berkwitz, A. Thompson, 271–284. London: Routledge.

3

CIRCULATIONS

Linked spaces and divergent temporalities in the Pāli world

Anne M. Blackburn

Introduction

In the last several decades, the term *network* has become central within the analytical repertoire of many disciplines in the social sciences and the humanities, including sociology, anthropology, history, political science, and religious studies. This chapter explores some of the strengths and weaknesses of *network* as an analytical term used by scholars interested in historical studies of processes and phenomena related to the Triple Gem (Buddha, Dhamma, Saṅgha) in the premodern Pāli world. I use the term *Pāli world* rather than *Theravāda Buddhism* in premodern contexts. In my usage, the Pāli world is a geographic space: connected and partly unified by Pāli language and textual traditions but retaining strong internal local and subregional differentiation; multilingual, as Pāli interacts with local and other trans-regional languages; characterized by statecraft strongly marked by understandings of *buddha-sāsana* rooted in Pāli-language textual materials but in a nonexclusive fashion; in which trans-regional connections presuming mutual intelligibility via Pāli language; and concepts were motivated by local aims. This chapter argues that the concept of "network" has some real but limited utility and proposes that investigating "circulatory processes" rather than "networks" offers the promise of greater subtlety and precision for historical studies of the Pāli world. I draw on materials from thirteenth- and fourteenth-century Sukhothai, a polity in northern Tai territories, to exemplify the limitations of network analyses and the relative advantage of thinking in terms of "circulatory processes."

Sukhothai[1]

For scholars interested in processes related to the expansion of the Pāli world, and the development of new political centers (Blackburn Forthcoming) and textual communities (Blackburn 2001) that were invested in Pāli-language *tipiṭaka*-related texts and *sāsana* histories, the inscriptions of Sukhothai from the first half of the second millennium A.D. are thought-provoking data. For the purposes of this chapter, I focus on two significant changes reflected by the Sukhothai inscriptional record. No exhaustive treatment of Sukhothai history or epigraphy is intended.[2] Over a period of roughly seventy years in the Sukhothai inscriptions, we find the intensifying presence of theories and themes rooted in Pāli-language texts related to *buddha-sāsana*, as well as a developing emphasis on Laṅkā as a privileged geographic location in the Buddhist world to

DOI: 10.4324/9781351026666-5

which Sukhothai monks and kings sought connection.[3] As the following examples make clear, the growing presence of theories and themes rooted in Pāli-language texts, and the increasing emphasis on connection to Laṅkā, did not entail the eradication of textual and material practices related to Khmer (and perhaps Mon) cultural spaces or the displacement of śāstric ideas with an intellectual lineage in Sanskrit textuality. However, the Sukhothai inscriptions valuably indicate the early second-millennium expansion of the Pāli world to include the emergent Tai polities of Sukhothai and Ayutthaya. Other epigraphic and literary evidence (not addressed here) signals a related process occurring at Chiang Mai. The Sukhothai inscriptions provide a rich context within which to reflect on the intellectual costs and benefits of using the idea of "network" to conceptualize how a particular locale—Sukhothai—came to participate more centrally in the Pāli world of the second millennium.

Sukhothai emerged toward the end of the thirteenth century as a Tai city-state (*müang*) with aspirations to control a number of what Chris Baker and Pasuk Pongpaichit (2017) call the "Northern Territories" along the Ping River system, which enters the Chao Phraya system and thence the Gulf of Siam and the wider Indian Ocean arena. Although earlier historians have described the rise of Sukhothai as an overthrow of Khmer imperial domination, Baker and Pasuk have recently convincingly built on earlier arguments by Michael Vickery (2010) indicating that substantial Khmer political control did not extend so far to the northeast, although there is evidence of Khmer royal engagement with sites near Sukhothai. Certainly, Sukhothai and other Northern Territories were part of a wider Khmer cultural sphere, hence the use of Khmer language, Khmer influences in the built environment, and the fact that Khmer titles persist in Sukhothai inscriptions of the thirteenth and fourteenth centuries. As indicated further later, Khmer practices of expressing sovereignty through interventions in the built environment likely continued to influence Sukhothai royal practice, even as the rulers of Sukhothai began to experiment with expressions of sovereignty informed by Pāli texts. The ongoing impact of Khmer ideas and practices was due in part to Sukhothai's periods of subordination to Ayutthaya—a powerful maritime polity in the Indian Ocean economy from the middle of the fourteenth century—and Ayutthaya's complex relationship to Angkor.

Our first royal inscription is the so-called Ramkamhäng Inscription, composed in or near 1292, during the reign of king Ramkamhäng (r. ?–1292?). After considerable controversy in the 1990s and early 2000s, this inscription is now accepted by scholars as our earliest Sukhothai inscription. I compare it with a cluster of royal and monastic inscriptions from several decades later, during the reign of King Mahā Dhammarāja I (1347–?). By the 1290s, the era of our first Sukhothai inscription, Buddhist ideas, *tipiṭaka* passages, and writing in Pāli language all had a deep history in parts of the Southeast Asian mainland, dating to the middle of the first millennium. Sukhothai Inscription 1 is our first extant inscription in a form of Tai language, and it has been the subject of much scholarly discussion as such. In the present context, I use it to develop a temporal comparison, indicating changes in the degree and manner in which elements drawn from Pāli textual culture appear within the Sukhothai inscriptions during the period ranging from the reign of Ramkamhäng to that of Mahā Dharmarāja I, over a period of approximately seventy years or two generations, and the degree to which authority and prestige are attributed to the island of Laṅkā. Sukhothai Inscription 1 uses a smattering of Pāli technical terms. It makes use of common Buddhist terms and titles, for instance. However, it does not incorporate substantial narrative content (stories, exemplary characters, etc.) from the textual corpus of the Pāli world. Moreover, the Buddhist elements are generic and could be drawn from Buddhist materials in any language: Ramkamhäng is said to know the *dhamma* and to follow an appropriate cycle of monastic ritual observances, such as *vassa* (the rainy season retreat for monks) and *kathina* (an annual robe offering ceremony). Sukhothai Inscription 1 does not explicitly attempt to argue for Sukhothai's place within a larger Buddhist geography; links to celebrated *buddha-sāsana* sites from the Indian mainland and Laṅkā are absent. It is not clear whence Ramkamhäng and his court drew these basic ideas and terms related to *buddha-sāsana* and monastic practice. The possibilities are greatly overdetermined, given the possible continued influence of Mon Pāli textual forms from the Lopburi area as well as flows into Sukhothai from locations further southwest such as Nakhon Si Thammarat indicated by the inscription itself.

While Sukhothai Inscription 1 is very direct, and not particularly graceful, much has changed by his grandson's reign. Mahā Dhammarāja I is referred to in a series of six royal inscriptions running from the 1350s into the late 1360s, and another from this later period composed by the highest-ranking Buddhist monk at Sukhothai at that time to commemorate the king's temporary ordination as a monk. There are also three inscriptions referring to the travels and *sāsana*-related activities of a high-ranking Sukhothai monastic named Si Sattha (Śrī Śraddhā), likely a former rival to the king. By this time, the inscriptional style has changed dramatically from that of Sukhothai Inscription 1, incorporating vastly more in the way of narrative and technical language from Pāli textual culture, and demonstrating more elaborate literary capabilities indebted to Pāli textual form. We also find royal prowess expressed in terms related to śāstric knowledge with roots in Sanskrit knowledge systems (Griswold and Prasert na Nagara 1992, 457–459; Blackburn 2017b). In the later inscriptions concerning Mahā Dhammarāja I and Si Sattha from the second half of the 1300s, narrative materials from the Pāli Buddhist corpus are deeply evident, including commentarial material and *vaṃsa* texts composed on Laṅkā, as Michel Lorillard has nicely demonstrated (2000). Lankan pilgrimage locations textualized through the Pāli vamsas were clearly known at Sukhothai. Other indications that Laṅkā served as one source (direct or indirect) for Pāli materials reaching Sukhothai include the fact that these later Sukhothai inscriptions reflect predictions that *buddha-sāsana* would decline over five thousand years, presented in a form close to that of *Manorāṭṭhapuranī*, a fifth-century Pāli commentary on the *Aṅguttara Nikāya* composed on the island of Laṅkā (Griswold and Prasert na Nagara 1992, 452–456). Such ideas of decline were incorporated into portrayals of Mahā Dhammarāja I as a king equipped to support his subjects' merit-making in the precious period before *sāsana*'s end. In addition, it is clear that the authors of the later Sukhothai inscriptions shared anticipations of the next Buddha Metteyya (Griswold and Prasert na Nagara 1992, 456–457), an increasingly popular narrative focus in Lankan Pāli texts composed around the turn of the second millennium CE. However, we should not assume that Laṅkā was the sole source of Pāli textual materials to the exclusion of other flows, especially given indications in the built environment that Sukhothai was connected to Pagan (Blackburn 2017a). Another indication of the growing presence of Pāli textuality at Sukhothai is the coincidence of images and motifs from the *jātaka*s (narratives of Gotama Buddha's past lives as aspiring Buddha) within later Sukhothai inscriptions—including one composed in Pāli by the then highest-ranking monastic of the realm—and the *jātaka* images of Wat Si Chum (Skilling et al. 2008) with Pāli captions. For instance, Inscription 6 composed in Pāli sometime in or after 1361 by the then leading monk of Sukhothai to celebrate the king's temporary monastic ordination, compares his monarch to *jātaka* heroes: "like Vessantara in generosity … like King Sīlava in morality" (Griswold and Prasert na Nagara 1992, 517). Inscriptions praising Si Sattha, likely dating to the 1370s, develop an extended comparison between this monk and the Buddha-to-be as Vessantara. For instance, Inscription 2 is striking for reporting Si Sattha's activities in a narrative style indebted to biographies of Buddha Gautama and to Gautama's previous life as Bodhisattva Vessantara; this monk is implicitly portrayed as a Buddha-to-be (Griswold and Prasert na Nagara 1992, 387–9).

Laṅkā is a strong presence in the inscriptions of this later reign, contrasting strongly with Inscription 1's relative disinterest in the wider geography of *buddha-sāsana*, two generations earlier.

Now monks associated with Lańkā are specifically sought by Sukhothai leaders; Lańkā is portrayed as a prestigious location within the perceived world of *buddha-sāsana*. Lańkā is also celebrated as a privileged source for Buddha relics used for protection and merit-making. In the Mahā Dhammarāja I inscriptions, sovereign authority is strongly linked to the king's ability to provide his subjects access to Buddha-relics. His capacity to do so is a public demonstration of the sovereign's fitness to rule, since—according to theories of sovereignty expressed in Pāli texts—Buddha-relics are understood to remain only in the company of those who deserve them (Trainor 1997). The installation of Buddha-relics at trade and military frontiers was a potent act. In the inscriptions, Sukhothai subjects are exhorted to make haste in offering *pūja* to the relics provided by the king. These relics are explicitly and repeatedly related to Lańkā, referred to as both Lańkādvīpa and as Sīhaḷa. For instance, Inscription 3 of 1357 discusses the consecration of the king, presents his royal title, and then describes a relic brought by him to one of the cities he sought to include within his kingdom:

> This precious relic is not a common one, but it is a real relic brought from far-away Lańkādvīpa. Some seeds from the *śrīmahābodhi* tree under which our Lord Buddha was sitting when he defeated the army of King Mārādhirāja and attained the omniscience of Buddhahood have also been brought here and planted behind this reliquary monument.
>
> (Griswold and Prasert na Nagara 1992, 449)[4]

Inscriptions describing Si Sattha also stress Lankan connections, emphasizing his pilgrimage travels to *sāsana*-related sites on Lańkā and gifts given to maintain Buddha-relic monuments there. Thus, a comparison of Sukhothai Inscription 1 with the cluster of inscriptions from the era of Mahā Dhammarāja I and Si Sattha show increasing emphasis Lańkā as a desirable location within *buddha-sāsana* and the impact of Pāli compositions composed on Lańkā. Although Tai and Khmer languages continue to dominate this epigraphic record (only one inscription is composed in Pāli from this period), we see that the textual culture of Sukhothai epigraphy rapidly incorporated Pāli materials, with an obvious debt to Lankan Pāli compositions, whether brought directly from the island or via other locations. The first half of the fourteenth century was clearly a critical period for incorporating the Northern Territories within the Pāli world (Blackburn 2018).

At the same time, it is likely that Mahā Dhammarāja I's choice to install Buddha footprints at locations of economic and military importance owed something to the rather recent history of Khmer imperial practice in the region and perhaps to understandings of Khmer sovereignty present in later fourteenth-century Sukhothai through Ayutthayan connections after Sukhothai became an Ayutthayan subordinate.[5] For instance, art historical evidence from the Sukhothai region addressed by Jean Boisselier (1969)—and more recently by Hiram Woodward (1994/5, 2005)—indicates the presence of Jayavarman VII-era (that is, late twelfth- and early thirteenth-century) construction at Sukhothai, not long before Sukhothai's emergence as an independent *müang*. These appear to have included images associated with the Angkorian king Jayavarman VII that yoked royal representation to cosmic Buddha symbols. The technique of making imperial territorial claims by installing such objects was not an innovation of Jayavarman VII but rather had a deeper history within the Khmer polity. It is not unlikely that the Khmer imperial expressive logic of conveying the combined force of royal and cosmological power through royally sponsored and strategically placed potent objects continued to shape the way Sukhothai soverigns expressed aspirations to expansive authority. Such logics, however, were adapted to encompass powerful Buddha-relics authorized by narratives composed on Lańkā and circulated within the expanding Pāli world.

Networks

The preceding discussion suggests a number of grounds for thinking that thirteenth- and fourteenth-century Sukhothai—the era in which the body of inscriptions just discussed was produced—could be analyzed fruitfully via a network analysis of some kind. The inscriptional corpus indicates that Sukhothai was a locale linked to other locations, that there were knowledge flows among these locations, and that changes in one location (e.g., Laṅkā or Ayutthaya) had causal impacts on another location (e.g. Sukhothai). Moreover, the inscriptions indicate the movement of various kinds of specialists among locations. When the inscriptions are mapped against other evidence from the region in this period, such as Indian Ocean trading practices, it becomes clear that the mobility of persons, objects, and ideas associated with the Triple Gem coincided with other movements occurring within the trading ecosystem of the Indian Ocean.

Three approaches to network analysis of the Sukhothai materials appear most promising, and I introduce them in the following. However, as the subsequent discussion indicates, in my view none of these approaches to the Sukhothai data (and other similar evidence from elsewhere in the premodern Pāli world) is adequate to the historical complexity we seek to study. Thus, the conclusion to this chapter proposes instead an analytical engagement with "circulatory processes," a conceptual framework better suited to our available evidence.

In my view, the three forms of network analysis with the greatest initial promise for the study of cases like Sukhothai are examining single networks created through bonds of trust or recognition, looking at multiple networks differentiated by function that intersect or overlap at hubs or nodes with causal impacts occurring from one network on another, and actor-network analysis examining the co-presence of animate and inanimate objects that combine to generate stable entities or enterprises. Among scholars of religion, historians, and historical anthropologists, a form of "network" analysis drawing on conceptions of group trust and recognition has proved influential. For instance, this usage has shaped scholarship on connectivity in the Indian Ocean region by scholars who have explored how shared religious affiliation and/or a shared place of origin facilitated the movement of goods and financial instruments across long distances.[6] Studies of more contemporary contexts have also drawn upon a related conception of "network" to analyze the role of religious affiliation in migration, suggesting that shared affiliation engenders relationships of mutual support in processes of transit and localization (Conermann and Smolarz 2015). Kenneth Dean has adapted the work of Charles Tilly to describe institutional connections in the South China Sea arena. He writes, for instance, of a "temple trust network" linking southern China and locations within what are now Singapore and Malaysia (2018). Dean portrays the institutional connections between Chinese temples nested within network relations. My own use of the term *network* in relation to nineteenth-century monastic communications between locations in what are now contemporary Sri Lanka, Burma/Myanmar, and Thailand did not foreground specifically the relationship between "religious affiliation" and "trust" (Blackburn 2010). Yet in some sense, I presumed the possibility of mutual recognition among those seeking the protection of the Triple Gem, a mutual recognition that might facilitate flows of information (e.g., about monastic lineage histories, or strategies for combatting Christian missionary activity) and conduce to shared goals (e.g., maintaining the vitality of *buddha-sāsana*).

Scholarly approaches to networks of trust and recognition have potential applicability to the Sukhothai inscriptions described earlier. For instance, one might refer to a "monastic network" or a "Buddhist network" in discussing the relay of interactions that appear to have played a role in the travel of Buddhist monks to and from Sukhothai. One could propose that the monastic dignitary from Mottama (Martaban), a coastal polity then located in territory now held within

Burma/Myanmar, referred to in King Ramkamhäng's Inscription 1, and the monk Si Sattha, who is the protagonist of several later Sukhothai inscriptions, were—as followers of the Triple Gem and/or as monastics—able to mobilize trust and recognition sufficient to secure their mobility across substantial distances, in times of unpredictable infrastructure for travel. Or, with reference to the repertoire drawn from Pāli texts that manifests with growing strength in the Sukhothai inscriptions between the era of King Ramkamhäng and that of King Mahā Dhammarāja I, one might invoke *network* in a different way, closer to the usage of Jason Neelis in his work on Silk Road Buddhist transmission (2011). Neelis draws centrally on the concept of "network" to portray mutually influencing agentive processes understood as affecting the transmission of Buddhist ideas and objects. This complex causation is discussed in terms of the co-presence and interaction of multiple networks, described as "religious," "economic," and "political." Here rather than emphasizing a particular characteristic that might support relations of trust and interdependence, Neelis's use of *network* appears closer to some form of systems theory involving linkages among hubs and nodes.[7] Returning to the Sukhothai epigraphic data, along these lines one might invoke the idea of a "Buddhist network" transmitting *sāsana*-related texts (oral and/or written) along with their human carriers and explain the viability of this network in relation to an "economic network" that characterized the Indian Ocean arena in the first half of the second millennium CE.[8] On this view the transmission of Buddhist phenomena along one networked set of interactions would be understood as enabled by an intersecting or overlapping series of trade-related interactions construed as another network. Sukhothai and the polities of Mottama and Ayutthaya could be understood as nodes operating simultaneously within a "Buddhist network" and a "trade network."

It would also be possible to approach the idea of "network" in relation to the Sukhothai data through a form of network theory articulated by Bruno Latour (1996, 2010). This to my knowledge has not been undertaken by any historian of Buddhism. In this view, the phenomenon under analysis is understood as the product of conditioning elements that must interconnect in a particular way to create the phenomenon in its stable form. The emphasis here is on maintaining a single scale of vision, such that the analysis does not depend on encompassing macro-scale concepts that—according to actor-network analysis—hide the immanent agencies productive of phenomena in the world. Thus, for instance, any one of our Sukhothai inscriptions would not be analyzed as expressive of a macro-level phenomenon such as "Buddhist kingship" but, rather, examined in terms of the co-constitutive elements ranging from building material to labor flow to Pāli-language ideational elements brought to the royal court by monastic literati. Or a public royal act such as the installation of Buddha-relics in a particular location could be understood in actor-network terms as comprising a theory of sovereignty linking kinship to the public provision of relics, the relics themselves, labor force, royal agent, royal clients, building materials, and so on.

Networks reconsidered

A critical question that arises in any analyses involving the concept of "network" is how the network is identified and labeled. A "network" is not a natural kind, of course, but a concept used for heuristic purposes in order to bring certain aspects of data into sharper visibility and to suggest certain relationships of cause or correlation. Although I have myself used the term *Buddhist network* in other published work, the term seems to me increasingly problematic, especially in relation to pre-twentieth-century data. In the first place, the term *Buddhist network* suggests an exclusive identity category at odds with historical forms of collective belonging related to Buddha, Dhamma, and Saṅgha. There is an abundance of data from locations in the

Pāli world showing that patrons of the Triple Gem often offered patronage and veneration to other ritual foci as well, such as Viṣṇu or the protective deity associated with particular topographic locations such as a mountain or royal city. Boundaries were sometimes drawn between Triple Gem practices and other forms (typically one was not simultaneously a follower of Mahā Jina and Gotama Buddha), but these boundaries were drawn less often, and less tightly, than modern understandings of discrete confessional religious communities would suggest. In other words, although as noted in the examples above one might be tempted to invoke the idea of a "Buddhist network," the cost of doing so arguably outweighs the benefits, since it distorts premodern data. For some historians, including myself, one intellectual aim is to identify and begin to understand the ways that individuals and groups articulated understandings of collective belonging (Blackburn 2010; see also Hansen 2018). Presuming "Buddhist" as a form of collective identification and using it for descriptive and analytical purposes as a modifier of the term *network* will often be at odds with the expressions of groupness (Cooper and Brubaker 2005) articulated by individuals at specific historical moments in the Pāli world.

The term *Buddhist network* also masks (although not intentionally) the historical fact that travelers looking to the Triple Gem for immediate protection and future security, did so cheek by jowl with persons characterized by other ritual and soteriological engagements, and that all those on the move were also marked by business, political, and/or familial interests. For instance, the ships on which Si Sattha traveled when moving between Sukhothai and Laṅkā were not vessels used solely for the movement of a Buddhist monk! As the geographic references in the inscriptions concerning him show, Si Sattha's travel depended on shifting trade and military relationships; a traveler like Si Sattha made do with the conveyances available at any point in time, and his movement occurred along with the travel of other persons with diverse motivations. What we know of trade in the Indian Ocean arena during this era strongly suggests that he would have traveled with followers of the Indian theist traditions, along with Muslims, in his attempt to undertake a pilgrimage to potent Buddha-relics in Laṅkā.[9] It is not unlikely that Muslims owned and/or captained one or more of the ships on which he traveled. Describing Si Sattha as moving along a "Buddhist network" would make these aspects of premodern Indian Ocean mobility harder to recognize, inadvertently reinforcing a historically misleading vision of compartmentalized confessional communities, and a "religious sphere" separated from other activities.

A related problem in the labeling of networks is identifying them by function-distinctive terms such as *religious*, *trade/economic*, and *political*. As noted earlier in the discussion of work by Neelis, such usage may in one sense be helpful toward the conceptualization of interactive processes within large and complex geographies. Yet distinguishing between networks in this way also brings significant risks of historical distortion. Identifying a distinctive domain as "religion" or "religious" is a rather late historical innovation—like "nation" and "ethnicity," "religion" is a modern concept that only became a widely shared "commonsense" term in the course of the nineteenth century. Moreover, it has often been conceptualized in ways strongly indebted to forms of Protestant Christianity (Masuzawa 2005). On account of its history, the term *religion* is vulnerable to anachronism and ill-suited to characterize many forms of ritual, institutional, and philosophical life in premodern contexts. Within the premodern Pāli world—as in other premodern contexts—there was no separation of a discrete arena of discourse and practice in the manner identified by the modern concept of "religion." Rather, we find the imbrication of forms of statecraft with a variety of protection rituals, as well as the patronage of ritual and literate specialists, often through elaborate public performance. Moreover, those involved in the transmission of soteriologies and protection rituals could also be carriers of information related to statecraft as well as valuable goods. Persons involved in the transportation of goods were simultaneously ritual practitioners who venerated one or more potent foci; they might also be patrons of ritual institutions.

To return to the Sukhothai examples, if we were to characterize the changing features of Sukhothai inscriptions on which I chose to focus earlier—more references to *buddha-sāsana* and sovereigns in ways influenced by Pāli texts and stronger rhetorical connections drawn to the island of Laṅkā—as the result of a "Buddhist network" or "religious network" supported or enabled by an "economic network" this would make it harder to see the implications of our available historical evidence. The data repeatedly shows the *co-constitution* of social authority, economic relationships, and Triple Gem–related practice. For instance, Maha Dhammarāja I erected public inscriptions celebrating kingship in *sāsana*-related terms borrowed from Laṅkā, as well as the Indian mainland and Angkor. He did so at geographic locations critical to Sukhothai's military security and commercial routes, likely conjoining notions of kingship related to Buddha relics expressed in Pāli texts with Khmer approaches to expressing sovereignty through royally sponsored landscape installations. The monk Si Sattha whose monastic status appears to have offered him access to multiple locations within the Buddhist world also attempted to leverage his position within elite politics at Sukhothai. His departure to Laṅkā from Sukhothai seems to have been timed for reasons of political vulnerability as well as merit-making; the pilgrimage itinerary responded to transportation opportunities shaped by a dynamic trading arena.

Thus, adapting network analyses rooted in both the trust/recognition framework and the multiple networks systems theory framework to the study of the premodern Pāli world entails certain risks in historical analysis, risks involving problems of anachronism, and the danger of taking too seriously empirically anachronistic heuristic distinctions between forms of activity designated as "religious," "economic," and so on. In addition to these areas of concern, there is another interestingly problematic feature of network analyses. They are ill suited to accommodate temporal complexity and causal processes occurring along multiple timescapes. This problem is particularly acute for actor-network analysis, but the difficulty also characterizes the other forms of network analysis discussed above. A network analysis along trust/recognition lines has the implicit potential to accommodate some matters related to temporality and memory inasmuch as the intragroup grounds for trust may include a historical sensibility that the group possesses shared history, and individuals may also gauge one another's trustworthiness through reflection on lineage, family history, and so on. However, this form of network analysis does not help us understand the wider conditions of possibility that have shaped the impulse to connect and then taking advantage of enhanced connection possible through trust and recognition. In other words, returning to one of the examples above, Si Sattha's Indian Ocean circulations may have been eased by his legibility to others as a Triple Gem follower or as a monastic, and interactions achieving this recognition might have included references to *sāsana* history. Yet via a trust/recognition analysis, we would not be well poised to understand the intersecting historical processes causing Si Sattha to set forth from Sukhothai (processes with shorter and longer temporal durations such as Sukhothai's changing place in Indian Ocean infrastructure or Mahā Dhammarāja I's accession to the throne). Nor would there be an opportunity to probe the ways in which past experiences (such as Si Sattha's experience as an elite youth and his family's military history) and anticipations of the future (including Si Sattha's aspiration to Buddhahood) helped shape Si Sattha's subjectivity (as best we have partial access to it through inscriptional evidence) and his chosen actions. In the systems theory network analysis, characterized by multiple networks sharing hubs and nodes, the emphasis is spatial rather than temporal. This kind of analysis may help us visualize how persons and phenomena come to be co-present in a particular location through intersecting and/or overlapping circuits of mobility, albeit at the risk of characterizing these persons and phenomena in misleading terms (see the previous discussion). However, focusing on relations occurring through hubs and nodes that bring more than one network into connection places the emphasis quite late in terms of causal processes. This approach is not well suited to evoking the deeper causal temporalities that have shaped the possibilities of intersection and connection. Moreover, the focus on network rather than persons participating in movement diverts attention that might be productively directed toward understanding how larger-scale historical processes come to bear on individuals, as well as how the way a person inhabits spaces of memory and anticipation shapes their acts in locations that might figure on a network map. Returning to the Si Sattha examples mentioned just previously, we again find ourselves with insufficient tools to understand his activities or context.

In actor-network analysis in the mode developed by Latour, such analysis is used to create a productive redescription of a present-tense phenomenon of some kind, a redescription that stresses the interactive agentive components required to create and maintain that phenomenon (such as an economic relationship, a technological form, or a theoretical articulation). Such redescription is intended to deconstruct larger-order descriptors understood by actor-network analysis to mask agentive relations by relying on artificial encompassing analytical categories. In undertaking this redescription, there is a strong and explicit emphasis on the temporality of the network itself to the exclusion of other temporalities (Law and Mol 1994; Law 2002). In such an analysis, our attention is focused on the present moment of the holding together of the phenomenon-creating/maintaining network rather than deeper temporal frameworks that reveal other causes, precursors, and meanings of the phenomenon in question. When Mahā Dhammarāja I installed footprint relics at strategic locations within the realm he aspired to control, invoking the forthcoming era of the next Buddha Metteyya, or when Si Sattha (or those crafting his inscriptional persona) portrayed himself as comparable to Gotama Buddha in pre-enlightenment lives and thus to a future Buddha, an actor-network analysis would help us to see the present-tense animate (e.g., the king, laborers, theorists of sovereignty) and inanimate (text models, mountains, stone) elements linked together to produce these inscriptions-as-artifacts. However, this perspective is not well suited to show how a such a moment of production is rooted in, and depends on, the invocation of the past and the anticipation of the future. Mahā Dhammarāja I's inscriptional projects are characterized by this temporal complexity and presume the capacity of subject audiences (readers, listeners) to interpret the present-tense artifact of the inscription within this larger temporal context in order for the artifact to take effect powerfully on them. This complex temporality is expressed for instance by the inscriptions' invocation of past kings, the deep time of *buddha-sāsana*, and the king's expressed ability to determine for his subjects where they stand within a timescape of promise and danger that extends between the lifetimes of past Gotama Buddha and the next Buddha Metteyya. Similarly, the inscriptions attending to Si Sattha invoke the memory of his ancestors in a manner that endows this monk with elements of royal prowess, and create for him the stature of a Buddha-to-be by describing him in terms taken from the *jātakas*; he is said to mirror the qualities of Gotama Buddha in his progression to Buddhahood.

Circulatory processes

How are we to write histories of the premodern Pāli world's process of coming-to-be, histories of the Pāli world's geographic expansion? Such work is immensely challenging, requiring a substantial understanding of multiple locales; attention to evidence often thought to characterize disparate fields (e.g., political economy, intellectual history, history of art, religious studies, etc.); and alertness to complex conditions of possibility for experimentation and innovation by individuals and collectives at particular conjunctures, and the terms in which such persons articulated their aims. Given the limited and challenging evidence at our disposal, it also requires a willingness to develop analyses across scales, developing an understanding of materials like the Sukhothai inscriptions discussed earlier as both causes and effects, made possible by and contributing to other occurrences within the Pāli world. In order to understand royal Sukhothai's growing investment in Pāli-language textuality, Lankan prestige, and visions of *buddha-sāsana* articulated from Laṅkā, for instance, and the manifestation of these interests in royal practice and the built environment, it helps to understand many other factors such as Sukhothai's relationships to other political formations, competing factions among Sukhothai elites, precedents for landscape intervention by rulers and strongmen at Sukhothai, and continuities or changes in trade and communication access between Sukhothai and locations both downriver and upriver. Many of these factors would not be caught from a network perspective, because of their temporal depth. At the same time, deep and historically sensitive investigation of discrete local environments will not suffice. We require also a way to identify and understand the ways in which specific combinations of local changes—changes occurring in more than one locale—alter the conditions of possibility for Triple Gem–related practices at other linked geographic locations. For instance, the expansion of Pāli-language technical terms and intertextual references connected to *buddha-sāsana* over a roughly seventy-year period running from the first inscription of King Ramkamhäng to those of King Mahā Dhammarāja I—changes that indicate innovation and experimentation in the practice of sovereignty at Sukhothai—were the result of complex shifts at multiple locations. The rising volume of Indian Ocean trade supported the emergence of new political formations at locations such as Mottama, Dambadeṇiya (a polity in west-central Laṅkā), and Ayutthaya. The combination of increasing trade connection and ambitious new political formations increased the speed with which *sāsana*-related elements traveled to Sukhothai from Laṅkā and coastal Burma. *Sāsana*-related elements such as theories of Buddhist sovereignty, styles of devotional practice, and cosmological arguments changed rapidly at Lankan locations owing to a variety of factors such as increasingly complex political administration, the growing presence of Sanskrit textual culture, and interactions between Indian theist and Triple Gem devotional forms. These new forms then traveled along Indian Ocean sea lanes and their linked riverine routes.

The concept of "network" cannot handle such levels of complexity. We need analytical language suited to representing dynamic processes at multiple locations that alter conditions of possibility at other multiple locations. We must be able to see how the impacts of such dynamic processes may be felt at specific locales on distinctive timescapes, without homogenization across a trans-regional environment. There must be room to see how new elements arriving at specific locales through interactive trans-regional processes interact with other processes (often deeply historical)—related to economy, statecraft, aesthetic preferences, cosmological understandings, and the like—already underway at those locales. Therefore, I propose that we explore the value of conceptualizing the expanding Pāli world in terms of "circulatory processes" rather than "networks." There are, of course, many ways of thinking about "circulation." Contemplating the complex causalities that characterized the premodern Pāli world, one finds considerable affinity with discussions of human biological processes: the human circulatory system is characterized by extremely complex local environments that exert dynamic effects on other such arenas through multidirectional flows, with both local and systemic effects. Provided that we are not tempted to identify and overvalue any one "heart" of the Pāli world, visualizing its history in terms of circulatory processes provides greater congruence between the heuristic concept used in description and analysis and the complex data available to us in the empirical record. Moreover, the fine-grained qualities of this conceptual formulation—drawing attention to the complex character of local arenas and far-reaching effects of changes within them—may encourage research scholars to seek new data, providing a more adequate understanding of many corners of the premodern Pāli world.

Notes

1 For fuller historical accounts of the examples discussed in this section, and complete citations, see Blackburn (2015) and (Forthcoming).
2 For a more complete discussion of my approach to Sukhothai history, see Blackburn (Forthcoming).
3 Sukhothai inscriptions are in Khmer and an early form of central Tai. I have thus relied on a series of translations, beginning with the work of Georges Cœdès (1924), modified by A.B. Griswold and Prasert na Nagara (1992; original publication dates in the 1970s). In addition, I have benefited from substantial consultation with Winai Pongsripian and Trongjai Hutangkura, who generously shared their more recent work with Sukhothai inscriptions. Dr. Trongjai kindly worked with me for two days in Bangkok to discuss translation matters. The more recent Thai translations retain more technical terms from Pāli and Khmer. See, for instance, Winai (1991, 2020).
4 See Note 3.
5 This argument is more fully developed in Blackburn (2017a) and Blackburn (Forthcoming).
6 For a critical review of this literature, see Trivellato (2009).
7 See also Neelis's (2011) useful literature review on "network" as a concept used within religious studies.
8 On the Indian Ocean trading ecosystem of this era in relation to monastic mobility, see Blackburn (2015).
9 A fuller bibliography on this aspect of the Indian Ocean ecosystem is available at Blackburn (2015).

References

Baker, C., Pasuk, P. 2017. *A History of Ayutthaya: Siam in the Early Modern World.* Cambridge: Cambridge University Press.

Blackburn, A.M. (Forthcoming) *Experimental Sovereignties Across the Pali World, 1200–1550.*

Blackburn, A.M. 2018. "*Pali Up-River: Thinking With Steve About the Work of Pali in Tai Territories.*" *Steven Collins Memorial Symposium*, 16 November 2018, University of Chicago.

Blackburn, A.M. 2017a. "*Lanka at Sukhothai: Towards an Interpretation of the Buddha Footprint Claims of Maha Dhammaraja I.*" *International Association of Buddhist Studies Conference*, University of Toronto.

Blackburn, A.M. 2017b. "Buddhist Technologies of Statecraft and Millennial Moments." *History and Theory* 56 (1): 71–79.

Blackburn, A.M. 2015. "Buddhist Connections in the Indian Ocean." *Journal of the Economic and Social History of the Orient* 58: 237–266.

Blackburn, A.M. 2010. *Locations of Buddhism: Colonialism and Modernity in Sri Lanka.* Chicago: University of Chicago Press.

Blackburn, A.M. 2001. *Buddhist Learning and Practice in Eighteenth-Century Lankan Monastic Culture.* Princeton: Princeton University Press.

Boisselier, Jean. 1969. "Recherches archéologiques en Thaïlande, II. Rapport sommaire de la Mission 1965." *Arts Asiatiques* 20: 47–98.

Cœdès, G. 1924. *Recueil des inscriptions du Siam, I.* Bangkok: National Library of Thailand.

Conermann, S., Smolarz, E., eds. 2015. *Mobilizing Religion: Networks and Mobility.* Berlin: EB Verlag.

Cooper, F., Brubaker, R. 2005. "Identity." In *Colonialism in Question: Theory, Knowledge, History*, ed. F. Cooper, 59–90. Berkeley: University of California Press.

Dean, K. 2018. "Whose Orders? Chinese Popular God Temple Networks and the Rise of Chinese Mahāyāna Buddhist Monasteries in Southeast Asia." In *Buddhist and Islamic Orders in Southern Asia: Comparative Perspectives*, eds. M. Feener, A.M. Blackburn, 99–124. Honolulu: University of Hawaii Press.

Griswold, A.B., Prasert na Nagara. 1992. *Epigraphical and Historical Studies.* Bangkok: Historical Society.

Hansen, A. 2018. "Buddhist Communities of Belonging in Early Twentieth Century Cambodia." In *Theravāda Buddhist Encounters with Modernity*, eds. J. Schober, S. Collins, 62–77. London: Routledge.

Latour, B. 1996. "Visualization and Cognition: Drawing Things Together." In *Knowledge and Society Studies in the Sociology of Culture Past and Present*, Vol. 6, ed. H. Kuklik. Bingley: JAI Press.

Latour, B. 2010. "*Networks, Societies, Spheres: Reflections of an Actor-network Theorist.*" *Keynote speech for the International Seminar on Network Theory: Network Multidimensionality in the Digital Age.* 19th February 2010, Annenberg School for Communication and Journalism.

Law, J. 2002. "Objects and Spaces." *Theory, Culture and Society* 19 (5/6): 91–105.

Law, J., Mol, A.M. 1994. "Networks and Fluids: Anaemia and Social Topology." *Social Studies of Science* 24 (4): 641–671.

Lorillard, M. 2000. "Aux origins du bouddhisme siamois [Le cas des buddhapāda']." *Bulletin de l'École française d'Extrême-Orient* 87 (1): 23–56.

Masuzawa, T. 2005. *The Invention of world religions, or, How European universalism was preserved in the language of pluralism.* Chicago: University of Chicago Press.

Neelis, J.E. 2011. *Early Buddhist Transmission and Trade Networks: Mobility and Exchange Within and Beyond the Central Borderlands of South Asia.* Leiden: Brill.

Skilling, P. ed. 2008. *Past Lives of the Buddha: Wat Si Chum: Art, Architecture and Inscriptions.* Bangkok: River Books.

Trainor, Kevin. 1997. *Relics, Ritual and Representation in Buddhism: Rematerializing the Sri Lankan Theravāda Tradition.* Cambridge: Cambridge University Press.

Trivellato, Francesca. 2009. *The Familiarity of Strangers: the Sephardic diaspora, Livorno, and cross-cultural trade in the early-modern period.* New Haven: Yale University Press.

Vickery, M. 2010. "Cambodia and Its Neighbors in the 15th Century." In *Southeast Asia in the Fifteenth Century: The China Factor*, eds. G. Wade, S. Laichen, 271–306. Singapore: National University of Singapore Press.

Winai, P. 2020. *Sukhōthai khadī: prawattisāt, čhārưk sưksā, lǣ nirukti prawat.* [Sukhothai Case Studies: History, Epigraphic Research, and Etymology]. Bangkok: Publisher unknown.

Winai, P., ed. 1991. *Pramūan čhārưk thī phop nai Prathēt Thai lǣ tāngprathēt.* [Corpus of Inscriptions, Part 7, A Compilation of Inscriptions Found in Thailand and Neighbouring Countries.] Bangkok: Office of the Prime Minister.

Woodward, Hiram. 2005. *The Art and Architecture of Thailand: From Prehistoric Times through the Thirteenth Century.* Leiden: Brill.

Woodward, Hiram. 1994/5. "The Jayabuddhamahānātha Images of Cambodia." *Journal of the Walters Art Gallery* 52/53: 105–111.

4
STATECRAFT
From Buddhist kingship to modern states

Patrice Ladwig

Introduction

We live in an era in which the state has become almost a universal norm. Despite the continuing existence of failed and fragmented states, from the early nineteenth century onward, communities all over the globe became increasingly engulfed by modern (nation-)states defined by territoriality, borders, and some sort of hegemonic political sovereignty. Amid the innumerable attempts to understand this massive transition, there has been extensive theorization of when, why, and how societies have developed into states. In earlier research, the (sometimes overdrawn) distinction between stateless societies and states was linked to the development of new agricultural technologies and the rise of larger administrative bureaucracies and durable institutions through the introduction of script (Goody 1986). The role of religion in early state formation has also been a prominent feature of research, and studies on sacred kingship have highlighted the evolvement of religious cults and cosmologies enabling that of larger social formations (Sahlins and Graeber 2017). This is the case with Theravāda Buddhism, as substantial research has been undertaken on the connections among politics, kingship, and statecraft in the Buddhist countries of South and Southeast Asia (see, e.g., Bechert 1966–1973; Obeyesekere and Reynolds 1972). More recent work has additionally highlighted the continuing relevance of Buddhism in modern nation-states (Harris 2001; Kawanami 2016).

This chapter reviews some of these accounts of the state and kingship in the context of Theravāda Buddhism in South and Southeast Asia but with an increasingly narrow focus on the very notion of statecraft in mainland Southeast Asia. Although addressing an equally broad concept such as politics and kingship, to which it is obviously connected, I propose that notions of statecraft reach beyond the well-researched topic of the interaction of *saṅgha* and kingship in Theravāda studies. By putting more emphasis on strategies and tactics of governing through ritual systems (Hocart 1970), I focus on the creation of ritual and spatial centers that acted as what could be called population accumulators and "cosmic systems of governmentality" (Sahlins and Graeber 2017: 24). Although we see rather fragmented processes of state building and community formation in the premodern era, I argue that the role of Buddhism in population management was crucial in laying the foundations of what would become the modern state, yet equally crucial is the fact that this was only possible through the thorough localization of Buddhism. In this perspective, the Indianization of Southeast Asia was based on

 DOI: 10.4324/9781351026666-6

an indigenization of Theravāda Buddhism and certain elements of Brahmanism. Both often fed on pre-Buddhist concepts of governance that led to the creation of larger economic and religious centers in the lowlands of mainland Southeast Asia.

The first section comprises a general overview of some of the classic works on Theravāda Budddhism and its political ideologies. Looking primarily at the circulation of texts and the introduction of monastic manuscript culture, we witness the creation of a Pāli and Sanskrit cosmopolis (Pollock 2006; Frasch 2017) constituting transregional social and political imaginaries based on sacred kingship. Although this emphasis on language and ideology as part of a larger Theravāda civilization has attracted a renewed critical interest in recent years (Schober and Collins 2017), other trends in research in Buddhist Studies have somewhat moved away from grand models of Buddhism, putting more emphasis on its localized forms beyond the contested Theravāda classification (ibid.). Therefore, the second section of this chapter takes a more detailed look at the localization ofTheravāda statecraft in Laos and bordering Tai-speaking areas (Thailand, southern Yunnan) from the fourteenth century onward. By moving away from the general "two wheels of the *dhamma*" model of Theravāda kingship whereby a partnership between the religious and the political order is seen to turn the wheel of the Law, and by exploring indigenous, pre-Buddhist systems of social organization of Tai-speaking groups in the area called *baan-muang* (village—principality), I seek to problematize the "Buddhism-as-civilization" writing of history from two perspectives. First, I argue that the widely applied *maṇḍala*-model (Wolters 1992: 126; Tambiah 1976) overlooks the heterogeneity of populations and the significance of local belief systems and thereby lends itself to an elite and Buddhist-centered writing of history. Second, I propose that some of the previous research derives from a unilinear Buddhist historiography, which presents the rise of states and statecraft as a normative and desirable evolution. By referring to what could be labeled the "dark" sides of Buddhist statecraft, such as slavery, taxation, and large-scale warfare, I take up James Scott's (2009) idea of a counterhistory from the perspective of state-evading non-Buddhist and partially Buddhist ethnic minorities occupying the highlands of mainland Southeast Asia.

The final part briefly discusses the significance of Buddhist statecraft in the modern era. Now deeply enmeshed in the ideology of the nation-state and modern forms of governmentality (Foucault 2007), and operating in political systems that have largely abolished kingship during the colonial era, I not only discuss here some of the ruptures modernity has provoked but also point to continuities. I locate the latter in the ritual aspects of Buddhist statecraft. While in the Theravāda world Buddhist kings are now often defunct or merely have representative roles, I argue that the cosmological manifestations of premodern kingship and statecraft are still very much alive. Despite the many transformations and historical ruptures caused by colonialism, modern revolutions, and the creation of multiple Buddhist modernities, state rituals that deal, for example, with the veneration of relics in contemporary Laos, show that we have not arrived in a purely secular Theravāda state. Returning to Hocart's (1970) theory of ritual as a form of sociopolitical organization, I argue that the state and its political workings are still grounded in the religious, albeit this connection is at times not directly observable and obvious.

Buddhist kingship and statecraft in the Pāli-Sanskrit cosmopolis

The association of the monk as an ascetic figure, the *saṅgha* and rulers has been a constant feature of the overlap of the religious order (Sk: *sāsanacakra*) and the "secular" realm (Sk: *ānācakra*) in Theravāda South and Southeast Asia. This orientation is grounded in the constitutive narratives of Buddhist kingship: in the *Aggañña Sutta*—a kind "Buddhist story of creation"—the Buddha outlines the evolution of the social and cosmic order, its structure, and the need for having kingship (Collins 1998: 627–34). This is supplemented by the *Cakkavatti-Sīhanāda Sutta*, which elaborates on the responsibilities of an ideal ruler (ibid.: 602–15) and can be understood as a kind of scriptural primer on kingship in the context of a story of moral, human, and cosmic degeneration. Although a plethora of other texts could be listed here, in this context, most narratives and histories that deal with Buddhist kingship refer to an ideological blueprint of statecraft in the story of the Mauryan king Aśoka, who ruled over large parts of India around 250 BCE. Aśoka is said to have fervently promoted Buddhism, and in this model of statecraft, the ruler was considered a wheel-turning-king and universal monarch (P: *cakkavatti*) standing at the apex of social organization. He grants the monastic order protection and supports it, while the *saṅgha* spreads the *dhamma*, which gives the leader legitimacy for his rule. Strong's remark that "throughout Buddhist Asia, the figure of Asoka has played a major role in concretizing conceptions of kingship and general attitudes towards rulers and government" (1983: 39) is valid for the kingdoms that developed in South and mainland Southeast Asia, and numerous Theravāda chronicles associated with Buddhist relics, temples, and statues refer to him. In early Buddhological research, as well as inside various Buddhist traditions itself, there is clearly a strong romanticizing tendency when it comes to Aśoka as a *rājadhamma* or *cakkavatti*, a king who upholds the *dhamma* and conquers the world by his benevolent righteousness. According to Sheldon Pollock, it "is unclear whether the Mauryan emperor even had a religious plan to spread the *dhamma*" (2005: 419). The ideology of the *cakkavatti* stresses a universal world ruler and a universal imperial form, but in reality, these very often remained only aspirations of transregional imperial rule. We deal here with very different forms of the early state in a continuum of various capacities of governance and administration. Kulke (1993), for example, suggests that this process of state formation in premodern India and mainland Southeast Asia runs through three phases: the local or chieftain phase, the regional and early kingdom phase, and finally the imperial phase, in Southeast Asia represented by superregional empires such as Angkor (ninth–fifteenth centuries) or Ayutthaya (1350–1767).

From the macro-perspective of historical sociology, Theravāda societies and their relation to politics appear as sharing "social phenomena which are common to several societies, more or less related to each other" (Durkheim and Mauss 2007: 61) or as a "family of societies" (ibid. 62). This has also been emphasized by Steven Collins (1998: 566), who suggests that they are characterized by "a shared belief and symbol-system among elites ruling translocal political formations, paradigmatically in a *maṇḍala* of client-kings around a central monarch, which naturalized the hierarchy of tribute-givers and tribute-takers." On a conceptual level of this understanding of politics and statecraft then lies the idea of the *maṇḍala* (circle; circle of states), understood by Tambiah (1976: 102f.) as a "galactic polity." A *maṇḍala*, as described in the Indian manual of statecraft, the *Arthaśāstra*, implies that these polities do not have fixed boundaries and territories like modern states but are fluid and might be involved in plurality of hierarchically ordered client relationships with varying degrees of independence and cultural heterogeneity.

However, beyond these larger conceptions of Theravāda kingship and *maṇḍala* states that have been discussed in the literature at length, the association of king, *saṅgha*, and state took on a variety of forms. For the case of northern Thailand, Swearer and Premchit (1978) have convincingly shown that over the course of 150 years (1350–1500), a broad variety of relations between the religious and political sphere can be discerned, including co-option, adaptation, and resistance. Moreover, on a textual level, kingship is not only embraced and glorified as in genealogical *vaṃsas* (see Berkwitz, this volume) but is also viewed critically in some parts of the textual universe. In order to secure the cooperation with, and the subordination of the monastic order, Theravāda rulers also initiated "purifications" of the *saṅgha* (*Katikāvatas*). These have been well documented for the case of Sri Lanka (Ratnapāla 1971) and Burma (Mendelson 1975).

Further tensions between these "two wheels of the *dhamma*" (king and *saṅgha*) could also be triggered by the large scale of the landholdings monasteries came to accumulate. According to Gunawardana (1979: 344) this led the Sri Lankan *saṅgha* to stand in "antagonistic symbiosis" with kings. In Burma, the latter also initiated purification measures when monastic property holdings reached a certain level, leading to veritable oscillating cycles of monastic accumulation and disciplining interventions (Aung-Thwin 1979).

Crucial for the at-times conflictual symbiosis of rulers and *saṅgha*, and new models of legitimation and statecraft as a whole, was indeed the introduction of written scripts through Buddhism. The adoption of Pāli and Sanskrit as languages implied that Buddhism, its literary works, and its technical-ritual treatises connected people to a larger—today one would say transnational—cultural and political world. As in South Asia (Pollock 2006: 15), rulers, lords, and kings in the Theravāda countries supported an ideological link of language and politics and, at their courts, sponsored monks, writers, and astrologers who composed works in Pāli, Sanskrit, and vernacular languages. This migration of peoples, ideas, and concepts created continuous trans-local patterns and interactions, which according to Steven Collins are based in the Pāli *imaginaire*, which he defines as "a mental universe created by and within Pāli texts, which remained remarkably stable in content throughout the traditional period." (Collins 1998: 41). This role of Pāli and Sanskrit also laid the basis for the transnational mobility of texts, ideas, and people across the Indian Ocean (Blackburn 2015), and enhanced Theravāda's great translocation from Sri Lanka to Southeast Asia between the eleventh and thirteenth centuries. Bagan, the first larger kingdom in Burma that flourished between the ninth and thirteenth centuries, was marked by a "cosmopolitan cohabitation and interaction of monks" (Frasch 2017: 72), creating a new center of Buddhism with Pāli becoming a *lingua franca* mediating between Mon, Sinhala, Burmese, Khmer, and other languages. The economic trade and cultural exchanges between Sri Lanka and Southeast Asia also involved a traffic in important relics, which were crucial for the building of cities as ritual centers, because "the protection, enhancement, and deployment of relics constituted a core technology of states" in South and Southeast Asia (Blackburn 2010: 319). This created a portable imaginary that Buddhicized the landscape and its inhabitants, making Hindu-Buddhist cosmology and its vision of kingship and governance universally transplantable.

But beyond this legitimizing textual world, relic cults, and royal genealogies that connected people in more or less far away places with each other and that contributed to the formation of principalities and larger states, was there also a corpus of texts and knowledge that provided direct *practical* knowledge (administration, economics, divisions of political offices etc.) for the management of a state and governance? Significantly, Brahmanism gave these rulers the new administrative vocabulary and concepts for organizing these kingdoms. Buddhism's vision of the political sphere provided legitimacy via its notions of kingship, but its scriptures contained little of what was of *direct practical use* for organizing bureaucracies and state institutions. Robert Lingat (1989: 152), looking at the organization of Buddhist kingdoms in Sri Lanka, mentions that Buddhist rulers and their advisors at the court surely did not have recourse to the Buddhist canon for questions of political organization but, rather, consulted independent literature, namely, that of technical treatises in Sanskrit such as the *Arthaśāstra* that explicitly dealt with these issues.

Theravāda Buddhism and its numerous forms that spread in Southeast Asia was therefore a major force that fueled political centralization and state formation. Important for the spread of Buddhism was also trade, and Assavavirulhakarn (2010: 19) remarks on the location of *maṇḍalas*: "The areas that sustained these maṇḍalas can be described as mainly riverine and lowland. They were situated at strategic points, mostly at nodes of intra- or extraregional trading centres, and usually located at the controlling point of a river valley that acted as a gateway to the hinterland beyond." Despite this limited reach, Theravāda Buddhism introduced new forms of population management in the lowlands, based on not only more complex divisions of labor but also steeper social hierarchies legitimized by the concepts of merit (see Schober and Langer, this volume). Paddy growers who settled around larger temple complexes and urban settlements could be taxed and drafted for military service (Scott 2009: 64f.). In these premodern forms of governance, the creation of trading points and ritual centers was of prime importance, and an overwhelming part of inscriptions deal with large donations made by kings. Monasteries, relics, land, and workers ("slaves") were given, and increased the fame and standing of kings. In areas where land was abundant but underpopulated (warfare in premodern Southeast Asia was usually about people, not land), Buddhism therefore acted as a "population concentrator" that allowed for taxation, revenue extraction, the building of armies, and the further conquest of other *maṇḍalas*. One could here develop a kind of political economy perspective on monasteries. Hermann Kulke (1993: 292), for example, attests for premodern Cambodia and Burma that

> monastic institutions ... provided imperial kings and their courts with an additional infrastructure.... It allowed the imperial courts, perhaps for the first time, a permanent and in some cases even a direct access to the sphere of local matters even outside the limited nuclear area which was under their direct political control.

However, one should not overestimate the administrative and bureaucratic strength of the kingdoms of premodern Southeast Asia, and Chutintaranond (1990: 92) rightly remarks that "in the case of Ayudhya, like in medieval South India, the terms 'centralized' or 'bureaucratized' are widely and inappropriately applied."

What then held these principalities and empires together in terms of governance and statecraft? Pollock states that "precious little that can be identified as 'Buddhist' can be found in their actual practices of governance ... if there is any determining religious dimension to rulership it seems to have been Brahmanical ritualism" (Pollock 2005: 415). Clifford Geertz, reflecting on the "theatre state" in nineteenth-century Bali, has advanced a similar, and even more radical, view. Large public rituals did not only support the state, but in his understanding, they *were* the state: "The state, even in its final gasp, was a device for the enactment of mass ritual. Power served pomp, not pomp power" (Geertz 1980: 13). Without giving any preference to direct economic explanations of the development of the premodern state (Buddhism as a religion of trade and urbanity) or the religious-culturalist reasoning of Pollock or Geertz, I argue that that these two went hand in hand. Taxable wet-rice growing settlements were created around monasteries and can therefore be seen as a simultaneous establishment of ritual communities that shared calendrical systems, repertoires of texts and narratives, and places of worship. If these were more Brahmanistic, Theravādin, or driven by pre-Buddhist beliefs remains another question, but I think that Hocart's statement that "population first condenses round the centre of ritual, not shops" (1970: 251) gives us a possible lead here. Like in Fustel de Coulanges's remarkable study *The Ancient City*, which showed the crucial part played by religion in the political and social evolution of Greece and Rome (de Coulanges 1867: 161ff.); *maṇḍalas* and cities with their temples and relics became centers of power, ritual and, worship. It was not only the economic or utilitarian that brought people together but also the more or less homogeneous systems of "ritual policy" (Kulke 1993: 286) that increasingly came to structure the communities living in the polities of the Pāli-Sanskrit cosmopolis.

Localizations: Statecraft in premodern Lao and Tai Kingdoms

According to the classic narrative I have just presented, Buddhism and Brahmanism fuelled a process of political centralization, brought scripts, a class of religious professionals, and new systems of supra-local administration. This narrative is certainly valid to some degree, but it also oversimplifies a complex set of *longue durée* processes that evolved within very diverse social and political structures. As Victor Liebermann (2003: 58) points out, Theravāda state formation was a hesitant, fragmentary, and slow process in mainland Southeast Asia.

In this section, I want to briefly explore how larger patterns of Buddhist kingship and statecraft were localized in premodern Laos, and other smaller principalities in northern Thailand, and southern Yunnan, populated by groups belonging to the Tai-Kadai language family. The case of Laos in general might indeed be well suited for exploring these localizations in more depth: the kingdoms that were located in the area that now mark the socialist nation-state of Laos, and evolved around the fifteenth-century represent the eastern limit of the expansion of Theravāda Buddhism in mainland Southeast Asia. Compared to larger polities such as Ayutthaya (fourteenth–eigtheenth centuries) or Sukhotai (thirteenth–fifteenth centuries), extended *maṇḍalas* covering a large lowland terrain could evolve but were more limited in their networks. The area is mainly composed of rugged and hilly terrain, which makes the establishment of large-scale cities, and extensive wet-rice cultivation, more difficult. Historical information on early Lao history is still rather scarce (Lorillard 2006), but what we can ascertain is that Buddhism did not erase previous social and political structures but actually merged with and thereby enhanced them. I first briefly outline some Buddhist-Hindu elements of statecraft, to then formulate a critique of the widely applied concept of *maṇḍala*, proposing that it often overlooks the interaction with indigenous patterns of political, social, and religious administration. The latter system, known still today by the term *baan-muang* in Lao and Thai, complicates the writing of a Buddhist history and underpins the multiple sources of early statecraft in areas marked by a plethora of ethnic groups and religious-ritual systems.

The early Lao kingdoms display the first clear signs of the Buddhicization of royal power around the mid-fourteenth century, when kings were labeled *cakkavatti*. The first hard evidence, however, for the development of Buddhism in Laos and the kingdom of Lan Xang (1354–1707) are the steles dating from the second quarter of the sixteenth century. These primarily mark the foundation of temples (Lorillard 2006: 392). Commissioned by King Photisarat (1505–1548) and King Setthatilat (1534–1571), they bear a strong mark of northern Thai (Lanna) Buddhism. A first wave of Buddhism probably coming from Lanna in northern Thailand reached the Luang Prabang area in Laos in the fifteenth century and a second in the sixteenth century. With the idea of rule linked to the *cakkavatti*, the first polities began to adopt prefix and suffix terms derived from Sanskrit, such as *nāgara* and *purā*, to form toponyms denoting centralization and urbanity. However, one again has to remark that the direct sphere of influence of the kingdom of Lan Xang probably has to be understood to be limited to the Mekong valley and other lowland areas. Maps that depict this and other kingdoms as covering a homogenous terrain are deeply misleading.

As noted earlier, it was not only Buddhist concepts of kingship and power based on merit and charisma that were influential here. It seems that vernacularized forms of the Indian *Arthaśāstra* (treatise on statecraft, economics, rule), the *nītiśāstra* (general maxims on right conduct), and the *dharmaśāstra* (general legal-religious duties) delivered for the most part the additional concepts and vocabulary for administration, politics and law. "Remixed" and transformed parts of these *Śāstra* can be found throughout the Theravādin mainland region of Burma, Thailand, Laos, and Cambodia. Louis Finot (1917: 140–146), for example, mentions a Lao manuscript version of the

Rājasavanī, probably drawing on the *nītiśāstra*. The Lao manuscript version is, according to Finot (1917: 140), "a political treatise" and shows the influence of Brahmanism in the political sphere. It is divided in three sections (king, government, and the duties of the king), and the section on the government first lists the *rājāparicāraka* (attendants, servants) and then seven elements of governance, such as ministers, fortresses, treasuries, armies, and diplomacy, among others. The latter correspond to the seven *prakṛti* found in Kautilaya's *Arthaśāstra*, and in his *saptāṅga* theory of state power, they appear as the constituent elements of the premodern *maṇḍala* state. Other important textual sources for statecraft are also to be found in Lao Buddhist law: the *thammasat luang* (the great law), a vernacular Lao variant of a *dharmaśāstra*, depicts the tenfold royal code (*dasavidha-rājadhamma*) by which a king should govern, and thereby ethicizes statecraft (Bouasysavat 1993). In a section labeled "laws of the civil hierarchy," the Thai *thammasat*—very similar in form and content to the Lao one mentioned earlier—also contains sections on the king, bureaucracy, administration, and on the mechanisms through which smaller tribute paying principalities were supposed to be governed (see Kourilsky and Ladwig 2017–18: 204–207). Other manuscripts and their modern transcriptions like *ratchasad* (Sk. *rājasāśtra*) contain further guidelines for governance and sections on the norms and duties of kings (Bouasysavat 1995). We know little about how these concepts were actually implemented on the ground, but they attest to the fact that Buddhism and Brahmanism brought new concepts of administration and statecraft.

But what does this vocabulary relating to pre-modern state-formation contained in Buddhist manuscript culture tell us about the interaction with indigenous patterns of administration and statecraft? What Georges Cœdès (1968) has labeled the "Indianized states of Southeast Asia" comprises a complex, and even today only partially understood, flow and transformation of elements of Brahmanism and Buddhism to mainland and insular Southeast Asia. Discussions following Cœdès have taken different turns, but one of the main points of critique has been that the Indianization model largely overlooked the *receptiveness* of certain societies to new concepts of rule and statecraft. The *cakkavatti-* and *maṇḍala*-model were heavily transformed as they were made to work in specific localities.

While we find clear evidence in manuscripts for the influence of Buddhist and Brahmanic concepts of statecraft in Lao history and documents, there is also ample evidence for a different, but related, system of administration and early statecraft that was in place before the arrival of Buddhism. Indeed, most documents and chronicles hardly mention the term *monthon* (Thai/Lao for *maṇḍala*) but instead refer to kingdoms and their administrative units as *baan-muang*. The term *muang* appears in different Tai languages to designate political and social units that constitute smaller principalities composed of villages (*baan*). This system of supra-village organization dates from the pre-Indianization era and can also be found among (partially nonliterate) Tai groups that have not been Buddhicized, such as the Tai Dam and Tai Daeng in northern Laos and the highlands of Vietnam as well as in faraway places such as Assam (Raendchen & Raendchen 1998). Condominas (1990) has called this the hierarchically ordered "system of emboxment" of Tai political organization. Significant here is that this socioreligious system at the foundation of early pre-Buddhist state building was based on cosmic principles that hierarchized indigenous spirits (*phi*), the latter playing an important role in Laos into the present-day (Holt 2009).

A glance of the pre-Buddhist political organization of *baan-muang* can be had in a category of manuscripts that convey a regulatory code still known today as *hit khong* (rites and rules). These rules were applied to a variety of fields including irrigation, kinship, and property. In the sphere of statecraft, the organization of the *muang* here emerges as a body politic, with Lao terms largely deriving from human bodies, houses, and agriculture: a diplomat is the ear of the *muang* (*hu muang*); the head of ritual affairs is its heart (*cai*) or seed (*kaen*), the wise man and counselor is described as its eye (*dtaa*), border guards as its door (*phratu*), the military chief as its wall (*faa*), and so forth (see Raendchen 2004: 409). Depending on author and locality, one finds little Sanskrit vocabulary in some of these manuscripts or a mixture of both. Interestingly, the Lao term for *maṇḍala* is hardly ever used, even in documents that show clearer signs of Buddhist and Sanskrit influence. However, in most general publications on the history of the region, *maṇḍala* has become the term that describes the premodern form of statecraft. The *maṇḍala* and *baan-muang* system do show a certain overlap in terms of hierarchy and divisions of labor, but few researchers differentiate between *muang* and *maṇḍala* with reference to their (initially) different cultural backgrounds (for an exception, see Grabowsky 2004: 4–14). Whatever form this mixture of Tai and Hindu-Buddhist concepts of statecraft may have taken, I agree with Wolters (1992: 10), who remarks that Indianization "brought ancient and persistent indigenous beliefs into sharper focus." Jana Raendchen (2004: 417) congruently comments on the meeting of this indigenous Tai social organization and Indian influences:

> With their ban-muang system the Lao, like almost all Tai, had developed a special "technology of state building" with great continuity in administration and external relations that could explain the sudden increase in power when additionally having taken over Indian concepts of the centralized state during the 13th/14th century.

This also led to a ritual integration of non-Buddhists living outside, or at the margins of these early states. They either had specialized roles in larger rituals in which spirit worship played a crucial role (Archaimbault 1973: 152) or were employed as border guardians, especially in the north of Laos, where contracts called *khong* between the Buddhist king of Luang Prabang and ethnic minorities were established (see Bouté 2017). As Edmund Leach (1954: 197f.) has outlined for northeastern Burma, egalitarian animist minorities *often became Buddhists and adopted ranked titles* but were also able to hold multiple religious and social identities. Therefore, with and beyond Buddhism, the *baan-muang* system was also based on the integration of non-Tai and non-Buddhist minorities. This has been shown by Volker Grabowsky and Wichasin (2007) on the indigenous history of northwestern Laos, and recently by Badenoch and Shinsuke (2013: 29) who conceptualize these *muang* as a "cosmopolitan area in which many sources of power, innovation and transformation intersect," partially with "Buddhist" elements, but more often in the context of the indigenous systems of rule and administration I have outlined earlier.

One also has to add that the power of Lao and Tai kingdoms, and in fact most of the kingdoms of mainland Southeast Asia, was limited to river basins and lowlands, only marginally integrating the non-Buddhist populations in the hills. Despite widespread forms of syncretism and religious adaptation (see Sprenger 2017, for the Lao case), not all indigenous populations adopted Buddhism, and both Buddhological research and modern nationalist writings can overlook this obvious fact. Buddhism's civilizational power was not always effective and seductive. According to James Scott, many ethnic minorities even rejected it, because they did not want to be integrated into the Buddhist paddy-states that were based on the fixation of populations, taxation, and warfare. Moreover, Buddhism—with its concepts of merit and power—brought steeper social hierarchies, at times at odds with the egalitarian social fabric of numerous ethnic highland groups of the region. Therefore, Scott postulates (2009: 10) that "civilization held little attraction" for these non-Buddhist minority groups. *Pace* the self-conscious narratives of the civilizing power of Buddhism, he suggests that these 'dark sides' of pre-modern Buddhist statecraft led some minorities to "actively resist incorporation into the state" (ibid., 19). Although Scott has been accused of generalizing in his account of *zomia*, the highland region of mainland

Southeast Asia, I see his work as giving us an interesting antidote to the self-adulation of Buddhist historiography and its contemporary nationalist reincarnations.

Theravāda Buddhism and modern statecraft

I started this chapter with the remark that the (nation-)state has become an almost universalized norm, and the multiple modernities that arose through colonialism and Western hegemony also provoked a rupture in the Theravāda world. The gradual rise of governmentality, to use the famous Foucaultian concept (Foucault 2007: 88), led to a deep transformation of the understandings and working of statecraft. This new "art of governance," according to Foucault, has its roots in the eighteenth century, when the active management of the state, its population, and the economy became a focus of European thinking (Foucault 2007: 108f.). Population and health politics, statistics (demography), educational apparatuses, policing, and the productivity-enhancing disciplining of society became dominant features of modern statecraft and spread through colonial rule. Taking this modernization paradigm as an implicit analytical framework, Edmund Leach (1973: 40) in an article on the post-colonial fate of Buddhist kingship in Sri Lanka and Burma, for example, states: "Fantasy apart, there is in fact very little in the present-day political organization of either Burma or Ceylon which derives directly from the traditional forms of pre-colonial centralized Kingship."

Is, then, nothing left of these premodern ideas of the Buddhist state and its forms of statecraft except fantasies of the past? I think that many Foucauldian approaches to governmentality and elaborations à la Leach are rather generalizing and represent a Eurocentric view, which overlook the complexity and heterogeneity of these processes. Although many of these features of statecraft I listed earlier were undoubtedly introduced through Western hegemony and colonialism, they obviously did not lead to a homogeneous world of states that has completely overwritten premodern forms of Buddhist governance. Although Buddhist institutions and systems of knowledge and governance were partially replaced by more secular and "rational" ones, this process led to multiple forms beyond the Western model. For the sphere of lawmaking and administration in Laos, Kourilsky and Ladwig (2017–18), for example, have shown that traditional Buddhist law was transformed by the French colonial regime but that this lead to a complex process of hybridization, in which Lao local elites had an active role and were not merely passive recipients of a modernization process. This could for sure be applied to many other fields, such as education, health, politics, and so forth, in a variety of countries and regions. Thus, although these modernization processes are also apparent when we explore the postcolonial and contemporary workings of statecraft in the Theravāda countries in South and Southeast Asia, we must not overemphasize the ruptures caused by modernity, Therefore, a narrative of loss and destruction of traditional Buddhist conceptions of the state through governmentality and secular powers is not adequate here, but we have to look at their transformative processes and their resignifications under the conditions of modernity and postcoloniality.

Then, although Leach's analysis quoted earlier is undoubtedly right regarding the institutions and figures of kingship in Burma, Sri Lanka, and many other Buddhist countries where it disappeared (with Thailand and Cambodia being the exceptions in the Theravāda realm), where can we then locate the enduring significance of models of kingship and Buddhist statecraft? Buddhism has not disappeared from politics, and propagators of Buddhist nationalism seem to postulate a historical continuity between traditional Buddhist states and its modern versions. Jonathan Spencer (1997: 9) claims that "indigenous ideas about kingship have continued to animate the political imagination in Sri Lanka, but without any kings to do the animating since the early nineteenth century." These political imaginaries have had a crucial influence through various forms of religious nationalism. Buddhism often became a resource of resistance to colonialism and then, in the postcolonial era, replicated this model, becoming a foundation for nation building. In many Theravāda countries, a new centralized model of Buddhism and its institutions was supposed to become a means for national integration. The establishment of a hegemonic national Buddhist culture ("To be Burmese is to be Buddhist," for example) often accompanied, and indeed went hand in hand, with the creation of modern forms of nation-states.

A good example here is Thailand, where Bangkok's central control over the nation over the nineteenth and twentieth centuries was thoroughly implemented through Buddhism. Local Buddhist traditions such as that of northeastern (Isan) and northern Thailand (Lanna) were to be homogenized, and millenarian movements broke out in these only partially integrated peripheries. The most famous example is here Khru Ba Sriwichai (1878–1938). Still today venerated as a "holy man" or "saint" (*nak bun* or *nak ton bun*) of Lanna, and associated with the revival of northern Thai culture, Bangkok believed that he was a leader of the millenarian revolt in the 1920s and 1930s and tried to curtail his influence through modern forms of *saṅgha* purification (see also Bowie and Hansen, this volume). Theravāda's "civilizing" power has also been instrumental for the "integration" of non-Buddhist ethnic minorities into the modern state, as, for example, documented in Thailand (Tambiah 1976: 434–435) and Laos (Ladwig 2016). However, the modern project of the homogeneous nation-state also creates problems, and violence and ethnic tensions in Sri Lanka and, more recently, in Myanmar, especially have been framed in Buddhist terms.

But given the absence of kingship in most contemporary Theravāda countries, what else remains of Buddhist statecraft except for its nationalist ideologies? I argue that a focus on the material manifestations of kingship beyond the figure of the king is crucial here. Right from the beginning Buddhist concepts of statecraft and rule were linked to the possession and ritual patronage of relics and powerful statues. In Lao and Thai history, "the possession of certain Buddha statues and relics, rather than kinship, was interpreted as conferring legitimacy and power to kings and rulers, because these statues were treated as the palladia of their kingdoms and principalities" (Tambiah 1982: 5). Even in countries where the Buddhist kingship was abolished by force, such as in Laos after the communist revolution in 1975, the significance of powerful palladia has not vanished. Instead of the Buddhist king, in contemporary Laos, the head of the state and of the communist party now opens the yearly ritual for the veneration of the Buddha's relic, supposed to be contained in the That Luang *stūpa* (see Figure 4.1) in Vientiane (Ladwig 2015).

Whereas in the past, the rite was believed to protect the *muang*, and increase the fertility of the rice fields, these properties have been repurposed. In a country that has undergone massive economic modernization in the last twenty years, the That Luang festival has now also become a large trade fair, with stalls and booths of companies encircling the central relic shrine. Monks I talked to during my numerous visits to the festival often mentioned the terms *development* and *prosperity*, thereby merging traditional notions of fertility and *dhammic* governance with modern economic aspirations. Thus, despite the discontinuities provoked by the abolishment of kingship, the rituals also seem to function without the institutional framework of Buddhist kingship, as the continuity of the cosmological underpinnings allows for adaptations. What might aid this process of cooption by the current Lao government is the fact that relics and statues are understood as having an agency of their own, which can be appropriated outside the framework of Buddhist kingship. If our only focus is on the person of the king, we run the risk of neglecting the role played by the objects themselves, enabling in some way their adoption by those powers having taken over from the kings.

Figure 4.1 Devotees gather for making offerings in front of the That Luang shrine. The festival has again become the most important state ritual in Laos, and high-ranking party politicians also attend it. Vientiane, 2015.

Photograph by the author.

This ritual governing of life and prosperity through relics is reminiscent of Hocart's work, invoked in previous parts of this chapter dealing with premodern Theravāda statecraft. When Hocart states that "ritual is a social activity and so requires an organization" (1970: 34), he is pointing up the central thesis of his writings: that ritual organization precedes and influences the structure of all social or political activities and institutions, and it aims at revitalization. For him, in modernity, religion and politics "seem to have parted, but they have not really done so; the common origin still operates in men's minds" (1970: 171). In rational forms of modern governmentality, in the Lao case of relic worship in state ritual, we also encounter a form of ritual as government. However, this now not only aims at ensuring the fertility of rice fields as in the past but also embraces the modern, capitalist economy as represented by the trade fair encircling the Buddha's relic. To conclude, on one hand, the rupture caused through the spread of modern, secular notions of statecraft cannot be denied (for Laos, see Ladwig 2011). Secular agendas, such as health politics, schooling, and the establishment of productivity-enhancing ideologies through global capitalism, seem, at first sight, to be no longer influenced by Theravāda Buddhism and its premodern notions of statecraft. On the other hand, however, the workings of the modern state cannot be separated from Buddhist conceptions, and its institutions have not become purely secular. One task of contemporary and future research is to uncover the religious foundations of seemingly secular forms of power and governance (de Vries and Sullivan 2006). Or as Carl Schmitt (1985: 36) famously phrased it, "[a]ll significant concepts of the modern theory of the state are secularized theological concepts." "All" is here a very ambitious claim, but perhaps only in this way, the present, but somehow hidden, streams of Theravāda statecraft in an only seemingly secular age can be discerned.

References

Archaimbault, Charles. 1973. *Structures religieuses lao (rites et mythes).* Vientiane: Vithagna.

Assavavirulhakarn, Prapod 2010. *The Ascendancy of Theravada Buddhism in Southeast Asia.* Chiang Mai: Silkworm Books.

Aung-Thwin, Michael 1979. "The Role of Sasana Reform in Burmese History: Economic Dimensions of a Religious Purification." *Journal of Asian Studies* 38: 671–688.

Badenoch, Nathan and Tomita Shinsuke 2013. "Mountain People in the Muang: Creation and Governance of a Tai Polity in Northern Laos." *Southeast Asian Studies* 2(1): 29–67.

Bechert, Heinz 1966–1973. *Buddhismus, Staat und Gesellschaft in den Ländern des Theravada-Buddhismus* (3 vol). Wiesbaden: Frankfurt a. M.

Blackburn, Anne. 2010. "Buddha-Relics in the Lives of South Asian Polities." *Numen* 57: 3–4: 317–340.

Blackburn, Anne. 2015. "Buddhist Connections in the Indian Ocean: Changes in Monastic Mobility 1000–1500." *Journal of the Economic and Social History of the Orient* 58: 3: 237–266.

Bouasysavat, Samlit. 1993. *Khamphi Pha Thammasat Luang: Kotmay Buhan Lao* [The 'Great Thammasat': Ancient law of Laos]. Vientiane: Project for the Preservation of Palm-leaf Manuscripts.

Bouasysavat, Samlit. 1995. *Khamphi Rachasat* ['The Treatise on Royalty']. Vientiane: Project for the Preservation of Palm-leaf Manuscripts.

Bouté, Vanina. 2017. *Mirroring Power: Ethnogenesis and Integration among the Phunoy of Northern Laos.* Chiang Mai: Silkworm Books.

Chutintaranond, Suneth. 1990. Mandala, Segmentary State and Politics of Centralization in Medieval Ayudhya. *Journal of the Siam Society* 78 (1): 89–100.

Cœdès, George. 1968. *The Indianized States of Southeast Asia.* Honululu: University of Hawai'i Press.

Collins, Steven. 1998. *Nirvana and Other Buddhist Felicities.* Cambridge: Cambridge University Press.

Condominas, Georges. 1990. *From Lawa to Mon, from Saa' to Thai: Historical and Anthropological Aspects of Southeast Asian Social Spaces.* Canberra. Department of Anthropology.

Coulanges, Fustel de. 1867. *The ancient city. A study on the religion, laws and institutions of Greece and Rome.* Boston: Lee & Shephard.

de Vries, Hent, Sullivan, Lawrence E., eds. 2006. *Political Theologies. Public Religions in a Post-Secular World.* New York: Fordham University Press.

Durkheim, Emile, Mauss, Marcel. 2007. "Note on the Concept of Civilisation." In *Techniques, Technology, Civilization*, ed. Marcel Mauss. New York/Oxford: Berghahn.

Finot, Louis. 1917. "Recherches sur la littérature laotienne." *Bulletin de l'Ecole francaise d'Extrême-Orient* 17(5): 1–219.

Foucault, Michel. 2007. *Security, Territory, Population: Lectures at the Collège de France 1977–1978*, translated by Graham Burchell. New York: Palgrave Macmillan.

Frasch, Tilman. 2017. "A Pāli cosmopolis? Sri Lanka and the Theravāda Buddhist ecumene, c. 500–1500." In *Sri Lanka at the Crossroads of History*, eds. Zoltán Biedermann, Alan Strathern. London: UCL Press.

Geertz, Clifford 1980. *Negara: The Theatre State in Nineteenth-Century Bali.* Princeton, NJ: Princeton University Press.

Goody, Jack 1986. *The Logic of Writing and the Organisation of Society.* Cambridge. Cambridge University Press.

Grabowsky, Volker, Wichasin, Renoo. 2007. *Chronicles Chiang Khaeng: A Tai Lu Principality of the Upper Mekong.* Honolulu: University of Hawai'i Press.

Grabowsky, Volker. 2004. *Bevoelkerung und Staat in Lanna. Ein Beitrag zur Bevoelkerungsgeschichte in Suedostasien.* Wiesbaden: Harrassowitz.

Gunawardana, R.A.L.H. 1979. *Robe and Plough: Monasticism and Economic Interest in Early Medieval Sri Lanka.* Tucson: University of Arizona Press.

Harris, Ian, ed. 2001. *Buddhism and Politics in Twentieth-century Asia.* London: Continuum.

Hocart, Arthur M. 1970. *Kings and Councilors: An Essay in the Comparative Anatomy of Human Society*, Chicago: University of Chicago Press.

Holt, John. 2009. *Spirits of the Place: Buddhism and Lao Religious Culture.* Honolulu: University of Hawai'i Press.

Kawanami, Hiroko, ed. 2016. *Buddhism and the Political Process*. New York: Palgrave Macmillan.

Kourilsky, Grégory, Ladwig, Patrice. 2017–18. "Governing the Monastic Order in Laos. Pre-modern Buddhist Legal Traditions and Their Transformation Under French Colonialism." *Buddhism, Law & Society* 3: 191–243.

Kulke, Herrmann. 1993. *Kings and Cults. State Formation and Legitimation in India and Southeast Asia*. Delhi: Manohar Publishers.

Ladwig, Patrice. 2011. "The Genesis and Demarcation of the Religious Field: Monasteries, State Schools, and the Secular Sphere in Lao Buddhism (1893–1975)." *Sojourn. Journal of Social Issues in Southeast Asia* 26 (2): 196–222.

Ladwig, Patrice. 2015. "Worshipping Relics and Animating Statues. Transformations of Buddhist statecraft in contemporary Laos." *Modern Asian Studies* 49 (6): 1875–1902.

Ladwig, Patrice 2016. "Religious Place Making. Civilized Modernity and the Spread of Buddhism Among the Cheng, a Mon-Khmer Minority in Southern Laos." In *Religion, Place and Modernity*, eds. Michael Dickhardt, Andrea Lauser. Leiden: Brill.

Leach, Edmund. 1954. *Political Systems of Highland Burma: A Study of Kachin Social Structure*. London: London School of Economics and Political Science.

Leach, Edmund. 1973. "Buddhism in the post-colonial political order in Burma and Ceylon." *Daedalus* 102 (1): 29–54.

Liebermann, Victor. 2003. *Strange Parallels: Southeast Asia in Global Context. c. 800–1830, Volume I: Integration on the Mainland*. Cambridge: Cambridge University Press.

Lingat, Robert. 1989. *Royautés bouddhiques: Asoka. La fonction royale à Ceylan*. Paris: Editions de E.H.E.S.S.

Lorrillard, Michel. 2006. "Lao History Revisited: Paradoxes and Problems in Current Research." *South East Asia Research* 14 (3): 387–401.

Mendelson, Michael. 1975. *Sangha and State in Burma: A Study of Monastic Sectarianism and Leadership*. Ithaca and New York: Cornell University Press.

Obeyesekere, Gananath, Reynolds, Frank, eds. 1972. *Two wheels of dhamma: Essays on the Theravada tradition in India and Ceylon*. Chambersburg: American Academy of Religion.

Pollock, Sheldon. 2005. "Axialism and Empire." In *Axial Civilizations and World History*, eds. Bjoern Wittrock, Johan Arnason, Shmuel Eisenstadt. Leiden/Boston: Brill.

Pollock, Sheldon. 2006. *The Language of the Gods in the World of Men. Sanskrit, Culture, and Power in Premodern India*. Berkeley/Los Angeles: University of California Press.

Raendchen, Jana. 2004. *The Socio-Political and Administrative Organisation of Müang in the Light of Lao Historical Manuscripts*, paper presented at the conference *The Literary Heritage of Laos*, Vientiane.

Raendchen, Jana, and Raendchen, Oliver. 1998. "Present State, Problems and Purpose of *baan-müang* Studies." *Tai Culture* 11(2): 5–11.

Ratnapāla, Nandasēna. 1971. *The Katikāvatas: Laws of the Buddhist Order of Ceylon from the 12th century to the 18th century*. München: Münchener Studien zur Sprachwissenschaft.

Sahlins, Marshall, Graeber, David. 2017. *On Kings*. Illinois: HAU/University of Chicago Press.

Schmitt, Carl. 1985. *Political Theology: Four Chapters on the Concept of Sovereignty*. Cambridge: MIT Press.

Schober, Juliane, Collins, Steven, eds. 2017. *Theravāda Buddhist encounters with modernity*. London. Routledge.

Scott, James. 2009. *On the Art of Not Being Governed. An Anarchist History of Upland Southeast Asia*. Yale: Yale University Press.

Spencer, Jonathan. 1997. "Post-Colonialism and the Political Imagination." *The Journal of the Royal Anthropological Institute* 3 (1).

Sprenger, Guido. 2017. "*Piglets* Are Buffaloes: *Buddhification* and the Reduction of Sacrifices on the Boloven Plateau." In *Changing Lives in Laos: Society, Politics and Culture in a Post-Socialist State*, eds. Vatthana Pholsena, Vanina Bouté. Singapore: Singapore University Press.

Strong, John. 1983. *The Legend of King Asoka*. Princeton: Princeton University Press.

Swearer, Donald, Premchit, Sommai. 1978. "The Relationship between the Religious and Political Orders in Northern Thailand (14th–16th Centuries)." In *Religion and Legitimation of Power in Thailand, Laos and Burma*, ed. Bardwell Smith. Chambersburg: Anima Books.

Tambiah, Stanley. 1976. *World Conqueror and World Renouncer. A Study of Buddhism and Polity in Thailand against a Historical Background*. Cambridge: Cambridge University Press.

Tambiah, Stanley. 1982. "Famous Buddha Images and the Legitimation of Kings: The Case of the Sinhala Buddha (Phra Sihing) in Thailand." *Res: Anthropology and Aesthetics* 4: 5–19.

Wolters, Oliver. 1992. *History, Culture and Region in Southeast Asian Perspectives*. Singapore: Institute of Southeast Asian Studies.

5

REFORM

Ideas and events in modern Theravāda reformism

Anne R. Hansen and Anthony Lovenheim Irwin

Introduction

Reform is such a persistent theme in the Theravāda that it constitutes a defining "idea" within the tradition. While pervasive as an idea, the numerous reforms enacted throughout Theravāda history are events that have taken widely different shapes and been motivated by reasons particular to their individual cultural and historical contexts. Our distinction between "events" and "ideas" comes from Charles Hallisey's understanding of the history of Theravādin councils (*saṅgīti* or *saṅgāyanā*), assemblies that have been held periodically to reinvigorate, purify, safeguard the transmission and teaching of the Buddha's Dhamma and/or for "decidedly impious" reasons, including whatever political and economic benefits religious reform might accrue to its sponsors or conveners (Hallisey 1991: 148). Hallisey argues for an approach to Theravāda reform—and Theravāda history more generally—that recognizes and takes account of the difference between "events" and "ideas." "Events," for Hallisey, are unique in that they are historically situated in specific circumstances that can bring about accidental and anomalous actions, meanings, and reactions. These events, however, do not occur in an ideological vacuum. Instead, they are related to and intertwined with "ideas," which are persistent patterns of norms and meanings that shape the actions of people and groups. While events and ideas are different, "the phenomena they refer to are inevitably interrelated," meaning that the influence and importance of "ideas," which serve as "frameworks of meaning," can inspire and authorize the emergence of "events" (Hallisey 1991: 136–137). Conversely, the historically specific contours of "events" keep big formative "ideas" valid and meaningful.

In the Theravāda, reform is a powerful idea that has resulted in a number of significant, but historically distinct events that have emerged as milesto nes throughout the history of the tradition. Hallisey argues that the interplay between ideas and events shows the "constructedness" of the Theravāda tradition and that the way ideas and events shape one another over time reveals how the Theravāda is a tradition "whose identity is continually being constituted and reconstituted" (Hallisey 1991: 137).

Premodern reforms, sometimes referred to by scholars as "purifications," had been enacted periodically since Buddhism became closely associated with the institution of kingship in the Aśokan period, often coinciding with the rise of new dynasties or following periods of warfare and social turmoil. Some of these reforms were sponsored by new rulers and centered on the

DOI: 10.4324/9781351026666-7

production of a new redaction of the scriptures or a heightened scrutiny of monastic discipline, at times resulting in cases of purging monks seen as too lax or impure from the monkhood. In other instances, a new ordination lineage might be imported from elsewhere in the Theravāda world to reinvigorate the Saṅgha's purity (Blackburn 2003).[1] Anthropologist Stanley Tambiah argues that many of these purifications were modeled on the paradigmatic reign of the third-century BCE king Aśoka and that such modeling simultaneously *made* that reformation the paradigmatic model that it came to be. As part of his strategy of political incorporation and governance, Aśoka supported the Buddhist Saṅgha and mounted religious purifications in order to strengthen both the state of religion and his own political position (Tambiah 1976: 54–72). Tambiah proposes an Aśokan model of elite-enacted Buddhist reform, of which there are many examples from the premodern period. In other words, the Aśokan reform was not only a seminal historical event, but it also became an idea of what reform might look like and what purpose it could serve leaders and states through periodic state-sponsored reforms that drew on it for inspiration.

In order to better understand how the very *idea* of reform might have helped animate historically specific reformist events in diverse periods, it is possible to break apart the large idea of reform into two main constellations of ideas centered on purity, namely, intertwining concerns with orthopraxy (correctness of practice) and scriptural hermeneutics. Attention to orthopraxy encompasses such issues as appropriate decorum for monks and laypeople and the depth and quality of their emotional, intellectual, and aesthetic situatedness on the Buddhist Path; the authenticity of ordination rituals and other types of consecrations; and the regulation of praxis through institutional organization and reorganization, the introduction or alteration of laws regulating the Saṅgha or monastic community, and laws regulating the relationship between Saṅgha and state. The second closely linked concern of Theravādin reforms has been with the authority and validity of *scripture* with respect to the definition, recitation, collection, preservation, transmission, correction, discussion, ritual performance, and translation of scripture. As Hallisey reminds us, Buddhist descriptions of councils suggest that not all of these concerns were enacted to the same extent or in the same ways across every council or other reforming event (Hallisey 1991: 144). Furthermore, anyone familiar with Theravāda history will immediately see that these two categories of concerns and sub-concerns overlap. Efforts to ensure the purity and authenticity of ordination and debates about how best to interpret the *Vinaya* (the part of the Buddhist scripture concerned with monastic regulation) blur into each other. A monk's or nun's demeanor, reputation for spiritual prowess, and ways of knowing and transmitting scripture are hard to separate. These concerns also map onto (but are not completely synonymous with) Pāli categories that Theravādins have used over the centuries to describe their central aims for reform: reinvigorating *paṭipatti* and *pariyatti*. *Paṭipatti* is the practice of the Dhamma, behavior or conduct that aspires to uphold moral or Dhammic teachings and values. *Pariyatti* refers to scripture (also known as Dhamma or *Dhamma-Vinaya*), scriptural study, and the transmission of knowledge contained in the scriptures. Attaining purity is key to these categories. Theravādins have multiple terms for referring to purification (including *pārisuddhi* and *visuddhi*), which is simultaneously an aspiration, outcome, ethos, affect, and aesthetic of *paṭipatti* and *pariyatti*.

In this chapter, we examine how the Theravāda was constituted and reconstituted in the modern era through a number of reform movements that unfolded in the nineteenth and twentieth centuries. Importantly, this era saw the emergence of reformism as a *pan-Asian* phenomenon, crossing Buddhist schools, sects, local and state boundaries, and continents within the context of modern developments in the realms of politics, ideology, and media. Some of the most salient themes and important historical hallmarks of this period included political centralization and state-making, colonial occupations, decolonization and nation building, shared conceptions of Buddhist prophetic temporality, the circulation of new scientific, religious and political theories, the impacts of state violence, and the emergence of new media forms such as print. In our analysis, these modern reforms were "events" conditioned by historically specific contexts and preoccupations that reflected and drew on the "idea" (or component ideas) of reform in Theravāda history: a framework of concern with the correlated issues of orthopraxy and scriptural interpretation. We show how this framework of reform was inflected through the modern period early on by new ways of accessing, articulating, and verifying knowledge. We also examine how modern Theravādins' concerns with purity interacted with, reflected, and were influenced by political changes that unfolded during the Cold War period, together with new developments in media and conceptions of subjecthood. In short, we argue that what was "modern" about reform movements in the nineteenth and twentieth centuries was not the aspiration to update, reinvigorate, or reinterpret Buddhism but, rather, a historically specific and broadly regional Buddhist engagement with modern ways of knowing, new technologies of textual production, and new conceptions of subjecthood that characterized reform events in this period.

For the purposes of this chapter, we employ *modern* as an imperfect but useful historical marker to designate a period extending roughly from the late eighteenth century through the early 1980s in the Theravāda world. The period begins with colonial expansion, the rise of print and the decline of manuscript culture, and ends as the regional wars and violence of the mid-twentieth century had begun to subside—and before the widespread introduction of the internet. We examine two connected waves of reform, a first wave from the late eighteenth century to the early twentieth century that coincided with the gradual entrenchment of colonial controls and a second wave emerging in the 1950s that reflected the aims and visions of Theravāda Buddhists in newly independent nations. Although our discussion is confined to considerations of how these factors played out in modern Theravāda reform movements in South and Southeast Asia, it is worth noting that comparable reforms were being instituted by Mahāyāna Buddhists in Vietnam, China, Korea, and Japan, in Islamic communities in the Southeast Asian archipelago and Buddhist and Hindu groups in India during this same period. Furthermore, it should be emphasized that reform itself was by no means an exclusively modern idea within the Theravāda. While modern reformers had specific concerns and constraints within which they operated, their reforms were part and parcel of the long history of reform as an idea within the Buddhist world.

New ways of knowing

The ethos of modern Buddhist reform movements in the Theravāda world is aptly conveyed in reformers' promotion of the *Kālāma Sutta*, a discourse included in the canonical *Tipiṭaka*. The *sutta* takes the form of a dialogue between the Buddha and a group of people from the Kālāma clan. The Kālāmas are confused about the conflicting teachings of various itinerant spiritual teachers they have encountered and go to the Buddha for advice on how to distinguish between true and false religious doctrines. After a series of questions aimed at helping the Kālāmas recognize their own powers of discernment, the Buddha exhorts them:

> Come, Kālāmas. Do not go by oral tradition, by lineage of teaching, by hearsay, by a collection of scriptures, by logical reasoning, by inferential reasoning, by reflection on reasons, by the acceptance of a view after pondering it, by the seeming competence of a speaker, or because you think, "The ascetic is our teacher." But when you know for yourselves, "These things are wholesome, these things are blameless; these things

> are praised by the wise; these things, if undertaken and practiced, lead to welfare and happiness," then you should engage in them.
>
> (Nyanaponika and Bodhi 1999: 66)

This *sutta* was often held up by modern reformist teachers and leaders as an example of the inherent rationalism contained in the Buddha's thought, which was seen as compatible with—and even anticipatory of—modern modes of reason. The *Kālāma Sutta* not only provided insight about how to evaluate different religions, they argued, but it also sketched out a hermeneutical approach to Buddhist scriptures: one should assess the validity of a given doctrine through reflection and personal application, remaining alert to the possibility that "tradition" had distorted the true spirit of the meaning. Prominent Buddhist reformer Prince Vajirañāṇavarorasa (1869–1921), son of the fourth king of the Chakri dynasty and eventual Supreme Patriarch of the Siamese Saṅgha, wrote that in reading Buddhist scriptures,

> I learned to make up my own mind, to select those passages which were acceptable to me and to reject, as if sifting out gold from sand, those which were unacceptable. One work which struck me was the *Kālāma-sutta* which taught one not to believe blindly and to depend on one's own thinking.
>
> (Vajirañāṇavarorasa 1979: 30)

Vajirañāṇavarorasa's comments emerge from a viewpoint current among elite reform-minded Buddhists in late nineteenth-century Bangkok: that the Buddha himself had promoted rationalism, that later refractors had inserted erroneous or fanciful interpolations and stories in the Buddhist scriptures, and that, in general, the Buddha's ideas had been presciently resonant with the discoveries and methods of contemporary science. In "sifting out gold from sand," Vajirañāṇavarorasa was also suggesting that some scriptural texts were more authentic than others in their adherence to the enlightened knowledge of Gotama Buddha.

Reference to the *Kālāma Sutta* was also prominent in the rhetoric of Theravādin reformers in Cambodia and colonial Ceylon. A favorite of reformist monks in Cambodia, the *Kālāma Sutta* was one of the earliest texts selected for translation and print in the first edition of Cambodia's new Buddhist periodical *Kambujasuriya* in 1925 by two of Cambodia's most important modernist scholar-monks, Braḥ Grū Vimalapaññā Uṃ-Sūr and Braḥ Mahā Vimaladhamm Thoṅ (1966: 7). And we can gain some sense of the powerful resonance of the *sutta* for Theravādin monk-scholars of the period from American abolitionist and author Moncure Conway's account of hearing the reformist monk Hikkaḍuvē Sumaṅgala Thera preach the *sutta* in the 1880s at Vidyodaya Pirivena, the monastic college he founded in Ceylon:

> he read in a clear sweet voice Buddha's plea for free thought. . . . At certain parts he was moved, his voice tended to intone, and his eyes rose glowing upon us, as if demanding homage for sublime ideas.
>
> (Conway 1906: 130–33)

Conway records that after Hikkaḍuvē's moving recitation, he and his Ceylonese host, Solicitor General of Ceylon Ponnambalam Ramanathan, noted the surprising but gratifying paradox that an ancient sermon "from a past of seventy generations" could be so in line with modern principles of rationalism "summoning man to rest his faith on his own reason" (Conway 1906: 133; Soma Thera 2008: 5–6).

A related wave of modern reforms took place in the 1950s and early 1960s as decolonizing Buddhists sought to regulate national Saṅghas, promulgate Buddhist values, reestablish older precolonial Theravāda networks, and build new regional and international organizations such as the World Fellowship of Buddhists. In this charged context of nation-building and the emerging geopolitical tensions among communist, democratic, and nonaligned ideologies and alliances, the *Kālāma Sutta* was again cited—this time for somewhat different reasons. During this period, the *sutta* was offered as evidence of the Buddha's emphasis on freedom of thought and religious freedom as innately Buddhist values.

Publishing the *sutta* in 1959 as the "Buddha's charter of free inquiry," the Sri Lankan missionary monk (*dhammaduta*) and scholar Kotahene Soma Mahā Thera wrote that the *Kālāma Sutta* "is justly famous for its encouragement of free inquiry; the spirit of the sutta signifies a teaching that is exempt from fanaticism, bigotry, dogmatism, and intolerance" (Soma Thera 2008: 4). Burmese missionary monk and scholar Sayadaw U Thittila wrote that since "now Asia is threatened with Communism ... every Buddhist must frankly face the incompatibility of the Communist and the Buddhist way of life," including its attacks on religion and "individual liberty of thought or deed" (Thittila 1948: 1–2). Buddhist intellectuals associated with the World Fellowship of Buddhists such as Thai princess Pismai Diskul argued that "there is nothing compulsory whatever in the Buddha's doctrine. The Buddha's instruction to the Kālāma people may be cited as confirmatory evidence" (Poon and Princess 1975: 5). Pronouncements like these were especially conspicuous during the Cold War period, when influential Theravāda Buddhists in Southeast Asia were being enlisted by the US State Department and other pro-capitalist actors to actively oppose regional communist movements. References to the *sutta* appeared in essays and speeches by prominent Southeast Asian politicians of the period. Sisowath Monireth in Cambodia wrote that the Buddha's insistence on "freedom of thought" in the *Kālāma Sutta* was unparalleled in the history of world religions and U Chan Htoon in Burma positioned Buddhism as an antiauthoritarian religion that promoted "an individualistic outlook" necessary for individual spiritual growth and a rejection of totalitarianism (Sisowath Monireth and Preah 1966: 32–33, 43–45; Chan Htoon 1958: 9):

> Buddhism requires that the freedom of the individual ... must never be subordinated to group interests which seek to mould him to a standardized pattern and so deprive him of the initiative necessary for his spiritual development. ...Buddhism is democratic, but makes no attempt to achieve a classless society, considering this to be an impossible condition. ...It is thus the antithesis of the totalitarian concept in which the individual has only a group-existence subordinate to the needs of the State.
>
> (Chan Htoon 1958: 9)

In his own extensive treatment of the *sutta*, Buddhadāsa Bhikkhu in Thailand (discussed later) used the text as part of his critique of all worldly (*lokiya*) political ideologies that lacked the insights stemming from a Dhammic perspective:

> In Buddhism there is no dogmatic system that pressures us to believe without the right to examine and decide for ourselves. This is the greatest uniqueness of Buddhism that keeps its practitioners from being anybody's intellectual slave. We Thais should never volunteer to follow the West as slavishly as we are doing now. Intellectual and spiritual freedom is best.
>
> (Buddhadāsa Bhikkhu 1988)

The widespread attention paid to the *Kālāma Sutta* by reform-minded monks and intellectuals in different Theravāda contexts during the nineteenth and twentieth centuries demonstrates why and how Buddhist reform discourses in the modern era have been described as exhibiting a shift toward rationalism. While "rationalism" is a concept that has been widely viewed as a prominent concern (and sometimes as an outcome) of European modernity, individual Buddhist reformers had their own frameworks for how to evaluate the validity of different ways of knowing, thinking, being, and acting. These evaluative frameworks drew on local or indigenous factors and inherited wisdom, such as the one we have seen in the *Kālāma Sutta*. During the reform period, they were also—unavoidably—in dialogue with European discourses about rationalism, science, historicism, and bureaucratic governance. In nuancing Buddhist understandings of reform, it is important to emphasize that for many modern Buddhists, rationalism did not necessarily signal a break in their relationship with spirits, gods, ghosts, ancestors, and other beings whose existence could be readily observed in the world. This is a notable contrast to some parts of the world where the privileging of rationalism as a condition for knowledge has been theorized by scholars as a disenchanting, demythologizing, and secularizing impulse.

As a central concern of modern reform movements, "rationalism" should be understood in the Dhammic terms in which it was cast by Buddhist thinkers and actors concerned with elucidating knowledge, reason, and ethics in the age of modern reforms. Rational thought, action, and speech were grounded in knowledge of the Dhamma—the Buddha's teachings that explained his insights into the nature of reality and right ways to live. Through practice and understanding of the Dhamma, practitioners would eventually attain enlightenment, which meant achieving recognition into the nature of reality and right ways to live.

While lesser examined than other movements of the same period such as nationalism, anticolonialism, or Marxism, Buddhist reformism was as much a pan-Asian phenomenon as these other movements. Although not all reformist movements and thinkers of the period were identical, they tended to share an interest in scripturalism (described in more detail later) and to demonstrate that the Buddha's Dhamma was compatible with modern science. At the same time that reform events across the Theravāda world shared these general goals and orientations, the different political and social contexts of the states in which reform movements developed during the colonial period shaped them in distinctive ways. For example, lay Buddhists became more influential in colonial Burma than in colonial Cambodia, where British and French colonial governments enacted quite different policies toward Buddhism; Buddhists in colonized Ceylon and independent Siam responded differently to challenges from European missionaries; Cambodian Buddhists adopted Thai reformist Thammayut practices more readily than Lao and Lanna (northern Thai) Buddhists who bristled against Bangkok's efforts at Saṅgha centralization and control of Buddhist ritual practice.

Modern religious reforms were also inseparable from the media in which their ideas were disseminated: from palm leaf manuscripts to billboards, radio and television broadcasts, cassettes and cinema, and even to the specific folds of monastic robes and photographic portraits of influential monks and teachers. The intentions and convictions of religious reformers were embodied in and promulgated to others through these different sources, and the impact and aims of reforms were sometimes a product of changing media technologies. For most of Buddhist history, reformation had remained an almost exclusively elite occupation enacted through the production of textual materials intended for Buddhist royalty and monastic literati. But with the advent of the modern period, media technologies changed and connected the world in unprecedented ways, opening up and fostering new possibilities for enacting and transmitting ideas of Buddhist reformation. One of the most dramatic technological advances tied to reformation in this period was the introduction of print, which became accessible to religious scholars in mainland Southeast Asia quite late relative to other parts of the world.

Finally, new forms and expressions of knowledge associated with Buddhist rationalism required new ways of being and thus new modes of subjectivity. In colonial and postcolonial contexts, rapidly changing understandings of the possible roles, rights, and obligations of individuals and new ways of conceiving of community began to emerge. One of the implications of reformist ideas was the notion that individuals had a responsibility to work for the welfare of "society." In colonial Cambodia, for example, this idea manifested as an ethical imperative for individuals to purify themselves in order to benefit society as a whole; in colonial Ceylon, activists began to argue that individual Buddhists had a responsibility to engage in social work for the benefit of others. The development of new bureaucracies and institutions meant that the Buddhist Saṅgha had to negotiate new relationships with governments and adapt to a climate in which there were other avenues for social mobility and prestige besides the monkhood. Along with the new forms of government ushered in during the early nineteenth and twentieth centuries, the altered ways of life associated with colonization, urbanization, industrialization, and mass transportation and communication all changed the ways in which people understood themselves, their relationships with each other and the state, and their possibilities for the future. Religious reforms both responded to these kinds of changes and helped shape them.

Scripturalism in Siam

In the Theravāda Buddhist areas then known as Siam, Cambodge, Burma, and Ceylon, reformists thinking about what it meant to be Buddhist at this time of change emphasized values of authenticity, rationalism, and historicism—priorities that scholars have grouped under the rubric of "scripturalism." Stanley Tambiah has defined the term in relation to the reformist Siamese king Rama IV or Mongkut (r. 1851–1868) as a "concern with finding the true canon, of understanding the truth correctly and discarding false beliefs and magical practices" (Tambiah 1976: 211). While Tambiah seeks to relate Mongkut's scripturalism to earlier Theravādin attempts to clarify orthodoxy and purify the religion, Steven Collins argues that scripturalism is a historically distinct modern religious attitude developed by Buddhist literati in reaction to a range of phenomena that converged in the mid-nineteenth century. Increased pressure from Western missionaries, the cultural prestige and rational practicality of European sciences, and the systematic dismantling of the networks of power and influence that made up the trans-regional world of elite Theravāda Buddhism by colonial encroachment led to a reorientation of how Buddhists conceived the effort to enact purification or reform (Collins 1990: 115, n. 51). Control of monastic decorum and behavior continued to be important to reformism but, in the modern period, was joined by an effort to assert authority over the religious actions of the laity, as well as a focus on the ethical and rational applications of Buddhist teachings. The teachings of the Buddha found in the early texts were touted as holding universal truths, as opposed to local meaning, and the elite began to highlight the ethical and moral value found within them, downplaying the magical and protective powers that they were often used to invoke.

In Siam, major Buddhist reforms reflecting scripturalist aims were initiated by Mongkut beginning in the 1830s while he was still a monk, through the introduction of a new Buddhist order called the Thammayut. He intended the Thammayut to enforce stricter disciplinary codes for its monks as well as to ensure that Thammayut monks had a much better knowledge of Pāli, the *lingua franca* of the Theravādin world in which the canonical scriptures were composed, than had been usual for Thai monks. He promoted and developed his scripturalist innovations through concrete means such as standardizing the system of ecclesiastical examinations and making them more rigorous. He also founded a printing press for the production and dissemination of Pāli works, with the result that they became more widely accessible than had been possible through previous manuscript practices.

Throughout, Mongkut was concerned with establishing the authenticity of Buddhist practices. This quest was based on what we might term a "Buddhist historicism" predicated on the proper understanding of and adherence to the *Vinaya*, the section of the *Tipiṭaka* that laid out the rules of monastic conduct. This historicism, in collaboration with the *Vinaya* became a crucial source of authority for reformers like Mongkut in determining whether local monastic practices, such as ordination ceremonies, robe styles, and ways of carrying alms bowls, conformed with early Buddhist prescriptions (Hansen 2007: 77–8; Reynolds 1972: 64–112, 214–216; Tambiah 1976: 200–219). Mongkut was not, however, obsessively tied to the *Vinaya*. In his quest to distill and ensure what he deemed to be authentic Buddhist practice, he notably embraced some monastic ceremonies and decorum unique to the Mon lineage, as well as some found within Buddhaghosa's later commentaries (Irwin forthcoming).

While most of Mongkut's reformist activities were carried out while he was a monk, his royal proclamations illustrate his concern not only for monastic decorum but also for the proper religious behavior of the laity. Most notably, a proclamation published in 1858 deals directly with the religious actions of the Thai laity in a way that shows Mongkut's growing concern for ethical universalism. The proclamation, often referred to as the "Proclamation on Religious Freedom," decrees that the Reign shall not prohibit individuals from believing in religions as they see fit and argues that every religion agrees upon universal ethical codes that are beneficial to both the individual and the state. It is notable that Mongkut begins his list of universal religious ethics with the five precepts, the ethical foundation of Theravāda Buddhist lay decorum. Later in the proclamation, there are echoes of the *Kālāma Sutta*, as Mongkut criticizes individuals who follow unlearned religious teachers, who compel them to perform extreme displays of faith. Mongkut specifically calls out a few notable cases of people who, in their fervor, "set themselves ablaze as a sacrifice to the triple gem, cut their throats and heads off as a sacrifice to the Buddha, or cut their flesh to collect their blood to put in oil lamps as a means of sacrifice" (Mongkut 2004: 209; Irwin 2011: 129–130). Chastising both the zealous devotees and monks who encouraged them, Mongkut argues that there is no mention of such acts in the Pāli scriptures, which proves that they are transgressive to Buddhism and the aims of the Reign. (Mongkut 2004: 208–211).[2]

The scripturalist reforms initiated by Mongkut spread from Bangkok to Cambodia during the nineteenth century. Beginning in 1848, the new Khmer monarch Ang Duong (r. 1848–1860), who had been a hostage prince in the Siamese court, turned to Bangkok for help in renovating Khmer Buddhism, importing *Tipiṭaka* texts as well as Thammayut-educated monks to aid his project. Ang Duong's son Norodom (r. 1864–1904) continued his father's efforts to reorganize and strengthen the Khmer Saṅgha by revamping Pāli exams for monks as well as centralizing Saṅgha administration. By the early twentieth century, building on Thai reformist ideas and aided by French colonial patronage, young monastic Khmer reformers began to advocate for a new approach to Buddhist learning and practice they termed "Modern Dhamma" (Hansen 2007: 13). This group of monks, including the charismatic Chuon Nath, were self-consciously experimenting with new forms of print expression as well as implementing new approaches to Buddhist learning. Most important, they wanted to ensure that practitioners—whether monks or laypeople—understood the scriptural words and ideas they were chanting and performing. While older memorization-based methods of learning resulted in many monks and laypeople not understanding what they were saying, the Modern Dhamma movement advocated scriptural study and comprehension that would bring one's behavior in line with Dhamma teachings. Rationalism for these Khmer monks was grounded in the intrinsic truth of the Dhamma. In translating the *Kālāma Sūtta*, for example, the monk-scholar Um Sūr wrote that even if one followed only the section of the sermon on avoiding harm, one "could not help but attain spiritual progress" (Thoṅ 1966: 2). The Dhamma could and should be empirically understood through personal observation and experience.

Mid-20th century reformers

The time period of the late eighteenth century through the early decades of the twentieth century saw major reforms in Burma and Ceylon as well as Siam and Cambodia. By the 1950s, Buddhist intellectuals emerging from the throes of colonialism who had been educated by the earlier generations of reformists asserted their own brand of reformist ideologies, institutional visions, and other projects that displayed deeply scripturalist values. These later reform discourses shared the historicist, rationalist, and demythologizing perspectives of the late nineteenth- to early twentieth-century reform movements but tended to rest on the interpretations or particular "discursive formations" of individual thinkers, were less identifiable as coherent movements, and were more contingent on local circumstances such as the development of new forms of nationalism and ethnic difference (Berkwitz 2006: 80). While some reformers of this period engaged in activities that promoted Buddhism as a means of developing the nation, others were critical of the aims and priorities of national religious institutions and their hierarchies. Many prominent reformers emphasized the importance of Buddhism as a resource for solving global problems, such as the prospect of nuclear war.

These reformers continued to persuade their followers that the study of Buddhist ethics was crucial for lay Buddhists as well as members of monastic orders. In many cases, they promoted not only the study of Buddhist scriptures in classical and vernacular languages but also meditation, a practice that had been largely confined to monks and nuns in previous periods. Starting in Burma and spreading across the region, lay meditation became increasingly popularized in parts of the Theravāda world during the twentieth century, a momentum that built on Burmese monastic leader Ledi Sayadaw's conclusion that "Buddha did not spend eons and eons accumulating his *pāramī* [perfection leading to enlightenment] to get this *ñāṇa* [wisdom] just for the sake of a handful of monks only. It is meant for all the sentient beings. So why shouldn't these teachings be made available to laypeople?" (Jordt 2007: 22–24). Regionally, the lay meditation movement was most influential in Burma, where its growth was supported by independent Burma's first prime minister, U Nu. Forms of lay meditation began to spread globally and, by the end of the century, gained currency among urban elites in Thailand. Although lay meditation did not hold the same kind of widespread appeal in Cambodia, small numbers of dedicated Cambodians and foreign supporters were introduced to meditative walking techniques by the activist monk Mahā Ghosānanda as part of his *Dharmayātra* (Dhamma walk) movement for reconciliation during the second Cambodian civil war (Poethig 2004: 197–212).

In the post-independence period, Theravādin reformists began to dismantle colonial-era constraints on Buddhism in the self-conscious sense of recovering and reimagining Buddhism's place in the world, what contemporary theorists have described as the ongoing work of "decolonization" (Shepard 2006: 5–10). Part of their efforts involved invigorating South and Southeast Asian Buddhist networks that had been curtailed by colonial restrictions on intra-regional travel and exchange and promoting the notion of Buddhism as a resource for global peace and antidote to Cold War dangers. In 1950, a Sri Lankan Pāli scholar named G. P. Malalasekera (1899–1972) founded the World Fellowship of Buddhists (WFB) to bring together Buddhists of all schools for fellowship and promulgate Buddhist teachings. Malalasekera was a fellow traveler of the Chinese reformer Tai Xu, who had also envisioned a global Buddhist movement (DeVido

2009: 420). The WFB was, in part, an outgrowth of the post-colonial flurry of preparations for the 1956/1957 *Buddha Jayanti*, the celebration of the twenty-five hundredth anniversary of the Buddha's *parinibbāna*. In 1954, Burmese Buddhists convened the Sixth Council, a dramatic event held in a cave, referencing the First Council in Buddhist history, to recite the Dhamma and launch a new redaction of the Buddhist scriptures and commentaries. The council, which convened an international group of Buddhist scholars, was timed to conclude as the *Jayanti* began in 1956. Celebrated within individual nations and internationally at a massive festival at Bodhgaya in India planned by representatives from different countries, the 2500th anniversary was a time of optimism and cosmopolitanism for Buddhists who understood the anniversary as a time of regeneration and renewal for spreading the Dhamma. In this post-independence moment, it was also an opportunity for countries with majority Buddhist populations to demonstrate their progress as new nations.

Although scripturalist values continued to deeply influence later twentieth-century Buddhist reformers, they were more willing than earlier reformers to reinterpret scriptures, reinvent practices, and draw on diverse international religious and philosophical influences such as Marxism and Gandhian nonviolence. Reformers like Buddhadāsa Bhikkhu in Thailand, U Nu in Burma, A. T. Ariyaratna in Sri Lanka, and Mahā Ghosānanda in Cambodia advocated humanist visions of the Buddha that cast Buddhism as resonant with scientific ideas, and they understood themselves to be revealing the true essence of Buddhism in the process.

Buddhadāsa Bhikkhu (1906–1993) is exemplary of the manner in which individual mid-century reformers both reflected and diverged from earlier scripturalist reforms. Buddhadāsa advocated a rigorous scholarly understanding of Buddhist scriptures and individual practice of meditation as a means for achieving individual and societal transformation. Buddhadāsa understood himself to be practicing a form of Buddhism close to the original Buddhism of early India, which he termed "pristine Buddhism," focused on nonattachment, non-self, *paṭicca-samuppāda* (the Buddha's teaching on the interdependence and reality of existence), and emptiness (Buddhadāsa Bhikkhu 1989). He differed from earlier Theravādin reformers in his incorporation of Mahāyāna ideas of emptiness and analyses of Marxist theories but always emphasized the importance of Dhammic values as crucial to the success of any political system. He drew on nature for inspiration for meditation and was a longtime advocate of Buddhist environmentalism as well as a critic of the Saṅgha hierarchy in Thailand and the country's system of monastic education (Swearer 2010: 167–172).

Similarly, individual Buddhists in other postcolonial countries critiqued the condition of their societies and advocated activism to address social problems, arguing for the importance of individual and collective understanding of the Dhamma as a means for transforming society. They recast bhikkhus as active participants in the political life of new nations and laypeople as members of civic organizations dedicated to spreading the Dhamma. The Burmese prime minister from 1948 to 1962, U Nu (1905–1995), combined politics with Buddhist revival. He set up a Buddhist Sāsana Council that initiated the Sixth Council, helped open a state-sponsored meditation center in Rangoon, and attempted to implement a Buddhist socialist political agenda that was based on the Buddha's teaching of the Eightfold Path. In Sri Lanka, A.T. Ariyaratne (1931–), a science teacher and layperson, founded a grassroots Buddhist organization for rural development in 1958 called Sarvōdaya, based on principles of voluntary mutual aid and peace activism. He urged monks to leave the confines of the monastery to engage in social work and rural development.

Mahā Ghosānanda's (1929–2007) transnational cosmopolitanism is representative of other reformers of this generation. He was educated in monasteries in Cambodia by Chuon Nath and other Khmer reformist teachers but came to social activism through the combined influences of

Buddhist reforms, his international education, and the impact of the communist Khmer Rouge control of Cambodia from 1975 to 1979 and its chaotic aftermath. He was sent to Burma to participate in the Sixth Council and then spent many years in India afterward, studying with Nichidatsu Fujii, the Japanese Buddhist follower of Gandhi. In 1965, he moved to Thailand to study meditation in Thailand under the Thai monk Ajan Dhammadaro, living as a forest monk for nearly fifteen years. After the fall of the Khmer Rouge, he learned about the extent of the violence and destruction in Cambodia from Khmer refugees pouring over the Thai border. He spent the next two and a half decades as an international spokesperson and advocate for peace and reconciliation in Cambodia. Like Ariyaratne, he wanted monks to move out of the temple and engage in social activism. And like Buddhadāsa, his Buddhist teachings emphasized *paṭicca-samuppāda* as the recognition of the fundamental interdependence of all sentient existence and the basis for mutual compassion (Chhath 2012).

Reform and media

It is no accident that modern Buddhist reforms in South and Southeast Asia developed in tandem with the growing availability and use of print. In the manuscript culture through which Buddhist knowledge was maintained and disseminated before the nineteenth century, manuscripts were regarded as sacred objects in themselves, not simply as vehicles for scripture. Buddhist texts were generally inscribed on ritually prepared palm leaves by monks or scholars adhering to devotional practices. Often they were commissioned by abbots or lay patrons and presented to monasteries or royal libraries, where they were kept in protective cloths or boxes and rarely consulted in spite of being highly valued. Scriptural stories and sutras were copied in fragments or rendered into loose vernacular versions, and canonical texts from the *Tipiṭaka* mingled on monastery shelves with astrology and divination manuals. The rise of print did not completely transform the sacrality with which the written word was perceived by Buddhists, but it allowed more people to have access to Buddhist texts. Interest in print by Buddhists was spurred on in some instances by Christian missionaries, who used printed pamphlets to disseminate their proselytizing messages. But the accessibility of print also coincided with Buddhist efforts to edit and disseminate new recensions of texts, especially the *Vinaya* in Sri Lanka, Siam, and Cambodia and the *Abhidhamma* in Burma.

Initial opposition to printing Buddhist scriptures by reluctant clergy disturbed by the threat to manuscript practices seems only to have occurred in Cambodia. But even in Cambodia, where printing was embraced relatively late, Buddhist publishing had begun to flourish by the 1920s. In addition to new critically edited editions of Buddhist scriptures (such as the *Kālāma Sutta*) Buddhists were printing periodicals that contained scriptural translations and commentaries as well as popular magazines, pamphlets of sermons, ritual manuals, and biographies of important monks. In both Cambodge and Ceylon, new texts referred to as *Gihi Vinaya*, addressed a variety of topics related to lay comportment, including how to eat, how children should treat their parents, how to behave in trains and buses, and proper ritual behavior (Gombrich and Obeyesekere 1988: 213–14).

Although print was the primary mode of disseminating new reformist values during this period, not every Buddhist was literate or had access to print texts and libraries, which were concentrated at least initially in urban areas. Some of the most visible late eighteenth- and nineteenth-century media communicating scripturalist values were monks' robes. Across the region, as monks sought to bring their practices in line with early Buddhism, a major controversy erupted regarding the proper way for monks to cover themselves. While this may not sound like a "modern" problem, in fact, clothing in general—for laypeople as well as monks—was a key site for negotiating what it meant to be a modern person in South and Southeast Asia during this period. Colonial subjects had to decide how and whether to adopt European fashions, including fashions that challenged indigenous notions of modesty or piety. Trade laws in some colonies made cloth manufactured in Europe prohibitively expensive and further ignited debates about clothing, as with Gandhi's *khadi* (homespun cloth) movement to protest British taxation policies.

Other visual media included the temples where Buddhists worshiped. As new building materials were introduced in the mid to late nineteenth centuries, new conventions concerning monastic architecture and temple decoration lent themselves to communicating new ideas. In nineteenth-century Siam, European painting techniques and styles such as multiple-point perspective and romantic landscape were first widely used for the creation of Buddhist murals. Unsurprisingly, the same royals behind much of Siamese Buddhist reform, Kings Mongkut and Chulalongkorn, were also instrumental in creating an identifiably modern Siamese temple aesthetic that eventually spread throughout the country (Irwin 2011: 135–191).

With new possibilities for travel and media dissemination, modern Buddhists could broadcast their images and messages more widely than ever before. Photographic portraits of famous monks became common in Buddhist publications, conveying to readers what a modern monk should look like. Dharmapāla's address to the international World Parliament of Religions in Chicago in 1893 was reprinted and widely reported on in US newspapers, as were the Cold War–era tours and diplomatic activities of later reformist monks such as Huot Tath from Cambodia. Newsreels of important ceremonies, such as the *Jayanti*, circulated not only within the Buddhist world but also in Europe and North America. By the 1950s and 1960s, Buddhist magazines and pamphlets were commonplace and often carried stories and photographs from the many international Buddhist conferences that were taking place around the world.

Modern Buddhist subjects

Modern Buddhist reforms did not extend their influence evenly over the populations of the countries in which they occurred; in the decades after reforms were implemented, many rural people in Thailand and Cambodia, for instance, might have felt very little effect from reforms intended to make Buddhism more relevant to modern practitioners. Reform movements were initially concentrated in monasteries and temple schools in urban areas until their ideas became mainstream. Later, when printed materials were widely accessible and other new media, such as architecture, cinema, and photography, were making their way into villages that were already undergoing socioeconomic changes, reform movements contributed to new visions of Buddhist subjects. By "subject," we mean the sense that people had of what it meant to act, relate, and live as a Buddhist, to have an identity as a Buddhist, whether lay or monastic, individual or collective.

Scripturalist thinkers tended to emphasize the historical lifetime of the Buddha as the most important source of authenticity and authority for Buddhist ideas about how to be Buddhist and what Buddhist subjecthood entailed. Thus, not only did the Buddha's historical biography take on standardized forms during the modern period in printed and visual biographies, but it was also "demythologized" to make the Buddha seem more human and more accessible as a role model. One example is a biography called the *Pathomsompōth* in Thai or *Paṭhamasambodhi* in Pāli (*The Buddha's First Enlightenment*) that circulated widely in the late nineteenth and early twentieth centuries in both Siam and Cambodia; the late nineteenth-century version was based on a version from the early part of the century, but in revising it, the Supreme Patriarch of the Thai Saṅgha, who was a member of the reformist Thammayut sect, deleted some of the mythical and miraculous elements of the Buddha's life story that had appeared in the older version (Swearer 1996: 320–325).

Within reformist circles, the paradigm of the ideal monk also shifted in this period. In Cambodia and Thailand, reformists championed monks who were well educated in the scriptures and who adhered to rigorous interpretations of monastic decorum and purity. Admiration for popular local monks who were skilled in acting out or dramatically retelling Buddhist stories, for example, was now redirected toward monks who were capable scholars of Pāli and who could preach authoritatively about canonical scriptures and commentaries (Bowie 2017). While members of local temples had once preferred to elect the most senior monks as abbots, monastic leadership and status were now connected to national Pāli exams and other official marks of distinction. Granted, not every community or monk embraced this new vision of the monk. Monks associated with the forest tradition in Thailand or older esoteric *boran* (ancient) meditation techniques in Cambodia, as well as village monks in some rural communities in northern Thailand and Laos, ignored the new norms for monk education (Kamala 1997; McDaniel 2008; Bizot 1976; Crosby 2013; Marston 2008; Harris 2005: 62–64). But the broader paradigm shift allowed educated young reformist monks such as Chuon Nath in Cambodia to rise to positions of authority and further fortify their viewpoints as new standards for orthopraxy and scriptural interpretation.

More dramatic than shifts in understandings of ideal monks, however, were the new conceptions of the laity. From a reformist viewpoint, individuals needed to purify their behavior, just as monks always had; the purity and well-being of the whole "society" (a new term that came into use in various Southeast Asian contexts during this period) depended on the moral purity of individuals. This conception was made evident in Mahā Ghosānanda's dictum: "A peaceful heart makes a peaceful person. A peaceful person makes a peaceful family. A peaceful family makes a peaceful community. A peaceful community makes a peaceful nation" (Chhath 2012: 60). Thus, in this new conception, the individual bore as much responsibility for the strength and well-being of Buddhism in society as the king and saṅgha once held. Perversely, in their Buddhist-infused communist worldview, the Khmer Rouge seemed to have adopted the idea that individuals must be made "pure" in order to create an effective society and purged those who were viewed as contaminated (Harris 2013: 60; Hinton 2002: 79–90, Marston 2002: 55–56). In each of the majority Theravāda Buddhist nations we have discussed, there was an equivalency made over time between "being Buddhist" and being a legitimate citizen of the nation. In the later part of the twentieth century, especially in Sri Lanka and Myanmar, the widespread acceptance of this equation in some areas contributed to prejudice or even violence against non-Buddhist citizens.

Conclusion

We see the modern era of Theravāda reform ending in or about the 1970s. Prior to this, while there were always different schools and factions of Buddhist interpretation, many of the reform movements of the period had exhibited similar trends. After that, the ways in which Buddhists were reinterpreting and developing Buddhism shifted away from the promulgation of the modern reform values of rationalism, scripturalism, new technologies of expression, and new modes of subjecthood examined in this chapter. The excitement of a shared decolonization of Buddhism that grew out of reformism in different parts of the Theravāda world—evidenced through the records of a plethora of regional exchanges, conferences, collaborative events, and collective activism (such as the early 1960s' WFB campaign to protest the Diem regime's harsh treatment of Buddhists)—came to an end as the local worlds of Theravādins began to diverge sharply.

By the 1970s, Cambodia, Laos, and the ethnic Khmer Theravāda Buddhist areas of southern Vietnam were engulfed in war. When these wars finally ended at different points between 1975 and the late 1990s (when the Khmer Rouge finally surrendered), war-tired populations were preoccupied with basic rebuilding. Rather than "reform," the revisions to Buddhism in these post-conflict areas initially took the form of carefully monitored state regulation, with a more extensive rebuilding of religious infrastructures occurring only later, as socialist government controls were loosened and economies began to expand (Kobayashi 2008; Thompson 2006: 137). In Sri Lanka, 1983 brought civil war and the intensification of a Buddhist nationalism, marked by ethnic and religious antagonisms between Sinhalese Buddhists and Tamil Hindus, that had been intertwined in different ways with reformist discourses since the 1940s (Berkwitz 2006, 2010: 174–181). While modern reforms of Buddhism, including an emphasis on scripturalism, were key political strategies under both the U Nu and Ne Win governments through the 1970s, Burma went through major political upheavals in the 1980s, and many members of the Saṅgha took to the streets to protest or sheltered dissidents during the uprising of 1988. After the fall of the Ne Win government in 1988, the State Law and Order Restoration Council (SLORC) took steps to severely repress Saṅgha political involvement (Schober 2011: 87, 107–108). In Thailand, some of the different strands of reformism that had been so important throughout much of the twentieth century were catalyzed into activism in the wake of the government's massacre of student demonstrators in October 1976. By the end of the 1970s, new modes of Buddhist activism had crystallized in Thailand, apparent, for example, in Sulak Sivaraksa's Thai socially engaged Buddhist network (Baskerville 2019: 236–251).

For all these reasons, the Theravāda Buddhist renovations, reinterpretations, and expressions that began to emerge in the 1980s seem to us to signal a new period in the Theravāda world shaped by markers of postmodernity, such as the rapid spread of the internet and social media, the rise in popularity of visual culture and virtual communication, globalization, the easing of economic and religious restrictions in the post-socialist, post-conflict societies, and the rise of Chinese political and economic power in the region. It is hard to know yet how best to characterize this new historical moment and whether there are reform *events* emerging in this new context that might be correlated to the Theravādin *idea* of reform.

Notes

1 We use *Theravāda world* here to refer to southern Asian Buddhist polities and communities, although Buddhists in southern Asia did not necessarily understand themselves to be "Theravādin" until the twentieth century. See Bretfield's chapter in this volume for a thorough discussion of the genealogy of this term. Most of our essay concerns the modern period when the term increasingly came to be adopted by Theravādins in South and Southeast Asia.

2 For a full translation of the proclamation, see Irwin (2011: 128–131).

References

Baskerville, J.T. 2019. *"Religion for Society": A Transnational History of Socially Engaged Buddhist Networks in Thailand.* Madison: University of Wisconsin Madison.

Berkwitz, S.C. 2010. *South Asian Buddhism: A Survey.* London and New York: Routledge.

Berkwitz, S.C. 2006. "Resisting the Global in Buddhist Nationalism: Venerable Soma's Discourse of Decline and Reform." *Journal of Asian Studies* 67 (1): 73–106.

Bizot, François. 1976. *Le figuier à cinq branches.* Paris: École française d'Extrême-Orient.

Blackburn, Anne M. 2003. "Localizing Lineage: Importing Higher Ordination in Theravādin South and Southeast Asia." In *Constituting Communities: Theravāda Buddhism and the Religious Cultures of South and Southeast Asia*, eds. J.C. Holt, J.N. Kinnard, J.S. Walters, 131–149. Albany, NY: SUNY Press.

Bowie, K.A. 2017. *Of Beggars and Buddhas: The Politics of Humor in the Vessantara Jataka in Thailand.* Madison: University of Wisconsin Press.
Buddhadāsa Bhikkhu. 1989. *Me and Mine: Selected Essays of Bhikkhu Buddhadāsa*, translated and edited by Donald K. Swearer. Albany: State University of New York.
Buddhadāsa Bhikkhu. 1988. "Help! The Kalama Sutta, Help!." translated by Santikaro Bhikkhu. https://www.dhammatalks.net/Books5/Bhikkhu_Buddhadāsa_Help_The_Kalama_Sutta_Help.htm. (Accessed 1/13/20).
Chan Htoon, U (Justice Thado Maha Thray Sithu). 1958. 'Address to the Sixteenth Congress of the International Association for Religious Freedom, Chicago, USA, August 1958.' Place of publication not identified: Union Buddha Sāsana Council Press.
Chhath, Linda. 2012. *Seeing the Angles, Step by Step: A Study of Mahā Ghosānanda, a Khmer Monk in Action.* Madison: University of Wisconsin Madison.
Collins, Steven. 1990. "On the Very Idea of a Pali Canon." *Journal of the Pali Text Society* XV: 89–126.
Conway, Moncure Daniel. 1906. *My Pilgrimage to the Wise Men of the East.* Boston and New York: Houghton, Mifflin and Co.
Crosby, Kate. 2013. *Traditional Theravāda Meditation and its Modern-Era Suppression.* Hong Kong: Buddha Dharma Centre of Hong Kong.
DeVido, Elise Anne. 2009. "The Influence of Chinese Master Taixu on Buddhism in Vietnam." *Journal of Global Buddhism* 10: 413–458.
Gombrich, Richard, Obeyesekere, Gananath. 1988. *Buddhism Transformed: Religious Change in Sri Lanka.* Princeton: Princeton University Press.
Hallisey, Charles. 1991. "Councils as Ideas and Events in the Theravāda." *The Buddhist Forum* II: 133–148.
Hansen, Anne Ruth. 2007. *How to Behave: Buddhism and Modernity in Colonial Cambodia, 1860–1930.* Honolulu: University of Hawai'i Press.
Harris, Ian. 2005. *Cambodian Buddhism: History and Practice.* Honolulu: University of Hawai'i Press.
Harris, Ian. 2013. *Buddhism in a Dark Age: Cambodian Monks under Pol Pot.* Honolulu: University of Hawai'i Press.
Hinton, Alexander. 2002. "Purity and Contamination in the Cambodian Genocide." In *Cambodia Emerges from the Past: Eight Essays.* ed. J. Ledgerwood, 60–90. DeKalb, Il: Southeast Asia Publications, Center for Southeast Asian Studies, Northern Illinois University.
Irwin, Anthony Lovenheim. 2011. 'Imagining Boundaries: *Sīmā* Space, Lineage Trails, and Trans-Regional Theravada Orthodoxy.' MA Thesis, University of Wisconsin-Madison.
Irwin, Anthony Lovenheim. (Forthcoming) "Changing *Sīmā*, Changing World." In Sīmās*: Foundations of Buddhist Religion*, ed. J. Carbine, E. Davis.
Jordt, Ingrid. 2007. *Burma's Mass Lay Meditation Movement: Buddhism and the Cultural Construction of Power.* Athens, OH: Ohio University Press.
Kamala, Tiyavanich. 1997. *Forest Recollections: Wandering Monks in Twentieth-Century Thailand.* Honolulu: University of Hawai'i Press.
Kobayashi, Satoru. 2008. "Reconstructing Buddhist Temple Buildings: an Analysis of Village Buddhism After the Era of Turmoil." In *People of Virtue: Reconfiguring Religion, Power and Moral Order in Cambodia Today*, eds. A. Kent, D. Chandler, 169–194. Copenhagen: NIAS Press.
Marston, John. 2002. "Democratic Kampuchea and the Idea of Modernity." In *Cambodia Emerges from the Past: Eight Essays*, ed. J. Ledgerwood, 38–59. DeKalb, Il: Southeast Asia Publications, Center for Southeast Asian Studies, Northern Illinois University.
Marston, John. 2008. "Reconstructing 'Ancient' Cambodian Buddhism." *Contemporary Buddhism* 9 (1): 99–121.
McDaniel, Justin. 2008. *Gathering Leaves and Lifting Words: Histories of Buddhist Monastic Education in Laos and Thailand.* Seattle: University of Washington Press.
Mongkut, King. 2004. *Prachum Prakaat Nai Rachakaan Tii Sii* [Collected Proclamations of King Mongkut]. Bangkok: Toyota Foundation.
Nyanaponika, Thera, Bodhi, Bikkhu. 1999. *Numerical Discourses of the Buddha: An Anthology of Suttas from the Aṅguttara Nikāya.* New York: AltaMira Press.
Poethig, Kathryn. 2004. "Locating the Transnational in Cambodia's Dhammayātra." In *History, Buddhism, and New Religious Movements in Cambodia.* eds. J. Marston, E. Guthrie, 197–212. Honolulu: University of Hawaii'i Press.
Poon, Pismai Diskul, Princess, H.S.H. 1975. *Thammai Khon Rao Tōng mī Sātsanā, A Being That is Human.* Bangkok: World Fellowship of Buddhists.

Reynolds, Craig. 1972. *The Buddhist Monkhood in Nineteenth-Century Thailand.* Ithaca and London: Cornell University.

Shepard, Todd. 2006. *The Invention of Decolonization: The Algerian War and the Remaking of France.* Ithaca and London: Cornell University Press.

Schober, Juliane. 2011. *Modern Buddhist Conjectures in Myanmar: Cultural Narratives, Colonial Legacies, and Civil Society.* Honolulu: University of Hawaii Press.

Sisowath Monireth, S.A.R., Preah, Samdech Krom. 1966. "Bouddha Sasana: Essai de Comprehension." *Banlȳ Buddhacakr* [Illumination of the Buddha-wheel], 26 (January–March): 29–49.

Soma, Thera. 2008. [1959] *Kalama Sutta: Buddha's Charter of Free Inquiry* (reprinted from *The Wheel Publication*, Volume 8). Kandy: Buddhist Publication Society. http://www.bps.lk/olib/wh/wh008_Soma_Buddhas-Charter-of-Free-Inquiry.pdf (accessed January 13, 2020).

Swearer, Donald K. 1996. "Bhikkhu Buddhadāsa's Interpretation of the Buddha." *Journal of the American Academy of Religion* 64 (2): 313–336.

Swearer, Donald K. 2010. *The Buddhist World of Southeast Asia* (2nd ed.). Albany: SUNY Press.

Tambiah, Stanley Jeyaraja. 1976. *World Conqueror and World Renouncer: A Study of Buddhism and Polity in Thailand against a Historical Background.* Cambridge and New York: Cambridge University Press.

Thittila, Sayadaw U. 1948. *Buddhism and the Personal Life.* London: The Buddhist Society.

Thompson, Ashley. 2006. "Buddhism in Cambodia: Rupture and Continuity." In *Buddhism in World Cultures: Comparative Perspectives*, ed. S.C. Berkwitz, 129–167. Santa Barbara, Denver and Oxford: ABC CLIO.

Thoṅ, Mahā Vimaladhamm. 1966. *Kālāmasūtr niṅ Parābhavasūtr* (3rd ed.). Phnom Penh: Buddhist Institute.

Vajirañāṇavarorasa, Somdetch Phra Mahā Samaṇa Chao Krom Phrayā. 1979. *Autobiography: The Life of Prince-Patriach Vajirañāṇavarorasa of Siam, 1860–1921*, translated and edited by C.J. Reynolds. Athens: Ohio University Press.

6

TRADITION

Nuns and "Theravāda" in Sri Lanka

Nirmala S. Salgado

Introduction

In December 2018 a large gathering of Buddhist monks and nuns was held in Vihāra Mahādevi Park in Colombo, Sri Lanka.[1] The park lies opposite the Department of Buddhist Affairs (DBA), a government office that oversees the needs of all the country's Buddhist monastics, excluding higher-ordained Buddhist nuns (*bhikkhunīs*), whom the state does not officially recognize.[2] A few hundred *bhikkhunīs* from around the country processed in a demonstration around the park. They, together with supportive monks, submitted a petition to DBA officials requesting that *bhikkhunīs* be accorded recognition as *bhikkhunīs* on their national identity cards (NICs). The government generally issues NICs to Sri Lankan citizens on request. Those cards are necessary to register for state exams, apply for passports, and vote but are not readily available to fully ordained nuns. Yet the question of *bhikkhunīs*' legal rights was not the only one at stake that day. At another level, the demonstration raised questions about the power of monastics vis-à-vis that of the state and how monastics and the state authorized "Theravāda" differently.

Here I focus on debates in Sri Lanka that have been formative in attempting to authorize who can say what about Theravāda. As Asad indicates, authorizing processes are intrinsic to the discourse and practice of religion and its representation (1993: 35–43). Sri Lanka is unique among so-called Theravāda countries in that it is seen not just as a country - whose supposedly pristine Buddhism is purportedly grounded in a continuous Pāli textual tradition, but also as a place to which *bhikkhunī* lineages throughout the world might trace their origins through the third-century BCE *bhikkhunī* Saṅghamittā to the first *bhikkhunī*, Mahāpajāpati Gōtamī (ordained by the Buddha himself). Although the (Theravāda) *bhikkhunī* lineage was lost in the last millennium, beginning in the 1980s, Buddhist nuns have become prominent in the Theravāda countries of Sri Lanka, Thailand, and Burma (Myanmar), attracting the attention of scholars and state authorities alike.[3]

It is not surprising that a heightened interest in the "status" of women in developing countries in the late twentieth century prompted an attentiveness to the higher ordination (*upasampadā*) of Theravāda Buddhist nuns. By the turn of the twenty-first century, procedures were in place in Sri Lanka to provide a Theravāda *upasampadā* for *bhikkhunīs* from around the world. However, the governments of Sri Lanka, Thailand, and Myanmar (Burma) have denied legal recognition to their *bhikkhunīs*, doing so at the insistence of Buddhist monks who claim that, in the absence

DOI: 10.4324/9781351026666-8

of a quorum of Theravāda *bhikkhunīs* for the *upasampadā*, a Theravāda *bhikkhunī upasampadā* is "impossible" (Kawanami 2007: 234–236; Seeger 2008: 160–163). Nevertheless, *bhikkhunīs* from Theravāda countries have forged ahead in the training and *upasampadās* of nuns (Ito 2012: 58 n. 8; Salgado 2013: 149–181). Meanwhile, in Sri Lanka in particular, householders who accept nuns as Theravāda *bhikkhunīs* have continued to support them regardless of such contestation (Mrozik 2014: 86). At the same time, some senior monks, ten-training-precept nuns (Sinh: *dasa silmātās* or *silmātās*), and state officials, claiming that the new *bhikkhunīs* are "Mahāyāna" or simply "illegitimate" because their founding ordinations were conducted by monastics from Korea and Taiwan, have continued to voice their disapproval of the *bhikkhunī* ordinations.[4] In Sri Lanka, Thailand, and Burma, the trope of "Mahāyāna difference" pitted against "Theravāda purity" has dominated discussions about *bhikkhunī* ordinations since the 1980s, raising the very notion of Theravāda to a prominence that it perhaps has not been accorded since the inaugural conference of the World Federation of Buddhists in 1950, a venue at which scholar-practitioners gave the term *Theravāda* new significance (Perreira 2012: 450–452). Evocations of a Theravāda tradition have been relatively recent in debates about Buddhist nuns, indicating, as Abeysekara points out, that certain claims, like those pertaining to an authentic Buddhism, are subject to particular contingent conjunctures or "a period … in which competing narratives and debates conjoin … to make centrally visible particular authoritative knowledges about what can and cannot count as Buddhism" (2002: 4 n. 10). In effect, the higher ordination of nuns in Theravāda Buddhism raises questions not just about Theravāda but about tradition itself. As Asad argues, disagreements, which are integral to a living tradition, are "not only about the substance of interpretation but also over where exactly the limits of a tradition lie" (2015: 169).

I want to consider how the very idea of Theravāda, grounded as it may seem to be in a Pāli textual tradition and lineage transmission, is not self-evident. What becomes important is how Theravāda is authorized as an authentic form of Buddhism, by whom, and when. My work, focusing on research conducted since the 1980s, underscores the contingent circumstances in which disputes about ordinations and lineages of Buddhist nuns are imbricated in particular relations of power. Sri Lankan Buddhist nuns of the late nineteenth and early twentieth centuries initiated a new renunciant practice. Although details of that practice were argued over intermittently, the question of nuns' Theravāda "authenticity," was not evoked as it has been in debates about recent *bhikkhunī* ordinations. Indeed, no question of Theravāda was evident in the initiation of the renowned Buddhist nun Sudharmachari (d. 1939), who has lineage descendants among *silmātās* to this day. Yet, Sudharmachari introduced a renunciant tradition that not only was unprecedented in Sri Lanka, but also marked a departure from the Burmese tradition in which she was first initiated (Bartholomeusz 1994: 93; Bloss 1987: 9–10; Salgado 2013: 112). The contrast between the reception in Sri Lanka of the initiations of Sudharmachari and her lineage descendants and that of the recent ordinations of Sri Lankan *bhikkhunīs* is telling. As we shall see, lineage descendants of Sudharmachari and other *silmātās* have drawn criticism for lacking a *Buddhist* (rather than a specifically Theravāda) authenticity.[5] However, by the 1970s, with the idea of Theravāda gaining prominence, the specter of Theravāda authenticity had assumed a new guise, setting the stage for framing controversies about the foundation and lineage tradition for a Theravāda *bhikkhunī* ordination, both in Sri Lanka and elsewhere. At the nub of these arguments was the supposed purity of *the* Theravāda tradition, defined in opposition to its Mahāyāna other. Such a use of Theravāda, however, depends not on what Theravāda putatively may or may not be (something always subject to debate) but, rather, on shifting configurations of power in a contestation for monastic and state authority.

Tradition

Scholars and practitioners often assume that the notion of a continuous Sri Lankan Theravāda tradition is traceable to ancient India (Holt 2017: 1; Gombrich 1988: 3). However, as Abeysekara points out, such a notion is misleading, given that "tradition" constitutes an ongoing process of contestation between less-than-disinterested stakeholders (2002: 74–100; 2018: 334). Today proponents and opponents of *bhikkhunī* ordinations seek the coherence and continuity of an identity grounded in interpretations of lineage and tradition. As Abeysekara reminds us, "[c]oherence is a discursively constructed idea" (2018: 338). In other words, an idea such as "Theravāda tradition," viewed as a coherent and continuous objective reality (whether by scholars or by practitioners), should instead be understood as a response to certain questions specific to particular contingent conjunctures. Let me begin by focusing on questions about nuns' monastic attire and disciplinary precepts, because they are indicative of a rethinking of "tradition." It is instructive to consider the debates (or lack thereof) about the nuns at the time of Sudharmachari (then referred to as female devotees, or Sinh: *upāsikā*s), since their lineage descendants (now called [*dasa*] *silmātā*s), like the Sri Lankan *bhikkhunī*s of today, can trace their practice to an inaugural initiation that was established by non–Sri Lankan monastics.

Monastic attire and training precepts generally serve to differentiate nuns from householders. Such differentiation, even as it emerged with the new visibility of *upāsikā*s and *silmātā*s, did not per se evoke the question of Theravāda authenticity. Yet monastic attire, bound up as it is with perceptions of public appearance and lineage tradition, has proved contentious in debating the so-called status of nuns as (Theravāda) *bhikkhunī*s in Sri Lanka, Thailand, and Burma. *Bhikkhunī*s, whose attire is relatively new and distinct in these countries, have, like the *upāsikā*s and *silmātā*s of Sri Lanka, pushed the limits of tradition by introducing a new attire for nuns. But the question of what constitutes "Theravāda"—central for the new *bhikkhunī*s—had no relevance to earlier debates about *upāsikā* and *silmātā* robes. Sudharmachari, who returned to Sri Lanka in 1905 after her initiation in Burma, may have worn "a white blouse and a yellow robe" (Bloss 1987: 11), although there is some indication that she and her students wore white with another color, such as salmon or brown (Salgado 2013: 114). Nuns I interviewed said that *silmātā*s did not assume a uniform colored attire of yellow or brown (without white) until about the 1950s. Over the years, their monastic attire has attracted attention for its increasing resemblance to that of monks. This sparked public opposition as early as the 1890s, and, more recently, in the 1980s and 1990s (Bartholomeusz 1994: 36–39; Salgado 2013: 115–116).

Those accusing *silmātā*s of observing an incorrect *Buddhism* had concerns similar to those of critics who faulted certain Sri Lankan monks for appearing to depart from tradition (Carrithers 1983: 126–127). The seemingly new forms of religious practice among monks and nuns did not evoke concerns about *Theravāda* authenticity, since the category of "Buddhism" (as opposed to other religions), rather than "Theravāda" (as opposed to Mahāyāna), was at stake. The foundational Burmese tradition to which Sudharmachari owed her ordination was simply accepted as authoritative, as was the *provenance* of the attire of the early nuns. Of course, one might point out that Burmese Buddhism is considered to be self-evidently "Theravāda" and that there is precedence for bringing monastic ordinations to Sri Lanka from Burma. But what is important to note is that the category of Theravāda as we understand it today was rarely evoked in Sri Lanka until after the 1950s (Perreira 2012: 443–457). Previously, disputes about correct monastic practice centered on what could count as Buddhism (in contrast to Christianity). As Scott and Malalgoda point out, "Buddhism" as a concept referring to a discrete "religion"—indeed, the Sinhala term for *religion* (*āgama*) itself—did not even arise until the encounter with Christian missionaries (Scott 1994: 188). I wish to highlight that even when a dispute purportedly claims to focus on correct Buddhist practice or a pure Theravāda *bhikkhunī* lineage, categories such as "Buddhism" and "Theravāda" are evoked in particular circumstances and defined in specific ways by individuals and the state in a bid to assert authority and power.

Let us now turn to questions about nuns' training precepts (Pāli: *sikkhāpada*), which are intrinsically connected to their renunciant (Sinh: *pävidi*/Pāli: *pabbajjā*) practice. Renunciant practice is generally differentiated from householder (Sinh: *gihi*) practice on the basis of an understanding of *sikkhāpada* and discipline (*vinaya*), which may be considered either "renunciant" or "householder." Here I want to point out that the provenance of *silmātā*s' discipline and training precepts did not come under scrutiny for Theravāda authenticity in the early twentieth century the way it has for recent *bhikkhunī*s. It is often forgotten today that *silmātā*s participate in an ordination ritual that had no known precedent before the initiation of Sudharmachari, to whom many of them can trace a direct lineage.[6] Sudharmachari received her first ordination from nuns in Burma. A lineage descendant of Sudharmachari informed me that Sudharmachari received a later ordination, into the ten renunciant precepts, from monks at the Malwatta chapter (Sinh: *pārśavaya*) in Kandy, Sri Lanka. What is interesting is not just that the Burmese ten precepts differ from those currently practiced in Sri Lanka or that the training precepts that Sudharmachari's lineage students continue to practice in Sri Lanka have no known precedent among Buddhist nuns, but also that those precepts were affirmed in the early twentieth century by monks of the Malwatta chapter of the Tooth Temple (also associated with the Asgiriya chapter). Those monks, custodians of the tooth relic of the Buddha, who worked closely with the state and other influential senior monks (Sinh: *mahānāyaka*s), authorized a new renunciant practice that attracted little or no controversy. Yet, today their lineage students at the same temple assert their claims to authority and power in another way: working closely with state officials and leading *silmātā*s throughout the country, they are now perhaps the strongest opponents of the *bhikkhunī* ordinations, arguing that the ordinations are "Mahāyāna," as are the new *bhikkhunī*s. Monks from this temple have rejected the (Theravāda) authenticity of the new *bhikkhunī*s even though the latter, like Sudharmachari and her students, have departed from tradition. It is telling that, although the monks of the Tooth Temple chose to ordain Sudharmachari and accept the new monastic practice that she introduced, the lineage students of those same monks now allege that Sri Lankan *bhikkhunī* ordinations subvert "tradition," as evidenced by the *bhikkhunī*s' new attire and the textual lineage of their *vinaya* precepts.

Though the growing visibility of the *upāsikā*s/*silmātā*s prompted debates about correct Buddhist practice, appeals to their Theravāda authenticity and their place in tradition were only invoked recently. In Sri Lanka in 2002, when the debate about the importance of Theravāda for *bhikkhunī* ordinations was at its height, a direct student descendant of Sudharmachari who opposed the higher ordination of Sri Lankan *bhikkhunī*s informed me that Sudharmachari took the renunciant ten precepts "according to the Theravāda way," even though the very idea of Theravāda had no known currency in Sudharmachari's time. Here we see a move to authenticate the practice of *silmātā*s in tradition as a means to counter the new *bhikkhunī* ordinations. But monastic advocates of those ordinations, while seeking to garner public acceptance of nuns' new disciplinary observances, have responded by construing the notion of tradition differently. Affirming the Theravāda authenticity of the recent *bhikkhunī* ordinations (traced through a continuing Pāli textual tradition and lineage to the ordination of Mahāpajāpati Gōtamī), they insist that it is the *silmātā*s, not the Sri Lankan *bhikkhunī*s, whose practice lacks grounding in tradition. Hence, in 2016, one monastic told me, "There is no *use* of the word *silmātā* in the *sāsana* [Buddhist dispensation]. The *usage* in the *sāsana* includes four words: *bhikkhu*, *bhikkhunī*, *upāsakā* [male devotee], *upāsikā*. *Silmātā* is a word for a householder, not a renunciant." This was an argument I had not heard when the inaugural *bhikkhunī* ordinations occurred. Then the dispute had centered on the Theravāda authenticity of the *bhikkhunīs*. Now proponents of *bhikkhunī* ordinations were turning the argument about tradition on its head, questioning the (textual) authenticity of a *silmātā* tradition. My point here is that it is mistaken to think about ideas such as "Theravāda," "Buddhism," and "tradition" as self-evident. Rather, they are concepts used in response to particular questions that arise in specific conjunctures. As Abeysekara, referencing Nietzsche, indicates, "Concepts have historical *uses*, with competing definitions and sensibilities in a genealogy" (2019: 10).

References to what constitutes Theravāda (and its Mahāyāna other) have become increasingly prevalent in Sri Lanka since the 1970s (Abeysekara 2002: 110–129). Affirming lineage continuity (in disciplinary precepts and monastic attire) has become essential to the new *bhikkhunīs*, whose ordinations were preceded by heated debates about Theravāda authenticity. The 1996 higher ordination of nuns at Sarnath, India, took place after Kusuma Devendra (ordained at Sarnath) had studied the Korean lineage tradition and determined that the "Korean *Dharmagupta Vinaya* tradition of Ordination was practically the same as the Theravāda tradition" and could be traced back through China and Sri Lanka to India (Kusuma 2012: 135). The Sarnath ordination of ten select Sri Lankan nuns was a dual ordination conducted by Korean *bhikkhus* and *bhikkhunīs* in the Korean language. The nuns had trained in Sinhala, studying Kusuma Devendra's Sinhala translation of the English translation of the Korean ordination procedure. The Sri Lankan ordinands underwent a Korean ordination, which incorporated marking their skin with joss sticks, wearing Korean monastic attire, and using the Korean language. Immediately after their dual ordination, the nuns were greeted by Sri Lankan monks who counseled them on how to observe practices specific to *bhikkhunīs*, many of which are in the Pāli texts. The senior Sri Lankan monks presented the new *bhikkhunīs* with the cut and sewn saffron robes of Sri Lankan monastics, thereby welcoming them into their monastic lineage. The Sarnath ordination received some public attention in Sri Lanka: newspaper reports included color photos of the Sarnath *bhikkhunīs* and their Korean mentors wearing Korean monastic attire ("Sasana History;" "The Ordination"). Some Sri Lankan monastics dismissed the event, whereas others refused to recognize the newly ordained nuns as Theravāda *bhikkhunīs*. Meanwhile, monastics under the leadership of Inamaluwe Sumangala, the head monk of the Dambulla Temple in Sri Lanka, lost little time in arranging a rival *bhikkhunī* ordination and spinning the story about Theravāda authenticity in yet another way.

Given that "Theravāda" has gained currency only since the 1950s, it is not surprising that the question of Theravāda authenticity arose with the recent *bhikkhunī* ordinations and not with the initiations of Buddhist nuns in the late nineteenth and early twentieth centuries. As we have seen, no such question was evoked in debates when Sudharmachari and her descendants first established a new practice for Buddhist nuns. However, the introduction of Sri Lankan nuns (as *bhikkhunīs*) has led to seemingly enduring questions about Theravāda tradition.

Contestation

The idea of a pure Theravāda tradition was used to reject *bhikkhunī upasampadās* in general and differentiate between lineages of Sri Lankan *bhikkhunīs* at the turn of the twenty-first century. Since then, *Mahānāyakas* who oppose the *bhikkhunī* ordinations have collaborated with government officials and *silmātās* to exclude *bhikkhunīs*' access to certain privileges accorded to other monastics on the grounds that their ordinations are Mahāyāna and not Theravāda. Let us now turn to how some Sri Lankan *bhikkhunīs* used that line of reasoning to discredit others. Here we shall see that opponents and proponents of the *bhikkhunī upasampadās*, in contesting notions of Theravāda purity, were also engaged in an assertion of power.

In February 1997, barely two months after the Sarnath ordination, which some leading *silmātās* had witnessed, senior *silmātās* and monks held a nationwide meeting in Sri Lanka to discuss the possibility of holding a *bhikkhunī upasampadā* there. A *silmātā* who had been encouraged to attend the meeting told me that "the Indian [Sarnath] ordination was Mahāyāna and that it would [now] be possible to establish the Theravāda ordination [instead] in Sri Lanka." Sumangala, upon accepting an invitation to be president of the newly established Sri Lanka Bhikkhunī Re-awakening Organization (SLBRO), immediately organized a *bhikkhunī* training program near Dambulla. Having observed the Sarnath ordination and witnessed two decades of dispute about the possibility of a Theravāda *bhikkhunī upasampadā*, senior monastics at the training program vociferously affirmed the Theravāda authenticity of *their* prospective *bhikkhunī* ordination. By July 1997, twenty-six *silmātās* had been ordained as novice nuns (*sāmaṇerīs*), with the intention that they receive the *upasampadā* in Sri Lanka. One *sāmaṇerī* training at the center that year buttressed claims to Theravāda authenticity in her upcoming *upasampadā* by stating, "It is the Theravāda *upasampadā* of Lanka that we are trying to establish, not the Mahāyāna. This [Theravāda *upasampadā*] is found nowhere else in the world." Evoking a Theravāda ideal about rooting the *sāsana* in the country, Sumangala announced that he planned to hold the initial ordination "on Sri Lankan soil." In doing so, he referenced the textual passage: "When a person born of parents who belong to Tambapaṇṇidīpa [Sri Lanka], enters pabbajjā [renunciation/ordination] in Tambapaṇṇidīpa, learns the Vinaya in Tambapaṇṇidīpa and recites the same in Tambapaṇṇidīpa, then will the sāsana take root in the land" (Adikaram 1953: 56). The romantic trope of a patch of virtuous soil grounding a Sri Lankan *bhikkhunī* lineage has since (perhaps unwittingly) been adopted in some ordination narratives, reinforcing the Theravāda authenticity of the ordinations organized by the Dambulla Temple in Sri Lanka (Cheng 2007: 19; Chuehmen 2007: 30).

However, that same idea became a point of contestation for the Sarnath *bhikkhunīs* who, having affirmed to me in 2004 (and more publicly later) the centrality of their inaugural ordination, argued that the text in question mandates holding ordinations for *bhikkhunīs* not *on* the soil of Sri Lanka but, rather, for those born *of* that soil (Kusuma 2008: 18). Though his plans changed, and he eventually held the ordination in Bodhgaya, Sumangala was keen to establish the ordination in Sri Lanka and did so without delay. The *bhikkhunīs* ordained in Sarnath helped train the twenty Sri Lankan (Dambulla) nuns for what is called the 1998 "International Full Ordination" in Bodhgaya—a dual ordination conducted by monastics from the Foguangshan (FGS) monastery in Taiwan. Unlike the Sarnath nuns, who donned Korean robes, the Bodhgaya-Dambulla nuns wore Sri Lankan monastic attire for their ordination. A newspaper depiction of them in familiar Sri Lankan robes provides a striking contrast to photos of the Korean attire worn by the Sarnath *bhikkhunīs* that had appeared the previous year ("Bak Pasalosvaka"; "The Ordination"). Soon after their international ordination, the Bodhgaya *bhikkhunīs* traveled to Sarnath, where, led by Sri Lankan monks and the Sarnath *bhikkhunīs*, they processed to a full-moon house (Sinh: *pōyagē*) to partake in a subsequent ritual, which some have called a second, or "Theravāda," *upsampadā*. Both the Sarnath ordination conducted by Koreans and the Bodhgaya ordination conducted by Chinese monastics followed the Dharmaguptaka *Vinaya*. Yet monastics ordained at the latter have often insisted on the Theravāda connection with China, not Korea, since Sri Lankan *bhikkhunīs* are recorded as having been the first to ordain Chinese nuns, in the fifth century CE. That the Chinese ordination lineage had spread to other countries, including Korea, was of little import to them. Opponents of the *bhikkhunī* ordinations voiced their criticisms of both the Sarnath and the Bodhgaya ordinations, parroting arguments that had been bruited about Sri Lanka over the previous two decades. Whereas some arguments reiterated variations of the old debate about the impossibility of resuscitating a lost *bhikkhunī* tradition (in creating new Theravāda *bhikkhunīs* from no Theravāda *bhikkhunīs*), others raised objections to an ordination ritual necessitating the *bhikkhunīs*' adoption of Mahāyāna robes and disciplinary precepts and the use of a language considered foreign to Theravāda. Among some *silmātās* and monks, the idea of Theravāda had become important as a criterion for excluding Sri Lankan nuns as *bhikkhunīs* altogether. Among Bodhgaya-Dambulla monastics, that same idea was used to reject the Sarnath ordination as Mahāyāna and establish their own seniority among Theravāda *bhikkhunīs* (Salgado 2013: 153–159).

Soon after their ordination, the Sarnath *bhikkhunīs*, who had to remain in India for some years, drew fire not just from *silmātās* and oppositional monks but also from Bodhgaya-Dambulla monastics. Some of the criticisms—such as that all the Sarnath *bhikkhunīs* had disrobed and had broken a contractual agreement to remain for five years in India before returning—were patently untrue. Without a spokesperson for them in Sri Lanka, all kinds of rumors swirled about them. My concern here is not to adjudicate the putative "facts" of the situation, but rather to highlight that some of the most trenchant criticisms of the Sarnath ordination were disseminated by monastics associated with Bodhgaya-Dambulla, who sought to establish their *bhikkhunī* lineage as the only authentically Theravāda one. Their promotion of the Bodhgaya-Dambulla ordinations circulated through multiple news networks in Sri Lanka, as well as through a pamphlet, *Higher Ordination and Bhikkhunī Order in Sri Lanka*, written by Bhadra, who had first been ordained at Sarnath but had had to leave India prematurely because of health issues. After returning to Sri Lanka, she was accepted for training at Dambulla and reordained there. Even though *bhikkhunī* ordinations of Sri Lankan nuns outside the Bodhgaya-Dambulla group may be traced to a Chinese ordination lineage, Bhadra's pamphlet, (whose contents have been disseminated well beyond Sri Lanka), emphasized the Theravāda authenticity of the Bodhgaya-Dambulla ordinations alone while drawing attention to the Mahāyāna character of the other *bhikkhunī* ordinations. Referring to a 1988 ordination of Sri Lankan nuns in Los Angeles, Bhadra stated that "those nuns were ordained by *bhikkhunīs* in Taiwan. But they were not accept[ed] as *bhikkhunīs* in Sri Lanka because Taiwan is a Mahāyāna country" (2001: 25). Furthermore, stating that the Sarnath ordination was "according to the Korean tradition," she drew attention to her own Dambulla ordination: "When the *Bhikkhunī* Order was re-established according to the Theravāda tradition at Dambulla, I ... followed the procedure to receive the Higher Ordination in the presence of the Sri Lankan *bhikkhu*[s] [and] *bhikkhunīs* according to the Theravāda Tradition" (29). Here we see how the use of "Theravāda" has effectively become a standard for validating some ordinations and not others.

The Bodhgaya *bhikkhunīs* returned to Dambulla within a few weeks of their 1998 ordination and ordained the *sāmaṇerīs* who had trained with them there. This was the first of three higher ordinations held in Dambulla that year. Invitations to apply for the training and the ordination, sent to *silmātās* throughout the country, served to highlight the Dambulla training center and its new initiatives ("Meheṇi Sasna"). Subsequent Dambulla *upasampadās*, held at least once a year, helped publicize the establishment of the Bodhgaya-Dambulla *bhikkhunī* lineage "on Sri Lankan soil," thereby affirming it as Theravāda. News of the ordinations appeared in the national newspapers and on TV. The 2007 inauguration of a private radio channel operated by the Dambulla Temple further assisted in spreading the word throughout the country. *Bhikkhunīs* ordained in Dambulla returned to their home communities in festive processions organized by household supporters, thus publicizing their *bhikkhunī upasampadās* in their immediate neighborhoods. The relatively rapid consecration of new *pōyagēs* at numerous *bhikkhunī* hermitages throughout the country facilitated their attendance at rituals considered obligatory for fully ordained monastics.[7] Bodhgaya-Dambulla monastics' activities left little doubt among prospective *bhikkhunīs* and their supportive householders that it *was* possible for Sri Lankan nuns to become Theravāda *bhikkhunīs*.

Some senior monks who had officiated at the Bodhgaya ordination and initially participated in the Dambulla ordinations began to notice how the exclusivist Theravāda rhetoric coming from Dambulla rendered their *bhikkhunī upasampadās* increasingly indigenous (Sinh: *dēsīya*) to Sri Lanka. In an effort to recognize the international character of *bhikkhunī* ordinations, they backed away from participation in the Dambulla ordinations and responded to those ordinations by bringing together Sri Lankan *bhikkhunīs* from the Korean (Sarnath) and Chinese (Bodhgaya) ordination lineages. In 2000, after a fifty-three-day training period at the FGS headquarters in Taiwan, twenty Sri Lankan nuns wearing Sri Lankan monastic attire received the ordination with the assistance of Sarnath *bhikkhunīs* (Chuehmen 2007: 30). In doing so, they initiated a Sri Lankan *bhikkhunī* lineage of nuns (henceforth the Sarnath-Taiwan-Neugala or S-T-Neugala lineage) that was connected to both Korean and Chinese monastics, some of whom continued to train and ordain *bhikkhunīs*, at the Neugala training center in Sri Lanka. In 2007, *bhikkhunīs* at Neugala began to hold annual *upasampadās*, and they have since continued to maintain close ties with monastics from both Sarnath and Taiwan (an FGS monastic served as the preceptor in their ordination ceremony as recently as 2012). Further consolidation of the Korean and Taiwanese *bhikkhunī* lineages in Sri Lanka occurred in 2003, when one ordination including *bhikkhunīs* from both Korea and Taiwan was held at the temple of Talalle Dhammaloka (a monk who had officiated at the Bodhgaya ordination), and another was held later in Anurādhapura by S-T-Neugala and FGS *bhikkhunīs*.

Monks and nuns have offered divergent slants on the Sarnath and Bodhgaya *bhikkhunī* ordinations. In the early years after the ordinations, when Sumangala had barred Bodhgaya-Dambulla *bhikkhunīs* from participating in certain rituals with the S-T-Neugala *bhikkhunīs* on the grounds of their Mahāyāna difference, nuns spoke to me of tension among leading *bhikkhunīs*, inclining them to prefer one ordination lineage to another. More recently, I learned that *silmātās* who had trained with one teacher-monk for decades were admonished not to take the Dambulla *upasampadā*, since, in order to take part, they would have to abandon their mentor-monk and acknowledge a new teacher in Sumangala. Criticisms of the Sarnath ordination, together with those of the S-T-Neugala lineage, persisted for some time. Bodhgaya-Dambulla *bhikkhunīs* claimed that the latter ordinations (unlike theirs) were Mahāyāna. Meanwhile, opposing *silmātās* and monks refused to recognize any Sri Lankan *bhikkhunī upasampadās*, because of such *upasampadās*' supposedly Mahāyāna antecedents. They argued that the (Mahāyāna) Sarnath ordination was a failure, as it appeared to have generated no lineage and that the Bodhgaya-Dambulla ordinations (also allegedly Mahāyāna) were led by a suspect and outcaste monk from the Asgiriya chapter, whom they accused of money laundering. As a monk I recently interviewed intimated, "Mahāyāna" in Sri Lanka had effectively become a label for any behavior that Buddhists there considered immoral or unacceptable.

Today, the notion of Theravāda as a marker that differentiates correct Sri Lankan Buddhist practice from the unacceptable Mahāyāna still carries weight among those refusing to acknowledge the (Theravāda) *bhikkhunī* ordinations of Sri Lankan nuns. Interestingly, sometime after their inaugural ordinations, the Bodhgaya-Dambulla monastics changed their tune; they began to collaborate with S-T-Neugala monastics. When we consider that *tradition* "is a name for an embodied debate in which opposing moral claims about what counts as religion, orthodoxy and truth are authoritatively … fought out" (Abeysekara 2002: 175), we begin to understand how claims about an authentic Theravāda lineage tradition, though made by monastics associated with the early Bodhgaya-Dambulla *bhikkhunī* ordinations, had lost currency by 2019.

Power

Opponents of the *bhikkhunī* ordinations have sought to assert their power by questioning the Theravāda "validity" of *bhikkhunī* ordinations. Questions of power, embedded as they are in relationships among Buddhist monastics, are intrinsic to the renunciant everyday of nuns as well as to a discursive tradition (Salgado 2013: 185–210; Salgado 2017, 2019). I now focus more closely on the Bodhgaya-Dambulla monastics who had initially planned to articulate an exclusive claim to a Theravāda *bhikkhunī* ordination lineage, contrasting their ordinations with those of the S-T-Neugala *bhikkhunīs*, and on how they reconstructed their initial views about "Theravāda" and "Mahāyāna" as they began to confront a more formidable opponent: the state. As is well known, no state with a Theravāda Buddhist majority has officially recognized Theravāda *bhikkhunīs*. In the late 1990s senior scholar-monks in Sri Lanka announced their nationwide opposition to the ordinations of Sri Lankan nuns, informing the country's president of their disapproval and arguing that, "in the absence of a Bhikkhunī Order in any Theravāda Buddhist country, ... no woman could be ordained as a Bhikkhunī nor a higher ordination ... given" ("Mahanayake Theras"). The Sri Lankan government has remained consistent in publicly rejecting the Sri Lankan (Theravāda) *bhikkhunīs*. Nevertheless, government officials have issued NICs and passports to some *bhikkhunīs*, effectively, if perhaps unwittingly, recognizing nuns as *bhikkhunīs*. Leading monks and *silmātās* who insist that a Theravāda *bhikkhunī* ordination is impossible have persistently questioned the practice of issuing NICs to *bhikkhunīs*. How and why the Bodhgaya-Dambulla monastics insisted on invoking a Theravāda mandate exclusively for their *bhikkhunī* ordinations soon after the inaugural ordinations—and later backed away from making such a claim—speaks to the place of "Theravāda" in a discursive tradition.

Monks are generally well positioned to confer the *upasampadā* on nuns in a single ordination ceremony and without the presence of *bhikkhunīs* (Bodhi 2010: 120; Anālayo 2017: 264–265). In Sri Lanka the consistent training of *sāmaṇerīs* and their dual ordination began at two centers: Dambulla (in 1998) and Neugala (in 2007). Some monks at other monastic centers sought the assistance of Bodhgaya-Dambulla *bhikkhunīs* and S-T-Neugala *bhikkhunīs* for the training and dual ordination of nuns at their home temples. Since the early 2000s, Sumangala had forbidden Bodhgaya-Dambulla *bhikkhunīs* from participating in specific rituals with *bhikkhunīs* from another lineage tradition. He hardly expected Bodhgaya-Dambulla *bhikkhunīs* to begin training *sāmaṇerīs* who had no plans to train and ordain in Dambulla. But a few such *bhikkhunīs*, either ignoring his misgivings or due to a miscommunication, proceeded to do so. In one instance, Bodhgaya-Dambulla *bhikkhunīs* who trained and ordained nuns (initially unbeknownst to Sumangala) were temporarily rejected from the Dambulla organization of *bhikkhunīs*. Sumangala, displeased that they had not consulted him in advance, was disturbed by what he perceived as their participation in an ordination that was supposedly held to accommodate the wish of a foreign donor.[8] Interestingly, those Dambulla *bhikkhunīs* were rebuked not for associating with a non-Theravāda or "Mahāyāna" ordination (even though the donor came from what might be considered a Mahāyāna country) but, rather, for neglecting to communicate with Sumangala and thus not acknowledging his authority and for engaging in what he viewed as a mercenary enterprise. Two later events attest to his downplaying of differences with the S-T-Neugala monastics—events that were to lead to a rapprochement between the Bodhgaya-Dambulla monastics and others that might have been inconceivable earlier.

Some years after the establishment of annual *bhikkhunī* ordinations in Dambulla, Bodhgaya-Dambulla teachers training *sāmaṇerīs* for the annual higher ordination were confronted with an unforeseen complication. Just weeks before the scheduled Dambulla *upasampadā*, they observed that some *sāmaṇerīs* had not fulfilled all the qualifications for the ordination.[9] Hence, those *sāmaṇerīs* were informed that they were ineligible for the *upasampadā*. But long-term householder-supporters of the *sāmaṇerīs* had already made elaborate arrangements to welcome the new *bhikkhunīs* back to their hometowns. Withholding the ordination from them would have resulted in disastrous consequences, compromising the authority of the venerable nuns in question as well as the good repute of the Dambulla *bhikkhunī* training program. As a last resort, monastics at Dambulla allowed the assistance of senior nuns from the S-T-Neugala lineage who had already trained and ordained their own *sāmaṇerīs* for the *upasampadā*. With the approval of senior Dambulla monastics, those nuns agreed to take the Dambulla *sāmaṇerīs* under their wing, and, after a brief training period, proceeded to ordain them. The Bodhgaya-Dambulla monastics were grateful to the S-T-Neugala *bhikkhunīs* for their assistance. Thus, the "Theravāda-Mahāyāna" opposition that the Bodhgaya-Dambulla monastics had initially demarcated to maintain the purity of their lineage vis-à-vis that of the S-T-Neugala nuns was conveniently sidestepped to accommodate more immediate concerns and practical needs.

Another important event testifying to a rapprochement between the Bodhgaya-Dambulla and S-T-Neugala monastics was an ordination ceremony that took place some years after Bodhgaya-Dambulla monastics had initiated legal proceedings against the state for its refusal to issue NICs to *bhikkhunīs*. As a young woman, the ordinand had had close connections with Tooth Temple *mahānāyakas*. Kusuma served as a preceptor for the ordination, which included *bhikkhunīs* from the S-T-Neugala and Bodhgaya-Dambulla lineages as well as monks from Asgiriya and Malwatta. Though the ordination was not conducted at Dambulla, it was graced by the presence of Sumangala—in itself a statement of incipient reconciliation between Bodhgaya and S-T-Neugala monastics. Consequently, it made waves among *bhikkhunīs* from both lineages who reported this to me. The new *bhikkhunī*, well positioned to question the senior Tooth Temple monks about their opposition to the ordination of Sri Lankan nuns, proceeded to do so. It is likely that Sumangala, in attending the ordination of this *bhikkhunī*, sought not just her support but also that of the S-T-Neugala nuns in contesting the state's position on the NIC.

Sri Lankan *bhikkhunīs* who were ordained in Sarnath, Bodhgaya, and Taiwan were initially issued NICs stating their names and *bhikkhunī* titles. When opponents of the *bhikkhunī* ordinations objected, pointing out the discrepancy in issuing government identity cards to *bhikkhunīs* who were not recognized by the state, DBA officials, under pressure from powerful *mahānāyakas*, stopped including the title of *bhikkhunī* on NICs. Between about 2000 and 2002, *bhikkhunīs* and their *sāmaṇerīs* in training were generally issued *silmātā* titles in lieu of *bhikkhunī* ones. Additionally, the procedure for obtaining an NIC was made more difficult for *bhikkhunīs*: as part of the application process, they now had to submit a written request for approval of their NIC to their local *silmātā* organization. In some cases, that meant *bhikkhunīs* had to obtain the approval of an unknown, if not hostile, community of *silmātās* in order to be legitimized by the state. At the time of writing this chapter, a *bhikkhunī* or her *sāmaṇerī* pupil may receive an NIC (bearing a *silmātā* title) only if she has first obtained a letter of approval from the head *silmātā* of her district, although some *bhikkhunīs* have informed me that the NIC was denied to them regardless. The state, together with monks who have opposed the *bhikkhunī* ordination and, with the assistance of *silmātās*, has effectively excluded Sri Lankan *bhikkhunīs* from receiving NICs on the grounds that their *upasampadā* is not Theravāda. That the question of the NIC impacts all *bhikkhunīs* in the country and has not been resolved satisfactorily is likely one reason that Sumangala began working with the S-T-Neugala *bhikkhunī* lineage. He has also begun to collaborate with the monk Kirama Wimalajoti, whose *bhikkhunī* training center is led by a *bhikkhunī* who trained under Kusuma and received ordination in Taiwan. For Sumangala, the question ofTheravāda authenticity has begun to focus less on denouncing competing *bhikkhunī* lineages and more on what the state will (not) allow. Perreira notes that, at the conference of the World Federation of Buddhists in 1950, "the unanimous decision to abandon the use of Hīnayāna in favor of Theravāda ... proved to be most far-reaching both as a conceptual tool in organizing, unifying, and simplifying the Buddhist world and for its rhetorical power in re-centering the very foundations of that world by effectively shifting them from India to [Sri] Laṅkā" (2012: 451). The *upasampadā*s of Sri Lankan *bhikkhunī*s attest to how the notion of Theravāda has become incorporated into the very panoply of the state.

By December 2018, *bhikkhunī*s from the Dambulla and S-T-Neugala lineages had begun collaborating to make an appeal for the NIC. At a national meeting in March 2019, a new National Organization of *Bhikkhunī*s was established. Unlike the previous, Dambulla-based national organization of *bhikkhunī*s, which had included only Bodhgaya-Dambulla monastics, the new organization includes *bhikkhunī*s who can trace their lineages to founding nuns ordained at Sarnath or Taiwan as well as at Bodhgaya or Dambulla. Though they still conduct their higher ordinations separately, the *bhikkhunī*s of different lineages are slated to meet about every three months to discuss common concerns, including the question of the NIC. The idea of a pure Theravāda lineage, once a bone of contention in the lineage dispute among *bhikkhunī*s, has become less relevant to that dispute as monastics have united to confront a state that refuses to legally accept their *upasampadā*.

Concluding remarks

The *upasampadā*s of the late 1990s focused on ordaining Sri Lankan nuns as Theravāda *bhikkhunī*s. One reason that Sri Lankan monastics initiated procedures for those *upasampadā*s was their concern that Sri Lankan women who wished to lead the lives of nuns could not do so as *bhikkhunī*s unless they were initiated into a Mahāyāna order and its practice. (Some Sri Lankan nuns were known to have already taken that route.) That the absence of a Sri Lankan *bhikkhunī* order would encourage women to "seek refuge in other faiths" was a concern the Cultural Affairs Minister shared publicly in 1999 ("State Will Recognize"). That may explain why, as one interviewee informed me, the state had issued NICs bearing the title *bhikkhunī* (until the early 2000s). The idea of what Mahāyāna is—apart from its difference from Theravāda and its association with East Asian Buddhism—is not self-evident. Although there have been misunderstandings among Sri Lankan monastics about so-called Mahāyāna beliefs and practices (Cheng 2007: 176–181; Salgado 2013: 267, n. 42), that has not been my concern here. Rather, my focus has been to underscore that the very idea of "Theravāda" and its "Mahāyāna" foil relates to assertions of power—and to who may authorize what can or cannot count within a tradition in particular contingencies. Over a century ago, without quibbling about the question of Theravāda or lineage continuity, the monks of the Tooth Temple authorized the inception of a new mode of life for nuns. Today the monks of that same temple affirm their power via the state by refusing to recognize *bhikkhunī*s for their apparent lack of Theravāda lineage continuity.

Questions about the Theravāda authenticity of the *upasampadā*s of *bhikkhunī*s from Sri Lanka and other countries, such as Thailand and Myanmar, are inevitably imbricated in the authoritative power of monastics and the state. Such questions about power, intrinsic to religion in general, test the very limits of tradition while engendering new possibilities in the practice of Buddhist nuns. A Sri Lankan monk recently shared with me his thoughts about the use of "tradition" in reference to the *bhikkhunī upasampadā*. He explained that, while one could raise questions about Theravāda purity in contesting ordination procedures, and lineage continuities, the evocation of tradition (*sampradāya*) in debates about *bhikkhunī upasampadā*s, was but a pretext. He saw no point in the scattershot arguments for and against the *upasampadā* that appeal to (Theravāda) tradition. He referred to the *Kālāma Sutta* stating: "The Buddha said that one should not chase after tradition. What has happened is that we are stuck in 'tradition.' ... There would be no problem [Sinh: *gäṭaluwak*] if people were to think about what they really want, without spinning the tale of tradition. One has to eradicate that [tradition] from one's thinking." Tradition, as he suggests, is hardly traditional.

Notes

1 I am grateful to Paul Westman, Indira Salgado, Carol Anderson, Joseph Walser, Robert Launay, Martie Reineke, Stephen Berkwitz, Ashley Thompson, Daya Wickramasinghe, and Robert Green for their assistance. A 2014 Robert H. N. Ho Collaborative Research Grant, a 2017 Augustana College Faculty Research Grant, and a 2017 David E. Nudd Fund Grant contributed toward funding my research.

2 By "monastics" I mean Buddhist monks and nuns with or without the higher ordination. I have not used honorifics and titles (e.g., Thera, *bhikkhu, bhikkhunī* etc.) for monastic names. I have also not used diacritics for names of individuals. No disrespect is intended.

3 When I speak of "Theravāda countries" in general terms, I do so in the conventional sense accepted by scholars and practitioners today, even though such nomenclature is imperfect. By "nuns" I refer to *bhikkhunīs* as well as female renunciants who do not have the *upasampadā*.

4 *Silmātās* are celibate Buddhist nuns and usually live together in community; however, they differ from *bhikkhunīs* as they are not fully ordained. Although many *bhikkhunīs* today were once *silmātās*, there are significant numbers of *silmātās* who do not wish to become *bhikkhunīs*. For more on why this may be the case, see Salgado (2013: 180).

5 In such contexts, "Buddhism" may be understood as being opposed to other religions, such as "Christianity," whereas the more recent nomenclature of "Theravāda" is defined by its "Mahāyāna" other.

6 Bartholomeusz observes that Sudharmachari was not the first Sri Lankan Buddhist nun. However, the initiation and religious practice of Sudharmachari were notably different from those of the earlier nuns.

7 The year 2002 saw the completion of nine *pōyagēs* built throughout the country exclusively for the use of Bodhgaya-Dambulla *bhikkhunīs*. By 2017, a total of sixteen *pōyagēs* had been constructed for them, thus putting into practice Sumangala's plans for establishing the ordination "on Sri Lankan soil" within a very short time after the initial Bodhgaya ordinations. By 2019 there were eighteen *pōyagēs* for Bodhgaya-Dambulla *bhikkhunīs*.

8 In this instance, the foreign donor had requested an opportunity to observe a *bhikkhunī* ordination while visiting Sri Lanka.

9 Interviewees informed me that these were minor requirements that may not have been adequately communicated to the *sāmaṇerīs*.

References

Abeysekara, A. 2002. *Colors of the Robe: Religion, Identity, and Difference*. Columbia: University of South Carolina Press.

Abeysekara, A. 2018. "Review of Schober, J. and Collins, S. (eds), *Theravāda Buddhist Encounters with Modernity*." *Journal of Buddhist Ethics* 25: 333–370.

Abeysekara, A. 2019. "Protestant Buddhism and 'Influence': The Temporality of a Concept." *Qui Parle* 28 (1): 1–75.

Adikaram, E.W. 1953. *Early History of Buddhism in Ceylon; or, "State" of Buddhism in Ceylon as Revealed by the Pāli Commentaries of the 5th Century A.D.* Colombo, Sri Lanka: M.D. Gunasena.

Anālayo. 2017. "Bhikkhunī Ordination." In *Vinaya Studies*, 221–307. Taipei: Dharma Drum.

Asad, T. 1993. *Genealogies of Religion: Discipline and Reasons of Power in Christianity and Islam*. Baltimore: Johns Hopkins University Press.

Asad, T. 2015. "Thinking about Tradition, Religion, and Politics in Egypt Today." *Critical Inquiry* 42 (1): 166–214.

'Bak Pasalosvaka Poya: Buddha Gaya Upasampada Ceremony.' *Daily News* (Colombo), April 11, 1998, p. 19.

Bartholomeusz, T.J. 1994. *Women under the Bō Tree: Buddhist Nuns in Sri Lanka*. New York: Cambridge University Press.

Bhadra. 2001. *Higher Ordination and Bhikkhuni Order in Sri Lanka*. Dehiwala, Sri Lanka: Sridevi.

Bloss, L.W. 1987. "The Female Renunciants of Sri Lanka: The *Dasasilmattawa*." *Journal of the International Association of Buddhist Studies* 10 (1): 7–31.

Bodhi, B. 2010. "The Revival of Bhikkhunī Ordination in the Theravāda Tradition." In *Dignity and Discipline: Reviving Full Ordination for Buddhist Nuns*, eds. T. Mohr, J. Tsedroen, 99–142. Boston, Wisdom.

Carrithers, M. 1983. *The Forest Monks of Sri Lanka*. Delhi: Oxford University Press.

Cheng, Wei-Yi. 2007. *Buddhist Nuns in Taiwan and Sri Lanka: A Critique of the Feminist Perspective*. London: Routledge.

Chuehmen. 2007. "The Right to Be Ordained as Bhikṣuṇs." Unpublished Manuscript.

Gombrich, R.F. 1988. *Theravāda Buddhism: A Social History from Ancient Benares to Modern Colombo*. London: Routledge & Kegan Paul.

Holt, J.C., 2017. *Theravada Traditions: Buddhist Ritual Cultures in Contemporary Southeast Asia and Sri Lanka*, Honolulu: University of Hawaii Press.

Ito, Tomomi 2012. "Questions of Ordination Legitimacy for Newly Ordained Theravāda Bhikkhunī in Thailand." *Journal of Southeast Asian Studies* 43 (1): 55–76.

Kawanami, H. 2007. "The Bhikkhunī Ordination Debate: Global Aspirations, Local Concerns, with Special Emphasis on the Views of the Monastic Community in Burma." *Buddhist Studies Review* 24 (2): 226–244.

Kusuma. 2008. "How I Became a Bhikkhunī." *Sakyadhita International Association of Buddhist Women* 16 (2): 16–18.

Kusuma. 2012. *Braving the Unknown Summit: The Autobiography of Ven. Bhikkhuni Dr. Kolonnawe Kusuma*. Colombo, Sri Lanka: Akna.

'Mahanayake Theras Disapprove Bhikkhuni Order.' *Sunday Observer* (Colombo), April 12, 1998, p. 12.

'Meheṇi sasna yaḷi sirilak pihiṭa vū vagayi!' (The Dispensation of Ordained Women Is Established again in Sri Lanka!). *Dinamiṇa* (Colombo), March 12, 1998, p. 15.

Mrozik, S. 2014. ""We Love Our Nuns": Affective Dimensions of the Sri Lankan Bhikkhunī Revival." *Journal of Buddhist Ethics* 21: 57–95.

'The Ordination of Dasa Sil Matas.' *Daily News* (Colombo), Jan. 23, 1997, pp. 16–18.

Perreira, T.L. 2012. "Whence Theravāda? The Modern Genealogy of an Ancient Term." In *How Theravāda Is Theravāda? Exploring Buddhist Identities*, eds. P. Skilling, J.A. Carbine, C. Cicuzza, S. Pakdeekham, 443–571. Chiang Mai, Thailand: Silkworm.

Salgado, N.S. 2013. *Buddhist Nuns and Gendered Practice: In Search of the Female Renunciant*. Oxford: Oxford University Press.

Salgado, N.S. 2017. "Tradition, Power, and Community among Buddhist Nuns in Sri Lanka." *Journal of Buddhist Ethics* 24: 369–399.

Salgado, N.S. 2019. "On the Question of "Discipline" (*Vinaya*) and Nuns in Theravāda Buddhism." *Religions* 10 (98): 1–23.

'Sasana History Made at Sravasti.' *Daily News* (Colombo), Dec. 21, 1996, p. 20.

Scott, D. 1994. *Formations of Ritual: Colonial and Anthropological Discourses on the Sinhala Yaktovil*. Minneapolis: University of Minnesota Press.

Seeger, M. 2008. "The Bhikkhunī-Ordination Controversy in Thailand." *Journal of the International Association of Buddhist Studies* 29 (1): 155–183.

'State Will Recognize Bhikkhuni Order Only If Mahanayakas Approve.' *The Island* (Colombo), July 1, 1999., p. 2.

PART II

Practices/Persons

7

MERIT

Ritual giving and its cultural mediations

Juliane Schober

Among Burmese Buddhists, and indeed throughout the Theravāda world, an invitation to participate in rituals is often followed by a common intention, "let's make merit" (B.: *kutho ya-aun*). Making merit is a central feature in the repertoire of Theravāda Buddhist practices that gives expression to the religious agency of laypeople seeking ethical rewards for virtuous deeds in order to ensure prosperity in this and future lives. Especially merit-making that accrues from the performance of generosity, a virtue that according to the Vessantara Jataka, the future Buddha perfected in his penultimate life, is a constitutive element in the social reality of Theravāda Buddhist communities.

This chapter explores the work of merit and the practices of generosity (*dāna*) in cultural contexts of Theravāda civilizations. I argue that merit-making is not merely about good or bad ethics. Rather, it is best understood as a social practice, discourse, and cultural mediation about ethical conduct and giving. In the Theravāda-dominated countries of Myanmar, Thailand, Laos, Cambodia, and Sri Lanka, where Theravadins constitute a majority of the population, merit-making and the ethics of giving are integral to the production of social capital, authority, and hegemony. In historical and traditional contexts, merit-making practices often involve giving and produce social hierarchies. Merit-making communities sharing in such ritual performances therefore live within a field of merit or social power. As promising career paths beyond the *saṅgha* become increasingly attainable for young people in contemporary Myanmar, merit-making practices are also changing. Monks (*saṅgha*) are no longer the sole sources of merit for laypeople, as new forms of giving are becoming popular among socially engaged Buddhists and others whose religious practice emphasizes the welfare of others (P.: *parahita*). While the emphasis on *parahita* practices is still quite recent in Myanmar, making merit by serving others is a more established practice elsewhere in the Theravāda world where modernity has already fundamentally restructured social relationships and mobility.

Yet defining just what merit is has been challenging. In conversations, the Pāli scholar Steven Collins declared provocatively that merit (P.: *kusala*, B.: *kutho*), despite its frequent mention in Pāli and vernacular Buddhist literature, could not be seen, had no material reality, and therefore did not exist. My essay concludes with a discussion of previous explanations of merit-making to foreground merit's socially mediated qualities over its material forms. In contrast to earlier research on Buddhist altruism and on the material value of the gift and its circulation, this

DOI: 10.4324/9781351026666-10

chapter looks at merit-making as the performance of ethical discourse practices. Following Talal Asad (1993, 35), I argue that merit-making is central to Theravāda societies because its performance creates the very conditions for experiencing Buddhist truths. Indeed, merit-making as ethical discourse creates social capital and institutions that facilitate the mediation of cultural flows through social networks that embody authority and define authenticity.

The perfection of giving in the Vessantara Jātaka

The most prevalent form of merit-making is the performance of generosity through acts of giving. Making merit through acts of generosity is a prominent motif in narratives that extol the virtue of giving. Perhaps most popular among them is the Vessantara Jātaka in which the future Buddha perfects the virtue of generosity (*dāna*). This story, which is the last of the Ten Great Jātakas, tells the penultimate life of the future Buddha as the Prince Vessantara. Well known in many versions throughout the Theravāda world, the story is a significant part of Theravāda moral knowledge and offers a paradigm for lay Buddhist practice as countless versions of the story share important descriptions of the performance of giving. Heir to a prosperous kingdom, Vessantara excels in giving away the sources of his power and the people most dear to him: the white elephant that ensures the rain and the prosperity of the kingdom, his horses, and kingdom and, living as an ascetic in the forest, his wife and his children. The performance of extreme generosity caused the hero to lose his royal power, his kingdom, and even his wife and children. And yet, all these are restored to him when the villains in the story reveal themselves to be not incarnations of evil and avarice they appear to be but, in fact, divine beings whose interventions merely enable Vessantara to perfect his quest for generosity. In the end, the hero returns from his exile in the forest to regain his family and kingdom.

The Vessantara Jātaka as Buddhist literature offers at once an invitation to contemplate generosity as moral virtue and as epic, tragedy, comedy, melodrama, and even utopia, all as commentaries on the hero's quest for ethical perfection. For Steven Collins (2016), the Vessantara Jātaka has immense literary value as it offers many ways of reading and recounting the perfection of generosity and illustrates the interpretive range narrative harbors for storytellers and audiences alike. Episodes of this *jātaka* story are performed in public recitations, in entertaining and even buffonic theater routines (Bowie 2017), depicted in temple paintings and in manuscripts (Handlin 2016), and enacted in rituals and processions (Lefferts and Cate 2016). These examples show that cultural understandings of ethical values like merit-making, giving, and generosity not only inhabit the religious imaginations of Theravāda Buddhists in significant ways but that they also are subject to unending iterations and interpretations in a variety of social contexts. The practice of giving is mediated and refracted in all kinds of social, ritual, and narrative contexts.

Making merit

Living an ethical life is the foundation for acquiring merit. While monks should not be attached to the rewards merit will bring in the future, for laypeople, the accumulation of merit over time ensures one's rebirth in an abode free of suffering and misfortune; empowers one to obtain a prosperous, peaceful life; and ultimately leads to insight into enlightenment. In ethnographic terms, individual merit-making is based on the performance of Theravāda ethical values, such as observing the Eightfold Noble Path that leads to the cessation of suffering and requires practicing right view, right thought, right speech, right action, right livelihood, right effort, right mindfulness, and right concentration. Merit can also be gained by venerating icons like images, relics, *stūpas*, and other material forms that embody the Buddha's teachings

(Dhamma). In fact, a donor of a Buddha image, *stūpa* or other object that is a perpetual source of merit for others is recognized in Burmese as Owner of Merit (*kutho shin*), the highest title a layperson may achieve.

Merit further accrues from venerating sources of merit like one's teachers, parents, and accomplished, disciplined monks whose virtuous practice has led them to become a source of merit for others. In other words, being mindful of one's social position and acting respectfully towards others, in short, being a good person, is in and of itself a meritorious life. Inasmuch as Buddhists are encouraged to create sources of merit that reflect their own good deeds and offer to others the opportunities for merit-making, people are discouraged from being "greedy" about merit-making by resisting to share such deeds with others. Refusing help when cooking meals for monks is one example that illustrates such greed. Similarly, making merit for purely social or political reasons without some degree of personal sacrifice is also frowned on. Yet, no one would deny that true generosity simply engenders and accrues merit for the donor, regardless of whether they intended the outcome.

All Buddhist rituals involve acts of communal giving by donors and their communities. Ritual giving is a uniquely structured mode of interaction in Theravāda cultures and, in Marcel Mauss's terms (2002), a "social fact" shaped by the flow of donations and their distribution to rightful recipients. The forms of merit-making that are socially most prominent center on the performance of giving as a demonstration of one's generosity. Laypeople who provide for the needs of a monk, such as the items required for his ordination or for his daily livelihood earn the title of "*taga*" (donor). Frequently, this term designates an ongoing relationship with a particular monk whom the donor regularly supports. Such relationships are significant since Theravāda monks, unlike monks in other Buddhist traditions, may not provide for their own livelihood and thus depend on donations from their lay supporters. In contrast to other Buddhist traditions, donations to maintain monastic livelihoods are a central requirement in Theravāda practice where monks depend on *dāna* for their subsistence.

All forms of merit-making rituals, regardless of the scale of performance, involving regular donations of food to monks or be they major ritual events, include an official act of giving by a donor or group of donors and an acknowledgment of accepting donations by members of the *saṅgha*. The ritual structure of giving underscores the ethical value attached to lay generosity and its significance in perpetuating the Buddhist dispensation (*sāsana*). Monks who practice with discipline and in accordance with the Vinaya are a source of merit to lay donors seeking to make merit. Donations to monks are given in a proscribed manner and donations are publicly validated by those present. For the ritual exchange to be valid, Burmese lay donors and monks must formally acknowledge both the gift and its acceptance. Public validation of the gift has important legal ramifications for Theravādin monks who depend, at least in principle, entirely on lay support for their livelihoods. Failure to witness the public acts of giving and accepting can imply an improper donation that can compromise the status of the donor and of the recipient monk who can be accused of having committed theft, a grave infraction (*pārājika*) against Vinaya rules that can lead to expulsion from the *saṅgha*.

Burmese Buddhists often say that the material value of the gift is less important than the future rewards merit-making generates. They mostly focus on indications that the intentions of the donor's generosity are genuine. A gift given with pure intentions will bring the most merit to the donor, regardless of its material value. Many considerations shape how much merit donors may gain on account of their generosity. For instance, a modest gift by someone with little means but pure intentions given to a highly deserving recipient may bring much greater rewards in the future than gifts donated by a wealthy person who lacks pure intentions. Alternatively, donations given to unworthy monks who do not practice monastic discipline (*vinaya*) do not generate merit for the donor. A wealthy person is expected to give more than a poor person. The performance of religious, ethical, and cultural values, rather than the material value of the gift, determines the success and social benefit of merit-making.

Sharing one's merit with others at the conclusion of rituals multiplies its benefits for the donor and for those who share in his or her meritorious deed (Schober 1996). Sharing of merit ensures a prosperous society in the future and ideally moves donors and their dependents toward an eventual transcendence of this world through enlightenment. At the end of such rituals, all good deeds are enumerated, along with the lay donors who contributed them. Affirmations are recited for all people who have contributed to this deed, all who are present and rejoice in this generosity, and finally all sentient beings at all levels of existence, while bells and gongs are rung and chants of "*thadu, thadu, thadu*" (well done) carry the news of good deeds even to those who are not present at the places where merit was made. Those faraway sentient beings and, ultimately, all beings at every level of existence will be able to rejoice in the merit made, because all rituals end with sharing merit throughout the Buddhist universe so that "all beings may attain enlightenment eventually."

Merit is conceptualized as an immaterial return for performing good deeds that translate into blessings and social capital for those who give freely and generously. Selflessness in the performance of generosity is important to the recognition of the social capital merit brings to donors. Those who are seen to be giving merely because they seek religious and social benefits are rumored to be actually selfish and greedy. For that reason, giving freely without attachment and sharing with others the labor and benefits of performing meritorious rituals are important elements in merit-making rituals. Although giving an anonymous gift is not a common practice, "robes falling from the sky" (*mo-bo-cha kahtein*) is one way of donating robes to a monk at the end of the Buddhist lent that exemplifies giving without attachment to the rewards of making merit. A donor will seek out a monk—any monk—to present robes to him to demonstrate having no attachment to one's merit.

Merit derived from the practice of generosity will ensure prosperity and well-being in the future. Wealth and status are understood as the fruition of meritorious deeds in the past and therefore are seen as manifesting status, prestige, and power in the present. Who can engage in merit-making is determined by one's status and power in the present, of past moral action and future prosperity. In his essay on freedom and bondage during the Konbaung dynasty in seventeenth-century Burma, F. K. Lehman (1984) shows that only "free men" (B.: *kun-daw*) who are taxpaying royal subjects have the agency to make merit, a legal attribute of their status as subjects of the king. Indentured people, pagoda slaves, and members of a household cannot make merit on their own accord. They cannot sponsor donations to monks, monastic buildings, or Buddhist images. They depend on their patrons, heads of households, and "owners of the merit" (B.: *kutho shin*) for opportunities to contribute to merit-making rituals. Because royal subjects provide members of their households with opportunities to make merit, household members, reminiscent of citizens of the state under the military junta during the 1990s, are perpetually indebted and obligated to their "owners of merit" (*kutho shin*), to whom they owe gratitude and allegiance for providing opportunities for merit-making and, with that, opportunities for a prosperous future. Hence, participating in another household's merit-making activities creates indebtedness to the owner of that merit, illustrating the hegemonic expressions of merit-making rituals and the social hierarchies that inevitably emerge.

Theravādins will perform merit-making rituals on behalf of their departed relatives. Burmese laypeople will commemorate anniversaries of departed parents and relatives by making donations to monks in order to make merit for them now that the departed reside in another realm where they may be unable to make merit. Not knowing whether their rebirth led to realms of suffering, perhaps in the form of hungry ghosts who inhabit liminal spaces, provides an added incentive for the surviving family members to make merit in ritual settings. During the dedication of merit at the conclusion of the ritual, the donor will state their wish that the merit from this ritual will accrue to their departed relatives.

In Laos, such ritual occasions are marked by feeding the dead, especially ghosts who may suffer from hunger because they are unable to feed themselves in their new form of rebirth. Patrice Ladwig (2012: 119) writes that "Buddhism plays a major role in the upkeep of these relationships through ritual exchanges with the dead," who remain intrinsic to the working of society. For many Buddhists, the act of giving to monks is a way to feed the dead for whom members of the *saṅgha* act to transmit and transfer the merit made on their behalf (Keyes 1983; Ladwig 2012: 120). "The deceased are a focus of ritual attention ranging from everyday acts of food donations to monks to larger festivals," Ladwig notes (2012: 120) and concludes that social relationships permeate the boundary between the living and the dead and that interactions between the living and the deceased are embedded in "a larger ritual economy" (Ladwig 2012: 137).

Not much can be said about Theravāda Buddhist civilizations without touching on the practice of generosity (*dāna*) as a constitutive element in a ritual economy of merit and the cultural hegemonies it creates within and among communities. Making merit is not only an ethical practice of individuals or households but figures prominently in the social life of communities. An ideal Theravādin society (*pativēda sāsana*) envisions social life to be replete with countless sources of merit like monks who ideally embody enlightenment, kings who rule justly in accordance with the Buddha's teachings, and ordinary people who live prosperous lives free from danger, calamity, war, and misfortune. Such acts of sharing the benefits of ethical performance with others create a field of merit where multiple sources of merit are present. Such conceptions account for a conceptual hierarchy of place where some locations are deemed more auspicious and powerful than others. These sensibilities about the presence of sources of merit explain why one finds small pagodas erected in seemingly out-of-the-way places, such as the edge of a rice field or along a forest path where people find refuge and seek to make merit by reciting incantations or practice meditation. Likely the most culturally persuasive form of merit-making is through the performance of rituals that establish communities that share in making and benefiting from merit and thus enact visions of an ideal society. Unlike other abodes of rebirth where making merit is rare, the dispensation of the Buddha (*sāsana*) affords humans many opportunities for making merit. Fields of merit can also dispel danger. For instance, during the Japanese occupation of Burma, residents of Mandalay sought refuge at Yanhkin Hill, a range of hills outside the city that is home to forest monks and Buddhist wizards. Its name denoted a hill free from danger.

In 1994 and again in 1996, the military junta in Myanmar enjoined the Ministry of Religious Affairs to orchestrate nationwide donation drives in support of the journey of the Buddha's Tooth Relic from China to Burma (Schober 1997). This continuous state-sponsored merit-making ritual was reminiscent of earlier ones performed during U Nu's celebration of the 2,5000th-anniversary celebration of the Buddhist dispensation. The extended journey of the Tooth Relic through Myanmar created multiple, overlapping, and ultimately coercive communities of merit who were ritually indebted to the military regime for providing access for the nation to be in the presence of the Buddha's physical remains. Crowds of Burmese Buddhists sought to make merit by venerating the relic and making donations to support its journey throughout the country. After extensive planning and orchestration by the Ministry of Religious Affairs and orchestrated implementation of a six-week-long procession of the relic and its entourage through the Burmese heartland, *dāna* flowed in from all sorts of social groups, including wealthy individuals and collectives of civil servants and ordinary citizens. It financed the perpetuation of the *sāsana* as a national project, underscoring the religious power and authority of a military regime that afforded its citizen subjects the opportunity to make unparalleled merit by donating to the Buddha's Tooth Relic. Even though perhaps somewhat hesitant to participate, most Burmese donors had little choice in evading the social pressures to contribute as the state newspaper listed daily the amounts and items donated and the names or donors. While all meritorious donations are generally publicly recorded, the daily tally published in the state-run newspaper revealed the political pressures particularly on people of social prominence to contribute to this state ritual. These included not only Burmese citizens, but also foreign dignitaries, embassy staff, and international organizations, along with non-Buddhist ethnic groups. While this national ritual accomplished several objectives for the military regime, it turned the nation and its territory into a field of merit for the benefit of its citizens, legitimated its political authority as a protector of the Buddhist religion, and demonstrated the junta's righteous Buddhist rule. The staging of this series of rituals venerating the presence of the Tooth Relic in Myanmar took place during a decade, the 1990s, when the military junta in power sought to consolidate and legitimate its power by acting as the patron of important Buddhist rituals. Against this coercive background, few dared to voice resistance and rare expressions of doubts about the authenticity of the relics were merely whispered.

Merit-making and institution building

The ethical practice of giving is at the core of Theravāda social fabric because making merit through ritual giving (*dāna*) shapes social relations. Ritual donations made to monks, ascetics, and other sources of merit can range in scale from local and communal levels to national ones. The discursive practices mediated by the performance of ethical virtue and acts of giving create cultural flows that lead to the establishment of merit-making communities, produce systems of allegiance, and form hegemonies. These flows also lead to building Buddhist institutions like monasteries and their networks, amplify the charismatic appeal of monks who are able to raise large amounts of money, and even contribute to the construction of pilgrimage sites which at times embody power and merit only to be abandoned as donations flow to new sources of merit (Schober 2001).

It is common for donations to monks, especially famous ones, to generate a secondary exchange in which the flow of donations (*dāna*) is redistributed within monastic networks. For instance, a *kaṭhina* ceremony, the giving of robes at the end of the Buddhist Lent, might generate many more robes than a famous monk, and even the monks in his monastery, will be able to use. In such cases, the surplus of donations received are then distributed to less wealthy monasteries affiliated with this monk. The sharing of material gifts received by monks and their redistribution through monastic networks can form the basis for building monastic institutions, for promoting the Dhamma, or for implementing a socially engaged agenda by supporting schools, hospitals, civil projects, relief efforts, development initiatives, and educational campaigns. This abundant flow of donations, in turn, mediates the charisma of monks who use their wealth, influence and power to build monastic institutions, branch monasteries, and regional, national, and even global networks of institutions and donors. Charismatic, powerful monks thus are significant nodes in the social flows of merit and donations. Redistribution of surplus donations can have a profound economic impact not just on local patterns of consumption, assistance for the needy, and strengthening institutions but also on regional and even global networks of giving.

Two examples demonstrate how the mediation of merit and its circulation in networks of Theravāda communities produce an ethical discourse, institutions, social networks, and communities through which authority structures and the political aspirations of donors are advanced. Ritual donations made to monks, ascetics, and other sources of merit can range in scale from local and communal levels to national ones. The Mahasi Meditation Center, a transnational institution centered in Yangon, with branches throughout the country and even abroad, was established through cultural and material flows of generosity during the second half of the twentieth century. Its founding abbot, Bhadanta Sobhana Mahathera (1904–1982), rose to prominence during the 1950s with the support of Prime Minister U Nu. Eventually, his monastic network grew to encompass more than three hundred meditation centers that followed his meditation method. A national institution, the Mahasi meditation centers came to train mostly urban laypeople in insight meditation techniques that certified specific levels of attainment for its practitioners in their quest for enlightenment. During its apex in the 1980s, the Mahasi meditation center network attracted middle-class meditators, many of whom were civil servants. After the passing of its founding abbot, disputes among his successors and rumored financial scandals began to undermine the reputation of the Mahasi meditation centers.

The rise to fame and influence of U Nyanissara (b. 1937), abbot of Sitagu Monastery, began in the early 1980s when he accepted donations to build a hospital for members of the *saṅgha* and an infrastructural project to supply clean water to hundreds of monasteries and nunneries on Sagaing Hill. His charisma was enhanced by his reputation as a venerated preacher who was then an outspoken critic of the military regime. The Sitagu Sayadaw went on to build a monastic university at his home monastery in Sagaing and eventually agreed to direct the International Theravāda Buddhist University in Yangon that previously had been under the Ministry of Religious Affairs. In defiance of the military dictatorship, he organized massive relief efforts after the Nargis cyclone in 2006 that killed and displaced more than one hundred thousand people in the lower delta region. His many missionizing travels abroad included Austin, Texas where he built another monastic complex. More recently, he has been a supporter of anti-Muslim sentiments in Myanmar. In 2019, he bemoaned that the UNESCO designation of Bagan as a World Heritage Site placed its ancient pagodas under the influence of Muslims who, in his mind, had been placed in charge of these UN activities. These stories show that the cultural flows mediated by merit and *dāna* forge close and complex connections among Buddhist monks, politics, and politicians, including conservative hardliners in the Union, Solidarity, and Development Party who support policies hostile to Muslims in Myanmar.

The reversal of the flow of donations by refusing to accept donations invokes the implosion of Theravāda social orders. Strikes as the refusal of gifts comprise transgressions of the structures of exchange that invalidate the roles of actors within the system. The events of September 2007 that led to the protest movement called the "Saffron Revolution" followed an abrupt government decision to stop subsidies for natural gas in order to mitigate an impending economic crisis. This precipitated a sharp increase in fuel costs and the overall cost of living for most Burmese. A major uprising against military rule and these unfair economic policies precipitated a reversal of traditional ritual practices between the *saṅgha* and its lay supporters through which Theravāda hegemony is constituted. The effects of the state's economic policies were seen as the failure of the military regime to live up to traditional Buddhist expectations of good governance, empowering the monks' moral position against the government. Sporadic confrontations, including labor and civil rights unrests and monks clashing with local police escalated into a nationwide ban by monks to accept donations from members of the military regime or any of their family members.

"Turning over one's alms bowl" (*thabei' mauk*) is the Burmese idiom designating the *saṅgha*'s refusal to confer religious, social, and political legitimacy on certain lay supporters. This boycott is tantamount to banning from the Buddhist field of merit any lay supporter who acted to the detriment of the *sāsana*. The traditional pattern of giving to monks is disrupted and the flow of *dāna* and merit-making is stopped by a formal act of the *saṅgha* that is legally binding under monastic law (*pattam nikkujjana kamma*) that mandates the entire *saṅgha* to refuse donations from unworthy donors until they show remorse and apologize to the monks. Some monks stated that their protest marches were motivated by their desire to give voice to the economic hardship their lay supporters endured. Skyrocketing costs of living jeopardized the welfare of lay supporters and placed financial strain on some monasteries by increasing the number of poor already living in monastic compounds. The plight of the poor not only limited donations to monasteries but also became a growing economic liability for the *saṅgha* as an institution. Monasteries became a refuge for the sick, indigent, and homeless and, by default, functioned as a social safety net in many local communities. This traditional function of monasteries has taken on new significance in the context of modern, socially engaged Buddhist practices (Schober 2011).

Monks began to organize protest marches in major cities like Yangon and Mandalay and in provincial towns like Sittwe and Pakhokku, where influential monasteries are located. Initially, the columns of marching monks in Yangon were flanked by laypeople who formed a human chain on either side to protect them as they made their way through crowded areas, signaling popular support for the courageous demonstrations of these monks. The largest protests occurred in Yangon in the days leading up to September 26, 2007, when close to one hundred thousand people, mostly monks and nuns, marched to protest of the military junta and its economic policies. Across the nation, close to three hundred thousand Buddhist monks joined their protests and openly contested the secular power of the state over issues of social injustice. During the following night, the state asserted its military coercion over the moral claims of the *saṅgha* with a violent crackdown on protesters (Schober 2011). Enacting *pattam nikkujjana kamma* creates extreme social tension which community leaders and senior monks usually seek to de-escalate to avert violent confrontations. The power of monks made evident in their refusal to accept donations from members of a military regime provoked a social and political crisis that only underscores the centrality of giving and merit-making within the Theravadin social fabric.

Contemporary flows of merit-making in the service of others

Increasingly popular merit-making practices emphasize service to others (*parahita*). These communal organizations have their historical antecedents in Myanmar's mutual aid societies (B.: *wunthanu*) and mobilize support in response to specific humanitarian needs. In doing so, these aid organizations redirect the cultural flows of generosity away from traditional or charismatic sources of merit and toward people in need. While monks and monasteries continue to have a role in organizing donation collection and the distribution of aid, the ultimate recipients of the collected donations are laypeople in need, rather than members of the *saṅgha*. The practice of *parahita* therefore constitutes somewhat of a departure from traditional merit practices. Like *vipassanā* mediation, performing *parahita* is a distinctly contemporary practice of merit-making that empowers laypeople to become benefactors in the welfare of others. The practice of *parahita* approximates generalized forms of exchange that produce egalitarian social relationships. Participants expect to gain merit from their contributions to social welfare, the merit they gain is a function of their intentions. In contrast to traditional merit-making, performing social welfare does not involve the *saṅgha* as a recipient of donations.

Over the past decades, Myanmar has experienced a devastating disaster in the cyclone Nargis and later opened up to global economic and political networks. Both of these large-scale events have inspired a new ethic and vision for the future, especially among young people in Myanmar. The former has underscored the need to care for the suffering, indigent, and poor. The latter has allowed for the pursuit of new careers and achievements to enable people to make merit by serving others in need (*parahita*). Both of these social factors are changing the production, circulation, and institutionalization of merit and the ways of consuming the labor of merit-making. The contemporary life offers young men new opportunities and prestigious career choices beyond joining traditional institutions like the *saṅgha*. This new reality inevitably threatens traditional forms of monastic authority and charisma while enabling new ways of making merit by mobilizing communities to directly alleviate needs of the indigent. Contemporary practices of giving therefore increasingly emphasize service to others in need (*parahita*). This shift in popular religious practice has an equalizing effect on the social status and capital of donors acting as a collectivity. This change affects fundraising strategies and the flow of donations to ethical causes and people in need and, ultimately, away from Buddhist institutions.

Mobilizing laypeople around the notion of selfless service appeals to a broad spectrum of Burmese and generates significant flows of material goods and their redistribution through various networks. Merit-making in the service of others can have a significant impact on communities in need of social welfare. For instance, many Burmese laypeople and monks organized donation drives to aid victims of Nargis in the aftermath of the cyclone's devastation of the lower delta region of southern Burma in 2006. Altruistic giving (*parahita*) also inspires and motivates many nongovernmental aid societies that emerged in the years following this disaster. The Free Funeral Society began its social work in the 1990s at the initiative of a well-known actor, Ko Thu, who offered to provide free funerals to anyone unable to afford funerary services (Mulung Hsu 2016). In the years that followed, his organization expanded into a nationwide network that provides free funerals as well as other social services. What motivates these volunteers is the performance of *parahita* and the future rewards of merit their selfless labor will bring. Other social groups, including the outlawed Ma-Ba-Tha known for its racial, nationalist, and anti-Muslim agitations that is now known by a new name, Buddha Dhamma Parahita, similarly appeals to people's desire to serve others in order to gain support for their agenda (International Crisis Group 2017: 17). Local chapters organize lay supporters to provide all types of social services to other Buddhists in their communities and see themselves as advocating especially the rights of women, thus demonstrating love for religion and country and dedication to *parahita* (Walton et al. 2015).

A third example of performing *parahita* blurs distinctions between monks and reportedly 2,400 resident lay yogi meditators. Since 2008, Sayadaw U Ottamarasara has developed the Thanlyin Thabawa Meditation Centre, a complex of 80 acres located a few miles south of Yangon. The abbot is known as a meditation teacher who attracts flows of *dāna* so that he can dedicate his work to social welfare. While few monks reside at the center, the ever-expanding complex is home to many different kinds of communities in need of the *dāna* this institution collects. The charisma of its founding abbot stems from his ability to attract donations, rather than any traditional forms of monastic practice like preaching, meditation, or scholarship. When I visited this monastery in 2019, the abbot was traveling abroad, but some wealthy donors from California nonetheless were there to make donations. The *dāna* collected supports several groups of residents, including indigent elderly who had retired there, hospice residents including cancer and mental patients, itinerant Western tourists, and a variety of others who had flocked to this meditation center because they were in need of meals, housing, or other services, all of which they received there freely. As a consequence, a village of fifteen thousand residents developed next to the meditation center as the abbot continues to acquire adjacent land with the donations he receives. The theme emphasized by the compound's leaders and residents was the abbot's seemingly limitless ability to attract donations to further his mission to perform *parahita*. His success in attracting *dāna* has enabled him to establish several subsidiary centers in Myanmar and abroad.

Theories of giving in a Theravāda Buddhist context

Anthropological writings on giving in Theravāda societies have focused on the material value of the gift, on the "free" gift as an alienated economic commodity, on the gift as sacrifice, and on the gift as a bad investment of resources. In the 1950s, studies on economic development and national integration (Pfanner and Ingersoll 1962) were critical of the "irrational choices" of Burmese Buddhists who invested their disposable incomes in donations to "unproductive" monks, expecting rewards in a future life rather than this one. Because of this, Theravādins were seen as wasting economic opportunities and lacking a Protestant work ethic. To the economist E. F. Schumacher (2011: 56ff.), however, this deferred expectation of Theravādins signaled detachment from material things and confirmed to him that "small is beautiful." Yet, as the grandeur and scale of architectural monuments produced throughout Theravāda history demonstrate, for Buddhist donors, giving freely and magnificently is beautiful.

Changing religious and ethical practices demand a critical appraisal of theories that explicate Theravāda Buddhist motivations and ask us to assess the degree to which past approaches remain compelling or, alternatively, how we might amend our scholarship to encompass new trends (Bowie 1998; Brac de la Perrière 2015; Sihlé 2015). Most of these scholars take their departure from Marcel Mauss's classic study on the gift, in which he proposes that giving is constitutive of human relationships and, ultimately, of society. He theorized that the manner in which gifts are reciprocated reflects the quality of social relationships and networks through which these items travel. Most important to Mauss, however, was the "spirit of the gift," by which he meant the mediated value of what is given and received.

Laidlaw (2000) sees the value of the gift as symbolic capital and notes that in Indian religions immaterial rewards are quintessential to ritual exchange. Yet, he also argues that a "free gift" does not create obligations between givers and receivers, a claim that does not hold up in Theravādin contexts in which giving creates social difference and obligations. Similarly, Strenski (1983) treats *dāna* as an unreciprocated gift circulating in a network of generalized exchange and fails to discern the hegemonic implications of generosity. By contrast, Carrithers (1983) cites the account of King Bimbisara's donation of the Deer Park near Benares as the first parcel of land given to the monastic community and recognizes that reciprocal lay–monastic exchanges of *dāna* and merit are necessary for a mendicant *saṅgha* to transform into a sedentary institution.

Ritual giving and its obligations within an economy of merit create a complex hierarchy of social relations, involving not just persons and things but also ideas about ethical virtues in the performance of social reciprocity. A great deal of social attention is paid to the disciplined performance of Buddhist precepts as a distinguishing marker of ethical virtue and different social status of monks and laypeople.

In the traditional Theravāda contexts in Myanmar, giving is restricted to the participation of donors and monks and creates reciprocal exchange relations in a stratified social system. This form of restricted exchange produces social differences wherein culturally perceived purity of the monastic sources of merit and of lay intentions are the significant variables mediating the ethical value of the exchange. At the core of this exchange lies the ethical value mediated in the ritual performance of generosity that makes merit for the donor, members of his family and household as well as others who contributed to the donor's efforts to make merit. The exchange between donors and monks is often carefully negotiated, especially when larger donations are involved, and more or less follows the steps described earlier to ensure public validation of the ethical reward donors receive for their practice of generosity, on one hand, and of the material gift received by members of the *saṅgha*, on the other. The public and ritual validation of these "social facts" renders the exchange legal. The central concern for participants in these ritual exchanges is not whether the gift is "free" but whether the donor is entitled to give it and practices generosity with pure intention and whether the recipient monk practices and observes *vinaya* rules sufficiently to be a proper source of merit.

In contemporary contexts, generalized flows of merit-making through social welfare networks foster egalitarian relationships that de-emphasize social difference. In contrast to the institution building of traditional merit-making practices, performances of *parahita* tend to address specific and contextually embedded social needs. This specificity enables social welfare groups to mobilize quickly and dissolve once urgent needs are met. *Dāna* is not a free gift as it creates expectations among donors of ethical rewards of merit that will lead to prosperity, wealth, influence, and power in the future. The material value of donations circulated in merit-making networks are therefore not alienated commodities. Rather, making merit creates and maintains Theravāda institutions, social networks, and civilizations.

References

Asad, T. 1993. *Genealogies of Religion: Discipline and Reasons of Power in Christianity and Islam*. Baltimore: Johns Hopkins University Press.

Bowie, K. 1998. "The Alchemy of Charity: Of Class and Buddhism in Northern Thailand." *American Anthropologist* 100 (2): 469–481.

Bowie, K. 2017. *Of Beggars and Buddhas, The Politics of Humor on the Vessantara Jataka in Thailand*. Madison: University of Wisconsin Press.

Brac de la Perrière, B. 2015. "Religious Donations, Ritual Offerings, and Humanitarian Aid: Fields of Practice According to Forms of Giving in Burma." *Religion Compass* 9 (11): 386–403.

Carrithers, M. 1983. *The Forest Monks of Sri Lanka: an anthropological and historical study*. Delhi: Oxford University Press.

Collins, S. 2016. "Introduction." In *Readings of the Vessantara Jataka*, ed. S. Collins, 1–36. New York: Columbia University Press.

Handlin, L. 2016. "A Man of All Seasons: Three Vessantara in Premodern Myanmar." In *Readings of the Vessantara Jataka*, ed. S. Collins. 153–182. New York: Columbia University Press.

Hsu, M. 2016. "Making Merit, Making Civil Society: Free Funeral Service Societies and Merit-Making in Contemporary Myanmar." *Journal of Burma Studies* 23 (1): 1–36.

International Crisis Group. 2017. Buddhism and State Power in Myanmar. Asia Report no. 290. Brussels: International Crisis Group, September 5.

Keyes, C.F. 1983. "Merit-Transference in the Kammic Theory of Popular Theravāda Buddhism." In *An Anthropological Inquiry*, eds. C. Keyes, F. Karma, 261–286. Los Angeles: University of California Press.

Ladwig, P. 2012. "Feeding the Dead: Ghosts, Materiality and Merit in the Lao Festival for the Deceased." In *Buddhist Funeral Cultures of Southeast Asia and China*, eds. P. Williams, P. Ladwig, 119–141.

Laidlaw, J. 2000. "A Free Gift Makes No Friends." *Journal of the Royal Anthropological Institute*, 6 (4): 617–634.

Lefferts, L., Cate, S. 2016. "Narration in the Vessantara Painted Scrolls of Northeastern Thailand and Laos." In *Readings of the Vessantara Jataka*, ed. S. Collins. 122–152. New York: Columbia University Press.

Lehman, F. 1984. "Freedom and Bondage in Traditional Burma and Thailand." *Journal of Southeast Asian Studies* 15 (2): 233–244.

Mauss, M. 2002. *The Gift: Form and Reason for Exchange in Archaic Societies*. London: Routledge.

Pfanner, D.E., Ingersoll, J. 1962. "Theravada Buddhism and village Economic Behavior: A Burmese and Thai Comparison." *The Journal of Asian Studies* 21 (3): 341–361.

Schober, J. 1996. "Religious Merit and Social Status among Burmese Lay Buddhist Organizations." In *Blessing and Merit in Mainland Southeast Asia*, eds. N. Tannenbaum, C. Kammerer, 197–211. New Haven: Yale Southeast Asia Monographs.

Schober, J. 1997. "Buddhist Just Rule and Burmese National Culture: State Patronage of the Chinese Tooth Relic in Myanmar." *History of Religions* 36 (3): 218–243.

Schober, J. 2001. "Venerating the Buddha's Remains in Burma: From Solitary Practice to the Cultural Hegemony of Communities." *Journal of Burma Studies* 6: 111–139.

Schober, J. 2011. *Modern Buddhist Conjunctures in Myanmar: Cultural Narratives, Colonial Legacies, and Civil Society*. Honolulu: University of Hawai'i Press.

Schumacher, E.F., 2010 (1973). *Small is Beautiful: A Study of Economics As If People Mattered*. New York: Random House.

Sihlé, N. 2015. "Towards a Comparative Anthropology of the Buddhist Gift (and Other Transfers)." *Religion Compass* 9 (11): 352–385.

Strenski, I. 1983. "On Generalized Exchange and the Domestication of the Sangha." *Man* 18 (3): 463–477.

Walton, M., McKay, M., Mar Kyi, Daw Khin Mar. 2015. "Women and Myanmar's 'Religious Protection Laws'." *The Review of Faith & International Affairs, Religion, Law, and Society* 13 (4): 36–49.

8

MEDITATION

Techniques and processes of transformation

Pyi Phyo Kyaw and Kate Crosby

Overview of meditation

Buddhist meditation entails a range of practices aimed to bring about self-transformation through the alteration of our responses, attitudes, ways of thinking, and—to varying degrees—physical makeup. The ultimate purpose of meditation is to free ourselves of defilements (*kilesa*) based in craving and delusion in order to attain *nibbāna*, freedom from the cycle of rebirth and suffering, *saṃsāra*. The defilements include temporary hindrances (*nīvaraṇa*), which obscure our mind and capacity to practice in any given moment, and fetters (*saṃyojana*), which bind us to *saṃsāra* over many lifetimes. Buddhist meditation is broadly divided into two aims, the development of the capacity of our mind to overcome the hindrances, *samatha*, literally "calm," and the unhooking of the deep-seated fetters through increasingly higher levels of insight, *vipassanā*. Different meditation subjects address different aspects of these two aims, their appropriateness depending on the character traits and level of development of the practitioner. The most well-known and universally suitable meditation topics are mindfulness of breath (*ānāpāna-ssati*), and the development of loving kindness (*mettā-bhāvanā*), but the variety of topics recorded in texts and pursued in practice is large, and there is an array of methods for each of them. Meditation is practiced at progressive levels from basic to advanced, the latter requiring significant commitment, experience, and expertise. While at the beginner level, meditation usually requires repetitive performance, more advanced levels often also entail a sequence.

Meditation can be practiced individually, or in groups, with regular practitioners moving between the two modes. As such meditation creates fluid communities, sometimes local but also international. While the type of transformation sought is often discussed in relation to spiritual values, meditation is also transformative in a broader sense, in terms of improving emotional and physical well-being in the present and ensuring a better state in the future. One of the ten wholesome actions, it is a merit-making practice, and short sessions may be integrated into the program of religious activities at Buddhist monasteries. The practice of meditation has varied in importance at different times historically and between different regions and lineages of Theravāda. In recent decades, it has influenced global culture, mainly in the form of Mindfulness, infiltrating multiple spheres of private and public life, spawning apps, online videos, and classes that reach across nations and religious affiliation.

DOI: 10.4324/9781351026666-11

Meditation is often assumed to be a primary practice for monks, one of their two traditional vocations as either meditator (*vipassanā-dhura*) or textualist (*gantha-dhura*). Nonetheless, many do not meditate, and other occupations have long been part of monastic life. While some Theravāda monks, nuns and laypeople pursue meditation as a regular commitment in their daily lives, others practise only on certain occasions or at certain periods in their lives; others never at all. Today, committed practice is more commonplace in Myanmar, among both monastics and laypeople. This is because of the distinctive response there to the threat posed to Buddhist practice and infrastructure by European colonialism in the nineteenth and early twentieth centuries. Leading monks taught that everyone had the responsibility to meditate to ensure Buddhism's survival and to make the most of the opportunity for spiritual progress while the Buddha's teaching was still available (Braun 2013; Kyaw 2014; Turner 2014). It has also become more popular in other Theravāda countries particularly since the second half of the twentieth century, when it began to be practiced among urban laypeople, a trend that has continued to increase as part of the global rise of faith-based and secular meditation globally. Meditation has also been reemphasized at previous crises in Theravāda history, such as the reforms of Buddhism in Sri Lanka in the twelfth and eighteenth centuries. Assessing its importance at such moments is challenging, because it is less visible to posterity than the textual revivals and construction or refurbishment of religious buildings that took place in the same context. Likewise, the extent of meditation practice in Theravāda history at any given moment is difficult to ascertain.

The aspects of meditation that we examine in this chapter are the stages of the path and the final goal in relation to the defilements, alongside wider advantages attributed to meditation including in global therapeutic contexts; textual sources of information about how to practice meditation from the Pāli canon onwards; the Pāli terms used in relation to meditation; meditation topics, particularly as found in the highly influential fifth-century *Visuddhimagga*; and how Abhidhamma provides a detailed map of the different aspects of practice and processes of transformation. We expand on the last topic, the relationship between Abhidhamma and meditation, to consider the main families of meditation practice of early modern and contemporary Theravāda; variation within and between them, in part relating to the use they make of Abhidhamma; and why some traditions of practice have survived and thrived in the modern period while others have not.[1]

The goal

To achieve the ultimate goal meditation must lead to radically transformative insights into reality in order to "see and understand the way things are" (*yathā-bhūta-ñāṇa-dassana*). These insights relate to understanding the interdependence of the conditioning factors that influence our experience. This experience is analyzed into various categories of components. The most familiar synchronic analysis of ourselves in a given moment is as the five aggregates (*khandha*), namely, "form" (*rūpa*), "feelings/sensations" (*vedanā*), "perception" (*saññā*), "mental formation" (*saṅkhāra*), and "consciousness" (*viññāṇa*). The most familiar diachronic analysis of how one moment and period of life leads to the next is the sequence of causality summed up by the twelve chains of "interdependent origination" (*paṭiccasamuppāda*). Underlying this interdependence are the three fundamental characteristics (*ti-lakkhaṇa*), of all phenomena, namely, "impermanence" (*anicca*), "suffering/ insecurity" (*dukkha*), and "no-self" (*anattā*).

Insights into these doctrinal truths bring about "long-term fundamental changes affecting many aspects of the person, such as perceptual, emotional, intellectual, spiritual, or behavioral patterns, eventually bringing about the anchoring of the person in more fundamental aspects of existence" (Eifring 2016: 9). This deep change in the nature, character, and perception of a person in Theravāda entails abandoning unskillful mental states and acquiring "noble" (*ariya*) positive or "beautiful" (*sobhana*) mental states, culminating in the realization of the truth of *anattā* and the attainment of liberation (*nibbāna*). Through this transformation, one ceases to be an "ordinary person" (*puthujjana*), stuck in the endless cycle of death and rebirth (*saṃsāra*), and enters the "noble path" (*ariya-magga*), progressing through four stages. The first is the "stream-enterer" (*sotāpanna*) who has gained a first glimpse of *nibbāna* and abandoned the first three of ten "fetters" (*saṃyojana*): identification with one's current embodiment (*sakkāya-diṭṭhi*), "doubt" (*vicikicchā*), and "clinging to precepts and vows" (*sīla-bbata-parāmāsa*). By weakening the next two fetters, "sensual desire" (*kāma-rāga*) and "ill-will" (*byāpāda*), one becomes the "once-returner" (*sakadāgāmī*), reborn as a human being no more than once. The "non-returner" (*anāgāmī*) has completely abandoned these first five fetters so is only reborn above the sense-desire realm of Buddhist cosmology, and matures to awakening there. The five remaining fetters are "attachment to the form realm" (*rūpa-rāga*), "attachment to the formless realm" (*arūpa-rāga*), "conceit" (*māna*), "restlessness" (*uddhacca*) and "spiritual ignorance" (*avijjā*). By abandoning these five one becomes an *arhat*, bringing all rebirths in *saṃsāra* to an end.

Alongside or even regardless of progress toward this goal, practitioners anticipate a range of other types of transformation from meditation, some of which are culturally specific, relating to understandings of health, current and future physical and mental well-being, cosmology, and the needs of the dead (Crosby 2014: 156–160; Cassaniti 2017). In modern therapeutic settings, there is less variety in the type of meditation practice and a narrower range of goals. There, mindfulness of the breath is the most common method, used as a simple calming practice to relax the body and quieten the mind so that the practitioner might be alert and aware of the present moment and their own condition at that moment. By offering an anchor for the mind to focus on breath, the practitioner is able to step back from entanglement in their ongoing thought processes, an outcome referred to as de-centering. This can be helpful in breaking the automatic, often repetitive, negative trains of thought that characterize anxiety and depression. Other advantages attributed to meditation include situational awareness, prosocial attitudes, and enhanced cognitive reserve in aging. Meditation is also of interest in the reduction of pain and symptoms of chronic illness.

The usefulness of meditation in secular, therapeutic contexts has increasingly been assessed using medical, cognitive, and social sciences. This means that practices originally aimed at transcendental transformation are scrutinized for effects they were not designed to deliver by systems of thought that do not subscribe to their original purpose.[2] The assessment of the validity of meditation is not unique to the modern period, however. Historically, the desired outcomes are described in detail in Abhidhamma, the vein of Theravāda learning that focuses on the components of reality, causality, and how change happens. Abhidhamma further unpacks the interdependence of causality noted earlier. Unlike meditation, Abhidhamma did not make the journey to the popular, global stage, although serious practitioners around the world have increasingly taken an interest in it because of its relevance to understanding experience and to offering a vocabulary for experiences often not encountered elsewhere.

Pāli terms concerning "meditation"

There are a number of Pāli terms used in relation to meditation. The word *bhāvanā* literally means "causing to become" or "cultivation" in the sense of developing skillful mental states through practice. The term *kammaṭṭhāna* literally means "place/object of work," referring to the individual meditation practices or subjects or to the practice of meditation more generally.[3] Many post-canonical Pāli and vernacular treatises on meditation have the name *kammaṭṭhāna* in the title. Meditation centers in Myanmar are referred to by the Burmese term *ka-ma-htan-yeik-tha*, "a pleasant shade for object of work."

Two other Pāli terms often associated with meditation are *samatha* and *vipassanā*. The term *samatha* means "calming," that is, the calming of physical and mental agitation and activity, particularly the discarding of unskilful mental factors that act as hindrances to progress along the path. The term *vipassanā*, often translated as "insight meditation," means "seeing through," "investigating," or "analysis," referring to the investigation into the true nature of things. The versatile nature of these two terms means they can be used in different ways.

Samatha and *vipassanā* are described in the *suttas* as the path (*magga*) to liberation (SN 43), the route by which one attains awakening. One can become an arhat by means of (1) *vipassanā* preceded by *samatha*, (2) *samatha* preceded by *vipassanā*, (3) *samatha* and *vipassanā* yoked together, and (4) the mind being seized by Dhamma excitement but then settling down, unified and becoming immersed in *samādhi* (AN 4.170).[4] In the canon, then, both *samatha* and *vipassanā* are important in the process of transformation, although the order does not matter. This is clear in the first three routes. The fourth route is when insight is the main trigger of enlightenment, but even so, at the last instance, *samatha* factors must assist with the full removal of certain defilements. While unskillful mental factors, rooted in greed, hatred, and delusion, can be weakened and temporarily suspended through *samatha* meditation, *vipassanā* is needed to uproot them. As Cousins highlights, only the order of the development of such qualities is variable: "in the longer term none can be neglected" (Cousins 1984: 65).

Samatha and *vipassanā* also refer to two broad techniques, mutually supportive for spiritual progress. The semi-canonical texts, the *Peṭakopadesa* and the *Nettipakaraṇa*, consider the path from the perspective of methods (*naya*) and see *samatha* and *vipassanā* as methods to overcome craving and ignorance respectively (Cousins 1984: 62). The primary aim of *samatha* meditation is to strengthen the agility and receptiveness of the mind, freeing it of hindrances, so that it becomes calm, unified and concentrated. In this way, one overcomes craving. The concentrated, still mind is then applied in *vipassanā* practice to dispel spiritual ignorance.

We also find *samatha* and *vipassanā* used to refer to concentration (*samādhi*) and wisdom (*paññā*), respectively (Ñāṇamoḷi 1999: 757, 836; Cousins 1984: 59; Kuan 2008: 57–58). While the identification of *samatha* and *vipassanā* with *samādhi* and *paññā* is less frequent in the *suttas*, it is standard in canonical and post-canonical Abhidhamma texts (Cousins 1984: 59). A practitioner still needs to develop *samādhi* in tandem with *paññā*, rather than in sequence, as each supports the development of the other in *samatha* or *vipassanā* meditation (Shaw 2020: 56).

These terms, i.e. *samatha* and *vipassanā*, are also now commonly applied to different meditation traditions, especially in relation to systems in or derived from Myanmar. In Myanmar, the term *samatha* has become associated with practices at the more 'magical', power-enhancing end of the spectrum of Buddhist meditation practices, such as Burmese *weikza*.[5] One purpose of *weikza* is longevity, to ensure that one will be present in the human realm rather than reborn in one of the cosmological realms less conducive to spiritual transformation, for the arrival of the future Buddha Metteyya. This reflects doubt in the possibility of enlightenment in the present day, given the declining state of the *sāsana* of the Buddha of our current era, Siddhattha Gotama. Meanwhile, *vipassanā* has become associated with the now-mainstream Burmese practices that began to emerge during the colonial period. *Vipassanā* lineages sought to prioritize salvific insight to ensure spiritual progress in this life, while the *dhamma* and spiritual attainments are still possible, given the anticipated disappearance of the *sāsana*.[6] The focus on quick results and a lack of requirement to become skilled in the calm and focused states (*jhāna*) developed through *samatha* techniques contributed to the relative accessibility of *vipassanā* practice, allowing it to be adapted to many contexts and environments. Modern Burmese *vipassanā* is now more widespread than other Theravāda techniques within Southeast Asia and globally.

An early and influential list of the qualities to be developed through meditation are "qualities that contribute to awakening" (*bodhipakkhiyādhamma*). There are thirty-seven of them categorized into seven sets (Gethin 2001: 21). Several qualities such as "concentration" (*samādhi*), "mindfulness" (*sati*), and "energy" (*viriya*) recur under the same or similar names within the seven sets. The word *samādhi* literally means "bringing together," "focus," or "concentration" and is developed by either focusing on a meditation object or being mindful of the present moment. The word *sati*, cognate with the verb *to remember*, means "mindfulness" or "awareness," referring to the heightened state of nonjudgmental awareness or seeing things from a detached perspective "as they really are." The word *viriya* means "effort," "energy," or "diligence." It gives one the sticking power to counter the hindrances to meditation and investigate one's skillful and unskilful aspects so that one is able to strive to achieve skillful actions and avoid unskillful ones. It therefore goes in tandem with wisdom (*paññā*). In Theravāda literature, these qualities are understood as both means and end (Gethin 2001: 351–352).

The word *jhāna* in Pāli texts may be translated as "meditative state," "meditative absorption," or "altered state of consciousness." It refers to the more refined, focused states of consciousness achieved through *samatha* meditation. There are different levels of *jhāna* which correspond to the mental states (*citta*) in the different heavenly realms of Buddhist cosmology, four *jhāna* that relate to the realm of form, which is above the realm of desire, then four formless *jhāna*, that relate to the higher, formless realms. Their traditional association with indirect benefits such as supernatural and psychic powers and the ability to visit the different realms of the Buddhist cosmos (Houtman 1990: 181–182) may be downplayed, ignored, or even explicitly rejected in the modern, globalized practice of Buddhist meditation, even when *jhāna* itself is valued.

Authoritative meditation texts[7]

While most Buddhist practitioners learn from teachers, the authority of the latter is supported by authoritative texts, from the Pāli canon to modern-day compositions in Pāli and vernacular languages. The most famous and most drawn-on canonical text is the lengthy *Mahāsatipaṭṭhāna-sutta* (DN 22; *Great Discourse on Establishing Mindfulness*), in the *Dīghanikāya* of the *Sutta Piṭaka*, a shorter recension of which, the *Satipaṭṭhāna-sutta*, is found in the *Majjhimanikāya* (MN 10). The commentary on the *Mahāsatipaṭṭhāna-sutta*, ascribed to the fifth-century Indian exegete Buddhaghosa, was highly influential in the nineteenth- and early twentieth-century revival of meditation in Burma. The *Mahāsatipaṭṭhāna-sutta* provides details of how to practice mindfulness on four meditation objects, namely, "body" (*kāya*), "sensations/feelings" (*vedanā*), "states of consciousness" (*citta*), and "objects of consciousness" or "constituents of reality" (*dhamma*). The last category allows for the inclusion of many other meditation subjects found elsewhere in the canon that are also developed in Abhidhamma literature. The *Karaṇīyametta-sutta* (SN 1.8; *Discourse on Loving-kindness*) is another important canonical text. Widely recited for its protective properties, it extols the benefits of extending to the entire universe the feeling of love a mother has for an only son. In addition to these *suttas*, the *Ānāpānasati-sutta* (MN 118), the *Sīlavanta-sutta* (SN 22.122), and the discourses on dependent origination from the *Nidāna* section of the *Saṃyutta Nikāya* also become the basis for later, often vernacular meditation manuals and traditions. The most significant post-canonical compendium of meditation is the *Visuddhimagga* (*The Path of Purification*), again ascribed to the Indian commentator Buddhaghosa, which has been influential throughout Theravāda history and has informed meditation globally.

The *Visuddhimagga* is divided into three books, the first on correct behavior (*sīla*), the second on concentration or meditation technique (*samādhi*), and the third on liberating insight (*paññā*). The middle section, containing forty primarily *samatha*-oriented practices, is the most well known.

Manuscript libraries throughout the Theravāda world, whether in temples or national collections, attest to a wide array of further meditation manuals and descriptive treatizes in Pāli and vernacular languages in their hundreds if not thousands. Only a fraction has been explored, let alone published, and most are difficult to date. In contemporary Theravāda Buddhist societies, works and talks by famous meditation teachers are also regarded as authoritative texts by their followers. A common feature of such vernacular texts is the way in which these meditation teachers draw on different layers of Theravāda literature. They may also incorporate an Abhidhamma-orientated understanding of the Dhamma found in the later layers of Pāli literature. This tendency to relate practice to such authoritative doctrinal texts provides the backdrop for a number of disputes and, in Myanmar, even court cases concerning meditation (Ashin and Crosby 2017).

Overview of meditation topics

One of the reasons for the *Visuddhimagga's* success is the order it brings to the wide variety of meditation topics found in canonical and commentarial texts.[8] It reduces and systematizes these into forty meditations that lead primarily to *samatha*, in its *Samādhi* section.

The forty meditation practices given in the *Samādhi* section of the *Visuddhimagga* are grouped into seven broad categories. Each is identified as leading to different levels of *samādhi* and *jhāna*. The first type is the *kasiṇa* "devices" or "visual objects" of which there are ten: earth, water, fire, air or wind, blue, yellow, red, white, space, and light. For earth or one of the colors, the practitioner uses a flat, often circular object. For the other objects, the device may be a pot of water, fire, the visible or tactile effect of wind, some kind of hole or space, and some kind of light. The practitioner gazes at the *kasiṇa*, quelling discursive thought, while repeating a phrase that aids total focus on the object, for example, "bright, bright" in the case of the fire. As he continues to focus on the object, his *samādhi* increases, and he develops the ability to maintain a mental image of the "sign" *nimitta* of the object, increasingly independent of the object. The strongest *nimitta* is the purified essence of the object, which he then learns to manipulate, for example, by expanding it. The ability to experience the highest level of *nimitta* reflects one's attainment of the highest level of *samādhi*, which is the precursor of the *jhāna* state of mind.

The second category is the decomposition of a corpse, broken down into ten stages from the bloating that occurs from a few days after death to the skeleton once all flesh has been consumed or rotted. The practitioner draws comparisons with their own body.

The third category consists of ten "recollections," *anussati*, on the Buddha, the Dhamma, the Saṅgha, often performed as a set of three; then moral conduct; generosity; gods; and the body, which is broken down into thirty-two components, death, the breath and peace. The four "divine abidings," *brahmavihāra*, are an extension of the love, *mettā*, taught in the *Mettā Sutta*, noted earlier. *Mettā* is the first. The other three types of love to be felt for all beings are pity or compassion, *karuṇā*, for those in distress; sympathetic joy, *muditā*, for those experiencing well-being or some kind of success, the opposite of jealousy; and *upekkhā*, equanimous appreciation.

The next set are the four formless *jhāna* that build on the four form *jhāna* by turning away from the material realm to increasingly unlimited and peaceful states: infinite space, infinite consciousness, infinite nothingness, and neither perception nor nonperception.[9] The final two meditation topics that finish our list of forty are the perception of repulsiveness in relation to food, *āhāre paṭikūlasaññā*, and meditation of the four primary elements: earth, water, fire, air, and how these relate to one's body.

The *Paññā* section is dedicated to practices aimed to bring the higher levels of transformative liberation based on insight into ultimate reality. The *Visuddhimagga* draws on Abhidhamma's analysis of reality into components or factors, *dhamma*, which fall into four categories. They are "materiality," *rūpa*; "states of consciousness," *citta*; "aspects of consciousness," *cetasika*; and "enlightenment," *nibbāna*. The *Paññā* section also discusses in detail the way in which these *dhammas* are interrelated and function in the context of meditation practice. Such discussion of the categories of ultimate reality could be seen as a scholastic exercise. However, most traditional practitioners would see this as a description of what they may experience at the advanced stages of meditation. Some meditation traditions in Myanmar, such as the Mahāsī and Pa-Auk traditions, apply it as a set of prescriptive instructions for *vipassanā* practice.[10]

Vipassanā meditation often emphasizes the use of a high degree of mindfulness (*sati*) because the practitioner pays attention to each passing sensory or mental object. There are thus many different meditation topics in the *vipassanā* practice, rather than focusing on and mastering of a single meditation object in the *samatha* practice. Other mental qualities such as *samādhi*, concentration, and *viriya*, energy, are also important to some degree. According to the *Paññā* section of the *Visuddhimagga*, a *vipassanā* practitioner, drawing on concentration (*samādhi*) that one has developed using the *samatha* practices, mindfully observes *rūpa*, *citta*, and *cetasika* in a systematic, detailed manner. One contemplates them constantly arising and falling away and analyzes them to be unsatisfactory and impersonal processes. In this way, the practitioner observes the nature and characteristics of the current bodily and mental experiences, and such discernment leads to increasing levels of *vipassanā*.

Meditation and Abhidhamma

Descriptions of meditation practice in the *Sutta* section of the Pāli canon primarily give instructions on how to begin to practice meditation. They also include standardized descriptive accounts of some significant meditative attainments such as the *jhāna*. We similarly come across instructions on how to meditate in meditation classes and on retreats, whether in a Buddhist or a secular Mindfulness context. The value of Abhidhamma in relation to meditation is that it offers a map or blueprint for the progressive and fundamental transformation that is being sought. While for Abhidhamma, the focus of the third major collection of texts that form the Pāli canon, is often referred to as scholasticism in Western writings on Theravāda, this is a misunderstanding. Abhidhamma describes in detail how progress is made on the path, particularly through meditative attainments. To support this, it identifies and explains the basic components of reality, how they mutually condition one another, and what one will experience if one successfully begins to bring about self-transformation. It provides labels for experience, explains those experiences, and allows practitioners and teachers to relate the early and progressive stages of the path to the ultimate goal. It also explains how materiality and consciousness work, which can offer a basis for relating experience to the fundamental functioning of one's body and mind. We can see this use of Abhidhamma in the *Visuddhimagga* which, while giving accessible descriptions of how to do meditation, also explains experience and attainments within an Abhidhamma framework. While Abhidhamma contains much technical vocabulary, often listed for brevity, and is therefore challenging to follow unless one has trained in it, it is very much there to support practice, by explaining experience and causality.

Kornfield observes that "there is probably more emphasis and use made of the Abhidhamma teachings in Burma [Myanmar] than in any other Buddhist country" (1977: 193). Myanmar's emphasis on Abhidhamma, like its widespread promotion of meditation, reflects its unique response to the crisis of the European colonial period. In their quest to protect their threatened religion Burmese Buddhists emphasized the preservation of Abhidhamma since it is regarded as the first part of the canon that will disappear as the religion declines. Abhidhamma was also emphasized for its importance in preserving transformative realizations (*paṭivedha*) since it explains the content of such realizations and meditation as the means to achieving them. It was this desire to ensure transformative insights while the Buddha's teaching was still accessible that led to the emphasis on those meditation practices leading to *vipassanā* in the Burmese meditation revival of this period. The two meditation teachers who did most to popularize the lay engagement in the first half of the nineteenth century in Myanmar were Ledi Sayadaw Ven. Ñāṇa (1846–1923) and Mūla-mingun Jetavana Sayadaw Ven. Nārada (1869–1955). The founder of the internationally famous Mahāsī meditation tradition, Sayadaw Ven. Sobhana (1904–1982), practiced under the guidance of the latter.

For the majority of Burmese Buddhists, the theoretical teachings as described in the law of dependent origination (*paṭiccasamuppāda*) and the more detailed explanations of causality found in the Abhidhamma play a crucial role in *vipassanā* practices. Meditation masters such as Ledi Sayadaw and Mohnyin Sayadaw Ven. Sumana (1873–1964)—whose reputations rested on their exceptional expertise in Abhidhamma—advocated that people learn it. For Ledi Sayadaw, Abhidhamma categories and concepts provide "the veritable 'dhamma tools' (*dhamma a chok' a ū*) [*sic.*] that enable a meditator to relate ultimate truth (*paramattha*) directly to perceptual experience as the means to awakening" (Braun 2013: 130–131). Burmese meditation masters such as Mohnyin Sayadaw, Saddhammaransī Sayadaw Ven. Kuṇḍalābhivaṃsa (1921–2011), and Pa-Auk Tawya Sayadaw Ven. Āciṇṇa (1934–) discuss the practical application of the *Paṭṭhāna*. The *Paṭṭhāna*, the seventh canonical Abhidhamma book, dedicated to the complex web of conditional relations between the constituents of reality (*dhamma*), can be used to examine the process of causality in *vipassanā* practice.[11] This importance of Abhidhamma for practice continues in contemporary Myanmar, with some meditators opining that in order to practice *vipassanā* meditation and develop insight knowledge, one must first have a foundation of theoretical knowledge about the *dhammas* (Khin undated: 90). Another Burmese meditation method that is heavily theory-based and informed by Abhidhamma analysis is the Mogok meditation tradition, founded by Mogok Sayadaw Ven. Vimala (1899–1962), whose method begins with the study of the law of dependent origination. In contrast, the meditation methods taught by Sunlun Sayadaw Ven. Kavi (1878–1952) and Theinngu Sayadaw Ven. Ukkaṭṭha (1913–1973) have practical approaches as one's starting point and prioritize experience and practice over theory.

In the past two decades, there has been an increasing interest in Abhidhamma among practitioners in other parts of Southeast and East Asia as well as Western countries. This is partly because of the increasing exchange of knowledge that occurred between Abhidhamma experts from Myanmar such as Ven. Dr. Nandamālābhivaṃsa (b. 1940) and practitioners from Asia and Europe. Moreover, the global outreach of some of the meditation traditions stemming from Myanmar such as that of the Mahāsi method, of the Goenka practice established by S. N. Goenka (1924–2013), Indian student of U Ba Khin, and of the Pa-Auk method has become more widespread, attracting both novice and experienced practitioners. Aided by Asian practitioners with expertise in Abhidhamma, connected through the network of fluid transnational communities that meditation creates, such practitioners have contributed to an opening up of what is otherwise an inaccessible, often abstruse topic. Members of the Samatha Trust set up in the United Kingdom in 1973, initially on the basis of the meditation teachings of former monk Nai Boonman (b.1932) from Thailand, have also taken a keen interest in Abhidhamma and contributed to its study and accessibility (Shaw 2019).

As in Myanmar, so in Thailand, practitioners sought to ensure that Buddhism would continue to survive in the face of the aggressive interests of Britain and France in the territories and commodities of the region. Buddhism was harnessed in the struggle for ongoing sovereignty. This contributed to the incremental reform of Buddhist education around a centralized monastic syllabus focusing on the *Sutta* and *Vinaya Piṭaka* from Mongkut (1804–1868) onward. Until there was a rekindled interest in the 1950s under Burmese influence, Abhidhamma was downplayed or ignored. The validity of meditation was increasingly assessed primarily against *sutta* texts.

An increased emphasis on administration in the Saṅgha also marginalized meditation practice for several generations. Nonetheless, in the northeast, the practice of living in the forests and pursuing an itinerant lifestyle dedicated to meditation died out only with the closures of the forests in the latter half of the twentieth century (Tiyavanich 1997). Only one teaching lineage is known to have survived, its history relatively well recorded after it spread both nationally and, from the 1970s, globally. It was founded by Ajan Sao (1861–1941), who had ordained within the reform branch of the Saṅgha established by Mongkut. Ajan Sao's student Ajan Mun (1870–1949), and his student in turn, Ajan Mahabua (1913–2011), popularized the Thai forest tradition both within Thailand and abroad. Particularly inspirational in the establishment of Thai forest monasteries internationally was their charismatic student Ajan Chah (1918–1992), who attracted large numbers of Western followers.[12]

While the meditation practitioners who received royal sanction in Thailand from the late nineteenth century de-emphasized Abhidhamma, the pre-reform systems of meditation for which we have evidence closely followed the map of transformation Abhidhamma had set out. Mongkut, while still a monk, studied this type of pre-reform meditation under his teacher, the supreme patriarch of the Saṅgha, but rejected it as too complicated and inconsistent with the parts of the canon familiar to him (Skilton 2019: 48). The modernization of Buddhist education and practice under Mongkut's successors had such an effect that by the early twentieth-century, pre-reform meditation had started to disappear to such an extent that publications of the 1930s, which sought to document it, labeled it *boran kammathan* (Thai, Pāli: *purāṇa kammaṭṭhāna*), "old meditation method."

This old method is only preserved in simplified and modernized forms in a few temple networks of Cambodia and Thailand today. Yet it is the only system of Theravāda meditation that we can trace back beyond the nineteenth century. We can follow it to the turn of the fifteenth and sixteenth centuries, when it was practiced by the supreme patriarchs of Laos, a tradition that continued until the eve of the Marxist revolution in 1974 (Choompolpaisal 2019: 156–157). It largely disappeared from Cambodia during the same decade under the Khmer Rouge, having already been marginalized under Thai and French colonial influence earlier in the century. In previous centuries, it was a different story. In the eighteenth century, for example, the king of Thailand sent a mission of monks to Sri Lanka to teach *boran kammathan* as part of the revival of Buddhism there. Cave temples were refurbished and redecorated with magnificent wall paintings for the students of *boran kammathan*. While its practice by a few seems to have continued into the twentieth century, new revivals of meditation in Sri Lanka were inspired mainly by Burmese *vipassanā* or by a return to such texts as the *Visuddhimagga*.

The relationship between *boran kammathan* and Abhidhamma is best documented in the manuals left behind by the Sri Lankan monks of the eighteenth-century revival. From their accounts, we see that changing one's consciousness from the unskillful to beautiful states is pursued step by step, in a process following each change in *citta* and *cetasika* set out in the careful analysis of causality detailed in Abhidhamma texts. The complexity of those processes of change is reflected in the complexity of the meditation, which requires thousands of different steps to reach its culmination. Particularly distinctive of *boran* methods is that they explicitly aim to transform not just the consciousness of the practitioner but their body, both *nāma* and *rūpa*.

The method for doing this involves drawing the *citta* and *cetasika* into the body through the nasal cavity and binding them with the elements that make up the body. The techniques for this process of internalization relate to other systems of bringing about physical change found in the broader culture, such as medicine and the premodern chemistry applied to the purification of metal. The loss of *boran* meditation in its fullest forms therefore probably owes as much to changes in the physical sciences during the modern period as it does to the marginalization of Abhidhamma: it disappeared with the loss of understanding of the processes of causality on which it was based.[13] The most widespread legacy of these practices is the modernized system developed by Candasaro Sot (1896–1956), abbot of Wat Paknam in Greater Bangkok, and taken up by the global network of Dhammakāya temples with its headquarters at Wat Phra Dhammakāya in Pathumthani outside Bangkok.

Conclusion

Our approach in this chapter has focused on how meditation offers mechanisms for self-transformation, and how these mechanisms relate to the main goal of Buddhism, to realize things as they really are. We have explained some of the key terms and concepts that express the Theravāda understanding of this reality and the relevant changes its realization entails. We have also identified the texts considered authoritative sources for the meditation techniques and stages that the practitioner should pursue.[14]

Progress toward the goal entails the step-by-step removal of defilements in the form of hindrances and fetters. The broader account of the path found in *sutta* texts provides the key goals, such as *samatha*, *samādhi*, *vipassanā*, and *paññā*, that one must develop in order to loosen the hold of the fetters that tie one to *saṃsāra* and reach the four stages of awakening. The processes of how the transformation of one's body and mind occur are detailed in Abhidhamma texts, which offer a more analytical consideration of causality and how to harness causal mechanisms to one's spiritual advantage. Abhidhamma provides the blueprint for the transformative processes, describes the experience and content of meditative attainments, and a offers a map for progress on the path. It both prescribes and accounts for stages of the practice and attainments. Providing examples of a range of practice families and lineages, looking at three main groups, Burmese *vipassanā*, the Thai forest tradition and pre-reform *boran* practice, has enabled us to see considerable variation in the use that different traditions make of the relationship between meditative experience and Abhidhamma.

Meditation as a lived tradition can only be traced back to the very end of the fifteenth century. Most contemporary practice traditions emerged in response to colonialism and modernity from the end of the nineteenth century or with the global interest that blossomed from the second half of the twentieth century. The extent to which these revivals were formed entirely on the basis of texts or linked to remaining traces of practice is as yet unclear. What we do know is that in Theravāda circles, close attention to the authoritative texts has shaped their current form and ensured that they are strongly rooted in the tradition. This does not mean that Theravāda meditation is rigid and unadaptable. Rather, it has an ability to adapt and transform itself to suit the social, political, and technological climate of the time. This continues to transform the way meditation practices are taught and transmitted as well as the narrative that frames meditation and its relevance to modernity. We can see this adaptability with the Burmese *vipassanā* movement in Myanmar and beyond, as well as the survival of the pre-form practices in modernized, more accessible forms.

The extent to which Abhidhamma has traveled with meditation varies considerably, falling out of favor as it did in Theravāda regions more influenced by the responses to modernity found in Thailand than those in Myanmar. Even in those traditions inspired by Burmese *vipassanā*, the significance of Abhidhamma has sometimes been de-emphasized and even lost, particularly when applied primarily to therapeutic contexts and performance-enhancement. This situation is changing as global meditation matures, with an increased consideration of Abhidhamma as a way of understanding and supporting meditative experience. We anticipate that this trend will continue as a consequence of the enhanced use of technology for linking people and groups internationally in response to the COVID-19 pandemic that began to restrict group meditation and retreats from early 2020. This has led to a wider availability and uptake of live and recorded talks about meditation and Abhidhamma, as well as to people pursuing retreats in their own homes linked to teachers and practice communities through online platforms, with some retreats attracting thousands of participants from all over the world.

Notes

1 See Crosby (2014, chap. 6), for an overview of meditation practices, techniques, and the historical contexts in which meditation is practiced in Theravāda Buddhism, as well as its modern application of secular contexts.
2 See McMahan (2017) for a comparison of the goals of Buddhist meditation traditionally in the monastic context and in the modern, secularized context.
3 On the development of the term *kammaṭṭhāna*, see Skilton (2019).
4 See Cousins (1984) on the four paths.
5 *Weikza* is the Burmese of Pāli *vijjā*, "knowledge," and its practitioners are referred to as *weikza-do*, (Pāli *vijjā-dhara*) "bearers of knowledge," a term translated into English as "wizard" or shortened to *weikza*. On multiple aspects of this subject, which remains relatively unfamiliar to students of Theravāda, see Rozenberg, Brac de la Perrière and Turner (eds.) 2014.
6 On the shared concerns that informed the development of radically contrasting approaches to meditation and Buddhism, from the ultra-traditional to the ultra-secular, see Crosby (2021).
7 See Shaw (2006) for an overview of the various kinds of meditations described in the Pāli canon.
8 For a useful summary and explanation of different meditation topics found in Pāli sources, see Shaw (2016).
9 For accessible accounts of the different *jhāna*, how to attain and recognize them, see Brasington (2015).
10 For the distinction between *samatha* and *vipassanā* meditation and the varied ways in which the details of Abhidhamma are related to meditation by different practice lineages, see Crosby and Kyaw (2021).
11 For examples of the ways in which the teachings in the *Paṭṭhāna* are related to *vipassanā* meditation, see Kyaw (2012).
12 For meditation teachers in the Thai forest lineage and sources about them, see Access to Insight (2013).
13 On the practice, history, and the disappearance of *boran kammathan*, as well as its relationship to other technologies, see Crosby (2020). On the varieties of practice and evidence for different lineages in Laos and Thailand, see Choompolpaisal (2019). On its enactment of Abhidhamma, see Crosby (2019).
14 On different varieties of Theravāda techniques and a discussion of changing attitudes to meditation in scholarship, see Kate Crosby, Andrew Skilton and Pyi Phyo Kyaw (eds.) 2019.

References

Access to Insight, ed. 2013. "Thai Forest Traditions: selected teachers." *Access to Insight (BCBS Edition)*, http://www.accesstoinsight.org/lib/thai/index.html. Retrieved 20 January 2021.

Āciṇṇa, Ven, Sayadaw, Pa-Auk Tawya. 2008. *Knowing and Seeing: Talks and Questions & Answers at a Meditation Retreat in Taiwan by the Pa-Auk Tawya Sayadaw*. 4th edition.

Anālayo, Bhikkhu. 2012. "*The Dynamics of Theravāda Insight Meditation*." In 佛教禪坐傳統國際學術研討會論文集, [*Buddhist Meditation Traditions: An International Symposium*], Kuo-pin Chuang (ed.), Taiwan: Dharma Drum Publishing Corporation, pp. 23–56.

Ashin, Janaka, Crosby, Kate. 2017. "Heresy and Monastic Malpractice in the Buddhist Court Cases (*Vinicchaya*) of Modern Burma (Myanmar)." *Contemporary Buddhism* 18 (1): 199–261.

Bodhi, Bhikkhu, ed. 2000. *Abhidhammattha Sangaha: A Comprehensive Manual of Abhidhamma. Pali text originally edited and translated by Mahāthera Narada.* Canada: BPS Pariyatti Edition.

Brasington, Leigh. 2015. *Right Concentration: A Practical Guide to the Jhānas.* Boston & London: Shambala.

Braun, Erik C. 2013. *The Birth of Insight. Meditation, Modern Buddhism, and the Burmese Monk Ledi Sayadaw.* Chicago: Chicago University Press.

Cassaniti, J.L. 2017. "'Wherever You Go, There You Aren't?': Non-Self, Spirits, and the Concept of the Person in Thai Buddhist Mindfulness." In *Meditation, Buddhism and Science*, eds. D.L. McMahan, E. Braun, 133–151. New York, NY: Oxford University Press.

Choompolpaisal, Phibul. 2019. "*Nimitta* and Visual Methods in Siamese and Lao Meditation Traditions from the 17th Century to the Present Day." In Kate Crosby, Andrew Skilton and Pyi Phyo Kyaw (eds.) *Contemporary Buddhism: Variety in Theravada Meditation* 20(1–2): 152–183.

Cousins, L.S. 1984. "*Samatha-yāna* and *Vipassanā-yāna*." In *Buddhist Studies in Honour of Hammalava Saddhatissa*, eds. D. Dhammapala et al., pp. 56–68. Sri Lanka: Nugegoda.

Crosby, Kate. 2013. *Traditional Theravada meditation and its modern-era suppression.* Hong Kong: Buddha-Dharma Centre of Hong Kong.

Crosby, Kate. 2014. *Theravada Buddhism: Continuity, Diversity, Identity.* Oxford: Blackwell-Wiley.

Crosby, Kate. 2019. "Abhidhamma and *Nimitta* in 18th-Century Meditation Manuscripts from Sri Lanka: A Consideration of Orthodoxy and Heteropraxy in *Boran Kammaṭṭhāna*." *Contemporary Buddhism: Variety in Theravada Meditation* 20 (1–2): 111–151.

Crosby, Kate. 2020. *Esoteric Theravada: The Story of the Forgotten Tradition of Southeast Asia.* Boulder, Colorado: Shambala.

Crosby, Kate. 2021. "The Shared Origins of Traditionalism and Secularist Tendencies in Theravāda Buddhism." In *Secularizing Buddhism. New Perspectives on a Dynamic Tradition*, ed. Richard Payne, 135–161. Boulder, Colorado: Shambala Publications.

Crosby, Kate, Kyaw, Pyi Phyo. 2021. "Transformation and Abhidhamma in Three Theravada Meditation Traditions." In *Illuminating the Dharma: Buddhist Studies in Honour of Venerable Professor KL Dhammajoti*, eds. Toschiichi Endo, Mingyuan, 29–50. Hong Kong: Buddha-Dharma Centre of Hong Kong.

Eifring, Halvor, ed. 2016. *Asian Traditions of Meditation.* Honolulu: University of Hawai'i Press.

Gethin, Rupert. 2001. *The Buddhist Path to Awakening.* Oxford: Oneworld. First Published 1992.

Gethin, Rupert. 2011. "On Some Definitions of Mindfulness." *Contemporary Buddhism: An Interdisciplinary Journal* 12 (1): 263–279.

Houtman, Gustaaf. 1990. "Traditions of Buddhist Practice in Burma." PhD Thesis. SOAS, University of London.

Jordt, Ingrid. 2006. "Defining a True Buddhist: Meditation and Knowledge Formation in Burma." *Ethnology* 45 (3): 193–207.

Karunadasa, Y. 2010. *The Theravāda Abhidhamma: Its Inquiry into the Nature of Conditioned Reality.* Hong Kong: Centre of Buddhist Studies, The University of Hong Kong.

Khin, Ohn. (Undated). *Datehti'-that Tanha-that (Killing Views and Craving).*

Kornfield, Jack. 1977. reprint 2007. *Modern Buddhist Masters.* Kandy: Buddhist Publications Society.

Kuan, Tse-fu. 2008. *Mindfulness in Early Buddhism: new approaches through psychology and textual analysis of Pali, Chinese and Sanskrit sources.* London and New York: Routledge.

Kyaw, Pyi Phyo. 2012. "*The Paṭṭhāna (Conditional Relations) and Buddhist meditation: application of the teachings in the Paṭṭhāna in Insight (Vipassanā) Meditation Practice*," *Conference Proceedings of the 2nd International Association of Buddhist University Conference: Buddhist Philosophy & Praxis.* http://www.undv.org/vesak2012/iabudoc/07PyiPhyoKyawFINAL.pdf.

Kyaw, Pyi Phyo. 2014. "*Paṭṭhāna* (Conditional Relations) in Burmese Buddhism." PhD thesis, King's College, London.

Kyaw, Pyi Phyo. 2019. "The Sound of the Breath: Sunlun and Theinngu Meditation Traditions of Myanmar." In Kate Crosby, Andrew Skilton and Pyi Phyo Kyaw (eds.) *Contemporary Buddhism: Variety in Theravada Meditation* 20 (1–2): 247–291.

Mahāsi Sayadaw. 2016. *Manual of Insight.* Translated by Vipassanā Mettā Foundation Translation Committee. Somerville: Wisdom Publications.

McMahan, D.L. 2017. "How Meditation Works: Theorizing the Role of Cultural Context in Buddhist Contemplative Practices." In *Meditation, Buddhism and Science*, eds. D.L. McMahan, E. Braun. New York, NY: Oxford University Press, pp. 21–46.

Nagasena, Bhikkhu. 2012. "The Monastic Boundary (*Sīmā*) in Burmese Buddhism: Authority, Purity and Validity in Historical and Modern Contexts." Ph.D. thesis, School of Oriental and African Studies, London.

Ñāṇamoḷi, Bhikkhu. (tran.) 1999. *The Path of Purification (Visuddhimagga) by Bhadantācariya Buddhaghosa.* Kandy: Buddhist Publication Society. 5th edition. First published 1956.

Rozenberg, Guillaume, de la Perrière, Bénédicte Brac, Turner, Alicia, eds. 2014. *Champions of Buddhism. Weikza Cults in Contemporary Burma.* Honolulu: University of Hawai'i Press.

Sharf, Robert H. 1995. "Buddhist Modernism and the Rhetoric of Meditative Experience." *Numen* 42: 228–283.

Shaw, Sarah. 2006. *Buddhist Meditation: An Anthology of Texts.* London: Routledge.

Shaw, Sarah. 2016. "Meditation Objects in Pāli Buddhist Texts." In *Asian Traditions of Meditation*, ed. Halvor Eifrig, pp. 122–144. Honolulu: University of Hawai'i Press.

Shaw, Sarah. 2019. "Tradition and Experimentation: The Samatha Trust." In Kate Crosby, Andrew Skilton and Pyi Phyo Kyaw (eds.) *Contemporary Buddhism: Variety in Theravada Meditation* 20 (1–2): 346–371.

Shaw, Sarah. 2020. *Mindfulness: Where It Comes From and What It Means.* Buddhist Foundations Series. Boulder: Shambhala.

Skilton, Andrew. 2019. "Meditation and its subjects: tracing *kammaṭṭhāna* from the early canon to the *boran kammathan* traditions of Southeast Asia." in Kate Crosby, Andrew Skilton and Pyi Phyo Kyaw (eds.) *Contemporary Buddhism: Variety in Theravada Meditation* 20 (1–2): 36–72.

Skilton, Andrew, Choompolpaisal, Phibul. 2014. "The Old Meditation (*boran* kammatthan), a pre-reform Theravāda meditation system from Wat Ratchasittharam: The *pīti* section of the *kammatthan matchima baeb lamdub*." *Aséanie* 33: 83–116.

Skilton, Andrew, Choompolpaisal, Phibul. 2017. "How to Deal with Wind Illnesses: Two Short Meditation Texts from Buddhist Southeast Asia." In *Buddhism and Medicine: An Anthology of Premodern Sources*, ed. C. Pierce Salguero. New York: Columbia University Press, pp. 425–430.

Turner, Alicia. 2014. *Saving Buddhism: Moral Community and the Impermanence of Colonial Religion.* Honolulu: University of Hawai'i Press.

Tiyavanich, Kamala. 1997. *Forest Recollections: Wandering Monks in Twentieth-Century Thailand.* Honolulu: University of Hawai'i Press.

9

REPETITION

Pāli iterations of ritual commitment, commentarial refrain, and assiduous practice

Christoph Emmrich

Repetition has emerged as a critical term in modern European philosophy, aesthetics, gender studies, and theology, from its early utilization in the critique of teleological models of memory (Søren Kierkegaard), history (Friedrich Nietzsche, Karl Marx), and the self (Sigmund Freud); its role in experimental modernist writing (Charles Péguy, Raymond Roussel, Gertrude Stein); and its centrality for critiques of authorship (Jacques Derrida) and representation (Gilles Deleuze) right up to helping conceptualize the order of music (Adam Ockelford), sexual difference (Judith Butler), and a theological ontology based on insistence (Catherine Pickstock). European and North American academic interest in Buddhist iterative forms of cosmology and time, particularly those inherent in concepts of rebirth and world renewal, has confined itself to the largely representational paradigm of the cyclical and the linear, at best using repetition to distinguish between the two (Collins 1998: 250–256). One of the aims of this chapter is to contribute, with the help of select passages from Theravāda texts, toward a shift from a geometrical and typological way of thinking about time to an event- and language-oriented one, involving speaker participation and linguistic self-reflexivity, repeating, so to speak, the insights of some of the authors mentioned earlier. The term *repetition* will allow us to think about time, not from a place outside of time from which types of time appear in lines and circles but from a time within time, the time between one repetition and the other, where time could be made explicit or may remain implied. It is a time that is thoroughly mediated by the linguistic practices, including translation, of Pāli, English, and other idioms, a mediation out of which, among many other things, the discourses of time, line, and circle have emerged.

In the study of Asian religions and literature outside of Buddhism, the interest in repetition in its literal sense has been modest, but longstanding. Maurice Bloomfield's early study on repetitions in the *Ṛgveda* (1916) was extended to Vedic literature by Jan Gonda (1959), to Śvetāmbara narrative literature by Klaus Bruhn (1983), and to the *Mahābhārata* by A. K. Ramanujan (1991) and has, more recently, led to multiple studies of "adaptive reuse" of textual material in Brahmanical literature (Freschi & Maas 2017). What all this research has in common is that it has relied on forms of repetition to explore the compositional principles behind the creation of religious texts. It has also helped develop our sensitivity toward the formal and

DOI: 10.4324/9781351026666-12

performative aspects of these texts and has allowed us to think more broadly about the how and why of saying and doing things again. What does it mean to say or do something again, how does it affect the meaning of what is said or done, and how does it, more generally, affect our understanding of meaning? What does it not just mean for, but do to the listener, the reader, or the reciter when they perform a repetition? What is achieved when someone does something again? These are questions particularly relevant in the repetitive world of religious practice, be the practice ritual, poetic, or philosophical.

Ritual

Every time someone pays obeisance to the Buddha chanting, whispering, or thinking *namo tassa bhagavato arahato sammāsambuddhassa*, "homage to the blessed, the worthy, the fully enlightened one," they are expected to do so not once but again—and one more time, in exactly the same wording. It is customary to subsequently ritually proclaim *saraṇaṃ gacchāmi*, "I take refuge," first to the Buddha, then, again, to the Dhamma, and, in a third declaration, to the Saṅgha. This set of utterances is then repeated two more times, adding, as one repeats, that one is doing so "also a second time," *dutiyaṃ pi*, and "also a third time," *tatiyaṃ pi*. The whole set is known as the *tisaraṇam*, the threefold taking of refuge, or the *tiratana vandanā*, the worship of the Three Jewels. Sets of thrice-recurring, more or less identical ritual utterances such as these, are, of course, a hallmark of ritual language not only across Buddhist communities but, indeed, around the globe and throughout history. The Upaniṣadic *oṃ śāntiḥ śāntiḥ śāntiḥ*, the Vaiṣṇava *rāma rāma rāmeti*, the Islamic triple *talāq*, and the Anglophone juridical *Oyez! Oyez! Oyez!* are only some of the best known. A devotee uttering a set of repetitions at the very beginning of a ritual event is particularly visible in Pāli liturgy. Moreover, it is striking that the last set of utterances is not merely made again twice, but the awareness of its recurrent nature is made explicit by counting the times it is repeated. The utterances are usually accompanied by the thrice-performed gesture of submission that has the devotees clasp their hands, kneel, and touch the ground with palms and forehead. What stands at the very beginning of what Theravāda Buddhists think, say, and do when they begin to act as such is self-reflexive repetition.

An early version of the Pāli refuge formula, *bhavantaṃ gotamaṃ saraṇaṃ gacchāmi dhammañ ca bhikkhusaṅghañ ca* (e.g. DN I 85,12-15), uttered by prominent legendary convertees, but only once, is elaborated on in the commentaries (DN-a I 229,18-234,22, MN-a I 130,35-135,22, AN-a II 107,7-112,29, and Khp-a 16-17). The exegesis unfolds "refuge" (*saraṇaṃ*) as referring to four things: (1) the surrender of self (*attasanniyyātanā*), (2) the condition of having '"that" (i.e., the Three Jewels) as one's main object (*tapparāyaṇatā*), (3) the acceptance of discipleship (*sissabhāvūpāgamana*), and (4) (homage by) prostration (*paṇipāta*). The commentaries list the four items, adding to each (e.g., DN-a I 231,17-31) the opening formula "From today onward, having performed the ..." (*ajja ādiṃ katvā* ..., as well as adding, only to (2) through (4) however, the concluding formula "with these words may you know me" (*iti maṃ dhāretha*). Although it is doubtful whether this version of the multiple refuge formula is anything more than commentarial hermeneutics (Bond 1982: 25), it still contains the element of iteration not contained in the root text and reminds one of the partial iterations found in the formula used during the taking of the precepts (*pañcasīla*, *upavāsa*, and *dasasīla*) by laypeople. In his reading of MN-a I 130,35-135,22 the modernist scholar and reformer Nyanaponika takes the commentary to record a more authentic version of the contemporary liturgical formula. His intention is to recover what he believes is the original meaning of the *tisaraṇa* formula being, representing "a vow," "perhaps a kind of initiation," a "venerable ancient practice" of which the current, thrice-repeated "thoughtless recital of the formula is a degradation" (Nyanaponika 1965: 17–18).

John Ross Carter, in contrast, points at the possible functions of repetition, addressing issues of cognition, formality, control, and affect:

> The recitation of the triple refuge is ritually structured in a threefold repetition to develop reflective alertness. This repetitive pattern sets the expression apart from routine patterns in normal discourse, serves to check a participant from running roughshod through a communal affirmation that has echoed through history, and tends to engender a sense of thoroughness in personal involvement.
>
> (Carter 1982: 4)

Carter's observation, while stressing the regulatory character of the mode of utterance, is still in line with Nyanaponika's reading of the *tisaraṇa* as a vow, which echoes the novitiation (*pabbajjā*) and ordination (*upasampadā*) rite where the intersubjective effect of triple recitation is even more explicit.

The threefold refuge formula as recited by laypeople already appears in the Theravāda *Vinaya*, in which the monks are instructed to make the candidates worship the feet of the monks, to raise their hands, and to thrice recite the prescribed words (Vin I 22,14-22). The Sri Lankan *Upasampadā-kammavācā* (UK) prescribes the same procedure, embedded in a series of further threefold repetitions (shared with the *Kammavācanā* of the Mūlasarvāstivādins, *evaṃ dvir api tṛr api*, Shōno 2019: 83). In fact, at the beginning of the ceremony, after kneeling down, the candidate asks thrice to be admitted as a novice (*dutiyam … tatiyam pi aham bhante pabbajjaṃ yācāmi*), requests the ordaining monk thrice (*tatiyavāraṃ*) to accept the robes for the novice candidate shall receive, and then asks thrice (*tatiyavāraṃ*) to receive the robes back. He obtains them and then asks thrice to be imparted the refuges and the precepts. The refuges are then, sentence by sentence, recited to him by the ordaining monk, with the candidate repeating each of them, one by one, starting with the threefold repetition of the *tisaraṇa*. In this specific context of ritual authorization, it is not only the text in itself that repeats. The repeated text needs to be repeated (once), with the utterance made by the senior monk echoing in the voice of the emerging novice and thus confirming commitment, submission, reliability, and the most basic degree of competence. At this point in the liturgy repetition as a form of interaction stops. The ten precepts, in fact, are prescribed to be requested and recited only once, as are the confirmation of receipt of novitiation, the asking for permission to rise, paying obeisance to his senior, asking for forgiveness, and the sharing of merit. The repetition of the formula returns only once with the twofold (or threefold) exclamation of *sadhu* (UK 3–9). Repetition appears as a framing device that opens and closes by heightening attention and demanding interaction.

This also applies to the prominent repetition featuring in the Theravāda *Pātimokkha* (Pāt 4,8-6,2 = Vin I 102,33-103,11; Pāt 6,4-6), which states that each question directed at the monks during the fortnightly purificatory ritual of the *saṃgha* concerning their current state of purity, namely, *kacci 'ttha parisuddhā* ("Are you pure in this?"), is asked thrice by the speaker (*tatthāyasmante pucchāmi … dutiyampi* pucchāmi … *tatiyampi pucchāmi*) and that the monastic remaining silent each time signifies that no offense has been committed while not revealing a committed offense right up to the third time (*yāvatatiyaṃ*) the question is asked qualifies as a conscious lie (*saṃpajānomusāvādo*). The repetition of the question, here, is instrumental in establishing whether the act of purposefully withholding information is performed by the monastic "who remembers" (*saramānena*, Pāt 6,1) their deeds, as the commentary adds, due to inactivity (*akiriyā*) regarding "the door of speech" (Pāt-a 26,4-5). Here, asking the monk about his status thrice is not about giving the possible perpetrator the time to come up with a confession but rather to ensure the level of consciousness, which involves memory, so that a possible infringement may not be dismissed as due to a mere lack of attention. Repetition here, as in many comparable cases also in the *Prātimokṣa* of other schools, where monastics are "requested and reminded two to three times" to desist from an action before it is called a transgression (e.g., Prebish 1996: 58, 60, 68–69, 85), cannot be simply an encore or potentially open-ended, but an iteration that is delimited by a prescribed set of times that need to be completed to firmly establish a potential breaching of the law and to validate an action. Repetition in the *tisaraṇa* and in the *pātimokkha*, performed either by the "candidate" or by the "examiner," either as a promise or as a prompt, thus functions in diverse ways within comparable contexts of recurring ritual confirmation.

The threefold repetition, however, also occurs outside the ritual-juridical performative context in the pericopes of the hagiographical passages of the canon, with a person, as if ritually, addressing another three times before the narrative carries on, usually leading to the exposition of a sermon by the Buddha. That involves mostly visitors requesting the Buddha to answer a question and the Buddha accepting an invitation only at the third request (e.g., MN II 103–104) or either initially rejecting the question (e.g. MN I 387; SN IV 306,16-307,2) or addressing the question more fully (e.g. DN I 211,6-212,9) only at the third exhortation. More often and more strikingly in narrative texts, however, the threefold repetition fails to have the desired effect and thus leads to a turn of events. That includes such prominent passages as Subaddha's request to speak to the Buddha before his *parinibbāna*, thrice refused by Ānanda before the Buddha overrules his disciple (DN II 149–150); Raṭṭhapāla requesting his parents thrice to consent to him going forth and being denied it as many times (MN II 56–57); the people warning the Buddha thrice, to no avail, about Aṅgulimāla (MN II 98); the Buddha, unsuccessfully, admonishing the unruly monks of Kosambi, thrice (MN III 153); and the Buddha thrice rejecting Mahāpajāpatī's request to personally accept her donation (MN III 253), to give only a few prominent examples. Mark Allon has shown that in the canon plot elements involving the display of respect are particularly heavy on repetition (Allon 1997: 79–80). The depictions of rituals of hospitality, including establishing the right timing, demonstrating determination and submission, and receiving permission for an encounter involving instruction, paralleling what is prescribed in the *kammavācā*, fall into the same category. The other cases too may be understood this way, with the threefold repetition being the form of ritualized address that defines the formally faultless request. The request may either succeed or fail and by its very iteration implies that there are strong reasons for it being rejected but would still be considered as having been adequately delivered. The thrice-repeated address would thus appear to be a feature of rule-driven behavior, similar to the contexts of worship and monastic law, but also as a narrative device that builds, maintains, and releases narrative tension, just as it slows down, stretches, and articulates the flow of the recited text.

Textual composition

Repetition extends beyond Theravāda liturgy and the framing of specific forms of discourse to textual composition in Pāli more generally. Large sections of the Pāli scriptures consist, famously, just as does much of the older Buddhist literature more generally, of passages of varying length that are repeated with no or minimal, if often crucial variations within one and the same text. In the history of the study of Theravāda literature, this feature has attracted both scholarly interest and censure. T. W. Rhys Davids was one of the first scholars to point at "the use of stock phrases" in the *Tipiṭaka*, as well as at "the habit of repeating whole sentences or even paragraphs, which in our modern books would be understood or inferred, instead of being expressed" (Rhys Davids 1881: xxiii). The pioneer of Pāli Studies was keenly aware of the importance of these repetitions, warning that any "curtailing destroys at least the form and the emphasis of the originals," pleading with the reader not to let "the wearisome form ... shut out the very striking ideas which these suttas contain," and recommending instead "a little judicious skipping" (Rhys Davids 1881: xxiv–xxxv). Léon Féer, in contrast, held the view regarding the Saṃyuttanikāya, next to the Aṅguttaranikāya and the Abhidhamma, the collection in which this phenomenon recurs most often, that "[t]he tiresome repetitions ... form so great a proportion ... that important abridgements are required." (SN V, v–vi). This particular kind of concern is likely to be as old as the putting into writing of a previously oral corpus. It led the early redactors of the text to deploy the particles *pe*, *pa*, and *la*, variant Pāli abbreviations of the formulaic *peyyāla*, which may derive either from Ved. *paryāya*, "going round"; or from *peya-alaṃ*, "suitable to be filled"; or from *pātum-alaṃ*, "worthy to be preserved" (Levman 2020: 113). In Pāli manuscripts, the term denotes passages that have occurred previously in the text, which those familiar with the relevant textual compositional principles may be able to supply and vary as required, even if sometimes it remains unclear what exactly is to be repeated (Gethin 2007: 366). Early European editors relied on this convention, sometimes intervening to a higher degree than Sinhalese scholars were comfortable with, or not always, stating whether the abbreviation was in the text or whether it was made by the editor (Norman 2006: 113–114). In contrast to Rhys Davids's early appreciation of repetition or the translations by I.B. Horner, who, in Kenneth R. Norman's words, "makes the stories ... even more repetitive than the Pāli justifies" (Norman 2006: 70), in more contemporary Pāli translation practice, repetition is perceived as something that needs to be avoided, if not to say repressed, at all cost. Richard Gombrich records himself proposing, to Walpola Rahula's great consternation, "that it would be sensible to print the Canon in far shorter form" (Gombrich 2018: 62). Translators like Maurice Walshe and Bhikkhu Bodhi make ample use of ellipsis points, the latter showing an understanding for the fact that "[r]eaders of the Pāli suttas are invariably irked and sometimes dismayed by the ponderous repetitiveness of the texts" (SN-transl. Bodhi 41). While Bhikkhu Bodhi consciously eliminates repetitions through rephrasing in narrative contexts but is more conservative in doctrinal ones (SN-transl. Bodhi: 42), Walshe goes so far as to resort to content summaries set in italics (e.g. DN-transl. Walshe: 301–304). It is a peculiar disinterest in form and the expectation that the translator should take care of Rhys Davids's "judicious skipping" on behalf of the reader may explain why late twentieth- to early twenty-first-century translations earn considerable praise for their abridgments on popular online book distribution sites.

Norman (2006: 70–73) himself retains some ironic ambivalence when he confesses that "[r]epetition reaches its highest (or lowest, depending on how you look at it) level in Pāli, in my experience, in the *Alagaddūpamasutta*" (MN I 130–142), in which an erroneous view is repeated twelve times while, at the same time, indicating that the study of repetition may be critical for our understanding of the formation and functioning of Pāli texts. The interest of Buddhist Studies scholars in repetition springs from the puzzlement that Buddhist texts rely so much more on this feature than comparable Brahmanical ones (Gombrich 1990a: 7). Rather than seeing it as a form of "primitive speech" (Gonda 1959: 347), Richard Gombrich (1990b: 24) sees the origins of repetition in Buddhist texts in their supposed stress on content at the expense of sound, while Georg von Simson maintains that textual repetition mirrors the Buddhist attention to cyclical cosmological patterns (von Simson 1977: 148, quoted in Allon 1997: 361). Other authors (Rhys Davids xxiii; Norman 1881: 65; Allon 1997) have tried to build their arguments on function. With the consensus being that repetition in canonical Pāli texts is connected to their oral beginnings, the most persistent opinion is that it functions as a tool for accurate textual preservation. In his groundbreaking study of formal aspects of canonical sutta prose passages, Mark Allon (1997: 363) proposes repetition to be a mnemonic tool suited for senior reciters with little prior textual training who did not profit from the professionalization of the high-performance Brahmin reciters acquired early in life. Bhikkhu Anālayo (2007: 9) goes so far as to assume a lack of training of the early reciters to explain the uneven transmission of some of the pericopal repetitions. Diverging from this line of thought, Gethin points out that the variations contained in the repetitions pose a different and not necessarily lesser challenge to those who memorize these texts. He takes up three more possible functions referred to by Allon: "getting the message across," "cultivating mindfulness," and "enhancing the aesthetic appeal of the texts" (2007: 382). Gethin concedes that repetitions may be intended to highlight key doctrinal concepts, maintaining that the minute variations require "a certain mental alertness and agility" as "a practice for developing the Buddhist meditative virtues of mindfulness and concentration" (Gethin 2007: 382; Gethin 1992: 167; cp. Kwella 1978: 173). On the other hand, Gethin seems to want to dismiss the functionalist approach altogether, when he writes: "What is driving the repetitions seems to be the very requirement to repeat" (2007: 382), in other words, "repetition for its own sake" (2007: 383). By gesturing at repetitions involved in praying the rosary, Gethin makes the important point that "broader religious practices can help us understand the possible functions of repetition in early Buddhist texts" (2007: 383), suggesting that these other contexts may open up different modalities of function shared by very diverse texts. Repetition, particularly of those passages marked by *pe* or *la* and in need of being supplemented by the reciter may be understood, Gethin suggests, as "a religious exercise" (2007: 384; cp. Gethin 1992: 156). It is Gethin's intuition that in the case of repetition purely functionalist models may yield limited results and that repetition may be a more general and more differentiated way of doing things. Resistance to functionalism is something rites share with texts that are meant to be beautiful or otherwise formally appealing and it is the aesthetic quality of repetition (following Hermann Oldenberg, Gonda, and von Simson quoted in Allon 1997: 362; Levman 2020: 209, 215), that we pursue next.

Possibly the most well-known case of repetition in which beauty and ritual outweigh the legal or the mnemonic is the refrain *maṅgalam uttamaṃ* that concludes every single verse of the *Mahāmaṅgalasutta* (Sn 258–269 = Khp 2,23-3,26). The word *maṅgalaṃ*, which in its utterance designates, announces, and performs auspiciousness, is in this form repeated 12 times. Its qualification with *uttamaṃ* ("utmost") identifies it as on a different level than that of more common carriers of good fortune. In fact, its association with the diverse practices it modifies marks it as qualifying all that pertains to "a comprehensive vision of the Buddhist religious life" (Hallisey 1995: 414). Just as in the introduction of the Sinhalese commentary the humans' and deities' repeated naming of the most diverse things as auspicious covers the entire cosmos of the mundane (Hallisey 1995: 416–417), so the repetition in the verses helps enunciate one after the other the many acts and states that lead to well-being conceived in the Buddhist way. Repetition helps list, assemble, and complete all that is good, calling out every item and both recommending and adorning each with the same recurring powerful ring. The performance of this text in purificatory and protective rites (De Silva 1980: 111–115) speaks of the effect its most persistent lines are expected to have. If we take one step further into poetic territory while remaining in the *Suttanipāta*, repetition recurs in a very different form in the genre of dialogues in verse that are so characteristic for canonical poetry. When Sabhiya approaches the Buddha for advice, his address in the first stanza is echoed in the response he receives in the second:

> 'I am the one who has come from far away, anxious and full of doubt,' / said Sabhiya / 'and who is anxious to ask questions. / You be the one who takes care of them for me. You are the one who has been asked: / answer my questions, gradually and being faithful to the *dhamma*.' //

'You are the one who has come from far away' / said the Lord, 'and who is anxious to ask questions. / I am one who takes care of them for you. I am the one who has been asked: / I will answer your questions, gradually and being faithful to the *dhamma*.' //

kaṃkhī vecikicchī āgamaṃ / iti Sabhiyo / pañhe pucchituṃ abhikaṃkhamāno / tes' antakaro bhavāhi me pañhe me puṭṭho / anupubbaṃ anudhammaṃ vyākarohi me // Sn 510
dūrato āgato si Sabhiyā / ti Bhagavā / pañhe pucchituṃ abhikaṃkhamāno / tes' antakaro bhavāmi ti pañhe te puṭṭho / anupubbaṃ anudhammaṃ vyākatomi te // Sn 511.

Here the ritualized thrice-repeated and finally granted request of the prose passages discussed regarding ritual is replaced by a play of reprise between requester and bestower of metrically repeated syllables in which the Buddha grants, in fact promises to comply, by rephrasing the request. The request is repeated to formulate agreement, while the difference repetition allows the poet to make, enunciates both asymmetry and opportunity, turns requesting into bestowing, and reminds the surprised listener of how intimately he who requests and he who bestows are connected.

The potential of repetition for the articulation of difference is more prominent in another poetic form that appears also in the *Suttanipāta* but finds its richest representation in the *Saṃyuttanikāya's Sagāthāvagga*. The long duet of Dhaniya, the cattle baron, and the Buddha (Sn 18–33) consists of alternating stanzas in which, analogous to the *Mahāmaṅgalasutta*, the refrain remains the same, but similar to the verses involving Sabhiya, the Buddha reprises what Dhaniya has sung, keeping the lyric's structure and syntactic units unchanged, replacing key elements, and turning the words of the householder into the world of the mendicant:

'I am the one whose rice is cooked, whose cow is milked,' / said the cattle herd Dhaniya, / 'I live on the bank of the Mahī with my kin. / The hut is covered. The fire is stacked. / So, rain, god, if you please.' //
'I am the one whose wrath is no more, whose stiffness is gone,' / said the Lord. / 'I spend one night on the bank of the Mahī / The hut is uncovered. The fire is out. / So, rain, god, if you please.' //

pakkodano duddhakhīro 'ham asmi / iti Dhaniyo gopo / anutīre Mahiyā samānavāso / channā kuṭi āhito gini / atha ce patthayasī pavassa deva // Sn 18
akkodhano vigatakhīlo 'ham asmi / iti Bhagavā / anutīre Mahiy'ekarattivāso / vivaṭā kuṭi nibbuto gini / atha ce patthayasī pavassa deva // Sn 19

Heinrich Lüders identified *pakkodano/akkodhano* and *duddhakhīro/vigatakhīlo* as puns (Lüders 1954: §85), and Norman pointed out that °-*khīlo* would work better metrically and semantically but may have been assimilated to °-*khīro*, strengthening the repetitive effect (Sn transl. Norman 154). Norman also remarks that *samānavāso* may be the corrupt form of *samāsavāso* (staying for six months), which would echo *ekarattivāso* (staying for one night) much more accurately. In Sn 22–23 "my attentive cowherd wife" (*gopī mama assavā*) recurs as "my attentive mind" (*cittaṃ mama assavaṃ*), in Sn 33–34 "enjoys" (*nandati*) is turned into "grieves" (*socati*), and in Sn 26–27 the stanza would repeat verbatim were it not for the negative particles that make "cattle" return as "no-cattle." In Sn 33–34 (= SN I 240,17-241,7), the role of the prompter is transferred from Dhaniya to Māra, requiring a rejoinder that not only projects the other, better life but one that also contradicts and defeats Māra, the ultimate distorter. Contradiction is the aim of the many verses (*gāthās*) of the *Mārasaṃyutta* and the *Devatāsaṃyutta* that feature various unnamed godlings, Māra, the Buddha, and several mendicants; that cover not only conduct but also matters of cosmology and eschatology; and that are composed in the same duet form. Here we find an inverted refrain, with the first two half-verses (*pādas*) repeated almost verbatim and the divergences getting more pronounced as the poem progresses:

> Nights and days never run out. / Life does not come to an end. / The life force of mortals circles onward, / like the rim of the wheel around the hub. //
> Nights and days do run out. / Life does come to an end. / The life force of mortals is wanting, / like the water of a stream that's merely a trickle. //
>
> *nāccayanti ahorattā / jīvitaṃ nūparujjhati / āyu anupariyāti maccānaṃ / nemīva rathakubbaran ti //*
> *accayanti ahorattā / jīvitaṃ uparuhhati / āyu khīyati maccānaṃ / kunnadīnaṃ va odakan ti //* SN I 242,18-243,4.

In this example, as in many others collected in the two initial chapters (*vaggas*) of the *Saṃyuttanikāya*, we find a somewhat more subtle form of repetition at work than in the mere negation of cattle as an impediment toward the holy life. When the stanzas contrast "Night and days never run out" with "Nights and days do run out," we must assume that there is more to the repetition than someone merely contradicting someone who got his facts wrong. Māra's lines are not about showing that Māra simply doesn't know better, but that his thinking is wrong because of his erroneous conception of the world and his resistance to the liberatory power of renunciation and that he does not mean well. The better way to read these verses is to assume that Māra and the mendicant are referring to the same thing in different ways. For stanza one, there will always be, and one will always live to see, another day. One could even say that the series of days and nights is one that never ends. On the other hand, every night and every day ends, as does the sum of days and nights of a human life, suggesting a sense of urgency, which is what stanza two is about. This deployment of double entendre is even more obvious in those poems in which there is no negation to signal the difference the repetition provokes. In one poem, both the deity (*devatā*) and the Buddha begin their respective stanzas with

> Life leads to the close, the life force is weak. / For the person who has been lead unto old age there are no defenses. / The person who perceives the horror that is dying /
>
> *upanīyatī jīvitam appam āyu / jarūpanitassa na santi tāṇā / etaṃ bhayaṃ maraṇe pekkhamāno* / SN I 4,8-11,14-16

But while the deity concludes:

> should perform meritorious acts that lead to happiness.' //
>
> *puññāni kayirātha sukhāvahānī ti* // SN I 4,12,

the Buddha's coda is:

> and who is looking for peace should avoid the ruse that is the world.' //
>
> *lokāmisaṃ pajahe santipekkho ti* // SN I 4,17.

Here, the awareness of "the horror that is dying" is shared by the two speakers and, as such, is worth repeating. This means, at the very least, that the speakers have diverging views as to what to do about a situation they seem to agree upon. But one could also argue that the *devatā*'s advice is based on a misreading of the world which only the Buddha's verse identifies correctly as representing the ultimate trap. In fact, the commentary (SN-a 23,14-15) explains that the deity says these words with, in its mind, the many eons of life in heaven brought forth by meditation and has the Buddha remark that "[t]his deity is presenting a discourse on liberation that does not qualify as real liberation" (*ayaṃ devatā aniyānikaṃ* [Burm. *aniyyānikaṃ*] *vaṭṭa-kathaṃ kathethī ti*), "pointing out to him [or her] the undoing of becoming" (*vivattaṃ assa dessento*).

If one were to understand repetition as an *alaṅkāra*, that is, as something that is an "improvement" intended to both beautify and fortify a text, "a magical-religious expedient" that "applies to a sacred state" (Gonda 1975: 265) rather than an "ornamentation" in the common sense of the word, as it is frequently translated, the closest poetic form these repetitions come to is the *yamaka*, or "doubling." In poetics, at the most basic level, it refers to the repetition of identical syllables within a verse or over a certain amount of verses. Its formal aspects are theorized as early as in Bharata's *Nāṭyaśāstra*, where *yamaka* is listed as one of the four *alaṅkāras*, as well as in Daṇḍin's seventh- and eighth-century *Kāvyādarśa* and in the Pāli *Subodhālaṃkāra*, in which, as if prefiguring the ambivalence of modern editors and translators of Pāli, *yamaka* is uneasily located somewhere between an *alaṅkāra* and a defect (*dośa*; Wright 2002: 324, 332). In its most elaborate and popular form, prominent in Sanskrit *citrakāvya*, or "flashy poetry" (Tubb 2014: 151), a *yamaka* requires an identical sequence of syllables to be repeated as a whole that allows for more than one parallel meaning depending on how the words are broken up. Gary Tubb points out that one of the functions of this kind of *yamaka* is to "provide a somehow more intense opportunity to examine a particular word or group of words." "[T]he repetition of the word," Tubb writes, "forces us to think twice about its significance"; in fact, "in every instance of *yamaka* we are compelled to find a distinct meaning to go with the second utterance of the sounds" (2014: 161). While the *yamaka* had been denied any value for the production of the main emotionally effective aesthetic flavors, or *rasas*, particularly involving the erotic, by theorists such as Ānandavardhana (Pollock 2016, 74–75), Tubb shows that its echolike, hypnotic quality, similar to poetic forms based on sound (*śabdālaṅkāra*), may indeed be accepted to support the *adbhuta*, or miraculous, *rasa*, to present "something striking, something spectacular" (Tubb 2014: 188; cp. Stainton 224–225). The verbatim or close to verbatim repetitions of the *Sagāthāvagga* quoted earlier neither qualify as examples of internal rhyme nor do they display the virtuosity expected from a *citrakāvya*. They also do not appear, as in the poems (*mahākāvyas*) studied by Tubb, as the occasional flash that startles the connoisseur. Yet, we find in the Pāli verses both the subliminal ring of the refrain and the rhetorical device that forces the listeners or the readers to repeat, to pause, and to think again, to realize, to their surprise, that the same turns out to be different and that the effect and message of the poem lies in recognizing that difference.

Doctrine

Our exploration of repetition so far has closely followed the form of texts and their practice, observing from outside the text, so to speak, what these texts are made to do. That has meant that repetition so far has been considered predominantly in its performative and textual embodiment, in other words, as what the text does, not as what it tells us texts or humans are doing. To better understand what it is that drives repetition it is imperative that we take a closer look at what the Theravāda texts themselves tell us about repetition. In introductory verses of the *Sumaṅgalavilāsinī* the commentator of the Dīghanikāya states what he sets out to do:

Without diverging from the consensus held by the seniors, who are the luminaries in the lineage of the seniors, / who are well-versed in explaining and who reside at the Mahāvihāra, / I, leaving aside the variously repeated meaning, I shall clarify the meaning for the sake of the happiness of the good folks and the longevity of the dhamma. /

samayaṃ avilomento therānaṃ theravaṃsappadīpānaṃ / sunipuṇavinicchayānaṃ mahāvihārādhivāsīnaṃ // hitvā punappunāgataṃ atthaṃ atthaṃ pakāsayissāmi / sujanassa ca tuṭṭhatthaṃ ciraṭṭhitattthañ ca dhammassa // DN-a I 1,21-24

With all the repetition we have run through so far, it may come as a surprise to encounter, on the part of a writer of Pāli, a critical attitude toward repeating. The commentator, in fact, seems to build his very enterprise on "leaving behind" (*hitvā*) elaborations of meaning (*atthaṃ*) that have been repeated (literally "arrived at," °-*āgataṃ*), "again and again" (*punappuna-*). The verses seem to say that the exegetical process consists in separating what has been repeated from what still needs to be clarified. It also implies that distinguishing the two involves "not diverging" (*avilomento*) from the normative consensus (*samayaṃ*) regarding the text's meaning. In other words, the commentator need not repeat to be faithful, just as it is a requirement of a commentary to say things that have not been said yet. That agrees with a verse in another commentarial opening which says that the commentator is "commenting according to meaning not previously [commented on] (*atthaṃ apubbam anuvaṇṇayanto*, Paṭis-a 1,22). It is also clear, however, that the commentarial work is seen as more complex than dismissing the repeated and just adding the new. A passage in the *Visuddhimagga* brings back repetition by claiming that the good commentator should proceed "by apprehending the meaning and, having returned again to that meaning, by explaining it in many alternative ways" (*atthaṃ saṅgāhantena tam ev' atthaṃ punarāvattetvā aparehi pi pariyāyantarehi niddisantena ca*; Vism 522,23-24). Commenting, thus, involves a kind of repetition different from repeating the already known and, rather, one that returns to the same word and each time produces an ulterior meaning. Our previous reading of the verse *hitvā punappunāgataṃ atthaṃ atthaṃ pakāsayissāmi* (DN-a I 1,23) was based on the Chaṭṭhasaṅgāyana's editorial intervention that places a comma after *punappunāgataṃ*, thus distinguishing between the repeated meaning, on one hand, and the to-be-clarified meaning, on the other. That is in agreement with the variant in the passage in verses opening the *Aṭṭhasālinī* which has the same phrase *atthaṃ pakāyissāmi* (Dhs-a 2,5). The density of stylistic repetitions in the verses in question (*therānaṃ theravaṃsa-*, *punappuna-*, *tuṭṭhatthaṃ ciraṭṭhitatthaṃ*) and *-āgataṃ* concluding the eight syllables of a double *pāda*, however, suggests that the repetition *atthaṃ atthaṃ* may be also, at least rhetorically, read together as "meaning by meaning," as in the phrase *taṃ pana tattha tattha pakāsayissāma* (commenting on the first *saṅgīti*; Vin-ṭ Vajir 4) and in the sense of "I will give the commentary on meaning in the order of [the individual] words (*padānukkamato eva karissām'atthavaṇṇanaṃ*; Dhs-a 2,10).

The phrase *tattha tattha*, which echoes in the alternative reading *atthaṃ atthaṃ*, falls, like *punappunaṃ*, into the category of expressions where the repetition of the word itself denotes an event repeated over time, just as in *divase divase* ("day by day," e.g., Thī 437) or *suve suve* ("tomorrow and after-tomorrow," e.g., Dhp 229a) but also like *thokathokaṃ* and *khaṇe khaṇe* in the verse

Gradually the wise man may, bit by bit, from instant to instant / polish away his own fault, like a smith the tarnish [that appears] on sterling silver. //

anupubbena medhavī thokathokaṃ khaṇe khaṇe / kammāro rajatasseva niddhane malam attano // Dhp 239, where Dhp-a III 340,13–14 explains *khaṇe khaṇe* as *okāse okāse*, "from one opportunity to the next." These examples help illustrate the way the commentary is intended to repeatedly deal with meaning as it proceeds to elucidate the Buddha's word: repetition means not a return of the whole, such as required in recitation, but a distinct, successive, persistent, ongoing, selective, yet comprehensive exegetical coverage of the material, word by word, meaning by meaning. What emerges here is another aspect of repetition: that involving a forward movement in which the cumulative effect repetition has on those participating in it is crucial, because it is only thus that the projected illumination can be achieved.

To clarify this further we need to look at the repetition of words the commentaries and manuals resort to when referring to repetitive performances. In the *Visuddhimagga*, *anupassanā*, or contemplation, is explained as being *purimañāṇaṃ anu-anupassanato* (Vism 290,34), which Ñāṇamoli translates as "because of … re-seeing successively (*anu anu passanā*) each preceding kind of knowledge" (Vism transl. Ñāṇamoli 283). In another explanation of *anupassati* as *anu-anupassati*, we find it glossed further, reminding one of the sequence of meanings in commentarial discourse, as *anekehi ākārehi punappunaṃ passatī ti*, "one sees again and again due to multiple signs" (Vism 642,13–14). Here Ñāṇamoli simplifies his earlier translation of *anu-anupassati* to "he sees always accordingly" (Vism transl. Ñāṇamoli 665). The exegesis of *anu* extends to more terms that carry the same prefix. When talking about the ten recollections (*dasasu anussatisu*), the *Visuddhimagga* states "Awareness [or memory] (*sati*) is re-collection because it arises again and again" (*punappunaṃ uppajjanato sati yeva anussati*, Vism 197,4–5), and the commentary adds: *anu anu sati anussatī ti*, literally, "'[r]ecollection' (*anussati*) is awareness [or memory] (*sati*) [understood as operating] along (*anu*) and along (*anu*)" (Vism-mhṭ 123). The commentary's use of *anu anu* extends to explaining concurrent occurrence (*anu anu pavattana*, Vism-mhṭ 268) in breathing meditation or the piecemeal fashioning (*anu anu byañjana*, Vism-mhṭ 15) of stipulating an erroneous whole out of parts in the perception process. The prefix *anu-* denotes consistent placement or movement along, or close to, an extended area, usually an imagined line of progression, or more abstractly, a rule or norm. That would mean that *anu* bears not only the meaning of "strongly, persistently, completely" (Sazaki 1986: 15–18) but already in itself, as Julian Pas has pointed out, "some degree of intensity, or methodical order, or repetition" (Pas 1995: 255). The commentarial analysis of verbal forms denoting key mental practices reveals that their very functioning is premised on repetition, that one cannot perceive or remember properly without doing it again and again at different times and with different mental objects and maintaining the same orientation and thus building the intensity and quality of the performance.

The assumption that these formulations are based on an understanding of repetition requires us to make one more crucial step. So far, this study has assumed, maybe naively, that the English term *repetition* does indeed capture something that is going on in Pāli texts and, even more consequentially, that Theravāda texts are in fact concerned with. In order to raise our terminological self-awareness, however, we should bear in mind that there is no single word in Pāli that adequately translates as the English *repetition* (EPD s.v. repetition). The terms *punarutti* (or *-utta*) or *punakaraṇa* refer to concrete cases of repeated speech (even tautology) and repeated action, and there is a range of compounds beginning with *puna-* that refer to specific events that can repeat, such as, in the eschatological context, *puna(b)bhāva*, "renewed existence," or *pun'āvāsa*, "repeating living," or refer to a recurring unit of time, such as *punadivase*, "on the following day," or *punavāre*, "another time," or specific actions such as *punapavāraṇa*, "a repeated or renewed offer" (DP s.v. *pun(ar)-*). Even the word *punarāvatti*, a variant of which *punarāvartanaya*, mediated through Sanskrit, is used in modern Sinhala for English *repetition*, in Pāli merely denotes *return*, usually to a place. There is, however, a Pāli term that has been translated with *repetition*, and that is *āsevana* (or *āsevanā*). The *Pali–English Dictionary* (PED s.v. *āsevana*) sees reason to differentiate between "practice, pursuit, indulgence," on the one hand, and "succession, repetition," on the other, while the *Dictionary of Pāli* (DP s.v. āsevanā) proposes to consolidate the meaning of *āsevana* as "assiduous practice; habitual cultivation." Strikingly, the influential translations of the *Visuddhimagga* (Vism transls. Pe Maung, Ñāṇatiloka, Ñāṇamoli, Maës) and of the *Abhidhammatthasaṅgaha* (Abhidh-s & Abhidh-s-ṭ transl. Wijeratne & Gethin), two texts in which this term figures prominently, all feature *repetition*, *Wiederholung*, or *répétition*. This divergence from the DP entry may give pause, as in most of the passages in question it may be debatable whether *repetition* or *habitual cultivation* would make for the more compelling choice.

As early as in the *Visuddhimagga āsevana* appears to denote a certain mode of practice that leads to a specific sought-for state. Satisfaction in the sense of *āsevana* (*āsevana āsevanaṭṭhena sampahaṃsanā pariyosānaṃ*;Vism 148,14–16) is what is implied in the first of the four meditative states (*jhāna*), for the *jhāna*'s *āsevanā* takes place in that moment (*yā c'assa tasmiṃ khaṇe pavattā āsevanā*;Vism 149,20–21) in which the meditator experiences the *jhāna*. This reads as if *āsevana* refers to maintaining that state, not necessarily to its repetition. The term is also used when explaining how the performance of a certain mental mode called "conformity and change-of-lineage" (*anulomagotrabhūnaṃ*) in a single cognitive series occurs through *āsevana*, which leads to the required change. That mental performance is compared to that of a person who pole-vaults across a stream and who may land staggering if he is lacking in *āsevana* (*aladdhāsevanatāya*) regarding that specific feat (Vism 673,30–32). Here again *assiduous practice* may be more adequate than *repetition*, with repetitive action being merely one requirement of exercising. This rendering of *āsevana* would even work well in the stock phrase in which the term recurs ever so often as the first element of the triad, it forms together with *development* (*bhāvana*) and *cultivation* (*bahulīkamma*), or variants thereof, in sentences such as "'Virtues of such kind lead to the absence of remorse for the mind, ... to *āsevana*, to development, to cultivation, to fortification (*evarūpāni sīlāni cittassa avippaṭisārāya saṃvattanti ... āsevanāya ..., bhāvanāya ..., bahulīkammāya ..., alankārāya ...*;Vism 50,26–30). However, already the *bahulī-* in the term *bahulīkamma* may refer both to volume and to frequency. That the texts do address the repetitive nature of *āsevana* becomes clear in descriptions such as the following regarding recollection: "Thus, though he has recollected by any of these eight signs, [his] consciousness obtains *āsevana* due to attention [paid] again and again (*iti imesaṃ aṭṭhannaṃ ākārānaṃ aññataraññatarena anussarato pi punappunaṃ manasikāravasena cittaṃ āsevanaṃ labhati*;Vism 238,29–31). Here, *āsevana* is not identical with, but is obtained through, repeated action.

As Caroline A. F. Rhys Davids in her 1900 translation of *Dhammasaṅgaṇī* 1354 (Dhs transl. CAF Rhys Davids 329) still renders *āsevana* as "the pursuing," we probably owe to Shwe Zan Aung to have introduced *repetition* in his and C. A. F. Rhys Davids's 1915 translation of *Kathāvatthu* 509,35–510,20. In a footnote to their translation he notes:

> *Āsevanā*, from *āsevati*, to serve over and over again ... is a difficult term to translate. In the *Compendium* (p. 192, § 12) we used "succession," but repetition or even retention, is in some ways better. The Burmese translators render by "repetition so as to form a habit"; hence habitual repetition. (Kv transl. Shwe Zan Aung & CAF Rhys Davids 294)

However, as Shwe Zan Aung points out, his translation of *Abhidhammatthasaṅgaha* 41,14, renders *āsevanapaccayo* with "[the relation of] succession," in the footnote he already adds: "More lit. 'repetition of an action.' It is used for 'recurrence [*sic*]" (ADS transl. Shwe Zan Aung 192, fn. 3).

The Burmese genealogy of the translation is confirmed by the *Tipiṭaka pāḷi mranmā abhidhān*, which reflects the vernacular commentarial, or *nissaya*, tradition. It not only gives (TPMA s.v. *āsevana*) "remaining in effect," "subsisting" (*mhī vai khraṅ*) as the main meaning but also includes, at the very bottom of a six-item list, "adding" (*thap kā thap kā*, literally "piling-on, piling-on"), "acting upon repeatedly" (*pru lup khraṅḥ*), and "repeating" (*thui mvamḥ khraṅḥ*).

The *āsevanapaccaya*, the twelfth of the 24 *paccaya*s, or causal conditions, which Shwe Zan Aung refers to, is explained in the *Visuddhmagga* to be "like the effort [made] on various past occasions (*purima-purima-*) regarding [the memorization of] books etc." (*ganthādisu purimapurimabhiyogo viya*, Vism 538,4-5), with *purimapurima-* echoing the use of the duplicated prefix *anu anu* discussed earlier. The commentary on the *Abhidhammatthasaṅgaha* is even more specific:

> *Āsevana* is [a process by which] something is pervaded by something similar, which [in contrast] is [already] excellent on the account of it being strong due to [previously acquired] mastery [and so the thing that is pervaded] becomes of the same kind [i.e. also excellent],—like the [recitation of] a book that has been constantly studied on various past occasions [affects] the [recitation of] the book on various future occasions.
>
> (*purimapurimaparicitagantho viya uttaruttaraganthassa kusalādibhāvena attasadisassa paguṇa balavabhāvavisiṭṭattasamānajātiyatāgāhaṇam āsevanaṃ*; Abhi-s-ṭ 186,23–25)

Nyāṇatiloka when explaining the "repetition-condition" (*āsevanapaccaya*) refers expressly to "just as in learning by heart, th[r]ough constant repetition, the later recitation becomes gradually easier and easier" (Nyāṇatiloka 1980: 143). Past repetition is the condition for the successful repetition of actions in the future. These passages identify neither *anu anu* or *purima purima*, nor the achieved habitual mastery with *āsevana*. Rather, *āsevana* understood as causal condition seems to be the power produced by repeated practice that explains how doing things again leads to mastery. In other words, if we were to translate *āsevana* with *repetition*, *repetition* would need to mean more than just "doing something again." One of the conditions of mastery is to do something again, but only after having already done it many times, which is why the commentary on the *Abhidhammaṭṭhasaṅgaha* also speaks of the mental impulsions of karmic volitions (*javana*) "acquiring *āsevana* again and again" (*punappunaṃ laddhāsevanāni*; Abhi-s-ṭ 147,3), in this case in the process of relinking (*paṭisandhi*) in the karmic flow from one birth to the next. In order to do things again drawing from one's mastery, *āsevana*, the power to repeat, can and needs to be reactivated again and again. This passage further shows that *āsevana* is also used on a much more basic level than just to explain competence. In fact, it is meant to explain aspects of the very functioning of *kamma*. The repetitive power of *āsevana* does not just lie in doing something again, but in the recurrence of the units of mental activity: "[I]t is only through two instances of conforming consciousness and not one alone that one achieves the causal condition of *āsevana* (*dvīhi anulomacittehi bhavitabbaṃ*; *na hi ekaṃ āsevanapaccayaṃ labhati*, Vism 675,22–24). *Āsevana* becomes relevant for explaining the emergence of possible causal events, or dhammas, based on the diverse powers inherent in the past of which *āsevana* is one (Abhi-s-ṭ 193,10). The serial arrangement of the smallest elements that constitute the mental karmic flow lends itself to an understanding of causation in which repetition plays a key role.

The Theravāda assumption that things can and must repeat on this most basic ontological level for karma to function has not remained unchallenged, as one reply to a heretic view in the *Kathāvatthu* proves. There the Theravādin has to contend with the challenge by certain heretics, vaguely called "Those of the Northern Path" (Uttarapāthakas), that "[a]s all dhammas are momentary and as, after something has been there only for an instant, [there is] nothing, that in fact performs *āsevana* (*āsevati*) as a causal condition of repetition, there exists no such thing as the causal condition of *āsevana*" (*tattha yasmā sabbe dhammā khaṇikā, na koci muhuttaṃ pi ṭhatvā āsevanapaccayaṃ āsevati nāma, tasmā natthi kiñci āsevanapaccayatā*, Kv-a 197,23–198,2). In other words, how can anything repeat, if what is expected to repeat is no longer there after enduring only for a single moment in time? Would not repetition through that which links the identical and the different across time imply the duration of something that is more extended than the singular momentary? The *Kathāvatthu* (Kv 618,18–620,3) responds by abandoning the level of *dhamma*s, returning to the level of conventional practice, and presenting a canonical passage (AN IV 247,8–248,13). The passage states that, if "repeated, developed, practiced frequently" (*āsevito bhāvito bahulīkato*) correct views, correct purpose, and so on lead to the deathless state, whereas killing, stealing, and so on lead to terrible births. The bad things, if done "very lightly" (*sabbalahu*, meaning, maybe, if repeated "less often" or done "just once"), lead to birth as a human whose life is bound to be short. Repetition happens and it matters, because living beings owe their future experiences to having done certain things more than once.

The place that we find ourselves in at the end of this study, the textual environment of Theravāda scholastic debate surrounding what may come closest to the English term *repetition*, is by no means intended to serve as a privileged place from which to review and reread the texts and practices previously discussed. There is no indication whatsoever that what the scholastic texts say about *āsevana* and the workings of the mind may in any way function as a master key to our understanding of what is going on in the commentators' exegetical method that resists repeating only to progress from word to word, in the *yamaka*-like verses of the *Suttanipāta* or the *Sagāthāvagga* that playfully allow the same to surprise us by becoming different, in the *Mahāmaṅgalasutta* that needs to repeat in order to name all that is auspicious, in the massive iterations that have helped build the corpus of the suttas, or in the seasonal or daily, lay or monastic scansions of confirmation and control or submission and devotion. On the contrary, as the example of the re-reading of books in the explanation of *āsevana* shows, it may be all these other practices that give meaning to rationalizations of how the mind works and, beyond that, meaning to each other. The beauty of an unexpected divergence may be hidden in rituals and texts that look all the same. Discipline and dedication may emerge out of a couplet varied ever so slightly. And the scholastic problem of the similar versus the same in mental repetition may allow us to think differently about how a good *yamaka* is composed or what makes for a successful ritual. Still, we need to also keep in mind that the rules for acting ritually, composing poetry, and explaining the mind are distinct and are kept distinct by the texts we study. Just as the English *time* may be a word too clunky or too overdetermined to be useful for exploring what is going on between doing something and doing something again and may itself become filled with new meaning when repetition asks us to think again, so repetition itself may be equally inadequate to capture the differences it claims to contain. And yet it has allowed us to collect and precariously assemble a range of practices that may do more than just be different from or reducible to the other. In fact, rather than using one to explain the other by positing either the synchronic regimentation of bodies or the momentary authority of the beautiful or the recursive agenda of mental cultivation as primary for this peculiar form of doing things, it may be more appropriate to understand each of these various instances of repetition as repetitions of the other.

References

Abhidh, S., Abhidh, S.T. 1989. *The Abhidhammatthasaṅgaha of Bhadantācariya Anuruddha and the Abhidhammatthavibhāvinī-ṭīkā of Bhadantācariya Sumaṅgalasāmi*, ed. Hammalawa Saddhatissa. Oxford: The Pali Text Society.

Abhidh, S. transl. Shwe Zan Aung = 1967. *Compendium of Philosophy*, translated by Shwe Zan Aung. London: The Pali Text Society.

Abhidh, S., Abhidh, S.T. transl. Wijeratne & Gethin = 2007. *Summary of the Topics of Abhidhamma (Abhidhammatthasaṅgaha) by Anuruddha. Exposition of the Topics of Abhidhamma (Abhidhammatthavibhāvinī) by Sumaṅgala*, translated by R.P. Wijeratne, Rupert Gethin. Lancaster: The Pali Text Society.

Allon, Mark. 1997. *Style and Function. A study of the dominant stylistic features of the prose portions of Pāli canonical sutta texts and their mnemonic function.* Tokyo: The International Institute for Buddhist Studies.

AN = *The Aṅguttara-Nikāya*, edited by Richard Morris, E. Hardy, & Mabel Hunt. 2nd ed. [1961] 1999.

Anālayo, Bhikkhu. 2007. "Oral Dimensions of Pali Discourses: Pericopes, other mnemonic techniques and the oral performance context." *Canadian Journal of Buddhist Studies* 3: 5–33.

Bloomfield, Maurice. 1916. *Rig-Veda Repetitions. The repeated verses and distichs and stanzas of the Rig-Veda in systematic presentation and with critical discussion.* Cambridge, MA: Harvard University Press.

Bond, George Doherty. 1982. "The Buddha as Refuge in the Theravāda Buddhist Tradition." In *The Threefold Refuge in the Theravāda Buddhist Tradition*, eds. John Ross Carter, George Doherty Bond, Edmund F. Perry, Shanta Ratnayaka, 16–32. Chambersburg, PA: Anima Books.

Bruhn, Klaus. 1983. "Repetition in Jaina Narrative Literature." *Indologica Taurinensia* 11: 27–75.

Carter, John Ross. 1982. "The Notion of Refuge (Saraṇa) in the Theravāda Tradition." In *The Threefold Refuge in the Theravāda Buddhist Tradition*, eds. John Ross Carter, Bond George Doherty, Edmund F. Perry, Shanta Ratnayaka, 1–15. Chambersburg, PA: Anima Books.

Collins, Steven. 1998. *Nirvana and Other Buddhist Felicities. Utopias of the Pali imaginaire.* Cambridge: Cambridge University Press.

De Silva, Lynn. 1980. *Buddhism: Beliefs and Practices in Sri Lanka* (2nd ed.). Colombo: Ecumenical Institute.

Dhs transl. CAF Rhys Davids = *A Buddhist Manual of Psychological Ethics*, translated by Caroline A. F. Rhys Davids. 3rd ed. Oxford: The Pali Text Society, [1900] 2004.

Dhs-a = *The Atthasālinī. Buddhaghosa's Commentary on the Dhammasaṅgaṇi*, edited by Edward Müller. Bristol: Pali Text Society, [1897] 2011.

DN-a = *The Sumaṅgala-vilāsinī, Buddhaghosa's Commentary on the Dīgha Nikāya*, edited by T. W. Rhys Davids and J. Estlin Carpenter. 3 vols. 2nd ed. London: The Pali Text Society, 1968–1971.

DN transl. Walshe = *Thus I Have Heard.* 1987. *The Long Discourses of the Buddha*, translated by Maurice Walshe. London: Wisdom.

DP = *A Dictionary of Pāli*, compiled by Margaret Cone. Vol. 3. Bristol: The Pali Text Society, 2020.

EPD = Buddhadatta Mahāthera. 1979. *English – Pali Dictionary*. London: The Pali Text Society.

Freschi, Elisa, Maas, Philipp A., eds. 2017. *Adaptive Reuse. Aspects of creativity in South Asian cultural history.* Wiesbaden: Harrassowitz Verlag.

Gethin, Rupert M.L. 1992. "The *Mātikās*: Memorization, Mindfulness, and the List." *In the Mirror of Memory. Reflections on mindfulness and remembrance in Indian and Tibetan Buddhism*, ed. Janet Gyatso, pp. 149–172. Albany: SUNY Press.

Gethin, Rupert M.L. 2008. "What's in a Repetition? On counting the suttas of the Saṃyutta-nikāya." *Journal of the Pali Text Society* 29: 365–387.

Gombrich, Richard. 1990a. "Recovering the Buddha's Message." In *The Buddhist Forum*, I, eds. Tadeusz Skorupski, pp. 5–20. London: SOAS University of London.

Gombrich, Richard. 1990b. "How Mahāyāna Began." *The Buddhist Forum*, I, ed. Tadeusz Korupski, 21–30. London: SOAS University of London.

Gonda, Jan. 1959. *Stylistic Repetition in the Veda.* Amsterdam: N.V. Noord-Hollandsche Uitgevers Maatschappij.

Gonda, Jan. 1975. *Selected Studies. Vol. II. Sanskrit Word Studies.* Leiden: E. J. Brill.

Kv transl. Shwe Zan Aung & CAF Rhys Davids = *Points of Controversy or Subjects of Discourse, being a translation of the Kathā-Vatthu from the Abhidhamma-Piṭaka* by Shwe Zan Aung and Rhys Davids. Oxford: The Pali Text Society [1915] 1993.

Kwella, Peter. 1978. "Some Remarks on Style in Some Buddhist Sanskrit Texts." *Indologica Taurinensia* 6: 169–175.

Levman, Bryan G. 2020. *Pāli, the Language. The medium and message*. Newcastle: Cambridge Scholars Publishing.

Lüders, Heinrich. 1954. *Beobachtungen über die Sprache des buddhistischen Urkanons*. Berlin: Akademie-Verlag.

MN = *The Majjhima-Nikāya*, edited by V. Trenckner. 4 vol. Oxford: The Pali Text Society, [1888] 1993.

Ñāṇatiloka. [1952] 1980. *Buddhist Dictionary. Manual of Buddhist terms and doctrines*. Kandy: Buddhist Publication Society.

Nyanaponika. 1965. *The Threefold Refuge*. Kandy: Buddhist Publication Society.

Oldenberg, Hermann. 1917. *Zur Geschichte der altindischen Prosa: Mit besonderer Berücksichtigung der prosaisch-poetischen Erzählung*. Berlin: Weidmannsche Buchhandlung.

Pas, Julian F. 1995. *Visions of Sukhāvatī. Shan-tao's commentary on the Kuan wu-liang-shou-Fo ching*. Albany: SUNY.

Pollock, Sheldon. *A Rasa Reader. Classical Indian Aesthetics*. New York: Columbia University Press, 2016.

Prebish, Charles S. [1996] 2002. *Buddhist Monastic Discipline. The Sanskrit Prātimokṣa Sūtras of the Mahāsāṃghikas and the Mūlasarvāstivādins*. Delhi: Motilal Banarsidass.

Ramanujan, A.K. 1991. "Repetition on the Mahābhārata." In *Essays in the Mahābhārata*, ed. Arvind Sharma, 419–443. Leiden: Brill.

Rhys Davids, T.W. transl. 1881. *Buddhist Suttas*. Oxford: Clarendon Press.

Sazaki, Genjun H. [1986], 1992. *Linguistic Approach to Buddhist Thought*. Delhi: Motilal Banarsidass.

von Simson, Georg. 1977. "Zur Phrase *yena … tenopajagāma / upetya* und ihren Varianten im buddhistischen Sanskrit." In *Beiträge zur Indienforschung. Ernst Waldschmidt zum 80. Geburtstag gewidmet*, ed. Heinz Bechert, 479–488. Berlin: Museum für Indische Kunst.

Sn = *Suttanipāta*, edited by Dines Andersen and Helmer Smith. Oxford: The Pali Text Society, [1913] 2017.

Sn-transl. Norman = *The Group of Discourses (Sutta-Nipāta)*, translated by K. R. Norman. 2nd ed. Bristol: The Pali Text Society, [1992] 2015.

SN = *Saṃyutta-Nikāya* edited by M. Leon Féer. 5 vols; vol. 1 edited by G.A. Somaratne. Oxford: The Pali Text Society, 1888–1998.

SN-transl. = *The Connected Discourses of the Buddha:* 2000. *A translation of the Saṃyutta Nikāya*, transl. by Bhikkhu Bodhi. Somerville: Wisdom.

Shōno, Masanori. 2019. "How to Become a Buddhist Monk. A Re-edition of the Gilgit Karmavācanā Texts." *Bulletin of the International Institute for Buddhist Studies* 2: 57–106.

Stainton, Hamsa. 2019. *Poetry as Prayer in the Sanskrit Hymns of Kashmir*. New York: Oxford University Press.

TPMA = *Tipiṭaka pāḷi mranmā abhidhān*. 22 vols. Rankun: Sāsanā reḥ ūḥ cīḥ ṭhāna puṃ nhip tuik, 1964–2017.

Tubb, Gary. 2014. "Kāvya with Bells On: Yamaka in the Śiśupālavadha; Or, 'What's a flashy verse like you doing in a great poem like this?'" In *Innovations and Turning Points: Toward a History of Kāvya Literature*, eds. Yigal Bronner, David Shulman, Gary Tubb, 142–194. Delhi: Oxford University Press.

UK = J. F. Dickson 1875. "The Upasampadá-Kammavácá Being the Buddhist Manual of the Form and Manner of Ordering of Priests and Deacons. The Páli Text, with a Translation and Notes." *The Journal of the Royal Asiatic Society of Great Britain and Ireland* 7 (NS), 1: 1–16.

Vism = *The Visuddhi-Magga of Buddhaghosa*, edited by C. A. F. Rhys Davids. London: The Pali Text Society, [1920] 1975.

Vism-mhṭ = *Visuddhimaggamahāṭīkā*. Chaṭṭha Saṅgāyanā CD-ROM Edition, Version 4. Igatpuri: Vipassana Research Institue, 1995.

Vism transl. Maës = *Buddhaghosa. Visuddhimagga. Le chemin de la pureté*, translated by Christian Maës. Paris: Fayard, 2002.

Vism transl. Ñāṇamoli = The Path of Purification. Visuddhimagga, translated by Bhikkhu Ñāṇamoli. Onalaska, WA [Kandy, 1975a] 1999.

Vism transl. Ñyāṇatiloka = *Visuddhi-magga oder der Weg zur Reinheit: die grösste und älteste systematische Darstellung des Buddhismus*, translated by Ñyāṇatiloka. 3rd ed. Konstanz: Christiani [München, 1931] 1975b.

Vism transl. Pe Maung Tin = *The Path of Purity: being a translation of Buddhaghosa's Visuddhimagga*, translated by Pe Maung Tin. London: Luzac, [1923–1931] 1971.

Wright, J.C. 2002. "The Pali Subodhālaṅkāra and Daṇḍin's Kāvyādarśa." *Bulletin of the School of Oriental and African Studies* 65 (2): 323–341.

10

FILIAL PIETY

Shades of difference across Theravādin traditions

Grégory Kourilsky

Introduction

If matricide and parricide are at the top of the list of the "five irremissible sins" (P. *anantariyakamma*), which make salvation impossible for the one who commits them (Sp II 444), Buddhist teachings as articulated in the Pāli canonical sources of the Mahāvihāra, in principle the authoritative texts of the tradition of Buddhism labeled as "Theravāda," are not normally seen as demonstrating much concern about filial piety. Although mentioned in places, devotion to parents does not count, for example, among the "perfections" (P. *pāramitā*) illustrated by the last ten lives (P. *jātaka*) of the Bodhisatta (Durt 2006: 239). This is hardly surprising for a religion that rests on the ethic of *karma* (P. *kamma*)—according to which the fate of a being remains strictly individual, resulting only from their actions in this or previous existences—and recommends, at least in its founding texts, the renunciation of filial and familial ties, often regarded as an obstacle on the path to liberation. One needs only recall the *Dhammapada* comparing the maternal bond to a tie that must be severed (Dhp 80), or the episode of Prince Siddhattha's "great renunciation" (P. *mahābhinikkhamana*) in which he abandons his kingdom, his parents, his wife and his son to follow his own path to Enlightenment. What little is known of other Indian Buddhist schools does not allow us to say that it was any different for their followers.

Yet Buddhism as practiced in Thailand, Laos, Cambodia, Burma, and Sri Lanka places—to varying extents—great value in filial piety (understood as to support and respect one's living parents or forebears, as well as to worship them after their death). Admittedly, Theravāda Buddhism is not unique in that respect. Both historically and in other Buddhist cultures the question of the relationship between the Buddhist ascetic ideal and the aspirations of ordinary society has manifested in a variety of ways. However, the fact that the Pāli canon is commonly perceived as the repository of the original doctrine taught by the Buddha certainly makes it more challenging to consider the value of filial piety and the ideal of Buddhist renunciation as anything other than in tension. The purpose of this chapter is thus to consider the place occupied by parents and ancestors in these Buddhist societies and to understand how, and to what extent, the latter have been able to harmonize social and familial accounts with the "Teaching of the Buddha" (P. *Buddhasāsana*), on which spirituality is understood to rest.

DOI: 10.4324/9781351026666-13

Filial piety in the Pāli scriptures

Although canonical writings in Pāli or in Sanskrit may present filial and family ties as obstacles for the faithful on the road to deliverance, Indian Buddhist practice does not require the faithful to renounce a sense of filial piety: if the Buddha intended to free himself from the values and constraints of a prevalent Brahmanism, he had to take into account the concerns of his fellow men, if only to better convert them to his teaching. Brahmanic society, today as in the time of the historical Gotama, places great value on the relationship between the faithful and their parents. In this connection, rites performed for the benefit of ancestors held an important place in India and they have been, in part, integrated into Buddhist practices, albeit in different forms according to place and time. Moreover, Brahmanism also requires the faithful to manifest devotion toward parents during their lifetime and to fulfill a certain number of duties toward them. The first of these duties is for a son to ensure his descent, thus guaranteeing filiation and the transmission of goods within the lineage, as well as freeing one's father from the congenital debt owed to his own ascendants, which his son then takes over on his own account (Dumont 1980: 16). The Buddha himself did not depart from this rule: he was married and the father of a young boy, Rāhula, when he left his palace to embrace the life of an ascetic. By this particular, potent example, no doubt, the writers of the Buddhist texts intended to show that Gotama's doctrine was not indifferent to the fundamental values of the Indian world.

Generally speaking, with the *Tipiṭaka* and its exegesis, Buddhist writers have tried to answer the questions that the individual was entitled to ask regarding the obligations imposed on them by traditional society. This led Buddhist texts to sometimes encourage a certain form of devotion to parents. In such instances, the Buddha ensures, however, the reappropriation of notions or customs already in use among the communities—primarily Brahmins. These were to be converted, in order to make them conform to his doctrine. An example of this process is a passage of the *Itivuttaka*, in which the Buddha takes over the notion of *Brahma-cariya* (conduct consistent with Brahman) but gives it a new definition. In the following extract, he considers respect for father and mother as one of the conditions for the "virtuous conduct" of an individual:

> Father and mother, O monks, are called 'Brahma'; they are called, O monks, 'pre-eminent deities' (*pubba-devatā*); they are also called, O monks, 'pre-eminent masters' (*pubbācāriyā*), and finally, monks, 'worthy of offerings' (*āhuneyyā*). What is the reason for this? Because, O monks, parents cover their children with blessings, they nourish them and are for them like a guide in this world.
>
> (It 110, AN I 62)

In an example from the *Aṅguttara-nikāya*, the Buddha answers the questions of a Brahmin about sacrifice. Keeping the Brahmanical terminology used by his interlocutor, he enumerates "three types of fire" (P. *tayo aggī*), which are parents, relatives, and recluses (AN IV 44). In the *Sigālovāda-sutta* (or *Siṅgāla-sutta*), the Buddha, or the Blessed One (P. *Bhagavant*) as he is regularly called in the Pāli canon, also analogously reinterprets the Brahmanic rite that consists in venerating the cardinal points and thereby encourages filial piety:

> In five ways, as a son of a house, a child must venerate his parents, towards the East [thinking]: "Having supported me, I must support them, I must carry out their tasks, I must maintain the lineage, I must take over the patrimony, I must, finally, make offerings for the benefit of my deceased parents (*petānaṃ*)."
>
> (DN III 189)

Canonical texts can also approach the subject of filial piety in a more direct way. The *Samacitta-sutta* (or *Kataññu-sutta*), for example, insists on the necessity, and the difficulty, of paying back the benefits received from one's parents:

> Monks, there are two [people] who cannot be paid back. What are they? His mother and father. Even if you carried your mother on one shoulder and your father on the other, and if you had to live like that for a hundred years, taking care of them, anointing them with ointment, massaging them, bathing them and rubbing their limbs, and even if they came to drop their excrement on you, you couldn't pay your parents back. Moreover, O monks, even if one establishes one's parents in supreme authority, reigning over the earth abundant in the Seven Treasures, one could not pay one's parents back. What is the reason for this? Because, O monks, parents grant many benefits (P. *bahukārā*) to their children: they bring them up, feed them and are a guide for them in this world.
>
> (AN I 62)

The *sutta* then takes a subtly proselytizing turn by explaining that only the parents' conversion to the Buddha's doctrine will enable the child to repay their debt. Here again the Buddha set an example, first by returning to Kapilavatthu to convert his father and then ascending to the heaven of Tāvatiṃsa to preach to his mother, Mahā-Māyā, who died seven days after giving birth.[1] In this connection, several canonical and paracanonical texts allude to the suffering endured by the mother during gestation and childbirth:

> Thus, monks, it is with great anxiety for her heavy burden that the mother, for nine or ten months, carries the foetus in the womb. Thus, monks, it is with great anxiety for her heavy burden that after nine or ten months, the mother gives birth [to the child]. When [the child] is born, she feeds it with her own blood; it is for this reason that the mother's milk is called, in the Ariya discipline, "the blood of life" (P. *lohitañhetaṃ*).
>
> (MN I 266)[2]

The subject of filial piety is further discussed in the *Mātuposaka-sutta*, in which the Buddha states that a monk can support his parents by sharing with them the fruits of almsgiving (Strong 1983: 175), or in the *Cīvarakkhandhaka* (Vin I), which contains a brief allusion to the question of a monk's duty toward his parents (Schopen 2007: 117–118). Mention should also be made of the *Petavatthu* and *Vimānavatthu* collections and their commentaries (Pv-a, Vv-a), in which several accounts relate how a *sāvaka* or fervent devotee comes, driven by a sense of filial piety, to the aid of their parents—from this life or a previous one—who were reborn in the state of "hungry ghost" (P. *peta*, < Sk. *preta*, Pv 17–19, 39, for example). The *Tirokuḍḍapetavatthu* Commentary (Pv-a 31f) is undoubtedly the most representative account of this theme. Bimbisāra, the pious king of Rājagaha, finds himself annoyed by a group of hungry *peta* who turn out to be deceased members of his relatives. He tries to comfort them with oblations, but his efforts are in vain: water and food disappear at the very moment the *peta* try to eat them. Bimbisāra reports to the Buddha, who explains to him that it is impossible to make offerings to the dead by direct means; on the other hand, if these are presented to the community of monks, the deceased will receive the fruit of the merit produced by this pious act and will thus be able to gain a new life under better auspices.

Also worthy of consideration are later Pāli works composed in mainland Southeast Asia, especially in the Lanna kingdom (in present-day northern Thailand) in the fifteenth and sixteenth centuries. Although it makes use mainly of the Pāli corpus of the Mahāvihāra, locally composed religious literature has from its beginning shown a predilection for the theme of filial piety. The *Jinakālamālī*, a Lanna chronicle composed in Pāli by Ratanapañña in 1516, for example, tells that the *Bodhisatta* went to Suvannabhūmi (i.e., the Indochinese peninsula) with the aim to bring gold from there to wait on his mother in comfort. As the ship was wrecked along their journey, the chronicle goes on, he carried his mother on his shoulders across the ocean, a deed sufficent for Brahma to recognize him as a future Enlightened One (Jinak 2). The story of the *Bodhisatta* saving his mother from a shipwreck is also found in other Pāli texts originating from or widespread in Southeast Asia, such as *Sotatthakī-mahānidāna*, *Tathāgatuppatti*, *Sambhāravipāka*, and *Mahāsampiṇḍa-nidāna*.[3]

The *Maṅgalatthadīpanī* of Sirimaṅgala, composed in Chiang Mai in 1524, dedicates five chapters—out of a total of 38—to filial piety and devotion toward one's forebears. Among them the most extensive is Chapter 11, the "Discourse on Supporting One's Parents" (*Mātapitu-upaṭṭhāna-kathā*). It begins by recalling the suffering of the mother, from the throes of gestation to the education of the child—here relying on the *Soṇananda-Jātaka* (Ja II no. 532). The text goes on to say that parents, through their efforts and sacrifices for the welfare of their child, are their "first benefactors" (P. *pubbakārī-jana*, "those who have done [the good] first"). Conversely, children are "[those] who must show them gratitude" (P. *kataññū-katavedīno*). *Mātāpitu-upaṭṭhānakathā* then lists the four types of "virtues" (P. *upakāra-guṇa*) that parents are endowed with and that must be recognized by their children, namely, the virtue of being "Brahma," "the first deities" (*pubba-devatā*), "the first masters" (*pubbācāriya*), and "worthy of offerings" (P. *āhuneyya*; It 110, see the earlier discussion). In return for the blessings received from one's parents, the practitioner must support them and looking after them (P. *upaṭṭhāna*), both during their lifetime and after death. Filial duty is also illustrated through the story of Bimbisāra and the *peta* from the *Petavatthu* aforementioned, and an additional argument drawing on the *Sabhramaka-sutta* and *Siṅgalasutta*. Sirimaṅgala finally insists on the difficulty to pay back one's parents', quoting widely the *Samacitta-sutta* (or *Kataññu-sutta*; AN II 62): even if one covers his father and his mother with tributes, the text says, even if one provides them with water and food, nappies and clothes, even if one anoints them with ointments, bathes them, washes their feet for a hundred years, the son (or the daughter) would not manage to repay their debt to them. Following the *sutta*, the commentator goes on to explain that only by converting the parents to the Buddha's doctrine will the child be able to repay the debt they have contracted toward them. The four other chapters of Maṅg-d dealing with the issue of filial piety are in the same vein, focusing on the related issues of "devotion" (viz. *Pūjā-kathā*, chapter 3), "kindness toward children" (viz. *Puttadārasaṅgaha-kathā*, chapter 12), "kindness toward relatives" (viz. *Ñātakasaṅgaha-kathā*, chapter 17), and "gratitude" (viz. *Kataññnutā-kathā*, chapter 25).

A number of Buddhist writings in Pāli therefore encourage devotion toward one's parents, during their lifetime as well as after their death. These remain, however, in a limited number compared to the Pāli corpus as a whole. One might see them as pledges given to those who might have been put off by an overly demanding doctrine and who hesitated to convert. Other sources, on the other hand, are more clearly reflective of lived Buddhism, showing a greater concern for filial piety in Theravādin societies.

"Sharing merit": Filial piety in Buddhist practice

Buddhism was not born in a vacuum. Despite obvious changes and evolution, Buddhist practice, as well as underlying conceptions and beliefs, appear to be a continuity of religious traditions that prevailed before the advent of Gotama's doctrine. In the Indic world as in Southeast

Asia,[4] Buddhism appears to have developed within the framework of Vedic, Brahmanical, and autochthonous systems of thought and representations. Contrary to what might be assumed, the relationship between these different religious traditions shows more continuities that ruptures, at least in terms of beliefs, conceptions, and practice. The notion of *karma*, for instance, was obviously not born with Buddhism but is an integral part of Indian thought as manifested in Hinduism and Brahmanism. Similarly, the question of the "sharing" of karma—understood here as a consequence of the act and not as the act itself—with a third person is already present in these religious currents.[5] This practice is connected to the idea, shared in both Brahmanical and Buddhist societies, that one's *karma* is connected to the *karma* of one's lineage—which obviously challenges the perception of *karma* as something stricly individual that comes through in canonical Buddhist scriptures. This conception of a collective and family *karma* considerably reinforces the weight of the merit and the faults accomplished, because an individual takes responsibility not only for their own condition but also for that of their ascendants and, eventually, descendants.

Therefore, it comes as no surprise that the production, sharing, or transmission of the results of meritorious acts to dead relatives is attested in the most ancient Buddhist practices. A large number of inscribed stelae on the Indian continent (in Barhut, Sarnath, Mathura, Bodhgaya, etc.) attest to the custom of offering merit in favor of parents, in particular the inscriptions of Ajaṇṭa, almost all of which (nineteen out of twenty-one) mention the father and mother of the donor as the beneficiaries of the gift (Schopen 1984: 116–8). Early Sinhalese epigraphy (ca. 200 BC) also mentions offering merit, sometimes specifically directed to the parents of the donor (Langer 2007: 180). The custom of dedicating merit to deceased members of one's family also appears very early in Southeast Asian epigraphy, both Brahmanic and Buddhist. For instance, a pre-Angkorian Sanskrit inscription by Bhavavarman II (639 CE) states that a donor had a statue erected "for the deliverance of his parents" (Sk. *pītāmātror vvimuktaye*; Cœdès 1904: 695–696). The inscription on the stele of Văt Prei Val (K 49, 664 CE), one of the oldest traces of the existence of Buddhism in Cambodia and even in the Indochinese peninsula, also mentions the acquisition of merit by ascendants of the donor of a pious deed.

Many later lapidary texts show that their patrons were often eager to share the fruits of meritorious deeds with their deceased relatives, whatever religious allegiance they claimed to have. This is the case, for example, of Angkorian king Yaśovarman, who established a cult "for the increase of the merits of one's parents" (K 323), or of later Angkorian king Rājendravarman, who intended pious works to "increase the merit" (Sk. *dharma vṛddha*) of his parents (K806; see Dumarçay, Groslier 1973: 207). Later, the Sanskrit inscription of Phimeanakas (K 484) shows that the definitive adoption of Buddhism at Angkor did not alter this dynamic by mentioning that the cult of *bodhivṛksa* was intended to enable devotees to gain merit on behalf of others. The exercise of filial piety through the sharing of merit is also attested in the Mon culture known as Dvāravatī (sixth–eleventh centuries), which is one of the earliest centers of Buddhism in the peninsula. For example, an inscription in Mon language dating back to the sixth century mentions the wish of a ruler to transfer merit to the living and the dead (Prapod Assavavirulhakarn 2010: 87). Another Mon inscription written in Sanskrit, found in Yasothon (northeastern Thailand) indicates that in the eighth century a dignitary offered jewelery and a forest to provide merit to his father.[6]

The later inscriptions of the Buddhist kingdoms of Sukhothai, Lanna, and Lan Xang attest to the persistence of this practice in the Theravādin context from the fourteenth century onward. Most have the function of commemorating a pious act, be it the foundation of a monastery, the installation of a Buddha image, or a religious building (*cetiya*, monastic cells, etc.) undertaken by a devotee who is often of princely rank. It is common for the donor to express the wish to share the merit of a pious deed with one or more ascendants. This offering of merit was almost systematic in the fourteenth and fifteenth centuries, and local Buddhism was already in harmony with the "animist" beliefs that prevailed in the region, as illustrated by the Thai language inscription of Văt Jāṅ$_2$ Làm$_2$ (EHS, 8),[7] dated 1384, in which a dignitary shares the fruits of his meritorious deeds with the "spirits" (Th. *phī*) of his deceased relatives. In the same vein, mention should be made of the two inscriptions—one in Thai, one in Pāli—of the Aśokārāma of Mahā-Dhammarājā II (1399 CE) in which the donor—here the widow of the late king—offers merit to her father, grandparents, and relatives (EHS, 2, I 36–142, II 66–81). The Văt Khemā inscription (1536 CE) similarily reports that a dignitary dedicated merit to his "masters, parents, ascendants and all members of [his] kin," especially those reborn in hell, as a *preta*, or as an animal in the hope of saving them from their sad fate (EHS, 15, II 13–18). Examples of this type abound throughout the Thai–Lao principalities.

The epigraphy of Middle Period Angkor, a time when Pāli Buddhism had become very influential in Cambodia, also contains numerous allusions to merit "offered" (Kh. *ta oy phala*) or "addressed" (Kh. *jūn* or *uddis puṇy*) to ancestors with the aim of delivering them from hell (Lewitz 1971: 94). Even in Burma, where orthodox Theravāda is supposedly more established, epigraphy bears witness to some similar cases. A lapidary text from Kyaukse mentions a temple erected jointly by a monk and his parents, obviously for them to get merit (EB III, 1, 70f),[8] while another, found in Pagan, mentions the dedication of a woman's merit to her grandparents and several of her relatives (Ray 2002 [1946]: 162).

Death rituals are of course the preferred occasion for offering or dedicating merit to one's parents and forebears. In all Buddhist societies, including those reputed to follow the doctrine of Theravāda more strictly (Sri Lanka, Burma), funerals and post-funeral ceremonies aim to ensure a better life for the relative in the afterlife (P. *paraloka*) while preventing his or her return among the living (Spiro 1967: 69; Langer 2007: 126–127). This may at first appear as contradicting Buddhist doctrine, according to which the fate of the deceased depends only on their own actions and not upon the performance of rites. On the other hand, these practices are in some respects similar to those of Brahmanic India. As a matter of fact, Buddhism in Sri Lanka, as well as in mainland Southeast Asia, has partly taken over the Brahmanical terminology, together with the entailed conceptions of death. The deceased is, for example, often described as *preta* (lit. deceased). In the Brahmanic context, this term refers to a recently deceased person, and as such contrasts with *pitṛ* (lit. father), which is used to qualify a relative who has acquired ancestor status. This is accomplished through the performance of Brahmanical funeral rites called *śrāddha*. In Pāli scriptures, however, *peta* does not refer to deceased in general but only to those who are reborn in the realm of the "hungry ghosts" (Langer 2007: 188). Yet funerals in Theravādin Buddhist societies, just as in Brahmanical India, aim to transform *preta*, which are possibly malevolent spirits, into strong and friendly ancestors (Renou, Filliozat 1985 [1947]: 367). Here the presence of the monks replaces that of the Brahmins. The offerings made to them on such occasions produce merit that can be "passed on" to the deceased relative through the recitation of dedicated Pāli chanting—some of which is based on the stanzas of the *Tirokuḍḍa-Petavatthu* (Langer 2007: 64; Kourilsky 2015: 205–206):

> May this be for my relatives! May the relatives be happy!
> Just as the rivers full of water fill the ocean full,
> even so does what is given here benefit the dead.
>
> (Pv 4)

In ancient sources as well as in contemporary religious life, the term *uddissa*—whose orthographic forms may vary—appears to be at the centre of expressions designating the offering or the sharing of merit with others, especially with deceased relatives. This term derives from the Sanskrit term *uddiśati* (to designate, to indicate, to prescribe), which was used in this sense very early in India, as can be seen from epigraphic sources (e.g., the inscriptions of Ajaṇṭā, see Schopen 1984: 118) or the corpus of *Dharmaśāstras* (see Wezler 1997: 574). The term can be found in Pāli in the form *uddissa*, a gerund of the verb *uddissati*, itself presumably derived from the verb *disati* (to grant [something to someone], < *p. ud-disati*). In canonical and postcanonical literature, *disati* is declined in various ways, such as *[dakkhiṇam] ādisa*, *uddassayī*, *ādiseyya*, and so on. As the form *uddissa*, it appears in particular in the *Pāṭikasutta* (DN III 1f.) and in the *Paramatthadīpanī* (Pv-a). We see the term employed frequently in Southeast Asian texts, as in the Middle Khmer epigraphic expression noted earlier, *uddis puṇy*.

Another word is *pattidāna* (giving [of merit]), which is actually the term used in the Commentaries to refer to the gift of merit (Langer 2007: 166). This term is also found in later Pāli literature, such as the *Abhidhammatthasaṅgaha* (ca. 11th c.; Abhidh-s 34) and the *Maṅgalatthadīpanī* of Sirimaṅgala. The *Sabbapattidāna-gāthā* is chanted by Thai and Cambodian monks during ceremonies dedicating merit to the dead (Kourilsky 2015: 162).

Generally speaking, the corpus of Mahāvihāra is far from being unequivocal about the sharing or dedication of merit, especially for the benefit of deceased parents. On one hand, it is explicitly denied in some texts, such as the *Kathāvatthu*, which considers it to be heresy (Premasiri 2001: 157). On the other hand, a number of canonical and paracanonical texts give it some legitimacy. In the *Mahāparinibbāna-sutta* (DN II 72f), for instance, the Buddha himself asserts that it is possible to share merits with deities, while its commentary (Sv II 542) suggests that this sharing is also possible with deceased relatives (Gombrich 1971: 207). Another example is the *Petānaṃnikāya* (AN III 43), which twice mentions the fulfillment of merit for the benefit of parents (*petānaṃ kālakatānaṃ dakkhiṇaṃ anuppadassati*, he will dedicate the merit of his offerings to those [of his parents] who have died and are in a state of *peta*). In similar terms, the *Siṅgala-sutta* (or *Sigālovāda*°) considers offerings to deceased parents as one of the five duties that a child has to fulfill toward their parents (see the previous discussion). The *Dhammapada* Commentary also contains a story in which an ogress (*yakkhinī*) received merit because her son in a previous life had recited the *Dhamma* on her behalf (Langer 2007: 172). But it is undoubtedly the *Petavatthu* and its commentary that contain the most explicit allusions to the offering of merit. In most stories of this collection, the Buddha not only confirms but also prescribes to the faithful the production of merit on behalf of deceased relatives—on the condition, however, that they live in the world of the *peta* (Pv-a 27). Obviously the aim of this collection is to promote the liberality of the faithful toward the Saṅgha by arguing that, without its intercession, the offerings addressed to the dead will not reach their goal. In short, the community of monks is the nodal point of a circuit of exchange between the living and the dead. Although it seems to differ from orthodoxy on this point, Buddhists in Laos, Thailand, Cambodia, Burma, and Sri Lanka have mainly relied on this collection to legitimize the practice of *uddissa*.

Filial piety as a Buddhist virtue

If the paying of debts to ancestors is indeed a duty in the Indian traditions and is not absent from canonical Pāli scriptures, filial piety holds a particularly important place in Buddhism of mainland Southeast Asia.

Regional epigraphy, which for a greater part celebrates the foundation of a religious building (temple, reliquary, monastic repository, etc.), suggests that honoring one's parents with filial piety has been the main motivation of their initiators over the centuries, regardless of place and time. In Brahmanic temples, the god is honored by the faithful, who, in return, expect protection for their deceased relatives and an improvement in their lot in the afterlife (Dumarçay,

Groslier 1973: 206). In Buddhist monuments, if the terms have changed and the statues of deities have been replaced by those of the Buddha or *bodhisattvas*, the ideology remains, and it is a rebirth in good conditions—if not *nirvāna*—that one wishes for one's ancestors. Not only are Buddhist monasteries memorials built in honor of deceased relatives, but their aim is also to provide a home for them or even to maintain their cult. In the Thai kingdom of Ayutthaya, for instance, monasteries were traditionally erected on the site of a princely cremation or the royal residence of a deceased king (Cœdès 1940: 336). The same is true in the northern Thai kingdom of Lanna, where, according to chronicles, several Buddhist buildings were built around a mortuary complex or on the site of cremation (see Jinak 141–142). Similarly, Lao chronicles tell us that, in many cases, monasteries were established to preserve the remains of a deceased member of the royal lineage (Lorrillard 2003: 188). Later inscriptions, as well as vernacular religious literature, suggest that this practice was not limited to the aristocracy but was also shared with commoners.

Erecting or commissioning the manufacture of a Buddha statue can also be an act of filial piety. The ideology that emerges from many inscriptions found on Buddha pedestals is straightforward: it is about producing merit, hoping to gain a favorable rebirth for oneself and one's family while manifesting liberality toward one's deceased ancestors. In certain cases, a statue of the Buddha or of one of his disciples is installed on a receptacle housing the ashes of the dead, which illustrates the connection existing between religious images and the cult of parents or ancestors (Kourilsky 2015: 223f).

More generally, parents and ancestors hold a central place in the religious life of Buddhists in mainland Southeast Asia, especially in that of the Khmer, the Thai and the Lao. This is visible even in the most common religious events, such as the daily offerings made to the monks during their morning alms round (*piṇḍapāta*). The main purpose of giving alms to monks is, indeed, to provide merit to one's dead relatives, who are believed to reside beneath the surface of the earth. Accordingly, donors pour lustrous water on the ground while monks recite appropriate Pāli verses (Kourilsky 2015: 187f).

The regional cycle of "Twelve Month Ceremonies," which are generally celebrated on each full moon day, provides other opportunities to give merit to dead relatives. In this regard, the most significant is the "Festival for the Dead" (Kh. *bhjuṃ piṇḍ*, L, *puñ khao$_2$ pratăp tin*, Th. *jiṅ prēt*), which is celebrated in Cambodia, Laos, and some parts of Thailand, during the month following the entering of the Buddhist lent. Whereas this festival is unknown in the Buddhist traditions of Sri Lanka and Burma, it does have a counterpart in the Chinese Buddhist tradition, namely, the *Yúlánpén* festival (Sk. *Ullambana*). On these occasions, the public reading of homiletic texts (Kh.-Th. *Ānisaṅs*[9]) is particularly significant, telling the story of Mahā-Moggallāna—a main disciple of the Buddha—going to hell to save the departed that have been reborn as *preta* (P. *peta*, Th.-L. *phī phēt*, Kh. *prēt*). The latter beg Mahā-Moggallāna to exhort their living descendants to perform meritorious acts for their benefit. It is after Mahā-Moggallāna's report that the Buddha, according to this legend, instituted this very festival. This echoes the Chinese legend of Mùlián (Sk. Maudgalyāyana) saving his mother from hell—a feature that also appears in some Southeast Asian narratives—which is likewise at the core of the *Yúlánpén* festival.[10]

A number of other *Ānisaṅs* texts related to death and funerals have as their specific subject the duty of gratitude toward parents. Some *Ānisaṅs* take over the story of Bimbīsāra questioning the Buddha as to the means of paying tribute to his dead parents, drawn from the *Petavatthu*. Examples are the Lao "Advantage of Offering Rice by Lot" (*Ānisaṅs khao$_2$ salāk*), which is related to another annual festival, and the Khmer "Advantage of Saving the Hungry Ghosts" (*Ānisaṅs prēt*). There is also the "Advantage of Repaying the Kindness of Parents" (*Ānisoṅ guṇ marḍā piḍā*), widespread in Laos and Northeast Thailand (Kourilsky 2015: 491f),[11] whose Khmer counterpart is 'The Advantage of [Reflecting on] Virtues and Wrongdoings" (*Ānisaṅs guṇ niṅ dos*; Bernon 2008: 13). Both extensively depict the good deeds parents do toward their children and exalt the virtue of repaying their kindness.

Vernacular Buddhist literature likes to recall that the Buddha himself did not depart from this obligation, as can be seen in various narratives relating the Blessed One's journey to the heaven of the "thirty-three deities" (P. *Tāvatiṃsa*), which he undertook in order to pay back the "price of rice and milk" received in early childhood. Narratives like *Paṭhamasambodhi* (a Southeast Asian biography of the Buddha written in Pāli) or the *Mālālaṃkāra-vatthu* (the Burmese version of the *Tathāgata-udāna*), as the Lao vernacular *Dē̆n nāṃ nŏm mè̄* (lit, to pay in return for mother's milk) and the Khmer *Mātā-guṇa-sūtr* (lit. the *sūtra* on the mother's legacies), rely on commentarial and later Pāli works relating the ascension episode to Tāvatiṃsa, but they give it a particular depth and flavor. The Master's descent from the Heaven of the Thirty-Three is often represented in Southeast Asian Buddhist art, such as on the walls of the temple of Ānanda in Pagan (12th c.), and on countless numbers of murals inside and outside temples in Thailand and Laos. Some scholars have recognized in the towers of the Bayon, in Cambodia, a representation of the great miracle fr this be for my relatives om Śrāvastī, when the Buddha, immediately after his return, appeared everywhere at once, whirling like many sparkling suns (Dumarçay, Groslier 1973: 289). In Thailand and Burma, after the rainy season, there is a festival celebrating the return of the Blessed One from Tāvatiṃsa after three months of absence and the supreme virtue of repaying his mother's kindness. In Cambodia, the "Ghost Festival" (Kh. *bhjuṃ piṇḍ*, see the previous discussion) ends with the recitation by monks of verses recalling the Buddha's teaching of the Abhidhamma to his mother out of gratitude and to pay the price of the milk he had suckled (Fuchs 1991: 72).

Indeed, Southeast Asian traditions emphasize the fact the Buddha shows his gratitude to Māyā by preaching the "Seven Books of Abhidhamma," a feature that is only briefly mentioned in Pāli commentarial literature. For example, *The Seven Books of the Abhidhamma*, a compendium of the Abhidhamma known in Thai, Lao, and Khmer, starts with the Buddha's ascent to Tāvatiṃsa, as does the *Aṭṭhasālinī*, Buddhaghosa's commentary on the *Dhammasaṅgaṇī*—the first book of the Abhidhamma. The vernacular text emphasizes the Buddha's determination to fulfill his filial duty toward his mother and to "save" her by teaching her the *Abhidhamma*, a feature absent in Buddhaghosa's work.

This episode very likely explains how the Abhidhamma came to be conceived in local Buddhism as an allegory of filial piety. Indeed, copying or ordering a copy of the Abhidhamma is particularly recommended to produce merit for relatives, living or dead. This is explicitly indicated in the colophons of some manuscripts pertaining to vernacular Abhidhamma texts, where donors express the wish to repay their mother's or father's kindness or to help them escape from hell (Kourilsky 2015: 588f). The use of reciting the Abhidhamma in order to save one's parent is also attested in epigraphic sources (e.g., *K. 264*, at Pre Rup temple, Angkor, 17th c.; Pou 1994: 39). Likewise, tradition requires to "recite the *Abhidhamma*"—in fact, just the *mātikā* (tables of content)—during mortuary ceremonies. This singular virtue assigned to the *mātikā* is linked to the tradition that attributes to each book of the Abhidhamma the creation of a part of the human body so that reciting *Dhammasaṃgaṇī* makes it possible to erase the faults committed by the eyes, *Vibhaṅga* those committed by the ears, and so on (Finot 1917: 78).

Although tradition specifically links the Abhidhamma to filial piety, it is locally assumed that ordering the copy of any Buddhist manuscript can help saving one's parent from a bad rebirth, and it is customary to have a manuscript copied as part of funeral ceremonies for the benefit of the dead. It is then wrapped with the piece of cloth previously placed on the coffin of the deceased and which was previously used in the death rituals called *paṃsukūl* (Philavong 1967:

195). In Cambodia, manuscripts can be burnt during cremations, or enshrined in reliquaries with the remains of the deceased (Becchetti 1994: 52). In Burma, a tradition in the families of dignitaries burning the clothes of relatives to make ink for writing Buddhist texts was considered a mark of filial piety (Veidlinger 2006: 96). Again, the Buddhist custom in Laos and Thailand of printing and distributing "volumes of cremation souvenirs" (Th. *hnăṅ sịị anusạn ṅān śab*) is intended to produce merit for the deceased.

But the most effective way—for a boy or man—to manifest filial piety is to ordain as a *bhikkhu* or a novice. Khmer, Thai, and Lao Buddhists accept that the primary motivation for one to become a monk is to give merit to one's parents. This idea is foreign to the classical texts of the Mahāvihāra tradition, in which the Buddha may certainly at times praise respect for parents but never equates the ordination with an act of filial piety. Even in China, where filial piety is an exalted virtue, ordination is not, in itself, considered as such. Rather, it is *in spite of* his status as a monk—which theoretically precludes him from his family duties—that the Chinese *bhikṣu* can possibly continue to exercise filial piety, because he could convert them or cleanse their sins as he receives clothing and food from their hand (Granet 1998[1922]: 211). In mainland Southeast Asia, however, ordination is unambiguously seen as an act of filial piety. Ordination is usually not left to the initiative of the applicant but to that of his parents, which explains that the merit is theirs. A number of *Ānisaṅs* texts praise the advantages and merits of "having ordained" (Th., L. *hai*$_2$ *pvaj*, Kh. *paṃpuos*) their child, as well as the *Paramatthamaṅgala*, a Pāli work composed in Thailand (Cicuzza 2012: 361–366). The *Maṅgalatthadīpanī* also supports this idea, arguing that "in becoming a monk (*pabbajita*), one is freed from the debt" (*api ca pabbajantena nāma anaṇena bhavitabbaṃ*) owed to one's mother and father.

The idea that the worshipper has incurred a "debt" to their parents is fundamental to Buddhism in much of the Theravāda world. Within Khmer, Thai, and Lao Buddhist communities, this notion is widely expressed through the term *guṇ* (P., Sk. *guṇa*) which, although borrowed from the vocabulary of ancient India, has been subject to local reinterpretations. In Pāli texts, the common meaning of the word *guṇa* is "virtue," "benefit," or "merit."[12] This term has locally been given an additional meaning, as it also refers to the "body components"—also referred to with the Pāli word *ākāra*—that progenitors pass on to their offspring during gestation. Here the term *guṇ* takes, by extrapolation, the meaning of "legacy" or "debt" held by parents toward their child:

> *Kesā* hair, *lomā* body hair, *nakhā* nails, *dantā* teeth, *taco* skin, *maṃsaṃ* flesh, *nhāru* nerves, *aṭṭhi* bones, *aṭṭhimiñjaṃ* marrow, *vakkaṃ* kidneys, *hadayaṃ* heart, *yakanaṃ* liver, *kilomakaṃ* pleura, *pihakaṃ* spleen, *papphāsaṃ* lungs, *antaṃ* intestine, *antaguṇaṃ* mesentery, *udariyaṃ* undigested food, *karīsaṃ*, food residues, *matthake* head, *matthaluṅgam* brain. These twenty-one components are the "Father's legacies" (*pitu-guṇa*) and constitute the Earth-element (*paṭhavī-dhātu*). *Pittaṃ* bile, *semhaṃ* phlegm, *pubbo* pus, *lohitaṃ* blood, *sedo* sweat, *medo* grease, *assu* tears, *vasā* sebum, *kheḷo* saliva, *siṅghāṇikā* nasal mucus, *lasikā* synovia, *muttaṃ* urine. These twelve components are the "Mother's legacies" (*mātā-guṇa*) and constitute the Water-element (*āpo-dhātu*).[13]

These "components" actually correspond to the stereotypical lists found in canonical and post-canonical texts when describing the human body parts, referred to as of the *dvattiṃsākāra* (the 32 components; (Khp 2, MN III 90, AN III 323, AN V 109, Vibh 82, 193–4, DN II 293, DN III 104–105, Vism 242f). In the Mahāvihāra tradition, however, *dvattiṃsākāra* are not linked to parents but are only meant to emphasize the composed and perishable nature of the human body, thereby illustrating the notion of "non-self" (P. *anatta*).

The Southeast Asian conception, moreover, covers a symbolic dimension, linking the number of "components" inherited respectively from the father (21) and the mother (12), with the duty to ordain as a novice (P. *sāmaṇera*) at twelve years old, and then as a *bhikkhu* at the age of twenty-one.[14] Indeed receiving the *pabbajjā* (i.e., to ordain as a *sāmanera*, or novice) enables the faults of one's mother to be redeemed, and the *upasampadā* (i.e., the higher ordination as a *bhikkhu*, or monk) the ones of one's father (Finot 1917: 81). Esoteric readings also connect the mother's and father's "legacies" with consonants of the Pāli alphabet, or with the first syllables of the mantra *namo buddhāya* (homage to the Buddha)—namely, NA = *mātāguṇa*; MO = *pituguṇa* (Lagirarde 1994: 68).

To "recollect parents legacies" (*raṇik/raṃlk guṇa pitā mātā*) is actually part of the monk's religious life. First, monks recite the *dvattiṃsākāra* in the assembly hall during the morning prayers, while reflecting on the "legacies" (*guṇa*) of the mother and father. The ancient tradition required the monk to do so also in the early morning as he put on the different parts of his monastic cloth (P. *cīvara*). This was a meditation exercise that reproduced the elementary gestures during intra-uterine gestation, in particular the march of the breath. To symbolically reproduce, by a series of ascetic practices, the sufferings of the mother during the period of gestation and childbirth is actually at the core of the local meditation tradition that some scholars refer to as the "*kammaṭṭhān* tradition."[15] Sleeping only in the sitting position represents the discomfort experienced when the mother was pregnant; not sheltering from the sun represents the pain endured when "being in the fire" after giving birth, and so on. Such penitential trials could be done in the solitude of meditation sessions or in collective rituals such as the Great Probation festival (P. *mahāparivāsakamma*), which takes place at the end of the rainy retreat (Bernon 2000: 475–6; Zago 1972: 285).

The theme of a mother's concern for her child and the torments of pregnancy and childbirth that she undergoes, as well as the vicissitudes of education, although already present in canonical scriptures (viz. *Soṇananda-jātaka*, *Mahātaṇhāsaṅkhayasutta*), has undergone a specific development in Southeast Asian Buddhist traditions. It is included in a number of vernacular treatises and narratives such as the *Mūl braḥ kammaṭṭhān*, *Dhammatrai* (or *Braḥ Dhămm Sām Trai*), *Pavarabandha* and *Gavampatti-sutta* (Lagirarde 1994: 73f).

Finally, not only the torments of the mother but also those of the father still appear in certain formulas to "recall vital spirits" (*sū₁ khvăn*) in Laos and Thailand (Kourilsky 2015: 485–486). These incantatory formulas can be considered as the ultimate stage in the process of the localization of canonical writings, as they are removed from their original purpose.

Conclusion

It has been shown earlier that the notion of filial piety is not absent from the Buddhist teachings of the Theravāda, as they are recorded in the Pāli canon, and especially in commentaries and later works. Moreover, Indian traditions have left evidence that this notion was part of religious concerns over centuries, especially for lay followers. The act of dedicating merit to parents was accepted in the practices of the oldest Buddhist schools (Mahāsaṅgika, Sarvāstivāda, etc.), as well as in Vedic and Brahminic India, and should not be attributed to a later development in Mahāyāna. It would be a bridge too far, however, to state that devotion toward one's parents or the cult of giving to dead relatives was ever considered to be at the forefront of Buddhist teachings. Rather, it seems that admitting filial piety into the religious life of Buddhist societies was a precondition for the Doctrine to be accepted among the population. It is well known that proponents of the Doctrine in China had to show ingenuity and flexibility in order for it to be accepted by a Confucian society that saw in Gotama a "barbaric man" precisely because he disregarded filial feelings and duties (Étiemble 1986 [1956]: 194). In contrast, many Buddhist communities in the Theravāda world consider devotion toward parents, forebears, and ancestors to be at the core of religious life and undoubtedly belonging within the teaching of the Buddha. Giving alms, building a monastery, casting an image of the Master or a saint, commissioning a copy of a manuscript, receiving ordination, practicing meditation, participating in annual festivals—all kinds of pious deeds—are opportunities to pay homage or provide assistance to parents and ancestral spirits, with whom the fruits of these actions will be shared. In Thailand, Laos, and Cambodia, as well as in Burma and Sri Lanka, filial piety and ancestor worship were hardly seen as an issue regarding the Buddhist doctrine. While Indian and Chinese Buddhist scholars had to demonstrate that it was possible to be a pious child *despite* being a Buddhist, it has always been widely assumed, within Theravāda societies, that a good Buddhist *must* be a pious child. This shade of difference is significant.

Notes

1 This episode appears in several Pāli texts, including the *Dhammapada-aṭṭhakathā*, *Jātaka*, *Aṭṭhasālinī*, *Sumaṅgalavilāsinī*, and *Buddhavaṃsa*.

2 Also worthy of mention is the episode where the Buddha expresses his filial piety toward Gotamī Mahāpajāpatī, his foster mother (Ap II 529). Nevertheless, the Buddha's sense of filial piety is quickly overturned so that at the end of the story, Gotamī prostrates herself before the Buddha, for it is she who is ultimately indebted to her son.

3 Javier Schnake, personal communication.

4 Although the orientalist tradition tends to include Southeast Asia in the "Indic world," there are grounds for distinguishing these two cultural areas. The process of "Indianization" that characterizes most parts of Southeast Asia was not a process of acculturation per se. Rather, Indian cultural traits have mainly been adopted at a formal level. Their visibility (in terms of material evidence as well as in vocabulary and conception) has certainly concealed but not erased autochthonous cultural substrata, as well as Chinese imprint.

5 This notion is, for instance, present in the *Mahābhārata*, the *Purāṇas*, the *Upaniṣads*, as well as in the *Dharmaśāstras*. It is also the subject of lengthy argumentative discussions in the Indian school of philosophy of *Mīmāṃsā* (Shastri 1963: 340).

6 http://www.sac.or.th/databases/inscriptions/inscribe_detail.php?id=330.

7 *Epigraphic and Historical Studies* (A. B. Griswold and Prasert na Nagara, cf. bibliography).

8 *Epigraphia Birmanica* (C. Duroiselle and C. O. Blagden, cf. bibliography).

9 P. *Ānisaṃsa*, "advantage," here referring to rewards in terms of merit. Also known in Laos and Northeast Thailand as *Slaṅ* (celebration).

10 For an in-depth comparative study on "death festivals" in Southeast Asia, and regarding Chinese *Yúlánpén*, see Kourilsky (2015: 199–444).

11 For a French translation of this text, see Kourilsky (2007: 43–70).

12 The term comes from Sanskrit where it first means "rope," "thread," and, by extension, "subdivision," "component," and "constituent."

13 Extract from a Lao version of the *Mūl Braḥ kammaṭṭhān*.

14 The Indochinese tradition enumerates twenty-one solid components, instead of twenty in the Mahāvihāra tradition. This is because it breaks down the last element of the canonical list, that is, *matthake matthaluṅgaṃ* (lit. the brain in the skull), into two distinct "components" (viz. brain *and* skull).

15 On this tradition, see Lagirarde (1994), Bernon (2000), Crosby (2013), and, above all, François Bizot's works (1976–2000). See also chapter by Crosby and Kyaw in the present volume.

References

Becchetti, Catherine. 1994. "Une ancienne tradition de manuscrits au Cambodge." In *Recherches nouvelles sur le Cambodge*, ed. F. Bizot, 47–62. Paris: EFEO.

Bernon, Olivier de. 2008. "La littérature des 'avantages' (ānisaṅs) dans les bibliothèques monastiques du Cambodge," unpublished draft, 18 p.

Bernon, Olivier de. 2000. "Le rituel de la 'grande probation annuelle' des religieux du Cambodge." *Bulletin de l'École française d'Extrême-Orient* 87 (2): 473–510.

Cicuzza, Claudio. 2012. "The Benefits of Ordination according to the *Paramatthamaṅgala*." In *How Theravāda is Theravāda? Exploring Buddhist Identities*, eds. P. Skilling, J.A. Carbine, C. Cicuzza, S. Pakdeekham, 335–369. Bangkok: Silkworm Books.

Cœdès, George. 1904. "Inscription de Bhavavarman II, Roi du Cambodge (561 *śaka*)." *Bulletin de l'École française d'Extrême-Orient* 4: 691–697.

Cœdès, George. 1940. "Études cambodgiennes. II." *Bulletin de l'École française d'Extrême-Orient* 40 (2): 315–349.

Crosby, Kate. 2013. *Traditional Theravada meditation and its modern-era suppression*. Hong Kong: Buddhist Dharma Centre of Hong Kong.

Dumarçay, Jacques, Groslier, Bernard-Philippe 1973. *Le Bayon. Histoire architecturale du temple. Inscriptions du Bayon*. Paris: EFEO.

Dumont, Louis. 1980. "La dette vis-à-vis des ancêtres et la catégorie de *sapiṇḍa*." *Puruṣārtha* 4: 15–37.

Duroiselle, Charles, C. O. Blagden. 1928. *Epigraphia Birmanica, being lithic and other inscriptions of Burma, Volume III, part I*. Rangoon: Government Printing.

Durt, Hubert. 2006. "On Gratitude in Japanese Buddhism." *Japan Mission Journal* 60 (4): 238–242.

Étiemble, René. 1986. *Confucius*. Paris: Gallimard (Fifth edition 1956).

Finot, Louis. 1917. "Recherches sur la littérature laotienne." *Bulletin de l'École française d'Extrême-Orient* 17: 1–218.

Fuchs, Paul. 1991. *Fêtes et cérémonies royales au Cambodge d'hier*. Paris: L'Harmattan.

Gombrich, Richard. 1971. *Precept and Practice. Traditional Buddhism in the Rural Highlands of Ceylon*. Oxford: Clarendon Press.

Granet, Marcel. 1998. *La religion des Chinois*. Paris: Albin Michel (first edition 1922).

Griswold, A.B., na Nagara, Prasert 1992. *Epigraphic and Historical Studies*. Bangkok: The Historical Society.

Khamphun Philavong 1967. *Gū$_1$ mịi bāṃ bĕn pun kusŏn khaṅ Buda parisăḍ (Manual for Buddhists to Accomplish Merit)*. Vientiane: Phone Phra Nao Monastery (in Lao).

Kourilsky, Gregory. 2007. "Note sur la piété filiale en Asie du Sud-Est theravādin: la notion de *guṇ*." *Aséanie* 20: 27–54.

Kourilsky, Gregory. 2015. "La place des ascendants familiaux dans le bouddhisme des Lao," PhD dissertation. Paris: École Pratique des Hautes Études.

Lagirarde, François. 1994. "Textes bouddhiques du pays khmer et du Lanna: un exemple de parenté." *Nouvelles Recherches sur le Cambodge*, ed. F. Bizot, 63–77. Paris: EFEO.

Langer, Rita. 2007. *Buddhist Rituals of Death and Rebirth. Contemporary Sri Lankan Practice and its Origins*. London and New York: Routledge.

Lewitz, Saveros. 1971. "L'inscription de Phimeanakas (K. 484). Étude linguistique." *Bulletin de l'École française d'Extrême-Orient* 58: 91–103.

Lorrillard, Michel. 2003. "The Earliest Lao Buddhist Monasteries According to Philological and Epigraphical Sources." In *The Buddhist Monastery. A cross-cultural survey*, eds. P. Pichard, François Lagirarde, 187–198. Paris: EFEO.

Pou, Saveros. 1994. "L'offrande des mérites dans la tradition khmère." *Journal asiatique* 282: 391–408.

Assavavirulhakarn, Prapod 2010. *The Ascendency of Theravada Buddhism in Southeast Asia*. Bangkok: Silkworm Books.

Premasiri, P.D. 2001. "Significance of the ritual concerning offerings to ancestors in Theravāda Buddhism." In *Buddhist Thought and Ritual*, ed. D.K. Kalupahana, 151–158. Dehli: Motilal Banarsidas Publishers.

Ray, Niharranjan 2002. *An Introduction to the Study of Theravada Buddhism in Burma. A Study in Indo-Burmese Historical and Cultural Relations from the earliest Times to the British Conquest*. Bangkok: Orchid Press (first edition 1946).

Renou, Louis, Filliozat, Jean. 1985. *L'Inde classique. Manuel des études indiennes*, tome 1. Paris: Adrien Maisonneuve (first edition 1947).

Schopen, Gregory. 1984. "Filial Piety and the Monk in the Practice of Indian Buddhism: A question of 'Sinization' viewed from the other side." *T'oung Pao* 70: 110–126.

Schopen, Gregory. 2007. "The Buddhist *Bhikṣu*'s Obligation to Support His Parents." *Journal of Pali Text Society* 29: 107–136.

Shastri, Dakshinaranjan. 1963. *Origin and Development of the Rituals of Ancestor Worship in India*. Calcutta, Allahbad, Patna: Bookland Private Limited.

Spiro, Melford E. 1967. *Burmese Supernaturalism. A Study in the Explanation and Reduction of Suffering*. Englewood Cliffs, NJ: Prentice-Hall.

Strong, John. 1983. "Filial Piety and Buddhism: the Indian antecedents to a Chinese problem." In *Traditions in Contact and Change*, eds. P. Slater, Donald Wiebe, 171–186. Waterloo (Ontario): Canadian Corporation for Studies in Religion.

Veidlinger, Daniel M. 2006. *Spreading the Dhamma: Writing, Orality, and Textual Transmission in Buddhist Northern Thailand*. Honolulu: University of Hawai'i Press.

Wezler, A. 1997. "On the gaining of merit and the incurring of demerit through the agency of others: I. Deeds by proxy." In *Lex and Litterae: Studies in Honour of Professor Oscar Botto*, eds. S. Lienhard, I. Piovano, 567–589. Alessandria: Edizioni dell'Orso.

Zago, Marcel. 1972. *Rites et cérémonies en milieu bouddhiste lao*. Roma: Università Gregoriana.

11

LAITY

Status, role, and practice in Theravāda

Asanga Tilakaratne

Introduction

The fact that there is a discussion on the laity and the nature of their religious practice assumes that there is another group against the practice of whom their practice has to be understood. Theravāda Buddhism has been considered as predominantly a monastic tradition as a result of which the subordinate position of the laity has been recognized from its early stages. The beginning of Mahāyāna as a new school in the history of Buddhism has, at least partly and likely erroneously, been attributed to this character of the early Buddhist tradition.

This historical aspect of the evolution of the laity in Buddhism has been studied by a number of scholars, and hence, I do not revisit the same (Warder 2000: 175–194). Instead, what I do in this chapter is to study the contemporary Theravāda lay practice, with reference to Sri Lanka and Myanmar in particular. In the course of this discussion, I also make brief comments on "diaspora" Theravāda practice of the Theravāda Buddhists who live outside the traditional Theravāda countries and the Theravāda practice of its new Western adherents and the "Navayāna" (New Vehicle, Ambedkarian) Buddhists in India.

Recent academic constructions of the laity in Theravāda

Modern scholars of Theravāda often make a sharp distinction between the laity and the monastics. Max Weber, whose influence on the subsequent sociologists and anthropologists of Theravāda Buddhism is beyond doubt, perceives the earliest form of Buddhism as constituting individual seekers of nirvana for whom "salvation is an absolutely personal performance of the self-reliant individual" (Weber 1960, 213). Such a salvation is gained only by those who have given up household life and the social aspects associated with it. The laity did not belong in this salvation scheme, and they had only a limited role. According to Weber (1960),

> [i]n the parish doctrine the status group of "house-dwelling people" in a manner somewhat similar to the tolerated infidels in Islam, existed only for the purpose of sustaining by alms the Buddhist disciple who aspires to the state of grace until he has reached it. ...Material support of the holy seekers fell on the laity and ultimately this alone constituted the highest merit and honor available to the *upasaka* (adorer).
>
> (214)

DOI: 10.4324/9781351026666-14

Weber's characterization has been developed in Spiro (1982), in which two forms of Buddhism, "nirvanic Buddhism," which is a religion of radical salvation, and "kammatic Buddhism," which constitutes "proximate" salvation, are developed along with what he calls "apotropaic" and esoteric forms. In the course of his detailed study of Buddhism in Burma, Spiro develops these two categories as exclusively applicable to the monastic community and the laity respectively.

What is problematic is not necessarily the two categories of Buddhism but attributing them exclusively to the two groups, nibbanic to the monastics and the kammatic to the laity. The early Buddhist discourses (e.g., AN I 69, DN III 167) refer to the broad classification of householders and renouncers—*gihi* (or *gahaṭṭha*) and *pabbajita*. Householders did not mean only those who followed the Buddha. It is a generic term used to refer to all householders, or all nonmonastics in general, whether they were the followers of the Buddha or not. Apart from these two types, there are yet another two found in the discourses referring exclusively to those who were committed to following the Buddha, namely, *upāsaka*, the male followers, and *upāsikā*, the female followers. They formed two parts of the four groups of the followers of the Buddha (also including monks and nuns) who, at least technically, were considered to be equal partners in the Buddhist community. The two terms seem to have been used to single out the particular Buddhist identity among many householders.[1] *Upāsaka*, by definition, is one who "takes refuge" in the Buddha, the Dhamma, and the Saṅgha (AN IV 220).

When it comes to the realization of the ultimate goal of nirvana, however, the preference was always for the monastic group whose mode of life was "open [unhindered] like sky" relative to the householder life which was perceived as "full of obstacles" (DN I 63, SN II 219). According to a statement found in the *Suttanipāta* (verse 221), a text belonging to the earliest phase of the Pāli canon, a layperson, like a colorful peacock that cannot match the speed of a simple-looking swan, cannot be compared to a sage who leads a life of contemplation in the forest.

Although the relative disadvantages of the household life were clearly recognized, this did not mean that the nirvanic goal was totally beyond them. There is evidence to support that the Buddha treated all the four groups as soteriologically equal.[2] Furthermore, there are reports of a number of laymen and -women who reached higher states in the path and who also mastered or even taught the Dhamma to monastic members.[3] This demonstrates that the exclusive attribution of kammatic Buddhism to the laity and nibbanic to the monastics, in all probability, is not correct at any stage of the historical existence of Buddhism. However, as we will see in the course of this discussion, in contemporary practice, lay Buddhist behavior has taken a turn toward "nibbanic Buddhism," challenging the popular characterization of Buddhist religious behavior through distinctions such as lay/monastic and kammatic/nibbanic.

The lay Buddhist as donor

In ancient Indian society, it was quite normal for "*śramaṇas* and *brāhmaṇas*" to rely on the laity for their daily existence. While it is recorded that there were preferences among people for particular religious groups, the general tendency appears to have been that people gave alms to religious mendicants without discrimination. There is abundant evidence that the Buddha and his disciples too made use of this readily available system for their survival. What is considered in this context, however, is not this general religious practice but how within Buddhism the role of the laity as donor developed. It is understandable that all could not choose the monastic life by giving up their household and social obligations. Those who opted to remain as householders were naturally expected to support those who left household life. King Bimbisara of Magadha is reported to have made the first donation to the Buddha and his monastic followers by dedicating a Bamboo Grow (Veluvana) for them to stay in (Vin I 39). Gradually, as discourses and the Vinaya record, there were rich donors such as Anathapindika, and Visakha, who donated dwellings to the Buddha, and his disciples and became lifelong supporters of the *sāsana*.[4] The three people mentioned here were *upāsakas* and *upāsikās* who had attained the first stage of the path, namely, stream-entrance, nevertheless remained lay, meaning that while Bimbisara continued to be the ruler of Magadha, Anathapindika, and Visakha continued to be a successful businessperson and a rich housewife respectively.

"The Advice to Sigala" (Sigālovāda-sutta, DN III 180–183) contains material to determine how the role of the laity was perceived within the Buddhist tradition. In this discourse, the Buddha teaches Sigala, a young householder, what later came to be known as "lay discipline" (*gihi-vinaya*) which includes, among many other matters, the proper behavior toward six social groups, among which is "ascetics and brahmins" (meaning dedicated religious people). According to the discourse, a householder should minister to religious people in five ways, among which is providing them with their worldly needs. The reciprocal duty of the monks toward the laity is to provide ethical guidance to them, in particular, to reveal the path to heaven, which is the more realistic goal for those who have household obligations to fulfill.

What modern scholars starting from Weber described as lay religious practice in Buddhism, namely, the accumulation of merits aiming at better rebirth in the next life, has remained generally true for lay practice within Theravāda from the ancient times to the present. Of the three or ten types of meritorious acts, donation (*dāna*), virtue (*sīla*), and meditation (*bhāvanā*), the first is most practiced and most loved. Also it is the first among the virtues that enable one to become a Buddha. The discourses have many references to people inviting the Buddha and the Saṅgha for meals. In the medieval Pāli literature of Sri Lanka, such works as *Sahassavatthu-pakaraṇa* and *Rasavāhini* are dedicated to elaborating on this lay practice of giving alms. The overall emphasis of the works of this genre is how people gained much in return after their death by giving the Saṅgha even a small thing or by giving during difficult circumstances such as famine.

It is not an exaggeration to say that donation (of meals to the Saṅgha) is the main religious act of the laity in Theravāda today. In Sri Lanka, where the monks usually do not go for alms from house to house, people undertake to provide the resident monks of the village or nearby monastery with meals on a monthly basis, once in three months, or annually. In countries like Myanmar and Thailand, where thousands of monks collect alms daily, the donation of meals and other requisites (such as toothbrushes, soap, etc.) to these daily alms-seekers constitute a key element of the daily religious life of those people.

The *kaṭhina* ceremony (marking the conclusion of the rainy season observance), usually falling in October–November, is an occasion in which the laity's donor role appears in its highest degree. In all traditional Theravāda countries this occasion is celebrated with colorful processions amid many festivities with singing and dancing. This is perhaps the most precious meritorious act in which the laity try their best to supply the monks and the particular monastery with every imaginable article needed for daily existence. In Myanmar, it is common during this period to see people traveling to monasteries in rows of vehicles with these various articles to be donated hanging all over the vehicle so that all those onlookers may rejoice in their meritorious act.

Dāna is practiced by diasporic Theravāda Buddhists in very much the same manner as they practiced at home. They provide meals to the monastery of their choice wherever they happened to be. It is interesting to see how they have adjusted themselves to practicing their religion in new situations with new lifestyles. In a big city like Los Angeles, where everyone is busy working or studying away from their homes on weekdays, they bring the midday meal of the resident monks a day earlier and keep it overnight in the refrigerator to be taken out and consumed by the monks the next day. Although this is not strictly in accordance with the monastic rules concerning stocking cooked food, both monks and laypeople have adjusted themselves to the new situations.

Giving meals and other requisites is not the only kind of donation practiced by Theravāda Buddhists. They donate money for various activities of the monastery and for the needs of the monks, such as the construction of new buildings and new pagodas, renovation of old buildings, and medicine and other requisites of the monks. In addition, diaspora Buddhists also give money for the monthly rent or the mortgage of the buildings where they house their monasteries until they collect enough funds to purchase or build their own place. Offering money to paint pagodas in gold color or offering actual gold to gild pagodas is a popular form of donation of the Buddhist laity in Myanmar. Once at Shwedagon pagoda in Yangon I saw a group of people, apparently simple villagers, going around the pagoda holding some flags and chanting. I was told that they were announcing their donation of some amount of gold to the pagoda and were asking others to rejoice in their meritorious deed, which, in itself, is a meritorious deed in Theravāda belief. Another form of donation unique to Myanmar, although not unknown in other Theravāda countries, is to sponsor a young monk or a nun[5] in their education (which is discussed in more detail later). Among many other forms of donation, organized events of donation of blood are quite commonplace in Sri Lanka and well patronized, and in addition, newspapers often report instances of organ donation by the survivors of the deceased.

Spiro who did his field research in Myanmar (then Burma) in the early 1960s has discussed the generosity of the Myanmar Buddhists. He refers to Crawfurd, who wrote in 1834 that the prosperity of any section of Burma is to be judged "not by the comforts or luxuries of the inhabitants or the reputable appearance of their habitations, but by the number, magnitude, splendor and actual conditions of its temples and monasteries" and says that "Crawfurd's observation is as true today as a hundred and fifty years ago" (Spiro 1982: 401). In fact, what was true when Crawfurd wrote in 1834 and when Spiro did his field research in early the 1960s remains substantially true even today.

The lay Buddhist meditation practice

In his study of kammatic and nibbanic Buddhism Spiro (1982) has shown how ordinary (Theravāda) Buddhists in Myanmar show preference to *dāna* over *sīla* and *bhāvanā* (103ff.). According to him, "meditation is found only infrequently in Burma, and even less frequently in other Buddhist societies" (54). This observation is corroborated in more recent research on Ledi Sayadaw and the popularization of Vipassana meditation in Myanmar by Erik Braun (2013). Spiro's remark that meditation is found even less frequently in other Buddhist countries is substantiated by Sri Lankan experience, studied by George Bond (1992), in which a larger majority of both monks and laypeople sit for meditation only sporadically.

It is on this background that the phenomenon discussed in this section, the current lay Buddhist meditation practice, becomes interesting. In traditional Buddhist societies, the general belief was that meditation is to be practiced by monks alone. This does mean that at least some laypeople did not practice meditation. What is new in lay meditation is that the laity who only occasionally practiced meditation, adopted it as an important part of their religious life. The new attitude to religious life within which this shift of emphasis took place, in the context of Sri Lanka, has been described by Gananath Obeyesekere as "Protestant Buddhism."[6] The following account captures the basic import of this concept:

> The utility of the label "protestant Buddhism" lies in its double meaning. It originated as a protest against the British in general and against Protestant Christian missionaries

> in particular. At the same time, however, it assumed salient characteristics of that Protestantism. We shall further explore the Protestant character below. Here it suffices to say that Protestant Buddhism undercuts the importance of the religious professional, the monk, by holding that it is the responsibility of every Buddhist both to care for the welfare of Buddhism and to strive himself for salvation. The traditional monastic monopoly in withdrawal from the world is called into question, while those monks (the majority) who do not become meditating hermits are criticized for lack of social involvement. The distinction between *Saṅgha* and laity is thus blurred, for religious rights and duties are the same for all.
>
> (Gombrich and Obeyesekere 1990: 7)

What is significant in this analysis for the present purpose is the new responsibility assumed by the laity, namely, striving for one's own salvation without the involvement of the monk. In both Myanmar and Sri Lanka this happened as a response to colonialism, but how it happened and the specific local conditions under which it happened are not the same.

It is in Myanmar that the modern *vipassanā* meditation movement started and from where it went to the rest of the Theravāda countries and to the world at large. According to Erik Braun, who studied the Burmese beginning of this movement extensively (2013, 2014), it is very closely connected to the loss of hope and frustration felt by the Burmese people when their last king Thibaw was dethroned and the kingdom was captured by the British on November 25, 1885. People took this event as marking the beginning of the deterioration and the ultimate demise of the *Buddha-sāsana*. It is to arrest this pending disaster that Ledi Sayadaw (1846–1923), the main architect of the movement, started popularizing the practice of meditation and the studies of Abhidhamma, not only among the monks but, more specifically, among the laity as well (Bechert 1984: 154). Meditation and the study of Dhamma by both monks and the laity, and Dhamma-preaching by the monks were the means of this revolution of the religiosity of the people. In Braun's words,

> [i]n less than 75 years, from 1886 to the mid-1950s, meditation had grown from a pursuit of the barest sliver of the population to a duty of the ideal citizen.
>
> (2014)

In Myanmar, although this happened as a protest against colonialism, it was not protestant in its other sense, in the sense of rejecting the authority and guidance of the monks, as it was the case in Sri Lanka. As we will see shortly, in Sri Lanka, the meditation introduced by the Burmese monks was opposed by some segments of Sri Lanka monks.[7] In Myanmar, the practice was adopted by both monks and the laity.

The new *vipassanā* meditation was introduced to Sri Lanka in the mid-1950s, along with *Buddha Jayanti*[8] celebrations by a group of Burmese monks who were invited to the country by a group of powerful lay Buddhists with the blessing of the then Prime Minister of the country, John Kotalawela. Lanka Vipassana Bhavana Samithiya (Lanka Insight Meditation Society) was formed for this purpose, and a center for meditation was established in Colombo. A salient feature of the new meditation movement was that it was sponsored by an English-educated elite group of Sinhala Buddhist people. In addition to the Burmese monks, there were a few Sri Lankan monks who had received training in Burma to continue the work. A leading monk associated with the movement from its inception was Kahatapitiye Sumathipala who established a center at Kanduboda, close to Colombo. With the increasing popularity of the movement, more centers were established in many parts of the island. A larger majority of the practitioners at these centers are still laypeople even though the instructor is usually a monk.

Another lay meditation movement still flourishing was started by some laypeople who received training under two eminent monks, Kadawadduwa Jinavamsa (1907–2003) and Matara Sri Nanarama (1901–1992), who were the pioneers of *Kalyani Yogashrama Sansthava* mentioned earlier and much revered meditation teachers. A leading lay meditation teacher associated with this group, a pupil of Matara Sri Nanarama, was Mitra Vettimuni (1951–2019), an elite businessman turned meditator who popularized *vipassanā* meditation among the urban professionals. Godwin Samararatne (1931–2000) was another lay meditation master who taught at Nilambe Meditation Centre and had a considerable lay following both local and foreign. Gamini Priyantha (b. 1966), who has a significant lay follower base, is influenced by the practice of Matara Sri Nanarama and teaches at Colombo and its suburbs.

Since the phenomenon of new Theravāda lay meditation has been studied in detail by many scholars, I do not repeat their discussions (Bond 1992: 130–176; Swearer 1970; Gombrich 1983). What is highlighted in all these discussions is how this phenomenon was started as lay movements and has remained so. Today, the number of lay meditators has increased from its early phase in the 1950s, and the Protestant Buddhist outlook, which made the phenomenon of lay meditation possible, remains the same, not as an active criticism of the monks but as something tacitly accepted. It is true that the laity criticize the monks for their lack of discipline, involvement in party politics, and growing worldliness. But these criticisms do not amount to a rejection of the monks. It is interesting to note that the Vinaya Vardhana Movement, which Kemper (1978) described as "Buddhism without Bhikkhus," had a sizable following several decades ago but is now no longer visible.

Meditation discussed so far as a characteristic of the Theravāda lay practice, however, has not been able to change the overall picture of the religious behavior of the laity, which is characterized by the accumulation of merit for which the reliance on monks is essential. With such new developments as lay meditation practice, the advancements in knowledge, the rise of secularism, and the advancement in communication, one might have expected the traditional and popular religious practice to recede. Paradoxically, not only has this not happened, but the appeal for ritualistic Buddhism also has increased. In Sri Lanka, one can see large-scale meritorious deeds such as offering hundreds of thousands of flowers to the Buddha, lighting eighty-four thousand oil lamps, all guided by the Buddhist monks, taking place practically every full moon day.

This general picture remains equally true for the Southeast Asian Theravāda. In particular, in Myanmar, as noted by writers such as Spiro some six decades ago, the accumulation of merits by such means as giving meals and requisites to the monks and nuns, offering flowers to the Buddha, going on pilgrimages to sacred places, and building monasteries remain the main religious preoccupations of the laity. The status of the monks remains unchallenged. Even though occasionally one may hear an elder complaining about the deterioration of the spirituality of the society, an outsider is bound to be amazed by the religiosity of the laity of Myanmar.

In Sri Lanka, as well as Myanmar, Buddhist modernism was started as a reaction/response to the Protestant religion introduced by the British. However, unlike in Sri Lanka, Myanmar Buddhists do not seem to have absorbed the features of Protestant Christianity. The *vipassanā* meditation movement, as we noted earlier, was started by monks who have remained meditation teachers. It is a fact that Myanmar produced some well-known lay meditation teachers such as U Po Thet (Saya Thatgyi; 1873–1945), his pupil U Ba Khin (1889–1971), and his pupil S. N. Goenka (1924–2013). But all these lay teachers were trained and inspired by the great monastic meditation masters to whom they always remained respectful. At the same time, however, by teaching meditation while remaining within family life, the last two, in particular, brought *vipassanā* meditation down to earth, paving the way for *vipassanā* to become a world practice.

Study of the Dhamma by the laity

A phenomenon associated with meditation is the need for Dhamma knowledge in one who practices it. This does not mean that no knowledge is involved in giving dana or performing other kinds of meritorious deeds. But usually *dāna*, which has a ritualistic element, is performed under the guidance of one's elders or simply under those who know better. The practice of meditation, however, is different. Although meditation is usually practiced under the guidance of an expert meditation teacher, the very fact that one makes a decision to embark on practicing meditation, and continuing with it is a result of one's knowledge about one's own life, the nature of *saṁsāra*, and knowing and feeling the need to practice meditation in order to realize the goal. This explains why mostly the lay *vipassanā* practitioners came from urban educated backgrounds who simply transported their habit of reading for knowledge to their religious practice.

In modern Theravāda societies, people usually get knowledge of the Dhamma by listening to Dhamma sermons and reading books on Dhamma. In the early modern period (and to some extent even now), the Dhamma sermons were highly ritualistic acts that would usually last for the whole night.[9] With the arrival of radio first and television next, today, Dhamma sermons are frequent occurrences and have become much shorter, usually lasting only for one hour or even less. As a means of getting knowledge, however, listening to Dhamma sermons cannot be said to be very effective because in traditional Theravāda societies people would listen to Dhamma mainly to accumulate merit and not to gain knowledge.[10]

Reading Dhamma books by the laity is a modernist development. But mastering the Dhamma by means of reciting has been integral to the Buddhist tradition from the very beginning. This is because the very nature of the Buddhist practice required the practitioner to have the necessary knowledge. Since knowledge (*pariyatti*) preceded practice (*paṭipatti*), both the monks and the laity had to have knowledge. In the ancient times, when the learning was transmitted orally, naturally the monks who preserved the texts orally had knowledge and the laity had to depend on them for their Dhamma knowledge.

If in the premodern period the laity did not have much knowledge in the Dhamma and if they had to rely on the monks for their Dhamma knowledge, this was not because there was any prohibition against the laity mastering the texts but rather due to circumstances that made textual knowledge not easily available for the laity. The Canon clearly seeks to demonstrate that the Buddha had a very open attitude toward his teaching. In a society in which the Upaniṣadic esoterism was very powerful, the Buddha is said to have clearly rejected "inner and outer" associated with religion and remarked that he did not keep the "teacher's [closed] fist" when he taught (*Mahaparinibbāna-sutta*, DN II 100). It is noted that he not only said that the Dhamma shines when it is open and not when it is hidden (AN III 283) but also encouraged disciples to ask questions about the Dhamma (*Mahaparinibbāna-sutta*, DN II 155).

All these suggest that there is in principle not any opposition in Theravāda to the learning of the Dhamma by the laity. It is only a result of historical circumstances that in Theravāda the laity was less learned than the monks. We must not forget in this context that, according to the *Mahāvaṁsa* (33: 102, 103), the ancient chronicle of Sinhala Buddhism, at a very early stage of its history, Theravāda tradition committed the word of the Buddha to writing, which speaks for its openness toward the texts. This openness can be contrasted with the Brāhmanic attitude toward their sacred texts: the Brahmins never allowed their texts to go outside their own caste and were never enthusiastic about committing the texts into writing.

This classical Theravāda attitude to textual knowledge notwithstanding, it appears that during the early modern era, there were some monks who seemed to have thought that the

Buddhist canonical texts should not be printed and published. One significant example is Yatramulle Dharmarama, who taught Pāli to T. W. Rhys Davids (1843–1922), the founder of the Pali Text Society that published the Pāli canon in Roman characters. When the latter proposed this idea, it is said that the learned monk did not approve. But interestingly there were other Buddhist monks who thought differently, and it is they who encouraged Rhys Davids to go ahead in his project and even supported him financially to carry on his work (Wickremeratne 1985: 151–152).

More recent efforts in Theravāda Buddhist countries to translate the Pāli Canon into local languages are partly a result of recognizing the need for laypeople to have access to the *Dhamma*. In Sri Lanka, it started in the mid-1950s and was completed in the early 1980s. Due to the archaic character of the language of this translation now, there is a government-sponsored project to translate the Pāli Canon into simple Sinhala. One A. P. de Soysa, a Buddhist layman with a legal background, translated the entire Pāli Canon into Simple Sinhala marking a milestone in the Dhamma knowledge of the laity, for the laity (and monks as well). Commenting on the situation in Myanmar, however, Dhammasami has pointed out that "the Burmese themselves … see no need for such a translation, as they have always turned to the Saṅgha for an understanding of the canonical texts" (Dhammasami 2018: 188).

In addition, we must mention here numerous Dhamma and Abhidhamma classes and *sutra* discussions conducted by monks at their monasteries, as well as at lay Buddhist organizations, for the dissemination of Dhamma knowledge among the laity. Such acts indicate a major shift of the monastic attitude toward the Dhamma knowledge of the laity. Laypersons, for their part, have been even more enthusiastic about learning the Dhamma ever since the Buddhists started owning printing presses in the latter part of the nineteenth century. The first Sunday Dhamma school was started at Vijayananda Pirivena, Weliwatta, Galle (Sri Lanka) in 1895. Subsequently, Young Men's Buddhist Association started in 1898 undertook to run Sunday schools for Buddhist children where they could receive formal knowledge in the Dhamma.[11] Today in Sri Lanka during daylong programs run for the laity who observe eight or ten precepts on full-moon (*poya*) days, usually a learned Buddhist layman is invited to give a Dhamma talk in addition to several Dhamma sermons by monks. Laypersons with a high Dhamma knowledge are becoming a regular feature in Theravāda Buddhism.

In Myanmar, as we saw earlier in the discussion, monks have been teaching Abhidhamma to laypeople for a long time. It is quite typical for many Burmese laymen and -women to sit various Dhamma examinations conducted by the government as well as by various lay and monastic organizations. Still, this number, contrasted with the number of monks who sit these examinations, represents a minority. Undoubtedly young monks, as well as nuns (*Thila Shin*), constitute a larger majority of the educated of the society. In Myanmar, the laity, who usually do not have much time or opportunities to acquire deep knowledge in the Dhamma, have found a way to compensate for this. It is by supporting materially the education of young monks (and nuns). Although this can happen in any Buddhist country, the Myanmar practice stands out by its widespread popularity. The support of the laity comes in many ways: by way of providing textbooks for study, by bearing all costs related to education including travel within and outside the country, and so on. Usually a young monk has one or more lay benefactors to provide this support. These laymen and -women are very often father and mother substitutes for these monks who have left their parents and relatives to live in places far away from their own native places.

While the overall system is undoubtedly beneficial for both the donor (by accumulating merits) and the receiver (by gaining knowledge), there can be unhealthy effects too. Dhammasami (2018: 180–183) highlights two such developments. The donors push monks to pass as many examinations as possible to derive a sense of pride that the monk they support is doing really well. On the part of educational institutes, they have much competition among themselves to recruit as many students as possible and produce top results in examinations so that they can win wealthy supporters:

> The two teaching monasteries in Burma with most students, the Mahagandhayon, Amarapura, founded by Ashin Janakabhivamsa and the New Ma-Soe-Yein, founded by Ashin Sirindabhivamsa in Mandalay, share between them more than 4000 resident monks and novices. The huge numbers of students and consequent high rates of examination success have drawn many wealthy donors to these two monasteries.
>
> *(Dhammasami 2018: 181)*

According to the same source, there are twenty-one Buddhist colleges and universities in Myanmar out of which only three get support from the state and the remaining eighteen centers are sponsored by the laity for whom the support for monastic education, among other things, is a means of acquiring merits.

To conclude this part of the discussion on the Dhamma knowledge of the laity, we must refer to the *Navayāna* (New Vehicle) Buddhism, based on Theravāda, initiated by Bhim Rao Ambedkar in the middle of the last century in India. Ambedkar's decision to embrace Buddhism along with several hundreds of thousands of his fellow Dalits was carefully thought out.[12] He wrote his *The Buddha and His Dhamma* to serve as the manifesto of the new Buddhism he envisaged. This book presents Buddhism from both modernist and socialist points of view informed by a strong sense of social justice. In this sense, *Navayāna* marks the beginning of a form of rationalist Buddhism in which the distinction, as well as equality between monks and laymen, is maintained, the distinction insofar as their ways of life and the mutually beneficial existence is concerned, and equality due to the fact that both share the same Dhamma (455). In Book III, part I, discussing "His Place in His Dhamma," Ambedkar begins by saying that "the Buddha claimed no place for Himself in His Own Dhamma" (213). Hence, it would be unimaginable for Ambedkar to envisage the Buddhist laity depending on the monks.

Since a larger majority of the followers of *Navayāna* Buddhism remain illiterate and materially poor, the rationalist reading of Buddhism developed by Ambedkar could still be considered a far cry. Nevertheless, with a fast-growing community of educated and professional *Navayāna*, Buddhists in many parts of India, including Maharashtra, where there are several millions of them, Ambedkar's new Buddhism is responding to new challenges. A relatively new development among these educated *Navayāna* Buddhists is their interest in the study of Pāli language. In places like Mumbai, Pune, Aurangabad, and Nashik (in Maharashtra), there are Pāli classes, some conducted by the academic staff of the regional universities. This move seems to be resulting from two reasons: one is political, namely, that Pāli is reckoned as the language of Buddhists, and hence, it is held that Buddhists should focus on Pāli, not on Brahmanic Sanskrit. This Pāli language factor has become an important aspect of developing a Buddhist identity among these new followers of Buddhism. The other reason seems to be "Protestant," namely, learning Pāli as a means of accessing the original discourses of the Buddha, including the Abhidhamma texts, the study of which has gained popularity among these groups lately.

Concluding remarks

As a part of concluding remarks, it is necessary to determine the place and the role of women in what is discussed in this chapter. What is said in this discussion on laity is basically applicable to both men and women. However, In Theravāda lay Buddhist practice, including meditation, as perhaps in religious practice in general, women appear to outnumber men. As Gombrich and Obeyesekere (1990: 234) have noticed, in almost all monasteries (in Sri Lanka), there are women's societies the main function of which is to look after the sustenance of the monks whereas men's societies look after things like the construction of buildings and organizing public events. In Myanmar practices associated with *Nat* (spirit) beliefs, which are shared by a larger majority of Buddhists, are usually attended by women, namely, by the mother of the family (Bechert 1984: 155). Although the overall social and educational standards of women in Buddhist societies remain relatively higher still there are certain restrictions. For instance, in Sri Lanka, although the historical legend is that the Buddha's Tooth Relic was brought to the country by a woman—Princess Hemamala—by hiding it in her hair, the prevalent practice is that women are not allowed to enter the inner chamber where the relic is housed. In Myanmar, the space closest to the object of worship is reserved for the monks and the males. Such traditions coming from the past, by far, seem to be tolerated tacitly.

A prominent feature in Buddhist modernism started toward the end of the nineteenth century was the reduction of the traditional gap between the monks and the laity. The following statement occurring in a *Memorial of the Saṅgha of Ceylon to King Edward VII* of 1904 suggests that the Saṅgha during this period was quite concerned about the new development:

> The Buddhist *Saṅgha* … form an integral part of the religion itself and are entitled to equal adoration with the Buddha and the Dhamma. The religion of the Buddha consists of only three elements of Buddha, the Dhamma and the *Saṅgha*, and nothing more. By the laws of the Buddha the laity form no part of religion. The *Saṅgha* are the only living representatives of Buddhism on earth.[13]

This emphatic assertion of the monks notwithstanding, the gap between monks and laypeople has become narrowed. Nevertheless, the latter, all over the traditional Theravāda world, appear to be heavily dependent on the former for their religious rites and rituals. Although the laity has criticisms of the Saṅgha about their weakened morality, the former is not prepared to follow religion without the latter. The Vinaya Vardhana movement in Sri Lanka, which strived to get rid of the Saṅgha whom they claimed to be corrupt, died down not because it "has fallen a victim to its own success" as Gombrich and Obeyesekere think, but, most probably, because the laity settled down to accept the Saṅgha as they were because the former felt that they could not do without the latter.

The *Vesak* greeting cards, which came as a result of Protestant Buddhism and once very popular in Sri Lanka, have disappeared almost completely with the popularity of social media. Although the lay practice of meditation was then a new development indicating the reduced role of the monk in the life of the laity, today, with the vast popularity of *vipassanā* meditation as a therapeutic measure, many laypeople practice meditation not to realize liberation from *saṃsāra* but to live happily in the *saṃsāra*.

Gods have been brought back to the sociopolitical scene with a new vigor, and it is quite commonplace today for people to smash coconuts before gods—a practice found in Sri Lanka—as a means of redressing injustice. Reading horoscopes, announcing the direction where Mara is on a particular day (so as to avoid that direction when leaving home for work or on an important mission), determining auspicious and inauspicious moments are some routine services provided in the early morning by many local TV and radio stations (in Sri Lanka) for their viewers and listeners. Examples of this nature seem to suggest that the laity in Theravāda today cannot be understood with reference to such categories as Buddhist modernism or Protestant Buddhism alone.

Notes

1 Gombrich (1983, 380) has noticed that "*upāsaka*" is used in contemporary Sri Lanka not to refer to any and every lay Buddhist but to one who is more religiously dedicated.
2 In the *Mahāparinibbāna-sutta* (DN II 104–106), the Buddha says to Mara that he will not pass away until all four groups of his followers master and practice the *Dhamma* equally well.
3 Among such people mentioned in the discourses are householder Citta, highest among the well-versed *upāsakas* in the *Dhamma* (AN I 26; SN IV 281–304), Siha, the army commander (AN IV 180–82) and Ugga (AN IV 208–212), and Khujjuttara, the highest among the well-versed *upāsikās* in the *Dhamma* (AN I 26).
4 Literally meaning the message or the teaching of the Buddha but referring to his religious organization.
5 In Myanmar, there are an estimated sixty thousand *Thila Shin* or Buddhist nuns (who are lower in status than *bhikkhunis* who do not exist in Myanmar) who also depend on the generosity of the Buddhist laity for their existence and education.
6 See Gombrich and Obeyesekere (1990: 6 note 7 and 202–240) for a detailed discussion of this concept.
7 Read Tilakaratne (2012a) for a comprehensive discussion on the nature and content of the debate resulted from this introduction.
8 Twenty-five hundredth anniversary of the Buddha's passing away celebrated during 1955–1956.
9 For a comparative study of new and old methods of Dhamma preaching, refer to Seneviratne (1999: 42–55). For *Vessantara-jātaka* recital among the Burmese Buddhists, which lasts for several days, refer to Tilakaratne (2012b: 101–104).
10 Listening to Dhamma is one of the ten meritorious deeds.
11 Presently these schools come under the Buddha Sasana Ministry of the government. Similarly, well-organized Dhamma school systems are not found in the other Theravāda countries.
12 Refer to Tartakov (2003) for an insightful discussion on this new form of Buddhism.
13 Cited in Bechert (1966: 67).

References

Bechert, Heinz. 1966. *Buddhismus, Staat und Gesellsschaft in den Landern des Theravada Buddhismus*, vol. I. Frankfurt and Berlin: Alfred Metzner.

Bechert, Heinz. 1984. "To be a Burmese is to be a Buddhist: Buddhism in Burma." In *Buddhism: Buddhist Monks and Nuns in Society and Culture*, ed. Heinz Bechert, 147–158. London: Thames and Hudson Ltd.

Bond, George E. 1992. *The Buddhist Revival in Sri Lanka: Religious Tradition, Reinterpretation and Response*. Delhi: Motilal Banarsidass.

Braun, Erik. 2013. *The Birth of Insight: Meditation, Modern Buddhism and the Burmese Monk Ledi Sayadaw*. Chicago and London: University of Chicago Press.

Braun, Erik. 2014. "Meditation en Masse: How Colonialism sparked the global Vipassana movement." *Tricycle* (Spring 2014).

Dhammasami, Khammai. 2018. *Buddhism, Education and Politics in Burma and Thailand: From the Seventeenth Century to the Present*. London: Bloomsbury Academic.

Gombrich, Richard. 1983.. "From Monastery to the Meditation Centre: Lay Meditation in Modern Sri Lanka." In *Buddhist Studies: Ancient and Modern*, ed. P. Denwood, A. Piatagorsky, 20–34. London: Curzon Press.

Gombrich, Richard, Obeyesekere, Gananath. 1990. *Buddhism Transformed: Religious Change in Sri Lanka*. Delhi: Motilal Banarsidass.

Kemper, Steven. 1978. "Buddhism without Bhikkhus: The Sri Lanka Vinaya Vardhana Society." In *Religion and the Legitimization of Power in Sri Lanka*, ed. Bardwell L. Smith, 212–235. Chambersburg: Anima Publishers.

Seneviratne, H.L. 1999. *The Work of Kings: The New Buddhism in Sri Lanka*. Chicago: University of Chicago Press.

Spiro, Melford E. 1982. *Buddhism and Society: A Great Tradition and Its Burmese Vicissitudes* (Second Expanded Edition). Berkeley: University of California Press.

Swearer, Donald K. 1970. "Lay Buddhism and the Buddhist Revival in Ceylon." *Journal of the American Academy of Religion* 38 (3): 255–275.

Tartakov, Gary. 2003. "B.R. Ambedkar and the Navayana Diksa." In *Religious Conversion in India: Modes, Motivations and Meanings*, ed. Rowena Robinson, Sathianandan Clarke, 192–215. New Delhi: Oxford University Press.

Tilakaratne, Asanga. 2012a. *Theravada: The View of the Elders*. Honolulu: University of Hawai'i Press.
Tilakaratne, Asanga. 2012b. "The Mahasi Sayadaw Method of Vipassana Meditation: An Abbreviated Path or a Misunderstanding?" In *Buddhist Meditation: Text, Tradition and Practice*, ed. Khammai Dhammasami, Charles Willeman, 55–78. Mumbai: Somaiya Publications Pvt. Ltd.
Warder, A.K. 2000. *Indian Buddhism*. Delhi: Motilal Banarsidass Publishers.
Weber, Max. 1960. *The Religion of India: The Sociology of Hinduism and Buddhism*. Glencoe, Illinois: The Free Press.
Wickremeratne, Ananda. 1985. *The Genesis of an Orientalist: Thomas William Rhys Davids in Sri Lanka*. Columbia, Missouri: South Asia Books.

12
DISCIPLINE
Beyond the Vinaya

Thomas Borchert

Normally, when thinking about Theravāda Buddhist monastics and discipline, scholars turn immediately to the Vinaya, the portion of the teachings of the Buddha focused on the rules that monastics are supposed to follow. There are three different *Vinaya*s currently in use in the contemporary world, and *saṅghas* of the Theravāda world follow the Pāli *Vinaya*. This version of the Vinaya is composed of two parts, the *Suttavibhaṅga* and the *Khandaka*. The former contains the list of rules the monks and nuns are to follow (the *Patimokkha*), as well as commentaries and narratives about these rules, while the latter contains discussions of various matters of monastic life. In the Pāli *Vinaya*, monks are responsible for following 227 rules, while nuns are to follow 311 rules. Novices are responsible for ten, and female renunciants, such as the *mae chi* of Thailand or the *dasa sil matā* of Sri Lanka, normally follow either eight or ten precepts. When they ordain, either as a novice or taking the "higher ordination" (*upasampadā*) monastics agree to follow these rules, and they form the core of what is meant to guide and shape monastic lives, a "yardstick for determining monastic etiquette and behavior" (Kusa 2007: 196).

Moreover, Vinaya texts have themselves become invaluable resources for understanding the complexity of Buddhist lives and communities. For the last three decades, scholars such as Gregory Schopen (2004), Shayne Clarke (2014), Petra Kieffer-Pülz (2014), and others have been mining different *Vinaya*s in an effort to open up the worlds that Buddhist monastics lived in. In doing so, they have helped us see that Buddhist monks and nuns held and bequeathed property, that they engaged in businesses practices, and that they had families. Using the *Vinaya*s, these scholars have shown that the worlds of Buddhist monasticism were far more complex than either scholars or the general public have imagined. More than heroic renunciants who were required to follow hundreds of rules, explorations of the *Vinaya*s have shown that Buddhist monastics were fully formed humans, with all the complex emotions that this entails.

Yet, while scholarship has done invaluable work in opening up our understanding of the worlds of Buddhist monastics, it has only gone part way toward helping us understand how it is that monks and nuns are disciplined. By disciplining, I am referring to the process or set of processes wherein monastics learn not just the content of what it means to be a nun, monk, or novice but also where and how a monastic subjectivity is formed. To be a monastic is to have a certain position in a society, and to fully inhabit that position, the practices and habits of monastic life need to be instilled and naturalized. Even as the rules of the Vinaya provide

DOI: 10.4324/9781351026666-15

central and important tools for communicating to monastics how they should act, there are limits to them. First, while it may seem obvious, they are only texts. They do not in and of themselves create agents that live according to their rules. Thus, it is necessary to understand the way they are learned and enforced, which parts are enforced, and how. Second, while clearly important for creating guidelines for the behavior of monastics, the Vinaya exists in specific contexts, along with other discourses, about religion and Buddhism, nationalism, and gender that also shape the ways that monastics should act. In this chapter, I argue that to understand how monastics are disciplined, we need to look at a much broader range of materials and contexts. While the Vinaya is certainly a part of this, we must also consider, the institutional, political, and communal contexts in which monastics not only learn the Vinaya, but they learn and ideally naturalize, what it means to be a proper nun or monk.

How to wear the robes

In order to show why this is necessary, I want to consider a poster I encountered in 2013 on the Chiang Mai campus of Mahā Chulālongkornrājavidyālaya University, one of the two Buddhist universities in Thailand. The poster shows a monk dressed in a neat fashion, standing straight and tall, his robe wrapped around one shoulder. A monk's bag hangs from his crooked arm, and a student badge is pinned to the outer robe draped over his single shoulder. The monk is standing in front of a tree and plants, perhaps to make it seem as if he was in a "forest" (although he was also standing on concrete circles common in urban gardens as places to walk in Thailand). The top of the poster states that its purpose is to remind monks and novices about "dressing properly according to the rules of the School of Pāli Studies" at the university, and it lists eight different rules about the way that monks should dress on the school's environs. They include commands that monks or novices should wear their robes "draped over one arm, with saffron robes," that the "end of the robe is five inches above the ankle," and that the belt and shoulder sash should be saffron." Other rules include a command to keep the head, mustache, and eyebrows shaved and the nails cut.

On the surface, there is little remarkable about this poster. These rules are reflective of the *sekhiya*, the training rules that are a part of the *Patimokkha* (Thanissaro 1994: 19). Indeed, in the *Entrance to the Vinaya*, an introduction to disciplinary rules written by the early twentieth-century supreme patriarch and prince of Thailand, Vajirañānarorasa, the first and second rules refer to the need for the under robe and the upper robe to be worn correctly. The prince-patriarch then explains that "to wear correctly means to wear the under-robe neatly, covering the navel at the upper edge but not reaching the chest; while the lower edge covers the knees to halfway down the calves but not reaching the ankle" (Vajirañānarorasa 1969: 204). In other words, the poster might be read as quoting a commonly used textbook that also reminds the students (all novices or young monks) that they should be neat and tidy when they are on campus. Although it does not say it explicitly on the poster, the implication is that neat robes are reflective of strong and vital discipline.

The robes are perhaps among the most identifiable aspects of Buddhist monastics, in Thailand and elsewhere in the Theravāda world. While a variety of institutions and communities such as the military, shave their heads either by regulation or standard practice the robes of monastics mark them clearly as set apart from the rest of society. The robes are so important that, in Thailand and Sri Lanka at least, when a monk is arrested for committing a crime, they must disrobe before going to prison (perhaps wearing white) because it is understood that the robes cannot be in jail (Reynolds 1994; Schonthal 2019a). The robes in other words represent both purity and the fundamentally set apart status of monastics.

Yet both this poster and Buddhist history suggest that neat robes are reflective of more complicated processes than simply remembering rules of proper action. In addition to harkening back to the *Entrance to the Vinaya*, the poster also distinguishes between insiders and outsiders. Monastic students are reminded to identify themselves with the university, by using a shoulder bag with a school logo and the school ID badge. Posters like these are common practice on Thai university campuses, where students are regularly reminded of the need to wear uniforms and to look "neat" (Thai: *riap roy*). This "neatness" is tied up with identification with the institution, saying in ways both implicit and explicit, that you are one of us. This is not all that different from moments in Buddhist history when monks debated over the proper way to wear their robes. While these debates, such as the one in Sri Lanka in the late nineteenth century over whether monks should wear their robes over one shoulder or two, were framed in terms of proper religious action, they were often also about group identity. In this context, Anne Blackburn has noted that

> [t]hrough the elements of dress, monks did (and do) identify their fellows and those with whom they might presume to find distance or disagreement. In response to elements of dress, lay patrons identify the monks with whom they are likely to find common cause on the basis of caste and/or perceived attainments of discipline."
>
> (Blackburn 2010: 92)

In other words, while on the surface the way to wear the robes is simply about knowing how to act as a monastic, I suggest that there is often if not always an institutional and thus political context to the way that monastics are trained to act, even if the interests of those politics are hidden in religious discourse (Lincoln 2012).

Monks behaving badly

The problem of undisciplined monastics is one that seems to be quite common. For example, in April 2019, there was a story in the *Bangkok Post* about a monk and a nun/*mae chi* who were arrested for possessing drugs that should not be in the possession of a monk (Methee 2019). The story did not give many details, nor did it need to. It is a well-worn tale that shows up in the Thai press (both English and Thai language), which might be categorized as "monks behaving badly." There are stories that are about monks who have been arrested for drunk driving (or public drunkenness), being caught in a sex ring or having sex (with either men or women), or embezzlement of some sort. Most notorious in recent years has been the story of Phra Nen Kham, a monk who came to prominence a half-dozen years ago when videos of him surfaced on YouTube with a Gucci handbag, Ray-Bans, and a private jet. There was much outrage at all of this: a monk should not act like this, that it was "inappropriate" (Thai: *may somkhuan*). This narrative of indiscipline and impropriety has become common in Thailand, but it is not limited to that country (see, e.g., *Colombo Telegraph* 2012).

What is useful about these stories is not the events themselves but the way that they portray monastics and the assumptions behind them. In Thailand, they are often accompanied by hand-wringing about the state of the Saṅgha, how monks don't act like they ought to (or used to), and the inability of the Supreme Saṅgha Council to govern monks. Significantly, they also assume that there is *a* standard for how monks should behave—according to the Vinaya—and their failure to do so is a failure of discipline. This failure of discipline is a crisis in and for the Saṅgha and, implicitly at least, a potential sign of the decline of the *sāsanā*.

These narratives tend to reinforce an image of what "real" Buddhism is, but in doing so, they also render invisible some aspects of Theravāda Buddhism in the twenty-first century. First, Buddhism (lay and monastic) across the Theravāda world, as well as within specific countries, is far more diverse than is normally portrayed within these narratives (if less commonly in academic scholarship). There are monastics who study, who meditate, who believe in magic, who don't believe in magic, who tell fortunes, who do office work, who teach, who believe that their vocations are in social work or organic farming, who believe their vocations are in performing rituals, who believe their vocations lie in communicating with the laity, who believe monastics should have a political voice, and who believe they should not. Official forms of Buddhism and quasi-official images (reinforced through the narrative of monks behaving badly) do not exhaust the way that monastics act in the world, how they think about it, or the way they view how monastics should attend to the teachings of the Buddha (*Buddhavacanam*), beyond a generalized veneration.[1]

Second, these articles are emerging at a particular historical moment (i.e., a contingent conjuncture) that has a clear impact on the way that Buddhism is understood or perhaps what is defined as legitimate forms of Buddhism. Within Thailand, the last two decades have been marked by conflict between different factions of elites. This conflict has manifested in mass mobilizations of the Thai populace, two coups (2006 and 2014), and years of military rule until the restoration of an elected government in 2019 (albeit one in which the military has an oversized influence; see Askew [2010] for discussion of the early years of these events). For the most part, Thai monks have sought to avoid overt participation in these politics. However, since 2014 the Thai state has increasingly made portions of the Saṅgha a target of its efforts to sanitize the nation, including the arrest of members of the Supreme Saṅgha Council in 2018. Ostensibly, the actions of the state are to rid the Saṅgha of corruption, yet it is also clear that the Thai state's surveillance is directed at monks that it sees as aligned with its enemies (Larsson 2019). There is a similar specificity to conditions in Sri Lanka and Myanmar, where the last half-dozen years have seen not only the end of a civil war and military rule, respectively, but also the emergence of an intense Buddhist nationalism wherein monks have fostered Islamophobic actions in each country.[2]

These politics intersect in an interesting way with what we might think of as the governance of monks within the "Theravāda secular." If we understand secularities in terms of an understanding of what counts as the proper space of religion in society, as well as the line between "religion" and "not-religion," then to follow the formulation of Mandair and Dressler (2011), "religion-making" from above is where the state establishes the rules for what counts as "religion." How actors respond to the state's formulations (actively or passively) is referred to as "religion-making from below." The specific conditions of religion and politics across the Theravāda world will impact what "religion-making from above" looks like in each nation-state and the formations of secularity. However, there are also important commonalities, such as the constitutional status of Theravāda Buddhism as the first among equals in Sri Lanka and Myanmar, the adherence to Theravāda Buddhism by the majority race or ethnicity, and a strong anxiety about the decline of the religion in the second half of the dispensation of the Buddha. Theravāda secularities shape the context in which monastics are disciplined, whether through external forces or self-disciplining practices.[3]

Understanding the context of Theravāda secularities allows (indeed requires) us to ask different kinds of questions about Buddhist formations. Over the last century, there has been a tendency to locate monastics, and particularly monks, as being at the heart of Buddhism. If you want to know about Buddhism in places like Laos or Myanmar, then you would need to know about monks. For example, when Julia Cassaniti, in a discussion of the formation of ethical selves in northern Thailand, asked villagers about Buddhism, they told her they knew nothing and that she should talk to the monks. In a telling moment of irony, these monks said that they did not know much about Buddhism and that she should go ask the monks in large urban temples (Cassaniti 2015). One might imagine that the urban monks would tell her to go to another set of monks, such as the ones who had official titles. The confusion between Cassaniti (who was interested in understanding what villagers knew and thought) and the villagers (who thought she wanted to know what "real" Buddhism was) reflects the assumption that monastics are the ones that matter. I suggest we need to be thinking about this differently.

Jessica Starling (2019) has shown the necessity of recalibrating our attention away from the front stage to the backstage of Japanese temple Buddhism. Doing so allows us to see that temple wives are not marginal to the practice of Buddhism but central to it, and that Japanese Buddhism should be really understood as functioning within a set of relationships (Starling 2019). Recalibrating our attention to see temple wives has the added benefit of allowing us to understand male priests more clearly, both who they are within the temple communities and how they rely on the labor of their wives in the construction of their authority. Following this, I suggest we need to similarly recenter the way we see Theravāda monastics. They are not the center of Buddhism, but they are a particular type of social actor that is at least partly separated from the rest of society by modern legal structures (see, e.g., Borchert and Darlington 2017/2018: 131–136; Schonthal 2016; Larsson 2016). While official forms of Theravāda Buddhism normally place monks at the heart of the religion, this has tended to obscure the fact that monastics are people (men within the majority of the Theravāda world) who have taken on a very particular type of profession. This profession provides them with some privileges (such as high status, access to education, and free food in most of the Theravāda world) and disadvantages (constraints on their activities as well as the ability to accumulate goods). Moreover, they are subject to training and disciplining and gendered and national discourses that overlap in some ways from those of lay Buddhists and are distinct from them in other ways. It is this sense of monastics as a particular type of actor within a larger whole that I suggest we need to understand more clearly.

Religious ideologies and practices within educational contexts

Monastics are disciplined within schools. In December 2002, I was visiting a group of monks in Sipsongpannā, who were doing a weeklong retreat. There were about fifteen monks, who were accompanied by two or three novices each, and they were all camped out in the worship hall (Dai: *wihān*) of a village temple a few miles outside of the capital of the region. There was not much to do during the afternoons of the retreat and on the afternoon that I was there, several senior monks decided to take the opportunity to work with some of the novices who were not students at their school. Their goal that day was to show the novices how to address monks they did not know in a polite fashion. In order to do this, they had a senior novice walk by them, making sure he bent his body in such a way that his head was lower than the monk's head. The senior novice then pretended to be a senior monk, and the junior novices practiced walking by him. When they were not low enough, one of the monks would tell him to go lower, or even physically push him down, until the novice's head and body were positioned "appropriately" below those of the senior novice. The retreat had become an impromptu school.

The first and most obvious way that men and boys are disciplined is in schools and other pedagogical contexts, such as the retreat. There are two different things taking place within these schools: first, novices and young monks are learning models of how to be a proper monk;

second, they are being physically trained in the subjectivity of what being a monk entails. This training may take place in a variety of contexts: informal village temples, formal schools, and even camps during school vacations (Borchert 2017: 8–9; Chladek 2017). Monasteries were the primary location of education in Buddhism and other fields of knowledge prior to the twentieth century, but since then, systems of monastic schools have emerged in relation to secular schools throughout South and Southeast Asia, sometimes as an additional form of public education, sometimes in competition with it (Chessman 2003; Samuels 2010; Dhammasami 2018; Borchert 2017).

While this is both intellectual and physical training, it is particularly the latter that I highlight here. Although the young men in these schools do learn about the life of the Buddha and the rules of the Vinaya, the material that they learn is often secondary to the physical ways that they are trained, and the bodily dispositions that they are asked to internalize. For example, Jeffrey Samuels (2004) suggests that novices in contemporary Sri Lanka learn proper monastic behavior not through the study of the teachings of the Buddha but through physical actions, of sweeping and cleaning the temple, and by worshipping the Buddha each day. The novices that Samuels talks to highlight that it was not what they studied but by internalizing "the way they were supposed to act" when they cleaned, walked, or talked to the teacher (964). As he says, "action functioned to mold the bodies of the novices within the monastic environment by restructuring the bodies and minds of the novices" through an "action-oriented pedagogy" (966). The physical and the cognitive often work together. Joanna Cook has suggested that in meditation retreats of female renunciants in Thailand (referred to as *mae chi*), the "ethical ideals of monasticism are actualized through the practice of meditation" (Cook 2010: 94). But it is also a concern with showing young men how to act properly and internalize the acts of getting dressed or walking like a monk (or novice) "should" act until this is naturalized (Borchert 2017: 110–112). Indeed, for new novices, or novices at Dhamma camp, making sure that they are neat and tidy (*riap roy*) in their bodily dispositions is a regular challenge (Chladek 2017: 66).

While this is a general process across the Theravāda world, it is also specific to different countries and Buddhist cultures. Some of the vectors of variation have to do with the state's role in the development of the education, local practices and concerns with Vinaya and the different actors that are involved in education. For example, in Sipsongpannā, the Chinese government has very little to do with the development of the educational system that the Dai-lue monks have developed, while in Thailand, the state has been involved in the educational system since the start of the twentieth century. In terms of local practices, adherence to Vinaya rules varies and this affects educational practices. In Sipsongpannā and northern Thailand, eating solids after noon is not uncommon for novices. Monks who are also teachers have told me that it is more important for students who are novices to have sufficient food for their studies.[4] Finally, the educational practices of Sipsongpannā often include former monks (*khanān*) as important supplementary pedagogical resources. In Thailand, monastic school teachers are a combination of laity and monks, and the funding for monastic high schools comes out of the national government budget. These local variations affect the ways in which novices and young monks are encouraged (or forced) to be one kind of monk or another.

Policing monastic bodies and appropriate activity

Since at least the middle of 2018, the state of monastic bodies has become a concern of the public in Thailand. First, around the middle of 2018, there was a whole series of stories that focused on an obesity "crisis" within the Thai Saṅgha. The articles pointed to statistics that suggested that as much as 40 percent of Thai monks were obese but that neither monks nor lay supporters noticed because monastic robes are not formfitting. The culprits identified were both a sedentary lifestyle, high-caloric foods, and especially sugary drinks. Monks apparently take in fewer calories than the average Thai man, but they also do less with those calories; specifically, they rarely exercise. Ironically, however, around the same time, a story circulated in both Thai and English language media about a monk who was too fit. This monk was incredibly buff, with prominent six-pack abs, and comments about this monk's social media posts ranged widely. Among the negative comments were that it was "inappropriate" (*may somkhuan*) for a monk to post these (or to exercise this way) because it displayed or inspired desire or that it would shake the faith of the people in the Saṅgha. The Thai National Office of Buddhism was concerned enough that it directed Buddhist protection groups to investigate the photos and find this monk (Khaosod 2018).

These stories suggest there is a lot of free-floating anxiety about the bodies of Thai monks. They are too fat or too thin. They act inappropriately in ways that are visible, and this is seen as a problem. When the monks at the Dhamma Summer Camps are working with the novices, they are highly concerned with making sure that the novices' robes are neat and in the right length. This is reasonable to the extent that these monks are responsible for the novices, but at the same time, I want to suggest that they are acting on a standard that can be ambiguous. People (lay and monastic, state and local community) have a vision of what a monk should look like and how he should act even if they do not always know where this aesthetic comes from. They find this aesthetic attractive (Samuels 2010: 34), but little understand how the aesthetic can vary across the Theravāda world.

It is worth asking where the aesthetics of a "proper" monastic body comes from. The people who are concerned about proper monastic behavior would no doubt claim that they are basing their complaints not on politics or anything mundane like that but on an understanding of how a monk should act that is from the *sāsanā*, the teachings of the Buddha. Yet there is very little within the Vinaya precluding for example exercise. When we look at something like the *Entrance to the Vinaya* from the early part of the twentieth century, which is the basis for many of the textbooks that are used in monastic high school, there are a number of statements out of which an aesthetic of bodily comportment could be extracted. It should be neat, the nails are to be cut, and hair neat (not unlike the poster from Mahā Chulālongkornrājavidyālaya). Moreover, in the section discussing the training rules, the prince-patriarch elaborates how monastics are to enter towns with "downcast eyes" or "laughing loudly." Indeed, he should go with "little sound," "not go fidgeting," or have "arms akimbo" (Vajirañāṇarorasa 1969: 206–208). There is attention to how one goes to the toilet, for example, walks in public, and interacts with laypeople. But the vision of well-mannered monks that can be extracted from the *Entrance to the Vinaya* is only part of the story about what proper action looks like for monks. It does not, for example, talk about exercise.

The relative absence of concepts of exercise from the Vinaya makes it difficult for monastics to know what is and is not appropriate in this aspect of physical activity. The accounts of monastic bodies being overweight or too fit suggest a desire for wellness for the Saṅgha but not a completely clear path to get there. This lack of clarity is born out in ethnographic materials from Thailand and Sipsongpannā. Monks and novices in these places participate in physical exercise, but they do so in ways that are constrained by varying views on the propriety of these activities. Casas (2017), for example, writes of Dai-lue novices in Sipsongpannā participating in basketball and soccer leagues but also that this is seen as a degradation of monastic norms (a point he argues against). In particular, he highlights anxiety that Thai monks who are patrons of the Chinese Theravāda Saṅgha ought not to see novices playing basketball (Casas 2017: 52). Dai-lue monks have told me that they shelved plans to construct athletic facilities for novices because they feared that Thai lay patrons would find it unseemly (personal communication, in Jing Hong, China, 2007). At the same time, however, Thai monks also clearly participate in exercise. In northern Thailand, it is not uncommon for *wats* to have fields in the back where monastics (primarily probably not solely novices[5]) have fields tucked away in the back for playing soccer, badminton, or other games (Chladek 2017/18: 56). That these fields are hidden suggests that there is tension between what activities are not appropriate and which are allowed but should not be seen.

Part of what this means is that the question of what a "proper" monastic body looks like, or what proper action looks like can vary across Theravāda communities, and so the effort to discipline these bodies will also vary. It is beyond the scope of this chapter to fully address the dynamic of propriety for Theravāda monastics, but there are two points worth highlighting as the site for future research. First, there is a complex dynamic between local and translocal conceptions of propriety. The Vinaya provides a key source for the latter, and images of how monks "should" act move freely across the Theravāda world electronically. Yet, the issue of exercise points to local rules and values having an important impact on standards to which monastics are held (Schonthal 2019b). I suggest we need to think more fully and comparatively about the interplay between the formal and informal, the local and translocal in understanding what is deemed as appropriate for Theravāda monastics.

Second, and relatedly, recent scholarship (Makely 2007; Chladek 2017; Casas 2017; Keeler 2017) has begun to consider the masculinities of monks. While on the surface the status of monks is because of their dedication to the Dhamma, it is also tied up with their renunciation of sex (Keyes 2007; Makely 2007; Keeler 2017). At the same time, significant parts of the Theravāda world practice temporary ordination; in these regions, time in robes may be less, or not only, about learning the teachings of the Buddha but also how to become a proper member of society ("cooked," according to my informants in Sipsongpannā)—really how to become a proper man. Yet like with exercise, there are both local and translocal ideals of the masculine that monks and novices may be subject to. For example, Creak (2011: 18) has demonstrated a "muscular Buddhis[t]" ideal in colonial and post-colonial Laos that is consistent with the monastic basketball players that Casas discusses (Casas 2017). On the other hand, Chladek (2017a: 135) has argued that Thai monastics are subject to much more complex notions of "proper" masculinity, and that the Saṅgha is a place where heteronormative masculinity is both reinforced and challenged. Even as it is clear that notions and aesthetics of monastic propriety are entangled with questions of masculinities, how these intersect in the disciplining process of male monastics within and across Theravāda societies remains to be fully researched.

Laity and monastic discipline

The third idea that we need to consider in understanding the disciplining process for Theravāda monastics is the role of the laity. We do not yet have a very robust understanding of how monastics interact with their lay supporters. Ethnographic accounts (including my own) tend to emphasize the distinctions between laity and monastics rather than their interactions. And yet, in places like Bangkok or other urban centers in Thailand, *wats* are located in the middle of neighborhoods, and novices and monks regularly interact with laypeople in both formal and informal ways. Many monks I have interviewed in Bangkok since 2014 have told me that the Saṅgha comes out of the lay community and holds many, if not most, of the same views as the laity. This suggests that the laity play an important role in the disciplining of monks in two different ways: first as an imagined other, and second as enforcers of particular standards.

Michael Chladek (2017b) has argued for a concept he refers to as the "imagined laity." He notes that when training novices as at summer Dhamma camps, monks will often encourage the young men to act in certain ways with reference to the laity, to their faith (*saddhā*), and their disappointment if the young men act out of line. That is, it is not a real, actual layperson's feelings but the vision of the laity and their imagined attitudes that matter. The "imagined laity" is a tool that monks use to train and discipline novices, but I have encountered monks who also use this idea. In the late 1990s, I was traveling with my wife in Thailand, and we visited a monk who was a friend of mine. When we said our farewells, my wife tried to shake his hand, which he ignored, but it clearly bothered him. Later he mentioned it to me, saying that "the people" do not like seeing monks with women. "It makes them feel bad. It is not attractive [*may suay*]." At the time, I took him literally, even though there were no laypeople around and interacting with us. Chladek's point, however, encourages a different interpretation. My friend was not referring to actual humans but rather to his imagination of them and what they might think about that interaction. In this reading, "the people" become a tool of self-discipline that the monk uses to remind himself of how he should (or thinks he should) act.

At the same time, however, laypeople also have a direct impact on communicating to monks (either explicitly or implicitly) about what kinds of things are okay or not okay. I have argued elsewhere (Borchert 2020) in giving monks some things and not others, lay supporters communicate directly what they see as appropriate or not. For example, several years ago, I witnessed a lay family give a monk in Bangkok a set of power tools as *dāna*. This was not a standard gift of course, but the monk later told me that he sponsored the construction of a temple in Northeast Thailand that a group of monks were building, and they needed the tools to continue their construction. The family was supporting the work of these monks, even if the idea of Theravāda monks with power tools is at least incongruous. Similarly, if we think about the trope identified earlier of monks behaving badly, there is a clear lay component to them. When monks drink at restaurants or drive cars under the influence, this often happens in semipublic spaces like restaurants. This means that there are lay Buddhists who support this, providing the monks with alcohol. In other words, they are neither critiquing the monks (at least to their faces) nor refusing to serve them but instead allowing/permitting monastic standards to be breached. This, in turn, creates new local standards for how a monk should act.

Conclusion: monks and smoking

I have suggested so far that in thinking about disciplining monks, we should look to schools, aesthetic visions of a "proper monk" monk, and lay articulation of communal standards in addition to the Vinaya. There are a number of ways that this analysis could and should be expanded. For example, there is a strong and important differentiation between public and private (inside the *wat* and outside) for monks—not least of which is that they do not have to wear their outer robe in the *wat*. Moreover, it is likely that the three mechanisms I have described are not equivalent across time and space. We could think about strong and weak forces of disciplining, the impact that mass and social media have on the images of monks that become hegemonic, the specific dynamics of state–civil society interactions across the Theravāda world, the history of the local Saṅgha and lay-Saṅgha relationships, as well as an individual monk's personal history. The point, however, is that monks are disciplined by wider social forces, whether this is done to them, or they are taught to do it to themselves. We see some of the issues coming together when we consider the tobacco-smoking habits of Thai monks.

In the first decade of the century, there was an effort to get monks to stop smoking cigarettes in Thailand. The campaign began with the annual birthday address given by the late king

Rama IX in 2003 in which he talked about the problem of smoking more generally. While the number of monks who smoked at the time is a bit unclear, studies suggested that between 25% and 45% of the monastic population smoked tobacco (AFP 2005; Chaveepojnkamjorn and Pichainarong 2005). After the king's address, the Supreme Saṅgha Council and the National Office of Buddhism established a committee to consider ways to reduce smoking with the Saṅgha. Among the actions taken were efforts to restrict smoking within temple grounds by both monks and laity, nicotine candies handed out at the Buddhist universities, and media campaigns directed to the Saṅgha to encourage monks to stop smoking and to the laity to encourage them to no longer give monks cigarettes as *dāna*. Monks I have interviewed about the campaign have described two different rationales for the campaign. First, because monks receive health care through the government, eliminating tobacco use is a public health problem. Second, smoking tobacco is a sign of addiction, even if it is not illegal, and it is more difficult for monks to be models for laity if they are themselves addicted to tobacco. These monks also described smoking as something that was discouraged by Saṅgha authorities but not actually proscribed.

The campaign entails many of the dynamics referred to earlier. Smoking tobacco is not an issue covered in the *Vinaya* because it is not an intoxicant. This means that the desire to limit monks smoking tobacco, as well as the tools used to encourage this type of disciplined behavior come from outside the Vinaya. The government is involved, as are the institutions that govern the Saṅgha, such as the Supreme Saṅgha Council and the National Office of Buddhism. Moreover, the reasons why monks should not smoke is entangled with the aesthetics of monastic bodies and propriety. While monks have told me that they should not smoke, because it makes them less effective moral exemplars, the language they use points to other issues. They describe monks smoking not as an "infraction" (*phit*) but as "unattractive" (*may suay*) as well as "inappropriate" (*may somkhuan*). This suggests that the visual of monks smoking matters, not just the act itself. Finally, laity are involved with this issue in at least two ways. First, monks refer to the laity as the reason for why they should not smoke, just as Chladek suggests when talking about the "imagined laity." Second, the fact that laypeople continue to provide monks with cigarettes (according to my monastic informants) suggests that many lay folk do not see this as a problem.

It should be stressed that the question of monastic smokers is at this point suggestive rather than conclusive. There has been very little research done on antismoking campaigns within the Thai (or any other) Saṅgha, and most of the energy within the Saṅgha itself seemed to have been expended in the first decade of this century. Yet what this relatively minor campaign points to are the complex ways that monks in Thailand are disciplined. The Vinaya is important of course, but only one of the factors that need to be considered if we want to understand how it is that monastics in Theravāda communities become disciplined. I have suggested here that it is also necessary to consider a broader range of materials in addition to the Vinaya. Disciplining is pedagogical process that entails rules, models of proper behavior, institutions for developing and fostering these models, and mechanisms for enforcement.

Notes

1 The implicit notion of "real" Buddhism is part of a universalist project that has naturalized notions of what religions should look like. Indeed, the emergence of Buddhism as a unified religion was a central part of that (Masuzawa 2005; King 1999). Instead of a universal object, I would argue that we should see Buddhism as an umbrella term housing a number of resources that individuals can draw on as they see fit, according to what appeals to them, or is seen as culturally legitimate.

2 For discussion of the wider politics of Thailand, see the essays in Pavin 2019; on the resurgence of Buddhism and ethnonationalism in Sri Lanka in the wake of the Civil War, see the essays in Holt 2016; and for a comparison of the emergence of Buddhist nationalisms in Myanmar and Sri Lanka, see Schonthal and Walton 2016.

3 The study of the forms of the secular within Buddhism as a whole remains understudied, especially in relation to the work of scholars of Islam. For a concise statement of how to think about secularism see Mahmood (2016: 5–6). Schonthal provides an invaluable discussion of the place of Buddhism in the Sri Lankan constitution (2016). See also Turner 2019 on Myanmar and Larsson 2019 on Thailand.

4 This contravenes one of the basic, and well-known, rules for novices (and fully ordained monastics as well). Precisely how common this is in the Tai world or beyond is unclear. In Sipsongpannā, this is sometimes seen as a sign of degradation of the discipline (Casas 2017). However, based on interviews with monks and novices in Bangkok and Chiang Mai, I suspect that it is simply more open in Sipsongpannā (see also Chladek 2017/2018: 55–56; Pannapadipo 2001: 56).

5 It is perhaps an obvious point, but novices are not subject to the same set of rules that fully ordained monks are. There is overlap between the ten precepts that novices are to adhere to and the 227 that fully ordained Theravāda monks must follow, but they are not the same. This means that what is appropriate for novices and fully ordained monks varies as well, although I would argue not as completely as we sometimes think.

References

AFP. 2005. "Buddhist Monks Find It Hard to Quit." *ABC Science*, 31 May. https://www.abc.net.au/science/articles/2005/05/31/1380995.htm, accessed January 3, 2020.

Askew, Marc, ed. 2010. *Legitimacy Crisis in Thailand*. Chiang Mai, Thailand: Silkworm Books.

Blackburn, Anne M. 2010. *Locations of Buddhism: Colonialism and Modernity in Sri Lanka*. Chicago, IL: University of Chicago Press.

Borchert, Thomas. 2017. *Educating Monks: Minority Buddhism on China's Southwest Border*. Honolulu, HI: University of Hawai'i Press.

Borchert, Thomas. 2020. "Bad Gifts, Community Standards and the Disciplining of Theravāda Monks." *Journal of Contemporary Religion* 35: 53–70

Borchert, Thomas, Darlington, Susan M. 2017/2018. "Political Disrobing in Thailand." *Buddhism, Law, and Society* 3: 113–156.

Cassaniti, Julia. 2015. *Living Buddhism: Mind, Self, and Emotion in a Thai Community*. Ithaca, NY: Cornell University Press.

Clarke, Shayne. 2014. *Family Matters in Indian Buddhist Monasticisms*. Honolulu, HI: University of Hawai'i Press.

Cook, Joanna. 2010. *Meditation in Modern Buddhism: Renunciation and Change in Thai Monastic Life*. Cambridge: Cambridge University Press.

Casas, Roger. 2017. "The Buddhist Basketball Association: Sport Practice and Cultivation of the Body among Tai Lue Monastics." *Asia Pacific Journal of Sport and Social Science* 6 (1): 46–60.

Chessman, Nick. 2003. "School, State, and *Saṅgha* in Burma." *Comparative Education* 39 (1): 45–63.

Chladek, Michael Ross. 2017a. *Making Monks, Making Men: the Role of Buddhist Monasticism in Shaping Northern Thai Identities*. Ph.D. Dissertation, University of Chicago.

Chladek, Michael Ross. 2017b. "Imagined Laity and the Performance of Monasticism in Northern Thailand." *Buddhism, Law and Society* 3: 45–78.

Chaveepojnkamjorn, W., Pichainarong N. 2005. "Cigarette Smoking among Thai Buddhist monks, central and eastern Thailand." *Southeast Asian Journal of Tropical Medicine and Public Health* 36 (2): 505–511.

Colombo Telegraph. 2012. "Drunken Chief Buddhist Monk: Bitter Truth Revealed with Wild Boar." *Columbo Telegraph*, 28 February. https://www.colombotelegraph.com/index.php/drunken-chief-buddhist-monk-bitter-truth-revealed-with-wild-boar/, accessed July 20, 2019.

Creak, Simon. 2011. "Muscular Buddhism for a Modernizing Laos." *The Journal of Lao Studies* 2 (2): 1–22.

Dhammasami, Khammai. 2018. *Buddhism, Education and Politics in Burma and Thailand: from the Seventeenth Century to the Present*. London: Bloomsbury.

Holt, John Clifford, ed. 2016. *Buddhist Extremists and Muslim Minorities: Religious Conflict in Sri Lanka*. Oxford: Oxford University Press.

Keeler, Ward. 2017. *The Traffic in Hierarchy: Masculinity and its Others in Buddhist Burma*. Honolulu: University of Hawai'i.

Keyes, Charles. 2007. "Sexy Monks: Sexual Scandals Involving Buddhist Monks in Thailand," paper presented at EUROSEAS 2007, Naples Italy, September 2007.

Khaosod. 2018. "Rong Pho. Phot. Sangthuk cangwat wa tua phra jo chik phaet, chi ben khwaam phit, 'loka-vajja'." 29 December. https://www.khaosod.co.th/special-stories/news_1889333, accessed April 10, 2019.

King, Richard. 1999. *Orientalism and Religion: Postcolonial Theory, India, and the 'Mystic East'*. London Routledge.

Kusa, Julian. 2007. *Crisis Discourse, Response and Structural Contradictions in Thai Buddhism 1990–2003*. Ph.D. Dissertation, Australian National University.

Kieffer-Pülz, Petra. 2014. "What the *Vinayas* Can Tell Us About Law." In *Buddhism and Law: an Introduction*, eds. Rebecca French, Mark Nathan, 46–62. Cambridge: Cambridge University Press.

Larsson, Tomas. 2016. "Buddha or the Ballot: The Buddhist Exception to Universal Suffrage in Contemporary Asia." In *Buddhism and the Political Process*, eds. Hiroko Kawanami, 78–96. New York: Palgrave Macmillan.

Larsson, Tomas. 2019. "Secularisation, Secularism, and the Thai State." In *Routledge Handbook of Contemporary Thailand*, ed. Pavin Chachavalpongpun, 278–290. London: Routledge.

Lincoln, Bruce. 2012. *Gods and Demons, Priests and Scholars: Critical Explorations in the History of Religions*. Chicago, IL: University of Chicago Press.

Mahmood, Saba. 2016. *Religious Difference in a Secular Age: a Minority Report*. Princeton, NJ: Princeton University Press.

Makely, Charlene. 2007. *The Violence of Liberation: Gender and Tibetan Buddhist Revival in Post-Mao China*. Berkeley, CA: University of California Press.

Mandair, Arvind-Pal S., Markus Dressler. 2011. "Introduction: Modernity, Religion-Making and the Postsecular." In *Secularism and Religion-Making*. edited by Markus Dressler and Arvind Mandair, 3-36. Oxford: Oxford University Press.

Masuzawa, Tomoko. 2005. *The Invention of World Religions; or, How European Universalism was Preserved in the Language of Pluralism*. Chicago: University of Chicago Press.

Methee Muangkaew. 2019. "Monk, Nun Arrested, Speed Pill Seized At Temple in Trang." *Bangkok Post*, Apri 1. https://www.bangkokpost.com/thailand/general/1659072/monk-nun-arrested-speed-pills-seized-at-temple-in-trang#cxrecs_s, accessed April 15, 2019.

Pannapadipo, Phra Peter. 2001. *Little Angels: the Real Life Stories of Thai Novice Monks*. Bangkok: Post Books.

Pavin, Chachavalpongpun, ed. 2019 *Routledge Handbook of Contemporary Thailand*. Oxon: Routledge.

Reynolds, Frank. 1994. "Dhamma in Dispute: the Interactions of Religion and Law in Thailand." *Law & Society Review* 28 (3): 433–452.

Samuels, Jeffrey. 2004. "Toward an Action-oriented Pedagogy: Buddhist Texts and Monastic Education in Contemporary Sri Lanka." *Journal of the American Academy of Religion* 72 (4): 955–971.

Samuels, Jeffrey. 2010. *Attracting the Heart: Social Relations and the Aesthetics of Emotion in Sri Lankan Monastic Culture*. Honolulu, HI: University of Hawai'i Press.

Schonthal, Benjamin. 2016. *Buddhism, Politics, and the Limits of Law: The Pyrrhic Constitutionalism of Sri Lanka*. New York: Cambridge University Press.

Schonthal, Benjamin. 2019a. "Buddhist Law Against the State? Thinking Again About Religion, Law, and Conflict." *Journal of the American Academy of Religion*. 87 (3): 662–692.

Schonthal, Benjamin. 2019b. "*The Monastery Rules, Lankan Style: A New Look at (not that) old Katikāvata-s*." Delivered at *Second International Conference on Buddhism and Law*, University of Buffalo. September 26, 2019.

Schonthal, Benjamin, Walton, Matthew J. 2016. "The (New) Buddhist Nationalisms? Symmetries and Specificities in Sri Lanka and Myanmar." *Contemporary Buddhism* 17: 1–35. doi:10.100/14639947.2016.1162419.

Schopen, Gregory. 2004. *Buddhist Monks and Business Matters: Still More Papers on Monastic Buddhism in India*. Honolulu, HI: University of Hawai'i Press.

Starling, Jessica. 2019. *Guardians of the Buddha's Home: Domestic Religion in the Contemporary Jodo Shinshu*. Honolulu: University of Hawai'i Press.

Thanissaro, Bhikkhu (Geoff DeGraff). 1994. *The Buddhist Monastic Code*, vol. 1.

Turner, Alicia. 2019. "*Colonial Secularism, Buddhism and the Continuing Violence of Burmese Women's 'Freedom'*." Presented at *Duke University*, February 2019.

Vajirañānarorasa, Somdetch Phra Mahā Somana Chao Krom Phrayā. 1969 [2512]. *The Entrance to the Vinaya* (Vinayamukha), Vol. 1. Bangkok: Mahāmakutarājavidyālaya.

13

FUNERALS

Changing funerary practices

Katherine A. Bowie

Across the Theravāda Buddhist world, funerals are often described as the most important of the life cycle rituals.[1] Within the philosophical canon of Theravāda Buddhism, death serves as a reminder of the Buddha's teachings on impermanence. Despite the canonical emphasis on non-self (*anatta*), most Theravāda Buddhists believe in rebirth, be it as humans, animals, deities or ghosts. Accordingly, both by listening to monks recite sacred texts and by offering gifts to them, funerals provide the living with opportunities to make merit to assist the deceased with a better rebirth. The ceremonies typically last several days but can extend across months and even years. As Bryan Cuevas and Jacqueline Stone note, "The performance of funerary and memorial ritual represents a chief social role of Buddhist clerics and strengthens ties between *saṅgha* and laity" (2007: 2). Nonetheless, even as late as 2007, Cuevas and Stone observe that, despite its centrality to Buddhist traditions, "until recently death has received surprisingly little attention in the field of Buddhist Studies" (2007: 3).[2]

Although rituals have been defined as "acts regularly repeated in a set precise manner," a historical perspective reveals that rituals change over time.[3] Like other rituals, Theravāda Buddhist funerary practices have undergone change.[4] A sixth-century Chinese account of the early Southeast Asian kingdom of Funan describes four methods of disposal of the dead: "(a) throwing the dead body into a flowing stream, (b) burning it to ashes, (c) burying it in the ground, (d) exposing it to the birds" (Wales 1992 [1931]: 159). However, today cremation is increasingly coming to typify Theravāda funerals in Thailand, Cambodia, Laos, Myanmar, and urban Sri Lanka.

Recognizing such variations invites a consideration of the broader historical processes leading to changes in Theravāda Buddhist funerary practices. These processes will vary in each country. This essay provides one such example by describing changes in funerary practices in central and northern Thailand over the course of the twentieth century. During the early decades of the twentieth century, the Bangkok court began expanding its administrative control, bringing once quasi-independent regions under its jurisdiction to form the modern nation-state of Thailand. Historically monks played important roles in education and other aspects of village life. Working through the Saṅgha Act of 1902 the court began to centralize control over monastic practice. However, notwithstanding earlier efforts, the Thai state did not gain political control over the northern Saṅgha until April 1936, when northern Thailand's

 DOI: 10.4324/9781351026666-16

most famous monk, Khruba Srivichai, was compelled to sign a document agreeing to abide by the 1902 Saṅgha Act. Srivichai had been detained under temple arrest in Bangkok since November 1935, during which time 340 of his disciples were forcibly disrobed.[5] Many of the disrobed abbots of northern temples were replaced by monks trained in Bangkok who began introducing changes in northern religious beliefs, many of which became manifest in funerary practices. These changes generated considerable controversy among northerners in subsequent years.

This chapter is divided into three sections. In the first section, I present an overview of shifting funerary practices in the central region over the nineteenth century that resulted in a standardized pattern of cremations by the early twentieth century. In the second section, I describe the pre–World War II funerary practices in the northern region that prevailed during Srivichai's lifetime, highlighting the very different positionality of temples. In the third section, I describe the changes that took place as Bangkok-trained monks gained influence. Although there are many possible elements of comparison, in each section I focus on four elements: the overall disposition of the deceased, the location, the timing, and the treatment of final remains. The essay draws on evidence from archival sources, the accounts of early explorers, and the work of fellow anthropologists, as well as my own interviews, oral histories, and participant observation over the course of four decades of research in Thailand. Because northern Thailand has long had particularly close relations with Burma, especially the Shan States, I also draw upon accounts of Burmese funerary rites.

Although I am focusing this essay on differences, the two regions shared some overall patterns that characterized the broader Theravāda Buddhist world. Overall, funerary practices reflected the major historical social divisions, differentiating funerary rites for monks, royalty, and commoners. Cremation typified monastic and royal funerals. Funerary practices also varied according to the manner of death, deaths by accident or in childbirth considered to be particularly inauspicious and even dangerous.[6] Today the division between auspicious and inauspicious deaths is becoming less relevant in determining the type of funeral held. Furthermore, patterned on royal and monastic funerals, today cremation is becoming increasingly the norm for commoner funerals as well. However, as this essay will show in the case of Thailand, contemporary practice in each country of the Theravāda Buddhist world emerges from a more complex religio-political history.

Central Thailand

In central Thailand, a region once known as Siam, cremation became normative by the early decades of the twentieth century. As H. G. Quaritch Wales writes in 1931, cremation

> is the means by which the vast majority of the Siamese people dispose of their dead, the exceptions being criminals, victims of cholera and smallpox, people who have been struck by lightning, and women who have died in childbirth, whose corpses are buried.
>
> (Wales 1992 [1931]: 137)

He adds, "Cremation is the only means of disposal of the remains of deceased royalty in Siam" (1992 [1931]: 137); the same was true for clergy. However, as this section shows, even as late as the turn of the twentieth century, commoners not only cremated their dead but also buried them or offered them to wild birds (typically vultures).

Of cremations, burials and bird-offerings

The earliest account of Siamese (Central Thai) funerary practice suggests that burial may once have been the norm among elites and bird offerings among the poor.[7] Ma Huan visited Siam at the beginning of the fifteenth century and left the following account, noting "whenever a man of wealth and standing dies, they take quicksilver and pour it inside of the abdomen (of the corpse) and bury it" (Ma 1970[1433]: 105). Ma (1970[1433]) continues:

> [W]hen one of the poorer classes dies, they carry the corpse to the wilds by the seaside, and place it on the edge of the sand; subsequently golden-coloured birds as large as geese–more than thirty, or fifty, of them–gather in flight in the sky; they descent [*sic*], take the flesh of the corpse, devour it completely, and fly away; [and] the people of the [dead man's] family weep over the bones which remain, then cast them away in the water and return home. They call this "bird-burial". They also invite a Buddhist priest to celebrate a mass, chant liturgies, and worship Buddha, and that is all.
>
> (105)

By the seventeenth century, it appears the elites had begun to prefer cremation. Simon de la Loubère (1969[1693]), who visited Siam in 1687, provides a detailed description of cremations, noting that someone who could not afford cremation at first buries the dead but later "causes the body of his Father to be digged up again, though a long time dead, to make him a pompous Funeral" (124). However, he adds that the poor "inter their Parents without burning them," or "expose them in the Field on an eminent place; that is to say on a Scaffold, where the Vulturs and the Crows devour them" (Loubère 1969[1693]: 125; for further details see 123–125).

In the early nineteenth century, British diplomat John Crawfurd (1987[1828]) records of his 1821 mission to Siam, "The only honourable funeral amongst the Siamese consists in burning the body, and the practice is very general" (321). If someone could not cremate the body, "either from poverty, or from the party dying at a distance," the body is "first buried, and afterwards, as soon as convenient or practicable, disinhumed, and consigned to the funeral pile" (1987[1828]: 321). Nonetheless, offering one's body to vultures appears to have become more popular among all the classes, linked not with poverty but with religiosity (e.g., Crawfurd 1987[1828]: 321; Pallegoix 2000 [1854]: 124–125). Wales explains,

> It used to be the custom in Siam at some time before cremation to cut off part of the flesh of the corpse immediately after death and offer it to the temple dogs and vultures on gold or silver dishes. This was only done by the wish of the deceased. ...It was given a Buddhist significance, and considered an act of great merit.
>
> (Wales 1992 [1931]: 160; see also Crawfurd 1987[1828]: 321)[8]

If in the early nineteenth century, offering oneself as charity to dogs and birds was a cross-class option, it seems by the turn of the twentieth century, it was limited to the poor and criminal class. As Ernest Young, a schoolmaster in Bangkok in the late nineteenth century, writes:

> Paupers and criminals are disposed of in a barbarous and revolting manner. At one of the city temples a flock of vultures, numbering over a hundred, is kept.[9] The vultures are repulsive dirty-looking birds who sit stolidly hour by hour upon the roof or walls of the temple, apparently without life or motion except when a body is brought for their repast. They become keenly excited at the prospect of the coming feast, for which, however, they must first do battle with the crowd of pariahs that also haunt the

vicinity of the same temple. They flock down with noisy croaking and great flapping of wings, but are beaten off by the attendants, who first prepare the body for the feast by cutting it open in different place with large sharp knives. They cast a few pieces of flesh to the dogs and then retire. In a second the body is hidden by the birds....

The meal over, the feathered cannibals return to their perches upon roof and wall. The relatives gather up the clean white bones, put them loosely in a wooden coffin, light wax tapers, and bearing the coffin with them, march three times round the funeral pyre. They then light the fire, place the coffin on the burning fuel, and scatter sweetly smelling incense in the leaping flames.

(Young 1982[1898]: 247–248;Younghusband 1888: 132–133; Dekeyser 1908: 127–129)

By 1924 the practice had ended, W. A. Graham writing that the custom "has been done away with and all such bodies are now cremated" (1924 Vol 1: 166). Similarly, Wales confirms that bird-offerings "long ago ceased to be the custom of royalty, and has now been prohibited by law in the case of commoners" (1992[1931]: 160).

Cremation at Mt. Meru on temple grounds

In Central Thailand, for commoners, as Sharp and Hanks write, "cremation always takes place at a temple" (1978: 164). The French Catholic bishop Pallegoix has provided one of the most complete accounts of a mid-nineteenth-century funeral typical of a commoner; both bird-offering and cremation were combined on temple grounds. After describing the initial preparations, he writes:

Then, to lugubrious sounds of clarinets, the coffin is placed in a big boat on a platform over which there is a dais. The relatives and friends accompany the convoy in several small *ballons*, bringing the deceased in procession to the temple where he must be cremated. Then, the relatives uncover the coffin and place the body in the hands of those who, by occupation, are charged with burning it for the price of a *tical* which they take care of placing in the mouth of the deceased. First, the burner washes the face with coconut milk and if the deceased has ordered before his death that he wanted to be eaten by vultures and crows, he dismembers it and throws the flesh to these birds of prey who do not leave the temples. When the corpse has been placed on the pyre, the fire is lit, the nerves being contracted the dead person appears to move and to roll to the middle of the flames. It is a horrible spectacle to watch.

(2000 [1854]: 124–125)

More specifically, the cremation takes place at "one of the temples which possesses a public 'Pramane [Phra Meru]'" (Young 1982[1898]: 246–247).[10] As the noted Thai scholar Anuman Rajadhon explains, "Meru is the name of the cosmic mountain where the gods of the Buddhists dwell. It forms the center of the universe," adding that "Indra, the King of the gods of Buddhism, lives in his glittering, golden mansion right on the top of the golden mountain, surrounded by similar golden mansions, smaller in size and grandeur, of the lesser gods" (1957: 65). In royal and monastic cremations, the deceased "does not die in the ordinary sense of the word but translates himself to the heavens" (Anuman 1957: 66; see also Crawfurd 1987[1828]: 318, 315–320). Although temporary Merus were specially built for monks and royalty to accommodate large crowds, permanent Merus were increasingly being built in temples across the central regions.

Delaying cremations, temple storage

With the increasingly popularity of cremations, delays became more common since cremations often involved considerable expense.[11] As Graham writes, "it sometimes happens that the whole of man's estate is dissipated by his heirs in their endeavours to gratify his spirit with a sumptuous burning" (1924: 165). Consequently, "as many as four or five years may elapse between the time of death and the actual cremation" (Kaufman 1960: 157). As a result, individual cremations in the central region were not staggered throughout the year but occurred typically "about April or May" (Graham 1924: 165), a time when "[t]he paddy has been sold, and relatively large sums of money are on hand" (Kaufman 1960: 159).

Although in the past bodies awaiting cremation were buried, it became more common to store them at the temples. Younghusband notes "hundreds of boxes "full of corpses in various states of decomposition" at one of the Bangkok temples he visited (1888: 132). According to Kaufman, bodies were typically kept at home for seven days, with friends visiting and monks invited to chant. "At the end of the seven days, the coffin is brought to the *wat* and kept in a special building called the *thikebsob*" (Kaufman 1960: 159).[12]

Cremains: kept in homes, chedi, or temples

After cremation, there were a variety of ways in which the cremains were handled.[13] Joost Schouten, writing of his trip in 1636 to Ayutthaya, notes that after the deceased is "burnt with fire, their collected ashes are afterwards anointed and buried near the Temples, a Pyramid rich and magnificent being erected over them; so that funerals are extremely expensive to the survivors, as well as honorable for the deceased" (1986[1636]: 143). Interestingly, Loubère noted these pyramidal structures or *chedi* were "Without any Epitaph" (1969[1693]: 124; see also Crawfurd 1987[1828]: 321).

In addition to the elite practice of constructing *chedi*, Central Thai also took cremains home.[14] In 1688, Loubère already noted the practice of bringing funerary urns (*kod*) home, writing, "Those that have neither Temple nor Pyramid, do sometimes keep at their house the ill burnt remains of their Parents" (1969[1693]: 124). Crawfurd suggests bringing urns home may once have been an elite practice for "persons of distinction" (1987[1828]: 321). However, by the mid-nineteenth century, the practice of keeping relic urns in homes appears to have been widespread. Pallegoix notes this practice in the mid-nineteenth century, writing, "When the combustion has ended, the relatives come to collect the main bones to place them in an urn kept at their house" (2000 [1854]: 124–125). Graham writes that these urns "may be seen in almost every house" (1924: 166; see also Young 1982 [1898]: 246–247; Plion-Bernier 1973[1937]: 41). Furthermore, "[o]n very particular occasions these remains are brought out and distributed about the rooms" (Young 1982[1898]: 246–247). This practice of keeping and reverencing funerary relics continued well into the twentieth century (e.g. Kaufman 1960: 161; Sharp and Hanks 1978: 166).[15]

Northern funerary rites

Unlike Central Thailand—where, by the early twentieth century, the deceased were cremated, their bodies stored in temples, and their cremains taken home or interred in temples—northern Thai kept death rites away from temples. Like Central Thailand, northern monks and royalty were "regarded as high-class persons by the people. When they died, it was believed they would be reborn in a better world or as a *deva* at different levels of heaven on Mount Meru" (Sommai and Dore 1992: 159). Thus, cremations were typical for the funerals of northern royalty and clergy. However, all cremations—for northern royalty, monks, and commoners—took place outside of temples. Only the bodies and cremains of monks were allowed inside northern temples.

Burial versus cremation

Despite the few existing nineteenth-century travel accounts suggesting northerners "cremate their dead except in cases of violent death" (Younghusband 1888: 130; Bock 1986 [1884]: 261), considerable evidence suggests a widespread practice of burials. The British explorer Holt Hallett, while noting cremations among the "Ping Shans," comments that "[b]urial, however, is still observed by the British Shans" (Hallett 1890: 49). The Lanna region was under Burmese rule for some two hundred years, from 1558 to 1774. Furthermore, northern Thailand was resettled over the course of the nineteenth century by war captives, taken primarily from the Shan States area of Burma (see Bowie 1996). In Burma, with the exception of monks and royalty, burials were customary (Graham 1924 Vol. 2: 259; Shway Yoe 1963: 589–596; Nash 1965: 156; Spiro 1970: 251).[16] As Milne summarizes, "Shans do not cremate their dead, only the bodies of monks are burnt" (1910: 86–97). Scott 1900: 326). Villagers I have interviewed in both Chiangmai and Lamphun Provinces confirm that they buried their dead as late as the 1970s. In the area where I conducted fieldwork, I personally attended both village burials and cremations in the 1970s.[17]

Charnel forest (paa chaa)*, not* temple Meru

Temples in northern Thailand have traditionally been considered as sacred grounds, as *"khuang kaew thang saam"* or "the area of the triple gems (i.e. the Buddha, the Dharma and the Saṅgha)." Corpses were seen as fundamentally polluted, inauspicious, or spiritually dangerous, and therefore inappropriate to bring into temple grounds. Furthermore, it is widely believed that *phii* (ghosts) cannot enter temple grounds; indeed it is a trope in Thai horror films that victims attacked by ghosts flee into temples for refuge.[18]

Accordingly, both burials and cremations took place, not in temples but rather outside the community in the "charnel forest" (*paa chaa* or *paa hio*), a practice that continues to the present day. The charnel forest is typically a forested area located to the west of the village boundary or at the "tail" of the village (*hang muubaan*).[19] Cityfolk removed their dead through a special gate, often located in the southwest corner of the city wall, for cremation or burial at the *paa chaa* outside the city. In Chiang Mai City, commoners who died in the city were taken out by Haiyaa Gate (the southwest gate today is called Suan Prung). Burmese shared these practices (e.g., Shway Yoe 1963: 593; Brown 1916: 22–23).

The same taboo also applied to royalty. Unlike in Bangkok, where the royal cremations were held inside the city walls, the cremations of northern rulers (*chao*) were held outside the city. However, royalty were not cremated in the same location as commoners, but at a separate area known as "*Khuang Men* (Meru)," typically located either to the north or east of the city (both were considered auspicious directions, north believed to be the direction of Meru and east associated with the rising sun). This field in Chiang Mai was located east of the city wall.[20] Monastic cremations were also not carried out in temples grounds but typically at special temporary Meru's built on a nearby open field given that these rites typically attract large crowds.[21] Monks could also be cremated at the community's *paa chaa*, albeit often at a separate part.

Corpses in homes, not temples

Northern funerals typically took place one to seven days after death, with the bodies kept at home until the final burial or cremation.[22] A monk from Srivichai's village said that in Srivichai's day funerals were very simple; the deceased was sprinkled with sacral water (*nam sompoi*) that had been blessed by the monks and removed to the *paa chaa*, often on the very same day with no further direct monastic involvement. Most villagers appeared to keep the corpses an average of three days. As Keyes summarizes, "[i]t is not common (in northern Thailand) to keep the corpse in the house for as long as (is done) in central (Thailand). At most it will be kept only for seven days" (1980: 8). Corpses of royalty were kept longer, but they were kept in their palaces of residence and not in the temples.

A mark of their high status, the only bodies that were kept in temples were those of monks (typically not in the central *viharn* but in the side *salabatr* hall). I have visited several temples in the north where the deceased abbot's body is being kept.[23] Although monks have been known to die in their temples and be kept there until their cremation, Srivichai insisted on being carried out from the temple to die in order to maintain the temple's purity.

Treatment of cremains

Unlike Central Thailand, northerners did not take cremains home or build commoner *chedi* on temple grounds. Bodies which were buried in the cemetery remained in unmarked graves. In cases of cremations, the bones were collected and put into a pot, which was then buried in the *paa chaa*.[24] Elsewhere in the north, villagers collected the bones and floated them down a river, yet others made sand *chedi* by the riverbanks. Some placed the cremains into firecrackers (this practice ended in Chiangmai City when shopkeepers objected to cremains landing on their roofs).

Indeed, far from wanting the ghosts (*phii*) of the dead to return home with them, upon leaving the charnel forest, funeral-goers dip their hands into a bowl of sacral water set out at the edge of the cemetery and wipe their heads. The reasons villagers gave me included concern about purifying oneself from the pollution of death or to keeping the spirit of the deceased or any of the other many ghosts there from following one home. *Phii* were seen as having the potential to cause harm to the living.

Unlike commoners whose cremains were buried in the charnel forest, royal cremains were interred not at a temple but in *chedi* built on the royal cremation grounds (*Khuang Men*, "Meru"). The ashes of Lamphun's ruling families (*chao*) remain to the present day in *chedi* located not in a temple but a gated area outside the city walls. The cremains of Chiangmai's *chao* were similarly interred at the *Khuang Men* east of the city wall. However, in 1908, when Chao Dara Rasmi, one of the wives of King Chulalongkorn (Rama V) and daughter of the Lanna king Inthawichayanon, returned after many years in Bangkok for a visit to Chiangmai, she relocated her forebearers' *chedi* from *Khuang Men* to Wat Suan Dok. Although Wat Suan Dok was then a deserted temple that lay outside the city walls, this decision and the decision to process the relics through the city, rather than around the outside, caused considerable controversy (Woodhouse 2009: 194–196).

Unlike commoners whose ashes were kept at a remove from one's home and community, the cremains of monks were considered sacred and the only ashes northerners considered appropriately kept within temples, typically located in the center of their villages. Thus, in addition to the enormous *chedi* (*phra that*) at northern temples believed to house the relics of the Buddha, many temples have much smaller *chedi* built to house the cremains of their abbots.[25]

Post-World War II changes

Funerary practices in Central and northern Thailand differed significantly prior to World War II, notably regarding the overall disposition of the deceased, the location, the timing, and the treatment of final remains. The 1902 Saṅgha Act centralized administrative control over the monastic order first in the central region, bringing an end to bird-offerings and burials in favor of temple cremations. Although the Saṅgha Act went into effect in the northern region in 1924, its implementation met with active resistance from northern monks. This resistance was finally overcome when the 340 monks and novices in Srivichai's lineage were disrobed and Srivichai was placed under temple arrest to compel his agreement to submit to the regulations of the Bangkok Saṅgha. As more and more monks trained in Bangkok or holding ecclesiastical positions within the national Saṅgha hierarchy took charge of northern temples, funerary practices began to change. Although urban temples led by Bangkok-trained abbots and patronized by government officials began the process, changes in funerary practices intensified across the northern region following World War II. As Sommai and Dore summarize northern practice, "[f]unerals today seem to be much influenced by the standardized patterns observed by Central Thai Buddhists, especially among urban people and government officials" (1992: 148).

In the central region, the primary change was the growth in crematoria and the commercialization of funerary rites. Tracing their rise to the decade after World War II in central Thailand (Wong 1998: 124), Deborah Wong writes, "Most temples now have crematoriums, which are tall stately buildings with ovens discreetly concealed inside a small room. Bangkok's landscape is punctuated by their tall, slender chimneys; even in the Thai countryside, nearly every temple has a small crematorium" (Wong 1998: 103). She notes that funerals "have become big business in Bangkok, and the customs surrounding death ritual are quite commercialized" (Wong 1998: 102–103). Temples that have made a business of funerals can have "anywhere from five to over thirty such halls surrounding the crematorium," and "it is not unusual for several funerals to be going on at once (Wong 1998: 112).[26]

The decades following the mass disrobings of Srivichai's disciples have seen major changes in northern funerary practice. The first important change is that cremation has become the norm. Furthermore, cremations are being increasingly elaborated and more expensive, from simple coffins once made from mats or scooped out logs (*hang muu*) to the addition of a simple decorative frame (*hang chang*) to incredibly ornate *prasat* (palaces). Bodies are now routinely being injected with preservatives. Villagers no longer serve local moonshine but increasingly more expensive store-bought alcohol such as beer. Growing numbers of monks are being invited. Funerary attendees now throw sandalwood on the pyre. Funerary wreaths are becoming more common and increasingly hosts provide mementos as gifts to attendees.[27] Northerners are also adding fifty-day and one-hundred-day post-cremation rites.

A second change has been the growing appearance of funerary *chedi* (called *kuu* in northern Thai) at temples and charnel forests.[28] Although many are unmarked, an increasing number now include the name, birth date, and death date; some even include photographs of the deceased. Initially the idea of commoner cremains being located within sacred temple grounds created controversy. The first funerary *chedi* appeared in urban temples with close ties to both Bangkok officials and monks who had studied at temples in Bangkok or who had received monastic titles through the monastic hierarchy centered in Bangkok. Temples aligned with Kruba Srivichai were resolutely opposed to cremains of any person other than their own abbot or other respected clergy; to this day, temples that maintained their lineages from Kruba Srivichai are far less likely to have any funerary *chedi* other than those of their abbots on their temple compounds. However, the practice of bringing cremains home never became routinized as part of northern rites and seems to be declining in the central region as well.[29]

A third major change is the growth of a funeral industry within northern temples, primarily those in urban and town centers. Unlike in the past when monks were invited to the home of the deceased, today, more coffins are brought to the urban temple for the formal rites prior to being removed for cremation. For many villagers, this too is an anathema since in their view, the deceased is not yet aware that they have died and wants to share the company of family and friends. Village rites entail villagers sleeping over, cooking for large crowds, and throngs of people eating, drinking, and gambling the nights through; in urban temples, the deceased is left alone in the funerary *salas*. Furthermore, this formalization of funerary rites has led to the demise of the northern tradition of bawdy sermons by "joking monks," in favor of monks chanting more somber texts (Bowie 2017). In sum, in the eyes of many villagers, such funerals are seen as more formal and hardly festive.

Nonetheless, for urban populations, this new service is greatly appreciated since they often do not have much space for large numbers of relatives and friends, to say nothing of the problem of parking cars and motorcycles. Furthermore, such temple rites are far less expensive. The monks typically chant for a couple hours in the evening, so the hosts do not need to be providing food beyond simple snacks and drinks. Because it is occurring at the temple, no alcohol is served. A basic service of three days, including renting the funeral *sala* and the subsequent cremation, costs about 10,000 baht (about US$330); the three-day funeral for a former village school principal cost about 300,000 baht (about US$9,930; the *prasat* and coffin alone cost about 50,000 baht or about US$1,650).

However, one element has remained resistant to change, namely, the Central Thai practice of holding cremations within temple grounds, and accordingly the idea of building crematoria on temple grounds. To this day, there is only one temple with a crematorium in Amphur Muang, Chiang Mai, namely, Wat BaPhaeng; its three crematoria were built after World War II and its monks are very quick to note that the land on which they are located is separate from the temple land (*baeng khaet*).[30] One temple in Amphur Mae Rim in Chiangmai Province has a newly created crematorium as part of its unique feature of accepting the bodies of those who have willed themselves as cadavers for the provincial hospital located there. More and more villages are discussing building Merus, however, not in the temples that are typically located in the center of the village community, but outside at their charnel forests.

As this comparison of Central and northern Thailand has shown, funerary rites have undergone different patterns of change. In the central region, in the early decades of the twentieth century, the practices of burial and bird-offerings ended and cremation at temple Merus had become the norm across classes. Because of the expense of cremations, corpses were increasingly stored in temples. Cremains were brought home or interred at temples. During this same period, northern Thai held both burials and cremations at charnel forests outside their villages. Northerners did not bring cremains home, and only monastic ashes were interred at temples. With the consolidation of Bangkok control over the northern region following the disrobing of Srivichai's lineage of monks, northern Thai funerary practices underwent significant changes. Although northerners adopted cremation voluntarily, the internment of commoner cremains on their temple grounds generated controversy. Today, although northern villagers continue to hold funerary rites at home, northern urbanites no longer observe the taboo against commoner corpses being housed at temples and are holding their funeral rites at temples. Nonetheless, the taboo against holding cremations on temple grounds has still largely been maintained across the northern region. The evidence of concrete differences in funeral practices described in this chapter provides tantalizing hints of further historical differences in interpretations of appropriate Buddhist practice across these two regions that await further study.

Today cremation is the norm across Thailand and most of the Theravāda Buddhist world. However, as this comparison of central and northern Thai funerary practice suggests, such a simple generalization about contemporary "Theravāda Buddhist" funerary practices belies the fact that each country has had its own complex political history of changing religious beliefs and funerary practices. Further comparative microhistorical studies of funerary rites are merited and may lead to further insights into the interrelationship between political and religious change across the Theravāda Buddhist world.

Notes

1 For example, Kaufman 1960: 156; Sharp and Hanks 1978: 164; DeYoung 1966: 69, 74; Tambiah 1970: 179.

2 Recent exceptions include Klima 2002; Williams and Ladwig eds. 2012; Davis 2016. Cuevas and Stone suggest that an important contributing factor "may lie in a perceived incompatibility of many Buddhist death-related practices with the doctrine of 'not-self' (Skt. *anatman*; Pāli *anatta*), the denial of any permanent essence, such as a soul" (2007: 5). Fundamental to the paradox of non-self is the belief in constant rearising or rebirth, prior to the attainment of nirvana. Given the veneration of his relics, the status of the Buddha himself is ambiguous.

3 https://www.merriam-webster.com/dictionary/ritual. Accessed August 13, 2019.

4 See Terweil 1979 for a pioneering comparative historical exploration of pre-Buddhist Thai funerary practices.

5 Srivichai died in 1939. For further details, see Keyes 1982; Bowie 2014a, 2014b; Cohen 2017.

6 Such unfortunate deaths typically involve burial (e.g., Crawfurd 1987[1828]: 321; Bowring 1969 [1857]: 141–142; Loubère 1969 [1693]: 125; Bock 1986 [1884]: 261; Young 1982[1898]: 247; Terwiel Barend 2012: 258–259).

7 Burials are described in Sri Lanka (Langer 2007: 62–69) and Laos (e.g., LeBar and Suddard eds 1960: 56).

8 Apparently a time of particularly intense religiosity, Crawfurd also notes self-immolation as a "solemn religious sacrifice of the highest order," hands "raised before his face, in an attitude of devotion," resulting in their relations "for ever after taken under the special protection of the sovereign" (1987[1828]: 322). In 1859, Cambodian king Ang Duong also had his body dismembered "as a final Buddhist act of generosity to animals" (Davis 2016: 50; see also Wales 1992 [1931]: 160). The Chinese traveler Cheou Ta-kouan believed that the "chief method of disposal of the dead in Cambodia was to expose them to the dogs and vultures," but Aymonier states that this practice was "always more common in Siam than in Cambodia" (Wales 1992 [1931]: 160).

9 This temple is likely Wat Saket (see also discussion in Bastian 2005 [1867]: 176).

10 The only exceptions are royal and monastic funerals for which special temporary Merus are constructed. Members of the Chakri dynasty have traditionally been cremated in Merus built in front of the Grand Palace (an area once called Thung Phra AdMeru). Following the 1932 overthrow of the absolute monarchy, royal cremations took place in temples but resumed with the death of King Ananda in 1946 (Plion-Bernier 1973: 50–51). For further accounts, see Pallegoix 2000 [1854]: 124–125; Bowring 1969[1857]: 99–100, 121–123, 142; Crawfurd 1987[1828]: 315–320; Bastian 2005 [1867]: 176–180; Graham 1924 Vol. 1: 164–166; Hallett 1890: 248; Bock 1986[1884]: 73–77; Wales 1992 [1931]: 137–168).

11 See also Plion-Bernier (1973[1937]: 31–42; Sharp and Hanks 1978: 165). By far the longest delays occurred with royal rituals, involving logs being sent down from northern Thailand (Pallegoix 2000 [1854]: 125–126). Because royal rituals were so costly, cremations for lesser royals were often held conjointly (Graham 1924: 165).

12 Poorer families did not conduct the fiftieth- and one-hundredth-day rituals and only invited monks for one or two nights only before storing the body (Kaufman1960: 159). Families with larger houses sometimes kept bodies at homes. As Plion-Bernier explains, "[l]ife continues around the corpse which is not an object of fear but of respect and before which one does not pass without making a *wai*, the hands joined" (Plion-Bernier 1973[1937]: 36).

13 The bones (relics) of the deceased are often treated separately from the ashes.

14 Writing over two centuries later, Bastian provides a fuller array of options, writing, "Following a cremation, the residual ashes are mixed with lime water and used to wash temple walls, or they are kneaded into a Buddha statue and buried under a pagoda, or they are preserved in a funeral urn" (2005 [1867]: 176).

15 In royal cremations, "[t]he bones not consumed by the fire are collected and reduced to powder. They are mixed with a little clay and of it small statues are formed and placed in a temple destined for this" (Pallegoix 2000 [1854]: 125–126). On royal cremains, see also Plion-Bernier 1973[1937]: 50; Wales 1992 [1931]: 171.

16 At his request, King Mindon was buried in 1878 (Shway Yoe 1963: 597–600). For accounts of a Shan ruler's funeral, see Adams 2000: 40; a monk's funeral in Burma see Shway Yoe 1963: 583–588; a monk's funeral in Kengtung, see Dodd 1923: 302. For accounts of northern royal funerals, see Bock 1986 [1884]: 261; Dodd 1923: 303–304.

17 Chinese (Hill 1992) and other ethnic minorities also buried their dead (e.g., Scott 1900; 528–529, 557, 588, 593, 604; Hallett 1890: 49, 175).

18 Northern villagers have often told me that to make merit for the dead, one must pour blessing waters (*yaat nam*) outside of temple walls. Shans and other northerners make offerings to monks for those with inauspicious deaths outside the temple because they "cannot enter the temple to collect the merit being made for them" (Eberhardt 2006: 65; Tannenbaum 1995: 151).

19 This pattern is also widespread outside of the central region (for northeastern Thailand, see Kickert 1960; Hayashi 2003: 164–189; Tambiah 1970: 183; Lefferts 1993: 117, 121).

20 This practice continued until 1908 when Chao Dara Rasmi relocated the royal cremains to Wat Suan Dok; thereafter, the cremations of northern aristocracy and its abbots have been held there (e.g., Sommai and Dore 1992: 152). Temporary Merus are built because Wat Suan Dok does not have a crematorium.

21 Ironically, despite Srivichai's beliefs, his cremation in 1946 took place at Wat Chamathevi, with high-ranking Bangkok officials in charge.

22 Those with accidental deaths were not brought home but buried without delay.

23 For a parallel development in Cambodia, see Marston 2006.

24 Cremation pot also buried in the Northeast (Tambiah 1970: 187).

25 In some cases, they mold the cremains into Buddha images.

26 Other changes are also occurring, for example, in music (Wong 1998), in religious texts (Terweil 2012: 251), in ordination (Kingkeo 1967: 118), and mourning customs (Pallegoix 2000[1854]: 125; Bastian 2005[1867]: 179; Bock 1986 [1884]: 73; Kingkeo 1967: 119; DeYoung 1966: 73).

27 Sharp and Hanks noted gifts for guests such as "a handkerchief, a bouquets of flowers, sometimes a book" (1978: 165–166); see also Olson 1992.

28 In northeastern Thailand, Hayashi also dates the practice of "making stupa-style tombs and interring the bones in temples" to about 1940 (2003: 168).

29 DeYoung writes that "this custom has been discontinued, for the modern Buddhist abbots do not approve of the family keeping the ashes of the deceased in the home" (1966: 72).

30 Earlier locals here also buried their dead.

References

Adams, Nel. 2000. *My Vanished World: The True Story of a Shan Princess*. Cheshire: Horseshoe Publications.

Anusaranasasanakiarti, Phra Khruu, Keyes, Charles. 1980. "Funerary Rites and the Buddhist Meaning of Death: An Interpretive Text from Northern Thailand." *Journal of Siam Society* 68 (1): 1–28.

Anuman, Rajadhon. 1957. "The Golden Meru." *Journal of the Siam Society* 45 (2): 65–73.

Bastian, Adolf. 2005 [1867]. *A Journey in Siam (1863)*. Translated by Walter Tips. Bangkok: White Lotus Press.

Bock, Carl. 1986 [1884]. *Temples and Elephants: Travels in Siam in 1881–1882*. Singapore: Oxford University Press.

Bowie, Katherine. 2017. *Of Beggars and Buddhas: The Politics of Humor in the Vessantara Jataka in Thailand*. Wisconsin: University of Wisconsin Press.

Bowie, Katherine. 2014a. "Buddhism and Militarism in Northern Thailand: Solving the Puzzle of the Saint Khruubaa Srivichai." *Journal of Asian Studies* 73 (3): 711–732.

Bowie, Katherine. 2014b. "The Saint with Indra's Sword: Kruubaa Srivichai and Buddhist Millenarianism in Northern Thailand." *Comparative Studies in Society and History* 56 (3): 681–713.

Bowie, Katherine. 1996. "Slavery in Nineteenth Century Northern Thailand: Archival Anecdotes and Village Voices." In *State Power and Culture in Thailand*, ed. E. Paul Durrenberger, 100–138. Yale University Southeast Asia Monograph #44.

Brown, R. Grant. 1916. "Death Customs in Burma." *Man* 16: 22–23.

Cohen, Paul, ed. 2017. *Charismatic Monks of Lanna Buddhism*. Copenhagen: NIAS Press.
Crawfurd, John. 1987 [1828]. *Journal of an Embassy to the Courts of Siam and Cochin China*. Introduction by David Wyatt. Singapore: Oxford University Press.
Davis, Erik W. 2016. *Deathpower: Buddhism's Ritual Imagination in Cambodia*. Columbia: Columbia University Press.
Dekeyser, Leon. 1908. *Notes de voyage, Japon, Iles Hawai, Chine, Siam*. Bruxelles: Severeyns.
DeYoung, John. 1966. *Village Life in Modern Thailand*. Berkeley: University of California Press.
Dodd, William Clifton. 1923. *The Tai Race: Elder Brother of the Chinese*. Cedar Rapids, Iowa: The Torch Press.
Eberhardt, Nancy. 2006. *Imagining the Course of Life: Self-Transformation in a Shan Buddhist Community*. Honolulu: University of Hawaii Press.
Graham, W.A. 1924. *Siam*. London: Alexander Moring Limited, De La More Press.
Hallett, Holt Samuel. 1890. *A Thousand Miles on an Elephant in the Shan States*. Edinburgh: William Blackwood and Sons.
Hayashi, Yukio. 2003. *Practical Buddhism among the Thai-Lao*. Kyoto: Kyoto University Press.
Hill, Ann. 1992. "Chinese Funerals and Chinese Ethnicity in Chiang Mai, Thailand." *Ethnology* 31 (4): 315–330.
Kaufman, Howard Keva. 1960. *Bangkhuad: A Community Study in Thailand*. New York: J.J. Augustin Incorporated.
Keyes, Charles F. 1982. "Death of Two Buddhist Saints in Thailand." *Journal of the American Academy of Religion, Thematic Series* 48 (3–4): 149–180.
Kickert, Robert. 1960. "A Funeral in Yang Terng, Changwat Ubol Northeast Thailand." *Journal of the Siam Society* 48 (2): 73–83.
Klima, Alan. 2002. *The Funeral Casino: Meditation, Massacre, and Exchange with the Dead in Thailand*. Princeton: Princeton University Press.
Langer, Rita. 2007. *Buddhist Rituals of Death and Rebirth: Contemporary Sri Lankan Practice and Its Origins*. London: Routledge.
LeBar, Frank, Suddard, Adrieene, eds. 1960. *Laos: Its People, its Society, its Culture*. New Haven: HRAF Press.
Lefferts, Leedom. 1993. "The Power of Women's Decisions: Textiles in Tai Dam and Thai-Lao Theravāda Buddhist Funerals." *Southeast Asian Journal of Social Science* 21 (2): 111–129.
Loubère, Simon de la. 1969 [1693]. *The Kingdom of Siam*. Introduction by David K. Wyatt. Kuala Lumpur: Oxford University Press.
Ma, Huan. 1970 [1433]. *Ying-yai sheng-lan: The Overall Survey of the Ocean's Shores' [1433]*. Translated from the Chinese text edited by Feng Ch'eng-Chun; with introd. notes and appendices by J.V.G. Mills. Cambridge: Published for the Hakluyt Society at the University Press.
Milne, Leslie. 1910. *Shans at Home*. With two chapters on Shan history by Rev Wilbur Wilis Cochrane. London: John Murray, Albemarle Street, W.
Nash, Manning. 1965. *The Golden Road to Modernity: Village Life in Contemporary Burma*. Chicago: University of Chicago Press.
Olson, Grant A. 1992. "Thai Cremation Volumes: A Brief History of a Unique Genre of Literature." *Asian Folklore Studies* 51 (2): 279–294.
Pallegoix, Jean-Baptiste. 2000 [1854]. *Description of the Thai Kingdom or Siam*. Translated by Walter Tips. Bangkok: White Lotus Press.
Plion-Bernier, Raymond. 1973 [1937]. *Festivals and Ceremonies of Thailand*. Translated by Joann Elizabeth Soulier. Bangkok: Assumption Press.
Kingkeo, Attagara. 1967. "The Folk Religion of Ban Nai: A Hamlet in Central Thailand." PhD Diss, Indiana University.
Schouten, Joost. 1986 [1636]. "A Description of the Government, Might, Religion, Customes, Traffick and other remarkable Affairs in the Kingdom of Siam." In *A True Description of the Mighty Kingdoms of Japan and Siam*, eds. Francois Caron, Joost Schouten. Bangkok: Siam Society.
Scott, J. George, with assistance by J. P. Hardiman. 1900. *Gazetteer of Upper Burma and the Shan States*. 5 vol. Rangoon: Government Printing Press.
Sharp, Lauriston and Lucien M. Hanks. 1978. *Bang Chan: A Social History of a Rural Community in Thailand*. Ithaca, NY: Cornell University Press.
Shway, Yoe. 1963. *The Burman: His Life and Notions*. New York: Norton Library.
Sommai, Premchit, Dore, Amphay. 1992. *The Lan Na Twelve-Month Traditions*. Chiang Mai: So Sap Kan Pim.
Spiro, Melford E. 1970. *Buddhism and Society: A Great Tradition and its Burmese Vicissitudes*. New York: Harper & Row.

Tambiah, Stanley J. 1970. *Buddhism and the Spirit Cults in North-east Thailand.* Cambridge: Cambridge University Press.

Tannenbaum, Nicola. 1995. *Who Can Compete Against the World?: Power-protection And Buddhism in Shan Worldview.* Ann Arbor: Association for Asian Studies.

Terweil, Barend. 1979. "Tai Funeral Customs: Towards a Reconstruction of Archaic-Tai Ceremonies." *Anthropos* 74 (3/4): 393–432.

Terweil, Barend. 2012. *Monks and Magic: Revisiting a Classic Study of Religious Ceremonies in Thailand.* Copenhagen: NIAS Press.

Wales, H.G. Quaritch. 1992 [1931]. *Siamese State Ceremonies: Their History and Function with Supplementary Notes.* Richmond, Surrey: Curzon Press.

Williams, Paul, Ladwig, Patrice, eds. 2012. *Buddhist Funeral Cultures of Southeast Asia and China.* Cambridge: Cambridge University Press.

Wong, Deborah. 1998. "Mon Music for Thai Deaths: Ethnicity and Status in Thai Urban Funerals." *Asian Folklore Studies* 57(1): 99–130.

Woodhouse, Leslie. 2009. "A 'Foreign' Princess in the Siamese Court: Princess Dara Rasami, the Politics of Gender and Ethnic Difference in Nineteenth-Century Siam." PhD Diss., University of California-Berkeley.

Young, Ernest. 1982 [1898]. *The Kingdom of the Yellow Robe.* Kuala Lumpur: Oxford University Press.

Younghusband, Lt. G. J. 1888. *Eighteen Hundred Miles on a Burmese Tat.* London: W.H. Allen & Co.

PART III

Texts/Teachings

14
CANONS
Authoritative texts of the Theravaṃsa

Peter Skilling

Texts have many lives and their value(s) depend on how we frame them and how we "canonize" them. This chapter examines the concepts of *canon* and *Pāli canon* and then broadens the scope to discuss the many canons that have coexisted within the Theravāda traditions, highlighting their fluidity and functionality with a focus on central Thai traditions. Canons are not static: they are flexible, living collections.

The idea of "canon"

A canon is an authoritative collection of socially and historically contingent texts.[1] A canon is "not a closed, absolute system … but a dynamic, evolving entity that can be reopened, reinterpreted, and reshaped" (Mitchell 2005: 20–21). There are religious canons, there are literary canons, and there are canons of the arts and many other fields. In education, canons are the mainstay of the curricula. They set the standards and determine the parameters of study and research. Their variety and complexity call for comparative, interdisciplinary approaches.

Heine and Wright cite two Western authorities to clarify the question of the Zen canon: "Zen does not have a canon in the formal sense of the term … [but it] recognizes a core of writings in the various genres as seminal resources for the expression of doctrine. As Harold Bloom shows in *The Western Canon*, the term canonicity does not necessarily refer to a fixed body of writings that assert a dogmatic sense of authority, but rather indicates the role of texts that express a compellingly creative and powerful message. Robert Alter points out in *Canon and Creativity*, 'A canon is above all a trans-historical textual community. Knowledge of the received texts and recourse to them constitute the community, but the texts do not have a single authoritative meaning, however many the established spokesmen for the canon at any given moment may claim that it is the case.' Alter goes on to show that 'although univocal meaning may be claimed, in the various traditions of canonical interpreters we find a tremendous diversity and range of viewpoints that are supported by the canon.'" (Heine and Wright 2004: 4–5)

Pāli Tripiṭaka and Pāli canon

Unlike Zen, the Theravāda tradition *does* have a formal canon, and Theravāda might be defined as a transhistorical and translocal textual community centered on the Pāli canon. Traditional

DOI: 10.4324/9781351026666-18

commentators discuss alternate meanings but favor authoritative single interpretations. The Pāli canon is one of several transmissions of the Buddha's teachings, and interpreters belonging to the eighteen (according to a traditional count) Buddhist schools tend to claim authority for their own school's versions against the others. This means that the mainstream Buddhist tradition is *not* univocal regarding the Buddha's teachings: the canons support a diversity and range of interpretations.

The scriptural heritage of the Buddhist schools evolved across South Asia for centuries, and each of the eighteen schools had its own scriptural collections. This produced a plurality of canons. The classical idea of canon became the *Tripitaka*: three (*tri–*) "baskets" (*piṭaka*) or collections of scriptures, one each for monastic discipline (*Vinaya*), discourses and dialogues of the Buddha (*Sūtra*), and systematized scholasticism (*Abhidharma*). These were redacted in early Middle Indic languages like Pāli and, with the increasing use of Sanskrit in Indian culture, the so-called Buddhist Hybrid Sanskrit-s. Only incomplete records of these canons survive, either as manuscript fragments in the original Indic languages or as partial translations into Chinese, Tibetan, and other languages.

It has long been a widespread assumption that the Pāli canon is not one among equals, not one of the *several* Buddhist canons of South Asian Buddhism but *the* canon, the one and only true canon. Through a concatenation of historical circumstances, including the British "discovery of Buddhism" in nineteenth-century Sri Lanka and the revival and development of transregional Buddhism, this collection has been privileged as the measure of *all* Buddhist literature, as the authentic canon of Buddhism as a whole. Here the Pāli collection wins by default because there is no competition: it is the only South Asian *Tripiṭaka* to survive. This chapter does not attempt to deal with the wide spectrum of Buddhist canons and restricts itself to the canons of the "Theravaṃsa" world.[2]

Canon formation

How was the Theravāda canon formed? The Theravāda and other Buddhist canons began orally and were only recorded in writing after several centuries. After the Master's passing, his monastic followers gathered to recite, collate, and redact his teachings. This was called a *saṃgīti* or *saṃgāyanā* (literally, chanting or singing together, here called a *convocation* or *convocation-recitation*). Pāli sources call this the original or root redaction (*mūlasaṅgaha*) while Indian thinkers like Vasubandhu (fourth century) and Bhāviveka (sixth century) call it the original or root recitation (*mūlasaṅgīti*). If there ever was a Buddhist canon, this would have been it: the canon agreed on at the first convocation. Nine centuries later, Vasubandhu lamented that by his time the root recitation was lost or at best fragmented (*mūlasaṃgīti-bhraṃśa*: Skilling 2010: 19 and 22). The Theravāda of Sri Lanka presents a radically opposite position. The Pāli *Chronicle of the Island* (*Dīpavaṃsa*) describes how the "schismatics" (i.e., the eighteen schools) "broke up the original redaction and made another redaction" (Skilling 2010: 22, 29) and maintains that the Theravāda was the sole non-schismatic school. This idea that is echoed by contemporary representatives of the tradition: "The Pāli Canon of Theravāda Buddhism, after two and a half millennia and six major rehearsals, has been generally recognised as the oldest, most original, most complete, and most accurate record of the Buddha's teachings still available today" (Payutto 2003: 1).

About a century after the first convocation, a second one was held at Vaiśālī to resolve differences that had arisen among the monastic orders. The two convocations constitute the foundations of monastic Buddhism and its scriptures. In the centuries to follow, new schools and orders developed, but for all of them, including the Great Vehicle, Buddhist history begins with the first two convocations. From that point on, each school held its own convocations and redacted its own canon and the traditions diverged. The history of the Theravādin canon is recounted in Pāli works like the *Manual of Buddhist Historical Traditions* (*Saddhammma-saṅgaha*, trans. B.C. Law). By the end of the eighteenth century, the learned Thai monk Somdet Phra Vanarat composed the *History of the Recitations* (*Saṃgītivaṃsa*) on the occasion of King Rāma I's ninth convocation, adding two Siamese redactions to the seven Indian and Sri Lankan councils of the Pāli sources to count *nine*. The Burmese enumeration differs. King Mindon (1808–1878, reigned 1853–1878) convened a *fifth* recitation, the last of the royal period, at Mandalay, where he had the whole *Tripiṭaka* engraved on marble slabs. After Burma became independent from Britain, Prime Minister U Nu (1907–1995) convened a *sixth* recitation in Rangoon, the capital of the newly formed Union of Burma, and published the Sixth Council edition of the *Tripiṭaka*. This edition was produced by the deliberations of learned monastics from international Saṅghas. Highly regarded, it is available electronically.

In this way, national Buddhist histories diverge. The Sri Lankan tradition counts *four* convocations. The Thai count is *nine*—seven Indian and Sri Lankan convocations plus two Siamese. The Burmese count is *six*, four Indian redactions plus two Burmese.

Materiality

Material canons are physical manuscripts and books. For several hundred years the Buddha's teachings were memorized and transmitted orally until they began to be written down in Sri Lanka, Gandhara, and elsewhere (the historical record is very sketchy: few contemporary documents survive except for the Gandharan manuscripts, some of which date to four or five centuries after the Buddha [first century BCE]). Gandhari manuscripts in the Northwest were written on birch-bark scrolls; in Sri Lanka, the Pāli canon was written down in manuscripts made from the long leaves of a species of the palm-tree family. Writing materials included brushes, styluses, pens, ink, and lampblack. Sri Lankan histories relate that the *Tripiṭaka* was written down on the island in the first century BCE. This means that scriptures were written down about the same period in Gandhara in the far northwest and Sri Lanka in the far south—and most probably at centers of Buddhist activity in between.

Manuscripts are sacred or holy objects because they enshrine the word of the Buddha. They are treated with respect and reverence according to codes and etiquettes of proper behavior; these are the same as those for images or relics of the Buddha or other sacred figures. Manuscripts are wrapped in fine cloth; they should be stored in a clean place, high up—above head level, if possible—and should not be laid on the ground or placed on a seat. A genre of literature extols the blessings and merits gained through the production of manuscripts, from gilding and embellishing them to protecting them with wooden covers, cloth wrappers, woven cords, boxes, or cabinets (Skilling 2017a). Everything connected with manuscripts is infused with an aesthetics of merit that ensures that manuscripts are things of beauty.

Writing systems

Which script was used to write down the first Pāli manuscripts? There is no record, but it is likely to have been a form of early Brāhmī, the script used for the earliest Sri Lankan stone inscriptions. No early Pāli manuscripts survive (with the anomalous exception of four *circa* eighth- and ninth-century *Vinaya* folios written in a north-Indian script found in Nepal). From the first centuries CE the use of writing took off in India and different cultures and areas developed their own scripts. Buddhist monastic communities established themselves across India and began to write their scriptures in contemporary local scripts. This included the

Theravāda Saṅghas who wrote Pāli in different scripts. As a result, there is no such thing as a *Pāli script* or a *Pāli system of writing*. Pāli was written in the letters of different regions of South and Southeast Asia and latterly in the roman script. Up to the nineteenth century, it was normal for an educated person to know several scripts and speak several languages. The various Indic scripts follow the same principles but the letters are pronounced differently. As a result, Pāli is pronounced differently in different cultures. For example, the simple formula of homage *namo tassa bhagavato arahato sammāsambuddhassa*—"homage to that one, the fortunate one, the worthy arhat, the truly and fully awakened Buddha"—sounds different in Sinhala, Mon, Khmer, Thai, or Burmese.

The Pāli canon was transmitted in manuscript form for two thousand years; it was only transferred into book format in the late nineteenth century when King Rāma V of Siam published a Thai-script Pāli Tripiṭaka. This, the first Pāli *Tripiṭaka* to be printed in book format, was soon followed by a Mon-script version printed in Thailand and by editions in the Burmese, Sinhala, Khmer, Devanagari, and other scripts. After one hundred years in book format, computer experts converted the *Tripiṭaka*s to digital formats which have become increasingly popular.

Problems with canons

The collection of texts that make up the Theravaṃsa canon was codified in Sri Lanka by the early centuries CE. It is redacted in a Middle Indo-Aryan language that the tradition calls Māgadhī, the language of the land of Magadha in North-Central India, but today is known internationally by another traditional designation, "Pāli," the "language of the scriptures." Generally regarded as closed and fixed, it is the only Indic language scriptural collection to survive in a complete state, at least in the shape defined a thousand years after the Buddha by the Theravādin master Buddhaghosa. By default, this became known as "the Pāli Canon" (or "canon"—both uppercase and lowercase are used with nuances in emphasis), "the *Tipiṭaka* (Pāli) or *Tripiṭaka* (Sanskrit)," "the Canon" (uppercase), or "the Buddhist Canon."

The notion of a canon is problematic in the study of Buddhism. The problem is not that there were no canons—we have seen that there was a plurality. The problem is the assumption that there has ever been an orthodox, pan-Buddhist canon, a single master collection of the Buddha's teaching—and that this is the Pāli canon. On the surface, this might seem fair enough: for Theravāda Buddhists and for scholars of all stripes, the well-preserved and widely accessible Pāli collection is a rich and nearly inexhaustible resource. One of the greatest records of the Buddha's teachings, it is an indispensable reference work—a *referential* or *working* canon.

The Theravāda canon: closed or open?

Was the Theravāda canon closed or open? Collins calls the Pāli canon a "closed list of scriptures" and goes on to state, "When compared with other extant collections of scriptures in Buddhism, I think the Pāli Canon is unique in being an exclusive, closed list" (1990: 89–91). This is a complex issue for which we have little ancient evidence. The notion of closure is, in fact, seen in the Sarvāstivāda literature, for example, in the complex system of tables of contents (*uddāna*) that mapped the structure of the school's *Tripiṭaka* and safeguarded against interpolation.

It is sometimes stated that the Theravāda canon was closed earlier than some of the other mainstream collections, like those of the Mahāsāṃghika or Sarvāstivāda schools, invoking Buddhaghosa's fifth-century list of the texts that constitute the Pāli *Tripiṭaka* as evidence. If we stop at the list, the Theravāda canon is indeed closed, but the list did not inhibit the development of nonclassical literature and practical canons (and likely was not meant to do so).

The question of closure is complicated by the fact that there are very few ancient records of the reception of canons or scriptures. The evidence that we have is late, from the premodern and modern periods, and it is socially stratified. To produce or sponsor a *Tripiṭaka* was a huge and expensive project and naturally enough the evidence bespeaks elite and court sponsorship. Lists of titles, royal orders, and royal questions reflect canons as conceived by the court.

Conceptual proliferation

The idea of canonicity spawns a plethora of linked concepts and terms like *pre-*, *post-*, *extra-*, and *non-canonical*. The idea of canonicity is exclusionist in that it divides textual products into "ours" and "theirs," "ours" and "others." This leads to judgmental labels like non-canonical, unorthodox, and apocryphal, spurious, and counterfeit and the exclusion, rejection, or marginalization of texts that do not meet the school's criteria. For the study of Pāli literature, it is more useful to regard these texts as didactic tools rather than forgeries. Noncanonical literature was produced to suit changing social needs and changing appetites of the literary imagination, leading to shifts in the patterns of production and reception.

The scope of the Theravāda canons includes a wealth of translated or vernacular canons. To treat the Theravāda canon as "Pāli-only" risks creating an artificial narrative—as if Pāli literature was created in a social and historical vacuum—that it was written and read by native speakers of Pāli living in "Pāli-land." Pāli literature was in fact created by people from many language backgrounds who lived in diverse societies across the map of South and Southeast Asia and interacted with other Buddhist and non-Buddhist traditions and languages. Pāli was the criterion of linguistic correctness, but it was not a national or state language. Like any culture or religion, Theravāda is a hybrid. This gives it vitality and interest, and it confirms the importance of Pāli for understanding the religious and cultural heritage of Theravāda through its many canons.

An overemphasis on canonicity masks the variety, diversity, and vitality of regional and vernacular cultures and conceals the degree of transcultural exchange and translation. It sidelines the continuous production of literature within the Theravāda traditions, a creative endeavor that has not been adequately recognized in modern studies. Pāli literature has no cut-off date. It flourished in Sri Lanka through the Polonnaruva period (eleventh to early fourteenth centuries); the Pyu, Mon, and Burmese used Pāli in Burma from an early date and from the Sukhothai to the Ayutthaya and Bangkok periods (approximately thirteenth to nineteenth centuries) Siam produced a vibrant Pāli literature in the shape of *jātakas*, *sūtras*, lives, and final liberations of Sākyamuni's disciples (*sāvaka-nibbāṇa*), biographies of Buddha images, chronicles, riddles, liturgies, panegyrics, and more. Vernacular or bilingual counterparts prove the functional popularity of some of these texts, such as sermon versions and the stories and rituals surrounding the thaumaturge Māleyya Thera (Phra Malai) and the *arhat* Upagupta, significant figures in the collective imaginations. These texts are confident in their authority as Pāli texts. The Siamese canon interacted with the narrative canons of northern and northeastern India. The texts are social documents, produced by communities with a shared imaginaire.

The Pāli texts did not develop in a closed or circumscribed world that was off-limits to outside ideas. The Pāli subcommentaries paraphrase and sometimes adopt the ideas of the influential Vaibhāṣika school of North India. The Pāli *Sārasaṅgaha* and the Sinhala *Nikāyasaṅgraha* list the titles of identifiable Mahāyāna texts. The riddles of the *Vidaddhamukhamaṇḍana*, moral maxims of the *Nīti* texts, and many of the narratives and are cultural translations of Indian works.

Modernity

In South and Southeast Asia, the colonial period brought changes in knowledge, cosmology, and technology. The introduction of the printing press brought new ways to present the Dharma stimulating new modes of study, lexicography, and edition. Most important, the translation of canonical texts into English began in earnest, conveying the teachings of the Buddha to new readerships worldwide.

The Pāli canon has enjoyed over a century of attention by modern scholarship; almost all of its contents have been edited in the roman script and translated into the English language. There are also modern printed editions and translations into the scripts and languages of South and Southeast Asia. The editions and translations are of varying quality and many would benefit from being done over again. The roman-script editions of the Pali Text Society, an organization that was founded in 1881, have become the canon for the study of Theravāda Buddhism in the west and (with reservations) worldwide. It is important to bear in mind, however, that before the modern period, the Pāli canon circulated largely in Sri Lanka and Southeast Asia and, to a limited degree, in South India. There is no evidence that it was widely known in South Asia as a whole, where other canons, particularly those of the Mahāsāṃghika, the Sarvāstivāda, and the Sāṃmitīya schools, were better known, or in the Northwest, where scriptures circulated in Gandhari Prakrit, written in a Semitic alphabet, Kharoṣṭhī. The canons of these schools were all authoritative in their own circles. The ideas, narratives, and practices recorded in the Pāli canon are those of the Theravaṃsa; they had a limited circulation in the premodern period. Only in the modern period, through the intellectual encounter with the vast British and French colonial enterprises, was the Pāli canon "upgraded" to a universal or "pan-Buddhist" status. At first, the Chinese *Āgamas* were left out of the picture, but in the last few decades, they have begun to take their rightful place.

Many canons: function and practice

The Pāli canon is the mainstay of Theravaṃsa practice, philosophy, and instruction. However, other canons developed within the school in response to changing social, religious, and ritual needs. These canons both draw on and supplement or complement the Pāli canon, and they even replace it in the sense that the extra- or supra-canonical texts are the ones that have been known and used by *saṅgha* and public in particular periods or in particular places. In this sense, they are functional or practical canons.

Canons can be local or regional or transregional, but given Buddhism's diversity, I doubt whether any single historical *canon* can be *universal*. The assorted canons may express universal ideas or mainstream thoughts of Buddhism, but there is no reason to suggest that any particular *version* of these is universal. Mapping the diverse types of canon socially, intellectually, historically, or literarily is no easy task because of their heterogeneity across the spectrums of time and space. They have developed in different Buddhist societies in South and Southeast Asia. Notions of canonicity depend on context; on place, period, and circulation; and on the choices made by educators and ritualists. In conceptual terms, the many canons include ideal/practical/functional, inclusive/exclusive, authentic/apocryphal, orthodox/unorthodox. There are canons of mental and spiritual cultivation (*bhāvanā*, *kammaṭṭhāna*), canons of philosophy (the interactive system of ideas laid down in the Abhidhamma), canons of art and aesthetics, and canons of medical lore. Ritual canons are the texts recited in ceremonies and rituals for blessing and protection, as well as the visual media of talismanic calligraphy. Curricular canons are the textbooks and manuals of monastic and lay education. Scholastic canons are the standard and definitive texts that authorities cite to support and illustrate their ideas. All of these canons interweave with the Pāli canon itself and with each other, as in the cases of the ancient and canonical *Collection of Miscellaneous Pāli Readings* (*Khuddakapāṭha*) or the *Four Recitation Sessions* (*Catubhāṇavāra*). The active use of the texts is their context, and this usage and this context determine their canonical status. Canons are more than lists of the major works of a literary or cultural tradition. To understand a canon is not simply to be able to recite a list of titles, just as to recite the titles of the great European novels does not mean to understand the European literary canon. It means to study the context, the whys and hows and the social, political, and historical change.

Canons change over time. The Pāli canon may seem fixed: Buddhaghosa's list does not change. But the collection and the texts are multifunctional, and they can serve many ends. Canons are perpetually contested, but that is another question. One may wonder whether the urge to fit everything into the right box is not a modern academic obsession, but in any religion questions of scriptural classification, of inclusion and exclusion, are never simple and are often disputed. One person's orthodoxy is another's heresy. The extent and contents of the *Tripiṭaka* were always a question, and Southeast Asian kings periodically asked learned monks to clarify the matter. Evidence of ideas of canonicity is found in inscriptions and scripture catalogues but the questions are never settled.

The inclusive Tripiṭaka

When a central Siamese king sponsored a *Tripiṭaka*, he had everything that was known to exist in Pāli copied. The project was divided into four groups: the traditional three *Tripiṭaka* divisions plus language and grammar. It included commentaries, subcommentaries, manuals, narratives, apocrypha—everything. A comprehensive scriptural collection like this is an inclusive *Tripiṭaka*; it was the rule in old Siam until the end of the nineteenth century. Only the book-format edition sponsored by King Rāma V (1853–1910) in the 1890s was, for the first time, a *Tripiṭaka* project trimmed down to thirty-nine volumes—a fraction of the texts of the inclusive *Tripiṭakas*. Later, in the reign of King Rāma VII (Prajadhipok, r. 1925–1935), the Thai *Tripiṭaka* was fixed at forty-five volumes (Syāmaraṭṭha edition, 1925–1928).

In premodern Burmese practice as well, the *Tripiṭaka* seems to have been an inclusive rather than an exclusive compilation. Inscriptions from Pagan in upper Burma dated 1223 and 1442 CE itemize donations of a wide range of texts that modern scholars would classify as canonical, paracanonical, extracanonical, and outside the known Pāli system entirely (titles that appear to be non-Theravaṃsa texts from North India; Than Tun 1998; Luce and Tin Htway 1976). The status of certain texts seems to be perennially uncertain or contested; these include the *Suttasaṅgaha*, *Nettipakaraṇa*, *Peṭakopadesa*, and *Milindapañha*. Similar conceptions were held in Cambodia. In 1857, near Angkor Wat in Cambodia, donors had a set of texts copied and donated to a local monastery. The titles are recorded in an inscription as "the sacred Tripiṭaka" (in Khmer, *phra traipidok*). Most of them do not belong to the Pāli *Tripiṭaka*; those that do are *jātakas* (which are equivocal in terms of canonicity), and the others are extracanonical and apocryphal. de Bernon notes that

> [t]he expression "holy Tripiṭaka" ... is used here to designate the sum total of texts mentioned on the stele, even though it is evident that the titles do not belong to the Tripiṭaka properly speaking. In fact, for Khmer Buddhists the notion of "Trai-piṭak," the "Three Baskets," embraces (Buddhist) religious literature in general, whether it is canonical, extra-canonical, apocryphal, or cosmological.
>
> (2012: 379)

Sponsorship

The societies of Southeast Asia were highly stratified, not by caste divisions as in India but by local hierarchies of power and influence. Only rulers and the nobility had the resources to sponsor such huge and costly projects as producing the *Tripiṭaka*. The description of the ninth (according to the Thai enumeration) recitation convoked by King Rāma I in Bangkok in 1788 illustrates how the production of a canon was an elaborate and high-profile ritual event (abridged citation from the *First Reign Chronicle*, trans. Flood I: 160–161):

> The monks gathered in the *ubosot* [*uposatha*] confessional hall of the Phra Sisanphetchayadaram Temple [known today as Wat Mahathat], according to the schedule set by the king. Both the king and the heir apparent went from the Grand Palace to the Temple in a procession, complete with their royal paraphernalia and fanfares of flutes and victory drums. They entered the confessional hall and rendered obeisance to the Three Gems. They then asked Phra Phimonlatham to call upon the deities in the midst of the assembly of Buddhist monks. The power of all the deities was convoked to support the success of the project of the great council. The monks were divided into four groups ... [to revise the *Suttanta*, *Vinaya*, and *Paramattha* (Abhidhamma) *Piṭakas* and the *Grammatical Treatises*]. ... The king and his younger brother, the heir apparent, went to the temple twice every day. In the morning they presented food to the monks at the temple's galleries. In the late afternoon they came out again to present drinking water, incense sticks, and candles.

Ritual canons of Siam

How does the *Buddhavacana* (the Buddha's words) function in society? The canon has the authority of the Buddha's word and interacts with daily life through ceremonies and sermons. We see this in expressions of homage, in the formulas of going for refuge to the Three Gems, and in the taking of precepts: all these use adaptations of canonical formulas. Verses of blessing and protection, texts recited at funerals: all draw their power from the *Buddhavacana* through the medium of recitation by the Buddhist order.

In the premodern Siamese kingdoms of Ayutthaya, Thonburi, and Bangkok, from the sixteenth to early nineteenth centuries, on the evidence of chanting manuals the received ritual canon—a canon by custom, a canon by convention—included inter alia the following:

The 7 Tamnan and the 12 Tamnan	Collections of blessings and protective chants also known as the *Cularājaparitra* or Lesser Royal Protection and the *Mahārājaparitra* or Greater Royal Protection
Tripiṭaka	The abridged, symbolic, or emblematic *Tripiṭaka* (Skilling 2016)
Abhidharma	The abridged, symbolic, or emblematic Abhidharma, also known as the *Seven Books of the Abhidharma*. Recitations of the highly condensed abridged *Tripiṭaka* and *Abhidharma* are symbolically or emblematically equal to recitations of the entire *Tripiṭaka* and Abhidharma
Sahassanaya	The *Thousandfold Method*, an excerpt of a long section of *Dhammasaṅgaṇī*, first book of the Pāli Abhidharma
Buddhaguṇa	A compilation of virtues of a Buddha (in Pāli)

Mahājāti	The *Great Rebirth Story* or *Vessantara-jātaka* (in Pāli and Thai)
Phra Malai	Story of the thaumaturge Mālaya Thera (in Thai), which connects the assembly to the next Buddha, Maitreya
Jambūpati-sūtra	*Sūtra on King Jambūpati* (in Pāli and Thai: Skilling 2009b: 30–32 and Skilling 2014a: 360–361)
Uṇhissavijaya	*The Victorious Crown* (in Pāli: Skilling 2009b: 32–36)

This collection was not a consciously constructed canon. It would have evolved naturally: texts that enjoyed ritual and social popularity became the texts of choice for recitation. Canon formation is not so much the result of reflection and selection than of functional weight. This active and functional canon would not have replaced or erased the *Tripiṭaka*. At any time, there would be scholars who were experts in the *Tripiṭaka*, like Dhammakitti, who, in fourteenth-century Ayutthaya, composed the *Saddhamma-saṅgaha* (Law 1963), like the unknown author(s) who compiled the *Handbook of the Tripiṭaka* preserved in South Thailand (Santi Pakdeekham 2017) and the *Garland of the Piṭaka* catalogues (*Piṭakamālā*) in North Thailand (Santi Pakdeekham 2011).

The culture of Lanna (present-day North Thailand) offers a range of examples of functional or ritual canons. One of these might be described as a calendrical or birth-year canon. A specific text is assigned to each year of the twelve-year animal cycle so that the individual's relation to significant texts is defined by their year of birth, and the devotee offers their text to make merit on appropriate occasions. The twelve-year calendar interacts with texts in other ways; for example, the animal years are associated with the thirteen chapters (*kaṇḍa*) of the *Great Life* (*Vessantara-jātaka*), and when it is recited, people sponsor their own specific chapter. There is a weekday canon, in which each day of the (eight-day) week has a text assigned to it, and on one's birthday, one may offer one's text to the temple. In one system, the seven texts are the seven books of the Abhidharma. There are also *gāthā*, verses, to be recited according to one's day of birth; each day has a numerical power and a color. These practices personalize the canonical texts by bringing devotees into a personal relationship with them through donation and recitation (Skilling 2013a: 229).

Sermons

The body of sermons is a canon in itself, and the individual sermons are often built around a canonical citation, such as pithy statements, verses, or promises of benefit and blessing. The canonical *Dhammapada* is a familiar source cited in tandem with the stories related in the fifth-century commentary: canon and commentary merge and have equal value. Sermons intersperse Pāli words or phrases to confer authority to the vernacular language.

Sermons seem to have been largely ignored in Western scholarship until recently, but it was through the medium of the sermon that *sūtras* circulated. In preliterate societies or cultures in which literacy was not developed, the sermon and oral instruction were the staples of education, and the learned were called "well-heard" or well-versed (*bahussuta*). Literacy and the circulation of the scriptures as printed books brought private reading and autonomous study. The canons of literate societies developed organically through sales, literary criticism, and deliberations of academies. Religious canons may be steered by the *saṅgha*, but they develop organically.

Vernacular canons

The numerous vernacular canons of the Theravādin tradition should not be counted in terms of the national or majority languages of modern nation-states. They are not national like the canons of German literature or Italian opera (which themselves are artificial and contested). The "state" traditions are not unitary or monolithic: different Vinaya lineages or different cultures had different concepts of canonicity and developed their own practical canons. They privileged different texts or introduced new texts to their curricular canons, for example, the Mahānikāya or Dhammayuttika in Siam or the different lineages of Sri Lanka, Arakan, or Burma. Periodic reforms of the education and examination systems and of liturgical practices led to changes in emphasis on different clusters of texts.

Burmese Buddhism is the interacting complex of the practices of Burmese, Mon, Karen, Shan, and other Tai groups. The map of Buddhist communities and cultures is the heritage of the precolonial royal periods in what are now Burma, Thailand, Laos, and Cambodia. The many Shan kingdoms have been merged in the Shan State (singular) and adjacent areas of Thailand, Laos and Yunnan. Many of the cultural and linguistic groups spill across modern borders. Thai Buddhist communities are found in the northern states of Malaysia, there are Tai groups in Assam in India, and there are Khmer communities throughout the Mekong delta region of southern Vietnam. These communities predate, often by centuries, the colonial-period mappings of Southeast Asia which gave rise to the present-day borders. Buddhism has always been porous, allowing and encouraging space for different linguistic and ethnic traditions. When King Rāma I (r. 1782–1809) of Siam held a recitation-convocation to restore the Pāli *Tipiṭaka*, he called on Thai, Mon, and Lao monks to participate. The scriptural heritage of present-day Thai Buddhism is written in the Central Thai, Mon, Lanna Thai, Northeastern Tai, and a variety of other scripts and languages.

Model canons

Canons are human and social products, made up of exemplary texts that have been chosen as models of ethics, conduct, and philosophy. They are also models for literary production. Nonclassical birth stories are modeled on the classical *Jātaka* collection, including the *Fifty Jātakas* of the Thai tradition. Apocryphal suttas like the *Jambūpati*—or *Nibbāna-sūtras*—are modeled on the canonical suttas, opening with the classical "This is what I heard" (*evaṃ me sutaṃ*).

Carved in stone: epigraphic canons

The earliest surviving Pāli manuscripts date at best to the fourteenth or fifteenth centuries CE; the vast majority belong to the eighteenth and nineteenth centuries. Although, as von Hinüber (*Handbook*, p. 4) notes, "the age of the manuscripts has little to do with the age of the texts they contain," for historical evidence of the use of Pāli, we have to turn to the epigraphic record. No early Pāli inscriptions have been found in Sri Lanka, but a number of (generally short) inscriptions are known from lower Burma, central Siam, and neighboring regions. In the ancient polity of Śrīkṣetra in lower Burma, a remarkable complete manuscript in silver was excavated from a *stūpa*, while inscribed slabs from central Siam and southern Cambodia also imitate the palm-leaf format (see Figure 14.1).

None of the inscribed texts bears a date; their age is determined palaeographically to the broad parameters of the fifth to eighth centuries CE. All of them are excerpts or citations from Pāli scriptures rather than original compositions. The Siamese corpus highlights the four truths

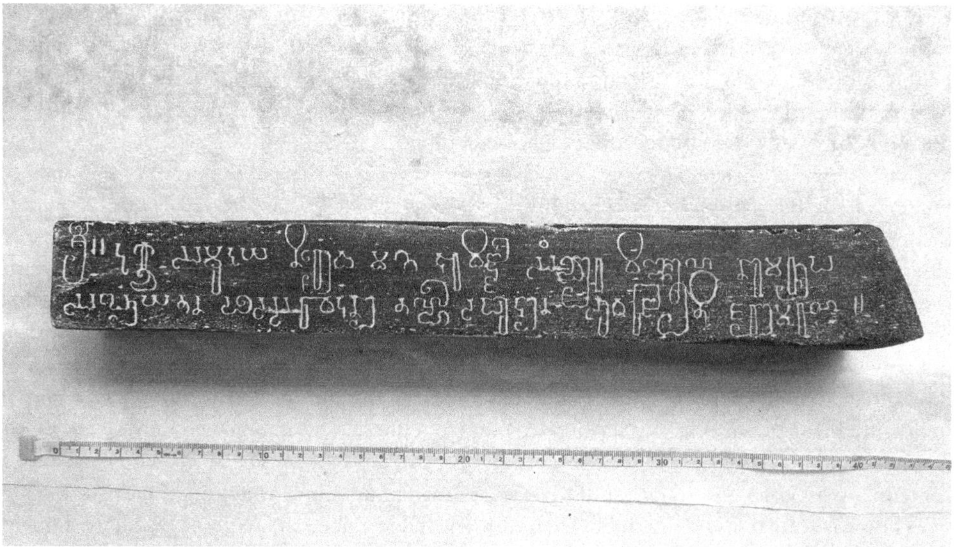

Figure 14.1 Stone bar inscribed on all four sides with Pāli texts, sixth to seventh century, from Nakhon Chaisi, Central Thailand; further details of provenance unknown.

Photograph courtesy Fragile Palm Leaves.

of the noble ones, especially the turning of the wheel of the Dharma, and conditioned arising, as well as the inspired utterances of the Buddha (*buddha-udāna*; Skilling, "Advent of Theravāda"; idem., "Theravaṃsa"). The *ye dhammā* stanza, an epitome of both the truths and conditioned arising, is common throughout the region, in Pāli, Sanskrit, and (in a few cases) Prakrit. It is the presence of these Pāli inscriptions that leads to the conclusion that the Theravaṃsa has always been present in the region—"always" meaning here from the early or even the earliest introduction of Buddhism to the region (Skilling 2019b). Later inscriptions from the reign of King Rāma IV (Mongkut 1804–1868, r. 1851–1868) on the wall that encircles the giant Phra Pathom Chedi in Nakhon Pathom include the full *Dhammapada* and *Suttanipāta*.

Inscriptions and narrative art help us to assess the circulation of texts and attitudes toward their canonicity. All traditions highlight the *Jātakas*, the previous lives of Gotama. This may be seen in the stone reliefs, terra cottas, and mural and cloth paintings in Pagan in Burma, in Sri Lanka and Thailand of varying periods, in the Pagan inscriptions referred to earlier, or in an inscription from Siem Reap Province, Cambodia, which enumerates twenty-seven texts donated by a monk to a monastery library in 1857 CE (de Bernon 2012: 391). The inscription states that the donor "had the sacred Tripiṭaka copied as recorded in this stone inscription" and goes on to list the titles of *Jātakas*, *Abhidharma*, *Jambūpati*, the *Three Worlds*, *King Milinda and Nāgasena*, and other texts, almost all vernacular Khmer compilations.

Early Buddhisms

The origins of the notion of early Buddhism lie in the age of imperialism, with the modernist and reformist thought of the end of the nineteenth century, and "rationalist" ideas about human progress and the evolution and decline of religions. The concept was influenced by contemporaneous currents in the study of Christianity that were concerned to separate out early Christianity from later forms with the idea that the early form was more authentic. By the early nineteenth century, European scholars developed a chronological view of the authenticity of forms of Buddhism. At first loosely called "early Buddhism"—or "primitive," "original," "pre-Asokan," or "presectarian" Buddhism—the notion took on increasing force as a frame for the study of Buddhism through the twentieth century.

Chronological theories were part of a historicist package in the earlier period of the study of religion. *Early Buddhism* has developed into an academic field and is now a keyword in an age that expects keywords. It has two aspects, one academic, the other ideological or quasi-religious, although the two are not easily disentangled. Whatever the case, some scholars and Buddhists took up *early Buddhism* as an attractive form of practice, a guideline for self-cultivation, that went beyond the historical and contemporary forms of the Theravāda, and early Buddhism has flourished under globalization to the point that it now stands out as an autonomous stream of thought and practice within modern and contemporary Buddhism. The term *early Buddhism* is frequently invoked without any serious attempt to define it, and it is not entirely clear exactly what it is. It is certainly not a religion, a sect, or a unified or centralized movement. It is not centered on a *saṅgha* or a leader, and it is nonregional, nonnational, and nonethnic. More often than not it is secular and demythologized. It might be described as a type of Buddhist thought and practice in progress, a loose association of groups who share modernist ideas, a no-frills movement that defines the Dharma as simple, practical, and reasonable.

The texts favored by its advocates amount to a "canon within the Pāli canon"—a selective or exclusivist reading of sources deemed to represent the Buddha's "true" or "authentic" teachings. Early Buddhism draws on two *Piṭakas*, the *Vinaya* and the *Sutta*, and usually does not regard the *Abhidhamma* as the word of the Buddha. Endorsed choices from the *Suttapiṭaka* include the four *Nikāyas*, certain texts of the *Khuddaka-nikāya* like the *Suttanipāta* (especially the *Aṭṭhakavagga* and the *Pārāyaṇa*), *Dhammapada*, *Udāna*, *Itivuttaka*, *Theragāthā*, and *Therīgāthā* (with an assortment of qualifications and reservations). In the earliest and still perhaps most common paradigm, early Buddhism is represented or defined by texts in the Pāli langauge; later developments show increasing historical maturity and include the *Āgamas* and the Gandhari texts.

In an article published in 1990, the late Steven Collins rejected the equation "the Pāli Canon = Early Buddhism" (Collins 1990: 89). What he calls a "realistic historical perspective" is this:

> Rather than pre-existing the Theravāda school, as the textual basis from which it arose and which it sought to preserve, the Pāli Canon—by which I mean the closed list of scriptures with a special and specific authority as the avowed historical record of the Buddha's teaching—should be seen as a product of that school, as part of a strategy of legitimation by the monks of the Mahāvihāra lineage in Ceylon in the early centuries of the first millennium A.D.

This is an important insight: the Pāli canon did not come first, but it was the *product* of editorial practices undertaken by the Theravāda school. This is equally true for all Buddhist schools for which we have any information: from the early period of oral transmission, canons were the products of group endeavors by teams of reciters. Rapid developments that took place in both *Āgama* and Gandhari studies since the 1990s have brought a sea change in Buddhist studies, expanding and deepening the very idea of early Buddhism (Allon 2018; Salomon 1999, 2018). The study of the ideological and scriptural development of Buddhism has had to adapt to more complex paradigms. It is no longer a simple question of "Theravāda—or early Buddhism—and the others."

The idea of a historicist or chronologically determined "early Buddhism" is absent in the literature of the Theravāda and other Buddhist schools; the closest idea might be that of the original or root redaction/recitation mentioned earlier. The origins of all eighteen schools lie in the same first convocation. We do not have much, or even any, information regarding how this fact was presented by most of the schools, but the information that we do have shows that the Sarvāstivāda and Vaibhāṣika streams of thought and those of the Theravāda tradition interpret the canonical development of Buddhism very differently. For the one, the root recitation is lost, fragmented, and incomplete, and this led to divisions in the Buddhist tradition. For the other, despite the attempts of other schools to falsify and impair the root collection, the root collection still survives as the canon of the Theravāda.

Traditional and modern scholars also have different views of the Pāli canon. Although the *Jātakas* were the mainstay of Theravāda Buddhism of Southeast Asia, modern scholarship, Eastern and Western, was unwilling or reluctant to accept them as authentic or early. It was the same for some other texts. The canonical credentials of the *Mahāsamaya-* and the *Āṭānāṭīya-suttas* (translated by Rhys Davids as the *Great Concourse* and the *Ward-rune of Āṭānāṭa*) might seem impeccable: they both belong to the *Long Collection*. Both contain lists of deities, mostly in verse, and both are regularly recited in the living Theravāda traditions. In the introduction to his translation of the former, T. W. Rhys Davids (1843–1922) writes, "The poem is almost unreadable now. The long list of strange names awakes no interest. And it is somewhat pathetic to notice the hopeless struggle of the author to enliven his unmanageable material with a little poetry. It remains, save here and there, only doggerel still" (Rhys Davids 1977: 282). The great and pioneering scholar's lack of enthusiasm is an example of how reception is never neutral—how Western scholars judged the canon by their own standards. The *suttas* are two of the most potent protections of Pāli literature, and to this day, they are chanted in Theravāda societies for protection and blessing—and, in the case of at least the latter, as an exorcism. The versions of other schools, such as that of the Sarvāstivāda, were also accorded high status. But once again, with its lists of supernormal beings and deities, its connection with exorcism and "superstition," it does not suit the palate of English Buddhists and is not high on the reading lists.

Liturgical collections are the functional canons of day-to-day Theravāda, and liturgical and ritual texts are those most familiar to both monastic and lay Buddhists. Intonation, melody, and rhythm are integral elements of liturgical canons that are transmitted orally by example and imitation. They remind us that the Buddhist scriptures were transmitted orally for three or more centuries before being written down. For several centuries, the transmission of Buddhism depended on the human memory and the human voice; it did not need any outside implements or technologies. The decision to use manuscripts brought the need for writing supports and instruments like ink, stylus, and brush, which, in turn, opened new avenues for making merit—the donation of writing materials and the copying of manuscripts.

The power of liturgy lies in its status as *Buddhavacana*, the Buddha's words, but *Buddhavacana* does not simply mean literal quotations from the Pāli canon. Glosses, summaries, paraphrases, and rewritings of canonical texts gain the status of *Buddhavacana*, a flexible category which according to the *Vinaya* includes what has been spoken by the Buddhas, by autonomous Buddhas, by auditors of the Buddha, by gods, and by sages—indeed, all that the Buddha says is well spoken, and all that is well spoken is the speech of the Buddha. The *ye dhammā* stanza, ubiquitous in the epigraphy of South and Southeast Asia, is not spoken by the Buddha but by one of his auditors (see Figure 14.2).

The chant called *Protection of the Aids to Wakening* (*Bojjhaṅgaparitta*) consists of verse summaries of three suttas from the *Connected Discourses*. The 271 stanzas of the *Pacification of Calamities* (*Uppātasanti*) draw on the power of canonical names—of Buddhas, realized monks and nuns,

Figure 14.2 Estampage of Angkor Borei Pāli inscription.

and a range of deities. The origins of the chant are uncertain—a Burmese tradition relates that it was recited in Chiang Mai in the fourteenth century to drive away the invading Mongols. It was selected for inclusion in a book of chants by Prime Minister U Nu of Burma in the 1950s, and an *Uppātasanti Pagoda* was erected when the army moved the capital to Naypyidaw in the first decade of the 2000s. Known in English as the Peace Pagoda, it was consecrated in 2009; 99 meters in height, it is only slightly lower than the grand Shwedagon Pagoda that graces the former capital of Rangoon. The chant, with some variants, was transmitted in the manuscripts of Lanna and central Siam (the latter as *Mahāsanti*), and it is recited today in some of Bangkok's temples. In this text, we see a transmutation of canonical elements into a Pāli verse and into architecture. The Pāli, liturgical, and architectural canons overlap as sources of power and protection.

The Ayutthaya canon (fifteenth to eighteenth centuries) included the *Vessantara-jātaka*, the *Nandopananda-sūtra*, the *Jambūpati-sūtra*, the *Phra Malai*, and the *Great Divine Mantra* (*Mahādibbamanta*). Only the first is canonical, or at least quasi-canonical. The *Taming of the Nāgas Nandopananda* is one of the eight events in Gotama's life summarized in the verses of the *Bāhuṃ*, one of the most popular auspicious and protective texts. All are victories or successes which bring good fortune—some from the canon and some from the commentaries—but each becomes canonical until the verses become a potent micro-canon packed with protective power. Protection comes through the power of what was *perceived* as *Buddhavacana*.

Canon and authority

There is a disjuncture between what modern scholars deemed or deem canonical and worthwhile and the texts that were and are actually *used*. A roman-script edition of the *Anthology of Suttas* (*Suttasaṅgaha*: HPL § 157), which may date to the twelfth century or earlier, was published in 1957, not in the United Kingdom by the Pali Text Society but in Calcutta by the Asiatic Society. It cites canonical suttas from four main collections (the four *Nikāyas*) including the *Great Assembly* from the *Long Discourses*. The *Miscellaneous Collection* is well represented by excerpts from the *Khuddakapāṭha*, the *Itivuttaka*, and the *Suttanipāta*. Citations from the *Dhammapada* and the *Vimānavatthu* are presented with their commentaries. There are three excerpts from the *Vinaya* and one from the *Book of Analysis* (*Vibhaṅga*) of the *Abhidhamma*. The subject matter and the source texts, with some significant exceptions, are not those on the standard reading lists of "early" or "original" Buddhism. Perhaps because of this the *Anthology* has not been translated into English and has been largely ignored. Cognate versions of some of the short sutras are, however, well known in the collections or treatises of other schools. Examples include the parable of the four mountains crushing down and the mountain of bones that are summarized in the verses of Nāgārjuna's *Friendly Letter* (*Suhṛllekha*).

The culture of the book

The written book was not exclusively associated with the Buddhist Dharma. There were also law codes, royal documents, medical treatises and recipes, poems and narratives, but the relationship with Buddhism was strong. Books were sacred. The *Legend of the Creation of the World*, a manuscript from southern Thailand, opens with homages to the Buddha and an invocation, and then states,

> If any woman or man wants to read or study this, they should first set up an altar and offer puffed rice, flowers, candles, incense, betel leaf and areca nuts, then place the book on the altar and then treat this book with respect. Success and well-being will follow.[3]

That to copy Dharma manuscripts was a highly meritorious act is emphasized in countless texts on the benefits of good deeds, most specifically those on "producing the *Tripiṭaka*" (*anisong sang phra traipidok*). This is exemplified in a verse found in the *Saddhamma-saṅgaha* and frequently placed at the end of manuscripts:

> Every single letter [in the Tripiṭaka] may equal an image of the Buddha:
>
> For this reason an intelligent person should write out the Tripitaka.
>
> As many as 84,000 Sambuddhas are there
> When the three Piṭakas are there.
>
> Each and every letter in the teaching of the world saviour [counts]
> Letter and Buddha image may have the same fruit.
>
> For this reason, an intelligent person who desires the three accomplishments
> Should write out, or have written out, the words of the Three Piṭakas as shrines of the Dhamma.

This powerful incentive to copy the scriptures is repeated in vernacular texts. For example,

> A person who offers palm leaves to the *saṅgha* so they can write down the Dharma gets the blessings of [rebirth for] six aeons [in heaven]. ...When a person writes out the Dharma and offers it to the monks: each letter equals a Buddha image and nothing can come anywhere near the blessing that each letter brings.[4]

Dharma was interpreted in the broad sense of Pāli and vernacular texts on the wide range of subjects of the "inclusive *Tripiṭaka*" and included nonclassical narratives, grammar and linguistics, and so on. The production of manuscripts contributed to the long life of the Dhamma and perpetuated the Buddha Sakyamuni's teachings.

On the other hand, to copy a manuscript for financial gain, in order to sell it, was considered a grave sin: "Anyone who writes the Dharma and sells [the book] suffers the result of this bad deed (*pāpa*) for 50,000 aeons. ...Anyone who writes the Dharma and sells it, creates evil that cannot be measured."[5]

^^^^^^

In the early Buddhism of India, the Theravādin *Tripiṭaka* was a canon among equals, one canon out of eighteen or more. The historical product of redaction by a single monastic and scholastic tradition, that of the Great Monastery of Sri Lanka, it is the precious record of the complete canon of one school in the original Indian language. It has been the foundation of Buddhism in Sri Lanka and Southeast Asia for over two thousand years and a rich resource for the study of Buddhist thought and practice. However, to treat it as *the* Buddhist canon reduces the diverse scriptural heritage of Buddhism to that redacted by a single school. This does not in the least mean that the canonical and post-canonical Pāli literature should be sidelined or displaced but, rather, that it should be seen in a broader context as a particular historical and literary instance of a Buddhist canon through balanced and critical assessments of early Buddhist canonical developments.

Freeing the "Theravāda canon" from the moorings of the "Pāli canon" opens space for appreciation of social and historical change and at the same time complicates the idea of canon immensely. Theravāda is not a monolithic tradition with a single and static canon and its head office in Sri Lanka. Letting the canonical cat out of the bag in which it has been confined by tradition and scholarship allows for the plurality of voices that is Theravaṃsa to speak up.

Acknowledgments

I thank Olivier de Bernon, Donald Lopez, and Trent Walker for their comments and for sending materials.

Notes

1 For reflections on canon, see Allon, "Formation of Canons;" Assmann, *Cultural Memory*, p. 102; Cabezón, "Scripture;" Collins "The Very Idea;" Crosby, *Theravāda Buddhism* (esp. Chap. 3); Harrison, "Canon;" Gethin, *Sayings of the Buddha*; Salomon, "Unwieldy Canon."

2 *Theravaṃsa* refers here to the broad mainstream of the Theriya or Sthāvira tradition; *Theravāda*, more specifically to the schools that developed in Sri Lanka, especially the tradition of the Great Monastery as codified by the fifth-century authority Buddhaghosa. I use the plural form *Theravādas* to signify the social, cultural, and linguistic plurality of the Theravaṃsa that developed historically in South and Southeast Asia.

3 *Tamnan sang lok: chabab ban pa lam*, from Pattani Province, southern Thailand: see *Wannakam thaksin wannakam khatsan*, Vol. 1, pp. 1–46. Citation from p. 7.
4 *Traiphum chabap ban krabi noi*, from Krabi Province, southern Thailand: *Wannakam taksin wannakam khatsan*, Vol. 1, pp. 47–97. Citations from pp. 94.26, 95.11.
5 *Traiphum chabap ban krabi noi*, pp. 94.7, 94.14.

References

Wannakam thaksin wannakam khatsan [Selected literature of the South]. 2005. Bangkok: Thailand Research Fund/Mahawithayalai Ratchaphat Surat Thani, 2548 [2005].

Allon, Mark. 2018. "The Formation of Canons in the Early Indian Nikāyas or Schools in the Light of the New Gāndhārī Manuscript Finds." *Buddhist Studies Review* 35 (1–2): 225–244. Reprt. in *Buddhist Path, Buddhist Teachings: Studies in Memory of L.S. Cousins*, edited by Naomi Appleton and Peter Harvey. Sheffield: Equinox, 2019.

Assmann, Jan. 2011. *Cultural Memory and Early Civilization: Writing, Remembrance, and Political Imagination*. Cambridge: Cambridge University Press.

de Bernon, Olivier. 2006. "The Status of Pāli in Cambodia: from Canonical to Esoteric Language." In *Buddhist Legacies in Mainland Southeast Asia*, ed. François Lagirarde, 53–66. Partis: École française d'Extrême-Orient.

de Bernon, Olivier. 2012. "Circulation of Texts in Mid-Nineteenth Century Cambodia: A new reading of Inscription K. 892 (Vatt Tā Tok, CE 1857)." In *How Theravāda is Theravāda? Exploring Buddhist Identities*, eds. Skilling, Peter, Jason A. Carbine, Claudio Cicuzza, Santi Pakdeekham, 371–399. Chiang Mai: Silkworm Books.

Cabezón, José Ignacio. 2004. "Scripture." In *Encyclopedia of Buddhism*, vol. 2, ed. Robert E. Buswell, Jr., 755–758. New York: Macmillan Reference USA.

Collins, Steven. 1990. "On the Very Idea of the Pali Canon." *Journal of the Pali Text Society* XV: 89–126. Rept. in *Buddhism: Critical Concepts in Religious Studies*, edited by Paul Williams, vol. I, London: Routledge, 2005, pp. 72–95. References are to the first edition.

Crosby, Kate. 2014. *Theravada Buddhism: Continuity, Diversity, and Identity*. Chichester: Wiley Blackwell.

Flood, Thadeus, Flood, Chadin, trans. 1978, 1990. *The Dynastic Chronicles, Bangkok Era, The First Reign. Chaophraya Thiiphakorawong Edition*. 2 vol. Tokyo: The Centre for East Asian Cultural Studies.

Gethin, Rupert. 2008. *Sayings of the Buddha: A selection of suttas from the Pali Nikāyas*. Oxford: Oxford University Press.

Harrison, Paul. 2004. "Canon." In *Encyclopedia of Buddhism*, vol. 1, ed. Robert E. Buswell Jr., 111–115. New York: Macmillan Reference USA.

Heine, Steven, Wright, Dale S., eds. 2004. *The Zen Canon: Understanding the Classic Texts*. Oxford: Oxford University Press.

Law, B.C. 1999. *A Manual of Buddhist Historical Traditions (Saddhamma-sangaha)*. [1941] repr. New Delhi: Asian Educational Services.

Luce, G.H., Htway, Tin. 1976. "A 15th Century Inscription and Library at Pagan, Burma." In *Malalasekera Commemoration Volume*, 203–256. Colombo.

Mitchell, W.J.T. 2005. "Canon." In *New Keywords, A Revised Vocabulary of Culture and Society*, eds. Tony Bennett, Lawrence Grossberg, Meaghan Morris, 20–22. Hoboken: Blackwell Publishing.

Payutto, P.A. 2003. *The Pali Canon: What a Buddhist Must Know*, trans. Somseen Chanawangsa. Bangkok: n.p.

Rhys Davids, T.W., C.A.F., trans. 1977. *Dialogues of the Buddha*. Part II [1910]. 4th ed. London: The Pali Text Society.

Salomon, Richard. 1999. *Ancient Buddhist Scrolls from Gandhāra: The British Library Kharoṣṭhī Fragments*. Seattle: The University of Washington Press.

Salomon, Richard. 2011. "An Unwieldy Canon: Observations on Some Distinctive Features of Canon Formation in Buddhism." In *Kanonisierung und Kanonbildung in der asiatischen Religionsgeschichte*, eds. Oliver Freiberger, Christoph Kleine, Max Deeg, 161–207. Vienna: Austrian Academy of Sciences Press.

Salomon, Richard. 2018. *The Buddhist Literature of Ancient Gandhāra: An Introduction with Selected Translations*. Somerville, MA: Wisdom Publications.

Santi, Pakdeekham. 2011. *Garland of the Piṭaka (Piṭakamālā)*. Bangkok and Lumbini: Fragile Palm Leaves Foundation/Lumbini International Research Foundation.

Santi, Pakdeekham, ed. 2009. *Jambūpati-sūtra: A synoptic romanized edition*. Bangkok and Lumbini: Fragile Palm Leaves (Materials for the Study of the Tripiṭaka, Vol. 4).

Santi, Pakdeekham. 2017. *Tamra Traipitaka: A Handbook of the Tipiṭaka.* (Materials for the Study of the Tripiṭaka, Vol. 13), Bangkok: Fragile Palm Leaves Foundation/Lumbini: Lumbini International Research Institute.

Skilling, Peter. 1997. "The Advent of Theravāda Buddhism to Mainland South-east Asia." *Journal of the International Association of Buddhist Studies* 20 (1): 93–107.

Skilling, Peter. 2009a. "Redaction, Recitation, and Writing: Transmission of the Buddha's Teachings in India in the Early Period." In *Buddhist Manuscript Cultures: Knowledge, Ritual, and Art*, eds. Stephen C. Berkwitz, Juliane Schober, Claudia Brown, 53–75. London: Routledge.

Skilling, Peter. 2009b. *Buddhism and Buddhist Literature of South-East Asia: Selected Papers by Peter Skilling*, ed. Claudio Cicuzza. Bangkok and Lumbini: Fragile Palm Leaves (Materials for the Study of the Tripiṭaka, Vol. 5).

Skilling, Peter. 2009c. "Theravāda in History." *Pacific World: Journal of the Institute of Buddhist Studies*, Third Series, Number 11 (Fall): 61–93.

Skilling, Peter. 2010. "Scriptural Authenticity and the Śrāvaka Schools: An Essay towards an Indian Perspective." *The Eastern Buddhist* 41 (2): 1–47.

Skilling, Peter, Jason A. Carbine, Claudio Cicuzza, Santi Pakdeekham, eds. 2012. *How Theravāda is Theravāda? Exploring Buddhist Identities*. Chiang Mai: Silkworm Books.

Skilling, Peter. 2012. "At the Heart of Letters: Aksara and Akkhara in Thai Tradition." In *80 that Mom Rajawong Suphawat Kasemsri* [Felicitation volume for MR Suphawat Kasemsri on his 80th Birthday], ed. Weerawan Ngamsantikul, 433–441. Bangkok: Rongphim Deuan Tula.

Skilling, Peter. 2014a. "Reflections on the Pāli Literature of Siam." In *From Birch Bark to Digital Data: Recent Advances in Buddhist Manuscript Research*, eds. Paul Harrison, Jens-Uwe Hartmann, 347–366. Vienna: Österreichische Akademie der Wissenschaften.

Skilling, Peter. 2014b. "Birchbark, Bodhisatvas, and Bhāṇakas: Writing materials in Buddhist North India." In *Eurasian Studies XII: Lecteurs et copistes dans les traditions manuscrites iraniennes, indiennes, et centrasiatiques / Scribes and Readers in Iranian, Indian and Central Asian Manuscript Traditions*, eds. Nalini Balbir, Maria Szuppe, 499–521. (Istituto per l'Oriente-Roma – Orientalisches Institut der Martin-Luther-Universität Halle-Wittenberg, Journal for Balkan, Eastern Mediterranean, Anatolian, Caucasian, Middle Eastern, Iranian and Central Asian Studies).

Skilling, Peter. 2015. 'Foreword' to *The Ten Great Birth Stories of the Buddha: the Mahanipata of the Jatakatthavannana, a book dedicated to H.R.H. Princess Maha Chakri Sirindhorn*, trans. Naomi Appleton, Sarah Shaw, xix–xxvi. Vol. I. Chiang Mai: Silkworm Books/Bangkok: Chulalongkorn University Press.

Skilling, Peter. 2016. "Chanting and Inscribing: The "Condensed Tripiṭaka" in Thai Ritual." In *'Guiding Lights' for the 'Perfect Nature': Studies on the Nature and the Development of Abhidharma Buddhism. A Commemorative Volume in Honor of Prof. Dr. Kenyo Mitomo for his 70th Birthday*. Tokyo: Sankibo Busshorin, (1)–(35) = pp. 928–962.

Skilling, Peter. 2017a. "Ānisaṃsa: Merit, Motivation and Material Culture." *Journal of Buddhist Studies Sri Lanka* XIV: 1–56.

Skilling, Peter 2017b. "The Many Lives of Texts: The Pancatraya and the Mayajala Sutras." In *Research on the Madhyama-agama*, ed. Dhammadinna. 269–326. Taipei: Dharma Drum Institute of Liberal Arts.

Skilling, Peter. 2017c. "Romance and Riddle: Buddhist narratives of Siam." In *Imagination and Narrative: Lexical and Cultural Translation in Buddhist Asia*, eds. Peter Skilling, Justin Thomas McDaniel, 161–186. Chiang Mai: Silkworm Books.

Skilling, Peter. 2019a. "Calligraphic Magic: Abhidhamma Inscriptions from Sukhodaya." In *Buddhist Studies Review*, ed. Lance Cousins. Reprint. In *Buddhist Path, Buddhist Teachings: Studies in Memory of L.S. Cousins*, edited by Naomi Appleton and Peter Harvey.

Skilling, Peter. 2019b. "The Theravaṃsa Has Always Been Here: K. 1355 from Angkor Borei." *Journal of the Siam Society* 117: 2.

Than, Tun. 1998. "An Original Inscription dated 10 September 1223, that King Badon Copied on 27 October 1785." In *Études birmanes en homage à Denise Bernot*, eds. Pierre Pichard, François Robinne, 37–55. Paris: École française d'Extrême-Orient.

15

ABHIDHAMMA

Theravāda thought in relation to Sarvāstivāda thought

Rupert Gethin

The nature of Abhidhamma

The term *abhidhamma* appears to have its origin in an expression found in the *Vinaya* and *Suttas*, "relating to the teaching" (*abhi dhamme*). The Abhidhamma can thus be understood as essentially a second-order exercise in presenting what the Buddha taught: historically it represents the attempts of the early generations of the Buddha's followers to draw out the system of thought implicit in the received discourses (*sutta*) of the Buddha. This enterprise resulted in the formation of a third division or basket of canonical texts, the Abhidhamma/Abhidharma Piṭaka. With reference to this collection of texts, the Theravāda tradition comes to understand *abhidhamma* as meaning the ultimate expression of the Buddha's teaching, directly expressing the truth understood by the Buddha's profound wisdom.

As such, Abhidhamma has been closely studied in the lands of Theravāda Buddhism from ancient times down to the present day. In part, this study has been sustained by the particular reverence shown to the Abhidhamma as the profoundest expression of the Buddha's teaching. This has manifested in the use of Abhidhamma texts in ritual, meditation and for protection. In Thailand, Cambodia, and Laos, the recitation of Abhidhamma is integral to funeral rites (Langer 2012); in Thailand, Cambodia, Laos, and Sri Lanka syllabic formulas encapsulating the essence of the Abhidhamma have been used for protection and in meditation practice (Swearer 1995; Cousins 1997; Crosby 2013); in Burma, the twenty-four causal relations of the *Paṭṭhāna*, the final book of the Abhidhamma Piṭaka, are recited for protection (Kyaw 2014: 22–24).

The initial development of Abhidhamma

While the Abhidhamma texts form a distinct class of early Buddhist literature, their production built on developments already found in the *Sutta* literature: (1) digests of lists and categories (the *Saṃgīti*—and *Dasuttara-suttas*); (2) the fundamental matrix (*mātikā*) or set of categories comprising basic Buddhist teachings, which informs the structure of the Saṃyutta-nikāya and includes dependent origination, the bundles, sense spheres, applications of mindfulness, right efforts, the bases of successful meditation, five spiritual faculties, the constituents of awakening and the eightfold path, and the four truths; (3) the refining and defining of technical terminology, exemplified in suttas dubbed "analysis" (*vibhaṅga* or *vedalla*).[1]

DOI: 10.4324/9781351026666-19

The production of the canonical Abhidhamma texts corresponds with the period of the emergence of the ancient Buddhist schools, of which the Sri Lankan Theriya (Sk: Sthāvira) or Theravāda was one. Tracing its roots to one of eight missions sent out from the Mauryan capital in Pāṭaliputra Pātiliputra to different regions of India by the monk Moggaliputta Tissa in the middle of the third century BCE, by the early centuries CE, the school flourished in Sri Lanka and southern India.

Buddhist tradition routinely talks of eighteen ancient schools, but this number is likely to be ideal: the ancient lists of schools do not agree in detail, while the status of some schools is unclear. In principle, each ancient school would have preserved its own characteristic version of the Tripiṭaka. What survives today, in an Indian language or in Chinese or Tibetan translation, is in broad terms the Vinaya Piṭaka of six schools (Theravāda, Mahīśāsaka, Dharmaguptaka, Sarvāstivāda, Mūlasarvāstivāda, and Mahāsāṃghika), the Sūtra Piṭaka of one school (Theravāda) along with significant portions of two other schools (Mūlasarvāstivāda and Dharmaguptaka), and the Abhidharma Piṭaka of three schools (Theravāda, Sarvāstivāda, and, probably, Dharmaguptaka).

A comparison of these texts reveals a substantial agreement among the ancient Buddhist schools with regard to the core contents of the Vinaya and Sūtra material. Regarding the latter, the great Belgian scholar of Buddhism, Étienne Lamotte, has observed that although preserved and transmitted by different schools, the Sūtra collections are not sectarian documents but the common heritage of the various schools (Lamotte 1988: 156). The same cannot be said of the Abhidharma texts. Here, although there is still much that is common in the general approach and underlying principles, we are clearly dealing with the different ways of drawing out the details of Buddhist thought developed by different schools. How many distinct Abhidharma systems existed in ancient times is unclear. Today we have substantial knowledge of only two: the Theravāda Abhidhamma, whose origins must lie in the north but which developed and flourished in the south of India and Sri Lanka, and the Sarvāstivāda Abhidharma, which set the Buddhist intellectual agenda in the north of India, directly influencing the development of schools of Mahāyāna Buddhist thought such as the Yogācāra, and became widely studied in China and Tibet. A comparison of these two systems allows us to discern the distinctive features of specifically Theravāda Buddhist thought.

Canonical Abhidhamma literature

The Abhidhamma Piṭaka of the Theravāda school survives complete in Pāli and comprises seven works, one of which, the fifth, is traditionally given an author other than the Buddha. The traditional order given in a fifth-century Abhidhamma commentary, the *Atthasālinī* (*Exposition of the Meaning*) is as follows (Tin 1920–1921 5): (1) *Dhammasaṅgaṇi* (*Enumeration of Dharmas*), (2) *Vibhaṅga* (*Analysis*), (3) *Dhātukathā* (*Discussion of the Elements*), (4) *Puggalapaññatti* (*The Conception of Persons*), (5) *Kathāvatthu* (*Points of Discussion*) by Moggaliputta Tissa, (6) *Yamaka* (*Pairs*), (7) *Paṭṭhāna* (*Causal Relationship*).

The Abhidharma Piṭaka of the Sarvāstivāda school comprises a quite different set of seven works which survive only in Chinese translation (with some Sanskrit fragments and one work in Tibetan translation).[2] Each work is associated with a particular immediate or later follower of the Buddha (Lamotte 1988: 184): (1) *Jñānaprasthāna* (*Foundation of Knowledge*) by Kātyāyanīputra, (2) *Prakaraṇapāda* (*The Treatise*) by Vasumitra, (3) *Vijñānakāya* (*Types of Consciousness*) by Devaśarman, (4) *Dharmaskandha* (*Compendium of Teachings*) by Śāriputra, (5) *Prajñaptiśāstra* (*Manual of Conceptions*) by Maudgalyāyana, (6) *Dhātukāya* (*Types of Element*) by Pūrṇa, (7) *Saṃgītiparyāya* (*The Comprehensive Recitation*) by Mahākauṣṭhila.

At first glance, surviving Abhidharma Piṭakas appear to have little in common. Closer scrutiny reveals some common ground. Thus the *Vibhaṅga* and *Dharmaskandha* are structured around a common set of topics: the five bundles (*khandha/skandha*), twelve sense-spheres (*āyatana*), eighteen elements (*dhātu*), dependent origination (*paṭiccasamutpāda/pratītyasamutpāda*), twenty-two faculties (*indriya*), four applications of mindfulness (*satipaṭṭhāna*), four right efforts (*sammappadhāna/samyakpradhāna*), four bases of success (*iddhipāda/ṛddhipāda*), four absorptions (*jhāna*), seven constituents of awakening (*bojjhaṅga/bodhyaṅga*), and the eightfold path (*magga/mārga*). Both the *Kathāvatthu* and the *Vijñānakāya* include sections concerned with the Abhidharma controversies of the issue of existence of dharmas in the past, present, and future and of the question of the status of the "person" (*puggala/pudgala*). In setting out lists of dharmas and types of consciousness, the *Dhātukāya* bears some comparison with the *Dhammasaṅgaṇi*.

What is striking is the wish, despite some opposition, to include these Abhidharma works in the category of "word of the Buddha" at the same time as acknowledging the role of both immediate and later followers in their production. Thus, according to the Theravāda account, the Buddha himself thought out all seven works of the Abhidhamma while seated in meditation in the fourth week after his awakening. For seven years, he kept them to himself but then taught them to his reborn mother and assembled gods in the Heaven of the Thirty-Three. At that time, he also taught them to Sāriputta, who, in turn, taught them to his pupils. Yet one work, the *Kathāvatthu*, is acknowledged only to have been expounded in full by the monk Moggaliputtatissa during the reign of the emperor Aśoka, some 150 years after the death of the Buddha. Similarly, Sarvāstivāda tradition associates three of its seven canonical Abhidharma works with certain of the Buddha's prominent and immediate disciples (Mahākauṣṭhila, Śāriputra, Maudgalyāyana); the remaining four works are associated with disciples who tradition suggests lived sometime after the Buddha, between the third and first centuries BCE.[3] Both the Theravādins and Sarvāstivādins counter the obvious objection that the attribution of Abhidharma works to disciples undermines their status as "word of the Buddha" by suggesting that the substance of the material comes from the Buddha himself and that the disciples in question only expanded on that or arranged it (Tin, 1920–1921: 4–7; Willemen, Dessein and Cox 1998: 221).

Precise dating of the canonical Abhidharma texts is not possible. It seems likely that they evolved and were developed over several centuries, from the mid-third century BCE to the mid mid-first century CE (Frauwallner 1995: 124–125; Cousins 2015: 132–133).

The development of Abhidhamma literature

From the early centuries CE, we see the production of various commentaries and manuals that complement the canonical works and act as aids to the study of their demanding systems of thought. In the south, on the island of Sri Lanka, various commentaries on the works of the Theravāda canon circulated in Sinhala Prakrit. In the late fourth or early fifth century, Buddhaghosa, a monk from, probably, southern India, initiated a project at the Mahāvihāra (Great Monastery) in Anurādhapura, the island's capital, to edit, collate, and render these commentaries into Pāli, in accordance with the consensus and traditions of the elders of the Mahāvihāra, giving us the Theravāda commentaries that survive today. These commentaries are substantially informed by Theravāda Abhidhamma theory. At the invitation of Buddhaghosa, an unnamed monk produced substantial commentaries on the first and second books of the Theravāda Abhidhamma, the *Atthasālinī* (*Exposition of the Meaning*) and *Sammohavinodanī* (*Dispeller of Delusion*), as well as the *Pañcappakaraṇaṭṭhakathā* (*Commentary on the Five Treatises*) on the remaining five books (von Hinüber 1996: 151). Buddhaghosa himself produced the *Visuddhimagga*

(*Path of Purification*), a comprehensive and, for the Theravādins, extremely influential digest of Theravāda understanding of the Buddhist path that includes a substantial section (Chapters 14–17) titled "The Foundations of Understanding" (*paññābhūmi*), which summarizes Theravāda Abhidhamma theory. In composing his *Visuddhimagga*, Buddhaghosa seems, in part, to have followed the format of an earlier work, the *Vimuttimagga* (*Path of Freedom*), a work that today survives only in Chinese and partial Tibetan translation. Its author was a monk named Upatissa, who probably belonged to a rival monastic lineage in Anurādhapura, the Abhayagirivihāra. Demonstrably Theravāda in its general Abhidhamma outlook, the *Vimuttimagga* nonetheless disagrees with Mahāvihāra positions on a number of issues, giving us a glimpse of an alternative Theravāda tradition of exegesis (Cousins 2012).

In the sixth and seventh centuries, important subcommentaries on the commentaries of the Abhidhamma Piṭaka were produced: Ānanda's *Mūlaṭīkā* (*Primary Subcommentary*) and Dhammapāla's (or Jotipāla's) *Anuṭīkā* (*Secondary Subcommentary*).

Besides these long and often difficult works, shorter "dexterous manuals" (*lakkhaṇa-gantha*) were composed. The earliest of these (fifth century) appear to be the *Abhidhammāvatāra* (*Introduction to Abhidhamma*) and *Rūpārūpavibhāga* (*Classification of the Material and Immaterial*), written in southern India by a monk named Buddhadatta. But the work that eventually came to supersede all others and is still used today as the preferred introduction to Abhidhamma in Theravāda countries is Anuruddha's (tenth-century) *Abhidhammattha-saṅgaha* (*Summary of the Meaning of Abhidhamma*), which in the space of some fifty pages covers the essential elements of Theravāda systematic thought.

Such manuals were designed to be memorized by the student, who would then receive further instruction from a teacher. The manuals thus acquired explanatory commentaries that summarized controversial and potentially contradictory points found in the voluminous and daunting Abhidhamma literature. In the twelfth century, Sumaṅgala, working in the capital of Laṅkā, now Polonnaruva, wrote commentaries to both Buddhadatta's *Abhidhammāvatāra* and Anuruddha's *Abhidhammatthasaṅgaha*. The first, the *Abhidhammavikāsinī* (*Elucidation of Abhidhamma*), at some 700 pages, is an exhaustive exposition of the issues discussed in the Theravāda exegesis of Abhidhamma. The latter, the *Abhidhammatthavibhāvinī* (*Exposition of the Meaning of Abhidhamma*), a mere 150 pages, is based on his teacher's earlier Sinhala summary, having in mind, it seems, "those who are frightened of books" (Wijeratne and Gethin 2002: 51). Another important summary of the Theravāda Abhidhamma is Kassapa's *Mohavicchedanī* (*Destroyer of Delusion*), written in southern India in Coḷa in the thirteenth century.

The production of Theravāda Abhidhamma literature continued in the kingdoms of Southeast Asia. The Burmese tradition of Abhidhamma studies dates back to at least the fifteenth century with the works of Saddhammajotipāla, a monk from Pagan who visited Sri Lanka, and Ariyavaṃsa, who wrote subcommentaries on the *Atthasālini* and *Abhidhammāvatara*. The sixteenth century saw the beginning of the production of Burmese vernacular Abhidhamma primers known as *ayakauk*. The particular Burmese fascination with the seventh book of the Abhidhamma, the *Paṭṭhāna*, seems also to date back to the seventeenth century (Kyaw 2014, 161–65). The Burmese tradition of learned Abhidhamma commentary continued into the twentieth century when the Burmese monk Ledi Sayadaw published his *Paramatthadīpanī* (*Explanation of the Ultimate*), an influential critique of positions advocated by Sumaṅgala's twelfth-century commentary on the *Abhidhammatthasaṅgaha*. In the sixteenth century in the Lanna kingdom (in what is now northern Thailand), the scholar-monk Ratanapañña composed the *Vajirasāratthasaṅgaha* (*Compendium of the Meaning of the Diamond Core*), an innovative work, combining riddle with Abhidhamma and other topics (Schnake 2021). His contemporary,

Ñāṇakitti, also composed a series of commentaries on the canonical Abhidhamma works and the *Abhidhammatthasaṅgaha* (von Hinüber 2000).

In the north of India in Kashmir, the Sarvāstivāda school also produced a series of important Abhidharma treatises with reference to their distinctive canonical Abhidharma texts. In the early centuries CE, the Theravāda Buddhist authors in the south seem unaware of the specific works being produced in the north, and vice versa, although there does seem to have been some familiarity with some of each other's characteristic doctrines and positions. However, it is clear that by perhaps the seventh century, works composed in North India, such as Vasubandhu's *Abhidharmakośa* (*Sheath of Abhidharma*), written in Kashmir in the fourth century, were also familiar to Theravāda scholar monks in the south, for the author of the *Abhidhamma-anuṭīkā* provides a lengthy counter to Vasubandhu's attempted refutation of the doctrine of immediate rebirth (see the following section).

The Abhidharma theory of *dharmas*

The Buddhist systematic thought of the Abhidharma rests on a basic distinction between two types of discourse. The discourses (*sutta/sūtra*) of the Buddha are regarded as his teaching applied to a particular situation, using terms figuratively and in accordance with everyday usage. The Abhidharma, in contrast, presents the Buddha's teachings without concession to time, place or audience, and in technical terms that are precisely defined to ensure analytical exactitude (As 21). The contrast between these two approaches coincides, in part, with other distinctions made in the texts between types of teachings. Some teachings are said to be expressed in terms whose meaning must be determined (*neyyattha/ñeyārtha*), while others are expressed in terms whose meaning is already determined (*nītattha/nītārtha*). Some teachings are expressed in conventional terms (*sammuti*); others are expressed in ultimate terms (*paramattha/paramārtha*). Underlying this is the basic Buddhist premise that the failure to see the world as it really is (*yathābhūtaṃ*) is what causes suffering. In principle, Abhidhamma is an attempt to use language exactly in an attempt to give a precise and full account of how the world is in order to assist the direct realization of the nature of things and so bring freedom from suffering.

Abhidharma can be seen as having three main areas of concern:

1 The reduction of the world to a set of fundamental mental and physical *dhammas* or "qualities," understood as the basic events or forces that combine to construct the world we experience. This exercise in reduction results in a kind of phenomenology of mind and body.
2 An account of how these fundamental *dhammas* or events interact according to different types of causal relationship. This includes the operation of *kamma*—how acts motivated by greed, aversion, and delusion and their positive counterparts (nonattachment, kindness, and wisdom) have pleasant and unpleasant results (*vipāka*)—as well as the analysis of the processes of perception and death and rebirth in different types of existence.
3 An analysis of the stages of the Buddhist path culminating in awakening

In the present context, there is only the space to say something about the first two.

The Abhidharma analysis of the world in terms of *dhammas* is a development from the analysis of the world in terms of five "bundles" (*khandha*) and six "sense spheres" (*āyatana*) found in the *suttas*. The sense spheres are understood as encompassing the totality of experience in terms of the six senses (sight, hearing, smell, taste, touch, mind), their corresponding objects (visible forms, sounds, smells, tastes, bodily sensations, ideas), and the types of cognition (*viññāṇa/vijñāna*) associated with each sense (cognition by way of sight, etc.), which gives a list known as the eighteen "elements" (*dhātu*). In the *suttas*, the five bundles refer to an analysis of the world in terms of (1) physical phenomena (*rūpa*), (2) feeling (*vedanā*), (3) recognition (*saññā/saṃjñā*), (4) volitional forces (*saṃskāra*), and (5) cognition. Thus in response to sense data, pleasant or unpleasant feelings arise, followed by a recognition of what has been perceived, which is the occasion for certain volitional responses leading to acts of body and speech; all this is framed by "cognition," that is, the sense of a subject experiencing an object. On the basis of indications given in the *sūtras* the Abhidharma texts of both Theravādins and Sarvāstivādins aim to give a full list of all possible types of *dharma* encompassed by the bundles. This involved in particular specifying the types of volitional forces in detail.

The overall concern is to give an account of the world without reference to a substantial "self" (*attan/ātman*), understood as an underlying, unchanging subject of experience. Thus instead of describing the world in terms of a self that now experiences greed, now anger, and so on, the world is described in terms merely of the succession of the qualities greed, anger, and so on. These qualities are connected not by an underlying substantial self but by different kinds of causal relationship.

Looking at the Theravāda and Sarvāstivāda lists of *dharmas* (see Table 15.1), we see that the starting point is a fundamental division between that which constitutes the "conditioned" (*saṃskṛta*) world that we ordinarily know and that which is outside and apart from this and therefore "unconditioned" (*asaṃskṛta*).

The unconditioned refers first and foremost to nirvana, which for both the Theravādins and Sarvāstivādins is a positive reality that eradicates all the defilements of the minds of those who reach the end of the Buddhist path. Theravādins refer to this reality as the "unconditioned element" (*asaṃkhata-dhātu*), the Sarvāstivādins as "cessation through understanding" (*pratisaṃkhya-nirodha*). The Sarvāstivādins posit two further unconditioned *dharmas*, cessation without understanding (*apratisaṃkhya-nirodha*) and absolute space (*ākāśa*). The former is a force that prevents the arising of *dharmas* that might arise but for the absence of causal conditions. The Theravādins and other critics regarded these two *dharmas* as unnecessarily concretizing what is merely conceptual.

Within the category of conditioned *dharmas*, there is a primary division between mind and body, between *dharmas* that are nonphysical (*arūpa*) and *dharmas* that are physical (*rūpa*). If pressed on the metaphysical question, the Theravāda and Sarvāstivāda Abhidharma systems are thus certainly dualist. Yet it is in good measure that phenomenological, not ontological, concerns inform much of their *dharma* analysis. Within the category of mental *dharma*s an important distinction is made between the bare sense of awareness (cognizing an object), termed *citta*, and associated mental activities, termed *cetasika* (Skt *caitasika*). The bare awareness that is *citta* is an abstraction that cannot by itself be aware of an object; to accomplish perception it needs the assistance of a minimum number of *cetasikas*, seven according to the Theravādins, ten according to the Sarvāstivādins. In addition to the basic divisions between body and mind, and *citta* and *cetasika*, the Sarvāstivādins introduce a class of dharmas termed "forces disassociated from mind" (*citta-viprayukta-saṃskāra*). The *dhamma*s of this class the Theravādins either pass over or conceive of in different ways. In sum, the Theravādins present *dhamma*s in terms of four ultimate categories (*paramattha-dhamma*), namely, mind, mentalities, matter, and *nibbāna*; the Sarvāstivādins in terms of five fundamental categories (*vastuka*), namely, matter, mind, mentalities, disassociated forces, and the unconditioned.

The *dharma* lists of both the Theravāda and Sarvāstivāda traditions are clearly the product of a process of discussion and debate about what to classify as a basic irreducible category. The early lists of both schools were open. The Mahāvihāra Theravādins eventually agreed on a list

Table 15.1 The dharma lists of the Theravāda and Sarvāstivāda Abhidharma compared. (Note that the traditional order has been adapted to facilitate comparison.)

Matter		*Mind*		*Mental Activities (unwholesome)*	
Theravāda (28)	**Sarvāstivāda (14)**	**Theravāda (1)**	**Sarvāstivāda (1)**	**Theravāda (14)**	**Sarvāstivāda (22)**
earth	earth	consciousness	consciousness	**universal (4)**	**universal (8)**
water	water	**Mental Activities (ethically variable)**		delusion	ignorance
fire	fire			shamelessness	shamelessness
wind	wind	**Theravāda (13)**	**Sarvāstivāda (14)**	recklessness	recklessness
eye	eye			restlessness	restlessness
ear	ear	**universal (7)**	**universal (10)**	*[occasional]*	inattentiveness
nose	nose	contact	contact		lethargy
tongue	tongue	feeling	feeling		faithlessness
body	body	recognition	recognition		sluggishness
visible form	visible form	volition	volition	**occasional (10)**	**occasional (4)**
sound	sound	concentration	concentration	greed	greed
smell	smell	attention	attention	view	*[= understanding]*
taste	taste	life	*[disassociated force]*	conceit	conceit
life	noninformative matter	*[neutral occasional]*	wish to act	hatred	aversion
femaleness	*[disassovciated force]*	*[wholesome]*	understanding	envy	*[secondary defilement]*
maleness		*[wholesome]*	mindfulness	stinginess	*[secondary defilement]*
heart base		*[neutral occasional]*	decision	anxiety	*[variable occasional]*
food				sluggishness	*[unwholesome universal]*
space	*[unconditioned]*	**occasional (6)**	**occasional (4)**	sleepiness	*[variable occasional]*
bodily information		thinking	thinking	doubt	doubt
speech information		examining	examining		**secondary (10)**
lightness		decision	*[variable universal]*		anger
softness		vigor	*[wholesome]*	*[unwholesome*	disparagement
readiness	*[disassociated force]*	joy	*[= feeling]*	*occasional]*	stinginess
accumulation	*[disassociated force]*	wish to act	*[variable universal]*	*[unwholesome*	envy
continuity	*[disassociated force]*	*[unwholesome]*	anxiety	*occasional]*	obstinacy
decay	*[disassociated force]*	*[unwholesome]*	sleepiness		cruelty
impermanence					deceit
					deviousness
					arrogance
					enmity

(*Continued*)

Table 15.1 (Continued)

Matter		*Mind*		*Mental Activities (unwholesome)*	
Mental Activities (wholesome)		**Disassociated Forces**		**Unconditioned**	
Theravāda (25)	**Sarvāstivāda (10)**	**Theravāda (0)**	**Sarvāstivāda (14)**	**Theravāda (1)**	**Sarvāstivāda (3)**
universal (19)	**universal (10)**	*[matter/universal]*	possession	*[matter]*	space
faith	faith	*[matter]*	nonpossession	nirvana	cessation by understanding
mindfulness	*[variable universal]*	*[matter]*	similarity of class		
[neutral occasional]	vigor	*[matter]*	unconsciousness		cessation without understanding
balance	equanimity	*[matter]*	attainment of unconsciousness		
shame	shame				
regard for consequence	regard for consequence		attainment of cessation		
nonattachment	nonattachment		life		
kindness	kindness		birth		
[wholesome occasional]	compassion		continuity		
tranquility of body and mind (2)	tranquility		decay		
lightness of body and mind (2)			impermanence		
softness of body and mind (2)			name		
readiness of body and mind (2)			sentence		
adaptability of body and mind (2)			syllable		
straightness of body and mind (2)	attentiveness *[= volition]*				
occasional (6)	*[= volition]*				
right speech	*[= volition]*				
right action	*[wholesome universal]*				
right livelihood	*[= feeling]*				
compassion	*[variable universal]*				
sympathetic joy					
understanding					

of seventy-two fundamental natural qualities (*sabhāva*). The Sarvāstivadins' list seems never to have been finally fixed, varying between seventy-nine and eighty-one.[4]

In so far as the Abhidharma taxonomies aim to provide a set of categories that allow for the description of all possible types of experience, they are simply descriptive of what there is. But at the same time they are normative insofar as certain *dharma*s are considered ethically wholesome (*kusala/kuśala*), certain unwholesome (*akusala/akuśala*), and others indeterminate (*avyākata/avyākṛta*).

Both the Theravādins and Sarvāstivādins conceive of the material world in terms of four primary elements that constitute its basic irreducible qualities: resistance (earth), cohesion (water), heat (fire), and motion (wind). Dependent on the four elements there occur secondary instances of matter with additional physical qualities: the physical bases of the five senses have the capacity to be sensitive to their respective objects; other instances of matter have the capacity to be seen, heard, tasted, or smelled. The elements themselves (either just three apart from water, according to the Theravāda, or all four, according to the Sarvāstivāda) are considered to constitute the sphere of touch in the form of the sensation of resistance, temperature, and movement. The additional items in the Theravāda list of material qualities are in part accommodated by the Sarvāstivādins under the category of disassociated forces or, in the case of space, the unconditioned. The Sarvāstivādins introduce a special type of matter that is "uninformative" (*avijñapti*), referring to the way significant acts of speech and body are carried invisibly in the body. This is rejected by the Theravādins as substantializing something that is purely conceptual.

Turning to the lists of mental activities (*cetasikas*) associated with episodes of consciousness, these are divided into *dharma*s that are ethically variable, unwholesome, and wholesome. There is a basic agreement on six of the universal activities that are the prerequisites of any instance of consciousness. The most striking difference is that the Sarvāstivādins include in this category "understanding" (*prajñā*) and "memory" (*smṛti*). For the Sarvāstivādins the former represents a fundamental disposition of the mind to form a view of the world, whether appropriate or not; for the Theravādins, it is an exclusively wholesome disposition to understand the world in terms of the four truths, namely, suffering, its cause, its cessation, and the way to its cessation. Similarly, the Sarvāstivādins take "mindfulness" (*sati/smṛti*) as a basic capacity of the mind to remember its object, while the Theravādins again see it as a distinctively wholesome attentiveness, that remains mindful of an object's nature. Nevertheless, both schools agree that when associated with the other qualities that arise in wholesome consciousness, mindfulness, and understanding become closely linked and play a special role in coming to a realization of the true nature of things.

In principle, the two schools are agreed that ignorance (*avijjā/avidyā*), shamelessness (*ahirika/āhrīkya*), recklessness (*anottappa/ anapatrāpya*), and restlessness (*uddhacca/audhatya*) are generally characteristic of unwholesome consciousness, which may then on occasion involve additionally either greed (*rāga*) or aversion (*dosa*), which each, in turn, may be associated with further unwholesome *dharmas*. However, the Sarvāstivādin overlay this conception with a scheme of six primary defilements—greed (*rāga*), ignorance (*avidyā*), aversion (*pratigha*), conceit (*māna*), views (*dṛṣṭi*), and doubt (*vicikitsā*)—and an extended list of secondary defilements (Gethin 2017).

Turning to the category of wholesome *dharma*s, most striking is the Theravāda list of six pairs (tranquillity, lightness, softness, readiness, adaptability, straightness of body and mind) where the Sarvāstivādins have only tranquillity. While the Sarvāstivādins do discuss these other qualities without distinguishing them as *dharma*s in their own right, their status as *dhamma*s in the Theravāda system highlights a distinctive emphasis on the phenomenology of mind and body in the process of meditation.

In fact, disagreement on which qualities to recognize as *dharma*s in their own right accounts for many of the differences between the two lists. Thus, for the Theravādins, "happiness" (*sukha*) and "joy" (*pīti/prīti*) are two distinct *dharmas*, whereas for the Sarvāstivādins, they are simply two different aspects of pleasant feeling. On other hand, the Sarvāstivādins see "anger" (*krodha*) as distinct from "hatred" (*dosa/dveṣa*), while the Theravādins see it as a particular manifestation of hatred. Such considerations also apply to other items in the Sarvāstivādin list of secondary defilements.

Other differences reflect particular positions taken in Abhidharma discussions. Thus, "sleepinesss" (*middha*) is for the Mahāvihāra Theravādins always unwholesome; for the Abhayagiri Theravādins, it is physical; but for the Sarvāstivādins, it may be unwholesome or wholesome. This difference seems to reflect disagreement about how to accommodate types of sleepiness induced by natural tiredness (Gethin 2017). For the Theravādins, since "anxiety" (*kukkucca/kaukṛtya*), which takes the form of regret directed toward past actions, is associated with unhappy feeling, it must involve aversion and therefore always be unwholesome. The Sarvāstivādins, on the other hand, while agreeing that anxiety involved unhappy feeling, allow that when it takes the form of regret for an unwholesome past action it should be regarded as wholesome.

The exercise of drawing up a list of *dharmas* understood as the basic elements out of which reality is constructed raised questions about what a *dharma* really is. In the first place *dharmas* are conceived as things that *happen*, that is, as momentary events. Lists of *dharmas* are attempts to identify the basic types of events that can occur. A *dharma* category comprises all instances that share a particular defining quality (*svabhāva*) or characteristic (*svalakṣaṇa*), such as the activity of being greedy or of hating (La Vallée Poussin 1988–1990: 57; Tin 1920–1921: 50; Karunadasa 2010: 12, 35). As what we find when we examine the subject and object of awareness closely, *dharmas* are conceived as in some sense the irreducible phenomena of experience. The Sarvāstivādins expressed the irreducibility of *dharmas* with reference to a distinction between two types of existence: nominal (*prajñapti-sat*) and real (*dravya-sat*), corresponding to conventional truth and ultimate truth. Similarly, the Theravādins make a distinction between concepts of things which are existent (*vijjamāna-paññatti*) and non-existent (*avijjamāna-paññatti*). Persons, men, women, trees, mountains, and so on exist nominally; they are concepts of things that ultimately do not exist; they are projected onto the truly existing *dharmas*. Greed, hatred and delusion, on the other hand, may be concepts (that is, conceptual names), but they are concepts that refer to things that truly exist.

The Sarvāstivāda use of the term *dravya* in the sense of "real entity," tended to undermine the conception of *dharmas* as fleeting events, and bring out a latent sense of the term *svabhāva* as "inherent existence." Such a conception of the ontology of *dharmas* was famously criticized by Nāgārjuna (second century CE) and followers of the Mādhyamika school of Buddhist thought, who suggested that it was incoherent to conceive of something that comes into existence dependent on conditions as having inherent existence. The term *dravya* is not used by the Theravādins in connection with the ontology of *dharmas*. This means that although the Theravāda ontology of a *dharma* must certainly be judged realist, it remained less explicitly so. It seems clear that the Theravāda Abhidhamma was not the main target of Mādhyamika critiques (Walser 2005, 226–28, 268–69).

Dharmas in action: causation, processes, and rebirth

In beginning to provide an account of the separate *dharmas* in action, Abhidhamma sets out a theory of possible classes of "consciousness" (*citta*), understood as basic momentary episodes of cognition, each consisting of bare consciousness (i.e., the sense of a subject who is aware of an object) associated with a set of mental activities (*cetasika*) that arise simultaneously directed toward the same object of awareness. These episodes of cognition are constituted by a minimum of eight *dhammas* according to the Theravādins or eleven according to the Sarvāstivādins; more complex episodes of cognition are constituted by upwards of twenty or thirty *dhammas*. Since it is possible to apply various principles to distinguish classes, different lists of the types of episodes of cognition are, in part, simply the result of a decision as to how fine to make the analysis. The two basic principles involve distinguishing episodes of consciousness as (1) wholesome (motivated by greed, aversion, and delusion), unwholesome (motivated by nonattachment, kindness, and wisdom), or indeterminate, and (2) belonging to the sense-sphere (the realm of ordinary experience), or the form or formless spheres (the realms of deep states of meditative concentration).

The developed Theravāda works with a system of eighty-nine classes of consciousness-episodes: eight types of sense-sphere wholesome, five types of form-sphere wholesome, four types of formless sphere wholesome, four types of transcendent wholesome, twelve types of sense-sphere unwholesome, thirty-four types of sense-sphere indeterminate, ten types of form-sphere indeterminate, eight types of formless spheres indeterminate, four types of transcendent indeterminate. The Sarvāstivāda texts seem not to provide such a full list, although a comparable list can, in part, be inferred. In discussing the basic combination of mentalities, Vasubandhu talks in terms of one broad class of sense-sphere wholesome *episodes of consciousness*, two broad classes of sense-sphere unwholesome, two broad classes of sense-sphere indeterminate, five types of form-sphere, and four types of formless spheres (La Vallée Poussin 1988–1990: 196–99).

The Abhidharma systems go on to analyze the different types of causal relationship that can operate between *dharmas*. On the basis of the *Paṭṭhāna*, the seventh book of the canonical Abhidhamma and "one of the most amazing productions of the human mind" (Warder 1980: 309), Theravādins elaborate an intricate web of causal connections through a system of twenty-four types of causal condition (*paccaya*), while the Sarvāstivādins have a system of six causes (*hetu*) and four conditions (*pratyaya*). Essentially, these sets of causal relations highlight how *dharmas* are conditions for other *dharmas* that arise either at the same time or subsequently. Thus the *dharmas* that make up a particular moment of awareness act as mutual conditions for each other, called "mutuality condition" (*aññamañña-paccaya*) by the Theravādins and coexistence cause (*sahabhū-hetu*) by the Sarvāstivādins. By way of "object condition" (*ārammaṇa-paccaya, ālambana-pratyaya*), these *dharmas* are also, in part, conditioned by the object of awareness. Furthermore, in the role of "contiguity condition" (*samanantara-paccaya, -pratyaya*), these *dharmas* are among the conditions necessary for the arising of another set of *dharmas* in the immediately following moment. If the instance of awareness constituted by the *dharmas* is wholesome (motivated by kindness, say) or unwholesome (motivated by hatred, say) it also has the potential to act as the "karma condition" (*kamma-paccaya*) or "cause of a karmic fruit" (*vipāka-hetu*) for *dharmas* that will arise sometime in the future. In this way, the Abhidharma elaborates one of its basic axioms, that nothing arises from a single cause, and no cause has a single effect (Ñāṇamoli 1964: 623; Willemen, Dessein, and Cox 1998: 28; T 28.885b).

Both the Theravāda and Sarvāstivāda Abhidharma also provide systematic expositions of the theory of "dependent origination" (*paṭiccasamuppāda/pratītyasamutpāda*). The twelve links can be seen as circumscribing three lives: actions conditioned by ignorance in the previous life condition consciousness, mind and body, sense faculties, sense contact, feeling, craving, grasping, and becoming in the present life; these, in turn, condition birth, old age, and death in the next. Alternatively, all twelve links are seen as operating from moment to moment: in each moment, we are born, live, and die.

This is closely related in the Theravādin Abhidharma to its account of the way the mind perceives and responds to objects of awareness, a distinctive feature which seems already assumed by the *Dhammasaṅgaṇi*'s system of eighty-nine classes of consciousness. It is common to both the

Mahāvihāra and the Abhayagirivihāra Theravāda traditions (Ehara 255–57). Two basic modes of the mind are distinguished: the mind that is active (*vīthi-citta*) in perceiving and responding to objects of consciousness and the mind that is inactive and at rest (*vīthi-mutta*), typically in deep, dreamless sleep. The inactive is termed *subconscious continuum* (*bhavaṅga*). Significantly, even when active the mind is said to momentarily rest in this inactive mode between each process of perception. When an object comes into the range of one of the senses, the mind stirs and turns its attention to the particular sense in question; it perceives the object and then begins to process and examine what it has perceived, before determining its nature; on the basis of this determination, the mind actively responds to the object in either a wholesome or unwholesome way; at the end of the process, the mind momentarily holds on to the object of experience before returning to its inactive state until the next object disturbs one of the senses. This is illustrated by various similes. To give one: A man sleeps beneath a mango tree; the wind disturbs the branches; a mango falls; he is disturbed, opens his eyes, and sees the mango; he grasps it, presses it, and smells it: "It is ripe for eating." He eats the mango; he swallows the last morsels, licks his lips, and goes back to sleep. The simile perhaps belies the fact that the processing of an object is understood to be rapid and a largely automatic and involuntary response. Nonetheless, each full process of perception is of moral significance.

The initial perception and apprehension of an object are said to occur in the form of episodes of consciousness that are the results (*vipāka*) of past action or karma. That is, at the initial moment of seeing, hearing, smelling, tasting, or touching something that is by nature "desirable" (*iṭṭha*), we experience a result of some previous wholesome act; at the moment of seeing, hearing, smelling, tasting, or touching something that is by nature "undesirable" (*aniṭṭha*), we experience a result of some previous unwholesome act. Our basic sense experiences thus come to us as the results of our previous karma and are beyond our immediate control. But in each process of perception the mind, having perceived and taking in an object, makes a decision as to how it will respond to the object experienced. It may decide to savor the object with greed, hatred, or delusion, or it may decide to do so with nonattachment, kindness, and understanding. At this point, a series of actively unwholesome or wholesome episodes of consciousness, termed *running* (*javana*), sow the seeds of karma that will bear future results (Cousins 1981). Our lives are seen as made up of countless numbers of these cognitive processes, which collectively determine the course of our rebirth.

The theory of *bhavaṅga* forms part of the Theravāda account of the process of death and rebirth. The *bhavaṅga* consciousness is essentially the state of mind that arises as the first episode of consciousness in any lifetime (in the case of human beings at the moment of conception in the womb), constituting the relinking (*paṭisandhi*) of mind and body at the beginning of a new life. This relinking is established as the immediate karmic result of the state of mind in the moment before death in the immediately preceding life. What is understood is that close to death significant acts performed during a lifetime come before the mind. Certain kinds of action—for example, certain types of murder—are regarded as so "weighty" that they cannot but come to mind at the time of death. In the absence of these, what tends to come to mind are habitual actions or actions done close to the actual time of death, but actions done in distant past lives may also come to mind. What in effect happens is that the dying person then relives this action in the last moments before death. The state of mind at the moment of relinking in the new life has this action as its immediate cause. The *bhavaṅga* state of a human being is understood to be the result of previous wholesome karma and is rooted in nonattachment, kindness, and sometimes also wisdom. Beings born as animals or in the hells, on the other hand, have as their *bhavaṅga* a much more basic type of consciousness that is considered the result of unwholesome action and is lacking in the wholesome roots (Gethin 1994).

For Theravādins and others (Mahīśāsakas, Dharmaguptakas, and Mahāsāṃghikas), rebirth is immediate. The last moment of consciousness in one life is followed in the next moment by relinking (*paṭisandhi/pratisandhi*), constituting the first moment of consciousness in the new life. The causal connection between the last moment of consciousness in one life and the first in the next life is illustrated by an echo or reflection (Ñāṇamoli 1964: 639). For the Sarvāstivādins and others (the Pūrvaśailas and Vātsīputrīyas), such an account of rebirth was problematic. How can a being's death in one moment in one place be causally connected to a being's conception in a quite different, perhaps far distant, place in the next moment? Rejecting the example of the causal connection between an object and its reflection, Vasubandhu argued at length in his *Abhidharmakośa* that there must be an intermediate being (*antarābhava*) which links the two lives. After death a being assumes a subtle form that is intangible and translucent but nevertheless prefigures the type of existence to which it is heading. A being remains in this intermediate state waiting for conditions to arise that are appropriate to its karmic destiny (La Vallée Poussin 1988–1990: 383–97). Some centuries later, the author of the *Abhidhamma-anuṭīkā* attempted to answer Vasubandhu's criticisms and defend a reflection as a valid example of causality operating across an apparent gap (Kv-anuṭ (B^e 1960) 120–24).

The Abhidharma analysis of the mind and body in terms of a series of causally interconnected *dharmas* arising and ceasing from moment to moment presented Buddhist thinkers with various theoretical problems associated with how to account for the continuity and reemergence of traits, tendencies, and habits when they are not constantly present. If, for example, anger and greed are not present in our minds what determines whether they will arise again? To arise again, surely they must remain somewhere in some latent state; otherwise, they would appear to arise again randomly. The different schools of Buddhism proposed various ways of explaining such issues, which there is not the space to discuss here in detail. But the Sarvāstivādins proposed in the first place that *dharmas* of the past and future should not be said not to exist; rather, they exist always, in the past and future as well as in the present; present existence is characterized, however, by activity. The Sarvāstivādins next proposed that two *dharmas*, "possession" (*prāpti*) and "nonpossession" (*aprāpti*) govern, which *dharmas* have the potentiality to become active or not in a given continuum of *dharmas*. When one experiences, say, anger, there is a "possession" (*prāpti*) of present anger; but when it is past, although there is no longer "possession" of present anger, there is still "possession" of past anger and the potentiality for it to become active again in the future given the appropriate conditions; if one were then to become a buddha, one would gain "nonpossession" of anger. Both "possession" and "nonpossession" are themselves *dharmas* included in the flow of *dharmas* that arise and cease from moment to moment and constitute a person.

For their part, the Theravādins seem to have referred such problems of personal continuity and karma and their results to their theory of the process of perception outlined earlier and, in particular, to the notion of the "subconscious continuum" (*bhavaṅga*). Between each active consciousness process the mind momentarily lapses into *bhavaṅga*, a basic state of consciousness that recurs throughout a being's life, defining a being's basic nature and influencing the nature of the flow of *dharmas* that constitute the lifetime of a given being. Thus, instead of understanding the continuity of character traits with reference to the presence of "possession" in the stream of *dharmas*, the Theravādins appear to appeal to a continually intervening state of mind. Such an approach bypasses the philosophical abstraction of the Sarvāstivādins and appears to have some affinity with the theory of the "store consciousness" (*ālayavijñāna*) developed by the Yogācāra school of Mahāyāna thought. Significantly, in trying to justify their theory, early Yogācāra thinkers cited the Theravāda notion of *bhavaṅga* (Gethin 1994: 31).

Conclusion

How should we characterize the Theravāda Abhidhamma in relation to the Sarvāstivāda system? First, there is a greater simplicity in its listing of *dharmas*. The category of forces dissociated from mind is rejected in favor of the basic categories of mind, mental activities, material form, and "the unconditioned." The list of unwholesome mental activities is more clearly related to the basic defilements of greed, hatred, and delusion. The single simplicity of the unconditioned element or *nibbāna* is related to the notion that knowledge of the Four Noble Truths is achieved in a single momentary flash of insight (*ekābhisamaya*), contrasting with the Sarvāstivādin notion that the four truths are known in a progressive series of cognitions (*anupūrvābhisamaya*). Thus, according to the Theravādin view, the suffering of *saṃsāra* (the first truth) is seen in the same moment as its cessation (the third truth), implying that nirvana is not to be thought of as existing in some other realm or at some other time from the here and now of *saṃsāra* (Cousins 1984).

The second broad distinctive feature of the Theravāda Abhidhamma is its theory of the process of perception, which is bound up with the scheme of eighty-nine categories of consciousness and the notion of the subconsciousness continuum (*bhavaṅga*). This systematically and comprehensively maps how *dhamma*s combine and interact in a stream of episodes of cognition; complemented by the system of twenty-four causal relations, the theory attempts to show how the processes of perception from moment to moment relate to the unfolding of actions and their results from life to life.

The overall effect of these two broad distinctive features of the Theravāda Abhidhamma is, I think, to render it less intellectually abstract than the Sarvāstivāda Abhidharma, which is more concerned with defending and elaborating its doctrinal positions on the ontology of *dharmas* in response to the criticisms of other Indian schools of thought, Buddhist and non-Buddhist. While it would be a mistake to suggest that Theravāda Abhidhamma thinkers consciously reject metaphysical positions in favor of a pure phenomenology, they remain less preoccupied with questions of ontology. In comparison with the Sarvāstivāda Abhidharma, the Theravāda Abhidhamma thus continues throughout its formative period (second century BCE–fifth century CE) to function more directly as a practical map for following and reaching the goal of the path to awakening (Cousins 1984: 104–107). This serves as a reminder that the Abhidharma generally—whether Sarvāstivāda or Theravāda—was always about something more than the ontology of *dharmas*.

Notes

1 On the formation of early Buddhist literature, see Gethin 1998: 35–58; Gethin 2008: xiii–xxvi.

2 Of the Abhidharma Piṭakas of other schools we have limited knowledge. A work that seems likely to constitute the Abhidharma Piṭaka of the Dharmaguptaka school survives in Chinese translation with the title *Abhidharma of Śāriputra* (*Shelifu apitan*; T 1548); it is relatively unstudied in modern scholarship. A *Vinaya* summary of the Haimavata school suggests that it had an Abhidharma consisting of five sections (T 24.818a); a work by the Chinese monk Jizang (549–643 CE) relates that the Vātsīputrīya school, which advocated the reality of the person (*pudgalavāda*), had an Abhidharma in nine sections, the *Abhidharma of the Characteristics of Dharmas* (*Faxiang pitan*) also associated with Śāriputra (T 45.9c). An Abhidharma-piṭaka of the Mahāsāṃghikas is also mentioned in ancient sources (Przyluski 1927, 210–212, 217; Bareau 1951, 9).

3 Chinese tradition lists the authors slightly differently, but the same principle holds true (Lamotte 1988: 156).

4 Chinese tradition fixed the Sarvāstivāda list as comprising seventy-five *dharmas*, but this is to, somewhat misleadingly, take the sphere of tangible objects as more fundamental than the four primary elements of earth, fire, water, and wind that constitute it.

References

Bodhi, Bhikkhu. 2007. *A Comprehensive Manual of Abhidhamma: The Abhidhammattha Saṅgaha of Ācariya Anuruddha.* (3rd ed.). Kandy: Buddhist Publication Society.

Cousins, L.S. 1981. "The Paṭṭhāna and the Development of the Theravādin Abhidhamma." *Journal of the Pali Text Society* 9: 22–46.

Cousins, L.S. 1984. "Nibbāna and Abhidhamma." *Buddhist Studies Review* 1: 95–109.

Cousins, L.S. 1997. "Aspects of Esoteric Southern Buddhism." In *Indian Insights: Buddhism, Brahmanism and Bhakti*, eds. Peter Connolly, Susan Hamilton, 185–207. London: Luzac Oriental.

Cousins, L. S. 2012. "The Teachings of the Abhayagiri School," in *How Theravāda is Theravāda? Exploring Buddhist Identities*, ed. Peter Skilling and others, 67–127. Chiang Mai: Silkworm Books.

Cousins, L. S. 2015. "Abhidhamma Studies III: Origins of the Canonical Abhidha(r)mma Literature." *Journal of the Oxford Centre for Buddhist Studies* 8: 96–145.

Cox, Collett. 1995. *Disputed Dharmas: Early Buddhist Theories on Existence: An Annotated Translation of the Section on Factors Dissociated from Thought from Saṅghabhadra's Nyāyānusāra.* Tokyo: The International Institute for Buddhist Studies.

Cox, Collett. 2004. "From Category to Ontology: The Evolution of Dharma in Sarvāstivāda Abhidharma." *Journal of Indian Philosophy* 32: 543–597.

Crosby, Kate. 2013. *Traditional Theravāda Meditation and Its Modern-Era Suppression.* Hong Kong: Buddha Dharma Centre of Hong Kong.

Dhammajoti, Kuala Lumpur. 2007. *Sarvāstivāda Abhidharma* (3rd ed.). Hong Kong: Centre for Buddhist Studies, University of Hong Kong.

Frauwallner, E. 1995. *Studies in Abhidharma Literature and the Origins of Buddhist Philosophical Systems.* (Sophie Francis Kidd, Trans.) (original work published 1964–1973). Albany, NY: State University of New York Press.

Gethin, Rupert. 1994. "Bhavaṅga and Rebirth According to the Abhidhamma." In *The Buddhist Forum*, Vol. III, eds. Tadeusz Skorupski, Ulrich Pagel, 11–35. London: School of Oriental and African Studies.

Gethin, Rupert. 1998. *The Foundations of Buddhism.* Oxford: Oxford University Press.

Gethin, Rupert. 2004a. "Wrong View (Micchā-Diṭṭhi) and Right View (Sammā-Diṭṭhi) in the Theravāda Abhidhamma." *Contemporary Buddhism: An Interdisciplinary Journal* 5: 15–28.

Gethin, Rupert. 2004b. "Can Killing a Living Being Ever Be an Act of Compassion? The Analysis of the Act of Killing in the Abhidhamma and Pali Commentaries." *Journal of Buddhist Ethics* 11: 167–202.

Gethin, Rupert. 2005. "On the Nature of Dhammas: A Review Article." *Buddhist Studies Review* 22: 175–194.

Gethin, Rupert. 2008. *Sayings of the Buddha: A Selection of Suttas From the Pali Nikāyas.* Oxford: Oxford University Press.

Gethin, Rupert. 2017. "Body, Mind and Sleepiness: On the Abhidharma Understanding of *Styāna* and *Middha*." *Journal of the International College for Postgraduate Buddhist Studies* 21: 254–216.

Hinüber, Oskar von. 1996. *A Handbook of Pāli Literature.* Berlin: Walter de Gruyter.

Hinüber, Oskar von 2000. "Lān2 Nā as a Centre of Pāli Literature During the Late 15th Century." *Journal of the Pali Text Society* 26: 119-137.

Jaini, Padmanabh S. 2002. *Collected Papers on Buddhist Studies.* Delhi: Motilal Banarsidass.

Karunadasa, Y. 1967. *The Buddhist Analysis of Matter.* Colombo: Department of Cultural Affairs.

Karunadasa, Y. 2010. *The Theravāda Abhidhamma: Its Inquiry into the Nature of Conditioned Reality.* Hong Kong: Centre of Buddhist Studies, University of Hong Kong.

Kyaw, Pyi Phyo. 2014. "*Paṭṭhāna* (Conditional Relations) in Burmese Buddhism." (PhD, King's College, London) https://kclpure.kcl.ac.uk/portal/en/theses/pahna-conditional-relations-in-burmese-buddhism(978ff34f-788d-468c-8292-d28b6cac0952).html.>

La Vallée Poussin, Louis de. 1988–1990. *Abhidharmakośabhāṣyam* (Leo M. Pruden, Trans.). (original work published 1923–1931). 4 vols. Berkeley: Asian Humanities Press.

Lamotte, Étienne. 1988. *History of Indian Buddhism from the Origins to the Śaka Era.* (Sara Webb-Boin Trans.). (original work published 1956). Louvain: Institut Orientaliste.

Langer, Rita. 2012. "Chanting as 'Bricolage Technique'': A Comparison of South and Southeast Asian Funeral Recitation.' In *Buddhist Funeral Cultures of Southeast Asia and China*, eds. P. Williams, P. Ladwig, 21–58. Cambridge: Cambridge University Press.

Ñāṇamoli. 1964. *The Path of Purification (Visuddhimagga) by Bhadantācariya Buddhaghosa.* Colombo: Semage.

Ñāṇamoli. 1987–1990. *The Dispeller of Delusion (Sammohavinodanī).* 2 vols. London: Pali Text Society.

Ronkin, Noa. 2005. *Early Buddhist Metaphysics: The Making of a Philosophical Tradition* (1st ed.). London; New York: RoutledgeCurzon.

Rospatt, Alexander von. 1995. *The Buddhist Doctrine of Momentariness: A Survey of the Origins and the Early Phase of This Doctrine up to Vasubandhu*. Stuttgart: Franz Steiner Verlag.

Schnake, Javier, ed. 2021. *Ratanapaññā's Vajirasāratthasaṅgaha and its Ṭīkā*. Bristol: Pali Text Society.

Swearer, Donald. 1995. "A Summary of the Seven Books of the Abhidhamma." In *Buddhism in Practice*, ed. Donald S. Lopez, 336–342. Princeton: Princeton University Press.

Tin, Pe Maung. 1920–1921. *The Expositor (Atthasālinī)*. 2 vols. London: Pali Text Society.

Walser, Joseph. 2005. *Nāgārjuna in Context: Mahāyāna Buddhism and Early Indian Culture*. New York: Columbia University Press.

Wijeratne, R.P., Gethin, Rupert. 2002. *Summary of the Topics of Abhidhamma and Exposition of the Topics of Abhidhamma*. Oxford: Pali Text Society.

Willemen, Charles, Dessein, Bart, Cox, Collett. 1998. *Sarvāstivāda Buddhist Scholasticism*. Leiden; New York: Brill.

16

VAṂSA

History and lineage in the Theravāda

Stephen C. Berkwitz

Vaṃsa, frequently translated as "chronicle," actually encompasses a broad range of historiographical texts found across Buddhist communities in southern Asia that identify with Theravāda monastic and literary traditions. The Pāli term *vaṃsa* carries the meanings of "bamboo" and "lineage," with the implication that the narratives of *vaṃsa* texts center around genealogies that relate a succession of influential actors and powerful objects that "made history" in those lands. It is important, moreover, to indicate that these Buddhist histories are *made* instead of "found." Historical narratives that forge connections between the Buddha and places in his native home of Jambudvīpa (or, roughly speaking, "India") with peoples and places outside of that ancient land engage in the imaginative and ideological work of imposing a sequence of selected events (chosen from an impossibly longer list of events) within a narrative structure that imposes coherence and meaning to those events as a whole. The historian Hayden White alerted us to the literary features of historical writing, how the author imposes the structure of a given story type upon certain events from the past so as to endow those events with the kinds of meaning that literary narratives render possible and understandable (White 1987: 44–45). Phrased differently, Buddhist *vaṃsa*s act to fashion narratives out of otherwise isolated historical events and, in doing so, lend broader and deeper significance to the past in relation to contemporary communities of Buddhists. Furthermore, it should be noted that some of these events are the fictive products of authors, crafted to serve the narrative work of historical storytelling and sometimes far removed from any putatively true or actual occurrence.

As a technical term that signifies Theravāda Buddhist narratives about the past, *vaṃsa* can be seen as a textual genre for Buddhist historiography distinctive to communities where Theravāda traditions predominate. Steven Collins has noted how *vaṃsa* was part of the literary genre of the *purāṇa* in India, texts fashioned out of genealogical lists and subsequently rendered by Buddhists to outline the genealogy and deeds of the lineage of the Buddha and his heritage (Collins 1998: 254–255). He argues further that *vaṃsa*s were texts that worked to interweave the timeless condition of Buddhahood with the chronological texture of the past, present, and future (Collins 1998: 256). Whereas Collins's interests were in the philosophizing about time contained in the canonical *Buddhavaṃsa* (*Chronicle of the Buddhas*) and the early sixth-century *Mahāvaṃsa* (*Great Chronicle*), the *vaṃsa* genre represents an even broader collection of interests and iterations.[1] It is necessary to recognize a diversity of forms and contents in Theravāda

DOI: 10.4324/9781351026666-20

Buddhist historiography, including the various languages utilized and the titles given to these types of works (Berkwitz 2004: 7). Many of the works with *vaṃsa* in their titles were composed in the Pāli language, but these were sometimes translated and adapted into vernacular language versions, while other works with or without the term *vaṃsa* in their titles were wholly original compositions in Sinhala, Burmese, Thai, and other languages.

Texts that can be included under the category of *vaṃsa* comprise historiographical works that emphasize the roles of the Buddha and his *sāsana* ("dispensation") in the development of culture and civilization in lands where the Theravāda monastic lineage and textual traditions held sway. Pāli and vernacular language histories were composed and located the Buddha's career, relics, and institutions throughout an expansive territory that coincides with the modern nation-states of Sri Lanka, Myanmar, Thailand, Laos, and Cambodia. Some of the Pāli *vaṃsa*s, such as the fifth-century *Dīpavaṃsa* (*History of the Island*), the tenth-century *Mahābodhivaṃsa* (*History of the Bodhi Tree*), and the thirteenth-century *Thūpavaṃsa* (*History of the Relic Shrine*) appear to have been based on ancient commentarial works (*aṭṭhakathā*) that are no longer extant (Berkwitz 2007: 5). In this view, early oral and written traditions about the establishment of the *sāsana*—especially relics—were incorporated into early commentarial texts, which, in turn, formed the basis for composing detailed narratives about the introduction of Buddhism into Sri Lanka. Other works from Sri Lanka include the twelfth-century *Dāṭhāvaṃsa* (*History of the Tooth Relic*), and a large number of Sinhala works composed between the thirteenth and fourteenth centuries, including the *Sinhala Thūpavaṃsa, Sinhala Bōdhivaṃsa, Daḷadā Sirita* (*Account of the Tooth Relic*), and *Sinhala Dhātuvaṃsa* (*History of the [Forehead-bone] Relic*).

Importantly, several of the Pāli works, including the *Mahāvaṃsa*, *Thūpavaṃsa*, and *Dhātuvaṃsa* are shown to have been transmitted to Southeast Asian lands, causing the Sri Lankan narratives to be modeled and adopted and remodeled by some local Buddhist histories. These latter Southeast Asian *vaṃsa* texts include the fifteenth-century *Cāmadevīvaṃsa* (*History of Queen Cāmadevī*), the sixteenth-century *Jinakālamālī* (*Sheafs of the Garlands of the Epochs of the Conqueror*), and the nineteenth-century *Saṅgītiyavaṃsa* (*History of the Recitals [of Pāli Scriptures]*) from premodern and modern Thailand, as well as the eighteenth-century *Vaṃsadīpanī* (*Explanatory Work of the Lineage*) and the nineteenth-century *Sāsanavaṃsa* (*History of the Dispensation*) from Myanmar. Despite the commonality of the term *vaṃsa* in many titles, the singularity of this textual genre can be overstated, and it has been more important rhetorically speaking to Sri Lankan authors than those in Southeast Asia. Other vernacular histories that can be formally included in the *vaṃsa* genre, although lacking the term, include works with the labels of *āvaliya* in Sinhala, *tamnan* in Thai, and *thathanawin* in Burmese.

Generally speaking, the *vaṃsa*s and related historiographical texts comprise narratives that describe how the Buddha used his psychic powers (*iddhi*s) to visit other lands and to resolve that his relics would one day be established in those places for local people to venerate and obtain blessings. Importantly, the spread of *vaṃsa* texts coincides more or less with the spread of Theravāda traditions. It may thus be argued that *vaṃsa*s were among the instruments used to define and propagate the Theravāda across southern Asia. Their historical narratives tell the story of how textual and ritual traditions associated with the Buddha's original disciples were transmitted and established outside of Jambudvīpa. They narrate the careers of Buddhist kings and Buddha relics, showing how they contributed to the founding of religious sites and the practice of religious worship in their respective lands. In other words, *vaṃsa*s deal with space as well as time, charting out when and where the Buddha's dispensation was preserved and transmitted by monastics in the Theravāda lineage with the assistance of royal supporters.

Expanding the Theravāda

The *vaṃsa* and related texts from southern Asia convey what could be called "Buddhist history," since they present narratives about past events that revolve around the transmission of the Buddha's *sāsana* in the form of teachings, monastic lineages, and sacred relics and images into new lands. The implied coherence and uniformity of this *sāsana* in literature belies what was surely a more heterogeneous network of loosely related monastic and lay communities (see Bretfeld, this volume). Over time, the dominant forms of Buddhism in Sri Lanka and peninsular Southeast Asia came to be known as "Theravāda" (Decrees of the Elder-Monks), although this designation came from the imagined associations of later monastic communities that made use of Pāli language texts and liturgies associated with the 500 *arahant*-monks who allegedly assembled and codified the Buddha's Word into the Pāli Canon shortly after the Buddha's demise (Skilling 2009: 64–65). As such, this notion of the Theravāda as a particular and privileged monastic lineage was originally fairly circumscribed in designation, only becoming expanded to characterize a broad-based Buddhist identity that includes laypersons around the twentieth century. Despite this fact, the *idea* of a Buddhist tradition linked to senior monks (*theras*) like Ven. Moggaliputta-tissa, the monk who led the formal purification of the Saṅgha under King Aśoka, and Ven. Mahinda, the monk who mastered and brought the Buddha's teachings to Sri Lanka, and that was traced down to the monks of the Mahāvihāra sect in Sri Lanka does seem to have been in operation since the early centuries of the Common Era (Gethin 2012: 55). Whatever the ways in which premodern Buddhists who affiliated with this tradition described and labeled it, it seems reasonable to conclude that one or more notions of a Buddhist tradition rooted in the teachings and lineage of renowned *theras* were fashioned and made available for people to identify with. Over the centuries, the *vaṃsa* literature played key roles in offering ways of conceptualizing monastic collectivities and the sense of belonging to a distinctive Theravāda lineage (Blackburn 2012: 276–277).

This idea of a singular monastic lineage and textual transmission that derives from the Buddha's original disciples was developed and disseminated by way of some Pāli commentaries and *vaṃsa* texts—literature that Peter Skilling (2009: 63) rightly notes was concerned with school formation and legitimation. The "origin story" of the *Samantapāsādikā* (All Pleasing), the Pāli commentary on the *Vinaya* books of monastic discipline and attributed to the fifth-century scholar-monk Buddhaghosa, contains a lengthy narrative that recounts how the Buddha's teachings were standardized by *theras* in three convocations or "councils," before being transmitted by an authoritative lineage of monks to Sri Lanka. The aim of this text is to demonstrate the continuity of the traditions of these monks and, in doing so, validate the Mahāvihāra monastic lineage that was currently in Sri Lanka (Jayawickrama 1986: xvi–xvii). This effort was expanded upon by the author of the *Mahāvaṃsa*, and both of these texts helped to guide a corpus of historical narratives that established these traditions of the *theras* as authentic and orthodox for later Buddhists in southern Asia. The Sri Lankan *vaṃsa* texts in particular assumed the role of developing and spreading this notion of a "proto-Theravāda" form of Buddhism encompassing the teachings and traditions passed down from the Buddha to his disciples and subsequently transmitted to other lands via the island.[2]

Accounts of the expansion of the Theravāda Saṅgha comprise important elements of Buddhist historiographical traditions. Sri Lankan *vaṃsas* often give attention to the journey of the *arahant* Mahinda to Sri Lanka, whereby he is credited with preaching the Dharma, converting the king, and establishing the proper sites for relics to be enshrined. The ordination of Sri Lankan monks and nuns by Mahinda and his sister Ven. Saṅghamittā is depicted by these texts as having extended an authoritative monastic lineage into Sri Lanka. These events are recounted, for example, in the *Sinhala Thūpavaṃsaya*, in which hundreds of members of the court and the royal harem are said to have been ordained and attained the state of *arahants* (those who have attained *nirvāṇa*) after only a few days (Berkwitz 2007: 157). In later centuries, texts in Southeast Asia sought to accomplish a similar goal and validate their own ordination traditions of monks and nuns within a lineage that derives from the Buddha's own disciples. For example, in northern Thailand, the fifteenth-century *Tamnān Mūlasāsanā Wat Pā Daeng* (*Chronicle of the Founding of Buddhism of the Pā Daeng Temple*) describes in detail how a Thai monk who went to study in Sri Lanka returned to Thailand and traveled around reordaining local monks in the linguistic and ritual traditions associated with the island. Not only did Ven. Ñāṇagambhīra bring back Buddha images, a Bodhi Tree branch, and Pāli texts to Thailand, he also reordained numerous local monks into what became known as the Sinhala order of monks (Premchit and Swearer 1977: 93–94). Despite the widespread influence of such narratives, other *vaṃsa* works composed in Southeast Asia disputed the claims of Sri Lankan traditions and asserted that an "unbroken" Theravāda lineage was introduced directly into their lands by journeys undertaken by the Buddha and his immediate disciples long ago (Pranke 2004: 138).

Whether the lineage was traced through Sri Lanka or not, the *vaṃsas* as a genre of Buddhist writing became key instruments in defining and expanding what would later be called "Theravāda Buddhism." Their narratives often include accounts of how the Buddha, his relics, and his teachings spread across southern Asia. In speaking of Buddha relics, John Strong (2004: 7) has described them as "extensions of the Buddha's biography," bringing his life story forward after his *parinirvāṇa* to include the travels and miraculous events of his sacred bodily remains. Likewise, *vaṃsa* texts can be said to be a means for extending the sphere of the Buddha's influence further in time and space. The spread of relics and images associated with the Buddha was facilitated by historiographical narratives that served to establish the affinities between those special objects and the Buddha himself (Berkwitz 2019: 7). These objects acquired significance by the narratives that ascribed them with the status of a "relic," often noting how they appeared in the world and their journeys before being established at a contemporary site of worship. The texts supplied accounts of how particular relics and images are related to the Buddha, providing testimony to their pedigrees as authentic and authoritative objects worthy of veneration (Trainor 1997: 78). When, for example, the *Mahābodhivaṃsa* describes how a branch from the Bodhi Tree Relic detached itself by the resolution of King Aśoka, was brought with great ceremony over the sea to Sri Lanka, conveyed by chariot to the capital city of Anurādhapura, and finally established in a shrine on the grounds of the Mahāvihāra monastery, the narrative serves to fix the relic in both time and space (Strong 1891: 158–161).

These relic journeys as conveyed by *vaṃsa* texts mirror in many ways the legendary accounts of how the Buddha traveled by air to certain locations in Sri Lanka and Southeast Asia. Theravāda textual traditions attribute extraordinary psychic powers (*iddhis*) to Fully Awakened Buddhas and *arahants*, including an ability to fly, and this enabled authors of *vaṃsas* to describe miraculous visits made by the Buddha to Sri Lanka and various kingdoms in Southeast Asia. The first chapter in the *Mahāvaṃsa* relates how the Buddha made three visits to the island of Sri Lanka, each time marking out places which would later become sites for relic shrines after his passing from the world (Geiger 2001: 3–9). Buddhist histories from Southeast Asia repeated the trope of the Buddha visit to describe how his *sāsana* was first introduced by him to local kingdoms. Many Northern Thai *tamnan* texts narrate visits that the Buddha paid to particular sites around the Lanna region to lay or deposit his own relics or footprints in places where previous Buddhas visited long ago (Lagirarde 2013: 85–86). Likewise, Burmese *thamaing* works describe how the Buddha visited various places in Myanmar, specifically in Arakan and the Mon country, to leave relics such as his hair for local devotees and to establish the roots of Buddhism in these lands (Leider 2009: 341). These Buddhist histories share an interest in showing how their local traditions and communities were connected with the Buddha and his *sāsana*. By depicting the Buddha as having traveled to distant lands to spread the Dharma and his relics, many *vaṃsa* texts worked to give the impression of a trans-local Theravāda tradition that was portrayed and authenticated by historical narratives. Even when the distinctiveness and singularity of such a Theravāda tradition could be questioned by competing orders (*nikāyas*) and regional variations in narrative accounts, the desire to acknowledge an unbroken lineage from the Buddha to contemporary monastic communities remained constant.

Another important feature of efforts by history writers to expand the boundaries of the Theravāda through time and space was to portray the spread of relics, images, and teachings of the Buddha in terms of predictions made by the Buddha or other awakened humans. A defining feature of Theravāda Buddhist histories is their tendency to assert that the establishment of sacred relics and images, as well as the *sāsana* more generally, in certain lands had been preordained. The Buddha and *arahants* are ascribed with the superhuman ability to see into the past and future, and thus they can predict which relics and images will be established where (Berkwitz 2019: 8). These predictions make it seem as if the *vaṃsa* accounts of how traces of the Buddha became established in distant lands were simply fulfilling what was destined to occur. Oftentimes, these predictions are attributed to the Buddha himself, and they reflect either his will or his intention to follow what previous Buddhas had done. At other times, awakened *arahants* like Ven. Mahinda are portrayed as guiding history by indicating what present and future kings should or should not do with relics and images.

Efforts to expand the Buddha's *sāsana*, and, by extension, the Theravāda that is charged with preserving and promoting it, are portrayed in many *vaṃsas* as the result of the Buddha's will as expressed in earlier eras. Works like the *Sinhala Thūpavaṃsaya* ascribe the spread of relics to a resolution of the Buddha to make his remains available for later generations to venerate and, as a result, attain the fruits of greater comforts in the present life and better rebirths in the future.

> Because our Buddha did not remain [in the world] for much time, desiring the welfare of the world and thinking, "My Dispensation has not been spread everywhere. Taking the relics that measure even a mustard seed from me when I have passed away in *parinirvāṇa*, making relic shrines in the places where people dwell, and enshrining the relics in caskets, the many beings who make offerings will enjoy the happiness of the divine world, the *brahmā* world, and the human world," he thus made a resolution for the dispersal of the relics.
>
> (Berkwitz 2007: 119)

Such narratives reinforce the idea that it was ultimately the Buddha who by the force of his will determined that his relics would be spread and established in the same lands where the Theravāda would be established—and also where, the *vaṃsas* claim, the Buddha himself may have visited in the past. Predictions in this way are said to guide human history according to the intentions of the Buddha (along with those of previous Buddhas held to exist in eras long ago), contributing to a sense that the Buddha had been compassionately concerned with the welfare of all beings and thus arranged the means through which later devotees could flourish and attain felicities after he was gone. An important effect of this historiographical stance is to make the readers and listeners of Buddhist histories feel grateful for being the beneficiaries of deeds done previously by those who penetrated the Dharma and spread the dispensation for their sake (Berkwitz 2004: 252). Some *vaṃsas* then display clear interests in fostering devotion and greater ethical awareness in their audiences.

Predictions made by Buddhas and *arahants* in *vaṃsa* texts make the course of historical events seem more intentional and coherent. These works fashion stories of the past in such a way as to make Buddhas appear to be directly responsible for the establishment of the Dharma, relics, images, and the Theravāda monastic lineage in kingdoms and countries across southern Asia. Examples abound of how earlier predictions set in motion a chain of events that brought people in premodern (and modern) Sri Lanka, Myanmar, Thailand, Laos, and Cambodia within the sphere of the Buddha's *sāsana*. The fourteenth-century *Sinhala Bōdhivaṃsaya*, for instance, relates at length how Ven. Mahinda tells a king how the four previous Buddhas—Kakusandha, Konagamana, Kassapa, and Gotama—all visited the island called "Laṅkādvīpa" and predicted that the great southern branch of the Bodhi Tree under which they attained their Awakening would in the future be established in the same place (albeit during different eons) in the future (Senadhira 1965: 189–197). Thus, not only has the most recent Buddha preordained that the Bodhi Tree Relic would be established on the grounds of the Mahāvihāra monastery for people to venerate, but the three preceding Buddhas made similar predictions, which indicates that a Bodhi Tree has been brought and established in the island of Sri Lanka numerous times. The allegedly predestined establishment of relics like the Bodhi Tree in places and by persons associated with the Mahāvihāra lineage would have reinforced the notion that the Mahāvihāra ethos and ideology were consistent with the Buddha's *sāsana*.

Southeast Asian *vaṃsa* texts contain similar predictions that describe how the establishment of relics and images in various kingdoms were frequently the results of the Buddha's will. The sixteenth-century *Tamnan Phra Chao Ton Luang* (Chronicle of the Grand Lord) relates how while the Buddha Gotama and an entourage of *arahants* were traveling around the Lanna kingdom in northern Thailand, he came across a spot where previous Buddhas had drunk some water, and he then predicted that in the future a large image of himself would be constructed and enshrined at that spot (Chiu 2017: 75–76). This particular *tamnan* thus connects the renowned Phra Chao Ton Luang image in Phayao with a prediction made by the Buddha much earlier, effectively consecrating the area as a future site for venerating a large Buddha image. Likewise, in the *Vaṃsadīpanī*, the *arahant* Gavaṃpati is said to have been given a prediction by the Buddha whereby after his own cremation, the monk will carry his thirty-three teeth as relics to Suvaṇṇabhūmi in lower Myanmar and reside there to help establish the *sāsana* (Pranke 2004: 131–132). This Burmese text reiterates the tropes of previous Theravāda *vaṃsas* by connecting the expansion of the *sāsana* in the forms of relics and monastic lineages to predictions the Buddha made previously.

Materiality and Theravāda

The descriptions of *vaṃsa* texts about how the Buddha and his *sāsana* were spread far beyond the land of his birth also gave material form to the traditions associated with the Theravāda. The expansion of the Theravāda relied on textual accounts of localized material expressions of the Buddha's sphere of influence in various parts of southern Asia. In other words, Gotama Buddha's dispensation was given tangible form in relics, images, shrines, and monasteries, all of which were often identified and located by *vaṃsa* narratives. Descriptions of these objects and the accounts of how they were found or built made it possible to encounter and recognize the *sāsana* in different lands. As material signs of an allegedly coherent Theravāda tradition that is fashioned by historical narratives in *vaṃsa* texts, the various relics, images, shrines, and monasteries mentioned therein collectively work to represent tangible expressions of an authoritative Buddhist tradition. These local and translocal histories used these sacred objects to constitute cultural landscapes oriented around Buddhist sites and to promote cultural hegemonies that set up hierarchies for ranking relics, images, monasteries, and their affiliated devotees (Schober 2003: 19). Buddhist *vaṃsa*s are thus frequently concerned with highlighting the special and extraordinary features of powerful objects that locate the Buddha's *sāsana* in particular places, places where devotees may venerate the Buddha, Dharma and Saṅgha with the sense of encountering and inhabiting a present that is connected to a revered past (Abeysekara 2019: 2–4).

Buddha relics and images are among the most important objects discussed by the authors of *vaṃsa* texts. The Theravāda tradition had established a threefold classification of relics by around the fifth century CE, consisting of corporeal relics, relics of use (such as the Bodhi Tree), and commemorative relics (such as Buddha images) that are supposed to receive devotion and that have their own kinds of shrines (Trainor 1997: 89). The *vaṃsa* narratives not only identify these special objects and relate their distinctive pedigrees, but they often also describe their beautiful appearances and miraculous natures. These historical texts in this way reinforce the perceived authenticity of these objects, supplying the narratives that make them seem more genuine and powerful. The power of these objects is derived from the accounts of how they can display the power of locomotion to travel on their own, the power to generate miraculous visions to devotees, and the power to confer great benefits on the devotees that worship them (Berkwitz 2019: 2). The relics' ability to move independently is confirmed by accounts that describe how they ascended into the sky and began to radiate six-colored rays of light in imitation of the living Buddha. This type of mobility and miraculous display is associated with the Bodhi Tree in the *Sinhala Bōdhivaṃśaya*, the Tooth Relic in the twelfth-century *Dāṭhāvaṃsa*, the Buddha's collarbone relic in the *Thūpavaṃsa*, and the frontal bone relic in the fourteenth-century *Sinhala Dhātuvaṃsa*, among other works (Berkwitz 2019: 12). By attributing relics with the ability to move and exhibit miraculous visions, the *vaṃsa*s suggest that these material objects can resemble and even substitute for a living Buddha.

Southeast Asian histories often feature sacred Buddha images that are empowered to control its movements and dazzle onlookers. These narrative descriptions of "image relics" include accounts of how images were carried to various locations by agents of kings for the sake of enhancing the reigns of the latter. Yet their mobility is also ascribed to their own intention, or as a factor of the resolutions of the Buddha or other awakened individuals at an earlier point in time. A fifteenth-century Thai work relates how the Sīhaḷa Buddha image "possesses supreme powers" and at one instance "got out of His seat and placed Himself in the air, and from Him sixfold rays were emanating in all directions" (Notton 1933: 27, 38). Meanwhile, in a sixteenth-century Pāli text, the renowned Emerald Buddha image in Thailand is also credited with miraculous power, having been enlivened as it were by the insertion of seven corporeal relics into the image, and subsequently making itself extremely heavy so as not to be carried away from a large city but instead allowing itself to be brought to a different city (Jayawickrama 1968: 142, 145). These narratives, although dealing with different relics, share an emphasis on relating their travels and miraculous powers. The Southeast Asian *vaṃsa* texts often focus more on Buddha images, although they can also reference bodily relics. In contrast, the Sri Lanka *vaṃsa*s concentrate on corporeal relics and *bodhi* trees, while giving relatively scant attention to image relics. In both cases, however, these Buddhist histories reveal the interests to glorify powerful relics that reinforce the coherence of a Theravāda tradition that connects peoples and lands with the Buddha and his *sāsana*.

The *vaṃsa* texts employ other strategies to circumscribe the Theravāda tradition with a material basis. These include narrating accounts in which relics, images, and texts become duplicated or multiplied, effectively working to spread their presence and influence to more places. The multiplication of sacred objects, either by miraculous or human means, represents a different model of relic distribution than that of division, whereby a collection of relics is apportioned into smaller amounts to be taken away and enshrined in different locations (Strong 2004: 156). Sri Lankan *vaṃsas* relate how a branch of the Bodhi Tree established in Anurādhapura suddenly generates five fruits, each of which then produces eight saplings that result in the quick appearance of forty bodhi trees that become planted at important sites around the island (Geiger 2001: 132–133). These ones are said to have been planted at monasteries at a distance of a league (*yojana*) apart throughout the island—an assertion that the *Mahābodhivaṃsa* suggests was "for the welfare and the happiness of the island's inhabitants everywhere" (Strong 1891: 162). The *Sinhala Bodhivaṁśaya* elaborates on this episode even further by specifying the places where the thirty-two additional saplings were planted on the island (Senadhira 1965: 235–236). By identifying the specific locations where Bodhi saplings were planted, the text depicts an island-wide sacred geography, where people may venerate the Bodhi Tree Relic in multiple locations.

Buddhist histories from Southeast Asia employ the trope of the multiplication of sacred objects by narrating how copies of revered Buddha images were made and then distributed to different locations to spread the good fortune and authority that they are held to bring to their surroundings. Stories of Budha images were very popular in Thailand from the fifteenth century to the late eighteenth century, whether translated from a Pāli original or composed in a vernacular language (Lagirarde 2015: 797). The account of the Sihiṅga Buddha image in the *Jinakālamālīpakaraṇaṁ* relates how multiple copies of the revered image were made during King Mahābrahma's reign, each one apparently just as worthy of veneration as the original image (Jayawickrama 1968: 125–126). The multiplication of this image allowed multiple kings and cities to possess it, lessening the perceived need to seize it in conquest like kings did with the Emerald Buddha. Analogous to the duplication and spread of Buddha images in certain *vaṃsas*, one also finds narrative references to the production of texts as a practice for defining and expanding an authoritative Theravāda tradition. While relating the history of the Emerald Buddha, the fifteenth-century *Ratanabimbavaṇṇanā* describes how the Pāli *Tipiṭaka* was brought to Southeast Asia with the jeweled image and then "spread out far and wide" across the continent (Notton 1932: 26). Furthermore, the *Tamnān Mūlasāsanā Wat Pā Daeng* concludes its narrative by calling on virtuous and wise ones to write down and practice the "root dispensation" that was brought from Sri Lanka to Lanna, further asserting that this particular *tamnan* text should be placed in every temple so that everyone will know the Buddha's teaching (Premchit and Swearer 1977: 110). The creation of duplicate copies of Buddha images and Dharma texts worked in similar ways to give rise to a more extensive geography of sacred objects.

In the process of describing the origins and journeys of the relics, images, and texts of the Buddha, *vaṃsas* also substantiate the Theravāda tradition by narrating the building of various religious monuments to house sacred objects and the monks who were ordained in the monastic lineage that purportedly derives from the Buddha's disciples. This duty to provide suitable homes for relics, images, and monastics often fell to kings. The accounts of kings who arranged for the building of such monuments became common features in the *vaṃsas*, and this type of royal deed became a key characteristic of a righteous king (*dhammarāja*) deserving of loyalty and support. The paradigmatic *dhammarāja* for the Theravāda was King Aśoka, whom the *vaṃsas* credit with having built eighty-four thousand relic shrines across his large empire. Subsequently, other Buddhist kings attempted to imitate this ideal, and the *vaṃsas* relate how their building projects gave a tangible presence to the Theravāda *sāsana*. The Pāli and Sinhala *Thūpavaṃsas*, for instance, include similar accounts that describe the building of the Great Copper-Roofed Mansion (*lōvāmahāpāya*) as a monastic residence and the construction of the Great Relic Shrine (*mahāthūpa*) in Anurādhapura (Jayawickrama 1971: 91–93, 136; Berkwitz 2007: 194–197, 245–246). These sites are treated as Buddhist landmarks in the *vaṃsas*, and they feature in these narratives as material instantiations of the *sāsana* in Sri Lanka. Likewise, the construction of relic shrines, image houses, and monastic residences by Buddhist kings in Thailand feature in the *Jinakālamālīpakaraṇaṁ* (Jayawickrama 1968: 147–149). When *vaṃsa* texts identify and locate shrines and monasteries within their historical narratives, their accounts of the establishment of the Theravāda across southern Asia become grounded in the physical landscapes of local Buddhist cultures.

Authority and Theravāda

The popularity of the *vaṃsa* genre in many Theravāda cultures may be deduced from the various purposes that such texts have served. The *vaṃsa*s worked to establish affinities between the Buddha and later generations of monastics and devotees, expanding the theoretical *sāsana* and its physical embodiments across southern Asian kingdoms outside of India. In this way, Buddhist historical narratives formed the basis for imagining oneself and one's community as being the beneficiaries of meritorious deeds done by the Buddha and other virtuous persons long ago. *Vaṃsa*s thus served to establish relationships with past actors that were held to generate favorable futures. At the same time, Buddhist *vaṃsa*s could also work to authorize royal and monastic lineages, making it seem as though the patrons and representatives of the Theravāda were directly affiliated with the Buddha and his early disciples. Some scholars have likened this function of the *vaṃsa*s with efforts to legitimate certain monastic orders and polities within hierarchies of their own making (Walters 2000: 152). While there is some merit to this argument, interpretations of *vaṃsa*s that reduce these texts to political tools are liable to overlook other uses of Buddhist histories in fashioning ethical relationships with past actors and devotional attitudes in the present. In other words, *vaṃsa*s should not be seen merely as instruments to legitimate various kings and monastic lineages as if they needed to secure the assent of their subjects and supporters by writing histories to bolster their power (cf. Pollock 2006: 522–523). One may instead choose to see these texts as involved with efforts to reaffirm an existing authority and to make the power and influence of the Theravāda and its royal patrons more widely known.

As noted earlier, a prominent theme in the *vaṃsa* genre is the alleged continuity between the Buddha's first disciples and the monks who preserve and disseminate the Dharma in southern Asian lands. These works posit the existence of authentic monastic lineages of elder monks (*theras*) in Sri Lanka and in Southeast Asian kingdoms deriving ultimately from the *arahants* at the First Council through Ven. Moggaliputta Tissa, the famed Elder-Monk who guided Aśoka in purging the Saṅgha of illegitimate monks (Gethin 2012: 30–31). This authoritative lineage becomes primarily associated with the Mahāvihāra order in the extant Sri Lankan *vaṃsa*s and many (but not all) Southeast Asian ones. By tracing this monastic lineage in an exclusive, coherent fashion down to Ven. Mahinda, the monk credited with introducing Buddhism into Sri Lanka in the third century BCE, *vaṃsa* texts confidently assert that the authentic Dharma and *sāsana* of the Buddha have been established correctly in the island.[3] To be sure, such a claim is better seen as a rhetorical rather than historical one, but it undergirds much of the self-image of Theravāda Buddhists as the proponents and preservers of the the Buddha's Dhamma. This assertion further enabled Southeast Asian Buddhists to link their own traditions to the Theravāda of Sri Lanka by receiving ordination lineages, Dharma manuscripts, relics, and images from the island. For instance, the Sihiṅga Buddha image that has served as one of the most important images in northern Thailand is said to have been crafted and worshipped in Sri Lanka before later being sent to Lanna at the request of a local king (Chiu 2017: 26–27). Similarly, Ven. Ñāṇagambhīra is credited in the *Tamnān Mūlasāsanā Wat Pā Daeng* with having gone to study the language and texts in Sri Lanka before returning to Thailand to establish the correct form of the religion there (Premchit and Swearer 1977: 91–92). Even among those Southeast Asian *vaṃsa* texts that claimed a direct transmission of the *sāsana* from Jambudīpa (i.e., India), the construction of a lineage of monks and pedigrees of relics that testify to an authentic Theravāda tradition was modeled after the historiographical conventions of Sri Lankan *vaṃsas*.

There are similar moves to establish the authority of local traditions in certain *vaṃsas* from Myanmar. The nineteenth-century *Sāsanavaṃsa* (*History of the Dispensation*), for instance, describes how a king in the Rāmañña country of lower Myanmar resolved to bring the "stainless" *sāsana* over from Sri Lanka by sending monks to the island for training in order to establish an authoritative lineage of monks (Law 1952: 50). The Burmese *Vaṃsadīpanī* describes how both monks and relics were received from Sri Lanka, and its author connects the flourishing of the *sāsana* in premodern Myanmar with its establishment in Sri Lanka. Significantly, the text also constructs its own independent lineage through the Elder-Monks Soṇa and Uttara, who were said to have traveled to Suvaṇṇabhūmi (identified by the Burmese with Myanmar) and established a unified lineage of Vinaya masters and teachers of the Dharma who never broke from the Theravāda (Pranke 2004: 133). And although this lineage is equated with the Mahāvihāra in Sri Lanka, the author of the text claims that it was actually established in Myanmar first. Whereas the *sāsana* became established in Sri Lanka after the Buddha passed away in *parinirvāṇa*, the *Vaṃsadīpanī* asserts that it was during the lifetime of the Buddha and his travels to Myanmar that the *sāsana* was established there (Pranke 2004: 138). Even though this narrative attempts to supplant the one that holds that Sri Lanka had become the center of Buddhism in the centuries after the Buddha passed away, it still accepts the premise that an authentic Theravāda tradition was established by monks, texts, and relics brought to other lands. In this way, this and many other historical texts accept the account of the *Mahāvaṃsa* that narrates how the Dharma was laid down at the First Council, heretical monks were removed from the Saṅgha at the Second and Third Councils, and the authentic texts and traditions of the Theravāda became transmitted during the time of Aśoka to Sri Lanka and other lands (Geiger 2001: 18, 26, 82).

In addition to authorizing a particular lineage of monks, the *vaṃsas* work to enhance the authority of certain kings by associating them with ancient royal genealogies and models of virtuous Buddhist kings (*dhammarāja*). Again, the *Mahāvaṃsa* outlines a list of kings in the genealogy of the legendary Mahāsaṃmata, the first king who established human civilization according to Indian Buddhist texts. The fourth-century *Dīpavaṃsa* (*Chronicle of the Island*) includes a lengthy list of kings, which includes that of Suddhodana, the father of Gotama Buddha, implying that the Buddha came from royal stock (Oldenberg 1992: 132). This *vaṃsa* goes further by portraying Sri Lankan kings as the descendants of the royal Okkāka genealogy that links them to the Śākya clan and makes them appear to be the kinsmen of the Buddha (Walters 2000: 117–118). When recent and contemporary kings who reign outside of India become linked to the Buddha and an authoritative royal lineage, Buddhist *vaṃsas* work to promote the authority of those monarchs by virtue of their direct and indirect associations with leading ancient kings.

While royal genealogies represented one way to enhance the authority of kings, the allusions made to righteous *dhammarājas* was another way to celebrate more local and sometimes recent kings mentioned in *vaṃsa* texts. Using the paradigmatic model of King Aśoka, who is depicted in Buddhist texts as a powerful and pious supporter of the Buddha's religion, the *vaṃsas* likewise celebrate certain kings in southern Asian lands for building relic shrines, image houses, and monasteries, as well as for embodying Buddhist virtues of generosity and morality by making generous donations to the Saṅgha and the poor. Sri Lankan *vaṃsas* often glorify kings such as Devānampiya-tissa (third century BCE) for welcoming Buddhist monks to the island and building monastic dwellings and shrines for the Bodhi Tree and other relics. King

Duṭṭhagāmaṇī (second century BCE) is another popular figure who is credited not only with dispelling foreign invaders but also with building more sites to promote the *sāsana*, including the Great Relic Shrine (Mahāthūpa). Works such as the *Thūpavaṃsa* praise the acts of merit performed by these kings, and in doing so promote a notion of kingship that later kings could imitate to enhance their own authority. Far from only serving to legitimate reigns, these narratives can also portray kings as ideal lay devotees who seek to venerate the Buddha by founding sites of worship, making extraordinary offerings to relics, and arousing morally productive emotions that give rise to meritorious deeds (Berkwitz 2004: 264–267).

The narratives about Southeast Asian kings in *vaṃsa* texts similarly praise the deeds and characters of Buddhist kings who are patterned after the *dhammarāja* ideal. The *Jinakālamālīpakaraṇaṁ* highlights the virtuous acts of King Tilaka in northern Thailand, who conducted ceremonies for dedicating the *sīmā*, or boundaries for monastic ordination, who listened to Dhamma sermons, who planted Bodhi Tree relics, who built monasteries, and who arranged for the establishment of relics such as the Emerald Buddha in his realm (Jayawickrama 1968: 136–140). The *Sāsanavaṃsa* likewise celebrates a large number of Buddhist kings in Myanmar for actively promoting the *sāsana* by building monasteries and relic shrines, as well as faulting other kings who neglected or harmed Buddhist monks (Law 1952: 106–109). The *Saṅgītiyavaṃsa* praises Thai kings who obtained the Pāli scriptures of the Buddha and who arranged for them to be edited, removing the corruptions that had accrued to these texts over time (Pakdeekham 2020: xxx–xxxi). Those kings who display their devotion to the Buddha and his *sāsana* are generously acknowledged and praised in the *vaṃsa*s. Texts that authorize the Theravāda also authorize the reigns of kings who promote this lineage of monks and the texts that are deemed to transmit what the Buddha himself founded. Such works thus provide models of action for current and future rulers, recording and augmenting a repertoire for the performance of kingship (Blackburn 2010: 320). By acting as sponsors of the Theravāda, Buddhist kings could earn recognition and esteem for their acts of merit that were held to strengthen the *sāsana* in their respective kingdoms.

Conclusion

The *vaṃsa* texts as composed in Pāli and literary vernaculars across southern Asia played a major role in constituting and spreading the idea of Theravāda Buddhism. This important genre of Buddhist literature supplied people with narrative accounts of how the teachings (*dharma*) and institutions (*sāsana*) founded by the Buddha came to be established in places far removed from the land of his birth. In the process of relating how the religion of the Buddha was introduced into Sri Lanka and peninsular Southeast Asia, the *vaṃsa*s and related texts provided seemingly historical evidence for the expansion of the Saṅgha, the *Tipiṭaka*, Buddha relics, and Buddha images from sources that are authentic and authoritative. It is the *vaṃsa*s, after all, that developed and codified the narratives from commentaries that trace the descent of monastic and textual traditions originating with the Buddha's disciples at the legendary First Council, relate the acquisition and enshrinement of relics, and praise leading kings and monks who were responsible for preserving and promoting the Theravāda.

One could argue, therefore, that those Buddhist traditions that come to be called "Theravāda" acquired their sense of coherence and authority from the *vaṃsa*s that narrated their origins and expansions across time and space. An illustration of how such a narrative worked to generate a sense of the Theravāda is found in the *Mahābodhivaṃsa*, wherein different Buddhist orders are identified, and the authentic lineage is distinguished from heretical ones.

> Among them, the Theravāda, starting out from the Meritorious [Buddha], being pure like a stream of water from the Heavenly River, being stainless like a crystal gem, and being unmixed among the monastic orders like a water drop from the leaves of a lotus flower, while pleasing the world of humans together with the deities, like the full moon to the flow of ambrosial liquid, came down to the present day.
>
> (Strong 1891: 97–98)

This assertion of the singularity and authority of the Theravāda goes far to demonstrate how *vaṃsa* texts were instrumental to efforts to identify the legacy of the Buddha and associate it with a particular and idealized transmission of monastic and textual traditions across southern Asian lands. Such an approach to retelling the history of Buddhism could also be used to reject allegedly unorthodox observances and the orders that practiced them while highlighting the purity of one's own traditions (Lieberman 1976: 141).

This idealized Theravāda form becomes associated with the Mahāvihāra lineage that took root, according to many of the *vaṃsas*, in ancient Sri Lanka with the arrival of Ven. Mahinda and his monastic colleagues. It must be said, however, that the Mahāvihāra tradition—in both its values and ideology—does not represent all forms of Theravāda Buddhism. Khmer forms of Buddhism, which possessed more tenuous ties to Sri Lankan traditions and did not produce or copy *vaṃsa* texts to the same degree as the people in Myanmar and Thailand, offered up a different model of the Theravāda. Indeed, Khmer forms of Theravāda with their Brahmanical and Tantric influences as seen in the appropriation of the Rāmāyana story and the esoteric meditative practices involving Pāli *mantras* and embryological visualizations depart in significant ways from the traditional Mahāvihāra forms contained in *vaṃsa* texts (Harris 2005: 91–95).

Nevertheless, across much of the premodern Theravāda world, the notions of predestined relics and images being brought to the kingdoms of pious kings by awakened monks were made widespread thanks to the circulation of *vaṃsa* texts and narratives. Similarly, their accounts of how the Buddha miraculously traveled to local sites in Sri Lanka and Southeast Asia, sometimes along well-worn paths traveled eons ago by previous Buddhas, served to deposit relics and sacralize lands distant from Buddhism's place of origins (Lagirarde 2013: 86). These *vaṃsa* texts taught people to recognize that they had been given access to authentic teachings, sacred objects, and institutions by the will of the Buddha and the efforts of other awakened monks. These works presented narratives that set up ways of being in the world that are relational in nature and historical in context. In this sense, the *vaṃsas* collectively shaped a vision of Buddhist history that connected present generations with past actors, and affirmed that Buddhist devotees could obtain good fortune and take steps toward liberation (*nirvāṇa*) as a result of deeds undertaken earlier by others and the effects of their own encounters with historical narratives (Berkwitz 2004: 64). Furthermore, the coherence and similarities found in the *vaṃsa* narratives as a whole would have surely contributed to a persuasive account of the prestigious and authoritative nature of the Theravāda lineage, variously understood and framed by their historical narratives. In the Theravāda, it may thus be said, history confers identity, and one's story up to now and in the future is held to be inseparable from the stories of what buddhas, monks, and kings have done long ago.

Notes

1 The use of the term *chronicle* for *vaṃsa* in these works is meant to illustrate how they are exceptional in comparison with *vaṃsas* that more closely resemble the genre of "history." According to White, the chronicle genre aspires to but falls short of full narrativity, since it fails to achieve narrative closure and simply ends without resolution in a story-like way (1987: 4–5).

2 It should be noted that the *vaṃsa* texts composed in Southeast Asia express varying opinions on how crucial the Sri Lankan Buddhist traditions were for the transmission of the Theravāda to Burmese, Mon, and Thai lands. In some cases, such as the eighteenth-century Burmese *Vaṃsadīpanī*, authors asserted that the Buddha's *sāsana* was imported directly from India (see Pranke: 2004).

3 See Bretfeld in this volume for a detailed discussion on Mahāvihāra claims of their exclusive connection with the Buddha's original *sāsana*.

References

Abeysekara, A. 2019. "Protestant Buddhism and 'Influence': The Temporality of a Concept." *Qui Parle* 28 (1): 1–75.

Berkwitz, S.C. 2004. *Buddhist History in the Vernacular: The Power of the Past in Late Medieval Sri Lanka.* Leiden: Brill.

Berkwitz, S.C. 2007. *The History of the Buddha's Relic Shrine: A Translation of the Sinhala Thūpavaṃsa.* New York: Oxford University Press.

Berkwitz, S.C. 2019. "Narratives of Buddhist Relics and Images." In *Oxford Research Encyclopedia of Religion*, ed. J. Barton. New York: Oxford University Press/Online Publication May 2019. doi:10.1093/acrefore/9780199340378.013.587.

Blackburn, A.M. 2010. "Buddha-Relics in the Lives of Southern Asian Polities." *Numen* 57: 317–340.

Blackburn, A.M. 2012. "Lineage, Inheritance, and Belonging: Expressions of Monastic Affiliation from Laṅkā." In *How Theravāda is Theravāda? Exploring Buddhist Identities*, ed. Peter Skilling, et al., 275–294. Chiang Mai, Thailand: Silkworm Books.

Chiu, A.S. 2017. *The Buddha in Lanna: Art, Lineage, Power, and Place in Northern Thailand.* Honolulu: University of Hawai'i Press.

Collins, S. 1998. *Nirvana and other Buddhist Felicities: Utopias of the Pali Imaginaire.* Cambridge: Cambridge University Press.

Geiger, W. 2001. *The Mahāvaṃsa: Or the Great Chronicle of Ceylon.* (reprint, 1912). Oxford: Pali Text Society.

Gethin, R. 2012. "Was Buddhaghosa a Theravādin? Buddhist Identity in the Pali Commentaries and Chronicles." In *How Theravāda is Theravāda? Exploring Buddhist Identities*, eds. Peter Skilling, et al., 1–63. Chiang Mai, Thailand: Silkworm Books.

Harris, I. 2005. *Cambodian Buddhism: History and Practice.* Honolulu: University of Hawai'i Press.

Jayawickrama, N.A. 1968. *The Sheaf of the Garlands of the Epochs of the Conqueror: Being a Translation of Jinakālamālīpakaraṇaṁ of Ratannapañña Thera of Thailand.* London: Pali Text Society.

Jayawickrama, N.A. 1971. *The Chronicle of the Thūpa and the Thūpavaṃsa: Being a Translation and Edition of the Vācissaratthera's Thūpavaṃsa.* London: Pali Text Society.

Jayawickrama, N.A. 1986. *The Inception of the Discipline and the Vinaya Nidāna: Being a Translation and Edition of the Bāhiranidāna of Buddhaghosa's Samantapāsādikā, the Vinaya Commentary.* London: Pali Text Society.

Lagirarde, F. 2013. "Narratives as Ritual Histories: The Case of the Northern-Thai Buddhist Chronicles." In *Buddhist Narrative in Asia and Beyond*, Vol. 1, eds. P. Skilling, J. McDaniel, 81–92. Bangkok: Chulalongkorn University.

Lagirarde, F. 2015. "Historiography: Thailand." In *Brill's Encyclopedia of Buddhism, Vol. 1: Literature and Languages*, ed. Jonathan A. Silk, 792–799. Leiden: Brill.

Law, B.C., trans. 1952. *The History of the Buddha's Religion (Sāsanvaṃsa).* London: Luzac & Co.

Leider, J.P. 2009. "Relics, Statues, and Predictions: Interpreting an Apocryphal Sermon of Lord Buddha in Arakan." *Asian Ethnology* 68 (2): 333–364.

Lieberman, V.B. 1976. "A New Look at the 'Sāsanavamsa'." *Bulletin of the School of Oriental and African Studies* 39 (1): 137–149.

Notton, C., trans. 1932. *The Chronicle of the Emerald Buddha.* Bangkok: Bangkok Time Press.

Notton, C., trans. 1933. *P'ra Buddha Sihiṅga.* Bangkok: Bangkok Time Press.

Oldenberg, H. 1992. *The Dipavamsa: An Ancient Buddhist Historical Record.* (reprint, 1879). New Delhi: Asian Educational Services.

Pakdeekham, S., ed. 2020. *History of the Pali Scriptures: Saṅgītiyavaṃsa by Somdet Phra Phonnarat.* Bangkok: Fragile Palm Leaves Foundation.

Pollock, S. 2006. *The Language of the Gods in the World of Men: Sanskrit, Culture, and Power in Premodern India.* Berkeley: University of California Press.

Pranke, P.A. 2004. *The Treatise on the Lineage of the Elders (Vaṃsadīpanī): Monastic Reform and the Writing of Buddhist History in Eighteenth-Century Burma.* PhD Dissertation. Ann Arbor: University of Michigan.

Premchit, S., Swearer, D.K. 1977. "A Translation of *Tamnān Mūlasāsanā Wat Pā Daeng:* The Chronicle of the Founding of Buddhism of the Wat Pā Daeng Tradition." *The Journal of the Siam Society* 65 (2): 73–110.

Schober, J. 2003. "Mapping the Sacred in Theravada Buddhist Southeast Asia." In *Sacred Places and Modern Landscapes: Sacred Geography and Social-Religious Transformations in South and Southeast Asia*, ed. R.A. Lukens-Bull, 1–27. Tempe, AZ: Program for Southeast Asian Studies, Arizona State University.

Senadhira, G. 1965. *Sinhala Bōdhivaṃśaya* (2nd ed.). Colombo: Abhaya Prakāśakayō.

Skilling, P. 2009. "Theravāda in History." *Pacific World: Journal of the Institute of Buddhist Studies* Third Series, no. 11 (Fall): 61–93.

Strong, A.A., ed. 1891. *Mahābodhi-Vamsa.* London: Pali Text Society.

Strong, J.S. 2004. *Relics of the Buddha.* Princeton: Princeton University Press.

Trainor, K. 1997. *Relics, Ritual, and Representation in Buddhism: Rematerializing the Sri Lankan Theravāda Tradition.* Cambridge: Cambridge University Press.

Walters, J.S. 2000. "Buddhist History: The Sri Lankan Pāli Vaṃsas and Their Commentary." In *Querying the Medieval: Texts and the History of Practices in South Asia*, eds. R. Inden, J. Walters, D. Ali, 99–164. New York: Oxford University Press.

White, H. 1987. *The Content of the Form: Narrative Discourse and Historical Representation.* Baltimore: The Johns Hopkins University Press.

17

MERIT

Ten ways of making merit in Theravāda exegetical literature and contemporary Sri Lanka[1]

Rita Langer

Introduction

The list of Buddhist precepts, which define behavior that is to be avoided, is well known and much written about. The commentarial list of ten ways of making merit *(puññakiriyavatthu)*, which define recommended religious and ethical behavior for Buddhists in positive terms, on the other hand, has received little comment in the scholarly literature.[2] Yet, as I shall discuss, the list is well documented in post-canonical Pāli texts and vernacular texts from South and Southeast Asia and today features prominently in Buddhist handbooks and sermons in Sri Lanka, Thailand, and Laos; it is also known in Myanmar and Cambodia.

This chapter examines how different texts and text genres understand the ways of making merit and what they reveal about the Buddhist practice past and present in Sri Lanka. The fifth-century Pāli commentaries and systematic Buddhist literature expanded the three canonical (DN III 218 et al) "primary" ways of making merit—generosity (*dāna*), morality (*sīla*), and contemplation (*bhāvanā*)—into a list of ten. A well-known verse in Sri Lanka lists them:

> *dānaṃ sīlañ ca bhāvanā, pattipattānumodanā*
> *veyyāvaccāpacāyañ ca, desanā sutti diṭṭhiju*
>
> (Generosity, morality and contemplation, [sharing of] and rejoicing in merit
> service and respect, teaching, listening and straightening [one's] views)

Poetic works (the tenth-century Pāli *Saddhamopāyana* and fifteenth-century Sinhala *Kāvyaśēkharaya*) expanded the list further to twelve ways of making merit. Other manuals such as the twelfth-century *Upāsakajanālaṅkāra* from South India and the sixteenth-century *Maṅgalatthadīpanī* from northern Thailand are content with the list of ten ways of making merit. Contemporary Sri Lankan handbooks, Dhamma schoolbooks, and fieldwork data reveal how the list of ten ways of making merit is received in Sri Lanka. What emerges from these sources is a formalization of the moral dimension that is characteristic of Theravāda developments in Sri Lanka and Southeast Asia.

DOI: 10.4324/9781351026666-21

Commentarial literature and systematic exegetical Abhidhamma texts

Three commentaries discuss the ten ways of making merit: the *Sumaṅgalavilāsinī* (Sv III 999–1000), Buddhaghosa's fifth-century commentary to the *Dīghanikāya*; the *Atthasālinī* (As 157–59), a commentary to the *Dhammasaṅganī* by an anonymous contemporary of Buddhaghosa, and the *Paramatthadīpanī*, the commentary to the *Itivuttaka* (It-a vol II 23–26) compiled in the late sixth or early seventh century by Dhammapāla (von Hinüber 1996, 136f). I summarize the definitions of the ten ways of making merit as presented in the *Sumaṅgalavilāsinī*, which is likely to be the oldest of the three commentaries. I then explore the rationale behind the expansion from three to ten ways of making merit, drawing on the other two commentaries:

1 *Generosity* (*dāna*) is defined (Sv 998) as volition (*cetanā*) occurring prior to giving, at the time of giving, and after. It is the recollecting with a happy mind which arises for someone who gives either the four requisites (robes, etc.) or the six sense objects (visible form, etc.) or the ten suitable offerings for ascetics and brahmins (food, etc.).[3]
2 *Morality* (*sīla*) is defined as volition that occurs in someone who goes to the temple thinking, "I shall go forth for the sake of fulfilling morality"; in someone at the time of going forth; in someone who has gone forth having fulfilled his wish; in someone reflecting on this thinking, "Good, good"; in someone taking on the restraint of the monastic code; in someone who contemplates the requisites, such as robes and the like; in someone who is restrained regarding the senses; or in someone who purifies their livelihood.
3 *Contemplation* (*bhāvanā*) is explained as volition that occurred in someone contemplating sense organs (eye, etc.), sense objects (visible form, etc.), and corresponding consciousnesses and feelings based on contact with the senses, recognition of the objects and so on, and old age and death as impermanent, suffering and not-self.[4] The explanation of the *Sumaṅgalavilāsinī* stops here with what is essentially *vipassanā* meditation.[5]

Under the heading of "ways of making merit" the *Sumaṅgalavilāsinī* looks at generosity, morality, and contemplation together and provides an explanation of how an act of giving can be understood in three different ways. The meritorious deed of giving is classified as "consisting of generosity" (*dānamaya*) when it is accompanied by either the reflection "I am giving food, etc." or by a more general contemplation on the perfection of generosity. The same act of giving can also be classed as consisting of morality (*sīlamaya*) when it is associated with the act of "making service a priority," which the subcommentary (*ṭīkā*) (Sv-ṭ III 267) explains as remembering that giving is a custom and practice of one's family. And again, it could be classed as consisting of contemplation (*bhāvanāmaya*), "having established knowledge of the way things perish and disappear" (*khayato vayato sammasanaṃ paṭṭhapetvā*). Other meritorious deeds, too, could presumably be classified in different ways depending on the mental frame at the time, but this is not spelled out.

4 Paying respect (*apaciti*) is illustrated with the example of someone who sees someone elderly, goes to meet them, takes their robe and bowl, and steps aside for them. The mention of robe and bowl indicates that the respect is being paid to a monastic but presumably the prescribed behavior would be culturally expected toward any elderly person.
5 Service (*veyyāvacca*), too, appears to be directed at monastics and the first example to illustrate this meritorious deed is someone collecting alms in a village for a senior monk. The second example is of someone reacting swiftly when asked to bring the monks' bowls. Both acts could presumably be done by either a layperson or a junior monk.

6 Sharing of merit *(pattanuppadāna)* is done simply by thinking, "May the merit be for all beings," after having done a meritorious deed of offering the four requisites.
7 Rejoicing in merit (*abbhanumodanā*) is done by expressing "joy in merit given by others" and saying, "Good, good!" The phrasing suggests that giving merit and rejoicing in merit are two connected events.
8 Teaching (*desanā*) done out of a desire to become a famous preacher and for personal gain does not result in great merit, but when done without desiring any reward is meritorious.[6]
9 Listening (to the teaching; *savaṇa*) should not be done out of desire to be regarded as faithful. It will, however, result in great merit when done by someone suffused with kindness and of a sensitive or gentle mind and with the view that "[i]t will be of great fruit for me."
10 Straightening one's views (*diṭṭh' ujjugata*) is explained (Sv 1000) simply as relevant to all three principal ways of making merit.[7]

The *Sumaṅgalavilāsinī* concludes the discussion by explaining that the ten ways of making merit are an expansion of the canonical set of three in so far as service and respect are included in morality and sharing and rejoicing in merit are included in generosity and teaching and listening are included in contemplation. When it comes to straightening one's view, the opinions are divided. The *Sumaṅgalavilāsinī* (followed by the *Itivuttaka* commentary) regards it as linked to all ways of making merit rather than as a way of making merit in its own right, but the *Atthasālinī* includes it in contemplation.

Abhidhamma works quote and build on the commentaries and are in style and content very similar. I briefly present some new perspectives and examples which these works provide concentrating on the seven additional ways of making merit. The *Abhidhammāvatāra* (Abhidh-av 3, v. 21–26), Buddhadatta's fifth-century work, presents the ten ways of making merit in the form of a verse (v. 21) which accounts for variation in terminology:

> Generosity, morality, contemplation, sharing of merit, service, teaching and rejoicing [in merit];
> straightening one's views, listening and respect—thus should the division of the ways of making merit be known.
>
> (*dānaṃ sīlaṃ bhāvanā pattidānaṃ, veyyāvaccaṃ desanā cānumodo*
> *diṭṭhujjutaṃ saṃsutī cāpacāyo, ñeyyo evaṃ puññavatthuppabhedo.*)

Verses 22–23 explain the ten ways of making merit as an expansion of the first three and like the *Atthasālinī* subsume straightening one's views under contemplation. Verse 24 explains that recollection (*anussati*), praise (*pasaṃsā*), and taking refuge (*saraṇattaya*) are included in straightening views.[8]

Anuruddha's *Abhidhammatthasangaha* (Abhidh-s 134ff), which is tentatively dated by Norman (1983, 151) to the end of the eleventh or beginning of the twelfth century but according to Gethin (2007, xiv) could possibly be as early as late sixth or early seventh century, is often described as superseding the *Abhidhammāvatāra*. The text does not go much beyond naming the ten ways of making merit, but its twelfth-century commentary by Sumaṅgala, the *Abhidhammatthavibhāvinī-mahāṭīkā* (Abhidh-s-mhṭ 134ff.), provides some interesting additional details. Respect should be done without expecting rewards such as robes, which indicates that monastics, as well as laypeople, are envisaged as paying respect. Rejoicing in merit should be practiced with a mind free of the stain of miserliness. The text also states that listening to the dhamma might inspire one to put into practice what one has heard and even to teach others.

Interestingly, the text also includes the study and teaching of blameless, ordinary subjects in the categories of listening and teaching respectively which is reminiscent of the inclusion of paying attention to ordinary, worldly jobs in the definition of contemplation (It-a 24). The *Abhidhammatthavibhāvinī-mahāṭīkā* provides a rationale for the groupings and explains that sharing of merit and rejoicing in merit are to be grouped with generosity, as all three have in common that they oppose envy and miserliness. Respect and service belong with morality as they have good conduct in common. The text quotes Dhammapāla's view that teaching, listening, straightening one's views, and contemplation form one category either because all four involve the practice of wholesome *dhamma*s or, because they all bring insight. The text also reports an alternative view that subsumes teaching under generosity, as the gift of *dhamma* surpass all gifts (Dhp 354) and reiterates that straightening one's views is relevant to all ways of making merit.

From three to ten ways of merit

The commentarial and Abhidhamma literature is not prescriptive in nature, but it reflects and reacts to existing practices and in turn influences and shapes them. The question is what does the expansion of the original three ways of making merit into ten reveal about Theravāda Buddhist practice?

There are many instances that suggest that the compilers of these texts broadened the definition of merit to include ordinary and common good behavior. The *Itivuttaka* commentary defines generosity not just as the giving of a suitable offering but also as giving help (*anuggaha*) and worship (*pūjā*). The commentaries take generosity beyond the narrow realm of asceticism and monasticism by including any offerings that are pleasing to the senses. The *Itivuttaka* commentary (It-a 24) included under the heading of *bhāvanā* "paying attention to ordinary, worldly jobs and crafts which are blameless," which goes beyond the definition of the *Sumaṅgalavilāsinī* and *Atthasālinī*. Some items in the expanded list such as listening (*savaṇa*) and teaching (*desanā*), too, represent everyday religious activities of ordinary people (laypeople and monastics) rather than a religious elite. The Abhidhamma texts broadened the definition to include the study and teaching of blameless subjects, thereby elevating the status of education in the process. The examples quoted to illustrate respect and service seem to be simply examples of everyday polite behavior. The exegetical literature fleshes out the definitions with more examples allowing glimpses into Buddhist everyday practice at the time. These texts, which were most likely compiled for and used by monastics, appear to be quite inclusivist by nature and sympathetic to laypeople who might not have the means to engage in lavish displays of generosity or the time or energy for sophisticated meditation practices. Simple good manners and mindful behavior are given the status of meritorious deeds

Some practices such as transference of merit (as it is often referred to in secondary literature) are not easily integrated into the Buddhist framework as they seem to go against the concept of personal responsibility. To be sure practice and doctrine do not have to be consistent, as Schmithausen (1986, 214) points out:

> In popular religious practice and doctrine, the notion of individual responsibility and the notion of merit transference could thus be alternatively emphasized according to the situation, without any conflict being felt.

Compilers of the early Buddhist texts opted to engage with the "transfer of merit" and integrated the widespread practice into the doctrinal framework.[9] The commentaries provide a rationale and solve the doctrinal issue of personal responsibility by introducing a two-way process: sharing of merit and rejoicing in merit. As both activities are defined as meritorious deeds in their own right both parties benefit without any merit actually "changing hands." While the *Sumaṅgalavilāsinī* had presented rejoicing only in the context of rejoicing of merit shared with all beings, the other two commentaries defined rejoicing more broadly to mean rejoicing in any meritorious deeds (As 158, It-a 25). The *Atthasālinī* adds two important aspects: the possibility of sharing merit with a specific person and the explanation that sharing merit increases it just as lighting a thousand oil lamps from one lamp increases the brightness of the first lamp. The prime occasions for sharing of merit with an individual are funerals or post-funerary rites such as the almsgiving on behalf of the dead (*matakadāna*). Sharing merit with the dead is still at the heart of the contemporary funeral rites in Theravāda countries today (Langer 2007, 156ff., Langer 2012) which might partially be due to the fact that it was given a doctrinal explanation in these early scholastic texts.

Poetic works and a lay manual

Unlike the commentarial and exegetical literature, the poetic works and the *Upāsakajanālaṅkāra* are more prescriptive in nature and extol the fruits (*phala*) and advantages (*ānisaṃsa*) of each of the individual ways of making merit in great detail.

The *Saddhammopāyana*, a Pāli poetic work in the style of a letter addressed to a fellow monk, is dated by Saddhātissa (1965, 33) to the tenth century, but von Hinüber (1996, 203) just states that its date is uncertain.[10] The later commentarial tradition attributed the work to Abhayagirikavicakravarti Ānanda Mahāthera and suggested its content was "diverging from the Mahāvihāra orthodoxy" (Von Hinüber 1996, 203). The text replaces (10) straightening one's views with three other elements (10–12) and comes up with a list of twelve ways of making merit:

Dānaṃ sīlañ ca bhāvanā pattipattānumodanā
desanā savaṇaṃ pūjā veyyāvaccaṃ pasaṃsanā
saraṇam anussati c'eva puññavatthūni bārasa. //213//

(Generosity, morality, contemplation, [sharing of] merit, rejoicing in merit;
teaching, listening, respect, service, praise;
taking refuge and recollection are the twelve ways of making merit.)

Apaciti/apacāyana is replaced with the term *pūjā*, which is defined (v. 221) as paying reverence and homage to persons of quality. The semantic fields of *apaciti/apacāyana* and *pūjā* overlap, and using them synonymously is not unusual. The *Mohavicchedanī*, Kassapa's twelfth- or thirteenth-century commentary on the *mātikās* of all seven canonical Abhidhamma texts, for example, illustrates physical expressions of respect (*apaciti*) with the examples of flower *pūjā* and worship and vocal expression of respect as *pūjā* consisting of praise (Moh 23).[11]

10 Praise is explained as creating gladness and strength in those doing meritorious deeds (v. 223).
11 Taking refuge is defined as going for refuge with a sense of shelter in the Buddha, Dhamma and Saṅgha and reverence of good qualities (v. 224).
12 Recollection (v. 225), which is usually defined as keeping in mind six objects (i.e., Buddha, Dhamma, Saṅgha, [one's own] morality, [one's own] generosity (*cāga*) and deities),[12] is extended in the *Saddhammopāyana* to include other wholesome deeds.

The *Saddhammopāyana* (Chapter VI, verses 211–262 and Chapter VII—XVIII, verses 263–587) devotes much space to the ways of making merit, but only sixteen verses are to do with their definition while the rest is devoted to the fruits (thirty-four verses) and the advantages (325 verses) of practicing these. The fruits come in three grades: least fruitful and pertaining to rebirth in *kāmaloka* (e.g., being popular, beautiful, and prosperous), middling and resulting in *brahmaloka* (e.g., rebirth in various higher realms), and best and leading to liberation (*mokkha*) (verses 260–261). As for the advantages, the amount of merit increases because the advantages of morality are inclusive of the advantages of generosity and the advantages of contemplation are inclusive of the advantages of generosity and morality.

The *Upāsakajanālaṅkāra*, Ananda's twelfth-century introduction to Buddhism composed in South India for the benefit of recently converted Buddhists (Agostini 2015, xii), is not a poetic work but is considered here as it draws heavily on the *Saddhammopāyana*. The text brings together interesting material from a great range of sources including the systematic Buddhists texts discussed above. The text devotes only nine pages (§§ 1–24) to the analysis of the ten ways of making merit but follows this with eighteen pages (§§ 25–66) on the advantages accruing from practicing them. The advantages of generosity which are at the lower end (wealth, harmony, joy, heaven) are included in the advantages of morality, which is described as the stairway to heaven and the door to *nibbāna*. The advantages of both generosity and morality are included in the advantages of contemplation which can lead to higher achievements such as higher knowledges, *brahmaloka*, and other heavens, and even Buddhahood. Examples of advantages of the remaining ways of making merit include rebirth in a wealthy family resulting from showing respect, having friends and retinue and achieving goals resulting from doing service, and happiness resulting from listening.

The *Kāvyaśēkharaya* is a sermon composed in Sinhala verse by Toṭagamuwe Rāhula in 1449 at the request of Queen Ulakuḍaya (v. 22). The text devotes only sixteen verses (of 887) to the ways of making merit and the reason might be the very broad scope of the *Kāvyaśēkharaya* (Holt 1991, 237):

> The *Kavyasēkharaya* is regarded by many as almost encyclopedic with regard to not only religious matters per se but with the problems of lay secular life. It articulates a medieval worldview on how the religious life is to be lived in the secular context.

The sixteen verses are part of a chapter in which the *paṇḍit*-minister Senaka (previous incarnation of the Buddha) advises the king on such matters as honoring gods, friends, and relatives; treating women and poor people well; not imposing heavy taxation; and more generally avoiding any of the eleven "unwholesome courses of action" (*akusalakammapatha*).[13] And at this point, the text turns to the same twelve ways of making merit that the *Saddhammopāyana* had listed.[14] It explains praise as to encouraging and energizing someone doing a meritorious deed and make them happy. The text (v. 53) defines taking refuge as a "royal wholesome act" but does not add much to the corresponding verse in the *Saddhammopāyana*. Recollection is explained as thinking of the advantages of wholesome deeds one has done. Rather than exploring the advantages accruing from the practice of the ways of making merit, the text then gives detailed advice on how to lead an ethical life more generally before returning briefly to a discussion of generosity, morality, and contemplation.

From ten to twelve ways of making merit

The three further ways of making merit to replace straightening one's views seem to have been prompted by the discussion as to whether straightening one's views was a way of making merit in its own right or an underlying condition to all ways of making merit—a view which the earlier commentaries (Sv1000, As 159, It-a 26) had quoted as an alternative. Furthermore, the *Abhidhammāvatāra* (v. 24) mentions, almost as an afterthought, that without doubt praise, refuge, and recollection are included in straightening one's view.[15] The *Abhidhammavikāsinī* (Abhidh-av-nṭ I 199 Be) attributes the list of twelve to the Mahāsāṅghikas and the Abhayagirivāsins and explains that it was created by eliminating straightening one's views and by incorporating the three additional items (Agostini 2015, 239). Ananda, the author of the *Upāsakajanālaṅkāra* who affiliates himself with the Mahāvihāra tradition (Upās Chapter X), explicitly rejects the list of twelve that was associated with the Abhayagirivihāra but treats praise, refuge, and recollection as aspects of straightening one's views. The twelve ways of making merit appear to be merely a different way of counting and presenting the ways of making merit but one that had a lasting impact.

In the process of establishing taking refuge and recollecting the six objects, great emphasis was given to the cultivation of faith. Taking the refuges and precepts is the starting point of every Buddhist ceremony in Sri Lanka. Making it a meritorious deed in its own right gives credit to the common act of placing faith in the Triple Gem. The six recollections are cultivating that initial faith by strengthening trust in the teachers and teaching (by recollection of Buddha, Dhamma, and Saṅgha), trust in oneself (by recollection of one's morality and generosity), and finally trust in the system that one can reach higher places (by recollecting the various classes of deities who achieved their existence through faith, morality, learning, and generosity (Vism VII, 6; 225). The deities correspond to the mind in various meditational stages (Gethin 1997) and are living examples of possible achievements. Recollection also has a practical application in the form of deathbed practices. The last object that comes to mind at the time of death is instrumental in determining the next rebirth, and the Abhidhamma texts explain three categories of objects (Bhikkhu Ñāṇamoḷi 1987, I 191f; Vibh-a 155f.)

A well-known example of recollecting one's own meritorious deeds on the deathbed is recorded in the *Mahāvaṃsa* (Mv 32.25–55), in which King Duṭṭhagāmaṇī (ca. 101–177 BC) summoned his scribe to his deathbed to read to him from his "merit book" (Langer 2007, 41f.). Even today, every effort is made by friends and relatives to assure that the mind of the dying person is directed toward the dhamma and positive thoughts including those of meritorious deeds, and there is evidence that keeping a merit book was still encouraged in the 1970s at least in some places (Langer 2007, 11). In the *Saddhamopāyana*, a large section under the heading of advantages of generosity (v. 278–304) deals with the impact that meritorious deeds can have on the death moment. The *Kāvyaśēkharaya* (v. 54) explains that *anussati* is to think of the advantages of wholesome deeds one has done, the commentary elaborates that this is effective in counteracting negative thoughts, an obvious advantage at the time of death. Defining taking refuge and recollection as ways of making merit gave weight to the cultivation of faith while broadening the definition of recollection to include recollection of one's own good deeds might have endorsed a common deathbed practice.

Another important aspect of the extended list is that it strengthens the link between merit and happiness. Joy and happiness feature highly in the description of Buddhist achievements—the first stages of *jhāna* meditation are accompanied by joy (*pīti*) and happiness (*sukha*)—and texts such as the *Sāmaññaphala Sutta* (DN I 47–86) emphasize happiness. As Gethin (2008, 6) remarks in the introduction to his translation of the *Sāmaññaphala Sutta*:

> The sutta sets this account of the path in a framework which presents it as an answer to the basic question (here posed by Ajātasattu): why embark on the difficult and demanding life of an ascetic? The answer the sutta seeks to give is, in short, not because it promises rewards after death, but because, more surely than any other way of life, it

> brings with it a secure happiness here and now: the freedom of the life of a religious wanderer (*samaṇa*); the happiness of a guilt-free conscience (*anavajja-sukha*) that comes with a life lived in accordance with moral precepts; the happiness of the composed mind (*avyāseka-sukha*) of one who is mindful in all he does; the joy, happiness, and peace of the *jhānas*....

By listing rejoicing and praise as ways of making merit our texts go one step further than the *suttas*. They do not just claim that doing meritorious deeds will make you happy, they make being happy and generating happiness meritorious deeds in their own right. The *Saddhammopāyana*'s definition of praise in terms of generating joy and happiness in someone doing meritorious deeds is close to rejoicing, which is defined as an act of giving joy to those who appreciate someone else's meritorious deeds (Saddh v. 229). Presumably both can occur together as observing someone doing a meritorious deed might first make the observer happy (by way of rejoicing) and then prompt them to praise the deed that, in turn, makes the doer of the meritorious deed happy. It is therefore not surprising that the text (Saddh v. 563) states that the advantages of praise are the same as those accruing from rejoicing. Defining happiness as a meritorious act is in line with a canonical passage (AN IV 88f; It 14f), which encourages monks not to be afraid of merit (*puñña*) as it is just another name for happiness (*sukha*).

Contemporary sources

The transmission of Buddhism in Sri Lanka has always been very oral in nature and looking at ancient and medieval texts does not tell us with any certainty what was actually transmitted. For the contemporary period, we have sources that are not only aimed at but also readily available to laypeople and the choice of topics and hands-on style reflect that. Most modern works start the discussion of the ten ways of making merit with the verse that I quoted at the beginning of the chapter. The earliest occurrence I could find of this verse was in an article published in 1884 in London by the Royal Asiatic Society (Ceylon Branch) by J. F. Dickson. Dickson, who worked for the Ceylon Civil Service from 1859 to 1885, starts his exploration of the "daily religion of the Buddhists of Ceylon" with a discussion of the ten ways of making merit (203–207), and his article picks up many of the explanations from earlier literature though without citing one; there are also some interesting ethnographic observations. I concentrate on the seven additional ways of making merit. Dickson (1884, 205) illustrates sharing of merit with the example of someone going on pilgrimage calling together his friends to share in his merit. Dickson also observes that sharing in the merits of another does not require an invitation. His examples of showing respect—offering flowers, incense, and food to the bodhi tree, *stūpa*, and Buddha image—would be equally fitting as illustrations for *pūjā*. In the context of straightening one's views, he makes reference to unwavering faith in the Triple Gem, which possibly harks back to an early understanding of the term *diṭṭhi* as akin to faith (Gethin 1992, 221). The rest of the article (207–236) is devoted to the description of four occasions for making merit (at the beginning of the rainy season, before death, after death, and in the form of offerings to the *saṅgha* or *caitya*).

Rērukānē Candavimala's (1949) *Bauddhayāgē Atpota*, translated into English by Silva (2014), was composed for a Sri Lankan Buddhist lay and monastic audience. Like the *Upāsakajanālaṅkāra*, it quotes Pāli verses and passages and retells stories from the commentaries. More than a third of the book (88 of 229 pages, pp. 93–181) is devoted to the ten ways of making merit that are presented as the positive counterpart to the ten *akusalakammapatha* (and other acts to avoid). There is also a separate chapter (fourteen pages, pp. 24–38) providing a definition and outlining the advantages of taking the refuges. The examples quoted for service include a story from the *Milindapañha* (Mil 3) about a novice and a monk at the time of the Buddha Kassapa. The monk had asked the novice repeatedly to clear away the rubbish. When he eventually did so, the novice evoked the merit of his service by making earnest wishes to always be reborn as a powerful being until his Nibbana and saying the right thing and being prompt in answering. The monk, in turn, was inspired to make an earnest wish to always be prompt in answering. They were reborn as King Milinda and Ven Nāgasena, respectively. Under the heading of respect, the text states that those of virtue are more deserving of respect than those of age and quotes the familiar *Dhammapada* verse (Dhp 109) listing advantages of respect. The section on sharing of merit provides the appropriate wording to use when giving merit to the dead, to gods, and to all beings and comments on the use of water pouring which symbolizes the act. Rejoicing is defined as the opposite of jealousy, and its result is minor or major depending on the nature of the original meritorious deed and the faith of the rejoicer. The section on listening points out that it is beneficial even without intellectual understanding retelling as examples well-known animal stories from commentaries and quotes A III 248 on the five advantages of listening which include straightening one's views. The section of straightening one's views warns against putting one's faith into auspicious sights and overemphasizing the effect of past karma on this life. The chapter on the ways of making merit concludes with reference to the above-mentioned canonical equation of merit with happiness.

Attuḍāvē Śrī Rāhula's (2000) *Bauddha Ädahilla* is one of many contemporary handbooks by that name or a similar name. The book is widely available and includes photographs of famous *stūpa*s and illustrations and provides the reader with contemplative verses in the section on meditation. This text is interesting as it contains only a very short, perfunctory subchapter (two pages out of a total of 307, pp. 213–215) on the ways of making merit. The chapter starts with the verse found in Dickson followed by the briefest of explanations of the three principal ways of making merit. For the remaining seven ways of making merit, the text merely provides a Sinhala translation of the Pali terms. There are, however, rather substantial individual chapters for generosity (Chapter X, 217–233), morality (Chapter IV, 25–58), and contemplation (Chapter XIII, 275–307), as well as chapters on veneration (*vandanā*, Chapter V, 59–118), worship (*pūjā*, Chapter VI, 119–150), and taking refuge (*saraṇagamana*, Chapter III, 13–24). There are no separate chapters on service, sharing of and rejoicing in merit, listening, and teaching. Clearly emphasis has shifted from the list of ten to only a few select ways of making merit while others did not receive much attention.

Finally, I want to explore how the ways of making merit are taught in the Dhamma schools that were founded in reaction to and modeled after Christian Sunday schools in modern Sri Lanka (Gombrich and Obeyesekere 1988, 205). The Dhamma schools are today an important feature in Sri Lankan Buddhist education, and according to Dhanapala (no year, 165), there are "9582 registered Dhamma schools throughout the island and 122084 volunteer Dhamma teachers. Over 1968093 Buddhist children attend the Dhamma schools" (Department of Buddhist Affairs: 2013). Students take classes on Sunday mornings and sit regular exams to test their knowledge of Buddhism. The relevant book which contains the chapter on the ten ways of making merit, *Daham Pāsala* grade 8 (2017), is aimed at thirteen-year-olds and has forty short chapters.[16] Topics range from explanations of *Dhammapada* verses and the Noble Truths to basic Pāli lessons and simple Abhidhamma explanations. The chapter on the ways of making merit takes up eight pages (out of 177, pp. 117–124), and I was told by a Dhamma schoolteacher that he spends about one hour on the topic. The chapter starts with the familiar verse and a brief rendering of the Pāli terms into Sinhala before the ten ways of making merit are discussed one by one. The sharing of merit with the dead and the gods is described as an ancient custom and rejoicing in merit is how the class of "ghosts living off what is given by others" (*paradattūpajīvin*) obtain merit; it is not just beneficial for the dead but for anyone alive as well.[17] Under the heading of service the usual activities are listed (services to the Triple Gem, elderly, sick, teachers) and paying respect to venerable persons, places and objects are defined as different "according to country, nation and religion." This is followed by the *Dhammapada* verse (Dhp 109) listing the advantages accruing from its practice. Teaching is explained as the best of all gifts and in the context of listening the text lists the Sinhala equivalent of the canonical list of the five advantages (A III 248). The explanation of straightening one's views points to right (*sammādiṭṭhi*) and wrong (*micchādiṭṭhi*) views. At the end of the chapter, there are five questions listed and question three asks students to name three ways of making merit that can be performed at the Dhamma school and to perform one of them.

In September 2018, I conducted semistructured interviews with participants from Colombo and a small village in the Gampaha district.[18] I asked the interviewees whether they were familiar with the ways of making merit and to give examples. All interviewees had heard about the list of ten ways of making merit either in Dhamma School or through sermons and some knew the verse (*Dānaṃ sīlañ ca bhāvanā* ...) as well. The three principal ways of making merit drew the liveliest responses and participants were far less certain of the remaining seven. Most participants knew that merit can be given to the dead, gods, and all beings (a very common practice in Theravāda countries), but the related practices of giving merit and rejoicing in merit also attracted speculations such as "merit can only be transferred by monks," "only about 50% of the dead can benefit from the merit," and "99% of the invisible beings who benefit from merit are of a particular class of hungry ghosts." The discussion of the next pair did not attract any unusual examples: service was defined by some as looking after and helping the elderly, sick, and poor (it was pointed out that monks, too, collect food for the poor). Others emphasized that service is not simply helping out a friend, but service is directed as those deserving respect such as monastics and teachers and *bodhi* trees and sacred monuments that house relics (Sk: *caitya*, Sinh: *sāya*).

The next pair, teaching and listening, prompted two elderly participants to reflect on how the practice of preaching has changed over the decades since the introduction of radio sermons. One participant pointed out that listening to the *dhamma* can be beneficial even for animals who lack intellectual understanding, and another suggested that reading, too, should be included in listening. Finally, most laypeople struggled finding examples for straightening one's views but maintained that Buddhists and non-Buddhists alike are capable of knowing good from bad. The monastic participants gave examples for right views such as accepting teachings regarding karma, cause and effect, and not-self. Examples of individual practice included giving alms to monastics, giving merit, listening to sermons, and feeding animals. It was striking that the laypeople all ranked the three principal ways of making merit first while the monastics unanimously ranked straightening one's views first. The monks also said they used the ten ways of making merit as a topic for sermons but not necessarily all of them together. One younger monk explained that the ten ways of making merit is a suitable topic for sermons on full-moon observance days (*poya*) but not for funerals but did not elaborate why this would be the case.

A characteristic Theravāda way of looking at merit

The list of ten and twelve ways of making merit discussed above appears to be unique to Theravāda sources. The Indian sources that have influenced the development of Mahāyāna Buddhism in China and Tibet reflect a different interpretation of the expression "ways of making merit" (*puṇyakriyāvastu*). Vasubandhu's fourth-century *Abhidharmakośa* and *bhāṣya* (vi.4ab and iv.11 ab) refers to seven material (*aupadhika*) and seven immaterial (*niraupadhika*) ways of making merit. Yaśomitra's sixth-century commentary (*Abhidharmakośavyākhya* 352–54) quotes a Sanskrit *sutra*, which lists the seven material ways of making merit: (1) a park for the Saṅgha, (2) a monastery in the park, (3) places to sit and sleep in the monastery, (4) permanent alms, (5) offering to a guest or someone who leaves, (6) offering to a someone who is sick or someone who attends to the sick, and (7) offering food to those who are cold and wet in bad weather and making sure they are comfortable after they have eaten.[19] The seven immaterial ways of making merit are: intense joy at hearing (1) that "the thus gone/come" (*tathāgata*) or a disciple is dwelling in some village, (2) that the *tathāgata* or a disciple is ready to come, (3) that the *tathāgata* or a disciple has reached the main road, (4) that the *tathāgata* or a disciple has reached this village road, as well as intense joy (5) at approaching to see the *tathāgata* or a disciple and (6) at hearing the *dharma*. And the final immaterial way of making merit is (7) taking refuge in the Buddha, Dharma, and Saṅgha and taking the precepts.[20]

The *Mahāprajñāparāmitāśāstra* (v pp. 2258–2260) mentions a different list of material ways of making merit that shows some overlap with the list of the ten items suitable as offerings to ascetics and brahmins (mentioned earlier). The *Mahāvyutpatti* (1699–1704), a glossary of Tibetan and Sanskrit terms compiled in the late eighth or early ninth century, lists five ways of making merit: the principal three, material ways of making merit, and a fifth category, *guṇya-puṇyakriyāvastu*, whose interpretation remains obscure.[21]

In talking of joy, hearing the dhamma, and taking refuge, these non-Theravādin extended lists of ways of making merit overlap in some respects with the Theravādin list. Nevertheless, it is clear, as I have illustrated here, that the list of ten ways of making merit is a formalization of the moral dimension of the way of making merit that is characteristic of Theravāda developments in Sri Lanka and Southeast Asia.

Conclusion

The list of ten ways of making merit has been widely known and referenced since the fifth century CE, yet it has attracted little scholarly attention. The earlier texts mentioning the list, the commentaries and Abhidhamma literature, were preoccupied with working out the mechanism of *kamma*. The technical nature of these texts indicates that they were likely compiled by and aimed at scholarly monastics. Nevertheless, by expanding the three principal ways of making merit into the list of ten, they show a remarkable understanding, accommodation, and recognition of everyday religious practices (such as "transfer of merit"), good manners (such as respecting elders), and even ordinary professions (the learning and teaching of blameless crafts and skills). In the *kāvya* literature and *Upāsakajanālaṅkāra* preoccupation with technical details gave way to elaborate lists of the various advantages of each of the ways of making merit. Again, the texts acknowledge everyday practices and furthermore lay great emphasis on cultivating faith and generating happiness. Finally, contemporary practical handbooks move away from emphasizing the advantages resulting from the ways of making merit to more practical advice on how to give gifts and so on. More recent handbooks give less space to the group of ten ways of making merit as a whole yet still devote separate chapters to some of them. My interviews reveal that not everyone may agree that good manners are of equal value to other meritorious deeds, yet the interpretation of merit as happiness seems to have truly caught on. The expansion of the three principal ways of making merit thus provides significant insights into the specifically Theravāda approach to merit.

Notes

1 I would like to thank Aindralal Balasuriya, Ven Hyo Eun, Mahinda Fernando, Rupert Gethin, Hiroko Kawanami, Gregory Kourilsky, Ven Wetara Mahinda, Mudagamuwe Maithrimurthi, Jasmin Mangalika, Nanda Senanayake, Arthid Sheravanichkul, Peter Skilling, Nimal Sriyaratne, Ashley Thompson, Trent Walker, and many others for their time and help in various ways. Any mistakes or inaccuracies are, of course, mine.

2 Gombrich (1991, 87) refers to a well-known verse listing ten ways of making merit (see the following discussion), and Crosby (2014, 119f.) provides her own examples for each of the ten ways of making merit from modern Theravāda countries; neither explores the history and background of this influential list.

3 *Cullaniddesa* 233 (§ 523), A IV 239, *Mahāniddesa* 273 for the ten suitable gifts.

4 The *Sumaṅgalavilāsinī* makes reference to the *Paṭisambhidāmagga* (Paṭis 236ff.).

5 The *Atthasālinī* (As 158) makes the point that the *samatha* meditation of the thirty-eight objects (*kammaṭṭhāna*) with the aim of achieving the *jhānas* should also be included here in the definition of contemplation as way of making merit.

6 The *Atthasālinī* adds that the good preacher makes freedom his priority, and the *Itivuttaka* commentary adds that he is intent on the welfare of others.

7 The *Itivuttaka* commentary makes reference to the canonical (MN I 403 et al) set of wholesome views (offerings exist, etc.).

8 See also Sumaṅgala's twelfth-century commentary (Abhidh-av-nṭ Be I 194–203 especially Be I 198).

9 Mil 294ff. allows giving merit but not demerit.

10 See also Saddhātissa 1965, 59–64 for a comparison of the *Saddhammopāyana* and the *Upāsakajanalaṅkāra*

11 The later works quote in the context of respect (*apacāyana*) the same well-known verse from the *Dhammapada* (Dhp 109) on the advantages of showing respect that the *Saddhammopāyana* (v. 549) quotes here in the context of *pūjā*.

12 Vism Chapter VIII adds a further four recollections (*maraṇasati, kāyagatāsati, ānāpānasati, upasamānussati*).

13 The standard lists of ten *kusalakammapatha* and *akusalakammapatha* are based on the five precepts, but the fifth precept regarding intoxicants is not represented (MN iii 46–50). *Saddhammopāyana* and *Kāvyaśēkharaya* extend the usual list of the ten by adding the consumption of intoxicants.

14 *Dan, sil, bāvanā / pindenu, anumodanā / baṇasanu, desanā / pidiyayuttan pudanu samanā // 40 // Karanu da vatāvat / pinkaru guṇa vänīmat / saraṇa, sihivīmat / dolos pin däna karava yāpat // 41 //.*

15 See also It-a 26.

16 The Dhamma school books are compiled by a committee and distributed to the temples directly. I am grateful to Ven. Wetara Mahinda, chief incumbent of the Kollupitiya Polwatte Pansala, and Dr. A. Balasuriya, who teaches in the Dhamma school, for providing me with a copy of the book.

17 Mil 294, see also Langer 2007, 164.

18 I conducted eleven interviews in English and Sinhala with participants (including four monks) ranging in age from thirty to eighty years and from the Colombo and Gampaha areas.

19 See Silk 2008, 213–217.

20 Chinese T26, k.2, p. 427c25–428c5, see also Bingenheimer 2013, pp. 38–41. This *sūtra* is also found in the Madhyamāgama (but not in the Pāli Canon) and is quoted or alluded to in various contexts, versions, or translations.

21 See also Lamotte (1980, p 2246) on a similar list of the five ways of making merit (again the fifth is unclear) in the *Mahāprajñāpāramitāsūtra*.

References

Primary sources and list of abbreviations

Abhidh-av = *Abhidhammāvatāra*. Edited by A.P. Buddhadatta, London, PTS, 1915–1928.

Abhidh-av-nṭ = *Abhidhammāvatāranavaṭīkā* = *Abhidhammavikāsinī*. Ed. by Aggamahāpaṇḍita Polvattē Buddhadatta, Ambalangoda 1961.

Abhidh-k-bh = *Abhidharmakośabhāṣyam* Ed. Pradhan 1967.

Abhidh-k-vy = *Sphuṭārthā Abhidharmakośavyākhya*. Ed. By Unrai Wogihara. Tokyo: Sankibo Buddhist Book Store. Abhidh-s = *Abhidhammatthasaṅgaha;* see Abhidh-s-mhṭ.

Abhidh-s-mhṭ = *Abhidhammatthasaṅgaha-mahāṭīkā* = *Abhidhamatthavibhāvinī* (Sumaṅgala). Edited by H. Saddhātissa, Oxford, PTS, 1989.

AN = *Aṅguttara-nikāya*. Edited by R. Morris and E. Hardy, London, PTS, 1885–1900.
As = *Atthasālinī*. Edited by E. Müller, London, 1979. PTS. For translation see: Pe Maung Tin 1976.
Bauddha Ädahilla. Edited by Attuḍāvē Śrī Rāhula, Nädimāla: Bauddha Saṃskṛtika Madhyasthānaya, 2000.
Bauddhayāgē Atpota (Rērukānē Candavimala 1949). Translated by D.J. Percy Silva, Handbook of the Buddhist, (Pokuṇuviṭa: Sri Chandawimala DhammaTreatises Preservation Board, 2014).
Cullaniddesa. Ed by W. Stede, London: PTS 1918, 1988.
Dhp = *Dhammapada*. Edited by K.R. Norman and O. von Hinüber, Oxford: PTS, 1994.
Dhs = *Dhammasaṅginī*. Edited by Müller, London 1978. For translation see Rhys Davids 1900.
Dhs-a = *Dhammasaṅganī-aṭṭhakathā* see As.
It = *Itivuttaka*. Edited by Windisch, London, 1975. PTS. For translation see Masefield, P. 2000.
It-a = *Itivuttaka-aṭ ṭhakathā* = Paramatthadīpanī II. Edited by M.M. Bose, London, PTS, 1934–1936.
KŚēkh = *Kāvyaśēkhara mahā kāvyaya* (Toṭagamuwē Śrī Rāhula, 1449). Edited R. A., Liyanārachchi, Colombo, Sri Lanka 2007.
MN = *Majjhima-nikāya*. Edited by V. Trenckner and R. Chalmers, London, PTS, 1888–1902.
Mahāniddesa. Ed. by L. de La Vallée Poussin and E.J. Thomas, London, PTS, 1916, 1917.
Moh = *Mohavicchedanī*. Ed. Ven. A.P. Buddhadatta and A.K. Warder, Oxford, PTS 1961. *Paramatthadīpanī II* see It-a.
Paṭis = *Paṭisambhidāmagga*. Ed. A.C. Taylor, London, PTS, 1905, 1907.
Saddh = *Saddhammopāyana*. Edited by Dr Morris. JPTS 1887, 35–169.
Sv = *Sumaṅgalavilāsinī*. Edited by T.W. Rhys Davids, London, PTS, 1886–1932.
Sv-ṭ = *Sumaṅgalavilāsinī-ṭīkā. Dīghanikāyaṭṭhakathāṭīkā Līnatthavaṇṇanā* ed. By Lily de Silva, London, PTS 1970.
Upās = *Upāsakajanālaṅkāra*. Edited by Hammalawa Saddhātissa, London, PTS, 1965.
Vibh-a = *Vibhaṅga-aṭṭhakathā* (= Sammohavinodanī). Edited by A.P. Buddhadatta, PTS, London, 1923.

Secondary literature and translations

Assaji, Ven Gantunē, et al. 2017. *Daham pāsala, 8 vana śrēṇiya*. Colombo: Department of Buddhist Affairs.
Bingenheimer, M., ed. 2013. *The Madhyama Āgama (Middle-length Discourses)*, Vol. I (Taisho Volume 1, Number 26).
Candavimala, R. 1949. *Bauddhayāgē atpota*. Boraläsgamuva, Sri Lanka: Śrī Candavimala Dhampustaka Samrakṣaṇa Maṇḍalaya.
Crosby, K. 2014. *Theravāda Buddhism: Continuity, Diversity, and Identity*. Chichester, UK: John Wiley and Sons.
Dhanapala, W.N. (n.d.) "A study of the role of Buddhist Dhamma school education in dealing with the issues of achieving millennium development goals in Sri Lanka," no place, p165f. http://www.icdv.net/2014paper/ws5_11_en__A_study_of_the_role_of_Buddhist_Dhamma_school_education_193629359.pdf.
Dickson, J.F. 1884. "Notes Illustrative of Buddhism as the Daily Religion of the Buddhists of Ceylon and Some Account of their Ceremonies before and after Death." *J.R.A.S. (Ceylon Branch)* 8: 203–236.
Gethin, R. 2008. *Sayings of the Buddha: new Translations by Rupert Gethin from the Pali Canon*. Oxford: Oxford University Press.
Gethin, R. 1997. "Cosmology and Meditation: From the Aggañña-Sutta to the Mahāyāna." *History of Religions* 36: 183–217.
Gethin, R. 1992. *The Buddhist Path to Awakening: a Study of the Bodhi-Pakkhiyā Dhammā*. Leiden: Brill.
Gombrich, R. 1991. *Buddhist Precept and Practice: Traditional Buddhism in the Rural Highlands of Ceylon*. Delhi: Motilal Banarsidass.
Gombrich R., Obeyesekere, G. 1988. *Buddhism Transformed: Religious Change in Sri Lanka*. Princeton: Princeton University Press.
Guruge, A. 1991 [1965]. *Return to Righteousness: a Collection of Speeches, Essays and Letters of the Anagarika Dharmapala*. Colombo: Ministry of Cultural Affairs & Information.
von Hinüber, O. 1996. *A Handbook of Pali Literature*. Berlin: De Gruyter.
Holt, J.C. 1991. *The Buddha in the Crown: Avalokiteśvara in the Buddhist Traditions of Sri Lanka*. Oxford: Oxford University Press.
Langer, R. 2007. *Buddhist Rituals of Death and Rebirth: A study of contemporary Sri Lankan practice and its origins*. Abingdon, UK: RoutledgeCurzon.

Langer, R. 2012. "Chanting as 'bricolage technique' a comparison of South and Southeast Asian funeral recitation." In *Buddhist funeral cultures of Southeast Asia and China*, eds. P. Williams, P. Ladwig, 21–58. Cambridge: Cambridge University Press.

Lamotte, E. 1980. *Le traité de la grande vertu de sagesse*. Vol. Tom. 5, Chapitres XLIX–LII, Et Chapitre XX (2e Série). Louvain: Université de Louvain, Institut orientaliste.

Masefield, P. 2000. *The Itivuttaka*. Oxford: Pali Text Society.

Ñaṇamoḷi, Bhikkhu (trans.) 1991. *The Dispeller of Delusion (Sammohavinodanī)*. London: Pali Text Society.

Norman, K.R. 1983. *Pāli Literature: Including the Canonical Literature in Prakrit and Sanskrit of all the Hīnayāna Schools of Buddhism*. Wiesbaden: Otto Harrassowitz.

Pe Maung, Tin. 1976. *The Expositor* (reprinted as one volume). London: PTS.

Rhys Davids, C.A.F. 1900. *A Buddhist Manual of Psychological Ethics of the Fourth Century B.C. Being a Translation now Made for the First Time from the Original Pali of the First Book in the Abhidhamma Pitaka Entitled Dhamma-Sangaṇi (Compendium of States or Phenomena)*. London: Royal Asiatic Society.

Saddhātissa, H., ed. 1965. "Introduction." In *Upāsakajanālaṅkāra*, ed. H. Saddhātissa, 1–122. London: PTS.

Schmithausen, L. 1986. "Critical Response." In *Karma and Rebirth: Post Classical Developments*, ed. R.W. Neufeldt, 203–230. Albany: State University of New York Press.

Silk, J. 2008. *Managing Monks: Administrators and Administrative Roles in Indian Buddhist Monasticism*, Oxford: Oxford University Press.

Silva, D.J.P. 2014. *Handbook of the Buddhist (Bauddhayāge atpota)*. Pokunuwita, Sri Lanka: Sri Chandawimala Dhamma Treatises Preservation Board.

Wijeratne, R.P., R. Gethin, (trans.) 2002. *Summary of the Topics of Abhidhamma*. Oxford: Pali Text Society.

18

BILINGUALISM

Theravāda bitexts across South and Southeast Asia

Trent Walker

Introduction

The geographic areas where Theravāda Buddhism thrives today—Sri Lanka and greater mainland Southeast Asia—have long been host to multilingual societies. The ritual, literary, and intellectual cultures of Theravāda Buddhism continue this polyglot heritage. Traditional learning is defined by skill in both Indic languages and local vernaculars. Itinerant ascetics, particularly on the Southeast Asian massif, master the borderlands between multiple dialects, cultures, and political spheres. Theravāda liturgies are rarely conducted in only one language; Pāli and local languages are deftly interwoven into a complex aural fabric.

The bilingual character of Theravāda Buddhism is no accident. It emerges from deliberate cultivation by Buddhist intellectuals in these regions over the past two millennia. The Theravāda transmission of texts is notably bilingual; scriptures in Pāli are often accompanied by vernacular translations and Pāli-vernacular bilingual texts, or "bitexts." A typical Theravāda manuscript library therefore contains Pāli scriptures and commentaries, bilingual Pāli-vernacular versions of those same texts, and texts composed in the vernacular that contain Pāli words and phrases. Some libraries may have a few titles in Sanskrit as well. What we call "Theravāda Buddhism" or "Pāli Buddhism" is not a monolingual heritage—it springs from a long encounter between classical Indic and local vernacular texts.

Yet this direct exchange between Indic scriptural languages and local vernaculars is rare elsewhere in the contemporary Buddhist world. Only among the Newar do Sanskrit and a local dialect (Newari) regularly appear side by side in the same manuscript, although the vernacular portions tend to transmit ritual instructions rather than translate the Indic liturgy (Gutschow and Michaels 2005: 153–175). There are limited examples of wholly bilingual Sanskrit-Tibetan manuscripts (Verhagen 2013: 325–327) and Nepalese-Sanskrit manuscripts with Tibetan glosses (Dimitrov 2006: 5). Bilingual Sanskrit-vernacular texts were also produced by other Buddhist cultures in the past, including the Khotanese (Maggi 2015: 863) and the Tocharian (Peyrot 2008: 83). But these are exceptions to the rule; most non-Theravāda parts of the Buddhist world no longer use bilingual Indic-vernacular texts.

How and why, then, did Theravāda Buddhists, especially during the second millennium, develop bilingual conventions for the transmission and performance of Buddhist texts? One might look north towards East Asia for comparison, where Literary Sinitic translations effectively

DOI: 10.4324/9781351026666-22

replaced Indic scriptures, but bilingual Sinitic-vernacular reading techniques flourished. Similar to the Tibetan canon, Chinese scriptural translations retain Indic words only in phonetic transcriptions of certain titles, spells, technical terms, and proper names. In China, Japan, Korea, and Vietnam, the Literary Sinitic of the translated canon became the accepted standard for exegetical and ritual purposes. On the other hand, bitextual presentations of Literary Sinitic, particularly in Japan (*kundoku*) and Korea (*sŏktok kugyŏl*), as well as new compositions in vernacular languages, accompanied the Chinese Buddhist canon throughout its history (Kornicki 2018: 157–186).

Indic scriptures, vernacular compositions, and Indic-vernacular bilingual texts comprise a roughly analogous mode of scriptural transmission in the Theravāda world. This chapter builds on scholarship about multilingual Buddhist texts in East Asia to consider different forms of bilingualism in Theravāda manuscript cultures, with a particular emphasis on what I call "Indic-vernacular bitexts." A "bitext," in the context of contemporary linguistics, comprises both a source text in one language and its translation into another. For the purposes of this chapter, an Indic-vernacular bitext is a bilingual text that stitches together portions in an Indic prestige language (usually Pāli but also Sanskrit in rare cases) and a local South or Southeast Asian vernacular, such as Arakanese, Burmese, Khmer, Mon, Sinhala, Tamil, Vietnamese, or various Southwestern Tai languages (Khün, Lanna, Lao, Lü, Siamese, etc.), typically in an interphrasal or interlinear arrangement.

In the first half of this chapter, I give an overview of the three primary steps—selection, analysis, and presentation—in the creation of Theravāda bitexts, based on a comparative study of bilingual compositions across South and Southeast Asia. The technical dimensions of these bitexts have previously been studied in isolation; I provide the first comprehensive view of what makes Indic-vernacular bitexts tick. This practical foundation serves as the basis for the second half of the chapter, in which I outline how these techniques gradually developed into a range of bitextual genres in first- and second-millennium Sri Lanka and Southeast Asia. Theravāda bitexts are much more interconnected across space and time than is commonly assumed. Their shared techniques and historical trajectories bring to life the currents of intellectual and linguistic exchange that have shaped this essentially bilingual religious tradition.

Creating bitexts: primary steps and techniques

Not all bilingual Theravāda books and manuscripts are bitexts in a strict sense. Most bilingual printed books with Pāli and vernacular texts in a parallel arrangement—including modern chanting guides, *Tipiṭaka* editions, and academic tomes—are not bitextual in the sense of combining Pāli and vernacular phrases. Other Theravāda books and manuscripts, including many in folded-paper (leporello) and short palm-leaf format, contain brief Pāli texts interspersed with vernacular ritual instructions. These, too, are bilingual rather than bitextual, since the Indic and vernacular portions do not purport to be grammatically linked.

Indic-vernacular bitexts, by contrast, bind together Pāli and vernacular portions into a single composition. Traditional Theravāda manuscripts, particularly those preserved on long-format palm leaf, are dominated by Pāli-vernacular bitexts that combine Pāli and vernacular portions in a phrase-by-phrase, sentence-by-sentence, or line-by-line arrangement. These bitexts are created through the three primary steps of selection, analysis, and presentation, each of which may include multiple possible techniques:

1 Selection
   1a Citation
   1b Invention

2 Analysis
  2a Parsing
  2b Amplification
  2c Rearrangement
  2d Annotation
  2e Gloss
3 Presentation
  3a Philological
  3b Exegetical
  3c Homiletic
  3d Poetic

The order of the steps and their attendant techniques reveals the logical method by which bitexts are created. All Indic-vernacular bitexts necessarily use all three primary steps, but which of the various techniques are employed depends on the linguistic background, cultural conventions, and intended audience of the author.

Selection

The initial step in creating a bitext is selecting and sometimes also directly quoting a particular passage in an Indic text. This passage may be a citation (1a) of an existing Indic text or an invention (1b) of an Indic text composed expressly for use in a bitext. Whether the selected passage is a citation or an invention, in nearly all cases, the Indic portion comes first and is thus treated as the source text. Although individual words and phrases may later be rearranged, Theravāda bitexts almost always proceed passage by passage through the existing or invented Indic source.

Citation

In the case of citation, selection entails choosing a passage that starts at the beginning of the existing source text, whether a single phrase or several paragraphs. Prior to this Pāli passage being analyzed and translated into the vernacular, it might be quoted in full. If complete quotations are not used, it is common to provide just the beginning and end of a given quotation, with the middle abbreviated by means of a *peyyāla* mark, typically *pa, pe*, or *la* (Gethin 2007: 383–384). During the third step of presentation, these quotations may be reduced or excised completely depending on the intended audience of the bitext.

Invention

When the source is invented rather than cited, the Indic and vernacular portions are penned by the same author. In some cases, the newly composed Pāli portions form a complete text that may be studied in and of itself. In most instances, however, an abbreviated style of presentation is adopted and the Pāli portions do not form a coherent text; the "missing" portions of the Pāli were not excised by the author but simply never existed in the first place. Invented bitexts signal to their audience that the authoritative diction of Pāli—perhaps even the words of the Buddha himself—form the basis for the composition at hand, even if no such Pāli source text exists. Such bitexts are widespread in Khmer- and Southwestern Tai–speaking cultures. A few bilingual works in Burma even invert the usual structure by applying normative bitextual techniques to create Burmese-Pāli bitexts, rather than Pāli-Burmese bitexts, in which the root text is the vernacular and its translation is in Pāli (Lammerts 2018: 93).

Analysis

The second step in crafting a bitext entails performing a reading and/or translation of the selected Pāli or Sanskrit passage. The techniques of analysis may be performed silently and invisibly ("reading") or in ways that are aurally or visually apparent ("translation") to a listener or reader. Analysis may include parsing the selected passage into its component parts (2a), amplifying implied or contracted Indic words (2b), annotating grammatical features of those words (2c), rearranging those words to fit vernacular syntax (2d), and providing Indic and/or vernacular glosses (2e).

Parsing

Since the cited passage typically contains many individual Pāli words, the sentence must first be "read" or dissected into its constituent components prior to subsequent stages of analysis. The author of the bitext must parse the passage into intelligible semantic units. In some manuscripts, the division of words is accomplished by the insertion of punctuation marks, including spaces. In other cases, Pāli words joined by the process of euphonic conjunction known as *sandhi* may be resolved into their basic components (e.g., *namatthu* becomes *namo atthu*). Parsing transforms the Indic passage from a sequence of phonetic syllables into a meaningful series of lexical items.

Amplification

Since Indic texts may contain many implied or contracted words and phrases, these need to be amplified or fleshed out during the process of analysis. Shortened clitic forms may be converted to full words (*va* to *eva* or *iva*; *ti* to *iti*, *me* to *mama* or *mayā*, etc.). Abbreviated or implied relative-correlative structures may be specified in their complete form (*tathā* ... becomes *yathā* ... *tathā* ..., etc.). Implied subjects, objects, and verbs are frequently added as appropriate. For instance, the opening *evam me sutaṃ* (Thus I have heard) of the *Maṅgala-sutta* might become *evaṃ ekenākārena* [or *ekena ākārena*] *me* [or *mayā*] *bhagavato samukhā sutaṃ idaṃ suttaṃ maṅgala-suttaṃ* (Thus, in this one way, I, in the Blessed One's presence, have heard this *sutta* called the *Maṅgala-sutta*). These amplifications all serve to make the grammatical structure of the Pāli as transparent as possible.

Rearrangement

The sequence of Pāli words and phrases may be rearranged to match vernacular syntax. None of the vernacular languages of Theravāda Buddhism cultures share the same word order as Pāli. Some, such as Burmese or Sinhala, are relatively close, while others, such as Khmer or Siamese, are significantly different. Moreover, the syntax of Pāli verse is quite free; even Pāli-Pāli commentaries on verse texts change the word order for exegetical purposes. Most, although not all, Pāli-vernacular bitexts engage in syntactical rearrangement to produce coherent vernacular readings.

Rearrangement may be marked in several different ways. The most common option is for the amplified version of the original Pāli passage to simply be written out in the vernacular word order. One Pāli-Siamese manuscript, shown in Figure 18.1, rearranges the amplified opening of the *Maṅgala-sutta* cited earlier as follows: *idaṃ sut[t]aṃ maṅgala-s[utt]aṃ me s[u]taṃ*

Figure 18.1 Pāli-Siamese manuscript in interphrasal format, with alternating Pāli and Siamese phrases (Sattaparitta, FEMC C.77.VII, detail of folio kī verso, line 5 and folio ku recto, line 1).

Photograph by the author.

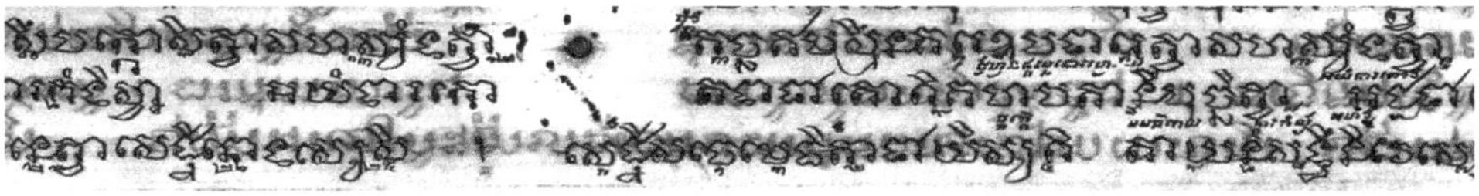

Figure 18.2 Pāli-Siamese manuscript in interlinear format, with alphanumeric rearrangement, Pāli amplification, and vernacular gloss (Dhammapadaṭṭhakathā, FEMC D.11.VII, detail of folio ṭhu verso, lines 3–5).

Photograph by the author.

bhagavato sumukhā evaṃ ekenākārena (This *sutta*, called the *Maṅgala-sutta*, I have heard in the Blessed One's presence thus, in this one way).

An alternative method of rearrangement uses interlinear annotations, usually in the form of numbers or letters, to indicate the proper sequence (see Figure 18.2). This new sequence structures both reading and translation: It is a perfectly legitimate way to read the Pāli passage, despite being tuned to the native syntax of a Sinhalese or Southeast Asian student of Pāli. It also matches the sequence by which each individual Pāli word needs to be glossed in order to create a fluent vernacular translation. With respect to the same example from the *Maṅgala-sutta*, the amplified passage would be numbered as follows to produce a Siamese reading: [6] *evaṃ ekenākārena* [3] *me* [5] *bhagavato samukhā* [4] *sutaṃ* [1] *idaṃ suttaṃ* [2] *maṅgala-suttaṃ*.

Annotation

Before glossing (2e) or translation proper may begin, there is often a crucial intermediate step. Annotation entails marking case, number, mood, tense, and other grammatical features of the Pāli with vernacular particles. Among major vernacular languages in Theravāda cultures, only Sinhala, an Indo-Aryan language like Pāli, has a morphological system for marking such grammatical features. Pāli-Sinhala bitexts therefore skip this step and move immediately to creating vernacular lexical glosses.

For Southeast Asian Pāli-vernacular bitexts, however, the annotation step is essential and sets them apart from ordinary vernacular texts. None of these vernacular languages has a comparable system of case; the function of nouns must be derived primarily from syntax (Enfield 2019: 18). Some Southeast Asian written languages have developed particles that mimic case-marking in Pāli. In Burmese, these particles are affixes that follow the noun; in Khmer, Khün, Mon, Lanna, Lao, and Lü, they mostly precede the nouns they modify. Selected examples are shown in Table 18.1. In Pāli-vernacular bitexts, such particles may be rigorously applied to mark Pāli cases; similar sets of particles can also be applied to mark grammatical number, mood, and tense (Walker 2018a: 337).

Table 18.1 Examples of grammatical annotation particles

Language	*Subject*	*Abbreviated Form*	*Plural*	*Abbreviated Form*	*Direct Object*
Khmer	*ṙī* + NOUN	*ṙī/ṙị*-like symbol	NOUN + *dāṃṅ ḷāy/dāṃṅ° hlāy°*	*da*	*nūv* + NOUN
Siamese	*ăn vā*$_1$ + NOUN	*ṙī/ṙị*-like symbol	NOUN + *dăṅ*$_2$ *hlāy*	*da*	*j̋ịṅ*$_1$ + NOUN
Lao	*ăn vā*$_1$ + NOUN	*ṙī/ṙị*-like symbol	NOUN + *dăṅ hlāy*	*dă°lā*	*yăṅ* + NOUN
Burmese	NOUN + *saññ*	*su/sañ*	NOUN + *tui'/tuiv'/tuiv*		*kui* + NOUN

The extent to which such markers are truly part of the vernacular language or are artificial technical particles is subject to debate (Okell 1965: 191–195; Khin 1999: 461–465). They tend to be more common in the literary registers of Southeast Asian languages, most notably that of Burmese (Okell 1965: 189–190). In Khmer and Southwestern Tai languages, for instance, there is normally no need to mark the subject or direct object of a given sentence with any special particle. However, Pāli-Khmer and Pāli-Tai bitexts will often meticulously mark Pāli nouns in the nominative (subject) and accusative (object) cases with specific technical particles. The formal or literary registers of all languages in Southeast Asian Theravāda cultures bear similar imprints of the Pāli-vernacular bitextual style.

Gloss

Glossing involves defining Pāli words and phrases with Pāli and/or vernacular glosses. Although less common, Pāli glosses nevertheless contribute to the distinctive aesthetic of bitexts. In Khmer, Khün, Lanna, Lao, and Lü manuscript cultures, a special vernacular particle is used to set off these Pāli glosses from the cited Pāli text (Khmer *moḥ*; Tai *moḥ vā*$_1$ or *măk vā*$_1$; transliteration throughout this chapter follows Walker 2018a xiii–xvii). Such Pāli glosses are then typically followed by vernacular glosses, which are not marked by a special particle. Returning to the *Maṅgala*-sutta example, *evaṃ* is glossed as *evaṃ* **moḥ** *ekenākarena* **ḍvay°**$_2$ **ākār ăn° nịṅ° grị̄ ḍai**$_2$ **savanā kār ɓăṅ** (thus, **that is to say**, in this one way**, in this one way, namely, the act of having listened**; FEMC C.77.VII, *kī* verso 5). The complexity of vernacular glosses varies depending on the term glossed and the intended audience of the bitext. The default is a simple translation of the Pāli word or phrase. As the next step reveals, however, such glosses may subsequently be abbreviated, expounded on, vividly elaborated, or set in ornate verse.

Presentation

After completing the analytical processes outline a reading and translation of the selected Indic passage, the author of a bitext then must choose how to present the analyzed passage for its intended audience. Some bitexts are written with monastic training in mind, others for elite patrons, still others for public recitation; each audience may have different practical and aesthetic concerns that shape the required presentation. I outline four techniques or modes of presentation here: philological (3a), exegetical (3b), homiletic (3c), and poetic (3d). These are not airtight categories; the modes may overlap for particular bitexts. Some passages in a particular bitext may receive a philological or exegetical treatment, while others may move in a homiletic or poetic direction.

Philological

Creating a bitext for the efficient linguistic study of a particular Indic source often relies on extensive abbreviation. A philological presentation may adopt special symbols for certain particles or glosses as well as elide some vernacular glosses entirely. Most such presentations are reserved for texts used for training in Pāli grammar and Pāli-vernacular translation. The bitext serves as an aid to the study of Pāli, and the intended audience is therefore either a private monastic reader or teacher. An abbreviated bitext for philological purposes may end up being less than a third vernacular material; in some cases, only scattered vernacular annotations are visible between the lines. Not all Theravāda cultures engage in such abbreviation in their written bitexts. Pāli-Sinhala bitexts do not appear to elide self-evident vernacular glosses; all Pāli words are translated into Sinhala. Moreover, since Sri Lankan bitexts do not use technical particles to mark grammatical features, there is little in the way of symbolic abbreviations.

By contrast, in philological presentations of bitexts in Laos and Thailand, elision of vernacular glosses for common Pāli words is widespread. In addition, a few common technical particles, including those for marking the nominative case and the plural number, are frequently notated through abbreviated forms (see Figure 18.1). This process soars towards its logical extreme in certain genres of Pāli-Burmese bitexts; William Pruitt documents nearly two hundred different forms of abbreviation in a single *Pātimokkha* bitext (Pruitt 1994: 235–241). In Khmer and Tai contexts, extensive abbreviation is generally restricted to treatises for monastic study rather than sermons for reading aloud to lay audiences. Philological treatments of bitexts typically occur with cited rather than invented Indic sources and are the only form of Theravāda bitext to favor an interlinear as opposed to interphrasal arrangement.

Exegetical

In contrast with philological presentations, a bitext tuned for exegetical purposes focuses not on linguistic acquisition or grammatical analysis but rather doctrinal exposition. This mode of presentation focuses on expounding Indic terms in accordance with scholastic conventions of the Pāli commentarial tradition, such as etymological reflections, rhetorical questions, citations of other texts, and refutation of competing viewpoints. Most exegetical bitexts feature extensive intertextual engagement with existing Pāli commentaries, explicitly demonstrating their fidelity to the Buddhist scholastic heritage. Like the monolingual Pāli commentaries they build on, many exegetical bitexts provide multiple contrasting interpretations of a single Pāli passage. In Tai bitexts, such alternative readings are marked with a local form of the Pāli *naya*, typically *năiy°* *nịṅ°* ("One interpretation states ..."). While bitexts are typically not a radical departure from monolingual Pāli commentaries, they may offer new lines of inquiry or emphasis (Walker 2018a: 351–361; cf. McDaniel 2008: 143; 153–154). In particular, Pāli-Burmese exegetical bitexts may feature an extended vernacular explanation (*adhippāya*) after the initial steps of introduction, citation, and analysis (Lammerts 2018: 95). Some Pāli-Sinhala bitexts may also quote at length from Pāli commentaries to elucidate their arguments (Blackburn 2001: 124–125).

Homiletic

Bitexts intended to be read aloud as prose sermons to laypeople often include far more vernacular than Pāli material. In the case of bitexts that cite existing Indic texts, much of the Pāli may be redacted in a homiletic presentation to make the sermon more accessible to lay audiences. If no existing source is present, an author of a bitext might choose to only compose enough Pāli needed for a particular audience. For sermons based on invented sources, the amount of Pāli included may be quite small beyond the first few passages. Whether based on extant or newly composed Indic sources, such sermons still retain the distinctive analytical techniques proper to bitexts. If the source is a known Pāli text, the vernacular portions tend to adhere to the norms of scholastic commentaries; authors of such bitexts generally do not insert idiosyncratic Pāli phrases or add details that veer from commentarial conventions (Walker 2018a: 370–373; cf. McDaniel 2008: 140–142). Authors of these homiletic bitexts nevertheless draw on the vernacular language to craft elaborate, engaging prose narratives and expositions that engage lay listeners while maintaining an explicit connection to Pāli scriptures.

Poetic

While most Theravāda bitexts are created to serve scholastic or didactic ends, a subset emphasizes their aesthetic qualities. Such bitexts focus on a poetic presentation, often as sermons for court or other elite lay audiences. These literary bitexts expand the vernacular glosses in accordance with the conventions found in both Indic and vernacular belles lettres. The poetic conventions employed in these extended vernacular glosses vary widely. In some cases, only the vernacular portions are crafted into verse, typically with established syllabic or rhyme constraints. In other cases, the Indic and vernacular portions may be merged into a single metrical structure. Like ordinary prose bitexts produced for sermons, poetic bitexts may elaborate on narrative and descriptive details for literary effect.

The steps and techniques outlined above are shared by the broader Indic commentarial tradition, especially monolingual Pāli commentaries. *Aṭṭhakathā* and *ṭīkā* select, analyze, and present Pāli passages anew. They frequently amplify implied or contracted Pāli words and provide scholastic exegesis or narrative elaboration. *Yojanā*, most of which were composed in second-millennium Southeast Asia, share a special emphasis on rearranging the syntax of Pāli texts and annotating their grammatical features (Kieffer-Pülz 2015: 432). *Pada-anvaya* (*pada-ānuma*), found only in Sri Lanka, are exclusively devoted to syntactic rearrangement, namely, changing the sequence of Pāli words to match the order for reading and translation in Sinhala (Bechert 2005: 28; cf. Godakumbura 1955: 352).

The techniques witnessed in Indic-vernacular bitexts thus reflect their close relationship with monolingual Pāli commentaries. Since these commentaries predate the earliest extant Pāli-vernacular bitexts, the Pāli *aṭṭhakathā* tradition and related Sanskrit scholastic practices are among the most important ancestors of Theravāda bitexts. But this model may not capture the complete historical picture. Since the now-lost Pāli-Sinhala Prakrit commentaries on the Pāli scriptures—the so-called *Sīhalaṭṭhakathā*—were the basis for the Pāli *aṭṭhakathā* commentaries, Pāli-vernacular bitexts were not necessarily a later development. This deeply intertwined relationship between monolingual and bitextual exegetical traditions brings us to a consideration of their historical development and diffusion across the Theravāda world.

Spreading bitexts: the diffusion of bilingual compositions

The three primary steps and multiple techniques shared across Pāli-vernacular bitexts demonstrate one dimension of their interconnected heritage. The historical processes by which these methods spread throughout South and Southeast Asia showcase another. Both dimensions point to the bilingualism at the core of Theravāda textual life.

The historical precedents for the bitextual genres witnessed in contemporary manuscript collections include Pāli, Sanskrit, and Sinhala Prakrit commentarial traditions as well as Indic-vernacular translation practices among the Khmer, the Mon, the Pyu, and other early civilizations of mainland Southeast Asia. As Sanskrit commentarial traditions fall outside the scope of this chapter, I focus on the earliest evidence for bitexts in each of the regions that now comprise the Theravāda world. I begin with the earliest surviving Sri Lankan examples (ca. 900–1200) before providing a survey of the major developments in mainland Southeast Asia from the first millennium to the present, including Old Khmer and Pyu proto-bitexts (ca. 500–1200) and early Mon and Burmese examples (ca. 1100–1500). These developments paved the way for the oldest extant Tai bitexts (ca. 1300–1700) and later variations among the Khmer, Tai Khün, Tai, Lü, and Vietnamese (ca. 1700–1950). This outline highlights the process of mutual influence and diffusion that shaped Theravāda bitexts up to the present.

Early Sri Lankan Bitexts, ca. 900–1200

Setting aside the lost *Sīhalaṭṭhakathā* commentaries, the earliest surviving Pāli-Sinhala bitexts were composed in the tenth century CE. These include both bilingual *gaṇṭhipada* (Sinhala: *gäṭapadaya*) and *sannaya* (also known as *sanna, sannē*, or sometimes *padārtha*). Although there is considerable overlap between the two genres, the former generally focus on "knotty" (*gaṇṭhi*) words, whereas the latter provide interphrasal glosses of entire texts. Both may engage in a range of exegetical commentary that goes beyond mere gloss (Blackburn 2001: 68). *Sannaya* generally reorders the syntax of the original to match the Sinhala order, such that the glosses form fluent sentences.

Examples of Sanskrit-Sinhala and Pāli-Sinhalese bitexts that may date from the tenth century include the *Kāvyādarśasannaya* (an interphrasal bitext of Daṇḍin's Sanskrit work on poetics, the *Kāvyādarśa*), the *Dhampiyā-aṭuvā-gäṭapadaya*, the *Jātaka-aṭuvā-gäṭapadaya*, and the *Mahābodhivaṃsa-gäṭapadaya* (bilingual exegeses of the Pāli *Jātaka-aṭṭhavaṇṇanā*, *Dhammapadaṭṭhakathā*, and *Mahābodhivaṃsa*, respectively; Dimitrov 2016: 144–145; 160–161; 454–455; Gornall 2017: 485). The *Siyabaslakara*, a ninth- or tenth-century Sinhalese adaptation of the *Kāvyādarśa* that includes a Sinhala-Sinhala *sannaya*, exhibits the same primary techniques of citation, analysis via rearrangement and gloss, and an exegetical presentation.

By the twelfth century, Pāli-Sinhala bitexts developed increasingly sophisticated forms of exegesis. Some of these followed in the footsteps of Vimalabuddhi's commentary on the *Kaccāyana-vyākaraṇa*, the *Mukhamattadīpanī*. Burmese recensions of this commentary enumerate a sixfold exegetical method (*sambandha*, *pada*, *padattha*, *padaviggaha*, *codanā*, and *parihāra*; Ruiz-Falqués 2015: 116). We could link *pada* (or *padaccheda*, following the Pāli-Lao reading of PLMP 08040102007_04, *ka* recto 5) to "parsing," *sambandha* to "rearrangement," *padattha* to "gloss," and *padaviggaha* (word analysis), *codanā* (objection), and *parihāra* (refutation) to various exegetical procedures. These techniques were instrumental in the "grammaticization" of both Pāli and Sinhala commentaries during this period, including the *Abhidharmārthasaṅgrahasannaya*, Sāriputta's bitextual version of the *Abhidhammatthasaṅgaha* (Gornall 2020). The spread of Sri

Lankan Buddhist texts to Southeast Asia during the early centuries of the second millennium assured that the exegetical approach of Pāli and Pāli-Sinhala commentaries influenced new compositions across the Indian Ocean as well.

Pyu and Old Khmer Proto-Bitexts, ca. 500–1200

In mainland Southeast Asia, many inscriptions, particularly during the second half of the first millennium, include portions in two or more languages, usually a classical Indic language (Sanskrit or Pāli) and a local tongue (Cham, Khmer, Mon, Pyu). However, in most cases, the classical and vernacular sections diverge: the Indic section may praise a deity in verse, while the vernacular prose documents what was donated to that deity. The Indic passage comes first, usually on the top portion of the inscription, while the vernacular lies below or on a different face.

One possible exception to this pattern is the Kan Wet Khaung Mound inscription, an unusual bilingual Sanskrit-Pyu text carved on the pedestal of a Buddha image found in central Myanmar, dated to the sixth century (Griffiths et al. 2017: 100–101). Unlike almost all other first-millennium bilingual Indic-vernacular texts, the Sanskrit and Pyu portions are arranged interphrasally, with a word or phrase in Sanskrit followed by a word or phrase in Pyu. Although many of the Pyu portions appear to be glosses, a recent study suggests that these glosses do not replicate the grammatical structure of the Sanskrit. Grammatical annotation is absent, with the possible exception of a particle for the plural number (Griffiths et al. 2017: 141–142). No amplification or rearrangement is attested, though it is likely that the Pyu portions contain various elaborations.

Hundreds of seventh- to fourteenth-century inscriptions containing both Sanskrit and Old Khmer portions appear in and around what is now Cambodia. In most cases, however, the two languages differ in both arrangement and substance. In the few cases in which they overlap in content, they are not arranged interphrasally and, as such, were not necessarily meant to be read in an explicitly dialogical relationship. Nevertheless, beginning in the tenth century, a handful of inscriptions feature close Khmer prose translations of Sanskrit verses (Chhom 2016: 319–340). The Khmer translations not only match the lexical structure of the Sanskrit but also echo the grammar. These Sanskrit-Khmer inscriptions engage in both vernacular gloss and grammatical annotation, including particles to express vocative, accusative, genitive, and plural attributes (*hai*, *nu*, *ta*, and *phoṅ*, respectively). Variations of these same particles are included in the more systematic techniques for grammatical notation that appear in Cambodia in the earliest known Pāli-Khmer bitexts hundreds of years later (Walker 2018a: 337).

Early Mon and Burmese Bitexts, ca. 1100–1500

Early Sanskrit-Pyu and Sanskrit-Old Khmer inscriptions hint at the existence of bitexts in both parallel and interphrasal arrangements, along with some of the techniques found in later compositions. However, it is not until the late eleventh or early twelfth century that unambiguous evidence appears for Pāli-vernacular bitexts in Southeast Asia. The earliest known example is the Pāli-Mon inscription from the pillars of the Shwezigon temple in Pagan, carved during the reign of Kyanzittha (r. 1084–1113; Luce and Shin 1969: 50–57). While the bulk of this massive inscription is solely in Mon, the first twelve lines contain a short Pāli verse followed by a rearrangement of the same passage into an interphrasal Pāli-Mon bitext (Blagden 1960: 93).

This passage displays the three primary steps and many of their attendant techniques. It begins with a selection of an invented Pāli verse. The verse is then analyzed through parsing, amplification, rearrangement, annotation, and gloss. The nominative case and aorist tense are marked with the technical particles *yaṅ* (Halliday 1923: 33) and *cin* (i.e., *cón*; Duroiselle 1913: 122). The presentation technique is largely exegetical, adding key details and explanations through rhetorical questions. Other presentation modes surface in Pāli-Mon bitexts (known as *naṃ* or *trāai*) from later eras (Griffiths et al. 2017: 104n118). By the twelfth century at the latest, it seems that nearly all the technical conventions for Pāli-vernacular bitexts in mainland Southeast Asia were already in place.

These bitextual techniques likely spread from Mon speakers to other linguistic groups in mainland Southeast Asia in the eleventh through thirteenth centuries. The earliest epigraphic evidence for a portion of a Pāli-Burmese bitext, known locally as a *nissaya* (Pāli *nissaya*; Sanskrit *niśraya*, "dependence" or "support," as in a crutch for reading an Indic text), dates to the late thirteenth century (Griffiths et al. 2017: 104n117). An inscription from 1442 lists a number of texts thought to be Sanskrit-Burmese *nissaya* (Lammerts 2018: 28–31).

Early Modern Siamese, Lao, and Lanna Bitexts, ca. 1300–1700

Bitexts were likely adopted by Tai-speaking groups from some combination of Mon, Khmer, Burmese, and Sinhala influences. By the middle of the second millennium, the core techniques had spread from the Mon and the Burmese to most Tai and Khmer groups, including those in Siam, Lanna, Laos, and Cambodia. The earliest surviving complete Pāli-Siamese bitext, a poetic version of the *Vessantara-jātaka* in several kinds of vernacular verse, was supposedly composed in 1482 (Walker 2018a: 364–367). The earliest securely dated Pāli-Lanna bitext was copied in 1552 (DLNTM 011903027_00), the oldest extant Sanskrit-Lanna bitext in 1578 (DLNTM 011318001_01), and the first known Pāli-Lao bitext in 1586 (PLMP 08040102007_04); the compositions themselves are presumably somewhat older.

Many of the earliest Lanna and Lao examples bear the term *nāmasăp°* or *săp°* in their title. *Nāmasăp°* may be related to Sanskrit **nāmaśabda*/Pāli **nāmasadda*, of uncertain meaning, but in all manuscripts known to me the final syllable is spelled *săp°*, meaning "to cut into pieces"; whether this is more apt than *śabda* (phoneme) is hard to say. Early Pāli-Tai bitexts sporting this term are based on canonical or commentarial Vinaya and Abhidhamma texts, use all five analytical techniques, and are presented in philological and/or exegetical modes. It seems reasonable to suppose that *nāmasăp°* bitexts were used exclusively for monastic study. Another large group of early Lanna and Lao bitexts adopt the term *nisrai* or *nissay*, comparable to *nissaya* in Burmese usage. Lao and Lanna *nissaya* are quite close to *nāmasăp°* in style (McDaniel 2008: 135). However, the term *nissaya* has a broader application, appearing in a wide range of bitexts copied prior to the eighteenth century, including Jātaka narratives, grammatical treatises, and *aṭṭhakathā* commentaries.

Starting from the early seventeenth century, the manuscript record provides evidence of Pāli-Tai homiletic bitexts that redact most of the Pāli portions or whose limited Pāli portions are invented. These include bitexts bearing the genre terms *vohān°*/*vohār°* (Pāli *vohāra*, "expression") and *ānisan͡°* (Pāli *ānisaṃsa*, "benefit"; i.e., sermons on the karmic boons of various pious acts); the oldest known manuscript examples of each date to 1666 (DLNTM 070710018_00; PNTMP 030306004_05). The term *vohāra* seems largely limited to Lanna; Pāli-Lao bitexts in a similar style are generally labeled *nissaya* instead. Early *vohāra* bitexts draw exclusively from known Pāli texts but use extensive redaction of the Pāli and elaboration of the vernacular to make them appropriate for sermons to lay audiences. Indeed, most *vohāra*, after a citation of the opening Pāli passage, insert the Pāli phrase *bho sādhavo* (All you good people!), followed by its vernacular translation, as an explicit nod to their audience. Pāli-vernacular *ānisaṃsa* texts, many of which predate later monolingual Pāli versions, use a similar style to *vohāra*. The crucial difference is that *ānisaṃsa* are not typically based on an existing Pāli text; the Pāli portions were apparently composed, or at least borrowed, by the author of the bitext. The bitextual format, including all of its technical conventions, allows *ānisaṃsa* to work as vernacular sermons that draw on the scriptural authority of the Pāli language.

Around this same period in Siam we find the earliest surviving evidence for philological Pāli-vernacular bitexts in an interlinear format. These take the form of inked or carved annotations in extremely small script, known as *khaam hvăt* or *tvă ksien* in modern Thai, that provide Pāli glosses and amplifications; vernacular glosses, grammatical annotations, and brief interpretive comments; and numbers or letters to denote exactly how the syntax is to be rearranged for a vernacular reading and translation (Walker 2018a: 373–377). Most of the texts annotated in this way are those emphasized in Siamese monastic examinations, including the *Kaccāyana-vyākaraṇa*, the *Dhammapada-aṭṭhakathā*, and the *Maṅgalaṭṭhadīpanī*. Hence, the annotations reveal how monks of the time actually studied Pāli texts. Similar annotations in both Siamese and Khmer are found in manuscripts in Cambodian collections copied as late as the early twentieth century (Walker 2018b: civ–cvi).

We also find seventeenth-century evidence for legal codes adopting aspects of Pāli-vernacular bitexts. The earliest available manuscript example is probably the *Garubhaṇḍa*, a Lao monastic law code copied in 1683 (PLMP 06018515002_02), of which certain parts are structured as a Pāli-Lao bitext. There is a Pāli or Pāli-Lanna manuscript on twenty-five types of monastic theft (*avahāra*) that was purportedly inscribed in 1472, though I was unable to verify this date (SRI 80.046.03.052–052). In Burma, the oldest extant Burmese legal code (*dhammasatttha*), known as the *Dhammavilāsa* and likely composed no later than 1637 or 1638, contains bitextual *nis-saya* passages (Lammerts 2018: 56–59). In Siam, some legal codes thought to be adapted from Mon sources likewise contain Pāli-Siamese bitextual portions, including the *Dhapmasātr*, likely composed sometime before 1805 (Baker and Phongpaichit 2016: 17–19).

Modern Khmer, Tai Khün, Tai Lü, and Vietnamese Bitexts, ca. 1700–1950

Pāli-vernacular bitexts, in both sacred and secular guises, eventually reached nearly all corners of the Theravāda world. Tai Lü (Dai Lue) and Tai Khün bitexts follow a similar pattern to the Lao and Lanna examples cited above. Even less is known about the precise nature of Pāli-Tai Nuea, Pāli-Shan, and other bitexts from Southwestern Tai-speaking Buddhist communities in the region, though bilingual manuscripts for rituals, medicine, and magic are abundant in these cultures. No Khmer-language manuscript survives in Cambodia from before the 1830s. Nevertheless, more recent manuscripts may transmit older Pāli-Khmer bitexts, generally in a redacted presentation, many of them dating from the eighteenth century or even earlier. During the incipient decades of Vietnamese Theravāda Buddhism in the mid-twentieth century, some translations were made of Pāli-Khmer bitexts, with limited Pāli phrases retained in the Vietnamese (Hộ Tông 1965: 8).

Theravāda bitexts today

Bitexts remain alive and well today as tools for monastic study, exegetical commentary, and public sermons. Contemporary Thai scholars distinguish between the fixed translation style associated with bitexts, *plè toy byañjanaḥ* (translating the letters), and a more natural style, *plè toy apthaḥ* (translating the meaning; Assanee 2012: 7). The term *plè yak sʹab(d)* (translating by citing words) implies a bitext in which the vernacular portions match the *plè toy byañjanaḥ* style. A opening verse presented first in Pāli and then in a dissected and rearranged bitextual style may also be known in Thai as *cuṇṇīyapad* (Pāli **cuṇṇīyapada*, perhaps "words to be cut into pieces"). Contemporary Khmer terms equivalent to Thai *p̃lè yak s̃ăb(d)* include *prè ṭoy lök săbd* (translating by citing words) and *prè lot prayog* (translating by jumping phrases), the latter of which explicitly invokes the distinctive technique of syntactical rearrangement (Walker 2018a: 319). *Samrāy* is a more general term for Khmer translations from Pāli, whether in monolingual or bilingual format.

The introduction of new Pāli pedagogies in the twentieth century, alongside the rise of novel vernacular literary genres, lowered the prominence of bitexts in some Theravāda societies, although their aesthetic prestige remains current. New intellectual endeavors provided alternative modes of erudition, exegesis, and eloquence, ideals long rendered by the production and performance of bitexts. Yet the legacy of bilingual composition still binds together much of the written heritage of Theravāda Buddhism and challenges us to view Pāli scriptures and commentaries as dependent on a specific set of shared bitextual techniques for successful transmission and performance.

Acknowledgments

The author wishes to thank the editors as well as Anne Blackburn, Chenxing Han, and D. Christian Lammerts for their detailed feedback. Assanee Poolrak, Alastair Gornall, Santi Pakdeekham, Peter Skilling, Tossaphon Sripum, Hunter Watson, and David Wharton patiently answered a range of questions. Research for this chapter was supported by a postdoctoral fellowship from the Khyentse Foundation.

Manuscripts cited

DLNTM 011318001_01 (http://lannamanuscripts.net/en/manuscripts/4475)
DLNTM 011903027_00 (http://lannamanuscripts.net/en/manuscripts/3700)
DLNTM 070710018_00 (http://lannamanuscripts.net/en/manuscripts/5982)
FEMC C.77.VII (https://www.tbrc.org/#!rid=W1FEMC021140)
FEMC D.11.VII (https://www.tbrc.org/#!rid=W1FEMC021193)
PLMP 06018515002_02 (http://www.laomanuscripts.net/en/texts/930)
PLMP 08040102007_04 (http://laomanuscripts.net/en/texts/6166)
PNTMP 030306004_05 (http://lannamanuscripts.net/en/manuscripts/4990)
SRI 80.046.03.052-052 (http://www.sri.cmu.ac.th/~elanna/Microfilm/index/index2e.html)

References

Assanee, Poolrak. 2012. *Năndopanăndasūtr gāṃ hlvaṅ: kār vigroḥ(h) śilpaḥ kār p̃lè lèḥ kalavidhī dāṅ vap̃ṇaśil(p̃)*. MA thesis. Chulalongkorn University.

Baker, C., Phongpaichit, Pasuk. 2016. *The Palace Law of Ayutthaya and the Thammasat: Law and Kinship in Siam*. Ithaca: Southeast Asia Program Publications, Cornell University.

Bechert, H. 2005. *Eine regionale hochsprachliche Tradition in Südasien: Sanskrit-Literatur bei den buddhistischen Singhalesen*. Wien: Verlag der Österreichischen Akademie der Wissenschaften.

Blackburn, A. 2001. *Buddhist Learning and Textual Practice in 18th-Century Lankan Monastic Culture*. Princeton: Princeton University Press.

Blagden, C.O. 1960. *Epigraphia Birmanica: Being Lithic and Other Inscriptions of Burma*, ed. Charles Duroiselle, Vol. 1, Part II. Rangoon: Superintendent, Government Printing and Stationery, Union of Burma.

Chhom, Kunthea. 2016. *Le rôle du sanskrit dans le développement de la langue khmère: Une étude épigraphique du VIe au XIVe siècle*. PhD thesis. École Pratique des Hautes Études.

Dimitrov, D. 2006. "Bilingual Sanskrit-Tibetan Glosses in a Nepalese MS of the Ratnaśrīṭīkā." *Newsletter of the Nepalese-German Manuscript Cataloguing Project* 2: 4–7.
Dimitrov, D. 2016. *The Legacy of the Jewel Mind. On the Sanskrit, Pali, and Sinhalese Works by Ratnamati.* Naples: Università degli studi di Napoli 'L'Orientale'.
Duroiselle, C. 1913. "Talaing Nissayas." *Journal of the Burma Research Society* 3 (2): 103–145.
Enfield, N.J. 2019. *Mainland Southeast Asian Languages: A Concise Typological Introduction.* Cambridge: Cambridge University Press.
Gethin, R. 2007. "What's in a Repetition: On Counting the Suttas of the Saṃyutta-nikāya." *Journal of the Pali Text Society* 29: 365–387.
Godakumbura, C.E. 1955. *Sinhalese Literature.* Colombo: Colombo Apothecaries.
Gornall, A. 2017. "Ratnamati et ses oeuvres." *Bulletin de l'École française d'Extrême-Orient* 103: 475–491.
Gornall, A. 2020. *Rewriting Buddhism: Pali Literature and Monastic Reform in Sri Lanka, 1157–1270.* London: University College London Press.
Griffiths, A., Hudson, B., Miyake, M., Wheatley, J. 2017. "Studies in Pyu Epigraphy, I: State of the Field, Edition and Analysis of the Kan Wet Khaung Mound Inscription, and Inventory of the Corpus." *Bulletin de l'École française d'Extrême-Orient* 103: 43–205.
Gutschow, N., Michaels, A. 2005. *Handling Death: The Dynamics of Death and Ancestor Rituals Among the Newars of Bhaktapur, Nepal.* Wiesbaden: Harrassowitz Verlag.
Halliday, R. 1923. "Slapat Rājāwaṅ Datow Smiṅ roṅ—a History of Kings. With Text, Translation, and Notes." *Journal of the Burma Research Society* 13: 5–67.
Hộ Tông. 1965. *Quí-vởớng vân-đạo.* Saigon: Theravada phật-giáo nguyên-thuỷ.
Khin, Sok. 1999. *La grammaire du khmer moderne.* Paris: Éditions You-Feng.
Kieffer-Pülz, P. 2015. "Vinaya Commentarial Literature in Pali." In *Brill's Encyclopedia of Buddhism*, Vol. I, eds. J. Silk, et al., 430–441. Leiden: Brill.
Kornicki, P. 2018. *Languages, Scripts, and Chinese Texts in East Asia.* Oxford: Oxford University Press.
Lammerts, D.C. 2018. *Buddhist Law in Burma: A History of Dhammasattha Texts and Jurisprudence, 1250–1850.* Honolulu: University of Hawai'i Press.
Luce, G.H., Shin, B.B. 1969. "Old Burma: Early Pagán. Volume One: Text." *Artibus Asiae, Supplementum* 25: 1–422.
Maggi, M. 2015. "Local Literatures: Khotanese." In *Brill's Encyclopedia of Buddhism*, Vol. I, eds. J. Silk, et al., 860–870. Leiden: Brill.
McDaniel, J.T. 2008. *Gathering Leaves and Lifting Words: Histories of Buddhist Monastic Education in Laos and Thailand.* Seattle: University of Washington Press.
Okell, J. 1965. "Nissaya Burmese." *Lingua* 15: 186–227.
Peyrot, M. 2008. "More Sanskrit – Tocharian B bilingual Udānavarga fragments." *Indogermanische Forschungen* 113: 83–125.
Pruitt, W. 1994. *Étude linguistique de nissaya birmans.* Paris: École française d'Extrême-Orient.
Ruiz-Falqués, A. 2015. *A Firefly in the Bamboo Reed: The Suttaniddesa of Saddhammajotipāla and the Grammatical Foundations of Theravāda Buddhism in Burma.* PhD thesis. Cambridge.
Verhagen, P. 2013. "Notes Apropos to the Oeuvre of Si tu paṇ chen chos kyi 'byung gnas (1699?–1774) (4): A Tibetan Sanskritist in Nepal." *Journal of the International Association of Tibetan Studies* 7: 316–339.
Walker, T.T. 2018a. *Unfolding Buddhism: Communal Scripts, Localized Translations, and the Work of the Dying in Cambodian Chanted Leporellos.* PhD thesis. University of California, Berkeley.
Walker, T.T. 2018b. "Siamese Manuscripts in Cambodian Collections." In *Inventaire provisoire des manuscrits du Cambodge, deuxième partie*, eds. O. de Bernon, et al., xcv–cvi. Bangkok and Lumbini: Lumbini International Research Institute and Fragile Palm Leaves Foundation.

PART IV

Images/Imaginations

19

VISUAL NARRATIVES

Buddha life stories in the "medieval Theravāda" of Southeast Asia

Samerchai Poolsuwan

Introduction

Characterizing the cultural landscape of Southeast Asia during the second half of the first millennium CE, as attested archaeologically and palaeographically, was the dissemination of the type(s) of Buddhism, strictly Pāli-based in terms of scriptural citations, over the western and central spheres of its mainland, that is, including the Pyu and Mon civilizations in central and Lower Burma as well as the Dvārāvati cultural domain in central Thailand (Stargardt 1995: 199–213; Skilling 1997a: 83–107; Skilling 1997b: 123–157; Skilling 2003: 87–112; Revire 2014: 216–237). Although suggested to be somehow associated with Theravāda, the Buddhism of this case remains enigmatic in terms of its origin(s) as well as affiliation(s) with any of the variety of schools existing in the so-called Theravāda domain during the period of concern (Ray 1939: 1–52; Luce 1974: 119–138; Skilling 1997a: 83–107; Stadtner 2008: 193–215). Also, it could not be simply equated or directly linked—beside the common adoption of Pāli as the designated religious language, in terms of ecclesiastic genealogy, canonical, and commentarial basis as well as observance of the *vinaya* rules by monks and nuns—with the "Theravāda" made familiar nowadays. The latter, rather monolithic in all the aspects mentioned, is more or less a product of the major religious reform conducted in Sri Lanka around 1165 CE, during the reign of Parākramabāhu I of Polonnāruva; the reform orchestrated a scriptural purification and the unification of all the Buddhist fraternities of the island, bringing them to adhere strictly to the one, Mahāvihāra tradition (Bechert 1993: 11–21). The latter is believed by its followers to be the purest form of Buddhism—that is, descended directly from the Third Buddhist Council, sponsored by the Mauryan king Aśoka of India during the third century BCE—and this is confirmed in the two famous chronicles of the School, the *Dīpavaṃsa* and *Mahāvaṃsa* (Sirisena 1978, Chapter 3). Set as a "new normal" for the Buddhist definition of Dhamma and conduct, the reformed Sīhaḷa Theravāda has become cosmopolitan by means of attracting followers widely and more or less continuously for almost a millennium in the Theravāda realm, mainly encompassing Sri Lanka and the major part of mainland Southeast Asia (Sirisena 1978: 58–81; Frasch 1998: 69–92; Frasch 2001: 85–97).

Later Mon and Pāli records, the fifteenth-century Kalyānī inscriptions of Dhammaceti, king of Pegu (Bago), in what is now Lower Burma, suggest that the reformed Theravāda could have been introduced into Southeast Asia for establishing its monastic lineage and communities at

DOI: 10.4324/9781351026666-24

Pagan, shortly after its revival in Sri Lanka, during the second half of the twelfth century. This reformed Theravāda movement was spearheaded by a missionary team of senior monks from Sri Lanka—led by Chapata, a Mon native originally from Lower Burma—who later either passed away, left the Saṅgha, or was in disputes with the other members of the team over observance of some *vinaya* rules. The phenomenon suggests that the reformed Sīhaḷa Theravāda, newly introduced to Pagan, did not survive for long. Prior to the period of concern, Pagan, with its civilization flourishing in Central Burma from around the mid-eleventh century, could have received its Pāli-based Buddhism first, as suggested by some later Burmese records, from the Mon center in Lower Burma, along with the latter's orthographic legacy, and perhaps also from Pyu progenitors (Luce 1969: vol. I, Chapters II–IV; Than Tun 1988: 23–45); the latter's knowledge of the Pāli sources is attested archaeologically (Stargardt 1995: 199–213; Skilling 1997a: 83–107). There was also, shortly afterward in the same century, as recorded in the *Cūḷavaṃsa*, an allied contact which could have allowed direct scriptural transmission from Sri Lanka to Pagan (Luce 1969: vol. I, 38–43). Propagation of the reformed Theravāda at Pagan during the second half of the twelfth century hints that the older Theravāda existing there might have been perceived, at least in the eyes of the Mahāvihāra reformists, as corrupt or far from uniform; from this perspective, the introduction of the "purer" form of the Buddhism was really a call to action.

The nature of the old Theravāda flourishing at Pagan prior to the coming of the reformed Sīhaḷa tradition during the second half of the twelfth century remains unclear. Being probably derived from the Mon and Pyu progenitors, on one hand, it could have been affiliated with the older Pāli-based Buddhism prevailing in the western sphere of mainland Southeast Asia during the first millennium CE.[1] On the other hand, a new influx of Buddhist tradition(s) through direct contact with Sri Lanka toward the end of the eleventh century could have added to the Theravāda variation or amalgamation characterizing the early Buddhist culture of Pagan.

There appears to have existed in Upper Burma a derivative of this old Theravāda that gained in popularity and royal patronage at Pagan during the thirteenth century. A number of epigraphic records of the period describe its ecclesiastic members as the monks of "*taw kloṅ*" (forest monastery); occasionally, the name "Arañ," most likely derived from *araññaka*, meaning "forest dwellers," was applied to them (Than Tun 1988: 85–100). The existence of *bhikkhunīs* and the laxity in the observance of some *vinaya* rules, in contrast to the reformed Sīhaḷa standard, was allowed in this Buddhist order. Also characterizing their establishment was the accumulation of wealth in terms of land estates, received either by donation or purchase. The rising and flourishing of the Arañ Buddhist *nikāya* in central Burma was the background to several attempts of reintroducing the reformed Sīhaḷa tradition of Buddhism to Pagan by successive groups of missionary monks (Frasch 1998: 69–97; Frasch 2001: 85–97; Gornall 2020: Chapter 10). However, none of them seemed to achieve enduring success over the Arañ. Deviation of the latter from the reformed Sīhaḷa orthodoxy is also confirmed by another, external but contemporaneous, piece of evidence contained in the *Mahānāgakula-sandesa*, a Pāli work composed in Sri Lanka during the mid-thirteenth century. It is a message from Thera Nāgasena of Rohana, in the south of Sri Lanka, sent to Thera Mahākassapa of Arimaddanapura (Pagan) inviting the latter, who was most likely the elder of the Arañ ecclesiastic lineage known under that very same name in inscriptions of the period, to initiate purification of the religion by following the reformed orthodoxy established in Sri Lanka during the reign of Parākramabāhu I (Sirisena 1978: 72–73; Gornall 2020: 215–20). The Sīhaḷa proposal of reform, however, may have failed given the fact that the Arañ maintained its prosperity and conventions at Pagan and elsewhere in central Burma until well after 1500, far beyond the Pagan period, as confirmed by a number of contemporaneous records (Than Tun 1988: 85–100).

Art historical evidence suggests that the Pagan-type of Buddhism could have been disseminated in the Buddhist network of Southeast Asia to cover the western and central spheres of its mainland, that is, Central and Lower Burma as well as northern and Central Thailand, prior to wide spreading of the post-reform Sīhaḷa orthodoxy newly introduced into the area from around the early fourteenth century onward (Samerchai Poolsuwan n.d.). In particular, the area of central Burma dominated by the Arañ seems to have staved off for more than a century the advance of the new Sīhaḷa orthodoxy. A major obstacle to the dissemination of the reformed Theravāda in Southeast Asia—from its inception in Sri Lanka around 1165 CE until the fourteenth century and well after, amid several reintroductions of the Buddhist tradition into the region—could have been the persistence of the matrix of interrelated local varieties of Pāli-based Buddhism. It is this matrix that I call here the "medieval Theravāda" of Southeast Asia. Probably most influential among these Pāli Buddhist traditions was that at Pagan, given its association with this major civilization that dominated the western sphere of the region, and probably, although to a lesser extent, its central sphere as well, from the mid-eleventh to the late thirteenth century.

This chapter attempts to understand the Buddhism of Pagan by exploring its mural traditions; these are seen as material manifestations of textual foundations as deployed within a specific cultural context. It will give particular focus to the illustration of the Buddha's life, which forms the most prominent narrative theme of the murals. Adorning the brick monument of the *gu-hpaya* (cave-temple) type, with hundreds of examples surviving in the Pagan area and as well the isolated clusters located in the middle Irrawaddy zone, the murals of the Pagan tradition, dating from the late eleventh to the late thirteenth century, constitute one of the largest and most complex bodies of Buddhist sacred art in existence. One of the major characteristics of the murals of the period, and in a broader sense of the Buddhist art of Pagan in general, is their strong affiliation, in iconographic and stylistic terms, with the postclassical center of Sanskrit Buddhism flourishing in northeastern India during the Pāla dynasty (from the eighth to the twelfth century), outside the Theravāda-dominated cultural realm (Luce 1969: vol. I, part B; Bautze-Picron 2003). At the same time, they show a strong connection, particularly in terms of visual narratives, with Pāli Buddhist literature (Luce 1969: Vol. I, Chapters XV–XIX; Ba Shin and Bohmu 1962; Samerchai Poolsuwan 2017: 255–294). The combination of these two major characteristics—which are not in concert conceptually and, as such, give the murals of Pagan their unique status—is puzzling in itself and requires a causative explanation in both cultural and political terms. The conceptual framing of my investigation seeks both to provide the murals with their appropriate textual background and to uncover their structural organization and associated symbolism. The broader aim is to enhance our understanding of the nature of the "medieval Theravāda," with Pagan providing one of its best-known examples. The present study shall also examine the downfall of Pagan Buddhism from the shadow cast on the art historical ground, particularly the decline of its mural tradition. This could have corresponded with the new influx of post-reform Theravāda from Sri Lanka into Southeast Asia from the early fourteenth century onward.

Visualization of the "Buddha's life" in early Pagan

Aside from being engrossed in the Dhamma and its associated philosophy expounded voluminously in early Pāli Buddhist literature, devoted followers of Buddhism could have found themselves to learn only little and fragmentarily about the personal life of the present Buddha Gotama, who had laid down the foundation of the teachings (Pande 1975; Rhys Davids 1975: 56; Winternitz 1977: 186). The narration of the Buddha's life has, however, played a major role in Buddhist art since its inception.[2] The only parallel to be found is in the subsequent stratum of Buddhist literature with its praise texts elaborately celebrating the Buddha's accumulation of *pāramī* (perfections) during his previous lives and episodes of his last existence leading to the most important episode of all, the Buddha's enlightenment. The *Lalitavistara* and, in a less orderly manner, the *Mahāvastu* comprise the major Sanskrit or hybrid Buddhist Sanskrit examples in this respect. Their Pāli counterpart could be found in *Nidānakathā*, the beginning part of the *Jātaka* commentary (*Jātakaṭṭhakathā*; for an English translation, see Jayawickrama 1990).

The latter Pāli source presents Gotama's story in three successive sections: the *Dūrenidāna*, the *Avidūrenidāna*, and the *Santikenidāna*. Contained in the first are stories of Gotama's previous existences in the course of four *asaṅkheyya* (incalculable number of eons) and a hundred thousand eons, during which he received the prediction of his future enlightenment from the twenty-four Buddhas of the past, that is, Dīpaṅkara and those subsequent Buddhas in chronological order; the future Buddha was afterward reborn as a chief *deva* of Tusitā Heaven. The *Avidūrenidāna* extends the Buddha's story to cover the early episodes of his last rebirth, as Prince Siddhattha, up to the moment of his enlightenment. As indicated in the text itself, the *Santikenidāna* is supposed to include episodes, taking place at various specific localities, from immediately after enlightenment to the moment of final departure, the *mahāparinibbāna*; in the *Nidānakathā*, however, it covers chronologically only from the seven weeks of meditation immediately following enlightenment to the Buddha's reception of the Jetavana Monastery donated by the rich man of Savatthi, Anāthapiṇḍika, in the third year after the enlightenment.

It is interesting to note that the *Nidānakathā* recognizes the core content of the text to which it belongs, that is, the account of the selected 547 stories of the Buddha's past lives, to also constitute another narrative theme of the *Santikenidāna* (a collection of the Buddha's stories after the enlightenment). This could be made logical given the notion clearly stated in the text that all these *jātaka* stories were individually told by the Buddha himself in a number of his preaching occasions, taking place at various specific localities, after the enlightenment. Since all the *jātaka* stories are grouped on the basis of their length, with the number of canonical stanza(s) describing each *jātaka* story, their organization in the text is not necessarily chronological.

Visualized in the earliest surviving murals at Pagan—those found adorning the interior of the Pātho-htā-mya Temple (monument 1605), dating probably from the last quarter of the eleventh century (Luce 1969: vol. 1, 302–303)—are complicated themes of the Buddha stories combined to account for a complete biography of Gotama in his last existence. The east-facing temple is a large and complicated brick structure with a square sanctum surrounded by a dark ambulatory corridor, housing a triad of colossal Buddha images made of brick and stucco. Access to the shrine could be made from the temple's entrance hall only through the passage cutting across the sanctum's corridor on its eastern side (for the architecture and layout of the temple see Pichard, Vol. VI 1995: 244–248). The murals of focus embellish the whole interior of the temple's sanctum and its surrounding corridor. Successfully identified by Professor Gordon H. Luce, the doyen of Pagan studies, is the series of narrative murals on the corridor's outer wall, with ink captions in Old Mon surviving to identify some of the narrative scenes; most likely based on the *Nidānakathā* account, the mural series, comprising twenty-four panels, proceeds clockwise from its start located in the east wall's southern section to chronologically accommodate narration of the early episodes of the Gotama's last existence up to the moment before his enlightenment, when the *bodhisatta* is approaching the Bodhi tree (Luce 1969: vol. I, 304–305). To complement Luce's study, I have reinvestigated the series of narrative murals of the corridor's inner wall, of which previous studies have led to confusion (Luce 1969: vol. I, 305; Bautze-Picron 2003: 158), to confirm that they are programmed to continue the outer-wall series; the inner-wall series, comprising twenty-eight panels (Figure 19.1), presents Gotama's

Figure 19.1 The Buddha's meditation (from right to left) during the second and third weeks after the enlightenment, second panel, inner wall series of the Buddha's life, Pātho-htā-mya.

All photographs included in this essay are by the author.

biography chronologically from the very moment of his enlightenment to his *mahāparinibbāna*, depicted as the last episode of the series (Samerchai Poolsuwan 2017: 258–266).

In total, the Pātho-htā-mya's corridor murals thus account for the stories belonging to the *Avidūrenidāna* and *Santikenidāna* sections of Gotama's biography, based on the *Nidānakathā*'s narrative categorization, however, with substantial extension (Samerchai Poolsuwan 2017: 258–266). It is unfortunate that the murals of the first three panels of the outer wall series—located on the corridor's eastern side, immediately after the entrance passage—are too damaged to allow any precise episodic identification. Located just before the episode of Gotama's birth, the three panels likely included the depiction of (1) "the first prophecy," when the *bodhisatta* as Hermit Sumedha receives the prediction for his enlightenment to come from the Buddha Dīpaṅkara; (2) the *bodhisatta* reborn as a chief *deva* of the Tusitā Heaven; and (3) the conception of the *bodhisatta* in the womb of Queen Māyā. If this interpretation is correct, the narrative murals of the Pātho-htā-mya's corridor series would have also accounted for the *Dūrenidāna*, although only briefly so in representation of the first two narrative panels of the mural series.

There are several series of complicated murals narrating the after-enlightenment life of the Buddha in the Pātho-htā-mya's sanctum. The mural scenes, each contained in a rectangular frame, are all inscribed; and the majority of them, however, are made repetitive in terms of their iconographic composition, with the Buddha in a seated posture flanked on both sides by his disciples. Based on Luce's systematic reading of the ink glosses accompanying the mural scenes, we can identify the narrative organization to comprise the following themes: (1) a series of selected episodes, probably based on the *Nidānakathā*, from the first sermon up to the Buddha's visit to the city of his father, Kapilavatthu (panels nos. 25–35 in Luce 1969: vol. I, 306); (2) miscellaneous post-enlightenment episodes that are not accounted for in the *Nidānakathā*, with only some of them arranged chronologically (scenes (i)—(xi) in Luce 1969: vol. I, 306–307); (3) a voluminous series of the Buddha's sermons grouped according to the *Dīghanikāya* and *Majjhimanikāya* of the Pāli *Suttapiṭaka* (Luce 1969: vol. I, 307–308); and (4) a series of incidents leading the Buddha to lay down the *Vinaya* rules for the *saṅgha* categorized according to the *Mahāvibhaṅga* account of the Pāli *Vinayapiṭaka*, to include the latter's following sections: *Saṅghādisesa*, *Aniyata*, *Nissaggiya*, *Pācittiya*, and probably *Pārājikā* (Luce 1969: vol. I, 308–309). The surviving ink glosses include a description of the event in question as well as the name of the specific locality where the event took place. Given the unarbitrary provision of such information, the mural series must be understood to logically follow the *Nidānakathā*'s tradition of creating the *Santikenidāna* narration of the Buddha's life. As guided by the text itself, the narration aims at selecting the episodes of the Buddha, of which the localities are all specified, to thematically constitute a variety of narrative collections all aimed at representing his life after enlightenment.

Another pertinent example is found at the Kubyauk-gyī Temple in Myinkaba (monument 1323), the construction of which is epigraphically attributed to Rājakumār during the first quarter of the twelfth century (Luce, Ba Shin, and Bohmu 1961: 277–284). Here, a complete series of the 547 stories of the *Jātakā*, largely in agreement with the Sīhaḷa recension, is depicted on the outer wall of the temple's ambulatory corridor (Luce and Ba Shin 1961: 331–362); since the depiction is presented as narrating the *Jātakā* itself—with an accompanying ink gloss giving the Pāli name and the *bodhisatta* of the story but not noting the occasion upon which the Buddha is telling the story—the narration may have represented the *Dūrenidāna* instead of the *Santikenidāna*. Arranged along the topmost row of the corridor's outer wall is the illustrative series comprising an elaborate narration of the whole *Nidānakathā* series of the *Avidūrenidāna* and *Santikenidāna* (Luce and Ba Shin 1961: 363–366). The *Nidānakathā*'s criterion for the *Santikenidāna*, thematically presenting the episodes that took place at various specific localities after enlightenment, was also probably adopted for the Buddha's preaching of the *Vinaya* rules, which took place in the seven chief cities, grouped and serially narrated in the murals of the upper register of the panels on the corridor's inner wall (Luce and Ba Shin 1961: 377–379).

The Buddha's realm created

The cult and iconography associated with the "Eight Major Episodes" of the Buddha's life were gradually developed in the Mahāyāna context of northeastern India during the Gupta and Pāla dynasties (Perimoo 1982; Huntington 1985: 46–61; Huntington 1987a: 55–63; Huntington 1987b: 56–68). They comprise (1) Nativity at Lumbinī; (2) Enlightenment at the Bodhi-tree, in now Bodhgaya; (3) First Sermon to the Pañcavaggiyā at the Isipatana Forest, near Varanasi; (4) Taming of Nālāgiri at Rājagaha; (5) Twin Miracles in Sāvatthi; (6) Descent from Tāvatiṃsa at Saṅkassa; (7) Monkey's Donation of Honey, probably in Vesāli (Huen Tsiang 1884: 68); and (8) Mahāparinibbāna in Kusinārā. Forming a coherent series, these episodes that took place at different localities showcase the complete biography of Gotama during his last existence, although in abbreviated form. Viewed from the context of sacred Buddhist geography, they were also linked with the establishment of the memorial sites for pilgrimage (Huntington 1987a: 55–63). Based on the standard iconography established during the Pāla dynasty, the "Eight Major Events" series of the Buddha is portrayed sculpturally with the central Buddha icon—normally made seated in the earth-touching pose under the Bodhi-tree, to signify enlightenment—flanked vertically on both sides, in a more or less symmetric fashion, and capped with smaller icons illustrating the other episodes of the series (Huntington 1987b: 56–68). The events are likewise depicted as a series in the period palm-leaf manuscripts of the *Aṣṭasāhasrikā Prajñāpāramitā*, the core text of Mahāyāna Buddhism (see examples in Saraswati 1977).

The Indian prototype of the Buddha's "Eight Major Events" eventually proved its popularity at Pagan by being prolifically, and almost faithfully, reproduced in both sculptural and mural forms. One major difference between the early Pagan examples and the Indian prototype concerns the iconography of the "Monkey's Donation" scene in which an elephant is additionally incorporated; this is most likely to allow its narrative compatibility with the Pārileyya episode, which took place near Kosambī, as described in the Pāli *Dhammapada* commentary. Given that all the other episodes of the series, apart from the "Monkey's Donation," could conveniently reference Pāli canonical and commentarial sources, it seems likely that Pagan's "Eight Major Events" series, although modeled after the Indian precursor, was perceived in the Theravādin literary context (Samerchai Poolsuwan 2017: 255–294). Early examples of Pagan murals illustrating the "Eight Major Events" of the Buddha under such iconographic and literary prescription are seen in the background of principal Buddha images representing the Buddha's enlightenment episode in Pagan temples 1580 (Loka-hteik-pan), 2103, and 2157, all dating probably from the first half of the twelfth century (Figure 19.2).[3]

One of the novel characteristics observed in the Buddhist art of Pagan is the combination of the Buddha's "Eight Major Events" series, as already described, with the other set of his serial episodes most likely derived from the *Jātakanidāna* account of his meditation during the "Seven Weeks" immediately following enlightenment. In its standard sculptural form, the earth-touching Buddha centering the composition represents simultaneously his enlightenment and first-week meditation; he is then vertically flanked in the inner circle of the composition with the other six-week meditation episodes—three on each side, in a more or less symmetric fashion (see examples in Luce 1969: vol. III, plates 401, 402b, 403 and 405). The iconographic arrangement thus suggests symbolization of the Buddha geography, a kind of Theravāda mandala, with the Bodhi-tree for together the Buddha's enlightenment and first-week meditation centering the two sacred geographic spheres: the inner sphere encompassing all the meditation stations, including the Bodhi-tree and its neighborhoods; and the outer containing the localities of his "Eight Major Events," all included within the Middle Country (Majjhimadesa) of the Great Southern Continent (Jambudīpa).

Associated with the previously described geographic symbolism, the "Eight Major Events" are juxtaposed with the "Seven Weeks" meditation series in the temple murals prevalent at Pagan during the thirteenth century (Samerchai Poolsuwan 2012: 377–397). The colossal sculpture presiding over a temple shrine—normally seated in the earth-touching pose, with the Bodhi-tree always depicted in the background—could symbolically represent the Buddha's enlightenment and his meditation in the following week. Portrayed in the temple murals to spatially encircle this cult image are, in the inner circle, the other episodes of the "Seven Weeks" series and, in the outer circle, the other "Eight Major Events" (Figures 19.3 and 19.4).

It is thus natural to find the enlightenment and first-week meditation of the Buddha always absent in mural representations. The depictions of the "Seven Stations" are always spatially arranged in the temple's shrine in such a fashion to best represent their directions from

Figure 19.2 "Eight Major Events" of the Buddha, Loka-hteik-pan temple (from top to bottom and left to right): Mahāparinibbāna (1st tier, damaged); coming versus departure of Māra, for the Enlightenment of the Buddha, also represented by the cult image itself (second tier); Taming of Nālāgiri versus Descent from Tavatiṃsa (third tier); First Sermon versus Twin Miracle (fourth tier); and Pārileyya versus Nativity (5th tier).

the Bodhi-tree, symbolized at the center of the temple's shrine. This could be based on the geographic descriptions of the "Seven Stations" contained in two commentarial sources: the *Nidānakathā* and the *Samantapāsādikā*. Numerous examples of the mural pattern could be found in Pagan, with one large cluster of them also located in Minnanthu,[4] the headquarters of the Arañ *nikāya* during the period of concern.

Also novel to Pagan during the thirteenth century, and truly extraordinary in its own way, is another mural program designed to serve the same symbolic function of creating the Buddha's realm. This second case, however, illustrates the Buddha's life more lavishly, with varieties of the other Buddha's episodes also incorporated. Only three representatives of the mural program have survived, in Pagan temples 85 (Thein-mazi temple), 658, and 659 (Winido temple);[5] the execution of the murals in these three sites is nearly identical, suggesting that they were made by the same group of designer(s) and craftsmen. Decorating the temple's square shrine that houses the principal Buddha image(s) in the earth-touching pose, the murals of focus occupy the wall space of the shrine, all gridded, only vertically along the lower half of its four corners; this is to leave most of the wall space to accommodate repetitive depiction of the past Buddhas,

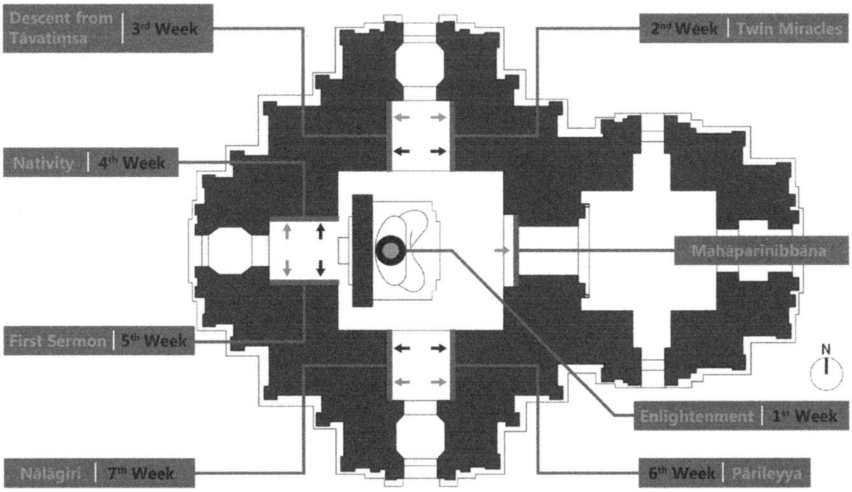

Figure 19.3 Symbolic arrangement of the cult images and the murals to represent "Majjhimadesa," centered at Bodhgaya, modeled after Pagan temple 664: "Seven Stations" in the inner circle and "Eight Stations" in the outer circle.

Figure 19.4 Twin Miracle at Sāvatthi (left) vis-à-vis Second Week Meditation at Animisa Cetiya (right), east wall of the north vestibule, Pagan temple 539.

each contained in a grid cell. There are eight mural panels, each with two or three columns of grid cells, illustrating Gotama's life. Based on the surviving ink glosses and iconographic composition, most of the mural scenes could be definitively identified (Samerchai Poolsuwan 2017: 255–294).

There are all together eighty mural cells to accommodate the narrative depiction of the Buddha's life; only some of them are arranged to depict the chronological events of the Buddha, while others contain independent episodes. Overall, the episodes are grouped according to locality. We see[6] twelve independent episodes at Rājagaha (E-wall, NE-corner), twelve serial episodes before the enlightenment at Uruvela (E-wall, SE-corner), eight serial episodes of Sujata preparing the cow-milk rice also at Uruvela (S-wall, SW-corner), eight serial episodes after the enlightenment at the residence of the Uruvela-Kassapa hermit (W-wall, SW-corner), eight serial episodes related to the Twin Miracle at Sāvatthi (W-wall, NW-corner), eight episodes before and after the enlightenment at Kapilavatthu (N-wall, NW-corner), and two independent episodes after the enlightenment at Vesāli (N-wall, NE-corner). The "Seven Weeks" serial episodes are separated into two groups: (1) the second to fourth weeks—at the stations to the northeast, north, and northwest of the Bodhi-tree—located on the N-wall of the shrine's NE-corner, and (2) the fifth to seventh weeks—at the stations to the east, southeast, and south of the Bodhi-tree—located on the S-wall of the shrine's NE-corner. This arrangement of the "Seven Weeks" stations likely represents the various sites' geographic directions with respect to the Bodhi-tree, based on indications in the *Jātakanidāna* and *Samantapāsādikā*. The "Eight Major Events" are dispersed here, in the shrine according to their locality, as described above, or in the temple vestibules. As usual, the Buddha's enlightenment and first-week meditation, represented by the shrine's central cult image, is omitted in the mural representation

The rise of the new Sīhaḷa order

It was toward the end of the thirteenth century that the Pagan dynasty practically lost its political hold over central Burma, due to the Mongol attack and subsequent internal discord (Than Tun 1988: 103–114). A century of war and political unrest followed, badly affecting religious activities, construction, and artistic creation that had formerly been prolific in the area. Epigraphic evidence shows that the Arañ Buddhist *nikāya* endured through this difficult time to resume its prosperity toward the end of the fourteenth century. Historian Than Tun has proposed that the monks of this Buddhist order—led by generations of strong successive leaders (after Mahākassapa), also making themselves suitable for royal patronage during the Pinya and Ava periods—played a pivotal role in revitalizing the farming activities of the area (Than Tun 1988: 103–114). This was based on recultivation of the land estates on a large scale—land either previously belonging to or newly acquired by them. The resource basis may have sufficiently supported the establishment and thus enhanced the continuity in central Burma of the Arañ Buddhist tradition. Affiliation of probably the later Arañ with the older art of Pagan is detectable in the persistence of several of the latter's elements and characteristics in the murals of Pagan monument 225 (an old brick monastery, currently named "Mya-daung-ok-kyaung," located in the Nyaung-U area to the north of the Old Pagan City), dated epigraphically to 1442 CE, as well those of Pagan monument 65 (a man-made meditation cave, currently named "Kyanzittha Umin," also located in Nyaung-U) stylistically dated to be a contemporary of monument 225 (Samerchai Poolsuwan 2015: 145–197).

Marking a watershed in the history of Theravāda in Southeast Asia was the rapid expansion, during the course of the fourteenth century, of the post-reform Sīhaḷa orthodoxy, freshly introduced from Sri Lanka into the region (Sirisena 1978: Chapters III–IV). This was to launch a firm establishment of the Theravāda orthodoxy, standardized after the reformed Sīhaḷa model, to be continuously preserved and transmitted in the geographic region up to our present time. Probably spearheading this religious movement—as recorded in the two northern Thai chronicles, *Mūlasāsanā* and *Jinakālamālī*—was the establishment, in 1331 CE, of the post-reform Sīhaḷa monastic center in Martaban, located in the Mon Country of Lower Burma. This center was founded by Udumbarapupphā Mahāsāmī, a senior *Thera* from the well-known Udumbaragiri Forest Monastery, a Mahāvihāra branch located south of Poḷonnāruva in Sri Lanka (Griswold and Prasert na Nagara 1972: 21–152). The tradition was later introduced—by a missionary team led by his disciples, Anomadassī and Sumana—to Sukhothai, probably from around 1341–1342 CE, and then Lanna from about 1369 CE onward. Sukhothai Inscription 2 also gives a lengthy account of another charismatic monk, Śrīśraddhārājacūḷamuni, who might have played a seminal role in germinating the new Sīhaḷa Buddhist tradition in the soil of Sukhothai. This was to happen after his long journey, first via Martaban and India to obtain reordination and follow a long course of study in a post-reform Mahāvihāra establishment in Sri Lanka. Around 1343–1344 CE, he returned to Sukhothai via Tenasserim, Phetchaburī, Rātchaburī, Nakhon Chaisri, and Ayodhyā (Griswold and Prasert na Nagara 1972: 21–152; see also Blackburn and Thompson in this volume, including on dating). His complicated routes reflect networks of communication between several Buddhist centers, including those located in Central Thailand.

Also recorded in the *Jinakālamālī* was the arrival, during the mid-1420s, of a missionary team of monks to launch the *upasampadā* (ordination) of the new Sīhaḷa order at Ayutthaya in central Thailand, in which Mahāthera Sīlavisuddhi, the tutor of the chief queen of king Boromarājā II of Ayutthayā (1424–1448 CE), and another *Thera* named Saddhammakōvida, received higher ordination (Ratanapaññā Thera 1968). This very king was the founder of Wat Rātchaburana established in the same decade (Khamhaikān Chāo-Krung-Kao 1967: 446). I describe in the following an important set of murals of the Buddha's life commissioned during the king's reign to adorn the interior of the crypt inside Wat Rātchaburana's main tower. Showing strong affiliation with the tradition and style of Sri Lankan Buddhist art, as opposed to Pagan's preexisting in the region, these murals appear to be a product of direct religious contact between Ayutthaya and the motherland of the new Sīhaḷa order during this decade.

Sunk deep in the mass of brick and laterite foundation of Wat Rātchaburana's main tower is a series of crypt chambers vertically arranged to house the relic(s) of the Buddha and various other sacred and auspicious objects. While most of these objects were looted in the twentieth century, the crypt's murals survive almost intact. At the most basic level, the symbolic murals representing the Buddha's life story adorning the crypt meant to house Buddha relics have their roots in the Sīhaḷa Buddhist tradition; this basic association of representing the Buddha's life story and relics is confirmed scripturally in the *Mahāvaṃsa* account (Geiger 1912: Chapter XXX), as well as archaeologically (Bandaranayake 2006: 73–79). On stylistic grounds, the Rātchaburana murals can also be perceived as closely related to Sri Lanka's long-standing traditions (Samerchai Poolsuwan 2014: 27–65). This is opposed to the Pagan example that, although adopting principally Pāli textual reference also most likely from Sri Lanka, is affiliated on stylistic and iconographic grounds with older Indian prototypes.

Three main narrative themes are found in these crypt murals: (1) a number of *jātaka* stories—although most likely selected from the Pāli *Jātakaṭṭhakathā*, with no accompanying inscriptional records—most could not be precisely identified; (2) a chronological series of the twenty-four past Buddhas, with their names all inscribed in conformity with the Pāli *Buddhavaṃsa* text; and (3) a detailed biography of Gotama in his last existence, most likely based on the *Jātakanidāna* and other Pāli texts (Samerchai Poolsuwan 2014: 27–65). Identifiable on iconographic grounds are the murals belonging to the last narrative theme, illustrating the following Gotama's episodes:

conception in the womb of Queen Maya; Nativity (probably—scene much eroded); the four treasure troops to miraculously come into existence at the time of the Gotama's birth; horse Kanthaka and his driver, Channa, in sorrow after leaving the *bodhisatta*; the Buddha's enlightenment and first-week meditation, represented by the same mural scene; the following six weeks of meditation scenes, each individually depicted; first sermon at Isipatana; taming of the Nālāgiri elephant; Pārileyya episode, with only the elephant present, probably based on the Pāli *Vinaya-Mahāvagga*; the *mahāparinibbāna*; and one out-group, a depiction of the Buddha's footprint enshrined on top of Sumana Mountain in Sri Lanka (Figure 19.5).

Although there are a number of scenes depicting the Buddha's activities that could not be precisely identified on iconographic grounds, none is compatible with the illustration of the Buddha descending from Tāvatiṃsa, normally executed in an easily recognizable composition. Thus, the murals are not intended to incorporate the complete "Eight Major Events" of the Buddha, the highly popular series seen in Pagan. In general, the Rātchaburana crypt-murals could be considered to represent a separate mural tradition, which, apart from sharing the same source of Pāli textual reference, has only a trivial connection with its preceding counterpart evidenced at Pagan (Samerchai Poolsuwan 2014: 27–65).

Figure 19.5 Buddha footprint on the summit of the Sumana Mountain in Sri Lanka, Rātchaburana's crypt murals.

Discussion

Thus far, I have demonstrated that the Pagan tradition of narrating the Buddha's life, as illustrated in the murals of the period, was primarily based on the standard Pāli canonical and commentarial sources. Although the Pāla iconographic elements—arisen in the Mahāyāna realm of northeastern India, centered spiritually at Bodhgaya—are noticeable in the murals of the period, likely they were also reinterpreted to suit Pagan's Theravādin context. That the murals of Pagan, and in the wider context, Pagan's art in general, take a strongly Pāla-inspired form is remarkable in itself, and it could have been somehow associated with Pagan's perception of the supremacy of Bodhgaya, the very spot of the Buddha's enlightenment. The symbolism evidenced in the structural organization of the Pagan murals, particularly during the thirteenth century, as detailed above, demonstrates this point. The phenomenon could be associated with a symbolic transposition of Buddhist spirituality from Bodhgaya—at that time entering a period of total decline due to severe Muslim attacks—to Pagan, then perceived as a new spiritual center reaching its supremacy in the Buddhist World.[7]

What seems to be extraordinary in textual terms at Pagan—also evidenced in the murals of the period, particularly during the thirteenth century—is the narration of stories that are not contained in any standard canonical or commentarial Pāli sources. Included in the murals of Pagan temple 585, located in Minnanthu, is an inscribed depiction of a young child, king Aśoka in his previous existence, donating a handful of dust for alms to the Gotama Buddha (Figure 19.6);[8] while the story could find a remote origin in an older Sanskrit text, the *Aśokāvadāna*, the mural narration might be derived from the more immediate source of the *Lokapaññatti*, an old Pāli work believed to be composed either in Burma or Sri Lanka (Saddhammaghosa Thera 1985: 96–97).

Depicted in the thirteenth-century murals of the Pagan tradition in temple number 69 in Sale is a serial narrative of three remote existences of Gotama: as a hermit teacher, jumping off the cliff to sacrifice his body to a tigress who was starving enough to swallow her own cubs; as a ship captain saving his mother from a shipwreck by carrying her on his shoulder while swimming in the ocean; and as a princess *bodhisatta* encountering Buddha Dīpaṅkara in his previous existence (Figure 19.7).

Although the first narrative could find its corresponding source in the Sanskrit *Jātakamālā* text (Āryaśūra 1971: 3–8), its inclusion in the series together with the other two *jataka* stories, both too remote to be accounted for in the standard Pāli *Jātaka* narration, more likely suggests the immediate source of the series to be derived from an old Pāli work, the *Sotaṭṭhakīmahānidāna*.[9] Being neither canonical nor commentarial in its own right, the latter text was composed by a *Thera* named Buddhaghosa at an unknown date, presumably in Sri Lanka; the text is, however, stated in the *Gandhavaṃsa*, a seventeenth-century Pāli work composed in Burma, to be authored by Cullabuddhaghosa, with a prefix used probably to distinguish him from the famous Buddhaghosa of the fifth century CE (Cullabuddhaghosa 1983: [14]–[37]; Minayef 1886: 63). The latter text provides a chronological narration of Gotama's previous and last existences—perceived in the text's own temporal framework, in contrast to the *Jātakanidāna*'s—to span the period of twenty *asaṅkheyya* and a hundred thousand eons, during which the *bodhisatta* had encountered in successive order the innumerable past Buddhas (see also Skilling 1996: 151–183; Derris 2000). With such temporal extension added to the narration of the *bodhisatta*'s path, the text is not strictly made to conform to the Pāli canonical-commentarial sources, that is, the *Jātaka-Jātakaṭṭhakathā* and the *Buddhavaṃsa-Madhuratthavilāsinī*.

Also evidenced in the murals of Pagan temple 447 (Le-myet-hna)—established in 1223 CE in Minnanthu, the Arañ's headquarters—is an inscriptional record providing some biographic

Figure 19.6 A young child Piyadassī, King Aśoka in his previous existence, donating a handful of dust for alms to Buddha Gotama, Pagan temple 585.

details on the first three Buddhas (Taṇhaṅkara, Medhaṅkara and Saraṇaṅkara) of the *Buddhavaṃsa* series, details not accounted for in the *Buddhavaṃsa* text itself, but found recorded instead in the *Sotaṭṭhakī* (Ba Shin and Bohmu 1962: 159–160). In the inscription of 1388 CE—located in Kyaukyit, Central Burma—we find a legendary account of Mahākassapa, the elder of the Arañ Buddhist *nikāya* during the thirteenth century, to contain the story, most likely derived from *Sotaṭṭhakī*, of the ten *bodhisattas* who shall become the future Buddhas after Gotama, of which one is equated with the previous existence of Mahākassapa himself (Than Tun 1988: 98). The text is also included in a 1442 CE epigraphic list of Buddhist scriptures donated to a monastery

Figure 19.7 Gotama in his remote existences, probably based on the *Sotaṭṭhakīmahānidāna* account (temple number 69 at Sale; from left to right): a hermit teacher sacrificing himself for a starving tigress; encounter of the ship's captain, who is saving his mother in the shipwreck, with the Mahābrahma God; encounter of the princess bodhisatta with Dīpaṅkara in his previous existence, a disciple of Buddha Purāna Dīpaṅkara; and Dīpaṅkara (in the same existence) obtaining a prediction for his enlightenment to come from Purāna Dīpaṅkara.

library in Pagan (Tun Nyein 1899: 37–47). These later pieces of evidence confirm continuity of the *Sotaṭṭhakī* knowledge, in the Buddhist context of Pagan until well after its dynastic period.

Approval in the Buddhist context of central Burma of some "unconventional" Pāli texts—bearing Buddhist narratives deviating from or not contained in the established canonical and commentarial Pāli sources constituting the core scriptures of the reformed Theravāda—could be logically considered another characteristic of the "medieval Theravāda" prevailing in the area, with the Arañ as its major known representative. In the broader context, the phenomenon might also provide a glimpse of the literary atmosphere of pre-reform Theravāda in Sri Lanka prior to the mid-twelfth century, even within the domain of Mahāvihāra orthodoxy. Based on accounts thus far provided of Central Burma's Arañ, we can suggest that Central Burma's Arañ comprised the following: (1) a Buddhist community truly well versed in Pāli literature, both "conventional" serving for the establishment of the reformed Theravāda and "unconventional" as could be a part of the older Theravāda; (2) as previously noted by historian Than Tun, a lax observance of some *vinaya* rules; (3) also based on Than Tun's investigation, a foundation in Central Burma dependent on the accumulation of wealth, particularly in the form of productive land estates; and (4) in the material sense, an association with the Pagan style of Buddhist art, widespread in central Burma and its neighboring regions.

Being a powerful kingdom, Pagan, during its dynastic period from the mid-eleventh to the late thirteenth centuries, could have exercised sovereignty over the whole of Lower Burma and probably other parts of Southeast Asia as well, although its power over these areas could have waxed and waned (Frasch 2002: 59–78). Religious transmission and exchanges likely accompanied its spread of power, allowing dissemination on an extensive scale of Pagan Buddhism, an old Theravāda represented materially by the form of the Buddhist art developed on the model of Pāla prototypes. The most notable image type on this model is the iconic representation of the Buddha wearing a pointed crown prevalent in Lower Burma, Haripunjaya in northern Thailand, and Central Thailand, all dating tentatively from the early centuries of the second millennium CE (Samerchai Poolsuwan n.d.). The Pāla characteristic is also included among those recognized by art historian Hiram Woodward as a signature of the old Hinayāna prevalent in central Thailand (Woodward 1997: 115–116; Woodward 2003: 166–171); Woodward perceives the latter, which he calls the "Ariya" Buddhist *nikāya*, as a continuum of the Dvāravatī Buddhist faith to be well extended into the period of Khmer domination over the area, also with Pagan contacts, between the eleventh and thirteenth centuries. Woodward's Ariya and the Pagan Buddhism explored in this chapter, with the "Arañ" serving as its major representative, constitute the currently best-known material components of the many variants of the "medieval Theravāda" of Southeast Asia.

To mark an end to the medieval phase of Theravāda in Southeast Asia could have been a series of heavy blows from the post-reform Theravāda orthodoxy from Sri Lanka in the area, to start its firm establishment in Lower Burma and then in the central and northern parts of Thailand from the early fourteenth century onward. To accompany the hegemony of the new Sīhaḷa order in the area was also the influx of the Sīhaḷa artistic and iconographic instruments, with obvious evidence in the Buddhist art and architecture of Sukhothai, Lanna, and Ayutthaya; the present chapter shows such influence in the murals of Wat Ratchaburana, Ayutthaya, dating from the first half of the fifteenth century. It is interesting to note that Central Burma could have been left as a backwater for spreading the new Sīhaḷa order until well after the fifteenth century; this could have been largely due to the relatively long-lasting success of the Arañ establishment (Samerchai Poolsuwan 2015: 145–197).

Acknowledgments

The author is grateful to the late U Aung Kyaing for his generous assistance with reading the mural inscriptions of Pagan and to Paritta Chalermpow Koanantakool, Donald M. Stadtner, and Nicolas Revire for their valuable comments on earlier drafts of this manuscript. This study was supported by Thammasat University Research Fund, Contract No. TUFT 2/2565.

Notes

1 One piece of evidence recognized by Luce as possibly representing the old Mon Theravāda is the presence at Pagan of a series of extra *jātaka* stories (*Velāma* 497, *Mahāgovinda* 498 and *Sumedhapandita* 499), materialized in art at the two Hpetleik pagodas; these tales come in addition to the known 547 stories accounted for in the standard (Sīhaḷa) version of the canonical *Jātaka* text (Luce 1956: 291–307; Luce, Ba Shin and Bohmu 1961: 277–417 (321–330)).

2 Starting from about the third century BCE, with the Buddha represented through symbols in narrative depictions of his life; the Buddha started to appear in anthropomorphic form in the Indian Buddhist art during the first few centuries CE, in association with the two major Buddhist civilizations: Gandhara in northwestern India, as well parts of the present-day Pakistan and Afghanistan, and Mathura, in now Uttar Pradesh, North India.

3 For dating the Loka-hteik-pan temple and its murals, see Ba Shin and Bohmu (1962): Chapter I.

4 To name a few of the major examples in the area are the Pagan temples 447 (Le-myet-hna), 534 (Sa-pwe-tin), 539 (Tayok-pyi), 663 (Mala-phyi) and 676 (So-hla-wun).

5 For the architectural details and layouts of the temples: Pichard (1992: vol. I, 159) (monument 85); Pichard (1994: vol. III, 152–155) (monument 658) and 156–160 (monument 659).

6 For details and systematic illustration of the mural panels, see Samerchai Poolsuwan (2017: 255–294); for complete illustration see Samerchai Poolsuwan (2016: 140–149).

7 For discussions on the significance of Bodhgaya in the Pagan context see also: Frasch 1998: 69–92; Brown 1988: 101–124.

8 Inscriptional identification provided to the author by the late U Aung Kyaing, former deputy director general, Myanmar Department of Archaeology.

9 While the Pāli *Jātaka* text accounts for the selected existences of Gotama during the past four *asaṅkheyya* and a hundred thousand eons, the three *Sotaṭṭhakī*'s *jātakas* of concern are to set forth the *bodhisatta*'s career to cover a period of twenty *asaṅkheyya* and a hundred thousand eons.

References

Āryaśūra. 1971. *The Jātakamālā (Garland of Birth-Stories)*, trans., J.S. Speyer. Delhi: Motilal Banarsidass.

Ba Shin, Bohmu. 1962. *The Lokahteikpan*. Rangoon: The Burma Historical Commission.

Bandaranayake, Senake. 2006. *The Rock and Wall Paintings of Sri Lanka*. Colombo: Stamford Lake (Pvt) Ltd.

Bautze-Picron, Claudine. 2003. *The Buddhist Murals of Pagan*. Bangkok: Orchid Press.

Bechert, Heinz. 1993. "The Nikāyas of Mediaeval Sri Lanka and the Unification of the Sangha by Parākramabāhu I." In *Studies on Buddhism in Honour of Professor A.K. Warder*, eds. N.K. Wagle, F. Watanabe, 11–21. Toronto: University of Toronto, Centre for South Asian Studies.

Brown, R.L. 1988. "Bodhgaya and South-east Asia." In *Bodhgaya: The Site of Enlightenment*, ed. Janice Leoshko, 101–124. Bombay: Marg Publications.

Cullabuddhaghosa. 1983. *Sotaṭṭhakīmahānidāna*, trans., Banjob Bannaruji. Bangkok: Wat Suthatthepvararam. [In Thai].

Derris, Karen. 2000. *Virtue and Relationship in a Theravādin Biography of the Bodhisatta: A study of the Sotaṭṭhakīmahānidāna*, Ph.D. thesis. Massachusetts: Harvard University.

Frasch, Tilman. 1998. "A Buddhist Network in the Bay of Bengal: Relations Between Bodhgaya, Burma and Sri Lanka, c. 300–1300." In *From the Mediterranean to the China Sea: Miscellaneous Notes*, eds. Claude Guillot, Denys Lombard, Rodenrich Ptak, 69–92. Weisbaden: Harrassowitz Verlag.

Frasch, Tilman. 2001. "The Buddhist Connection: Sinhalese-Burmese Intercourse in the Middle Ages." In *Explorations in the History of South Asia: Essays in Honour of Dietmar Rothermund*, eds. Georg Berkemer, Tilman Frasch, Hermann Kulke, Jurgen Lütt, 85–97. Delhi: Manohar.

Frasch, Tilman. 2002. "Coastal Peripheries During the Pagan Period." In *The Maritime Frontier of Burma. Exploring Political, Cultural and Commercial Interaction in the Indian Ocean World, 1200–1800*, eds. Jos Gommans, Jacques Leider, 59–78. Amsterdam: KITLV Press.

Geiger, Wilhelm, trans. 1912. *The Mahāvaṃsa or the Great Chronicle of Ceylon*. London: Pali Text Society.

Gornall, Alastair. 2020. *Rewriting Buddhism: Pali Literature and Monastic Reform in Sri Lanka, 1157–1270*. London: UCL Press.

Griswold, Alexander B., Prasert na Nagara. 1972. "King Lödaiya of Sukhodaya and His Contemporaries, Epigraphic and Historical Studies, No. 10." *Journal of the Siam Society* 60 (1): 21–152.

Huen Tsiang. 1884. *Si-Yu-Ki: Buddhist Records of the Western World*, vol. 2, trans., Samuel Beal. London: Trubner & Co.

Huntington, John C. 1985. "Sowing the Seed of the Lotus: A Journey to the Great Pilgrimage Sites of Buddhism, Part I." *Orientations* 16 (11): 46–61.

Huntington, John C. 1987a. "Pilgrimage as Images: The Cult of the *Aṣṭamahāprātihāryā*," Part I. *Orientations* 18 (4): 55–63.

Huntington, John C. 1987b. "Pilgrimage as Images: The Cult of the *Aṣṭamahāprātihāryā*, Part II." *Orientations* 18 (8): 56–68.

Jayawickrama, N.A., trans. 1990. *The Story of Gotama Buddha: The Nidāna-kathā of the Jātakaṭṭhakathā*. Oxford: Pali Text Society.

Khamhaikān Chāo-Krung-Kao. 1967. *Khamhaikān Khunluang-Hāwat lae Phrarātchaphongsāwadān Krung-Kao Chabap Luangprasōetaksōrnniti* (Testimonies of the inhabitants of Ayutthayā and its former king, Khunluang-Hāwat, and the Ayutthayā Chronicle of the Luangprasōetaksōrnniti version). Bangkok: Klangphittaya. [In Thai].

Luce, Gordon H. 1956. "The 550 Jātaka in Old Burma." *Artibus Asiae* XIX (3/4): 291–307.

Luce, Gordon H. 1969. *Old Burma-Early Pagan*, vol. I & III. New York: J.J. Augustin Publisher.

Luce, Gordon H. 1974. "The Advent of Buddhism to Burma." In *Buddhist Studies in Honour of I. B. Horner*, eds. L. Cousins, A. Kunst, K.R. Norman, 119–138. Boston: P. Reidel Publishing Company.

Luce, Gordon H., Ba Shin, Bohmu. 1961. "Pagan Myinkaba Kubyauk-gyi Temple of Rājakumār (1113 A.D.)." *Bulletin of the Burma Historical Commission* II: 277–417 (321–30).

Minayeff, J.P. 1886. "*Gandha-Vamsa*." In *Journal of the Pali Text Society*, ed. T.W. Rhys Davids, 54–80. London: Pali Text Society.

Pande, G.C. 1975. *Studies in the Origin of Buddhism*. Delhi: Mortilal Banarsidass.

Perimoo, Ratan. 1982. *Life of Buddha in Indian Sculpture (Ashta-maha-pratiharya): An Iconological Analysis*. New Delhi: Kanak.

Pichard, Pierre. 1992–1995. *The Inventory of Monuments at Pagan*, vols. I, III and VI. Paris: UNESCO.

Ratanapaññā Thera. 1968. *The Sheaf of Garlands of the Epochs of the Conquerer, Being a translation of Jinakāla mālīpakaraṇaṁ*, trans., N.A. Jayawickrama, Pali Text Society Translation Series No. 36. London: Pali text Society.

Ray, Nihar-Ranjan. 1939. "Early Traces of Buddhism in Burma." *Journal of the Greater India Society* 6 (1): 1–52.

Revire, Nicolas. 2014. "Glimpse of the Buddhist Practices and Rituals in Dvāravatī and Its Neighbouring Cultures." In *Before Siam: Essays in Art and Archaeology*, eds. Nicolas Revire, Stephen A. Murphy, 216–237. Bangkok: The Siam Society.

Rhys Davids, T.W. 1975. *The History and Literature of Buddhism*. Delhi: New Era Offset Printers.

Saddhammaghosa Thera. 1985. *Lokapaññatti*. Bangkok: Department of Fine Arts. [In Thai].

Samerchai Poolsuwan. 2012. "After Enlightenment: Scenes of the Buddha's Retreat in the Thirteenth Century Murals at Pagan." *Artibus Asiae* 72 (2): 377–397.

Samerchai Poolsuwan. 2014. "The Pagan-Period and the Early-Thai Buddhist Murals: Were They Related?." *SUVANNABHUMI* 6 (1): 27–65.

Samerchai Poolsuwan. 2015. "Buddhist Murals Illustrating Unusual Features in Temple 36 at Sale and Their Cultural Implications." *Journal of Burma Studies* 19 (1): 145–197.

Samerchai Poolsuwan. 2016. *Chittakam Phutthasatsana Samai Phukam: Rupbaeb Lae Khwammai Khong Sinlapa Haeng Sattha* (The Buddhist Murals of Pagan: Form and meaning of the Devotional Art), Vol. II. Bangkok: Thammasat University Press. [In Thai].

Samerchai Poolsuwan. 2017. "The Buddha's Biography: Its Development in the Pagan Murals vs. the later Vernacular Literature, in the Theravādin Buddhist Context of Southeast Asia." *Journal of the Royal Asiatic Society* 27 (2): 255–294.

Samerchai Poolsuwan. (Forthcoming) "The Buddha Sculptures of Tham Phra (Buddha Cave): Implications on understanding the Complex Religious Atmosphere of Western Thailand During the Early Second Millennium CE." In *The Emergence of Theravada in Cambodia*, eds. Hiram W. Woodward, Jr., Ashley Thompson. Singapore: NUS Press.

Saraswati, S.K. 1977. *Tantrayāna Art: An Album*. Calcutta: The Asiatic Society.

Sirisena, W.M. 1978. *Sri Lanka and Southeast Asia: Political, Religious and Cultural Relations from A.D. c. 1000 to c. 1500*. Leiden: E.J. Brill.

Skilling, Peter. 1996. "The Sambuddhe Verses and Later Theravādin Buddhology." *Journal of the Pali Text Society* 22: 151–183.

Skilling, Peter. 1997a. "The Advent of Theravāda Buddhism to Mainland South-east Asia." *Journal of the International Association of Buddhist Studies* 20 (1): 83–107.

Skilling, Peter. 1997b. "New Pāli Inscriptions from Southeast Asia." *Journal of the Pali Text Society* 23: 123–157.

Skilling, Peter. 2003. "Dvāravatī: Recent Revelations and Research." In *Dedications to Her Royal Highness Princess Galyani Vadhana Krom Luang Naradhiwas Rajanagarindra on Her 80th Birthday*, ed. Chris Baker, 87–112. Bangkok: The Siam Society.

Stadtner, Donald M. 2008. "The Mon of Lower Burma." *Journal of the Siam Society* 96: 193–215.

Stargardt, Janice. 1995. "The Oldest Known Pāli Text, 5th-6th Century: Results of the Cambridge Symposium on the Pyu Golden Pāli Text from Śrī Kṣetra, 18–19 Apr. 1995." *Journal of the Pali Text Society* 21: 199–213.

Than Tun. 1988. *Essays on the History and Buddhism of Burma*, ed. Paul Strachan. Arran, Scotland: Kiscadale Publications.

Tun Nyein. 1899. *Inscriptions of Pagan, Pinya and Ava*. Rangoon: Superintendent, Government Printing.

Winternitz, M. 1977. *History of Indian Literature*, Vol. I, trans., Jha Subhadra. New Delhi: Munshiram Manoharlal.

Woodward, Hiram W. 1997. *The Sacred Sculpture of Thailand*. Bangkok: River Books.

Woodward, Hiram W. 2003. *The Art and Architecture of Thailand*. Leiden: Brill.

20

ICONS

Standing out from the narrative in Theravādin art

Ashley Thompson

Setting the scene

"The term *icon* is loaded with implications," writes art historian Robert Brown toward the end of a thought-provoking essay examining the iconic function of *jātaka*, narratives of the Buddha's achievement of perfections over his past lives, painted and sculpted on and in South and Southeast Asian monuments (Brown 1997: 98). In Brown's simple sentence, I read discreet acknowledgment of the Christian heritage borne both by the term *icon* and by the many academic fields in which it operates, and glimpse a particular nod to the ever-extending body of work in the field of art history grappling with the term's pertinence in the interpretation of theory and practice in Buddhist worlds. To gaze intently at the "icon" in this field would be to open oneself and one's readers to the infinite, where, strictly speaking, nothing is seen, to reference Jean-Luc Marion's definition of the "icon" in opposition to the "idol" as cited in Jacob Kinnard's detailed discussion of a selection of the many extant discussions in primary and secondary sources on the "question of the presence of the Buddha in physical objects" (Kinnard 1999: 25–44). I can afford no more than a glimpse into Brown's glimpse here, as readers can by now, I hope, imagine and will follow Brown's lead in circumscribing discussions as he closes the essay in looping back around to his opening critique of what has proved to be, for scholars of Buddhist art of South and Southeast Asia, an impactful reading of early artistic representations of Buddhist narratives by art historian Vidya Dehejia (Dehejia 1990).[1]

Dehejia's reading is faulted by Brown precisely for its *reading*, that is to say for its presumption of a sort of equivalence between written text and pictorial representation, where the one (pictorial) effectively translates the original other (written) representation. In Dehejia's work, the different forms are seen to share semantic content and to engender a like process of accessing that meaning: reading. This vision of linear development, from the written to the pictorial, nonetheless posits a certain hierarchy of value in which the written serves as a point of origin and reference for the therefore derivative other. If the typology proposed by Dehejia for deciphering, describing, and organizing dominant early artistic modes of rendering Buddhist narratives makes, in Brown's words, "an important contribution" to art-historical analysis, Brown challenges Dehejia's qualification of the discerning subject as a "viewer." In Brown's reading, Dehejia's "viewer" shares more with the art historian-cum-museum-goer than it does with the

DOI: 10.4324/9781351026666-25

early Buddhist worshiper as apprehended by many modern scholars attempting to traverse time and space to see from within local eyes.[2] While noting that, on one level, Dehejia masterfully discerns the logics of composition, Brown calls for further attention to *jātaka* pictorial function in its inseparability from the processes by which meaning is had within ancient Buddhist milieu.

"I intend it [i.e., the term *icon*]," Brown (1997: 98) continues, "in a specifically Indic religious sense, simply as a form of the deity that is the focus of reverence and worship." Replacing the "viewer" with the "worshiper" triggers a gestalt shift whereby what scholars are first made to see as narrative becomes instead iconic. The *jātaka* representations that Brown studies are integral to monumental architecture. They are stories of the Buddha's past lives, but, Brown demonstrates, their very physical emplacement within the monumental space precludes "reading" by a "viewer." Instead, they are parts of a whole schema by which the Buddha is made present (*re*-presented) in the here and now to worshipers. Brown's analyses make evident that it is this sort of active re-presentation of the Buddha that is at work in the "specifically Indic" reverence for a form of the deity and that makes that form an "icon." Likewise, it is this relatively simple formulation of "icon," which deconstructs the opposition, and so the hierarchy, between copy and original, such that a representation of X is a *re*-presentation of X, that is at the core of my own usage throughout this chapter.

The "icon" in this sense maintains an existential relation with its original manifestation—in our case, the Buddha. This relation can be on the order of the Veronica, the quintessential Christian relic in which the image of Christ's face derives its potency from its supposed material contact with his actual face, and the existential relation between original and copy is manifest in their shared physical form. In many ways, with the help of relics and ritual, and as a type of relic itself, the anthropomorphic image of the Buddha can be likened to the Veronica. The relation can also be considered along the lines of the Peircean index, where the one physical form—take, for example, a footprint—depends on another—in this example, a foot—for its very existence. The Buddha's footprint contains in the here and now his past presence. From an art-historical point of view, the one (the present footprint) wills the other (the past-present Buddha) into existence. From a worshiper's point of view, the active willing agent is the walking Buddha making his presence manifest in the footprint. This particular form of the Buddha's presence is variously manifest today across South and Southeast Asian landscapes, repeatedly attesting at once to a singular historical event of object consecration itself attesting to a singular legendary event, when the Buddha is understood to have been then and there. Among the region's most famous footprints today are that of Sri Lanka's Śrī Pāda (Adam's Peak), Cambodia's Phnom Bakheng, Thailand's Phu Phra Bat, Luang Prabang's Phu Si, and Burma's Shwesettaw. These forms range from the amorphous (natural stone formations in the land) to the metonymically anthropomorphic (detailed sculptures in the round variously "impressed" into the land); each has been framed by architectural, legendary, ritual and often iconographic structures to appear as the enduring mark the Buddha has left on the land. The worshiper's perspective turns the art-historical analysis on its head of course, without, however, transforming the fundamental function of the index. But let me reiterate that the existential relation I am describing cannot be reduced to an impoverished understanding of representation as a conventional, pragmatic mode of rendering which underestimates the complexity of both "original" and "copy," as well as their relation in the contexts that concern us. The existential relation between the "original" manifestation (which is to say the "original" is itself always already a manifestation) and its re-presentation can be had in both the more or less mimetic anthropomorphic form of the Buddha mentioned earlier and in the abstract form of the *stūpa*. Just as relics can be embedded in both statue and *stūpa*, so, too, can stories of the Buddha's past lives be narrated around them to make or animate the relation. My doubling of representation and *re*-presentation is meant to emphasize what Kinnard identifies as a productive tension between the realm of representation per se and the realm of ontology at the heart of Buddhist art.[3]

On image-text relations

That the interpretive processes at work here, in ancient Buddhist contexts as in the modern day, are anything but simple is illustrated in Brown's closing analogy between the "iconized dharma" and the *jātaka* as "iconized word texts." The "iconized dharma" is the crystallization of a foundational Buddhist tenet, the *pratītyasamutpāda* (in Pāli, *paṭiccasamupāda*) or "dependent origination," into a four-line verse, the *pratītyasamutpādagāthā*, which becomes objectified in medieval India (ca. 600–1200 CE)—literally made into an object on the order of the funerary *stūpa*, or of the relic within the *stūpa*, or of the image which is like the relic assimilated with the funerary monument.[4] Just like Brown's *jātaka*-as-icon, the "iconized dharma" does not reference a pictorial translation of a text, a secondary derivative of an original, a mere illustration; instead, it names apprehension of the verse-tenet as icon, that is as an image whose veneration makes the Dharma present in the here and now. In Pāli traditions, the *paṭiccasamupāda* can be identified with the Dharma as a whole (Boucher 1991: 2 and 17, n. 4), the Buddha's teachings that stand in for the Buddha, notably during his absence from this or that place, and, irrevocably, after his entry into nirvana (Figure 20.1)

When inscribed on a statue of the Buddha, a practice well established in first-millennium Southeast Asia as seen in a corpus of statues from what is now Thailand, Cambodia, and Vietnam, the verse cannot be reduced to a text to be read but functions rather like the *jātaka*

Figure 20.1 Buddha statue inscribed with the "iconized dharma" or the "dharma relic" on its upper back and rubbing of the inscription. The statue was found around 1952 by Phra Dhammasenani, then abbot of Wat Mahathat, Ratchaburi, Thailand, at an abandoned temple in Tambol Lum Din, Muang District, Ratchaburi. The abbot had the statue transferred to Ratchaburi's Wat Mahathat, where it is still held. The statue no longer has its head. Seventh to eighth century. Present height (without head, feet, or base: 127 cm, maximum width 57 cm, maximum depth 21 cm; Skilling 2003: 274). Images after *Prachum silacharuk, Part 3* 2508 [1965]: figs. 2 ka and 2 kha. Another image of the statue with head in place and with other statuary moved to Wat Mahathat from the same site features on a Ratchaburi heritage website: http://rb-old.blogspot.com/2010/04/blog-post_4310.html.

on a *stūpa*, endowing the larger image with its very life.[5] As Peter Skilling (2003: abstract) notes, the *paṭiccasamupāda* verse is the "dharma-relic" par excellence. The apparent distillation of a fundamental teaching, which takes diverse, more or less elaborate discursive form across all Buddhist traditions, into the four-line verse is analogous with the apparent distillation of a scene or an episode or a sequence of episodes or even an entire *jātaka* tale to its bare essence. The hierarchized values implied in art-historical analyses that presume images to have been derived from texts meet a powerful challenge in this interpretive context that sees images and iconized word texts rather as embryonic, containing and maintaining the vital potentiality of Buddhahood.[6] There is a manifest equivalence between text and image at work here, but it is radically different from the model of translation with which we began in following Brown's critique of Dehejia's readerly viewer.

Skilling effectively extends Brown's reflections anchored in select sites in South and Southeast Asia to make a more general point about the *jātaka* function in relation to the Buddha image broadly defined—including the "aniconic" form of the *stūpa* as it will be discussed later. Skilling insists on the importance of understanding the *jātaka* as not just tales of the Buddha's past lives but, more precisely, as tales of the future Buddha's attainment of ethical "perfections" (*pāramitā*) over these many lives leading to his Awakening as the Gotama Buddha, or, as he is often called in scholarship on Theravāda Buddhism, the "Historical Buddha." The *stūpa*, Skilling (2008: 61–63) writes, is

> the repository of the Buddha's power and virtues, from his career as a *bodhisattva* [a being on the path to Awakening] over many lives, to his teaching career as an awakened Buddha in his final life, up to his death, embodied in the relics installed within the *stupa*.

The anthropomorphic image of the Buddha is no different from the *stūpa* in this regard as Skilling explicates it, nor, I would add, is it different from the Buddha himself:

> [the] physical form of the Buddha is the product of ethics, the product of merit. Since the image of the Buddha is meant to represent the idealized form of the Buddha, there is an intimate relation between *jātakas* and Buddha image. The *jātakas* have, in a sense, culminated in the image.
>
> (Skilling 2008: 68)

To see the image strictly as something to be seen is, in Skilling's Buddhologist eyes, nothing less than to manifest ignorance in the "history and function of Buddhist art" (2008: 80). That the narrative imagery can be made to be unseen must be itself seen in light of its function as integral to the body of the Buddha as such, which is to say to its iconicity as an object of veneration.

The manifest relation between image and text in Theravāda manuscript traditions points up another dimension of this critical paradigm. Images in manuscripts frequently do not serve to illustrate the texts which they nonetheless accompany; nor are they simply abstract décor.

Figure 20.2 exemplifies one telling mode of visual-cum-textual composition. This accordion-style, or leporello, manuscript is from Wat Khao Yi San, Samut Songkhram Province, western-central Thailand. Its use of a particular Khom script, a type of decorative writing derived from Old Khmer script and used in central and southern Thai sacred contexts, allows for dating the manuscript to the late eighteenth–early nineteenth century. The Pāli text is from the abbreviated *mātikā* of the seven books of the *Abhidhamma*, with the spread pictured here displaying the *Dhātukathā mātikā*. The flanking images are of the *Suvaṇṇasāma Jātaka*.[7] Skilling's

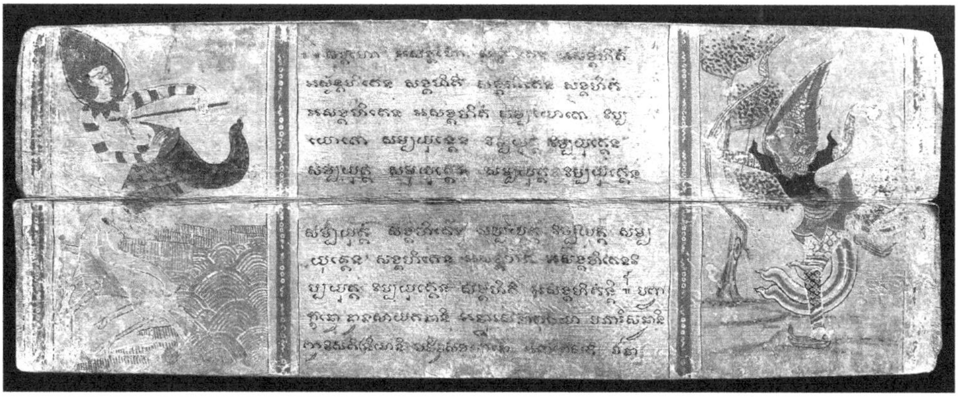

Figure 20.2 Spread of a late eighteenth–early nineteenth-century leporello manuscript held in Wat Khao Yi San, Samut Songkhram province, Thailand. (Wat Museum run jointly with Silpakorn University.) The text displayed here is the *Dhātukathā mātikā*; the flanking images are of the *Suvaṇṇasāma Jātaka*. Photograph by Somneuk Hongprayoon, courtesy Fragile Palm Leaves Foundation.

comments on this type of eighteenth- to nineteenth-century Thai leporello with *jātaka* imagery is illustrated in the 2008 volume cited earlier with a manuscript now held in the Asian Art Museum of San Francisco; they apply equally to the more modest manuscript of Figure 20.2, still held in a monastery setting. The *jātaka* paintings appear "in two vertical bands that flank the text. ...The accompanying text is not however that of the *jātakas*" (Skilling 2008: 72; see also image p. 73). For Skilling (2008: p. 72), this presentation of the *jātaka* demonstrates that the paintings "exist in their own right, as amplifications of the power and perfections of the Buddha." This is a somewhat strange formulation: they exist in their own right, yet they do so as amplifications of something else. The first clause distinguishes the painted *jātaka* scenes from mere illustrations of a text; the second affirms that they are nonetheless integral to something greater than themselves. In this description, the manuscript is thoroughly analogous to the monumental *stūpa* and the anthropomorphic Buddha statue in which the *jātaka* participate in the iconization of the Dharma.

I would amplify Skilling's analysis in noting the gestalt effect produced by the composition. The two painted panels on either side of the text on a given page (the spread composed of two pages, unfolded) are framed by decorative borders, with the framing enhancing the iconicity of each scene. The inner decorative border of each painted panel separates the flanking *jātaka* paintings from the central text, serving thus as borders *also* to the text. The two inner decorative borders are identical to each other but differ from the two outer borders, which are, in turn, identical with each other. When seen together, that is as belonging to the text rather than to their respective paintings, these "inner" borders of the paintings become outer borders of the text. That is, they frame the central text, enhancing *its* iconicity. Gazing at an unfolded page, we can see at once a singular framed image and a triptych. Variations on this particular compositional and framing practice, in which image and text become interchangeable via a logic radically different to that of illustration, by which I mean translation, can be readily observed in the British Library *Discovering Sacred Texts* online resource. See, for example, the eighteenth-century leporello from Central Thailand that contains a collection of Pāli extracts from the *Vinaya* and the *Abhidhamma*, along with a Pāli composition on the Buddha's virtues derived from a famous fifth-century Pāli commentary on the *Abhidhamma* by Buddhaghosa in Sri Lanka, the *Visuddhimagga* (British Library Oriental Manuscript Or 14068: https://www.bl.uk/

collection-items/animal-tales-mahabuddhaguna-birds-buddhist-texts). The paintings flanking the manuscript are of the last ten *jātaka*. The framing technique used in this manuscript, in which the inner borders are most prominent, singles out the *text* as image over the images themselves while also presenting the whole of an unfolded page as a triptych.

I note, finally, that the view of "reading" shared by both Dehejia and Brown is itself circumscribed within an academic discourse which risks stripping the practice of (1) its metaphysical—or shall I say meditative—dimensions to leave us readers as it were with a rather impoverished understanding of what it is that we do when our eyes move across the traces on a surface and (2) any contextual dimensions inflecting what a given reader at a given time in a given context is doing when they "read." In short, I am not sure that I know what reading is—no more or less than I know what it means to worship a Buddha image. To pursue reflections on what it is to read would bring us to further nuance distinctions Brown is evoking in this essay and to highlight also relations, for example, between the secular and the sacred; it would also, however, bring me further from my present circumscribed task to examine the icon in Theravādin art, even as this task presumes that, in giving body to transcendence of the material world, "art" itself—not unlike the Buddha—challenges such distinctions.

The aniconic and the anthropomorphic: ongoing issues in Buddhist art history

The term *aniconic* gained currency in early twentieth-century art-historical studies of the earliest instances of Buddhist art.[8] It is a misnomer insofar as what it names is not *an*-iconic, that is, a negation of the iconic, but rather an investment in it. Early "aniconic" Buddhist art includes a range of forms that index the Buddha without representing him anthropomorphically. These forms range from relatively simple signs, such as the footprint or the *stūpa*, to complex narrative scenes interpreted as presenting events in the Buddha's life story in which the Buddha is distinctly not represented in human form and this anthropomorphic absence is made evident by a variety of means, from symbolic stand-ins to empty spaces staged as such. This "aniconic" art is generally associated with monumental *stūpa*. If, to requote Brown, an icon, "in a specifically Indic religious sense" is "a form of the deity that is the focus of reverence and worship," "aniconic" Buddhist art is truly *iconic*, whether it comprises a singular emblem, a setting of that emblem within a narrative construct, or a narrative sequence in which the anthropomorphic figure of the Buddha is made conspicuously absent. The "aniconic" can be a distinct focus of worship and/or participate in the iconization of the monument of which it is a part. The "aniconic" in this early scholarly context was set in opposition to anthropomorphic representations of the Buddha. The interpretive focus has been twofold. On one hand, we see a predominantly historical investment, with scholars intent on identifying the earliest of early Buddhist art and establishing a chronological sequence from the aniconic to the anthropomorphic; on the other, we see a more interpretive investment in uncovering the causes behind both "aniconic" representation of the Buddha and the emergence of its perceived opposite in human form, be these causes geo-historical, sociocultural, ritual, or doctrinal. A more apt term for the "aniconic" in this context might simply be the *non-anthropomorphic*. Note, however, that insofar as it is only the "Historical" Buddha, who is not represented in human form in early "aniconic" Buddhist art, the term *non-anthropomorphic* does not adequately describe this category of art as a whole, which is fully figurative and often teaming with anthropomorphic figures, a context that, in fact, enhances the conspicuousness of the absence of the anthropomorphic figure of the Buddha. For this reason, also, the term *aniconic* as it can be used in art-historical writing more generally to designate nonfigurative art must be considered a misnomer for our specific topic here.

More than a century of debate on the topic has led to robust understandings of the geo-historical development of early Buddhist art, and to a widespread acceptance of the absence of any formal prohibition on anthropomorphic representation of the Buddha underpinning early practice. It has produced sophisticated understandings of the historical and conceptual dimensions of the evolution of early Buddhist art production, notably with work on funerary portraiture (DeCaroli 2015) and detailed accounts of the role of Buddhist narrative in integrating a pool of Indic auspicious signs, with the representation of the auspicious figure of the anthropomorphic Buddha as one outcome of this process (Karlsson 2000, 2006). The aniconic–anthropomorphic paradigm has in many ways been superseded with more complex, historically grounded frameworks for understanding early Buddhist art. Yet the paradigm haunts Buddhist art history still and not only in writing on early India. Brown, for example, is compelled to distance his usage with reference to first- and early second-millennia South and Southeast Asian *jātaka* representation from that embedded in the debates summarized earlier, adding a footnote to his simple definition of *icon*. "My use of *icon*," he writes, "is not intended to relate to this dialectic" (between "iconic" and aniconic" in writing about the early Buddhist art of India) (Brown 1997: 107, n. 86). The reasons for this haunting are no doubt multiple. In the following, I probe a few of these, in pointing up how Brown's usage might relate after all to this dialectic at the foundation of Buddhist art history insofar as his South and much later Southeast Asian materials render the dialectic in themselves and, in doing so, challenge established narratives of the simplicity of Theravāda and its art in its supposed singular focus on the "Historical" Buddha.

The *stūpa* and the anthropomorphic figure of the Gotama Buddha can be said to stand out as the principal mainstays of Theravāda artistic production over time and space. As the earlier discussion on *jātaka* tales, sculpted or painted as well as written, has, I trust, demonstrated, the *stūpa* and the Buddha image do not stand alone, but they are made to stand out. The *stūpa* is aniconic in the established usage of the term in Buddhist art history; that is, it renders the Sakyamuni Buddha in non-anthropomorphic form. In my view, all of Brown's case studies provide fine examples of the dialectic maintaining between the two forms, including in Theravāda settings. I will draw out a few salient points in this regard at one of Brown's chosen sites, Wat Si Chum of Sukhothai, to then consider Cambodia's Angkor Wat temple as transformed in the sixteenth century in light of these discussions. With these specific historical examples, I aim also to give some sense of how what might appear to be an abstruse theoretical construct of the icon—involving lofty ideas of presence and absence apparently far from the minds and experiences of average worshipers—actually takes mundane material form. In making the connection between debates on early Buddhist art and second-millennia Southeast Asian constructs, I do not mean to suggest that Theravāda maintains a privileged relationship to early Buddhist art in any straightforward historical sense. The relations are thoroughly ideological insofar as the *stūpa* and the image of the Historical Buddha can be said to evoke, in embodying, existential relations with the Buddha himself. It strikes me in fact that the work of these icons is more in tune with the complexities frequently attributed to Mahāyāna developments on visualizations and embodiments of the divine in *contrast* with the thus-perceived simple Theravāda. Kinnard's "quite tentative" contrasting characterization of the two is indicative in this regard, as it recognizes the reductive nature of the vision of Theravāda on which it nonetheless relies. Short of adequate interpretive frames, this is what Kinnard says:

> The Theravādin position, on its face at any rate, is relatively straightforward: the Buddha was an extraordinary man who lived in the sixth century BCE; he was endowed with certain extra-human powers, but was nonetheless a mortal who was born, lived and

> died. ...Therefore, to look for the presence of the Buddha in stones, relics, sculptures, etc., is to look in vain. These are merely reminders of the Buddha, and they thus serve to signify the Buddha who is himself no longer present, but whose life and teachings serve as both, to use Geertz' well known terms, a *model of* and a *model for* the ideal life. The Mahāyāna position is more difficult to summarize briefly.
>
> (Kinnard 1999: 26)

The "face" of Theravāda is of real import in this affair. It appeals to a certain historicity, an investment in an understanding of linear time by which a man lived and died, and whose life and death is commemorated by adherents centuries on. Theravāda, in this sense, embodies an investment in history as a linear, teleological narrative: as Siddhattha Gotama progressed to Awakening, so, too, do adherents progress in their lives commemorating his. The face of Theravāda is more than a façade covering up something else, something more complicated or illicit even, something heterodox akin to Mahāyāna as this sort of hesitant characterization of Theravāda tends to suggest. With a nod to Kinnard's own theorization of Mahāyāna constructs in this same chapter, I suggest rather that the tensions maintained in that very face are what *make* Theravāda and its icons. The "Historical Buddha" is as much a supernatural as a natural phenomenon. The perfections he legendarily achieved over many past lives led to the life of Siddhattha Gotama and his Awakening. Each of the characteristic marks the Buddha bears—*uṣṇīṣa* (cranial protuberance) on the head, *cakra* (wheels) on the palms, and so on—is linked to a "perfection" (Skilling 2008: 67–8). The latest in a line of Buddhas, he becomes an idealized figure, an exemplar, which is to say at once bearing and bereft of singular identity—an "icon" in and of himself to be venerated. The *stūpa* embodies another iteration of this tension between the historical and the ahistorical. The monument represents the end of the narrative, the Buddha's death, the disappearance of the natural figure. At the same time, however, it gives body and supernatural, ahistorical life to that figure. Relative to the spectacular artistic developments of Mahāyāna or Vajrayāna the figure of the Buddha and *stūpa* are simple indeed. Yet, as the following historical examples should demonstrate, they are, like Mahāyāna, not easy to summarize briefly. They too are "metapractical" objects on the order of the Mahāyāna materials described by Kinnard, "involving and invoking a range of strategies with which Buddhists could work through the incongruities and complexities" at hand (Kinnard 1999: 43–44).

The broader Theravāda narrative I will sketch out, linking Sukhothai's Wat Si Chum and Cambodia's Angkor Wat, aims to point up how ensembles of imagery—aniconic, iconic, and narrative not only in the conventional sense each of these terms has carried in Buddhist art history but also in their relations I have attempted to outline—embody remarkably coherent strategies. In turn, these strategies lend a certain physical and conceptual coherence to a vast region otherwise characterized by heterogeneous language use and topographies as well as political and cultural histories. I am not speaking directly to exchange networks by which people, objects, and ideas circulated, though these underpin to a degree my concerns which linger rather on aesthetic questions concerning the *work* that art does. On the surface, the image ensembles, at Wat Si Chum and Angkor Wat, are quite dissimilar. They differ markedly in architectural and artistic form, style, and manifest content. Each ensemble is thoroughly historically contingent, produced as a result of specific local historical events and contributing to the commemoration of these. They stand at a great distance from each other in time and space, north-central Thailand in the fourteenth century and northern Cambodia in the sixteenth century. To my mind, they point to two major inflections of premodern Theravāda on the mainland. The one, Wat Si Chum, can be said to be largely shaped through an orchestrated orientation to Sri

Lankan Buddhism, building on Angkorian constructs while nonetheless distancing itself from them; this comes with a pronounced investment in the Buddha's life stories. The other, Angkor Wat, is predominantly shaped by the Angkorian heritage of which the temple is an exemplary part; the sixteenth-century transformation of the temple evinces a pronounced investment in the Hindu god Viṣṇu's life stories, now serving to endow the temple-as-Buddhist-icon with new life. Still their different modes of expression share in a visual projection of Buddhist icons made to stand out as such by epic narratives in which the Buddha and Viṣṇu are, in varying ways, assimilated, a shared projection that makes each ensemble also stand out from local historical narratives to participate in what might be termed a Theravāda civilization transgressing contingencies of time and space.

Readers are encouraged to read the following in conjunction with Anne Blackburn's essay in the present volume examining how Sukhothai came to participate in the Pāli world of the second millennium. In a forthcoming monograph on Theravādin Buddhist kingdoms, Blackburn expands on this work tracking a shift from the discrete state-building focus of King Ramkhamhaeng's Buddhist expression in early Sukhothai to subsequent Sukhothai reigns characterized by sustained campaigns to emplot traces of the Buddha in Tai territories and a noted immersion in Pāli texts composed in Sri Lanka, to a subsequent predominant concern for monastic lineage in developments in Lanna (northern Thailand) and Bago (Burma). While Blackburn sounds the fine distinctions between these polities and their Buddhisms as they develop in time and space, she tracks a singular arc of development. In the following, I seek to add another piece to the larger premodern Pāli world in which Cambodia is also integral, though otherwise. Sukhothai might be seen as a sort of pivot linking and foreshadowing what will become, in one inflection, the Sri Lanka–Bago–Lanna arc traced by Anne Blackburn and, in another, the Cambodia–Central Thailand arc that we might be tempted to name Ramayanic Buddhism in ways that should become evident in the next section. The developments I examine follow on, in both historical and art historical terms, from those at Pagan described by Samerchai Poolsuwan in the present volume; they intersect with those he describes at Ayutthaya.

Re-presenting the Buddha: two historical examples

Wat Si Chum is a fourteenth-century Theravāda monastery outside the city walls of Sukhothai, one of three urban centers comprising the backbone of an eponymous premodern polity in what is now north-central Thailand. Sukhothai emerged in the thirteenth century as a Tai Buddhist power with a developing cosmopolitan outlook and regional prominence; this rise came in the wake of Angkor, the Khmer polity centered on the Angkor plain in what is now northern Cambodia from the ninth to thirteenth centuries. Angkor had expanded its reach into the area that would become the independent realm of Sukhothai by the late twelfth–early thirteenth centuries and ultimately contributed to its foundation, such that Sukhothai can be considered one of multiple inheritors of Angkor. Angkor had thrived on a largely Hindu political structure in which the gods Śiva and Viṣṇu figured prominently in royal cults and associated administrative structures. Buddhism was present over much of this period but came to prominence at court only in the late Angkorian reign of Jayavarman VII, which saw a flourishing of Mahāyāna and Vajrayāna expression underpinning political consolidation and expansion into what is now Thailand and Laos. Theravāda Buddhism became dominant at Angkor and elsewhere in Cambodia in the thirteenth and fourteenth centuries, developing at this time also in exchange with Sukhothai, Pagan, and other regional polities in ways that remain relatively obscure today.[9]

Wat Si Chum has been the subject of extensive research. This is in part for the unique configuration of the site's dominant architectural feature, what is referred to in the scholarly literature as a *mondop* according to Thai pronunciation of the Pāli *maṇḍapa*. The *mondop* is thought to have been built in the late fourteenth century around a preexisting colossal Buddha image. A narrow tunnel-like passageway was built into the *mondop*'s monumental walls, spiraling through a system of staircases from the floor level around the building up to its top. Stone etchings of one hundred *jātaka* tales, numbered and with legends, are fit into the ceilings and other select components of this passageway effectively encircling the Buddha image. Scholars were long misled in the interpretation of these *jātaka* plaques, and so of the site as a whole, by a conviction perfectly articulated by epigraphist–art historian team Griswold and Prasert na Nagara (1972: 77) in their seminal work on the architectural complex:

> Representations of Jātakas, more than any other category of Buddhist art, are intended for the edification of the general public; so it is certain that these were not made to be installed in a dark stairway where they could only be seen with the aid of a candle.

This widely held conviction led to interpretive acrobatics on the part of multiple scholars positing that the *jātaka* etchings were originally mounted on the exterior of Sukothai's Mahādhātu, the majestic city centre *stūpa*, only to be moved later to the eccentric *mondop* of Wat Si Chum. This interpretation has been discredited, both for the way in which the stone slabs have been shown to have been custom-made during the original construction of Wat Si Chum and for its premise that the very raison d'être of *jātakas* lies in being read—a premise convincingly challenged by Brown and Skilling as discussed previously. A massive, lengthy stone inscription in Thai language and script was found in Wat Si Chum's inner-wall passageway entrance; once thought, in conjunction with the *jātaka* hypothesis, to have belonged to Sukhothai's Wat Mahādhātu, it is now generally understood that the epigraph was found just where it belonged, at Wat Si Chum.

The *mondop* and *jātaka* of Wat Si Chum comprised one of the case studies presented by Robert Brown in his 1997 essay. Brown is most interested in the placement of the *jātaka* at Wat Si Chum, encircling the Buddha/monument yet out of easy sight in ways he shows to be comparable to the placement of *jātaka* at other Buddhist sites including the early twelfth-century Ananda temple at Pagan. The 2008 collective volume edited by Peter Skilling presents a comprehensive interdisciplinary review of the extant research on Wat Si Chum while also contributing new findings and interpretations of multiple dimensions of the site. I draw primarily from the work of Skilling, architectural historian Pierre Pichard, and art historian Pattaratorn Chirapravati in this 2008 volume to make a few further points (Skilling: 2008: 59–109; Pichard 2008: 41–57; Chirapravati 2008: 13–39).

The photograph in Figure 20.3 shows a view of the *mondop* today following multiple restoration campaigns in the twentieth century. It is a large stuccoed square brick structure on a massive stepped base aligned to the west of a brick terrace. The terrace is understood to be the remains of a *vihāra* (pronounced *wihan* in Thai) or worship hall, containing at its western end a pedestal for a Buddha image facing east, like the Buddha inside the *mondop* behind it. The alignment of a *vihāra* and *mondop* is common at Sukhothai, with variations including the addition of a *stūpa* behind the *mondop*, or a *stūpa* in the place of the *mondop*. The Wat Si Chum configuration is unusual in the Sukhothai context for the fact that the *vihāra* appears to have been closed at its western end such that the colossal figure of the Buddha visible through the peaked doorway of the *mondop* today would not have been readily visible as the configuration was originally conceived. A narrow space between the *vihāra* and the *mondop* nonetheless

Figure 20.3 Wat Si Chum, Sukhothai, Thailand: *mondop* preceded by pillared *vihāra* terrace and one of the one hundred engraved stone *jātaka* plaques from the staired passageway inside the *mondop* wall spiraling around the colossal Buddha image. This plaque represents in condensed form the *Maghadeva Jātaka*; it is pictured here in situ on the ceiling of the passageway inside the *mondop*'s southern wall; the next plaque can be seen above. *Mondop* photograph by author. *Jātaka* plaque photograph courtesy Thanaphat Limhasanaikul.

allowed access into the latter. The Wat Si Chum *mondop* is unusual in the context of other *mondop* structures at Sukhothai for a number of other reasons including its massive size and relatively unadorned exterior.

Pierre Pichard's detailed study of the structure makes a tentative but strong argument that Wat Si Chum's *mondop* was conceived as a sort of *stūpa*. Pichard reminds readers that it is unlikely that the term *maṇḍapa* was used during the Sukhothai period to refer to this structure or to like structures today called *mondop* in other period temple sites. The interchangeability between *stūpa* and *mondop* evidenced in the period site configurations described above itself comprises a first suggestion that this structure could have been a *stūpa* or at least associated with, if not veritably assimilated with, the *stūpa* concept.[10] The upper part of the inner walls of the *mondop* are tapered inwards. To Pichard, this indicates that the structure was originally conceived as a tall tower with a high corbeled inner structure but was left incomplete. Pichard cites possible local architectural models in the late twelfth- and early thirteenth-century Khmer sanctuary towers of Sukhothai's nearby Wat Phra Phai Luang and the square tower-shaped Lanna stupas some 300 kilometers to the north such as the famed Chedi Ku Kut at Wat Chamathewi in Lamphun first constructed in the mid-twelfth century. He additionally evokes the Satmahal Prāsāda in Sri Lanka's twelfth-century capital of Polonnaruva as a possible inspiration to monks returning to Sukhothai from the island. Whatever the specific inspiration might have been, assuming there was one, for this architectural historian the overriding image of Wat Si Chum's *mondop* is that of a *stupa*: "If, as generally believed, the large … Buddha image was there before the *mondop's* construction, a solid *stupa* would have been out of the question since an interior space was necessary around the image, but the general profile could be adopted nonetheless" (Pichard 2008: 53). The especially tight fit between the colossal Buddha and the monument enveloping it, along with the placement of the ensemble directly behind the enclosed *vihāra*, certainly renders the *stūpa* effect, in which the Buddha relic inside is more or less inaccessible. There is scant space for worship inside the *mondop*. The spatial relation between image and monument creates a dazzling effect for the worshiper on the ground who, once inside can behold the image little better than from the outside, that is to say they cannot behold the image per se, as a whole, but can only be impressed in a nearly literal manner by the monumentality of the Buddha's presence.

Inscription 2, from Wat Si Chum, datable to the latter half of the fourteenth century, is a remarkable text recounting the exploits of prince-become-monk Śrī Śraddhā.[11] The text opens and closes with a sort of précis of Śrī Śraddhā's good Buddhist works, including a focused reference to his construction and veneration of a *stūpa* housing a tooth relic and another housing a famous hair and neckbone relic in a forest monastery. Alternating between the first and third person, the text then tells us of the heroic acts of ancestors, whose sovereign titles were originally bestowed on them by Angkor at the foundation of Sukhothai and then of Śrī Śraddhā's own military prowess before leaving the princely world behind for the monastic order. The ebullient prose then records one pious work after the next, including multiple temple, bodhi tree, *stūpa*, and statue foundation and restoration campaigns, and culminating in an extraordinary, long account of relics performing miracles like fireworks in the sky, evidencing Śrī Śraddhā's extraordinary devout power. Throughout the text, Śrī Śraddhā's acts are associated with "acts of truth" (Pāli: *saccakiriyā*) by which the good works done, including that done in the recording of the vow, are explicitly formulated as building the meritorious path by which Śrī Śraddhā will become a Buddha. Chirapravati judiciously summarises convincing historical arguments for positing Wat Si Chum as the forest monastery named in the inscription and built by Śrī Śraddhā on a preexistent Theravādin site to house a newly introduced forest-dwelling Sinhalese monastic lineage (Chirapravati 2008: 19). The *mondop* with its *jātaka* engravings is assumed to have been among his many good works.

The text weaves in and out of Sukhothai and the neighboring Si Sajjanalai, Mottama (Martaban, a Mon polity on the Andaman coast), India and Sri Lanka, where Śrī Śraddhā appears to have been reordained, in ways that make it often impossible for the reader to discern exactly where this or that event is said to have occurred, and whether it occurred in fact or fiction. Griswold and Prasert na Nagara's (1972: 84–85) comments in this regard are informative on multiple levels:

> the author of inscription 2 is gushing, hyperbolic, at times long-winded and repetitive, at times hurried and elliptical to the point of obscurity. He jumps from one subject to another in a very confusing way, so that painstaking study is sometimes required to decide whether we are in Siam or in Ceylon or in India. ...Despite the oddities of the composition ... when we take the trouble to disentangle the succession of events and straighten out the topography it is one of the most informative we possess.

The authors skillfully do just this by reading Inscription 2 up against another epigraph in which the same Śrī Śraddhā recounts his travels with a slightly greater degree of chronological and topographical clarity. Other scholars have continued the quest to trace Śrī Śraddhā's exact trajectory, pinning down times and places to build a picture of monastic practices and regional exchange networks operating at the time.[12]

These are vital historical points, to which I would like to add reflections on the historical vision had by the text and its author as evinced in the text's very form. The interpretive acrobatics required to set Śrī Śraddhā's record straight is strikingly reminiscent of those long undertaken to explain the "hidden" *jātakas* of Wat Si Chum: they belie a process by which the logic of the interpreter prevails over the logic of the text. What if, then, the form of the text, with its tangled temporalities and twisted topographies, were to be taken on its own terms? The question pulsates throughout Griswold and Prasert's meticulous critical translation but remains unarticulated as such and so unanswered. Instead, following on from their authoritative depiction of the oddities cited earlier, we hear them go further to characterize the author as irrational (Ibid: 89); we hear them ask, in repeating and expanding on their initial depiction, "What of the author's hyperbolic style of writing, his repetitions and ellipses, his jumping about from one subject to another, his dream-like chronology and topography and his general absent-mindedness?" (Ibid: 90) As they attempt to pin down a series of acts recounted in the text to specific times and places we hear them preempt anticipated readerly objections with the argument that "order and continuity are not [the author's] strong points" (Griswold and Prasert na Nagara 1972: 127–128, n. 149). Yet, the shadow of a doubt in their own convictions of the authors' illogic emerges as they qualify their recurrent argument in this regard: "We believe this to be true; but the train of thought may be more complex" (Griswold and Prasert na Nagara 1972: 128, n. 49).

Here in this tiny footnote to a footnote, and as I will show, in like supplementary commentary, Griswold and Prasert are onto something essential to the understanding of Theravāda icons, something that adds another dimension to the historical interpretation that has thus far dominated critical work on the Wat Si Chum text. These are linguistic turns that themselves embody the condensation of time and space by which an icon embodies the powerful presence of the Buddha. The indiscrimination between times, present or past, and places, here or there, which has challenged translators for nearly a century is not only a result of an irrational author. It is rather structurally embedded in the Buddhist practices recorded as in the Buddhist practice of recording. Griswold and Prasert note, for example, the ambivalence embedded in the usage of Tai and Sanskrit verbs that can mean at once "to construct" and "to reconstruct";[13] in the usage of a Tai demonstrative meaning "that" or "there" (*dī nann*) to also or instead mean "this" or "here," an ambivalence which contributes to that of the positioning of the text's enunciating subject vis-à-vis the objects and events he describes in time and space;[14] and in the spectacular capacity for relics to self-reproduce such that duplicates, found, seen, deposited or venerated here and now, are indistinguishable from their "originals." Such questions of linguistic ambivalence bring the translators to concede to footnote a particularly thorny passage as "most likely" … "a kind of religious double-talk" in which a single phrase would reference at once *stūpa*s in Sukhothai and Sri Lanka, as if the one were "magically identified" with the other (Griswold and Prasert na Nagara 1972: 128, n. 149). Call it what you like—condensation, dreamlike or double-talk, the formal dimensions of the text, like those of the *jātaka*–Buddha–*stūpa* ensemble of Wat Si Chum, allow us to think how Buddhist art writ large, that is, text, image, and monument, itself thinks history, in conjunction with how modern scholars might seek to understand history with reference to it.

What is crystal clear from the inscription is that Śrī Śraddhā's life story is that of a *bodhisattva*, a being destined to become a Buddha who accomplishes good works, enabling the fulfillment of that destiny, and that "Sri Lankan" Buddhism comprises the model by which Buddhahood is to be achieved. In the life recorded in stone, Śrī Śraddhā effectively reincarnates the past Buddha in his past lives. As Blackburn has noted in the wake of the text's translators, the account of the transition from domestic to ascetic life mimics first that of Siddhattha leaving the princely fold for the ascetic life at the sight of pains and sorrows of the mundane life and then the *Vessantara Jātaka*, a tale of the past life of the Buddha as Prince Vessantara who gives away fortune, kingdom, and family in accomplishing the perfection of generosity (Blackburn: forthcoming). Here it is the technique of literary allusion which accomplishes the condensation of time and space, such that the tales of the accomplishment of perfection give Śrī Śraddhā's own present person the power of the Buddha-to-be.

This vision of Śrī Śraddhā as a *bodhisattva* is reiterated in a multitude of spectacular ways throughout the text. Early on we learn that his good works are explicitly channeled to promote the Sri Lankan model and intended to forge his predestined path to Buddhahood. The relic miracles are both caused by his devotion to Sri Lankan Buddhism and proof of his future Buddhahood. The two core elements of his formal name, Śrīśraddhārājacūḷamuni Śrīratanalaṅkadīpa, encapsulate his Buddhist person as it appears at the end of the text. The first can be literally rendered August (*Śrī*) Faith (*śraddhā*) Royal (*rāja*) Lock of hair left on crest of the head after shaving, mark of royal distinction (*cūḷa*) Ascetic (*muni*, also spelled *muṇi* in the text); as Griswold and Prasert note, the end compound *cūḷamuṇi* recalls *cūḷamaṇi*, the legendary "Hair-crest Jewel" of the Buddha encased in an eponymous heavenly *stūpa*.[15] The royal monk literally appears to merit this name when in the finale of the spectacular relic miracle performance, after Śrī Śraddhā has thrown himself "on the ground and offered [his] life as an irrevocable gift, vowing to uphold the religion of Laṅkādīpa [Sri Lanka]," two relics are physically embedded in him (Griswold and Prasert na Nagara 1972: 131). The first, a golden relic, circles his head in a propitious manner before landing on it to then install itself in his forehead; the second, a hair plucked from the Buddha's own head when living, lands and stays atop Śrī Śraddhā's own head. At this sight, the Sri Lankan onlookers and artisans Śrī Śraddhā had brought back to Sukhothai with him for the express purpose of building the Sri Lankan model on Tai land exclaim him to be a *buddhāṅga*, a Buddha element or seed or essence, which is to say embodying the remains and the potential of Buddhahood (Griswold and Prasert na Nagara 1972: 104 [Thai text Part II, l. 73]). "The reason they [the relics] performed such miracles," the text tells us, "was to show themselves to all the people, to cause them to help uplift the Dharma of Laṅkā[dīpā] as a great source of merit, and to make the Buddhist religion manifest."[16] The second core element of the epigraphic hero's formal name emphasizes this dimension of his person: he is the August (*Śrī*) Jewel (*ratana*) [of the] Island (*dīpa*) of Lanka.

The Khmer figure periodically in the text, in a sort of apposition, in contrast to the recurrent figuring of Sri Lanka in the position of inspiration and source. Ancestral political relations to the Khmer recorded in the opening of the biographical account are complemented by ancestral cultural relations evidenced throughout the text in its use of Khmer terminology.[17] When recording Śrī Śraddhā's efforts to "save the August Great Royal Reliquary" (*loek hai ka tāṃ braḥ mahādhātu hlvaṅ*) in a phrase combining Khmer, Thai, and Pāli terms, the text adds that "[t]he Khmer call it 'Great Buddha'" (Khmer: *braḥ dhaṃ*) (Griswold and Prasert, Tai text, Part I, ll.20–23). To my mind, it is not entirely clear to which monument this passage refers; and it is of note that the Khmer appellation *braḥ dhaṃ* is common (in modern usage and in Middle Khmer as we understand it) for Buddha images but not for *stūpas* themselves. Chirapravati and Skilling aim to close the long debates on this question in identifying the *braḥ mahādhātu hlvaṅ / braḥ dhaṃ* with the Dhanyakataka in Amaravati (in Andhra Pradesh, India) subsequently named in the text. Chirapravati makes a convincing argument in this regard, notably pointing to ongoing activity in the fourteenth century at this majestic *stūpa* first built in the third century BCE and to the concomitant reference in the Wat Si Chum text to the monument in question having once boasted "stone carvings of the five hundred … jātakas." (Chirapravati 2008: 19–20). The Dhanyakataka did indeed once boast hundreds of scenes of the life of the Buddha and *jātaka* tales sculpted on stone slabs on the inner face of its surrounding railing. Reviewing the epigraphic and art-historical evidence, Chirapravati argues that Śrī Śraddhā could well have visited the site (Chirapravati 2008: 19–20). I argue simply that this convincing historical identification might further serve to inform understandings of the overarching logic of the text and of the practices it records, including the practice of recording it performs, whereby what happens in the South Asian sites reputed for their ancient association with the Buddha is virtually inseparable from what happens in Sukhothai through Śrī Śraddhā's person. Indeed, though Wat Si Chum boasted stone carvings of only one hundred *jātakas*, Pichard calculates that the apparent conception of a tall tower could have well included an intended installation of another four hundred *jātaka* plaques in a passageway continuing to spiral up the monument.

An ancillary point to my point here is that while the text is overarchingly concerned with the Sukhothai-Sri Lankan/Indian relation, the Khmer somehow mattered. Why does Śrī Śraddhā take the time to tell us how the Khmer called the site "saved" from ruin by Śrī Śraddhā? Were Khmer-speaking pilgrims working alongside Śrī Śraddhā in Amaravati, restoring the stone carvings of *jātaka* tales before Śrī Śraddhā would return to Sukhothai to recreate his experiences there—including naming the Khmer name for an early Indian site there in the Wat Si Chum inscription? The possibility is intriguing. In any case it is of note that this late fourteenth-century Tai text discreetly tells us that the Khmer (name) mattered even as the people and the name were statedly, textually pulled into Sukhothai's Sri Lankan orbit.

A last note on Śrī Śraddhā's own dynamic identity will introduce us to our closing consideration of royal Cambodian Theravāda expression. The overarching identification of Śrī Śraddhā as a future Buddha is underpinned by periodic mention of his past Vaishnava lives. As a princely youth he makes a vow to become Rāma, an avatar of Viṣṇu.[18] Later, as a royal monk-*bodhisattva* he is called "Lord Kṛṣṇa," the very "person of Rāma and the god Nārāya(ṇa) who descended from heaven to be reborn and travel through the round of last transmigrations, wandering back and forth from birth to birth" (Ibid: 124). This identification of the *bodhisattva* Śrī Śraddhā as Rāma and Kṛṣṇa, avatars of the god Viṣṇu, also known as Nārāya(ṇa), is followed immediately by an enigmatic and fragmentary quotation: "'Mettaiyo ... Gotamo'," an appeal to Maitreya the future Buddha and Gotama the present Buddha in the singular Theravāda line. In other words, Rāma lingers in and is, in fact, reborn in the person of this (once princely now future) Buddha. It was not unusual for Buddhist kings to be seen in such a Vaishnava light, and the figure endures in the titulature and pageantry of Southeast Asia's remaining Cambodian and Thai monarchies. What interests me here are Śrī Śraddhā's parallel evocations, at Wat Si Chum, of his own (re)incarnation of the many lives of Viṣṇu and the Buddha as he works his way along the path to Awakening. Whether or not his relics are deposited in the *jātaka*–Buddha–*stūpa* ensemble of Wat Si Chum, we cannot be sure. The inscription does, however, ensure his ongoing life (Figure 20.4).

Angkor Wat temple was built on the Angkor plain in what is now northern Cambodia in the twelfth century under the reign of King Sūryavarman II. The *prāsād* (Hindu temple) was dedicated to the god Viṣṇu in association with the founder king for whom it would serve as a posthumous abode. No foundation stele has been found for Angkor Wat, nor do we know what statue originally served as the temple's central icon. The information just conveyed has instead come to us through the temple's twelfth-century sculpted reliefs which are predominantly Vaishnava, and short legends inscribed among these identifying representations of the founder king by his posthumous name, "Paramaviṣṇulok," "He who has gone to Viṣṇu's realm."

Significant transformations were made to Angkor Wat in the sixteenth century. The major components of this transformation were, first, the completion of Vaishnava bas-reliefs in the northeastern wings of the temple's third enclosure galleries. Associated short inscriptions tell

Figure 20.4 Angkor Wat, Siem Reap, Cambodia: temple seen from the west and panel from sixteenth-century reliefs on the eastern section of the northern third-level gallery enclosure plus one of the four Buddhas sculpted into sandstone blocks filling in the central sanctuary's doorways. Photograph of temple courtesy Kim Samnang. Photographs of Buddha in western entranceway and gallery bas-relief panel courtesy Phoeung Dara.

us that these reliefs were sculpted between 1546 and 1564 under the commission of *braḥ pād stac braḥ rāja oṅkār parama rājādhirāja rāmādhipatī parama cakravartirāja* to complete the "narrative panels" "left unfinished" by *braḥ pād mahāviṣṇulok.* The former title is notable in the present context for its Vaishnava orientation naming Rāma and his attribute as a wheel-turning monarch, the *cakra* disc; the latter serves to prove that the temple's founder king was remembered by his posthumous Vaishnava name some four centuries after the fact (Cœdès 1962). The dates correspond to the reign of a king more often known as Ang Chan, notably celebrated in the broader contemporary historical record and later local historiography for leading a Buddhist renewal of the Cambodian kingdom at the time (Groslier 1958; Vickery 1977: esp. 226–228). The twelfth-century reliefs of Angkor Wat's third enclosure include multiple stories of Viṣṇu and his avatars, as well as a historical depiction of King Sūryavarman II and his entourage in procession, and a depiction of beings transmigrating through heavens and hells, their destinies made to be seen as depending on actions committed in past lives. Representing narrative sequences highlighting the heroic actions of Viṣṇu and his avatar Kṛṣṇa, the sixteenth-century reliefs do indeed complete the twelfth-century narrative schema. Art historians have hypothesized, in fact, that at least portions of these later narrative compositions were sketched into the stone in the twelfth century such that Ang Chan's artisans had only to follow their lead (Boisselier 1962: 244; Giteau 1975: 93–111; Roveda 2002: 57).

The second major sixteenth-century transformation of Angkor Wat consisted in the closing off of the originally open central sanctuary: each of the four doorways was filled in with large sandstone blocks sculpted into a colossal standing Buddha. Seen in conjunction with two Khmer language inscriptions at the temple, this modification appears to have comprised the conversion of the central sanctuary into a *stūpa* in the late 1570s to contain the relics of King

Ang Chan's son under the commission of the latter's spouse and their son, now king in his father's stead, whose lengthy title also included Rāma; in the process, the four Buddhas of the central sanctuary-*stūpa* were assimilated with royal ancestors (Lewitz 1970; Thompson 1998). The works accomplished at the temple summit, along with the vows recording them, were explicitly designed to participate in the renewal of ancient Cambodian political power, now under the Buddhist banner. Written respectively in the first-person voice of the queen mother and in a third-person narration of her son, the king, these inscriptions declare themselves to be "vows of truth" (Sanskrit: *satyapraṇidhān*) in the same genre repeatedly cited by Śrī Śraddhā at Wat Si Chum. The operative vocabulary of "saving" (*loek*) an ancient temple in restoring it and in doing so "saving" the Buddhist religion, along with the interchangeability of "constructing" and "reconstructing" (here with the Khmer verb *sāṅ*) seen at Wat Si Chum (with the terms *phlūk* and *pratiṣṭhā*), likewise situate these sixteenth-century Cambodian works in a broad Theravādin politico-cultural complex. The good works in sixteenth-century Cambodia are conceived as enabling Maitreya's coming, but the emphasis is nonetheless on channeling them and the salvation of Buddhism to save the Cambodian kingdom as a whole. In contrast with the fourteenth-century Sukhothai materials discussed earlier, there is no overarching reference to Sri Lanka and no harping insistence on the *bodhisattva* nature of the royal actors.

For their apparently distinct religious orientations, the one Vaishnava and the other Buddhist, as for their asynchronous commissions, these two transformations to Angkor Wat have been consistently interpreted in more or less discrete terms—including by myself in a number of publications. The third enclosure's northeastern Vaishnava reliefs are understood to be the demonstration of a post-Angkorian Cambodian Buddhist king's respect for tradition. The later transformation of the central sanctuary into a *stūpa* with four Buddhas, on the other hand, is understood to comprise an expression of the transformed state of the kingdom in the name of Theravāda Buddhism. The two are presented as discrete if harmonious in the Cambodian context as an example of syncretism by which religious heritage is valued and incorporated into a specifically historically conditioned cultural complex. Art historian Madeleine Giteau's comments in the one monograph to date on post-Angkorian art are telling in this regard: "It is Braḥ Bisṇulok or Vishnu and the Brahmanic gods who reign on [Angkor Wat's] lower level, while the higher levels are dedicated to the Buddha" (Giteau 1975: 89). This is a perfect picture of syncretism as it has often been conceived in Cambodia, where one discrete religion is layered atop another. This is not entirely false, nor, however, is it the whole truth.

What I wish to suggest here, in closing, is that Wat Si Chum, along with its many avatars studied by Robert Brown et al., allows us to see late sixteenth-century Angkor Wat in more holistic terms. The Vaishnava narratives encircling the temple are, I believe, analogous, in sixteenth-century Cambodian terms, with the *jātaka* encircling other sites, working to endow the temple's central icon with its own life and effectively *iconize* the temple as a whole. As they tell the story of Viṣṇu's accomplishments over many lives, they endow the Viṣṇu-Buddha-King(s) in the body of the *stūpa-prāsād* that is Angkor Wat with its own powerful presence. This is akin to what George Cœdès (1992 [1936]: 267) said nearly a century ago with reference to the Angkorian-period mythological and historical narrative reliefs at Angkor Wat as well as at the Mahāyāna Buddhist Bayon temple:

> [the] presence of [narrative reliefs] on the walls of the temple animate him [the god understood to reside in the temple]. ...Just as a statue made according to the fixed rules and duly consecrated according to established rites, *is* the god himself, a bas-relief representing him in this or that episode of his legend contributes greatly to animating the temple with his real presence.[19]

In the late sixteenth century at Angkor Wat, there is no distinction between "Buddhism" and "Vaishnavism," let alone between "Theravāda" and its others; these are modern terms on which the paradigm of syncretism is built. On one critical register, the four-Buddha-*stūpa* ensemble at the summit of Angkor Wat is unmistakeably Theravādin, set as it is within a Pāli context anchored with reference to the Gotama Buddha and the future Maitreya and integral to a broader Theravāda world. But the Theravāda which emerges at Angkor Wat encompasses, amongst many other things, the so-called Historical Buddha *as* Rāma, and this Buddha-Rāma *is* also the Cambodian king and his avatars—past and future. This is to say that Cœdès's reading of relations among the narrative, central statue, and temple at Angkor Wat must be extended in terms of both theory and content to debunk once and for all any lingering notions that Theravāda is "relatively straightforward" (Kinnard 1999: 26). That the classical Cambodian version of the *Rāmāyaṇa*, whose composition dates to around this time, consistently refers to Rāma as a *bodhisattva*, proves my point. Without skipping a beat, Rāma is, like Śrī Śraddhā in his own account of others' exclamations before his miraculous relic-animating feats at Wat Si Chum, called the *buddhaṅkur*, a Buddha element or seed or essence, which is to say embodying the remains and the potential of Buddhahood. The Khmer Rāma is explicitly described in the Khmer *Rāmāyaṇa* as being "in the lineage of the Buddha" (*aṃ pūr tathāgat / baṅs bodhisambhār*), or, further telescoping temporalities, he is at times called the Buddha himself (Pou 1977: 87). In Angkor Wat, I mean to say, we have another iteration of the *jātaka*–Buddha–*stūpa* ensemble, where the life stories make the Buddha–*stūpa* anthropomorphic–aniconic ensemble the icon that it is.

Recent research by art historian Eric Bourdonneau and historian Grégory Mikaelian has highlighted another key element of sixteenth-century developments at Angkor Wat that link the temple at once to the ancient Angkorian *devarāja* cult, to Śrī Śraddhā's fourteenth-century Sukhothai and to the modern Phnom Penh and Bangkok courts while also demonstrating relations between the temple's sixteenth-century Vaishnava lower-level gallery reliefs and its summit. In short, the Brahmanic royal tutelary divinities of Angkor had found new embodiment in the *devālayamahākset*, "residence of the gods of the great sacrificial field," a temple set outside of Sukhothai's city walls within a monastery built on royal commission to host a leading visiting monk and his entourage from Mottama, who had himself resided in Sri Lanka—a monastery minutes away from Wat Si Chum. The sixteenth-century epigraphic record at Angkor Wat noted earlier tells us that the *stūpa-prāsād*'s upper terrace served as the assembly site of these same Brahmanic divinities who effectively oversaw royal initiation ritual; they also appear in the sixteenth-century lower-gallery bas-reliefs. And they have an enduring place in Cambodian and Thai court ritual today (Bourdonneau and Mikaelian 2020).

What we see at Angkor Wat is not a corruption of Theravāda or a syncretic outcome that can only be understood as "Cambodian Theravāda," in which the qualifier implies both the existence of a nonqualified, pure original thing that this one is not and a unique nationally bound thing known nowhere else. Even if what we see at Angkor Wat may be called Ramayanic Theravāda, it is important to remember that this *is* Theravāda just as much as what we see at Wat Si Chum is Theravāda—if Theravāda is anything at all. That is to say: Theravāda is only ever localized, even as it makes its place in broader worlds.

Notes

1 See also the 1997 monograph in which Dehejia develops on this 1990 article, along with Brown's 2001 review of the book in *Artibus Asiae* in which he reiterates both praise for Dehejia's work and a critique of that dimension of her approach which "treats the art as if it were on the walls of a museum or on the screen in a classroom" (Brown 2001: 357).

2 In addition to the synthetic critical work of Kinnard cited earlier, see Huntington 1990, 1992, and 2015, whose critique is also directed at Dehejia on bases shared with Brown to the degree that both seek a more distinctly emic perspective; Schopen 1987, 1991; DeCaroli 2015; and, for the now-classical studies of the very closely related question of Hindu vision: Eck 1981 and Babb 1981. I examine in further detail later Peter Skilling's insightful consideration of this question with specific reference to interpretation of *jātaka* tales but set within a broader critique of art-historical practice (Skilling 2008, esp. p. 80).

3 Kinnard 1999: 25–44. For the specific reference here to the Buddha made present "indexically" in "texts, images and relics and other icons and indices," see Tambiah 1984, ch. 14, p. 202, also cited in Kinnard. I have also grappled with these questions in other contexts: Thompson 2011, 2013, 2020.

4 Brown 1997: 99, reading Boucher 1991. A common rendering of the verse:

> *ye dhammā hetuppabhabvā tesāṃ hetuṃ tathāgato*
> *āha tesañ ca yo nirodho evaṃvādī mahāsamaṇo 'ti*
> (Those *dhammas* which arise from a cause
> The Tathāgata has declared their cause
> And that which is the cessation of them.
> Thus the great renunciant has taught.)
>
> (Translation from Boucher ibid., p. 6, cited by Brown 1997: p. 108, n. 89.)

5 On the image pictured here, held by Wat Mahathat, Ratchaburi, Thailand, see Skilling 2003: 274–5. A well-studied contemporaneous image is from Tuol Preah Theat in Cambodia's Kompong Speu Province and is now held by the Musée national des arts asiatiques Guimet, Paris, inventory no. MG 18891. See Baptiste and Zéphir, 2008: 20–21 and 27–28. The copious bibliography provided in this catalogue entry highlights the piece for its inscription, effectively making it "iconic" also in the more popular sense of the word. See also Skilling 2019, who likewise notes that the "usual function" of the *ye dhammā* verse is "to be installed in a stūpa, the foundation of a building, or a Buddha image" (Skilling 2019: 44). In his veritable corpus of studies on the verse, Skilling brings to light the remarkable corpus of first-millennium Buddha statues bearing *ye dhammā* inscriptions in Pāli, Sanskrit, and Prakrit to which I refer earlier. While this research demonstrates the participation of the verse in creating a common Buddhist culture across mainland Southeast Asia in the first millennium, the use of diverse languages likewise points up a diversity in monastic affiliations at this time.

6 For examination of dimensions of these questions in linguistic realms, see Gethin 1992, in which the truly interminable lists in Buddhist literature are considered for their matricial function: "Translators of Buddhist texts have often taken the word (*mātikā/mātṛkā*) to mean something like 'summary' or 'condensed content.' Although one would hesitate to say that this is incorrect, it is, strictly speaking, to put things the wrong way round, for it is the underlying meaning of 'mother' that seems to inform the use of the term here. A *mātikā* is seen not so much as a condensed summary, as the seed from which something grows. A *mātikā* is something creative—something out of which something further evolves. It is, as it were, pregnant with the Dhamma and able to generate it in all its fullness" (Gethin 1992: 161); and Crosby 2020, esp. ch. 4, who considers how Theravādin meditation practices treat language as a veritably bodily creative principle.

7 Thanks to Trent Walker for initially sharing this image and the details noted previously with me. On the Khom script, in an excellent introduction to the Khmer-Tai Buddhist manuscript culture of which this leporello is a part, see Walker 2018: 1–46, esp. pp. 20–21.

8 A number of the key texts reconsidering the early scholarship on early Buddhist art I summarize here are those by Dehejia, Huntington, and DeCaroli cited earlier. See also Karlsson 2000, 2006.

9 For more on the spread of Theravāda in Cambodia after Angkor, see Thompson forthcoming; and Walker forthcoming.

10 Early Theravādin architectural configurations at Angkor are strikingly similar in this regard, evincing the interchangeability of ancient sanctuary towers or *prāsād* with *stūpa* and, in limited cases, what has been referred to as a "treasury," which most resembles the Sukhothai *mondop* in physical terms. More extensive comparative work than that accomplished to date would no doubt be productive. See in particular Marchal 1918; Gosling 1996; Thompson 1998.

11 For a critical review of the extant scholarly work on dating the text and a reasoned hypothesis that the text dates no earlier than the late 1350s, see Blackburn forthcoming.

12 In addition to Skilling's 2008 edited volume, see Chapter 2 of Anne Blackburn's forthcoming monograph on Theravāda kingdoms.

13 Griswold and Prasert na Nagara 1972: 119, n. 109 (Part II, line 9 of inscription): Tai *phlūk*, where the term is actually used twice in a single passage associating the construction of a *stūpa* with the planting of flowering trees; and p. 127, n. 149 (Part II, line 27 or inscription): Sanskrit *pratiṣṭhā*.

14 The issues arise repeatedly throughout the text. See especially comments in Griswold and Prasert na Nagara 1972: 26, n. 146.

15 The titles appear with a range of small variations on a Pāli-Sanskrit mix of component terms in both Pāli and Sanskrit. I have given the Sanskrit spellings as regularized by Griswold and Prasert na Nagara 1972, p. 75 and note 2.

16 Ibid.: 133. This passage is somewhat ambiguous. Cœdès gives: "The reason for these miracles was to inspire all the people to go to Laṅkādvipa to contribute to making the religion prosper, which is a great and manifest source of merit in the religion of the Buddha" (my translation of Cœdès 1924: 74).

17 One example of the textual positioning of the Khmer in contrast with the Sinhalese comes in a passage which Cœdès translates as "He [Śrī Śraddhā] enjoys observing the prohibitions and meditating in the middle of forests and woods, losing himself there and without food (reduced to content himself with) fruits and roots, behaving in all manners according to the model of the Siṅhala (monks). The people of Kameradesa [the Khmer country] come (to Sukhothai) in search of higher learning" (Cœdès 1924: 64); and which Griswold and Prasert translate as "He [Śrī Śraddhā] likes to observe the precepts and meditate in the depths of woods and forests, absorbed in thought, forgetting to eat. [His usual food is only?] fruits and the roots of plants. His daily routine is [that of] Siṅhala in every way. He likes to wander about the country in search of wisdom" (Griswold and Prasert na Nagara 1972: 113, and note 58). The divergent interpretations hinge on the reading of one consonant as either *k* (in "the Khmer country," *kameradesa*) or *th* (in "wander about the country," *tameradesa*). The latter, while not naming the Khmer as coming to Sukhothai, nonetheless names Śrī Śraddhā's Sinhalese-like quest for wisdom in Sukhothai with the ancient Khmer term *tmer*, from *ter*, "to walk, travel."

18 The passage in question is slightly effaced, giving Harīḥr …, which is very likely Harīḥrakksa—Hariraksa, an epithet of Rama used in the Siamese *Ramayana*. See Griswold and Prasert na Nagara 1972: 166 and n. 89.

19 My translation. Cœdès's comments are explicitly meant to counter European aestheticization of Angkorian art as "art for art's sake," and in such they might be construed as foreshadowing Robert Brown's critique of Dehejia's interpretive paradigm discussed in the opening of the present essay. We are not however reinventing the wheel already perfected by Cœdès. First, Dehejia's reading does in many ways take into account local Buddhist modes of pictorial composition. And, crucially, the contemporary commentators I have elected to work with throughout this chapter advocate significant reconsideration of relations between text and image as perceived in much colonial scholarship. While Cœdès laments the supposed loss of master manuscripts thought to have dictated Angkorian sculpture to a T, from Brown to Skilling, as we have seen, Buddhist art can call for examination in its own right in the absence of any appeal to art for art's sake.

References

Primary Sources

British Library. (n.d.) *Discovering Sacred Texts* online resource, Buddhism. https://www.bl.uk/sacred-texts/collection-items?related_themes=buddhism.

Prachum silacharuk, Part 3. 2508 BE [1965]. Bangkok: Samnak Nayok.

Secondary Sources and Translations

Babb, L.A. 1981. "Glancing: Visual Interaction in Hinduism." *Journal of Anthropological Research* 37 (4): 387–401.

Baptiste, Pierre, Zéphir, Thierry. 2008. *L'Art khmer dans les collections du musée Guimet.* Paris: Édition de la Réunion des musées nationaux.

Blackburn, A. (Forthcoming) *Experimental Sovereignties Across the Pali World, 1200–1550.*

Boucher, Daniel. 1991. "The *Pratītyasamutpādagāthā* and Its Role in the Medieval Cult of the Relics." *Journal of the International Association of Buddhist Studies* 14 (1): 1–27.

Brown, R. 1997. "Narrative as Icon: The *Jātaka* Stories in Ancient Indian and Southeast Asian Architecture." In *Sacred Biography in the Buddhist Traditions of South and Southeast Asia*, ed. J. Schober, 64-109. Honolulu: University of Hawai'i Press.

Brown, R. 2001. "Review of V. Dehejia." *Discourse in Early Buddhist Art: Visual Narratives of India. Artibus Asiae* 61 (2): 355–358.

Boisselier, J. 1962. "Note sur les bas-reliefs tardifs d'Angkor Vat." *Journal Asiatique* 250 (2): 244–248.

Bourdonneau, É., Mikaelian, G. 2020. "L'histoire longue du *Devarāja*: *Pañcaksetr* et figuier à cinq branches dans l'ombre de la danse de Śiva." In *Rāja-maṇḍala: le Modèle royal en Inde*, eds. E. Francis, R. Rousseleau, vol. 37, 81–130. *Puruṣārtha*, École des hautes études en sciences sociales.

Chirapravati, P. 2008. "Illustrating the lives of the Bodhisatta at Wat Si Chum." In *Past Lives of the Buddha. Wat Si Chum: Art, Architecture and Inscriptions*, ed. P. Skilling, 13–39. Bangkok: River Books.

Cœdès, G., ed. and trans. 1924. *Recueil des inscriptions du Siam. Première partie: Inscriptions de Sukhodaya.* Bangkok: Bangkok Times Press.

Cœdès, G. 1992 [1936]. "Légendes indiennes illustrées par les imagiers du Cambodge." In *Articles sur le pays khmer 2*, 267–270. Paris: École française d'Extrême-Orient. (Re-edition from *Cahiers de l'École française d'Extrême-Orient* 6, :24–39).

Cœdès, G. 1962. "La date d'exécution des deux bas-reliefs tardifs d'Angkor Vat." *Journal Asiatique* 2: 235–248.

Crosby, K. 2020. *Esoteric Theravada: The Story of the Forgotten Meditation Tradition of Southeast Asia.* Boulder: Shambhala Press.

DeCaroli, R. 2015. *Image Problems: The Origin and Development of the Buddha's Image in South Asia.* Seattle: University of Washington Press.

Dehejia, V. 1990. "On Modes of Visual Narration in Early Buddhist Art." *The Art Bulletin* 72 (3): 374–392.

Dehejia, V. 1997. *Discourse in Early Buddhist Art: Visual Narratives of India.* New Delhi: Munshiram Manoharlal.

Eck, D. 1981. *Darśan: Seeing the Divine Image in India.* Chambersburg, Pennsylvania: Anima Books.

Gethin, R. 1992. "The Mātikās: Memorization, Mindfulness and the List." In *In the Mirror of Memory: Reflections on Mindfulness and Remembrance in Indian and Tibetan Buddhism*, ed. J. Gyatso, 149–172. Albany: State University of New York Press.

Giteau, M. 1975. *Iconographie du Cambodge Post-Angkorien.* Paris: École française d'Extrême-Orient.

Gosling, B. 1996. *A Chronology of Religious Architecture at Sukhothai, late thirteenth to early fifteenth century.* Chiang Mai: Silkworm Books.

Griswold, A.B., Prasert na Nagara. 1972. "King Lödaiya of Sukhodaya and his Contemporaries. Epigraphic and Historical Studies no. 10" *Journal of the Siam Society* 60 (1): 21–152.

Groslier, B.-P. 1958. *Angkor et le Cambodge au XVIe siècle d'après les sources portugaises et espagnoles.* Paris: Presses Universitaires de France.

Huntington, S.L. 1990. "Early Buddhist Art and the Theory of Aniconism." *Art Journal* 49 (4): 401–408.

Huntington, S.L. 1992. "Aniconism and the Multivalence of Emblems: Another Look." *Ars Orientalis* 22: 111–156.

Huntington, S.L. 2015. "Shifting the Paradigm: The Aniconic Theory and its Terminology." *South Asian Studies* 31 (2): 163–186.

Karlsson, K. 2000. *Face to Face with the Absent Buddha: The Formation of Buddhist Aniconic Art.* PhD diss, Uppsala University.

Karlsson, K. 2006. "The Formation of Early Buddhist Visual Culture." *Material Religion: the Journal of Objects, Art and Belief* 2 (1): 68–95.

Kinnard, J.N. 1999. *Imaging Wisdom: Seeing and Knowing in the Art of Indian Buddhism.* Oxon and New York: Routledge.

Lewitz, S. 1970. "Textes en khmer moyen. Inscriptions modernes d'Angkor 2 et 3." *Bulletin de l'École française d'Extrême-Orient* 57: 99–126.

Marchal, H. 1918. "Monuments secondaires et terrasses bouddhiques d'Aṅkor Thom." *Bulletin de l'École française d'Extrême-Orient* 18 (8): 1–40.

Pichard, P. 2008. "The *Mondop* at Wat Si Chum: New perspectives." In *Past Lives of the Buddha. Wat Si Chum: Art, Architecture and Inscriptions*, ed. P. Skilling, 41–57. Bangkok: River Books.

Pou, S. 1977. *Études sur le Rāmakerti (XVIe-XVIIe siècles).* Paris: École française d'Extrême-Orient.

Schopen, G. 1987. "Burial *Ad Sanctos* and the Physical Presence of the Buddha in Early Indian Buddhism: a Study in the Archaeology of Religions." *Religion* 17: 193–225. [Reprinted in G. Schopen, *Bones, Stones and Buddhist Monks. Collected Papers on the Archaeology, Epigraphy and Texts of Monastic Buddhism in India*, Honolulu, University of Hawai'i Press, 1997, pp. 114–147.]

Schopen, G. 1991. "Monks and the Relic Cult in the *Mahaparinibbana-sutta*: an Old Misunderstanding in Regard to Monastic Buddhism." In *From Benares to Beijing: Essays on Buddhism in Chinese Religion*, ed. K. Shinohara and G. Schopen, 187–201. Oakville, Ontario: Mosaic Press. [Reprinted in G. Schopen, *Bones, Stones and Buddhist Monks. Collected Papers on the Archaeology, Epigraphy and Texts of Monastic Buddhism in India*, Honolulu, University of Hawai'i Press, 1997, pp. 99–113.]

Skilling, P. 2002. "Some Citation Inscriptions from Southeast Asia." *Journal of the Pali Text Society* 27: 159–175.

Skilling, P. 2003. "Traces of the Dharma: Preliminary Reports on some *ye dhammā* and *ye dharmā* inscriptions in Mainland South-East Asia." *Bulletin de l'École française d'Extrême-Orient* 90–91: 273–287.

Skilling, P. 2008. "Narrative, art and ideology: *Jātakas* from India to Sukhothai." In *Past Lives of the Buddha. Wat Si Chum: Art, Architecture and Inscriptions*, ed. P. Skilling, 59–109. Bangkok: River Books.

Skilling, P. 2019. "The Theravaṃsa has always been here: K. 1355 from Angkor Borei." *The Journal of the Siam Society* 107 (2): 43–62.

Tambiah, S.J. 1984. *The Buddhist Saints of the Forest and the Cult of Amulets*. Cambridge: Cambridge University Press.

Thompson, A. 1998. "The Ancestral Cult in Transition: Reflections on Spatial Organization of Cambodia's early Theravada Complex." In *Southeast Asian Archaeology 1996. Proceedings of the 6th International Conference of the European Association of Southeast Asian Archaeologists, Leiden, 2–6 September 1996*, eds. M.J. Klokke, T. De Brujin, 273–295. Hull: Centre for Southeast Asian Studies, University of Hull.

Thompson, A. 2011. "In the Absence of the Buddha: "Aniconism" and the Contentions of Buddhist Art History." In *A Companion to Asian Art and Architecture*, eds. R. Brown, D. Hutton, 398–420. Hoboken: Blackwell.

Thompson, A. 2013. "Forgetting to Remember, Again: on Curatorial Practice and "Cambodian" Art in the Wake of Genocide." *Diacritics, Review of Contemporary Criticism* 41 (2): 82–109.

Thompson, A. 2020. "Anybody: Diasporic Subjectivities and the Figure of the "Historical" Buddha." In *Interlaced Journeys: Diaspora and the Contemporary in Southeast Asian Art*, eds. P. Flores, L. Paracciani, 113–127. Hong Kong: Osage Art Foundation.

Thompson, A., ed. (Forthcoming) *Early Theravadin Cambodia: Perspectives from Art and Archaeology*. Singapore: NUS Press.

Vickery, M. 1977. "Cambodia after Angkor: The Chronicular Evidence for the Fourteenth to Sixteenth Centuries." Ph.D. dissertation, University of Michigan, Ann Arbor.

Walker, Trent. 2018. *Unfolding Buddhism: Communal Scripts, Localized Translations, and the Work of the Dying in Cambodian Chanted Leporellos*. Ph.D. dissertation. University of California, Berkeley.

Walker, Trent. (Forthcoming) "Buddhism in Cambodia: 14–19th centuries." In *Brill's Encyclopedia of Buddhism*, vol. IV. Leiden: Brill.

21

AFFECT

Notes from contemporary Southeast Asian visual culture

Chairat Polmuk

Visualizations of the body and bodily remains are instrumental in Buddhist pedagogical thought, whether to impart its central doctrine of impermanence (*anicca*) or to arouse a sensorial experience of faith (*pasāda*—also translated as "serene joy") that enables acts of devotion and merit-making.[1] In this chapter, I draw on phenomenological accounts of the body—especially its material aspect—from both canonical sources and vernacular practices to explore the Buddhist notion of affect. Particularly, I find narratives of the Buddha's relics in the Theravāda Buddhist corpus extremely instructive for theoretical reflections on the significance of affective experiences in Buddhist thought. As physical traces of the Buddha, the relics capture Buddhism's pedagogical preoccupations with death, grief, and attachment. In practices such as *stūpa* worship or funerary ritual, the religious function of relics can extend beyond a soteriological domain—a realization of impermanence and a cessation of attachment—to an affective entanglement between the living and the dead, between the body and inanimate objects.

In examining these accounts on relics through the lens of affect, I propose to bring scholarship in Buddhist Studies into conversation with affect theory. Set in motion in the late 1990s, the field of affect studies presented a shared attempt to circumvent the privileging of language, representation, and structure during the heyday of the "linguistic turn" that shaped disciplinary trajectories of structuralism and poststructuralism since the early 1960s (Clough and Halley 2007; Gregg and Seigworth 2010). Affect studies scholars' critiques of discursive constructivism and their renewed attention to nonsignifying and embodied intensities are generally indebted to philosophical works of Gilles Deleuze and Félix Guattari and of their predecessors such as Baruch Spinoza and Henri Bergson (Massumi 2002). Deleuze and Guattari are often cited to define and distinguish the term *affect* from a more individuated and cultural designation such as emotion. Affect, according to the French philosophers, is a desubjectivized feeling that challenges the binary opposition between mind and body, subject and object, interiority and exteriority, the psychic and the social.[2]

In Buddhist accounts of relics I examine in this chapter, the evocative power of such material objects to forge sensorial experiences and a kind of attachment across time and space is in line with current theoretical expounding of affect. The power of relics to produce an affective relationship between human bodies and their nonhuman, material milieu, for example, can be understood through what cultural geographer Ben Anderson (2009: 80) calls "affective atmospheres," as he writes that

DOI: 10.4324/9781351026666-26

> [a]tmospheres are generated by bodies—of multiple types—affecting one another as some form of "envelopment" is produced. …Affective qualities emanate from the assembling of the human bodies, discursive bodies, nonhuman bodies, and all the other bodies that make up everyday situations.

Looking at contemporary Southeast Asian visual culture, I stress that affective relations are not purely visceral but aesthetically mediated and historically grounded. My analysis of references to—and representations of—relics in film and video installation by filmmakers Apichatpong Weerasethakul (Thailand) and Rithy Panh (Cambodia) proposes to delineate the ways in which Buddhist exegeses on relics of the Buddha provide a conceptual tool for understanding specific mechanisms and modalities through which the affective transmissions between the body and its material milieu are evoked and how such evocation enables us to attune our sensory experience to historical memory in its hazy and ethereal conditions.

Relics: temporal dialectics and affective attachments

Relics, by embodying the Buddha and his teachings (*dhamma*) in his absence, occupy a privileged place in the Buddhist temporal conceptions of impermanence. In his comprehensive study of relics in relation to the Buddha's biographic process, John Strong (2004: 11) writes,

> Buddhist eschatology thus tends to be a dialectic between themes of continuity and termination, and it is perhaps not surprising that relics, which similarly hold in tension themes of the disappearance of a Buddha and of his ongoing presence, should be featured in some of these scenarios.

This temporal dialectics of the relics, as we shall see, is integral to Buddhist accounts of eschatology and soteriology as much as of affective attachments.

In an account of the "final extinction" of the Buddha's bodily remains—an event known as *dhatu-parinibbāna*, the dialectic of impermanence and continuity is formalized in the context of eschatological transition. Referencing a Pāli commentary composed by the fifth-century Buddhist scholar Buddhaghosa titled *Commentary on the Anguttara Nikāya*, Strong outlines four successive periods of decline—each marked by the disappearance of Buddhist knowledges, practices, or objects—which finally leads to the extinction of the Buddha's relics. This includes the decline of people's ability to attain enlightenment, the loss of people's observance of moral precepts, the disappearance of knowledge of scriptures, and the vanishing of Buddhism's physical emblems, such as the monastic robe and the begging bowl (Ibid.: 222–223). In the final stage, the Buddha's corporeal remains, here specifically referred to as *dhātu-sārira* (a body of relics), will be consumed by fire until the last relic reaches "the state beyond conceptualization (*appaññattika-bhāva*)" (Collins 2010: 116). John Strong and other scholars, such as Steven Collins, understand this event as a marker of the transition between the "present" Gotama Buddha to the succeeding Metteyya Buddha. The destruction of the relics makes possible a sense of closure in the highly repetitive time of Buddhist cosmology. This idea of closure, however, is not completely unambiguous in other versions of the event in which the total destruction of the relics is omitted.[3] Reflecting on this ambiguity, Strong offers a concluding remark worth quoting at length:

> Almost by nature, relics toy with the opposition between "gone" and "not gone." On the one hand, they are, themselves, living entities: they can grow, they can emit rays of

> light, they can fly up into the air and perform miracles. ...On the other hand, they are also reminders of impermanence, of the death of the Buddha, of the end and destruction of his body, of the fact that it was split up into grains the size of mustard seeds and spread throughout the world, or buried beneath huge stupas, sealed into chambers, never to be opened again...until, of course, the end of the Buddha age, when Śākyamuni's relics will reemerge and all come alive once more. Only to "die" and disappear again. Only to make way for the next buddha and his relics. Put all together, then, the sides of this dialectical paradox make relics the powerful embodiment of the process of arising and cessation that characterizes all buddhas and all things.
>
> (Strong, 2004: 239)

While Strong first delineates the dialectic of continuity and discontinuity in the context of Buddhist eschatology, his conclusion that the relics embody "the process of arising and cessation" inherent in all animate and inanimate objects points toward a more generalized understanding of relics. I take this generalization as the basis for examining Buddhist affect and materiality in a more mundane setting. We might say, for instance, that our temporal and affective relations to objects can be viewed through a Buddhist lens in order to gesture toward an interplay between impermanence and continuity. The relics specifically elucidate these affective entanglements in the context of loss. In other words, the affective transaction between the body and the objects in Buddhist thought is expressed most explicitly and intensely when we witness the decay of desired or venerated objects, when an act of mourning or devotion delays the soteriological realization of impermanence and prolongs our attachments to such objects.

Scholars in Buddhist Studies have focused on relics and other related objects such as *stūpas*, Buddha images, and amulets as media that powerfully bind the past with present, the dead and the living, persons and things. In his analysis of Theravāda historical writing from thirteenth-century Sri Lanka in the *Sinhala Thūpavaṃsa*, Stephen C. Berkwitz posits that the text recounts a series of events related to the arrival of the Buddha's relics in Sri Lanka to evoke generalized emotions of serene joy (*pasāda)* and gratitude. In his attempt to reevaluate a conventional reading of the genre of *vaṃsas* as carriers of historical truth, Berkwitz highlights an emotive force of textual representations of relic veneration in transforming audiences into ethical subjects and thus constructing "a connection between remembering the past and performing ritualized *pūjā*, or devotional offerings, in the present" (2001: 155–173). Focusing also on an affective aspect of Buddhist textual and material practices, Andy Rotman (2003) applies Catherine MacKinnon's theoretical framework on pornography to examine the erotic power of objects such as relics, *stūpas*, and Buddha images in early Sanskrit Buddhist *Avadāna* texts that impel viewers to perform meritorious acts. Placing emphasis on the sensory response of viewers as they come into contact with such objects, the erotics of relics refers to affective intensities that animate social and ethical relations between persons and things.

The evocative power of relic media to forge affective attachments across space and time can also be found in Stanley Tambiah's pioneering work on amulets in modern Thailand in which he employs the Peircean notion of indexicality to conceptualize material, social, and economic exchanges enabled by such cultic objects. Regarded by Tambiah as the "sedimentation of power in objects," amulets embody the Buddha's or Buddhist monks' mystical power (*saksit* in Thai, from Pali/Sanskrit *saktisiddhi*) and perfections (*barami* in Thai, from Pali *pāramī*) before transferring them to devotees through existential contact as they circulate across the realm of material life and the marketplace. The indexical traces of important religious as well as historical figures, amulets work like archives as they make possible an intimate access to "condensed and objectified bits of the past" in the present (Tambiah 1984). Extending Tambiah's study of amulets as indexical symbols, Malcolm Eckel borrows Mikhail Bakhtin's concept of the "chronotope" (literally "space-time") to describe the way in which relics and other signs of the Buddha create a "place where space and time intersect to give a particular interpretive structure to a series of events" (Eckel 1992: 62). The interplay between the presence and absence of the Buddha inherent in his relics allows Eckel to parse the concept of emptiness (*śūnyatā*) in the Mahāyāna tradition, arguing that emptiness requires a locus (*āśraya*, also translated as "place," "standpoint," and "substratum") around which the Buddhist community shares interpretive as well as affective knowledge about the Buddha's absence.

While relics are essentially objects of vision (a passage from the *Mahāvaṃsa* reads, "when one sees the relics, one sees the Buddha"), the indexical qualities of such bodily remains also evokes a sense of touch. Or, to use the term by film studies scholar Laura Marks in a different context, relics provide a kind of haptic visuality from worshippers who come into contact with these objects whether through ritual practices or through textually and visually mediated forms.[4] As the Buddhist Studies scholars discussed earlier have shown, when the temporal dialectic of relics is no longer bound up with nibbanic time or epochal transition but unfolds in an ordinary time of material practice, affective attachments are prolonged and reinforced through veneration practices that evoke haptic experiences in audiences.

In what follows, I further expand this nondoctrinal approach by examining cinematic experimentations with the temporal features and affective potentiality of relics in the works of Apichatpong Weerasethakul and Rithy Panh. The filmmakers represent emergent voices of Southeast Asian artists whose works reckon with violent episodes of the Cold War that range from anticommunist killings to genocide. Art historian David Teh (2017) contends that these artists who by no means belong to a singular, unified movement share a commitment to take into account the "transnational revenants" that speak to the political violence and historical injustices. In his survey of contemporary cinematic reckonings with such revenants, Teh includes Apichatpong Weerasethakul's *Primitive* project (2009–2010) and Rithy Panh's *The Missing Picture* (2013), among other films and video art, as examples of the hauntological archive of the post–Cold War era. "The spectral moving images surveyed above," Teh concludes, "are haunted at every turn by the Cold War, both in their narratives and immanently, in their very media, the electronic vectors of an ideological contagion that drew the region together as such into a shared, regional present" (Ibid.: 195). Through the lens of Buddhist affect, I examine Apichatpong's and Panh's subtle deployments of Buddhist elements to interrogate a traumatic history of the Cold War in Thailand and Cambodia. More specifically, I pay close attention to their aesthetic remediations of relics and other related objects ranging from physical remains to archival images, from funerary objects to ruined landscapes, that shed light on Buddhism as comprising modes of affective memorialization of Cold War atrocities.

Remediating relics in Apichatpong Weerasethakul's affective history of the Cold War

Apichatpong Weerasethakul (b. 1970) is an independent Thai filmmaker well known for weaving Buddhist and other vernacular constructs with his critical mediations on modernity, national history, and sexual politics.[5] To elucidate how Buddhist notions of relics inform Apichatpong's depiction of an affective history of the Cold War, I turn to his short film, *Phantoms of Nabua* (*Phi Haeng Ban Nabua*, 2009), an inaugural piece of the *Primitive* project which revisits a history of anticommunist killings in a small village called Nabua in Northeast Thailand. The project was initially inspired by a text titled *A Man Who Can Recall His Past Lives* (*Khon raluek chat dai*), written by Phra Sripariyattiweti, a monk from Apichatpong's hometown in Khon Kaen

Province. In the book, the monk recounts the story of a man named Boonmee, who claims to have the supernatural ability to recollect his past lives as a water buffalo, a cow, a hunter, and a hungry ghost (*phi pret* in Thai, from Pali *peta*). This text belongs to a loosely defined genre of Buddhist literature; its narrative structure would not be unfamiliar to readers from other Southeast Asian Theravādin Buddhist countries.[6] The trope of rebirth figures significantly in the *Primitive* project's centerpiece and a Palme d'Or–winning feature, *Uncle Boonmee Who Can Recall His Past Lives* (*Lung Boonmee Raluek Chat*, 2010).

In *Phantoms of Nabua*, Apichatpong Weerasethakul transforms a mundane landscape—the rice field of Nabua—into a space of affective encounter and contingency through the remediation of relics. The film's establishing shot depicts a projection screen that has been set up in an open rice field at night. At one level, this mise-en-scène is reminiscent of open-air cinema (*nang klang plaeng*) made popular during the Cold War with the pervasive use of lightweight 16mm film and a mobile projector.[7] Far from being nostalgic, however, the invocation of this Cold War cultural relic is intimately linked to the haunting memory of political atrocity. The medium shot that follows reveals projected images on the screen: the *stūpa*-shaped charnel houses where cremated remains of the dead are kept for Buddhist mourning rituals (Figures 21.1a and 21.1b). Surrounded by flashing streams of lightning, the relic shrines appear as a turbulent interplay of light and shadow that intensifies the uncanny sense of a ghostly exposure. Framed by references to Buddhist modes of memorialization, the film thus rematerializes persistent memories of the Cold War as ambient phenomena and ephemeral affective relations.

(a)

(b)

Figure 21.1 a and b Projection of light from Buddhist reliquaries.

Screenshots from *Phantoms of Nabua*. Courtesy of Kick the Machine Films.

Apichatpong's remediation of funerary objects in *Phantoms of Nabua* resonates with these discussions of the temporal and affective dimensions of the Buddha's relics discussed earlier. The projection of light from the Buddhist reliquaries, for example, visually and materially foregrounds an affective relationship between the living and the dead made possible through ritualized or imaginative treatments of bodily remains. Through this cinematic experimentation with the vernacular practice of relic veneration, the film dislodges what will prove to be its central issue, embodied perception, an issue shared with Buddhist formal and informal theorization of relics, from questions of soteriology and moral economy to enact new possibilities for historical reconfiguration. By invoking an experience of haptic visuality, the film uses material remains to create a sense of nonlinear temporal entanglement between past and present rather than to convey any doctrinal lesson on impermanence or attachment. In this sense, the film rearticulates a melancholic attachment to remnants of the Cold War in a new manner by acknowledging and allowing this affective Buddhist relation to trauma and foregrounding it in the film's opening.

Emphasis on mediation, reflexivity, and playful performativity further marks Apichatpong's nondoctrinal Buddhist approach to relics. In the film, the haptic experience enabled by relics is filtered through a screen in a way that reflexively reveals a process of mediation. The screen positions an act of witnessing as a kind of visual engagement but not simply in representational terms. Immediately after we see projected images of the relic *stūpas* on the open-air screen, a group of male teenagers, the descendants of Nabua farmer communists, emerges onto the rice field and begins to kick a blazing football. Through simultaneous movements of light and of bodies, the film creates, for these nonprofessional actors and for audiences, a sensorial experience of witnessing that is embedded in the Buddhist practice of tactile visuality. Literalizing the Buddhist teaching about how we can be "touched" by objects and images through seeing, the film uses the technique of projection and embodied movement to create this kind of (visual) contact.[8]

Near the end of *Phantoms of Nabua*, the group of teenagers burns down the screen with the flaming football, and the projector behind the screen is revealed, shining directly onto us, the audience. This final scene simultaneously positions the teenagers of Nabua, and the audience as witnesses of an affective history that the film evokes through Buddhist memorial objects as well as Buddhist-infused spatiotemporal configurations. The incineration of the screen speaks to the precarious condition of Cold War memories and what it means to bear witness to ephemeral remains of the haunting past in the present.

In Apichatpong Weerasethakul's 2014 short video titled *Fireworks (Archives)*, the temporal dialectics and affective attachments central to Buddhist notions of relics are invoked through the remediation of archival images and Buddhist ruined landscapes. As suggested by its title, the video dramatizes the temporal dialectic of the ephemeral and the collectible and of destruction and commemoration through the use of the atmospheric matter of light and fire. This six-minute-long, single-channel video opens with a grainy black-and-white photograph of a man greeting his audience while surrounded by a group of uniformed officers. Although unidentified in the video, the photograph is quite well known to Thai audiences; it is an iconic photograph of a local leader of the communist movement in the Lao-speaking region in Northeast Thailand, Krong Chandawong, who was publicly executed without trial under a right-wing military regime in 1961. This redeployment of the photograph of the revolutionary leader offers us a glimpse of the marginalized history of the Cold War.

Reflecting further on the photographic archive as a "writing of light," to borrow from Eduardo Cadava (1997), the video then illuminates the screen with the exploding sparks of fireworks, transforming it into a surface for a luminous inscription. The flickering sparks of the fireworks foreground the materiality and movement of light, creating traces of time in space. The atmospheric quality of such luminous, flaming matter figures memories as flashes that, while threatening to disappear forever, leave mental impressions. The blazing fireworks contain a destructive force but also convey a kind of commemoration. As we will see, this commemorative atmosphere transforms the ruined space of a Buddhist temple into a site of haunting memory while the fireworks' illumination seems to bring the temple's bizarre animal sculptures drawn from Buddhist fables and local folktales to life.

In his account of a journey to Sala Keoku, a Buddhist temple near the Thai–Lao border where those animal sculptures are located, Apichatpong recounts the story of the local religious leader who commissioned the construction of the site during the Cold War. According to oral histories, the man was accused of being communist and was imprisoned by the military government. Some of the sculptures were searched and destroyed by the Thai army on the suspicion that he hid weapons inside those lifeless animals. Apichatpong remarks,

> The northeast is a region with a long history of revolts against the government. For me, Sala Keoku represents another kind of rebellion. It's rebellion to religious expression, to beliefs. The state doesn't recognize other religions, so Sala Keoku is like an outcast because it mixes all of these religions together. For me, the place is like an act of protest.[9]

By invoking Sala Keoku as an act of protest, Apichatpong posits the sculptural remnants as nonhuman witnesses to the violent past.

In light of this extradiegetic account, we might understand light and fire in relation to the archive on another level. By rekindling the remnants of destruction, the video constitutes an archive of ashes that enacts the possibility for belated mourning and witnessing.[10] Ash, as the relic of time and the texture of memory, thus evokes not only the visual experience of a dwindling light but also the tactile experience of diminishing heat. This haptic quality of media indicates a nonmonumental and noneventful configuration of memory that hinges on the theoretical Buddhist temporal dialectic of ephemerality and continuity figured prominently in accounts on relics.

If the self-annihilating image of ash already indicates the ephemeral and incomplete nature of the archive, Apichatpong further emphasizes this by explicitly and playfully invoking the Buddhist doctrine of impermanence. The video features a wandering couple who navigate and immerse themselves among those lifeless animals. The woman is taking a photograph of the sculptures, casting on them a red light from her camera flash. The illumination of light here reveals a process of documentation, recording, and archivization through the writing of light. Later on, we witness them mimicking the sculpture of a skeleton couple that depicts the Buddhist meditative practice known as *asubha kammaṭṭhāna*, the practice of meditating on corpses or images of corpses to discern the illusoriness and impermanence of flesh (Figures 21.2a and 21.2b).

This direct reference to Buddhist teachings of impermanence should not be understood in a didactic way. Rather, it should be linked to Apichatpong's experiment with the atmospheric medium of light and fire to meditate on the relics of history. In line with Apichatpong's configuration of the relic-archive as ephemeral and fragmentary, we might read this imagery of decay as a nonlinear temporal conception of history and a reflective meditation on the loss of the Thai political left which has gone unmourned in an official rite of public commemoration. Mobilizing the Buddhist temporal dialectic of endurance and impermanence to meditate on post–Cold War affective histories, Apichatpong, introduces a unique form of attachment to the wounded past—an attachment that resists both the fetishization of trauma and the blissful foreclosure of historical injury.

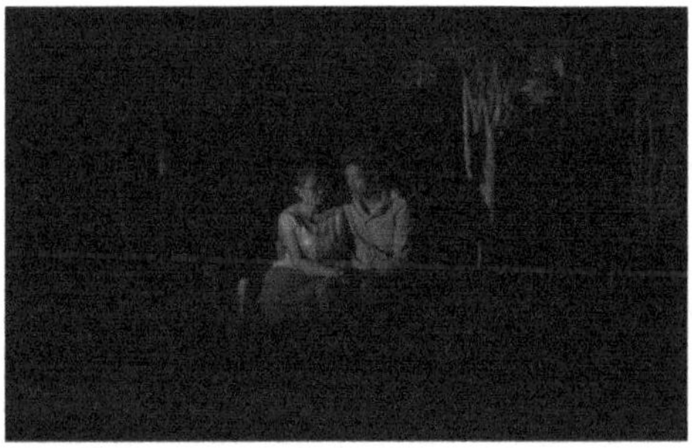

(a)

(b)

Figure 21.2 a and b The Buddhist *memento mori* as a site of endurance and impermanence.
Screenshots from *Fireworks (Archive)s*. Courtesy of Kick the Machine Films.

Relics that bind: Rithy Panh's *The Missing Picture* and the affective trace of the Cambodian genocide

A Khmer Rouge survivor who spent eleven years as a refugee in France (where he attended a film school), Rithy Panh returned to Cambodia in 1990 and began to excavate the country's wounded history through filmmaking. Panh's *The Missing Picture* (2013), a winner of Cannes's Un Certain Regard and an Academy Award nomination in the Best Foreign Language Film category, showcases the director's continuing commitment to personal and collective experiences of the genocide.[11] Panh's aesthetic investment in the history of the Cambodian genocide can be situated within a broader context of cultural restoration, psychological reparation, social reconciliation, and transitional justice in the aftermath of the war. At the same time, his cinematic rematerialization of the genocidal past is also informed by Buddhist beliefs and practices, especially his evocation of bodily remains through the elemental medium of clay in *The Missing Picture* and his allusion to the rag robe or dustheap robe (*paṃsukūla*) in his 2017 operatic co-production, *Bangsokol* (from Pali *paṃsukūla*), to denote death, mourning, and rebirth in the wake of the genocide.

Rithy Panh's *The Missing Picture* opens with images of cinematic detritus: scattered piles of corroded film canisters and discolored celluloid strips housed in a shabby, dusty room. Uncoiled, the old film strips reveal recorded images of a Cambodian classical dance performance that speak to a parallel history of Cambodian cultural restoration and film production in the pre–Khmer Rouge period of the 1950s and 1960s.[12] Shifting from this "missing picture" of a Cambodian cultural history, the film depicts the making of a clay figurine representing Panh's father that

Figure 21.3 Clay sculpting and sensory memory.
Screenshot from *The Missing Picture*. Courtesy of Rithy Panh and Catherine Dussart Production.

evokes a keen sense of touch. "I want to hold him close," narrates the voiceover as those anonymous hands tenderly paint the clay figure—an ordinary act of creation in the aftermath of mass destruction that poignantly links an individual's grief with collective loss (Figure 21.3). Through the invocation of decaying cultural artifacts and ephemeral recollection objects, the film creates what the Holocaust historian James Young (1993) calls "the texture of memory." Nonetheless, whereas Young's inquiry into the material aspect of memory pivots on monumental forms of remembrance (i.e., Holocaust memorials in Europe, Israel, and the United States), Panh's film dramatizes the fragility of memory in post-genocide Cambodia through a Buddhist-inflected reconstruction of the past in a strikingly nonmonumental and impermanent form.

Writing on contemporary art in Cambodia in the early 2000s, Ashley Thompson (2013) demonstrates how the overarching emphasis on the Khmer Rouge in curatorial practice and artistic production has raised concerns about the perpetuation of a Western fantasy of Cambodia as a site of loss and trauma. In her critique of this fantasy promoted by Western media and museum discourses, Thompson turns to Buddhist commemoration as a culturally specific response to the Khmer Rouge tragedy. Reflecting further on Buddhist spirit shrines in Roka Kaong temple in which scattered remains of Khmer Rouge victims are gathered for Buddhist memorialization, Thompson notes,

> This spontaneous assimilation of the Khmer Rouge dead with the Buddha-image-as-reliquary, facilitated by the artistic staging, gave the dead new life as they were symbolically reincorporated into the samsara, the cycle of life, death, and rebirth from which the unburied dead are excluded and so condemned to forever wander the world as famished, unclothed ghosts.
>
> *(Ibid.: 89)*

Proposing a middle path between a complete erasure and an evidentiary display of the remnants of war, Thompson identifies Buddhist material culture as a vernacular mode of commemoration and as an affective form of artistic remediation of the genocidal history. In his essay, Rithy Panh (1999: 30) shows his attentiveness to this Buddhist belief as he writes: "In Cambodia, they say people who've died a violent death can't be reincarnated, that the souls of dead people who haven't had a religious funeral and burial wander the earth forever, haunting the living." How, then, does the Buddhist notion of relics inform Panh's use of clay figurines to represent death and to stage the work of mourning?

Panh's poetic deployment of clay figurines can be considered a subtle invocation of relics in the Buddhist material culture Thompson describes. The film's inaugural mise en abyme, which depicts a figurine of the dead father, vehemently evokes a temporal trope of rebirth: "With clay and with water, with the dead, with rice fields, with living hands, a man is made." In this way, the elemental medium of clay embodies a cycle of death and rebirth, the dissolution of the flesh into dust, and the reconfiguration of life through the earthly material. The materiality of clay itself allows for the meditation on the passage of time in relation to an affective experience of mourning. In its fragility and malleability, clay captures a cyclical sense of time and temporal duration. A mixture of the elements of earth, water, air, and fire, clay often represents the human body—its creation and decomposition—in various myths of origin.[13] This is evident in a burial scene toward the end of the film. A clay figurine is placed in a freshly dug hole in the ground before grains of soil start covering his body and face. Once the whole body is totally covered and under the earth, the same clay corpse reemerges and the burial continues (Figure 21.4a and 21.4b). His visual uncanniness is accompanied by the voice-over: "Mourning is difficult; there is no end to the burial." The unending burial here denotes the mass destruction during the Khmer Rouge regime that makes mourning a daunting task. It also suggests the temporal duration of mourning that enables us to navigate the ruined landscape of loss, to sense the texture of memory, and to forge an affective engagement with fragmented remains of the past.

Panh's reference to Buddhist narrative and practice can also be found in the film's harrowing depiction of the Khmer Rouge's evacuation of Phnom Penh in which he cites lines from an oft-cited Khmer text in verse, the *Buddh Daṃnāy* (*The Predictions of the Buddha*). As archival footage of the desolate capital takes us through debris of urban ruination, a lyrical voice-over narration begins to reiterate the Khmer Rouge's legitimating discourse: "The city is impure. The city is corrupt. It is emptied within hours. Two million people are thrown onto the roads." This is ironically juxtaposed with the Khmer Rouge's utopian vision of pre-capitalist society which ultimately leads to a tragic history. An enigmatic passage from the *Buddh Daṃnāy* is cited to reframe political atrocities, linking the Khmer Rouge's mass destruction to the Buddhist epoch's eventual devastation. The film's voice-over comments:

> The revolution is pure.
> No room for humans.
> Now Phnom Penh can be filmed,
> Like in the prophecy of *Puth Tumneay [Buddh Daṃnāy]*:
> "Houses with no occupants,
> Streets with no pedestrians,
> Stairs no one will climb,
> Flowing rivers of blood."

Loosely based on a Pāli sutra, the *Buddh Daṃnāy* is structured by a Buddhist temporal conception of cosmic epochs or *kalpa*, "a vast cycle of temporality associated with cycles of the

(a)

(b)

Figure 21.4 a and b The unending burial.
Screenshot from *The Missing Picture*. Courtesy of Rithy Panh and Catherine Dussart Production.

dissemination, practice, and decline of the Dhamma, the teachings of the buddhas on 'what is right' and also with the generation, degeneration, destruction, and rebirth of the universe itself" (Hansen 2008: 57). In Cambodia, the text has become an enduring framework through which Khmer Buddhists interpret collective experiences of violence, suffering, and injustice. During the Pol Pot period, variegated versions of the *Buddh Daṃnāy* reemerged as an explanation for the downfall of Cambodian society, especially regarding the eradication of Buddhist institutions and practices, which resonates strongly with the prophecy concerning the destruction of Buddhism by *tamil* (transcribed as *tmil* in Hansen's work, from the ethnonym "Tamil" and designating "enemy" in Khmer, in this case "enemies of Buddhism" or nonbelievers) at the end of a cosmic epoch (Ibid.: 56–62).

While the Buddhist framing of the Khmer Rouge atrocity is hardly Rithy Panh's invention—it is rather a citation of popular religious discourse surrounding the historical event—the visual reiteration of the lines of the Buddhist prophesy in *The Missing Picture* reanimates Buddhist-framed interpretations of the genocide in a new aesthetic context. By invoking the *Buddh Daṃnāy*, Panh provocatively relates the Buddhist conception of temporal corruptibility to the film's aesthetic of decay, the mobilization of material corruption to pollute the Khmer Rouge's ideological underpinnings. The film's invocation of Buddhist narratives of epochal devastation powerfully and satirically figures the destructive force of the Khmer Rouge's dogmatic notions of revolutionary purity and spatiotemporal cleansing. In contrast with violent forms of temporal purification, *The Missing Picture* evokes the Buddhist-informed topos of the relics of time that testify to past terror and its affective residues.

In 2017, Rithy Panh collaborated with the composer Him Sophy in the production of an opera titled *Bangsokol*, a reference to a monastic robe made from the shrouds of abandoned corpses. According to a Pāli text on merit attained in relation to the "dustheap" robe, the *Paṃsukūlanisaṃsaṃ* (*The Account of the Advantages of the Dustheap Robe*), the Buddha originally obtained his robe from a piece of cloth used to wrap the body of the unborn fetus of a deceased young mother. As the Buddha collected the cloth, the putrefying fetus and placenta fell to the ground. In this vivid account, the dustheap robe recalls an amniotic sac and a shroud at the same time and thus "concretizes the rite of passage from the death of one buddha to the birth of the next" (Strong, 2004: 218–220). In everyday practice, this story of the origins of the monastic robe may serve as a reminder to Buddhist monks of impermanence and of the suffering of death and rebirth.

This temporal and affective dimension of the *paṃsukūla* relic is discussed in the study of Cambodian Buddhism by the French ethnologist François Bizot, well known for his memoir as a Khmer Rouge survivor. In the late 1960s and early 1970s, Bizot conducted research on Buddhist practices in Cambodia and wrote a sustained analysis on the *paṃsukūla*. In it, Bizot suggests that the *paṃsukūla* represents a "symbolic womb" and that a ritual centering on this object—especially the healing ritual in which a patient is covered with a shroud while the *paṃsukūla* chant is intoned—can be understood as a process of revivification. While sequences concerning the *paṃsukūla* figure in funerary ritual, they can also constitute healing and life-prolongation ceremonies. In studying the ritual practice and associated texts in Khmer, Thai, and Lao, Bizot underscores a distinction between esoteric practices and "orthodox" traditions that diminish the death/rebirth symbolism to instead highlight the merit-making dimensions of the practice in which robes are offered to monks.[14]Along these lines, I understand this vernacular practice as an extension of the canonical account of the Buddha's dustheap robe in which the temporal dialectics and affective attachments of the relic are central to the conveyance of Buddhist soteriology.

Bangsokol, a libretto composed by Buddhist Studies scholar Trent Walker, references the *paṃsukūla* to convey the realization of impermanence that leads to a blissful state of enlightenment:

> The white *bangsokol* shroud
> lays upon everyone's body.
> A person of virtue may roll it up
> To make it into a robe, intoning thus:
> "How transient the elements of life!
> Their nature is just to arise and pass away.
> Having emerged, they soon disappear.
> Their complete cessation is peace."
> Once this skin is shed, bliss arises,
> relieving all pain, and pollution,
> taking you far away from misfortune
> to tread the path towards happiness.[15]

Drawing on the death/rebirth symbolism of the *paṃsukūla*, the libretto continues, "Alas, my souls, stop your wandering! / Let go of this sadness and strife / Walk forward, come here, follow the sounds, the sounds of music, to take rebirth."[16] Instead of putting an end to *saṃsāra*, this operatic rendition of the Cambodian genocide is concerned with samsaric, repetitive time—the possibility of rebirth—that speaks to the generative dialectic between destruction and survival, between attachment and letting go, and which already lies at the center of scriptural and ritual exegeses concerning the sartorial relic of the Buddha.

In *Bangsokol*, as in *The Missing Picture*, Rithy Panh posits relics as the ties that bind the living with the dead, the past with the present. Relics are the traces of time and the matter of mourning, providing a unique aesthetic mode for activating and sensing the past—tangible yet ephemeral, intimate yet unfamiliar, belated but also becoming. Panh's poetic take on mundane materials through implicit and explicit references to Buddhist accounts of relics creates the texture of memory and foregrounds the affective experience of touch in the process of mourning that ultimately gestures toward a renewed pathway toward reinhabiting the ruined space of post-genocide Cambodia.

Conclusion

Through the notion of relics, I have delineated how visual materials from Southeast Asia enable a kind of affective transaction between the body and its material milieu across space and time. These affective engagements are crucial to artistic interventions in post–Cold War Southeast Asia in which remnants of the violent past continue to haunt the present. As can be seen from the work of Apichatpong Weerasethakul and Rithy Panh, filmic remediations of Cold War relics—be it of the bodily remains, the deteriorated photographs, or the ruined landscape—stage our encounters with those objects, intensify their affective pull, and attune our senses to their mundane yet haunting qualities. Their works exemplify the vital new strain of aesthetic and political interventions among contemporary artists and filmmakers who mobilize Buddhist modes of affective memorialization to address the urgency for historical accountability and justice regarding political violence during the 1950s and the 1970s. This includes, for instance, Lao filmmaker Xaisongkham Induangchanthy, whose short film *Those Below* (*Tok Khang*, 2016) remediates debris of war such as unexploded ordnances to recount the continuing impacts of the American secret war from the 1960s to 1970s, and Cambodian artist Vandy Rattana, who documents the lingering effects—and affects—of the same event in Cambodia through a series of videos and photographs of scarred landscapes in his exhibition, *Bomb Ponds* (2009). In his 2015 short, *Monologue*, Rattana meditates on the death of his sister, a victim of the Khmer Rouge regime, through his imagined dialogue with her at the ground under which five thousand people were buried during the Pol Pot era. Dwelling on the space and time of decay, these post–Cold War media archives deploy Buddhist temporal features to yield a unique account of endurance that allows for an embodied experience of belated witnessing.

In bringing the field of Buddhist Studies into conversation with theories of affect, this chapter has demonstrated how Buddhist concepts of relics offer a sustained exegesis and a culturally specific framework for probing affective potentialities of material objects. Taking its cues from scholars who look beyond pedagogical instrumentalization of affect and the body, my analysis of contemporary Southeast Asian visual culture further extends this nondoctrinal aspect of Buddhism to an investigation of history and politics. Films and video art discussed in the chapter instantiate the way in which contemporary artists incorporate nondoctrinal elements of Buddhism to interrogate a history of oppression rather than to convey Buddhist pedagogy. The incorporation of Buddhist elements into artistic practices reveals how the Buddhist-inflected temporal dialectics of impermanence and continuity open up possibilities for ethical and affective engagements with historical trauma and for articulations of novel forms of aesthetic and political imaginings.

Notes

1 For a discussion on textual representations of the female body to deplore sexual desire and to convey the tenet of impermanence, see Liz Wilson, *Charming Cadavers: Horrific Figurations of the Feminine in Indian Buddhist Hagiographic Literature* (Chicago: University of Chicago Press, 1996). For a discussion on visual practice and faith, see Andy Rotman, *Thus Have I Seen: Visualizing Faith in Early Indian Buddhism* (Oxford: Oxford University Press, 2009).

2 As Deleuze and Guattari write, "[p]ure affects imply an enterprise of desubjectification" and "[s]imilarly, feelings become uprooted from the interiority of the 'subject,' to be projected violently outward into a milieu of pure exteriority that lends them an incredible velocity, a catapulting force: love or hate, they are no longer feelings but affects. See Gilles Deleuze and Félix Guattari, *A Thousand Plateaus: Capitalism and Schizophrenia* (London: Continuum, 2004), 392–393.

3 Strong cites the *Nandimitrāvadāna*, a non-Theravādin text translated by the Chinese monk Xuanzang in which the Buddha's relics are depicted as gradually disappearing into the earth instead of being completely destroyed by fire. See Strong, *Relics of the Buddha*, 225–226.

4 Laura Marks uses the term *haptic visuality* to describe the ways in which the affective potentiality of images should not be limited to the optical since visual media such as film produce bodily sensations beyond vision. Marks specifically looks at films by diasporic directors in which objects and images in the films possess a kind of fetishistic power to recall memories of home and displacement. See Laura Marks, *The Skin of the Film: Intercultural Cinema, Embodiment, and the Senses* (Durham: Duke University Press, 2000).

5 See, for example, Arnika Fuhrmann, *Ghostly Desires: Queer Sexuality and Vernacular Buddhism in Contemporary Thai Cinema* (Durham: Duke University Press, 2016); May Adadol Ingawanij, "Animism and the Performative Realist Cinema of Apichatpong Weerasethakul," in *Screening Nature: Cinema Beyond the Human*, eds. Anat Pick and Guinevere Narraway (New York: Berghahn Books, 2013), 101–105; and Anders Bergstrom, "Cinematic Past Lives: Memory, Modernity, and Cinematic Reincarnation in Apichatpong Weerasethakul's *Uncle Boonmee Who Can Recall His Past Lives*," *Mosaic: A Journal for the Interdisciplinary Study of Literature* 48,4 (2015): 1–16.

6 For example, in his essay on rebirth memory in Cambodia, Erik Davis traces this literary and cultural phenomenon in canonical Buddhist texts in which the Buddha's recollection of past lives is instrumental to understandings of suffering and ultimately spiritual liberation. In popular cultural imagination and practice, the lived experience of past life recollection significantly diverges from the Buddhist pedagogical paradigm and performs different social functions, especially with regard to the reconstruction of social fabrics beyond death. See Erik W. Davis, "Kinship Beyond Death: Ambiguous Relations and Autonomous Children in Cambodia," *Contemporary Buddhism* 16, 1 (2015): 127–128; and Erik W. Davis, "Between Forests and Families: A Remembered Past Life," *People of Virtue: Reconfiguring Religion, Power, and Morality in Cambodia Today*, eds. David Chandler and Alexandra Kent (Copenhagen: NIAS Press, 2009), 128–144.

7 The popularity of the 16mm film between the 1950s and 1970s (often periodized by film scholars as the "16mm era") was a result of the shortage of the 35mm film in the aftermath of World War II. The more mobile and lightweight projecting equipment made the 16mm film widely accessible in the countryside and gave rise to provincial spectatorship. See May Adadol Ingawanij, "Figures of Plebeian Modernity: Film Projection as Performance in Siam/Thailand," *Southeast Asia Program at Cornell Bulletin* (Fall 2014): 10–16.

8 Citing a well-known dictum, "seeing the relics is seeing the Conquerer (i.e. the Buddha)," Steven Collins succinctly notes that "so long as relics exist, so long can the Buddha be seen; but when the relics disappear, such sight (*dassana*, another term with an extensive psycho-theology in Hinduism, as Sanskrit *darsana*, but with no systematic counterpart in Pali) comes to an end; the Buddha finally nirvanizes, this time for ever, when his relics become invisible, by going to the state beyond conceptualization." See Collins, *Nirvana*, 115–117.

9 Paul Dallas, "Apichatpong Weerasethakul by Paul Dallas," *Bomb Magazine* (October 2015), http://bombmagazine.org/article/8429107/apichatpong-weerasethakul, accessed April 29, 2016.

10 See Jacques Derrida, "Poetics and Politics of Witnessing," in *Sovereignties in Question: The Poetics of Paul Celan* (New York: Fordham University Press, 2005), 68. Derrida writes, "Ash, this is also the name of what annihilates or threatens to destroy even the possibility of bearing witness to annihilation. Ash is the figure of annihilation without remainder, without memory, or without a readable or decipherable archive."

11 Panh has extensively explored the subject in his previous films such as *Bophana: A Cambodian Tragedy* (*Bophana, une tragédie cambodgienne*, 1996), *One Evening After the War* (*Un soir après la guerre*, 1998), and *S-21: The Khmer Rouge Killing Machine* (*S-21, la machine de mort khmère rouge*, 2003). In 2006, Panh co-founded the Bophana Center in Phnom Penh, an archive of visual materials and a training center for a new generation of Cambodian filmmakers.

12 See Ingrid Muan and Ly Daravuth, eds., *Cultures of Independence: An Introduction to Cambodian Arts and Culture in the 1950s and 1960s* (Phnom Penh: Reyum, 2001). More recently, the topic of cultural loss has been taken up in independent films such as Davy Chou's *Golden Slumbers* (2012) and John Pirozzi's *Don't Think I've Forgotten: Cambodia's Lost Rock and Roll* (2015).

13 The famous line from *Genesis* reads, "Then the Lord formed a man from the dust of the ground and breathed into his nostrils the breath of life." A Buddhist myth of origin can be found in the *Aggañña-Sutta* (*Discourse on What Is Primary*), which recounts a story about luminous beings who consume the earth-essence and become human beings. See Steven Collins, "The Discourse on What Is Primary (*Aggañña- Sutta*): An Annotated Translation," *Journal of Indian Philosophy* 21, 4 (December 1993), 301–393.

14 François Bizot, *Le don de soi-même: recherches sur le bouddhisme khmer III* (Paris: École française d'Extrême-Orient, 1981). See also Erik Davis, "Binding Mighty Death: The Craft and Authority of the Rag Robe in Cambodian Ritual Technology," in *Deathpower: Buddhism's Ritual Imagination in Cambodia* (New York: Columbia University Press, 2016), 149–151.

15 *Bangsokol: A Requiem for Cambodia*, BAM Howard Opera House and Cambodian Living Arts, December 15–16, 2017. It should be noted that at the theater, this verse was printed and placed on each audience's seat, together with a white cloth representing the *bangsokol* shroud. During the performance, audiences were asked to cover their shoulders with the white cloth.

16 This formulaic summoning of the souls draws from a traditional Khmer ritual text known as "calling the souls" or *hau pralung*. See Ashley Thompson, *Calling the Souls: A Khmer Ritual Text* (Phnom Penh: Reyum, 2004).

References

Anderson, Ben. 2009. "Affective Atmospheres." *Emotion, Space, and Society* 2: 77–81.

Bergstrom, Anders. 2015. "Cinematic Past Lives: Memory, Modernity, and Cinematic Reincarnation Apichatpong Weerasethakul's *Uncle Boonmee Who Can Recall His Past Lives*." *Mosaic: A Journal for Interdisciplinary Study of Literature* 48 (4): 1–16.

Berkwitz, Stephen C. 2001. "Emotions and Ethics in Buddhist History: The *Sinhala Thūpavaṃsa* and the Work of Virtue." *Religion* 31 (2): 155–173.

Bizot, François. 1981. *Le don de soi-même: recherches sur le bouddhisme khmer III.* Paris: École française d' Extrême-Orient.

Bruno, Giuliana. 2002. *Atlas of Emotion: Journeys in Art, Architecture, and Film.* London: Verso.

Cadava, Eduardo. 1997. *Words of Light: Theses on the Photography of History.* Princeton: Princeton University Press.

Clough, Patricia, Halley, Jean, eds. 2007. *The Affective Turn: Theorizing the Social.* Durham: Duke University Press.

Collins, Steven. 2010. *Nirvana: Concept, Imagery, Narrative.* Cambridge: Cambridge University Press.

Collins, Steven. 1993. "The Discourse on What Is Primary (*Aggañña-Sutta*): An Annotated Translation," *Journal of Indian Philosophy* 21 (4): 301–393.

Dallas, Paul. "Apichatpong Weerasethakul by Paul Dallas." *Bomb Magazine* (October 2015), http://bombmagazine.org/article/8429107/apichatpong-weerasethakul. Accessed April 29, 2016.

Davis, Erik. 2009. "Between Forests and Families: A Remembered Past Life." In *People of Virtue: Reconfiguring Religion, Power, and Morality in Cambodia Today.* eds. David Chandler, Alexandra Kent, 128–144. Copenhagen: NIAS Press.

Davis, Erik. 2016. *Deathpower: Buddhism's Ritual Imagination in Cambodia.* New York: Columbia University Press.

Davis, Erik. 2015. "Kinship Beyond Death: Ambiguous Relations and Autonomous Children in Cambodia." *Contemporary Buddhism* 16 (1): 125–140.

Deleuze, Gilles, Félix Guattari. 2004. *A Thousand Plateaus: Capitalism and Schizophrenia*. London: Continuum.

Derrida, Jacques. 2005. "Poetics and Politics of Witnessing." In *Sovereignties in Question: The Poetics of Paul Celan*, eds. Thomas Dutoit, Outi Pasanen, 65-96. New York: Fordham University Press.

Eckel, Malcolm. 1992. *To See the Buddha: A Philosopher's Quest for the Meaning of Nothingness*. Princeton: Princeton University Press.

Fuhrmann, Arnika. 2016. *Ghostly Desires: Queer Sexuality and Vernacular Buddhism in Contemporary Thai Cinema*. Durham: Duke University Press.

Gregg, Melissa, Gregory J. Seigworth, eds. 2010. *The Affect Theory Reader*. Durham: Duke University Press.

Hansen, Anne. 2008. "Gaps in the World: Harm and Violence in Khmer Buddhist Narrative." In *At the Edge of the Forest: Essays on Cambodia, History, and Narrative in Honor of David Chandler*. eds. Anne Hansen, Judy Ledgerwood, 47-70. Ithaca, NY: Cornell Southeast Asia Program.

Massumi, Brian. 2002. *Parables for the Virtual: Movement, Affect, Sensation*. Durham: Duke University Pres.

May Adadol, Ingawanij. 2013. "Animism and the Performative Realist Cinema of Apichatpong Weerasethakul." In *Screening Nature: Cinema Beyond the Human*. eds. Anat Pick, Guinevere Narraway, 91–109. New York: Berghahn Books.

May Adadol, Ingawanij. 2014. "Figures of Plebeian Modernity: Film Projection as Performance in Siam/ Thailand." *Southeast Asia Program at Cornell Bulletin* Fall: 10–16.

Muan, Ingrid, Ly Daravuth, eds. 2001. *Cultures of Independence: An Introduction to Cambodian Arts and Culture in the 1950s and 1960s*. Phnom Penh: Reyum.

Panh, Rithy. 1999. "Cambodia: A Wound That Will Not Heal." *Unesco Courier* 52 (12): 56–65.

Rotman, Andy. 2003. "The Erotics of Practice: Objects and Agency in Buddhist *Avadana* Literature." *American Academy of Religion* 71 (3): 555–578.

Rotman, Andy. 2009. *Thus Have I Seen: Visualizing Faith in Early Indian Buddhism*. Oxford: Oxford University Press.

Strong, John. 2004. *Relics of the Buddha*. Princeton: Princeton University Press.

Tambiah, Stanley. 1984. *The Buddhist Saints of the Forest and the Cult of Amulets: A Study in Charisma, Hagiography, Sectarianism, and Millennial Buddhism*. Cambridge: Cambridge University Press.

Teh, David. 2017. *Thai Art: Currencies of the Contemporary*. Cambridge: The MIT Press.

Thompson, Ashley. 2013. "Forgetting to Remember, Again: On Curatorial Practice and 'Cambodian Art' in the Wake of Genocide." *Diacritics* 41 (2): 82–109.

Thompson, Ashley. 1996. *The Calling of the Souls: A Study of the Khmer Ritual Hau Bralin*. Clayton, Australia: Monash Asia Institute.

Wilson, Liz. 1996. *Charming Cadavers: Horrific Figurations of the Feminine in Indian Buddhist Hagiographic Literature*. Chicago: University of Chicago Press.

Young, James. 1993. *The Texture of Memory: Holocaust Memorials and Meaning*. New Haven: Yale University Press.

22

DEITIES

Supernatural forces in Theravāda Buddhist religious cultures

John Clifford Holt

Before addressing the specific nature of deities and supernatural forces in Theravāda Buddhist religious cultures, there are important preliminary discussions to address, the first of which concerns the term or category of "deity" itself and its suitability for understanding the nature of the divine or supernatural within Theravāda Buddhist religious cultures. The English term *deity* is etymologically related to Latin *deus* and Greek *theos*, but also to Sanskrit and Pāli *deva* or *devatā*, from which the Sinhalese in Sri Lanka derive *dēviyō*, and the Thai-Lao *thewada*. These terms actually signify various types of exalted deities, but none of them equates with the nature and function of Judeo-Christian, Islamic, or Hindu radically transcendent conceptions of the divine, such as Yahweh, Allah, Viṣṇu or Śiva. In some Theravāda contexts, the power of the Buddha may be appealed to directly to help assuage conditions of suffering in this world, or faith in the advent of the future Buddha Maitreya can provide a hope for an auspicious rebirth in the distant future, but unlike the Judeo-Christian, Muslim, and Hindu conceptions of high gods, the Buddha is not an omnipotent creator deity standing outside of and in judgment of human history. Perhaps because of this crucial difference, some commentators, especially early nineteenth-century European armchair scholars, have sometimes labeled Buddhism as "an atheistic creed." This is hardly the case.

Second, in each of the Theravāda religious cultures under consideration, there are other forms of supernatural forces that are to some degree either disembodied in nature or non-anthropomorphically envisaged. These include the *phi* of Thailand and Laos, some *neak ta* in Cambodia, and various forms of *nats* in Myanmar. These supernatural figures are qualitatively not *devas* or deities in the same definitive sense, especially because they do not always exert their powers benevolently within the Buddhist understanding of moral economy, but they are, nevertheless, powerful supernatural forces in their own right and, at times, can function positively in response to the entreaties of Buddhist devotees.

Third, the nature, degrees of relative importance, and extent of assimilation of deities, particularly of Brahmanical or Hindu origins, varies considerably from one national or ethnic Theravāda Buddhist context to another. What can be identified as Theravāda Buddhist religious culture is unique wherever it is found on the ground.[1] Monolithic constructions of the religion need serious qualifications or should be avoided entirely. The same is true in this specific instance regarding the relative importance of deities in different cultural contexts.

DOI: 10.4324/9781351026666-27

Fourth, in Pāli canonical literature, a host of Brahmanic deities are present or alluded to in various textual moments, but in general, they are usually seen as bystanders to the central narrative events and doctrinal or ritual explications with which these texts are more concerned. Perhaps the most visible of these deities often present in the background is Indra, or Sakka, who as the *devarāja* (king of the gods) is featured prominently in a number of *Jātaka* stories as making sure that the Buddha's trajectory of spiritual perfection unfolds in a progressive manner. Important and conspicuous as he is, his function, as with all deities, is always subsidiary to the Buddha.

In the various national Theravāda contexts, *deva*s of Hindu or even Mahāyāna origins seem to appear more prominently in Sinhala, Thai, and Khmer constructions of Buddhist religious culture than in, say, the Lao or Burmese. While their presence in the Thai and Khmer contexts is undoubtedly derived from their ubiquity and centrality to ninth- through thirteenth-century Angkor civilization, whose conceptuality of kingship and polity, not to mention written language and ritual, became in many ways paradigmatic for the Lao and central Thai,[2] the assimilation of Hindu *deva*s has been, perhaps, most completely rendered in the Sinhala Sri Lankan context. It is this instance of a historical *longue durée* that is now addressed.

Buddhist *Devas* in Sri Lanka

The religious culture of Sri Lanka provides an excellent context for discussing what can make for a specifically "Buddhist deity." Indeed, sometimes the Buddha himself is referred to as *devātideva*, or the "god beyond the gods," located beyond the apex of the karmically determined pantheon of deities, the supernatural figures who do the Buddha's bidding in relation to assuaging suffering (*dukkha*) in this world. Obeyesekere (1983, 59) has made the interesting observation that "while the Buddha is made into a kind of god, the god is made into a kind of Buddha." In fact, most deities in Sinhala Buddhist religious culture are understood to be on the path to Buddhahood themselves and to have been provided with warrants (Sinh. *varama*) by the Buddha to assist in compassionately assuaging the conditions of suffering encountered by Buddhist devotees (Holt 2003, 179). In this sense, then, they are soteriologically significant, and by virtue of their perceived intimate relation to the Buddha and his mission, they are unmistakably "Buddhist" in their perceived raison d'être.

Nātha *dēviyō*, whose original identity was none other than Mahāyāna *bodhisattva* Avalokiteśvara, whose cult thrived from the eight through the eleventh century largely in the south and south-eastern littorals of the island (based on an analysis of surviving sculpture; Holt 1991, 72–90), eventually became regarded as the "god of Senkadagala" (the oldest name for the city of Kandy, the late medieval upcountry royal capital of Sri Lanka) and ultimately as the tutelary deity of the dynasty of Kandyan kings from the late sixteenth through the early nineteenth century. Nātha also came to be regarded as one of the four guardian deities (Sinh. *satara varam dēvi*) of the Kandyan kingdom in this late medieval period. His central *dēvālaya* (deity shrine), the oldest remaining architectural structure in the city of Kandy today, is located adjacent to the *Daḷadā Māligāva* (Temple of the [Buddha's] Tooth-Relic) and the former royal palace, and it became the ritual hub for annual rites celebrated throughout the kingdom. But of greater significance is the fact that Nātha finally came to be identified as the deity who would eventually be reborn as Metteyya (Sk. Maitreya; Sinh. Maitri), the future Buddha following Gotama's dispensation who will again make known the *dhamma* for the soteriological benefit of those reborn during his time (Holt 1991, 214–215.) As such, Nātha is regarded by many devotees as the highest and most virtuous of the Sinhala deities ranking immediately below the Buddha Gotama at the apex of the divine hierarchy.

Like the *dēvālayas* dedicated to other higher deities in the Sinhala pantheon, Nātha's shrines field petitions from the faithful on *kemmura days* (Wednesdays and Saturday mornings), the most inauspicious times of the week when people are more likely to feel the greatest need for divine compassion (P. *karuṇā*). Compassion has remained the divine trait most commonly associated with him since his introduction to the island as Avalokiteśvara. The iconography of Nātha images in his *dēvālayas* dating from between the fourteenth and the eighteenth centuries remains consistent with Avalokiteśvara's, insofar as he is always depicted with a Buddha in his crown, indicating not only his near Buddha status but also his unequivocal identification with the soteriological path. His current epithet of Nātha derives from Lokanātha (lord of the world), a name often given to Avalokiteśvara wherever his cult spread throughout South and Southeast Asia (Holt 1991, 41). Significant for the religion as a whole, relevant to the needs of local people where his shrines are located, Nātha epitomizes the nature of Buddhist divinity insofar as he responds compassionately to the immediate existential needs of his petitioners while simultaneously embodying and symbolizing their future soteriological hopes. He is both *laukika* (present-this-worldly) and *lokottara* (future-other-worldly) significant. Indeed, the performance of meritorious acts of positive karmic efficacy by laity is often motivated by the desire to be reborn in Maitri's future time. Often, merit derived from these karmic actions is ritually transferred to deceased family members so that they might gain rebirth in Maitri's era too. This motivation for rebirth during Maitri's era is not limited to the Sinhala Buddhist context but can be found in virtually all other Theravāda oriented religious cultures as well (Holt 1993).

Hindu *devas* were introduced to Sri Lanka from at least the second half of the first millennium, but especially so following the late tenth-century invasion of South Indian Cōḷa armies that decimated Anurādhapura, the longstanding Sinhala royal capital and center of Buddhist monasticism for thirteen centuries (third century BCE–tenth century CE), located in the north-central region of the island known as the *rājaraṭa* (king's country). The subsequent establishment of Polonnaruva as the new capital by the Cōḷas in the eleventh century, about 120 kilometers to the southeast, witnessed an increasing presence of Hindu cultic life, both Śaiva and Vaiṣṇava. The Theravāda Buddhist monastic chronicle, the *Mahāvaṃsa*, especially the sections written in the twelfth- and thirteenth-century Buddhist Polonnaruva period, is replete with many references to Śaiva and Vaiṣṇava deities and practices as it describes the courtly culture of those Sinhala kings who had displaced the Cōḷas in Polonnaruva. Polonnaruva became a great center of power, home not only to a Buddhist monastic *pirivena* (school of higher learning) of some ten thousand resident monks, some of the most resplendent sculpture in the history of Sri Lanka's religious culture, but also the venue of Śaiva and Vaiṣṇava temples and sculpture in the classic South Indian style as well (Holt 2003, 36). Judging from archeological remains in this context, Hindu and Buddhist cultic practices seemed to have been celebrated separately at this time.

In the politically chaotic centuries following the fall of Polonnaruva in the thirteenth century, when many mercenaries were imported from south India to engage in various battles for political hegemony, many Hindu literary and cultic traditions were also introduced at all levels of Sinhala society, from village to court. It is during this particular historical period that a wholesale acceleration of the assimilation of Hindu deities and their worship into a Buddhist rationalized and hierarchically arranged pantheon and cosmos began to take place and processed within ritual contexts. The rationale for this hierarchy, and thereby the manner in which specific deities were understood, was articulated through an understanding of moral economy. The formula for this understanding was simply this: deities are who they are, and do what they do, on the basis of what they have done: the karma they have performed. Karma has empowered them. The more compassionate and beneficial these gods are in relation to their devotees, the further along the path to Buddhahood do they advance. To illustrate their storied careers leading to their contemporary positions of divine power to respond to their devotees' petitions, a vast literature of mythic narratives was formulated accounting for their great past deeds. It is within these narratives illustrating the positive karmic efficacy of their exploits that the perceived dynamics of a moral economy are revealed. At the base of this understanding is the belief that these deities have been enlisted and sanctioned to do work in the world warranted ultimately by the Buddha.

A prime example of assimilation from Hindu to Buddhist context is the *deva* Viṣṇu, ostensibly one of the most important and elevated deities in India's evolving Hindu religious culture. Within the context of Sanskrit and Indian vernacular literature and across the broad spectrum of regionalized Hindu cultic activity, Viṣṇu has a commanding presence. For his devotees, and the devotees of his ten avatars, especially Kṛṣṇa and Rāma, Viṣṇu is the eternal deity who periodically re-creates the world. For the more philosophically minded, he is the embodiment of *brahman*, the fundamental reality or force of this world beyond its variegated and everchanging observable material forms (*māyā*). Periodically, he descends to take the form of an *avatar* (divine incarnation) to restore the order of *dharma* when its efficacy has waned and chaos threatens the well-being of the world. Eventually, when the world is beyond hope at the end of the *Kaliyuga*, the last of four great eons comprising a *kalpa* (temporal world cycle), existence devolves back into his cosmic body, mythically imagined as resting in a dreamlike state during intervals between *kalpa*s.

Viṣṇu's grand profile as one of the highest, if not for some the highest deity in the Hindu cosmos, was not lost on Sinhala Buddhists. There is literary and ritual evidence of the popularity of the epic *Rāmāyana* from the Polonnaruva period forward, but especially during the seventeenth- and eighteenth-century period of the Kandyan kingdom (Holt 2003, 225–246). Of greater importance was the conflation of Viṣṇu's identity with the indigenous deity Upulvan; for, it is this historically earlier Sinhala deity who provides much of the color for what eventually became the "Buddhist Viṣṇu." Of chief importance in this regard is the *Mahāvaṃsa*'s account of what happened at the time just after the Buddha's enlightenment experience. The Buddha

> spoke to Sakka (Indra) ... :"Vijaya, son of Sīhabāhu, is come to Laṅkā from the country of Lāḷa, together with seven hundred followers. In Laṅkā, O lord of the gods, will my religion be established, therefore carefully protect him with his followers and Laṅkā."
>
> When the lord of the gods heard the words of the Tathāgata, he from respect handed over guardianship of Laṅkā to *the god who is in colour like the lotus*.
>
> ... And all the followers of Vijaya came to him and asked him: "What island is this sir?" "The island of Laṅkā," he answered. There are no men here, and here no dangers will arise." And when he had spoken so and sprinkled water on them from his water vessel, and had wound a thread around their hands, he vanished into the air.
>
> (*Mahāvaṃsa* 7: 8; 55; emphasis mine)

In the preceding passage, there are two salient points to emphasize. The first is that "the god who is in colour like the lotus" is a glossed translation of Pāli *devass' uppalavaṇṇassa*. In a footnote to this passage, Wilhelm Geiger, the *Mahāvaṃsa*'s translator, said simply: "That is, Viṣṇu." This assertion, however, is entirely anachronistic, and perhaps this reference to the deity Upulvan that is inherent in this Pāli passage is itself a later interpolation; for, there is no further notice of Upulvan in Sinhala or Pāli literature or inscriptions of any kind until a ninth-century royal inscription, and Upulvan does not seem to gain widespread notoriety until the dissemination of the well-known "Myth of the Sandalwood Image," originating from Devinuvara, and articulated to account for the spread of the Upulvan cult into Sri Lanka's upcountry in the late thirteenth and early fourteenth centuries (Holt 2003, 95–96). Moreover, the eventual conflation of Upulvan and Viṣṇu does not seem to have been affected until the seventeenth century.

The second point of significance is much more straightforward: that Upulvan's act of sprinkling water and tying a thread around the hands of Vijaya's followers is regarded widely as a primordial instantiation of the practice of *pirit*, the ritual of protection par excellence in later Sinhala religious culture that captures one of the basic virtues associated with Viṣṇu: protection. Taking both of these points into consideration, Viṣṇu has been later identified with the original mythic and ritual acts of divine protection accorded to the Sinhala people in Sri Lanka.

But who is Upulvan more specifically and what is the legacy of his cult for the later "Buddhist Viṣṇu"? The following summarizing passage concisely reveals the answer to this question.

> [T]he cult of Upulvan originated amidst Buddhist people most likely in the southern extremities of the island [in the region of modern Devinuwara]. What seems clear is that every notice pertaining to his cult in the Buddhist tradition (the *Mahāvaṃsa-Cūlavaṃsa* or inscriptions left by various Sinhala Buddhist kings) is politically related or politically motivated. He appears as the [protective] guardian deity of the Sinhalas and their religion in the *Mahāvaṃsa* colonization myth of Vijaya; he is the patron deity and namesake of an important regional town [Devinuwara] apparently established in the ninth century by a Buddhist king or contender for the throne; he is thanked by a royal pilgrim (Prince Vīrabāhu) after strategic military victories in the 13th century; he is recognized as one of the "four guardian deities" of the island in the fourteenth century Gampola era; his cult is lavishly patronized by royalty in the 15th c. Kotte period, and he is recognized in 15th c. century *sandēśa* literature as perhaps the most powerful of all the gods (*devarāja*), as one of the most frequently appealed to for divine assistance to benefit the state.
>
> (Holt 2003 100–101; brackets mine here)

The later conceived "Buddhist Viṣṇu" was the beneficiary of this legacy while the cult of Upulvan per se disappeared almost entirely from active propitiation subsequently.

Viṣṇu's relation to the protection of the state was further intensified during the Kandyan period, especially during the reigns of the last six kings who royally endowed Viṣṇu *dēvālaya*s throughout the kingdom, especially the shrines located in proximity to the royal palace, and at Hangurankheta, Gadaladeniya, Lankatilaka, and in Alutnuwara, where for some time Viṣṇu was known locally as "Alutnuvara Dēviyō." During this time, an extensive Sinhala literature recast Viṣṇu's divine exploits within the idiom of the moral economy of karma. He was even regarded in some texts as the future Rāma Buddha. But most significant of all, Viṣṇu came to be known popularly as the guardian protector of the *Buddhasāsana* (Buddhist tradition), a type of "minister of defense" (Holt 2003, 23). It is this important development that was read back anachronistically into the *Mahāvaṃsa* passage about Vijaya's arrival in Sri Lanka cited earlier. Eventually his cult became as thoroughly integrated into local Sinhala religious culture as any other deity on the island (Holt 2003, 24). Indeed, Buddhist villagers in rural Sri Lanka would be surprised to learn that Viṣṇu could be anything other than a Buddhist deity, that his origins derived from Hindu India. Viṣṇu became a paradigmatic symbol of protection, from the level of the village to the state and to the veritable Buddhist tradition in Sri Lanka itself.

This assessment of the "Buddhist Viṣṇu" provides an opportunity to compare and contrast Buddhist conceptions of the divine, specifically Viṣṇu, with the Hindu in order to bring more clarity into the discussion of what constitutes a Buddhist conception of *devas*. Rather than being understood as the cosmic creator of existence who also abstractly embodies the fundamental power of existence, the "Buddhist Viṣṇu" has been subordinated to the soteriological regime of the Buddha. He has become primarily a divine protector of the people, the state, and the monastic community, all understood as destined to sustain the Dhamma of the Buddha. He no longer stands over against the conditioned world of rebirth (*saṃsāra*) but is an active participant in sustaining those whose ultimate religious goal is to transcend it. Viṣṇu is envisaged as being on this same path, and his success in abetting the Buddha's prophecy is what enhances his own progress. Insofar as he is best known now for his role as the protector of the *Buddhasāsana*, his profile is consonant with the consistently asserted modern constitutional responsibilities of the Sri Lankan state[3] to provide special protection to the Buddhist religion. This conception of divinity is far more politically entwined and more thoroughly this-worldly than the Hindu. Yet it is not separate from soteriological significance insofar as not only Viṣṇu is regarded as being on the soteriological path himself but his chief function also is to guard the means by which that soteriological path can be traversed.

The *Phi* of Thai-Lao Buddhist religious culture

Phi may not be regarded as *devas* or deities per se, but they represent a very important and contrasting type of conception of the supernatural in Buddhist Thailand and Laos, and they bear some similarities to the *neak ta* spirits of Cambodia and some *nats* in Myanmar. In Sri Lanka, *devas* and lesser supernatural figures have been thoroughly integrated into what is clearly a Theravāda Buddhist religious episteme. Many deity shrines, including those not found specifically within the precincts of Buddhist temples, are impressive autonomous institutions supervised by socially prestigious lay administrators (*basnāyake nilames*), supported historically through royal endowments of land, and operated by a cadre of full-time specialist priests (*kapuraḷas*) who regularly offer liturgical petitions on behalf of Buddhist laity to deities whose powerful and attractive anthropomorphic likenesses form the focus of devotional attention within highly symbolically decorated *sanctum sanctora*.

By contrast in northeastern Thailand and Laos, the representation of supernatural *phi* is subtle and almost always aniconic.[4] There are virtually no artistic traditions of sculpting anthropomorphic images of *phi* or portraying their mythic or supernatural exploits in temple mural paintings. While diminutive spirit houses for *phi* are regularly positioned near the boundaries of premises for many commercial establishments (usually hotels and guest houses in urban areas like Vientiane and Luang Phrabang in Laos), the shrines for village guardian *phi* are usually humble sheds or ramshackle canopies located in the forest outside the boundaries of the village with little or no symbolic representations, or their presence is indicated simply by a pole or pillar placed at a central location in the village, often in front of the house of the village headman. Some *stūpas* (such as That Dam in central Vientiane) or sacred trees within *vats* (temples) are also regarded as the abode of *phi*. However, there are no freestanding buildings "housing" *phi* within which petitioners can enter to offer their invocations or petitions. Nor will one find full-time administrative or priestly specialists overseeing the wellbeing of a local village *phi* cult or orchestrating an open public ritual at regularized weekly or monthly timings. There may be an annual or semiannual public ritual in honor of the *phi ban* (village spirit), but any other interaction with the village guardian spirit or other *phi* is totally dependent on individual, private initiative, and the availability of part-time ritual specialists.

The relative lack of an iconic tradition for the representation of *phi*, the relative lack of social administration related to the cult, and the relative paucity of public ritual orchestration are sure indications of a relative lack of institutionalization of the *phi* cults in general (Condominas 1973,

254). Yet there is no doubt that the various cults of *phi* are related intimately to a number of important social institutions: beginning with the family household and then extending to private or commonly held village fields, the village *vat* (monastery), the village itself, collections of villages (*muang*), regional chiefdoms, kingdoms, and even the institution of Theravāda Buddhism itself.[5] They may also be associated with particular natural phenomena such as rivers, ponds, caves, or mountains. *Phi* are the spiritual forces linked to specific places. But particularly in Laos, *phi* as supernatural phenomena seem to be significantly more nebulous in nature and function than the *devas* of Sri Lanka, the *nats* of Myanmar, and *neak ta* in Cambodia.[6]

An especially relevant example of "relative lack of institutionalization" is illustrated by the typical spirit house one finds in Lao and Thai urban centers. In contemporary Laos, spirit houses are often constructed so that they resemble miniature Buddhist *vats*. This style of spirit house would, in itself, seem to indicate the domestication of the *phi* cult within a religious culture now dominated by Theravāda Buddhism. Yet there is no image of any kind to be found within the "Buddhist-*vat*-inspired-and-styled spirit house." The spirit house remains an empty dwelling, precisely because the spiritual force that it symbolically represents refuses, ultimately, to be permanently embodied; for the *phi* are actually, within the Lao purview, not essentially personages at all. Rather, they are fundamentally bodiless or "post-embodied" forces, wills, or powers of jurisdiction. So, it would appear that the *phi* of Lao religious culture, unlike the *devas* in Sri Lanka, have not been subjected to, at least not to the same extent, the powerful processes of "Hinduization or Buddhicization" that have contributed significantly to the anthropomorphizing of spirits or minor deities in other nominally Buddhist religious cultures. Although some Lao literature entertained by the elites became coated with a Buddhist moralizing, the popular religious culture of the Lao was never subjected as intensively to the kind of matchmaking identification process between indigenous deities and Hindu gods or Buddhist *bodhisattvas*. Moreover, the *phi* cults have not been subjected to the process of karmic rationalization either. Historically, then, the *phi* cults of the Lao, and the regions of Thailand that are historically of ethnic Lao origins, have remained relatively less acculturated ("sanskritized" or "buddhacized") and have retained their own ontology of power based primarily on power of place.

Consequently, what one doesn't see in play within Lao religious culture, as one does see very clearly in the Sinhala Sri Lankan context, is a thoroughly Buddhistic rationalization that serves to interpret various aspects of popular religion. In Sri Lanka, one can expect to find a variety of ballads, poetry, and/or mythologies, in written or oral forms, explaining, from a Buddhist perspective, how it is that particular deities or spirits have risen to a current status of great power because of how, in the past, they have accumulated vast loads of merit through virtuous exploits, thereby earning warrants from the Buddha himself to dispense power on behalf of the Dhamma to deserving suffering people within a certain region or throughout the country as a whole. In Laos, there are no claims made that any *phi* is regarded as spiritually or morally advanced or a potential candidate for *nibbāna*. Their power, rather than being understood as unambiguously good or morally based, while often protective in nature, is also understood to be potentially destructive if not, at times, malevolent. For *phi* can be of many kinds. Rather than begging a comparison to the *devas* of Sri Lanka, the power of *phi* is more reminiscent of the power of *yakṣas*, a power to be feared because it is ambivalent in nature and less morally informed or engendered. The power of *phi*, therefore, seems less domesticated, less morally guided, less "buddhisticly" channeled, more intrinsic rather than cultivated, and therefore more to be feared because of its ambiguity.

While Theravāda Buddhism in Laos may have become the authorizing religion of the Lao royal courts beginning in Luang Phrabang as early as the late fourteenth or early fifteenth century CE, and while the monastic *vat* eventually became the veritable hub of the *ban* (village) in ethnic Lao cultural areas, the popular religious culture of the Lao in the form of *phi* cults was never provided with a Buddhistic ontology. Along with the related cult of the *khwan*, "vital spirits" or "souls," the cult of the *phi* maintained its own basic conceptual ontology, relating to and sometimes informing but, at the same time, understood apart from Buddhist conceptuality or in a complementary relation to it.[7] Some Western scholars have characterized the relationship between Buddhism and the spirit cults in Lao religious culture as "blended;" still others have used terminology in which Buddhism is seen as "encompassing" or "subordinating." Rather than finding a sustained interpretive Buddhist understanding of *phi* on the basis of Buddhist conceptuality, the converse is actually more likely to be found among the Lao: Buddhist conceptuality, symbol, and ritual tend to be understood at the popular level of Lao culture through the prism of the indigenous religious substratum constituted by the cults of *phi* and *khwan*. Following the French historian of religions Paul Mus, this archaic ontology reverberates or resonates with the same kind of indigenous religious culture or substratum out of which Buddhism, itself, within its own native Indian religious milieu, originally emerged.[8]

In his classic study of *Buddhism and the Spirit Cults of North-east Thailand*, Tambiah (1970: 332) had written that villagers "view malevolent agents more as disorderly forces emanating from the unpredictable external non-human world or the world of the dead than as originating amongst the living contemporary fellow villagers and kin." This observation helps to explain why Buddhism and the spirit cults remain two separate forces in play. *Phi* represent powers from an extra human supernatural plane of existence, and because their powers were not regarded as of human origins, their forces are, therefore, somewhat uncontrollable and require the expertise of a specialized ritual practitioner. Because the actions of *phi* are unpredictable, they fall outside the Buddhist regime of karma, the inexorable principle of cause and effect. Since the powers of *phi* are regarded as phenomena operating outside the cause-and-effect expectations of karmic retribution, *phi* are not necessarily influenced or placated by the ethical behavior of human beings.[9] Their power cannot be controlled through the moral power of karma. Rather, the expressions of their power are more a matter of caprice or, at best, ritual cajoling. Thus, the protective power of *phi* is more likely to be elicited through bargaining and bribes than by undertaking ethical action to please them. Or they may be cajoled not by the ethical power of karmic actions but by the superior magical power that is often associated with Buddhist Pāli *mantras*, Pāli inscribed amulets, and the like. The punishing power of *phi* is also just as likely to be elicited by neglect, by not showing proper respect for their jurisdiction than by unethical behavior in relation to other human beings.

Regarding how aspects of Buddhist religious culture have been interpreted through the prism of the *phi* cult, there are several examples that can be briefly noted. Every *vat* in Laos has a *vat phi* worshipped within the temple sermon hall. It is often none other than the original founding abbot of the temple, akin in function and substance to a *phi ban* (village spirits who are often understood as the original inhabitants or "grandparents"[10] of the village). Second, familial or national *stūpas* are almost always believed to be the abode of a jurisdictional *phi*. They are identified with ancestors of the family, or even with the spirit of the nation (as with the That Luang in Vientiane). And perhaps most controversial, the Prabang image of the Buddha, the image that functioned as the palladium for the Lao Lan Xang kingdom historically, was vested with the kind of power that would be analogous to a *mandala phi*. Its power could be elicited or activated in defense of the kingdom in times of threat. In each of these instances, the ontology of spirits can be seen in operation, an understanding of generative power that renders the ritual and material culture of Theravāda Buddhism within an alternative interpretive frame of reference[11] but one, nonetheless, remaining of vital importance to Lao and Thai Theravāda Buddhists for whom an awareness of a boundary between Buddhism and spirit cults is largely missing.

Nats of Burmese Myanmar

Regarding yet another different conceptualization of the supernatural, *nats* are a category of supernatural beings that is quite eclectic, insofar as their types seem to overlap somewhat with *devas* or *devatās* in Sinhala Buddhist culture, and with the *phi* among the Thai-Lao. Some *neak ta* among the Khmer in Cambodia may also be classified as overlapping in this fashion. *Nats* are basically of three types. First, those that, like some *phi*, are forces associated with natural phenomena such as rivers, forests, or rice fields. These are clearly, like *phi*, jurisdictional and protective. Second, some *nats* very clearly resemble *devas*, some of them directly derived from Hindu culture, whose main function is to protect the *Buddhasāsana* and to assist devotees in their encounters with *dukkha*. A classic visual material expression of these *devas* is found atop the boundary walls protecting the famous thirteenth-century Shwezigon Pagoda in Pagan. The profile of these *devas* is similar to the "Buddhist Viṣṇu" of Sri Lanka. Third, *nats* known collectively as the "37 *nats*" are potentially malevolent forces who have been provided with a mythic or quasi-historical biography that explains their transformations from human to supernatural (Spiro 1967, 42). The brief discussion that follows focuses on this third type; for, these are the most well-known and ubiquitous *nats* in Burmese culture, although few people are actually able to identify all of them and their enumeration varies from locale to locale, despite royal efforts in the eighteenth century to certify their identities in uniform fashion.

Because this type of *nat* is potentially dangerous, the "37 *nats*" are often objects of propitiation. Before entering their jurisdictions, quiet and brief petitions are offered to mollify potential harmful outbreaks. Why these *nats* are bent toward violence and misfortune is suggested by accounts of their earlier human lives, when they were murdered, executed unjustly, or died in very unfortunate circumstances. It is their fury that is now channeled into aptitudes for malevolence, which can strike capriciously for the unsuspecting. It would seem difficult to relate them to positive religious virtues, especially because their cultic celebrations sometimes involve a license to transgress. Spiro (1967, 140–142) went so far as to describe the social behavior of devotees at *nat* festivals as "symbolic opposition to Buddhist values," similar to festivals like Carnival in Christian contexts or *holi* in Hindu, types of ritual reversals in which a release from normative social repressions is expressed. But, in fact, there is a thoroughly Buddhist explanation for the malignant behavior of these *nats* that most Burmese ascribe to since the quality of one's consciousness is so crucial to the rebirth process (it is consciousness [P.: *viññāṇa*] that transmigrates from one birth to another), a violent death presages, or makes very much more likely, what becomes a very unfortunate and dangerous rebirth. In Cambodia, this kind of death is known as "dying in the street" in juxtaposition to "dying at home" (Holt 2017, 240–249). It is not uncommon in all Theravāda Buddhist religious cultures for family members and friends to assuage their dying loved ones in a manner that helps produce mental tranquility during the last moments of life. This is done in the belief that it will ensure smoother transitions to rebirth either in the human realm or in a supernatural afterlife. Here, Buddhist conceptuality (consciousness transmigrating) and indigenous conceptions of spirits have been wedded. The former explains the latter. And it indicates how Buddhist religious culture in Myanmar, as in Sinhala Buddhist Sri Lanka but not so much among the Lao Buddhists, functions as the means by which the supernatural can be explained. The "37 *nats*" died while their minds and dispositions were terrified. They now live out the legacy of that trauma.

The cultic posture assumed in relation to these *nats* is therefore quite defensive or preventative owing to their negative predilections. But they are also propitiated during virtually all life-cycle rites: at birth, at *pabbajjā* (monastic novice ordination), marriage, and death. They may also be venerated simply at different stages of the agricultural cycle. In each of these cases, a *nat* is formally addressed "to evoke assistance ... or, more typically, to avoid his anger" (Spiro 1967, 108). But there are also *nat pwes*, public ritual celebrations that involve singers and orchestras to perform music associated with a particular *nat* that tells of his tragic past and current powers. More important, shamanic ritual specialists are hired to become possessed by the *nat* and then express his will and expectations (Brac de la Perriere 1989). Festivals in honor of one of the "37 *nats*" may be local, regional, or national and are usually held on an annual basis. The most famous national annual festivals are held for the *nat* Min Mahagiri at Mount Popa southeast of Pagan and for the Taungbyon Brothers in Taungbyon north of Mandalay. For Burmese Theravāda Buddhists, the cultic celebration of *nats* is simply a necessity, another means of controlling the forces produced by the karmic dynamics that swirl through samsaric existence.

Conclusion

These various patterns of supernatural conceptions within these Theravāda Buddhist cultures seem to have evolved on the basis of many historical and political factors. One is the degree to which Theravāda, the authorizing religion of kingship, was able to penetrate the grassroots level of religious culture in villages and in peripheral realms of respective kingdoms. For example, Laos itself has always been an especially remote region of Southeast Asia where Theravāda did not arrive with any force at the grassroots level until at least the sixteenth century, less than five hundred years ago. By comparison, Buddhism has been present in Sri Lanka and Myanmar for more than two millennia. Moreover, the comparative weakness of Lao's royal political regimes to exercise cultural hegemony in relation to peripheral regions beyond its capitals made village populations much less likely to be aware of, or conform to, the orthodoxy and orthopraxy of Theravāda or to adopt exclusively a Theravāda epistemic regime. Instead, they remained, as they have to this day, thoroughly subsumed in a worldview in which *phi* remain active powers in their daily lives that require careful attention and respect (Holt 2009, 232–258). A related factor may be attributed to the more intensive types of Hindu cultural migrations that occurred in Sri Lanka, Myanmar, and Angkor, whereby Hindu cults were thoroughly transmitted and took root before being transformed and assimilated under the canopy of Theravāda conceptuality.

Notes

1 It is also actually more common to hear religious people in these national or cultural contexts refer to their religion as Sinhala Buddhism, Burmese Buddhism, Thai Buddhism, Lao Buddhism or Khmer Buddhism, and so on rather than to Theravāda per se (Holt 2017, 3–4).

2 Perhaps the most visible legacy of Hindu *deva* presence through assimilation is the manner in which the kings of Bangkok's Chakri dynasty are enumerated as Rama, the current being designated as *avatar* number 10.

3 See Article 9 of Sri Lanka's current constitution and its extensive discussion in Schonthal (2016).

4 In other regions of Thailand, especially Central Thailand, and even in the Northeast, there is now a pattern of placing an image resembling the Hindu deity Brahma within spirit houses.

5 In some ways, the cult of Nang Thoranee, although not a *phi* per se, functions as a protective cult for the *Buddhasāsana*, functionally akin to Viṣṇu's role in Sri Lanka.

6 Harris also agrees: "[T]he *phiban* [village deities of Laos] are geographically more specific and functionally less well-defined" (Harris 2005: 257; brackets mine). Indeed, the fact that they are more "geographically specific" is a key insight in recognizing their archaic yet continuing function for Lao religious culture.

7 Condominas (1973: 272) also saw the relationship in this very same way: "this common religious core [of the spirit cults] has been penetrated only superficially by exogenous world religions, and has been less than profoundly affected by other cultural elements taken over seemingly *in toto* by the peoples of Southeast Asia" (brackets mine).

8 The art historian Robert De Caroli (2004) has also recently argued cogently that the rise of Buddhism, at least insofar as it can be understood through a study of sculpture and popular literature (especially the *jātakas*), needs to be understood within the context of a religious culture dominated by spirit cults.

9 Davis (2016) does not find this true in contemporary Cambodia, where the ability of Buddhist monks to bind the wild and dangerous power of spirits depends on their moral bases of power, what he calls "Deathpower."

10 This attribution may signal the residual presence of ancestor veneration present within the substratum of religious culture throughout Southeast Asia.

11 For a full discussion of these phenomena, see Holt (2009, 46–53 and 250–258).

References

Ang, Cholean. 1988. "The Place of Animism Within Popular Buddhism in Cambodia: The Example of the Monastery." *Asian Folklore Studies* 47: 35–41.

Brac de la Perriere, Benedicte. 1989. *Les rituels de possession en Birmanie: du culte d'état aux cérémonies priveés.* Paris: Éditions Recherche sur les Civilisations.

Condominas, Georges. 1973. "Phiban Cults in Rural Laos." In *Change and Persistence in Thai Society*, eds. William Skinner, A. Thomas Kirsh, 252–273. Ithaca, NY: Cornell University Press.

Davis, Erik. 2016. *Deathpower: Buddhism's Ritual Imagination in Cambodia.* New York: Columbia University Press.

De Caroli, Robert. 2004. *Haunting the Buddha.* New York: Oxford University Press.

Eberhardt, Nancy. 2006. *Imagining the Course of Life: Self-transformation in a Shan Buddhist Community.* Honolulu: University of Hawaii Press.

Ebihara, May. 1968. "Sway, a Khmer Village in Cambodia." Ph.D. dissertation, Columbia University.

Gombrich, Richard. 1971. *Precept and Practice: Traditional Buddhism in the Rural Highlands of Ceylon.* Oxford, UK: Oxford University Press.

Gombrich, Richard, Gananath Obeyesekere. 1988. *Buddhism Transformed: Religious Change in Sri Lanka.* Princeton, NJ: Princeton University Press.

Harris, Ian. 2005. *Cambodian Buddhism: History and Practice.* Honolulu: University of Hawai'i Press.

Holt, John Clifford, ed., and U.P. Meddegama, trans. 1993. *The Anāgatavaṃsa Desanā: The Sermon of the Chronicle-to-be.* Delhi: Motilal Banarsidass.

Holt, John Clifford 1991. *Buddha in the Crown: Avalokiteśvara in the Buddhist Traditions of Sri Lanka.* New York: Oxford University Press.

Holt, John Clifford. 2003. *The Buddhist Viṣṇu: Religious Transformation, Politics and Culture.* New York: Columbia University Press.

Holt, John Clifford. 2009. *Spirits of the Place: Buddhism and Lao Religious Culture.* Honolulu: University of Hawai'i Press.

Holt, John Clifford. 2017. *Theravāda Traditions: Buddhist Ritual Cultures in Contemporary Southeast Asia and Sri Lanka.* Honolulu: University of Hawaii Press.

Kapferer, Bruce. 1983. *A Celebration of Demons.* Bloomington: Indiana University Press.

Mahāvaṃsa or the Great Chronicle of Ceylon. 1950 Trans, and ed. Wilhem Geiger. Colombo: Ceylon Government Department of Information; originally published by the Pali Text Society in London, 1912.

Masefield, Peter. 1986. *Divine Revelation in Pali Buddhism.* Boston: George Allen and Unwin.

McDaniel, Justin. 2011. *The Lovelorn Ghost and the Magical Monk: Practicing Buddhism in Modern Thailand.* New York: Columbia University Press.

Mus, Paul. 1975. "*India Seen from the East.* Trans. from the French by I.W. Mabbett, ed. I.W. Mabbett and D.P. Chandler. Monash: Monash University Centre of Southeast Asian Studies; originally published as "Cultes indiens et indigenes au Champa"." *Bulletin de l'École française d'Extrême-Orient* 33 (1933): 367–410.

Obeyesekere, Gananath. 1983. *The Cult of the Goddess Pattini.* Chicago: University of Chicago Press.

Padma, Sree. 2019. "Are *Satara Varan Devi* Sinhala Buddhist Deities? Vibishana, a Case Study." In *Sagar* (South Asia Institute, University of Texas at Austin), 26: 92–119.

Poree-Maspero, Eveline. 1951. "Le ceremonie de l'appel des esperits vitaux chez les cambodgiens." *Bulletin de l'École française d'Extrême-Orient* 45 (1): 145–183.

Schonthal, Benjamin. 2016. *Buddhism, Politics and the Limits of Law: The Pyrrhic Constitutionalism of Sri Lanka.* Cambridge, UK: Cambridge University Press.

Spiro, Melford. 1967. *Burmese Supernaturalism*. Englewood Cliffs, NJ: Prentice-Hall.
Strong, John. 2004. *Relics of the Buddha*. Princeton: Princeton University Press.
Tambiah, S.J. 1970. *Buddhism and the Spirit Cults of Northeast Thailand*. Cambridge, UK: Cambridge University Press.
Thompson, Ashley. 1996. *The Calling of the Souls: A Study of the Khmer Ritual Hau Bralin*. Clayton, Australia: Monash University Centre of Southeast Asian Studies.
Zucker, Eve. 2013. *Forest of Struggle: Moralities of Remembrance in Upland Cambodia*. Honolulu: University of Hawai'i Press.

23

MONS

Creating a narrative of the origins of Theravāda

Patrick McCormick

Constructing an image: Mons in Southeast Asia

Seeing "the Mons" as a people of Theravāda Buddhism, as the first Theravāda Buddhist civilization of Burma and Southeast Asia, or as the people who brought Theravāda Buddhism to the rest of Southeast Asia is to recast an ambiguous, contingent past through a series of "modern," colonial-era practices of creating knowledge and the ensuing categories. Each of these terms, *the Mons*, *Theravāda*, *Buddhism*, *Burma*, and *Southeast Asia*, is a historically contingent product of modernity with little depth beyond 150 years and are not simply natural given categories of thought. A British technology of governance, the classification of the peoples of the newly conquered colony of Burma by language, led to the creation of "races" based in the new colony. Colonial conquest imposed definite borders on the new colony and thus created another new subject. At the same time, a similar mania for classification, this time situated in a wider European conversation on "religion," created new religions and religious categories, including "Hinduism" and "Buddhism," the latter further divided into "Theravāda" and "Mahāyāna," among others.

Each of these new subjects became objects of study, sites of history (the bound territories in which history occurred) or agents in history (racialized actors), and subject to further processes inherent in the logic of their emergence. Race emerged out of Romantic nationalism, which associates each race with its own history, territory, language, culture, and sometimes religion. One of the primary concerns of "history" in this context, whether of a race or of territory delimited as a kingdom, colony, or country, is to establish origins, or the point in time when that race or territory "emerged" into history in the shape it has today.

The British created nothing out of whole cloth. The British (who themselves in the nineteenth century were a recently emerged subject) did not arrive on the scene and conjure subject races out of thin air, nor was it they who sowed dissent among those races and subjects where only harmony across difference had existed before. Rather, the British usurped local prerogatives to write and interpret local pasts. In Burma—even if renamed Myanmar, it is still the same colonial-defined construction—local scholars and intellectuals have largely come to accept those British terms and practices, in particular the reorganization of language, culture, and difference under the boundaries of "race" (rechristened "ethnicity" during the twentieth century), and the reconfiguration of history as the search for origins. *Origins*, in this sense, points to the

DOI: 10.4324/9781351026666-28

moment when a race—a racial subject—emerged as an actor in a historical narrative, usually the narrative of the origins of a kingdom or country. In the process of adopting these practices and categories, local scholars and intellectuals have taken forward a central concern of precolonial historiography, the lineage of the *sāsana* (now reconfigured as "Theravāda Buddhism"; Skilling et al. 2012), and the connection of local kingdoms and rulers to the *sāsana*, whether as patrons, purifiers, or as descendants of supra-local patrons and purifiers located elsewhere in (what we now call the Theravāda) Buddhist cosmopolis (Pollock 2006; Goh 2014). Today, the intellectuals of one of those newly emerged races, the Mons, have come to understand and define themselves through an assertion ("the Mons have the first Theravāda Buddhist civilization of Burma and Southeast Asia") that is couched in colonial and postcolonial terms, each an interpretation and rearticulation of local experiences.

Spatial constraints allow me to explore just one aspect of this conjuncture: how the association between Mon and Theravāda came to hold definitional importance to Mon intellectuals in their projects of writing and interpreting their own history. Tracing this process involves crossing unexpected territory, at least if the traveler is following the premises of race or ethnicity: modern stories of Mon origins are deeply intertwined with Burmese-language sources, not only to the origins of "Burma" but also, disconcertingly, with the country now called Thailand. Even if the story of Mon origins as local scholars and intellectuals create and retell it finds its own origins in the emergence of British categories and practices, that story remains only loosely connected to ongoing conversations taking place largely outside the country about archaeology, race, or ethnicity and "Theravāda" among cosmopolitan scholars.[1]

Cosmopolitan scholars and the search for Mon origins

Despite decades of studying nationalism and deconstructing ethnicity, such heuristic terms as *the Mon* remain in common use. Inherent in an ethnonym is the idea of a coherent people who have their origins in a particular time and place. It is not clear that the cosmopolitan "scholarly gaze" treats this association with the reservation it deserves: Robbins Burling, an anthropologist and linguist who worked extensively in Southeast Asia and Northeast India, has pointed to the absurdity of asking, for example, "When did 'the French' begin?" Yet questions of origins have become so naturalized in the study of Southeast Asia that cosmopolitan scholars rarely question it. Local scholars have taken up the quest for them with great seriousness (Burling 2012: 49–62). The origins of the Mons are intertwined with the spread of "Theravāda" Buddhism to a region now called "mainland Southeast Asia" through Mon intermediaries. Local scholars see Theravāda Buddhism as the purest and best form of Buddhism, and they take great pride in this association. The corollary is a suspicion of and hostility toward any attempts to untangle or historicize what are, after all, terms situated in a recently emerged discourse, here, "*the Mons*" and "*Theravāda*."

Nevertheless, the origins remain a compelling question. Where did the Mon come from, or said another way, when did the Mons first appear? Archaeological, art historical, and linguistic evidence serves to answer such questions. For most of the ancient peoples of Southeast Asia, this evidence includes inscriptions and various physical artifacts, especially temples and shrines. Scholars see the sixth century CE as the starting point of Mon civilization, which was when the first inscriptions in the earliest form of the Mon language appeared in what is now Central Thailand, at the same time that inscriptions in Khmer appeared a bit farther east. These Old Mon inscriptions are associated with such religious objects as votive tablets or "Buddhist sealings" and *dharmacakras* or "wheels of the law" (Skilling 2019). Such objects render the Mon past legible and so seemingly mark the emergence of the Mons into history and therefore the Mon people (Brown 1996).

Of crucial importance here is an equation so naturalized as to be self-evident and unremarked, at least in English-language scholarship: language is equated with ethnicity, so evidence of a language is taken as evidence of an ethnicity, usually in the sense of indicating the ancestors of a group existing today (McAuliffe 2017). To historicize this association, consider whether the appearance of (Classical) Latin inscriptions in Spain would be taken as evidence of "the Spanish" there. Many take the appearance of a language as evidence for ethnic emergence.

Earlier generations of cosmopolitan scholars, most prominently French archaeologist and historian Georges Cœdès, built a narrative of the "Indianization" of Southeast Asia based on how Mon- and Khmer-language inscriptions appear in close association with artifacts bearing clear Indic connections (Cœdès 1968). Mon-language inscriptions appear with Pāli-language inscriptions, suggesting a "Theravāda Buddhist cosmopolis" (Pollock 2006; Thompson 2016). As a result, there has emerged the idea that the Mons were the first Theravāda Buddhists of mainland Southeast Asia, who were responsible for transmitting Theravāda Buddhism to the rest of the region. That same early generation of scholars thought that the linguistic and art-historical evidence also indicated an entire cultural complex, which they associated with an empire, called Dvāravatī. Cœdès and Quaritch Wales were some of the first to write about Dvāravatī in these terms (Wales 1969). Perhaps physical and linguistic proximity between the Khmers and the Mons led many to assume that the Dvāravatī was the same kind of entity as the Khmer or Angkor "empire."[2]

Around the turn of the second millennium CE, our story of the Mons becomes more complicated. Mon language inscriptions and artifacts continue to appear until about the thirteenth century throughout what are now the Central, North, and Northeast regions of Thailand and even over into what is now Laos. Sometime in the tenth to eleventh centuries CE, art and architectural styles, which the highly influential British scholar G.H. Luce attributed to the Mons, start to appear in Pagan in the form of Buddhist temples. Mon- and Burmese-language inscriptions appear at about the same time in the eleventh century.

In recent years, cosmopolitan scholars have begun the important work of revisiting the foundational interpretative work of the early founders of modern, high-colonial Burmese historiography, attempting to move historiographical conversations into the postcolonial. Michael Aung-Thwin (2005), for example, questions many of the ethnic attributions and associations that Luce and others claimed and which have become set in proverbial stone. From a linguistic perspective, Pagan falls considerably to the west, both of all earlier Mon-related finds and, more generally, from the center of gravity of most of the Austroasiatic languages, the family to which Mon belongs. The usual reading of such geographical dispersion has simply been that the Mons had a wide-ranging presence. Another reading is that local peoples (here, the people of Pagan) associated the Mon language and cultural forms with the prestige and power of Buddhism and expressed themselves through that trans-local medium with the assistance of experts invited there.[3] Luce saw Pagan as the beginning of Burma—ancient in its lineage, new in its conception—so Pagan was the locus of the emergence of the Burmese language, people, and culture. That emergence was predicated upon the presence of the Mons and Theravāda Buddhism at that founding. Pagan thus establishes the prestige of Burma as a particular inheritor of the Theravāda tradition. Even if similar Theravādin practices or lineages stand behind other countries, such as Thailand or Cambodia, the lineage of Burma is thus one of the most ancient. As I explore in the following, the cosmopolitan concern with Theravāda and Burma is—wittingly or not—caught up in the discourse of legitimation, precedence, and a narrative of purity, many of the same concerns of local precolonial historiographies.

Local historiographies of "origins" before the colonial encounter

This cosmopolitan narrative is not anything like that found in local historiographies before the colonial era, in the sense that local historiographies were not concerned with origins or the various subjects that emerged in the colonial moment: the Mons, the Burmese, Theravāda Buddhism, and Burma. In a grammatical sense, none of those terms occur in the subject position. Rather, local narratives concerned the lineage of the *sāsana* (a preconfiguration of the latter-day "Theravāda Buddhism") of the "Mon lands," with latter polities in the place that became Burma. We must first, however, deal with the tricky nature of local sources and fraught questions of textual lineage, the former of vital interest to the "proper" practice of history, and the latter often a fetish of historian and Pāli scholar alike. Before briefly reviewing the development of a particular narrative as a way to understand local historiographies, however, we must deal with the tricky nature of local sources. The quest to recover a precolonial local historiography—at least one based solely on Mon-language sources, taken as representative of "Mon historiography"—involves questions of "authenticity," transmission across languages, and complex, interdependent textual lineages.

A common expectation is that the Mon past will have come down to the present in the Mon language through ancient Mon texts written in "Monland," understood as a sort of kingdom-empire in what is today Lower Burma. The preponderance of history-related texts in the Mon language is extant in the form of a two-volume book, the *Rājāvaṁsa Kathā*, printed in the Mon community of Pak Lat in Siam in the early twentieth century (Candakanta 1912). In other words, the "primary" texts of "Mon history" are artifacts of modernity.[4] Based on linguistic evidence, the component texts of the *Rājāvaṁsa Kathā* were partly composed around the time of printing, while other sections were taken from written predecessors, either in Mon or Thai (McCormick 2011a, 2011b). No manuscript of any of the component texts are extant in Burma or Thailand today in the exact form as in the *Rājāvaṁsa Kathā*. A lack of exact antecedents, however, reflects not the inauthenticity or unreliability of the *Rājāvaṁsa Kathā* but, rather, reminds us of the extent to which textual lineages—even those of religious texts in a classical language like Sanskrit or Pāli—also incorporate change, "improvements," even oral elements, with each inscription (McCormick 2010; Veidlinger 2006).

Mon-language accounts

I consider a few "retellings" of one of the earliest narratives concerning the people we think of as Mons from a local perspective. I use the term *retelling* because it suggests but one iteration of a narrative, without the specter of degradation from a pure "original" inherent in the term "*version*." The first I consider is perhaps not the oldest, but it is the retelling that has served as a site of elaboration over the centuries.

The first retelling is but a brief blurb in the Kalyāṇī Inscriptions erected between 1476 and 1478 to record King Dhammacetī's purification of the local *sāsana* in his kingdom of Haṁsāvatī, or Pegu/Bago.[5] The stone plaques, written in Pāli, commemorate the purification and describe why Dhammacetī sent local monks to Laṅkā to be reordained in the more orthodox Mahāvihāra tradition there. The inscriptions start with earlier examples of monarchs undertaking purifications of the *sāsana*, such as King Aśoka. After the narrative of the trip to Laṅkā, the text concerns details of the new ordination ritual.

The incident of interest falls towards the very beginning of the inscriptions in a section outlining the history of the *sāsana* in and around Haṁsāvatī. The text speaks of its arrival in

"Rāmañña lands." I offer my translation of a recent Mon-language text, Nāy Indaka's *Prakuih Trāy Lik Tma? Kalyāṇī* (*Nissaya Treatise on the Kalyāṇī Inscriptions*):[6]

> When Manuhaw [Manuhā] or Sūriyakumā, also called *Smiṁ Uparājā*, ruled, the Rāmañña lands truly had little power. It is the truth [that it happened] 1600 years from the time that the Noble Buddha entered *nibbāna*.
>
> After a long time, after three ages had passed, the vast Rāmañña lands were destroyed and split through the looting and stealing of thieves and dacoits. It came about that the soldiers of seven *smiṁ* brought to straitened circumstances the noble *sāsana* in the Rāmañña lands, which had become weak through eruptions of skin diseases, destructive floods, hunger and starvation. Because of this weakness, the monks and clergy living in the Rāmañña lands were not able to practice fully the *sāsana* [nor maintain] the *pariyatti* or *piṭika* in peace.
>
> In 1600, or 419 [1057 CE] in the local system, after three ages, King Anawrahta, who had power over the country of Bakāṁ [Pagan], also called Arimaddana, arranged for a group of monks and clergy, together with the three *piṭika*, to be brought and have them preach in Arimaddana, also called Bakāṁ.
>
> (Indaka 131, translation by author)

This section of the narrative continues that over a hundred years later, the king of Pagan visits Laṅkā in the company of a novice from Rāmañña lands, where they conduct another ordination ritual before eventually returning to Pagan. The narrative speaks of transmission of teachings between various places—Pagan, Laṅkā, and Rāmañña lands—and the ordination lineages connecting them through individuals. It also fixes the connection between Rāmañña lands and the *sāsana* at an early date, around the end of the first millennium CE.

We can pause to note carefully what terms the passage does and does not speak in. The passage speaks of leaders in the polysemous term <SMIṀ>, which can signify a "king" in the European sense, down through a local leader or warlord, just as does its Burmese-language analogue *mìn*. Nor does the Mon text speak of "kingdoms," "Buddhism," "Burma," or "Monland." Rather, it speaks of place and land: <TWUIW RAḤ GLAḤ TI RĀMAÑÑA>, "Rāmañña area (and) land," and <ṬHĀN TWUIW RAḤ GLAḤ TI RĀMAÑÑA>, "Rāmañña place, area, (and) land." The term *Rāmañña* is a "Pālicization" of the native Old Mon term for "Mon," written <RMEÑÑ>.[7] These two phrases are equivalent to the better known Pāli term *Rāmaññadesa*, which many have taken as a political entity equivalent to Dvāravatī or Angkor rather than the "land(s) of the Rāmañña" which the native expression encompasses.

Burmese-language accounts

Burmese language sources continue the narrative in a much-expanded form. The last line of the above rendering is of particular interest: up to that point, the *sāsana* had become well established in the Rāmañña lands, suggesting that in those lands were both orthodoxy (correct texts and views) and orthopraxy (correct practices). Then the *sāsana* weakens. This last line suggests that the *sāsana*, or at least the canon in the form of the *piṭaka*, and members of the *saṅgha* or clergy, went from the Rāmañña lands up to Pagan. This one line became ever more elaborated, ever more vivid in detail: retellings appear in Burmese-language court-sponsored histories several centuries later, including U Kalà's *Mahā Yāzawin Gyì*, compiled in 1730; *Twìnthìn Myanmā Yāzawin Thit*, eighteenth century; and the *Hmannàn Mahā Yāzawindaw Gyì*, compiled in 1829.[8]

Histories of the *sāsana*, including the *Thāthanālinkāra Sādàn* (late eighteenth century) and U Pyinnyāthāmi's *Thāthanawunthá* (mid-nineteenth century),[9] also retell these events. Suffice it to say that there is a high degree of intertextuality among these retellings. The reigning king would order the *yāzawin* (often glossed as "court chronicles") to be updated, and so a committee of scholars would consult older sources to compose a "new" chronicle, at times including texts or narratives from other languages.

The eighteenth-century context of the retelling in the *Mahā Yāzawin Gyì* differs from that of the fifteenth-century Kalyāṇī Inscriptions.[10] Now, Anawrahta Mìn Zàw of Pagan is in conversation with Shin Arahan, a monk advising him on how to encourage the *sāsana* to flourish in his kingdom. Shin Arahan observes that Anawrahta does not have the *piṭaka* or any Buddha relics but that he can ask for them from Thaton, a country that does. Anawrahta prepares suitable gifts and sends them down to make a request. Manuhā, king of Thaton, becomes exceedingly angry on hearing the request and refuses. Anawrahta himself becomes angry and decides to attack Thaton:

> Anawyahta called together all the war heroes in the country, and sent forth land and water forces, including 800,000 ships and a million soldiers. Included in the land forces were the four great warriors Kyanzitthà, Nga Htwèi Yù, Nga Lòun Let Hpe, and Nyaung Ù Hpì, who were sent to the front line. They set off with Anawyahta holding the rear. The land forces consisted of 800,000 elephants, 800,000 horses, and eight million soldiers. The boats had not even finished setting off from Pokkarāma [Pagan] when the front of the forces reached Pegu [close to Thaton], nor had the rear land forces finished leaving Pokkarāma when the front reached the outer villages of Thaton.
>
> (U Kalà 1962: 20, translation by author)

Despite their overwhelming size, Anawrahta's forces cannot gain victory because Manuhā has used "magic"[11] to protect the city. After they dispose of the cut-up body parts used in the magic, Anawrahta's forces are victorious. Anawrahta takes possession of Manuhā, his children, wife, and courtiers and loads the "bejewelled relics which the line of kings of Thaton had worshipped" and the *piṭaka* on the backs of thirty-two white elephants to carry them back to Pagan. A lengthy description of various groups of artisans and specialists of Thaton follows, including makers of canon and guns. He enshrines the relics, places the *piṭaka* in a bejeweled *prasāda* (a sort of pavilion) and has the *saṅgha* preach.

Out of the merest mention of texts and monks being brought to Pagan has grown an account of full-on attack ending in the total vanquishing of Thaton and its civilizational accomplishments. This retelling reflects the contemporary environment: not only have artisans been arranged into groups, not a feature of Pagan-era social organization, but we also hear of gun- and canon-makers.

Continuities nevertheless do run through the retellings separated by over two hundred years: the narratives are premised on what today would be called "Buddhist cosmology" or take place in a universe in which events reflect karma and the teachings of the Dharma. The Mahā Yāzawin Gyì speaks in a Burmese Buddhist vocabulary of power: *hpòun*, "power, glory, influence"; *dagò*, "power, potency"; and the Pāli loanword *anúbaw*, "dignity, power, magnificence."[12] Key here is an understanding of Manuhā's defeat as the result of his karma, since his use of magic suggests either a desperate ploy to prop up waning power or was a karmic consequence of the magic, which involved dismemberment.

Narratives in circulation: colonial-era Mon texts

A brief look at two retellings from the texts of the *Rājāvaṁsa Kathā* reveal how these narratives are in conversation with Burmese-language retellings. The first appears in the *Uppanna Sudhammavatī* (*Arising of Sudhammavatī*) text of the *Rājāvaṁsa Kathā*.[13] At the end of the text appears the following:

> When *Smiṁ* Manuhaw reigned, he had as his queen Naṅgaladevī, daughter of the *smiṁ* of Pachālaraḥ. *Smiṁ* Manuhaw was master of thirty white elephants, and of a rat-eggplant drum. All the *smiṁ* in his line had been glorious owners of this drum. During his reign, Nuratā Jaw [Anawrahta Mìn Zàw][14] rose to power in Bakāṁ and heard tell that Manuhaw's line was no more. He came down and surrounded Sadhuim [Thaton], then brought back Manuhaw, monarch of Sadhuim. Thenceforth the fifty-seven successions in the line of Sadhuim were broken off.
>
> (Candakanta 1912: 25, translation by author)

The details may differ yet again, but the story operates in the same universe, as the symbols of karmic accumulation in the form of the white elephants and the unidentified "rat-eggplant" drum indicate. This retelling gives little detail of violence, although it clearly has occurred. In fact, the text does not explicitly mention either texts or monks being taken to Pagan.

The second retelling is similarly short, found this time in the far lengthier text concerning the ruler Rājādhirāj, a ruler, military, and culture hero whose story has been retold over the centuries in Mon, Burmese, and Thai:[15]

> *Smiṁ* Manuhaw, Lord of Thirty-Three White elephants and *Smiṁ* Nawrathā Maṅ Jaw, Lord of Sixteen White Elephants, became *kalyāṇamitta*[16] under a *eugenia* tree named *Jammarukho* and swore an oath [of friendship] before Indra. Later there was a war attacking Sadhuiṁ. *Smiṁ* Manuhaw sent a royal letter to Nawrathā Maṅ Jaw, who sent down four brave soldiers to help in the fight. When they won, *Smiṁ* Manuhaw sent a woman up [to Pagan] to give to Nawrathā Maṅ Jaw.
>
> (Candakanta 1912: 310)

Here is a radically different depiction of relations, couched less in terms of location and more as two rulers, who have formed a bond of friendship with each other. There is a war not between the two named rulers but with an outside force (from the context, the Krom or Khmers). This retelling also makes no mention of texts or monks. The exchange of a "woman"—likely a princess—is ambiguous: she may represent an act of reciprocity, with Manuhā thanking Anawrahta for his help, or she may be an indication of subordination, in that the exchange of royal daughters is often an act of fealty in Southeast Asia.

This second retelling highlights the complex layering of chronology in dealing with this narrative. The Kalyāṇī Inscriptions themselves were put up in the late fifteenth century but record events (at least the events related to the Rāmañña lands and Pagan) from the middle of the eleventh century CE. The retelling from the Rājādhirāj narrative occurs in the context of Rājādhirāj, leader of Haṁsāvatī in the mid-fourteenth century, dealing with a diplomatic crisis. He has received a provoking letter from Min Gaung (r. 1400–1421), leader of Ava or Inwa (1364–1555) and is considering how to respond. One of his advisors cites what had happened between Anawrahta and Manuhā as a possible model for action. To reiterate, the actual site of recording of the retelling, the *Rājāvaṁsa Kathā*, comes from early twentieth-century Siam.

The plurality of the retellings suggests a fluid narrative, only loosely interconnected, each liable to change according to contemporaneous circumstances, including political and religious interests.

A new normativity: British creations of national pasts

Beginning with the first Anglo-Burmese war in 1824 through to the end of colonial control in 1948, the British wrought profound changes in the conception and practice of history. With each successive war, culminating in the takeover of the rump Konbaung dynasty in Mandalay in 1885, the British wrested ever-greater control over the writing of history out of the hands of locals. The courts were displaced as the site of the production and interpretation of local pasts. Similarly, the role of monasteries as a site of production of religious histories also waned. Instead, the desks of a handful of British scholars and administrator-scholars became the preeminent site of Burmese historiography. These figures include Arthur Purves Phayre (1812–1885), Godfrey Eric Harvey (1889–1946), John Sydenham Furnivall (1878–1960), Gordon Hannington Luce (1889–1979), and Daniel George Edward Hall (1891–1979).[17] The latter two were instrumental in developing the study of history at places like the newly established Rangoon University, founded in 1878. The move also marked a professionalization of history, which became a subject of academic inquiry that Burmese could now study and receive degrees in. The rise of the university under colonial rule also meant that English became the preeminent language of intellectual life in the colony, and even in historical research, retains that position to this day, at least in terms of the salience of English-language interpretation.

History itself was an emerging field of inquiry in Britain and Europe in the nineteenth and early twentieth centuries and was deeply imbricated in emergent nationalist discourses. The language of history was inflected with the vocabulary of races (later developing into "ethnicities" in the English-speaking world), nations, and territories. Scholars in Europe were writing new kinds of histories, one which often sought to establish the ideal of one "nation," "race," or "people" sharing one language, one culture, one territory, and therefore one past. These new histories reflected an ideological shift—at least in western Europe—away from the political formation of the empire, with its mismatch between languages, peoples, territories, and pasts, towards the seemingly rational, unified nation-state.

British historians sought to create a "national" history for the new territory, albeit one contingent on British colonial control. This new national history involved the creation of new historical subjects and actors: first "Burma" itself, as a coherent and territorially demarcated site for history. This new "Burma" displaced the looser, expanding and contracting *maṇḍala*-based histories from before the colonial period (Wolters 1997). These scholars also spoke in terms of new "national" subjects not only in the sense of anyone from the colony but also more narrowly in the sense of coherent, bounded, exclusive, unified "races" who shared the same past (even if, as in many cases, that past had yet to be discovered). These new racial subjects were the Burmans, Mons, and Pyus, and over time, all the other 135 "national races" emerged, with more continuing to make claims for recognition. Thus, also emerged racial history—the history of each race, confined to a delineated territory, whether a kingdom or a colony.

To return to the narrative of Thaton and Pagan, under the British, the events were further reworked, being placed in a European historiographical frameworks and emergent religious categorizations. The British gave the events a title, the "Sack of Thaton," with *sack* recalling the successive attacks on Rome by Germanic barbarians, a trope familiar from British classical education and here fitting nicely with a British view of "the Burmese" as warlike, late-coming Romans to "the Mons" as early bearers of religion and culture, who were thought weak. Luce and his local interlocutor Pe Maung Tin published a partial translation of the *Hmannàn Mahā Yāzawindaw Gyì* (itself based largely on U Kalà's *Mahā Yāzawin Gyì*) as the *Glass Palace Chronicles* in 1923. D. G. E. Hall, whose influence is still strong both inside and outside the country, wrote in 1950 an interpretation of the events, seeing them as seminal:

> Directed by Shin Arahan, Mon monks spread far and wide the doctrine of Hinayana Buddhism. Pali, the language of the Tripitakas, became the sacred language of the Burmese. The Mon alphabet was adopted, and Burmese became for the first time a written, not merely a spoken language.
>
> The conquest of Thaton in 1057 was a decisive event in Burmese history. It brought the Burman into direct contact with the Indian civilizing influences in the south and opened the way for intercourse with Buddhist centres overseas, especially Ceylon. The possession of the Pali scriptures revolutionized his outlook: they supplied him 'ready-made, with a complete mental outfit' (Luce). They introduced him to the Buddhist ethic, which, as monasteries and teachers multiplied throughout the land, began to exert its moral force, to restrain his more barbarous impulses, and to liberate him from the worst of his animistic practices. [18]
>
> (Hall 1950: 16)

Here Hall speaks in racial categories, with races as subjects, in striking distinction to their absence in precolonial narratives. Racial thinking of the nineteenth and early twentieth centuries reflected social Darwinism, embodied in the notion of "national characters." In the colonial context, these characters marked the degree of civilization of a race and what they were fit for (soldiers, farmers, businessmen) or whether they could be granted independence. Equally important is that Hall speaks not in terms of *sāsana* or even religion but specifically of Hīnayāna Buddhism and its fitness for the people of Pagan. The larger cosmopolitan historiographical context of Hall's comment is that local sources speak of "heretical" practices at Pagan, which cosmopolitan scholars have tentatively identified as "Mahāyāna." The possibility of British and European approval of (rational, Protestant-like) Theravāda in contrast to (irrational, Hindu-inflected, Papist-like) Mahāyāna inflecting that line of cosmopolitan interpretation must be put aside for another occasion.

What quickly followed was that local scholars themselves adopting these British ideas and interpretations and began to reconceptualize local histories in their light. Through English-language publications, often in the form of school textbooks, this new kind of history spread throughout society. One typical example is that of the work of Ba Shin, a leading figure in Burmese historiography during the twentieth century, offers a typical interpretation of the Sack of Thaton in his *History of the Union of Burma*, written in 1953:

> The Myanmā of Pagan, in addition to their own natural law which was their own original belief system, also believed in *nat* worship. They accepted and believed Hīnayāna, or Southern Buddhism, which the Pyu in Thamaya had followed; and Northern Buddhism, called Mahāyāna, which came into Burma from the north and had become changed and corrupted. Such a corrupt belief system would not have been satisfying for the developed Myanmā people. Therefore, Anawrahta, as leader of an advanced people, looked for a more suitable and proper belief system. At the time of his search, a Mahā Thera named Shin Arahan had arrived in Pagan from Thaton to proselytize. In Thaton prospered Southern Buddhism, which was purer than the Buddhism of Pagan.
>
> (Bo Ba Shin 1953: 43–44)[19]

Ba Shin's take on the Burmans (here called by their more formal name, "Myanmā") is more flattering than those of Hall or Harvey, but he ends up telling a similar story couched in similar terms: the Sack of Thaton was a civilizing moment, a foundational moment if not the very beginning of Burma as reconceived of as the preeminent site of the Burman or Myanmā people. Both "the Mons" and "the Burmans" were present and participated at that foundation, albeit in unequal roles. The terms in which he sees Hīnayāna and Mahāyāna are clear, with Mahāyāna decidedly inferior. Ba Shin also makes reference to yet another emergent categorization of religion, "*nat* worship" (although not stated but understood as "animism"). Local historiographies had taken up the banner of Theravāda and promoted it with vigor.

As a foundational moment, this new retelling of the Sack of Thaton has taken on great importance in current Mon-language historiography. The "Sack" enshrines the position of the Mons as having had civilization, and most importantly, Theravāda Buddhism before the Burmans. Once the narrative shifted away from tracing the lineage of orthodox practice, to becoming a story with a title that records the founding of the newly imagined nation, starring two subject races, a next step was to view the conflict as fundamentally racial. Indeed, many Mon and other minority intellectuals take the Sack of Thaton as indicative of long-standing racial enmity in the country. Many Mon scholars view attempts to displace the Mon from the early history of Burma with deep hostility, as they read Michael Aung-Thwin doing in his *Mists of Rāmañña*.

Local adaptations

While British scholars introduced new terms and categories, it was actually local scholars who, in internalizing the new terms and categories, carried forward their earlier historiographical concern with lineages and purifications, this sealing the association between the Mons and Theravāda. The British and other Europeans created and introduced the categorization of local religious practices into separate orders of Hīnayāna (in recent decades, rechristened "Theravāda"), Mahāyāna, Hinduism, and *nat* worship or animism. Overall, however, British historiography was more concerned with the mundane, the secular. In this new historiography of Burma, new subjects provided new causality: the Burmans and the Mons had always been at war in Burma because of their racial difference. Much less important was the purity of practice and texts, which in the precolonial historiography offered if not a causality, more a correlation between events. The signs of the workings of karma were everywhere evident, indicating the rise and fall of figures in cycles of arising and decaying. A central feature of post-enlightenment historiography is after all a secular, rational, unenchanted reading (or, better, creation) of the past.

Local scholars and intellectuals, however, were not mindless subjects simply replicating the historiography, nor is the addition of local inflections a matter of imperfect learning or mimicry. Rather, local scholars' "take" on the new colonial historiography was to see continued concern with the *sāsana* (albeit in a new guise) as central to their own narratives of the Burmese and Mon pasts. Theravāda, for these local scholars, has represented a superior form of Buddhism with none of the "corruptions" or "changes" apparently inherent in Mahāyāna, and as such, is a noblest and excellent part of their self-understanding. A point for future consideration would be to analyze further the interactions among British, local, and then cosmopolitan scholars taking up this local concern with Theravāda in their work on the country, Buddhism, and various Burmese ethnic groups in succeeding decades.

Notes

1 Scholars trained in the Euro-American tradition, usually writing primarily for a similarly international audience, in contrast to the "local" scholar, usually writing in a local language for a local audience. "Cosmopolitan" accommodates "local" scholars who have acquired an education abroad or who teach and write outside their home countries.

2 In recent years, that understanding has been reassessed to a number of small probable polities, which had little superordinate political structure.

3 The widespread use of English in Burma today perhaps parallels the situation in Pagan: a widely used language with almost no local body of native speakers.

4 British linguist and father of Mon Studies, Harry Shorto, repeats a common idea that there are few Mon-language historical texts because they were destroyed in the fall of Haṁsāvatī or Pegu in the late eighteenth century (Shorto 1961: 63–72). The *Rājāvaṁsa Kathā*, *Nidāna Ārambhakathā*, and the "Pak Lat Chronicles" are all names for the same text.

5 I use the Pāli term (*thāthanā* in Burmese pronunciation) rather than the gloss *religion* to ease the burden of that loaded term.

6 Indaka (1984). A *nissaya* is a bilingual text with a few lines of Pāli immediately followed by a vernacular rendering. I have chosen this text over Taw Sein Ko's "standard" translation from Pāli into English (Taw Sein Ko 1892: 7–9) because as an interlocutor of the high colonial period, he makes use of the new English-language categories.

7 Myanmar Unicode is still not compatible with most word processors. Because of the marked discrepancy between script and pronunciation, I have provided a transliteration. The Old Mon pronunciation was something like */rəmaɲ/ or */rəmɔɲ/ until perhaps the thirteenth century. Over time, the <R> was dropped, and the graphic form <MAN> appeared, reflected in the modern pronunciation /mo̤n/. See Shorto (1971: 325).

8 For details of the people and committees involved in the creation of these texts, see Hla Pe (1985: 52–67) and Aung-Thwin (2005: 142–144) and throughout.

9 Pāli scholars will recognize in these the Burmese pronunciations of *Sāsanālaṅkāra*, Paññāsāmī, and *Sāsanavaṁsa*, respectively.

10 The following summary is based on my reading of Ù Kalà (1962: 19–23).

11 Burmese *payàwgá*, from Pāli *payoga*. "Sorcery" or "witchcraft" are also possible renderings.

12 The first two terms seem to have a connotation of power based on an accumulation of merit; indeed, the etymology of *dagò* suggests the "(incense) smoke of donations." For a fuller discussion of these first two terms and their gendered aspects, see Keeler (2017).

13 Linguistically, this appears to be a fairly typical eighteenth-century text.

14 This Mon form becomes clearer in light of Written Burmese <ANORATHĀ MAṄḤ CO>, which preserves an earlier pronunciation of /ʔənɔrət^{h}a màn jò/

15 The linguistic evidence of this section of the Rājādhirāj narrative suggests that much of it was written around the time of publication in the early twentieth century.

16 The Pāli term here, "virtuous friend." The Mon is actually <KAÑÑĀMIT>; the change of /ly/ to /ññ/ is not a process in Mon phonology but is in Thai, suggesting that this word came through Thai.

17 This list is not exhaustive. The British did not wholly replace everything that went before them, nor did they work alone. Some of their local interlocutors, protégés, and intellectual heirs include Taw Sein Ko (1864–1930), Pe Maung Tin (1888–1973), who worked extensively with Luce, Htin Aung (1909–1978), and Than Tun (1923–2005).

18 Despite the late date, his interpretation here reflects ideas formed in previous decades during his stints as a lecturer at Rangoon University. Here he echoes much of the sentiments of Harvey in Harvey ([1925] 2000: 28–29).

19 Apparently, Ba Shin was Muslim, so his role in promoting these new categories of religious thought are remarkable.

References

Aung-Thwin, Michael. 2005. *Mists of Rāmañña: The Legend That Was Lower Burma*. Honolulu: University of Hawai'i Press.

Ba Shin (Bo). 1953. *Myanmā Naingngandaw Thamàing* [History of Burma] (5th ed.). Rangoon: Pyithu Alì Pounhneittaik.

Brown, Robert L. 1996. *The Dvāravatī Wheels of the Law and the Indianization of South East Asia.* Leiden: E.J. Brill.

Burling, Robbins. 2012. "Where did the question, "Where did my tribe come from" come from?" In *Origins and Migrations in the Extended Himalayas*, eds. Toni Huber, Stuart Blackburn, 49–62. Leiden: Brill.

Candakanta (Nai). 1911/1912. *Rājāvaṁsa Kathā*, vol. 1–2. Pāk Lat: Siam.

Cœdès, George. 1968. *The Indianized States of Southeast Asia.* Honolulu: East-West Center.

Edwards, Penny. 2003. "*Re-locating the interlocutor: Taw Sein Ko and the triangulation of colonial knowledge*," in *Traditions of Knowledge in Southeast Asia*, conference proceedings, 17–19 December 2003, Yangon, Myanmar, pp. 1–46.

Goh, Geok Yian. 2014. *The Wheel-Turner and His House: Kingship in a Buddhist Ecumene.* Dekalb: Northern Illinois University Press.

Hall, D.G.E. 1950. *Burma.* New York: Hutchinson's University Library.

Harvey, G.E. 1925/2000. *History of Burma.* New Delhi: Asian Educational Services.

Hla, Pe. 1985. "Burmese historiography: the source, nature, and development of the Burmese Chronicles." In *Burma: Literature, Historiography, Scholarship, Language, Life, and Buddhism*, ed. Hla Pe, 52–67. Singapore: Institute of Southeast Asian Studies.

Indaka, Nai. 1984. *Prakuih Trāy Lik Tma? Kalyāṇī* [Nissaya Treatise on the Kalyāṇī Inscriptions]. Mudon: Lwī Mān Htaw Monastery.

Kalà, U. (Hsayā Pwà, ed.). 1962. *Mahā Yāzawin Gyì*, vol. 1. Rangoon: Hanthawadi Press.

Keeler, Ward. 2017. *The Traffic in Hierarchy: Masculinity and its Others in Buddhist Burma.* Honolulu: University of Hawai'i Press.

McAuliffe, Erin. 2017. *Caste and the Quest for Racial Hierarchy in British Burma: An Analysis of Census Classifications from 1872–1931.* MA Thesis. International Studies: Southeast Asia, University of Washington.

McCormick, Patrick. 2011a. "The position of the *Rājāvaṁsa Kathā* in Mon history-telling." *Journal of Burma Studies* 15 (2): 283–304.

McCormick, Patrick. 2011b. "Mon converging towards Thai models." In *Austroasiatic Studies: Papers from ICAAL 4, Mon-Khmer Studies Journal Special Issue No. 2*, ed. Sophana Srichampa, Paul Sidwell, 81–97. Canberra: Australian National University: Pacific Linguistics.

McCormick, Patrick. 2010. *Mon Histories: Between Translation and Retelling.* PhD Dissertation, University of Washington, History Department.

Pe Maung, Tin, G.H. Luce. 1960. *The Glass Palace Chronicle of the Kings of Burma.* Rangoon: Rangoon University Press.

Pollock, Sheldon. 2006. *The Language of the Gods in the World of Men: Sanskrit, Culture, and Power in Premodern India.* Berkeley: University of California Press.

Shorto, Harry. 1971. *A Dictionary of the Mon Inscriptions from the Sixth to the Sixteenth Centuries.* London: Oxford University Press.

Shorto, Harry. 1961. "A Mon genealogy of kings: Observation on the *Nidāna Ārambhakathā*." In *Historians of South East Asia*, ed. D.G.E. Hall, 63–72. London: Oxford University Press.

Skilling, Peter. 2019. "Many lands of gold." In *Suvarnabhumi, the Golden Land: The New Finding for Suvarnabhumi Terra Incognita*, eds. Bunchar Pongpanich, Somchet Thinapong, 191–218. Bangkok: GISTDA.

Skilling, P., Carbine, J., Cicuzza, C., Pakdeekham, S. 2012. *How Theravāda is Theravāda: Exploring Buddhist Identities.* Chiang Mai: Silkworm Books.

Taw Sein, Ko. 1892. *The Kalyāṇī Inscriptions Erected by King Dhammacetī at Pegu in 1476 AD, Text and Translation.* Rangoon: Government Printing.

Thompson, A. 2016. *Engendering the Buddhist State: Territory, Sovereignty and Sexual Difference in the Inventions of Angkor.* London: Routledge.

Veidlinger, Daniel. 2006. *Spreading the Dharma: Writing, Orality, and Textual Transmission in Buddhist Northern Thailand.* University of Hawai'i Press.

Wales, H.G.Q. 1969. *Dvaravati, the Earliest Kingdom of Siam (6th to 11th Century Ad).* London: Quatrich.

Wolters, O.W. 1997. *History, Culture, and Region in Southeast Asian Perspectives.* Ithaca: Southeast Asia Program Publications, Southeast Asia Program, Cornell University.

INDEX

Page numbers in **bold** indicate tables, page numbers in *italics* indicate figures and page numbers followed by n indicate notes.

Abeysekara, A. 100, 101, 103
Abhayagiri 20, 25, 30–31, 33–34, 236
Abhidhamma 129, 227; and filial piety 164; initial development of 227–228; literature 228–231; and meditation practices 133–137; theory of *dharmas* 231–240
aesthetics: of art 312; of bodily comportment 188, 190; of Buddhist path 84; of film 330, 334, 337, 339; of Pāli language 49; of repetition 145, 148; of texts 276, 278; as trans-regional process 67
affect: and attachment 329–330, 338; of impermanence 329; of objects 329, 339; of Pāli chanting 53; purification as 84; repetition as 142; theory 327; and trauma 332, 335, 339
Abhidhammatthasaṅgaha 151, 152, 230–231, 259
Aggañña Sutta 71, 340n13
Allon, Mark 143–145
Ambedkar, Bhim Rao 178
amulets 329
Anālayo, Bhikkhu 144–145
Ānandavardhana 148
Anawrahta, King 359–361
Ang Chan, King 320
Angkor 65, 72, 160, 313, 344
Angkor Wat temple, Cambodia 311, 312, 319–322, *320*
aniconic Buddhist art 310–311
Anurādhapura 21, 31, 106, 229, 246, 250, 345
Arañ Nikāya 288, 296
arahant/arhat 3, 129, 246–248
Ariyaratne, A. T. 92
Asad, Talal 99, 100, 116
āsevana (repetition) 150–152
Asoka/Aśoka, King: council of 45; as devotee 246; legends of 299; missions of 27; model of 72, 250, 252; purifications of 84, 245, 358
Association for Asian Studies 7
aṭṭhakathā (commentaries) 4, 5, 23, 32, 244, 278
Atthasālinī 228–229, 258, 259, 261
Aung, Shwe Zan 151
Aung-Thwin, Michael 357, 364
authenticity 94, 100, 103–104, 108–109, 116, 220, 358; of relics 120, 249; *see also* tradition
authority, *also* authorization: assertion of 100–102; and canon 84, 210, 216, 220, 222–223; of images 250; of kings 33, 61, 252; of meditation teachers 131; of monks 10, 45, 123, 174, 186; and Pāli language 44–47, 52, 213, 217, 282; political 119–120; of reformers 90, 94; of ritual 142; of Sri Lanka 59; and Theravāda 251–254
Ayutthaya 59, 63, 75, 163, 222, 297

Ba Shin (Bo) 363–364
baan-muang system 76–77
Bagan 73, 121; *see also* Pagan
Bareau, André 22, 24, 26
bhāvanā (contemplation) 129, 151, 257, 258, 260
bhikkhunīs (higher-ordained Buddhist nuns) 99–109; *see also nuns*
bi-texts: contemporary 282–283; creation 272–278; diffusion 279–282; Pāli-vernacular 51–52, 271–283
Bizot, François 338

Blackburn, Anne 47, 184, 313, 317–318
Bodhgaya (-ā) 18, 92, 104, 109, 160, 292, 299
Bodhi, Bhikkhu 144
Bodhi Tree 61, 160, 246, 248, 250, 264, 293
bodhisatta/bodhisattva: Avalokiteśvara 344; identification of deities as 349; identification of monk with 317–319; murals of 291; narratives of 299–300; perfections of 156; Rāma as 322; royal actors as 321; saving parents 159; veneration of 163
book, culture of 223–224
boran kammathan 95, 135
boundary markers *see sīmā*
Brahmanism 73, 76, 157
Braun, Erik 173, 174
Brown, Robert 305–307, 311, 314, 321
Buddha images 5, 249–251; in early Pagan 289–292, *291*; footprint *298*, 306; in his remote existence *301*; iconography of "Eight Major Episodes" 292–296, *294*; *see also* icons
Buddha relics 249, 327; destruction of 328–330; and kings 61, 65; in films of Apichatpong Weerasethakul 330–333, *331*; Footprint Relics 66, 306; housing of 200, 247; installation at frontiers 61; journeys of 73, 246–247; narratives about 244; power of 79, 249, 316–318, 327; representations of 297; self-reproductions of 317; Tooth Relic 119–120, 179, 248; in work of Rithy Panh 334–339
Buddhadāsa Bhikkhu 87, 92
Buddhadatta 230, 259
Buddhaghosa 4, 45, 90, 131, 245, 328
Buddhavacana 216, 221, 222
Buddhavaṃsa 243, 297, 299

cakkavatti (wheel-turning monarch) 72, 75–76, 320
Candavimala, Rērukānē 264–265
canon(s): and authority 222–223; epigraphic 218–219, *219*; model 218; notion of 209, 212, 214–215; ritual 216–217; sermons 217; sponsorship/production of 216; vernacular 218; *see also* Pāli canon
Carter, John Ross 142
Cassaniti, Julia 185–186
cetiya see stūpa (funerary monument)
Chan Htoon, U 87
Chapata 288
Chiang Mai 59, 199, 221
Childers, R. C. 46
Chirapravati, Pattaratorn 314, 316, 318–319
Chladek, Michael Ross 189–191
Christianity 64, 101, 175, 219
chronicles *see vaṃsa* (chronicles/genealogical literature)
circulatory processes 66–68
citta (consciousness) 131, 133, 135, 232, 236, 238–239, 258, 351
classification 71, 171, 215, 249, 355
Clifford, James 1
clothing 93–94; monastic robes 183–184; nuns' monastic attire 101
Cœdès, George 76, 321, 322, 357
Collins, Steven 3, 7, 20, 43, 72, 115, 116, 212, 220, 328; and "Pāli imaginaire" 46–47, 73; on scripturalism 89
Colombo 174
colonialism 78, 88, 128, 136, 174, 355; *see also* meditation practices, in response to colonialism and modernity; reform(s), during colonial period
consciousness: *bhavaṅga* 238–239; classes of 236–237; in meditation 131; and rebirth 239, 351; as results of karma 238; states of (*citta*) 131, 133, 236; through repetition 142, 151; transformation of 135–136; types of **233**, 235, 237; *viññaṇā* 128
contemplation *see bhāvanā*
Councils 83, 252; First 253; Sixth 92; Third 287
Cousins, Lance S. 22, 26

Dambulla Temple 104–105
dāna (generosity) 115–117, 125, 257; advantages of 262, 263; definitions 258, 260; of kings 252; practice of 118–119, 172–173, 257
Dāṭhāvāṃsa 51
decolonization, and reform(s) 84, 91, 95
Dehejia, Vidya 305–306
deity (term or category) 343
Deleuze, Gilles 327
democracy 87
demythologization 94
dependent origination *see pratītyasamutpāda*
devas (deity): rebirth as 199, 290; in Sri Lanka 344–348
dēvālaya (deity shrine) 344, 347
dhamma (teachings) 44; Abhidhamma theory of 231–239; in action 236–239; iconized 307–308, *307*; lists of Theravāda and Sarvāstivāda traditions **233–234**; material culture of 6; study by laity 176–178
Dhammaceti, King 49, 358
Dhammapada 156, 217, 220, 265
dhammarāja 250, 252, 253
Dhammasami, Khammai 177–178
Dharmakīrti, Jayabāhu 28, 30–32
Dharmarama, Yatramulle 176–177
Dīpavaṃsa 15, 22–27, 31, 252
dispensation *see sāsana*
diversity: perception of 18; *see also nikāya*
doctrine, and repetition 148–153
donors, among laity 171–173
Duṭṭhagāmaṇī, King 253, 263

early Buddhism 93, 219–222, 224
Eckel, Malcolm 329–330
Eightfold Path 92, 116, 227, 229
elaboration, cultural 48–49
encompassment, cultural 49–51
Engaged Buddhism 96, 115, 120, 122
epigraphy: of Angkor 161; in Burma 161; in Pāli 49; Sinhalese 160; Sukhothai 61; *see also inscriptions*
esoteric 95, 166, 254, 338
Eurocentrism 78; *see also* Western

filial piety 156; and Abhidhamma 164; in Buddhist practice 159–162; as Buddhist virtue 162–167; and ordination 165; in Pāli scriptures 157–159, 166
Finot, Louis 75–76
Foucault, Michel 78
Free Funeral Society 123
funerary monument *see stūpa*
funerary practices: bird offerings 196–197; burial 196, 199; changes in 194–204; charnel forests 199; *chedi* 200, 201; commercialization 201, 202; cremains 200; cremation 195–199, 203; post-World War II 201–203

Gavaṃpati 248
Geiger, Wilhelm 346
gender 183
generosity *see dāna*
Gethin, Rupert 23, 24, 27, 145, 259, 263–264
Ghosānanda, Mahā 91–93, 95
ghosts 119, 158, 161, 194, 199–200, 265–266, 331, 335; *see also phi*; *nats*; *neak ta*; *peta*; spirit
giving: ritual 117, 124; theories of 124–125; *see also dāna*
Goenka, S. N. 134, 175
Gombrich, Richard 144, 179
governance/governmentality: of Aśoka 84; Buddhist forms of 73–74, 79, 121; European discourse of 88, 355; pre-Buddhist 71–72; modern 78; and ritual 80; texts on 76
Griswold, A. B. 317, 318

Hall, Daniel George Edward 362, 363
Hallisey, Charles 1, 83–84
haptic experience 330, 332, 333
Heim, Maria 4
Heine, Steven 209
heresies: "teaching of the Blue Robe" 32, 38n57; Vaitulyavāda 30–33; Vājiriyavāda 32
hermeneutics 84, 85
Hikkaḍuvē Sumaṅgala 86
Hindu: cosmology 73; literature 50; notion of the divine 343–345, 347; political structure of 77, 313; rituals 351; thought 160
historicist/historicism/historicity: agenda of scholars 19, 220; of early Buddhism 220; in European discourse 88; idea of canon 4; in reform movements, 89–91
historiography: British creations 362–364; Burmese-language 359–360; colonial-era Mon texts 361–362; Mon-language 358–359; Theravāda Buddhist 243–244
history, professionalization of 362
Hocart, Arthur M. 74, 80
Horner, I. B. 144
householders 102, 108, 146, 171–172

icons 305–306, 310; image-text relations 307–310
image(s): anthropomorphic 310–311; of crowned Buddha 302; donation of 5, 167, 251; as equivalent to written letters 223–224; as icon 306; and kings 251–252, 358; multiplication of 250; narratives of 248–250; power of 249, 350; as relics 249; and text-relations 307–310
impermanence, doctrine of 4, 194, 327, 333, 338
indexical/indexicality, of amulets 330; of Pāli language 44, 52–54; or relics 330
Induangchanthy, Xaisongkham 339
inscriptions: Buddhist identity in 18, 21; donative 160, 163, 215; Kalyānī 287, 358, 361; and kingship 65, 74, 347; languages of 5; in Mon language 356–357; in Pāli 52, 218–219; Sanskrit-Khmer 280; Sukhothai 58–63, 65, 67; of *Tipiṭaka* 49; as vows of truth 321; *see also epigraphy and stele*

Jayavarman VII, King 61, 313
Jetavana 20, 31, 33–35
jhāna 131–132, 151, 264
Jinakālamālī 244, 250–251, 253, 296–297

Kālāma Sutta 85–88, 109
Kandy 102, 344
karma/*kamma*: in Abhidhamma 231, 267; collective 164; and conditions for experience 238; of deities 345; and ethics 156; in historical events 360, 364; moral economy of 347; notion of 160; overemphasis on 265; repetition of 152
kammatic Buddhism 171, 173
Kathāvatthu 15, 152, 162, 229
kāvya (poetic literature) 148, 267, 279
Kāvyaśēkharaya 257, 262, 263
Khmer Rouge 93, 95, 135, 335, 337
kingship, Buddhist: in Pāli-Sanskrit cosmopolis 71–74; in premodern Lao and Tai kingdoms 75–78
Kinnard, Jacob 305, 311–312
Kornfield, Jack 133
Kulke, Hermann 72, 74

labor, 63, 71, 74, 118, 121, 123; *see also* slaves
laity: conceptions of 95; in contemporary Theravāda 170–180; as donors 171–173; and meditation practices 91, 173–175, 179; and monastic discipline 189–190; study of Dhamma by 176–178; women 178–179
Lanka Insight Meditation Society 174
Lanna: bitexts in 281–282; Buddha image in 251; Buddha visits to 246, 248; funerals in 163, 199; local traditions of 75, 79; Pāli works from 53, 158–159, 230; resistance to Bangkok 88; ritual canons of 217, 313
Lan Xang, kingdom of 75, 160, 350
Lao Buddhist law 76
Latour, Bruno 63, 66
Leach, Edmund 77, 78
Ledi Sayadaw 91, 134, 174
literacy 64, 93, 217
Literary Sinitic translations 271–272
Lokapaññatti 50–51, 299
Loubère, Simon de la 196, 198
Luang Prabang 75, 77
Luce, Gordon H. 290, 292, 357, 362

Magadha, and Pāli language 44–45, 48, 212
Mahābodhivaṃsa 28, 246, 250
Mahā Dhammarāja I, King 59–61
Mahā Ghosānanda 91–92, 95
Mahasi Meditation Center, Yangon 121, 133–134
Mahāvaṃsa 15, 22, 25, 31, 34, 176, 244, 252
Mahāvihāra: historiography 35; lineage of 21, 25, 28, 251; monastery 246, 248; monks 4, 245; *nikāya* 16, 35; orthodoxy of 20–22, 25, 30, 248; pure tradition of 287–288, 358; texts 156, 162, 220, 229
Mahāyāna, idea of 109, 363; merit-making in 266–267; iconography of 298; as heterodoxy 106, 312
Mahinda 4, 30, 45, 245, 251, 254; legend of 22
Maitreya/Metteyya 66, 130, 319, 321, 322, 343–345
Malalasekera, G. P. 91–92
maṇḍala (circle; circle of states) 71–75, 77, 293
Mandalay 122, 211, 362
manuscript(s): age of 211–212, 218; bilingual 271, 272, 282; burning of 165; canonical 212; culture 76, 85; epigraphic 218; iconization of 309; images in 116, 293, 308–310; libraries 132, 271; for making merit 164, 167, 221, 223–224; materiality of 211; of practical canons 47; as sacred objects 93, 211; transmission of 251
Marxism 88, 92, 135
Martaban/Mottama 62, 67, 297, 316
masculinity 189
materiality 133, 211–212, 248–251, 329, 336
Mauss, Marcel 117, 124
media: manuscripts 211; and reform(s) 93–94
meditation practices 127–128; and Abhidhamma 133–137; authoritative texts 131–132; goal of 128–129; lay 91, 173–175, 179; and Pāli language 53; Pāli terms for 129–131; in response to colonialism and modernity 128, 136, 174; *samatha* 130–131; *vipassanā* 130–131, 133, 173–175; *see also* Buddhaghosa; *Visuddhimagga* (Path of Purification)
merit/merit-making: Abhidhamma texts on 259–260; on behalf of the dead 160–162, 166, 194, 261; commentaries on 258–259; contemporary sources on 264–266; cultivation of faith 263; defining 115–116; donating to monks 117, 120–122, 171–173; and institution building 120–122; listening 259–260; paying respect 258–260; poetic works on 261–262; recollection 261, 263; rejoicing in 259, 261; in service of others 122–124, 258, 260; sharing of 118–119, 159–162, 259, 261; straightening one's views 259; as taught in Dhamma schools 265–266; teaching 259; ten ways of 257–268; transference of 260
Meru, Mount 197–199, 202
Milindapañha 215, 219, 265
military 61, 65, 74, 118–121, 183, 185, 332–333
mindfulness: applications of 227, 229; cultivating 145; culture of 127, 133; meditation 127, 131; objects of 131, 133; in therapeutic settings 129; in Theravāda thought 235
modernism, Buddhist 175, 179
Moggaliputta Tissa 228–229, 245, 251
monasteries: building of 120–121, 175, 251–253; for deceased 163; Dhamma teaching at 177, 187; donations to 173; histories of 251, 362; international 135; and *sāsana* 248–249; social services of 122; women's societies at 179
monastic code *see Vinaya*
monastic community *see saṅgha*
monastic lineage *see nikāya*
monastics: bodies of 187–189; duty toward laity 172; formation 182–184, 186–187; physical exercise 188; and questions of power 107–109; robes 101, 183–184; and smoking 190–191; and the state 99–100, 107–109, 185; undisciplined 184–186
mondop (maṇḍapa) 314–316
Mongkut, King 89–90, 94, 135, 219
Mons, in Southeast Asia 355–356

morality *see sīla*
Muslims 64, 121, 123, 299

Nāgārjunakoṇḍa 21–22
Ñāṇābhivaṃsa 44
Nātha *dēviyō* 344–345
nationalism: Asian 88; Buddhist 78, 91, 96, 185; discourses of 183; and race 355
nats, of Burmese culture 351–352; *see also* ghost; *neak ta*; *phi*; *peta*; spirit
Navayāna (New Vehicle) Buddhism 178
neak ta, of Cambodian culture *see* ghost *nats phi peta* spirit
Nepal 2, 211, 271
network(s) 62–66; as analytical term 58, 63–64
nibbāna: as *dhamma* 232; insight of 240; and meditation 127; realization of 129; of relics 328; *see also* nirvana
Nidānakathā 290, 292
nikāya (monastic lineage): concept of 16–18; genealogies 22–33; genealogy of *Dīpavaṃsa 26*; in Theravāda 247
Nikāyasaṅgraha 15, 27–33
nirvana: for ancestors 163; of the Buddha 29, 247, 307; as ultimate goal 170–171; as unconditioned 232, 240
Norman, Kenneth R. 144, 146, 259
Nu, U 91, 92
nuns 2; attire 101, 104; authenticity of 100, 102; giving to 175; legal rights of 99; and meditation 128; monastic disapproval of 107–108; in *nikāyas* 16; ordination of 99–100, 103, 105–106, 109, 245–246; protests by 122; rules given to 182; training precepts 102; *see also bhikkhunīs*
Nyanaponika 141–142
Nyāṇatiloka 152

Obeyesekere, Gananath 173–174, 179, 344
ordination: and filial piety 165; lineages 103, 106–109; *see also nikāya*
organization and reform, and Pāli language 43, 47–51
origins: local historiographies of 358–362; search for 355–357
orthodoxy: disputed 106, 215; Mahāvihāra 16, 261, 301; of Rāmañña 359; and scripturalism 89; Sīhaḷa 288–289, 296; as Theravāda claim 23, 302, 352
orthopraxy 84, 85, 95, 352, 359

pabbajjā (novice ordination) 102, 104, 142, 166, 351; *see also* ordination
Pagan 357; Buddhism of 289; murals 290–296, 298–302; *see also* Bagan
painting: cave temple 135; of *jātakas* 116, 219, 309; of *phi* 348; and texts 309–310; use of European techniques 94
Pāli canon 2, 4, 44, 209–210; closure 212–213; and early Buddhism 220–221; and filial piety 157–159, 166; formation 210–211; idea of 46–47; materiality 211; in modernity 214; translations 177; writing systems 211–212
Pāli language: authoritative tradition 43–47; as classical language 45–46; epigraphy 49; indexical power of 43, 53; as language of Magadha 45; and meditation practices 53, 129–131; and organization and reform 43, 47–51; and performative rituals 52–53; as root language 44–45; and Sanskrit 45–46, 50, 73; as spoken by the Buddha 4, 44; use as sacred 2, 43
Pali Text Society 177
Panh, Rithy 328, 330; *The Missing Picture* 334–338, *335*, *337*
parahita (service of others) 122–124
Parākramabāhu I, King 28, 32, 48, 287–288
pāramī/pāramitā (perfections) 5, 156, 290, 305, 308, 312, 329
paritta (protective chants) 53, 221
pariyatti (scriptural knowledge) 44, 84, 176, 359
patipatti (practice) 84
Pātho-htā-mya Temple 290–291
Pātimokkha 142–143, 182–183, 277
Paṭṭhāna 134, 230
peta/preta (hungry ghost) 158, 161–163
Perreira, T. L. 3, 108–109
Phayre, Arthur Purves 362
phi/phii 199–200, 343, 352; of Thai-Lao culture 348–350; *see also* ghost; *nats*; *neak ta*; spirit
photograph 88, 94, 201, 265, 332–333, 339
Phnom Penh 322, 336
Phra Malai 213, 217, 222
Pichard, Pierre 314–316, 319
pilgrimage: to sites of Buddha's life story 292; and intra-religious encounters 18; and merit-making 120, 264; to relics 64; sites mentioned in *vaṃsas* 60; in Sri Lanka 53, 61
Pollock, Sheldon 72, 74
Polonnaruva 213, 230, 297, 315, 345
Poon Pismai Diskul, Princess 87
postcolonial 78, 89, 92, 356–357
pratītyasamutpāda/paṭiccasamupāda (dependent origination) 128, 134, 227, 237, 307
Prasert na Nagara 60, 61, 68n3, 317, 318
Premchit, Sommai 72, 201

print: of Buddhist texts 86, 144, 212, 358; and Dhamma knowledge 177, 214, 217; and literacy 93; and merit-making 165; opposition to 93, 176; rise of 85, 88–89, 93; subjects of 94; *see also media*
procession 119, 197, 216, 320
purity, *and* purification: modern forms of 79, 89; of nuns' lineage 108; revolutionary 337; of robes 183; of Saṅgha 28, 72–73, 84, 124, 245; of *sāsana* 33, 287–288, 358; of society 95; of Theravāda 85, 100, 109, 254

race/racial thinking 123, 185, 355, 362–364
Rajadhon, Anuman 197
Rāma (deity) 320, 322, 347
Rāma I, King 216, 218
Ramanujan, A. K. 140
Rāmāyaṇa 254, 322, 346
Ramkamhäng/Ramkhamhaeng, King 59–60, 313
Rangoon 211, 222; *see also* Yangon
Rationalism/rationalization: of Ambedkar Buddhism 178; of the Buddha 86, 89; Buddhist 89, 91; concept of 88; of Europe 89, 362–363; in governance 80; of popular religion 349; and progress 219; reform value of 95
Rattana, Vandy 339
reform(s): during colonial period 88; and decolonization 91; as idea 83–84; and media 93–94; mid-20th-century 91–93; and modern Buddhist subjects 94–95; modern movements 85–89; premodern 83–84; scripturalism in Siam 89–91
refuge: merit in taking of 259, 261–263, 265; of monasteries 122; Pāli formula 141–142, 216; threefold 142; for women 109
relics *see* Buddha relics
religion, as term 64, 101
renunciants: female *see* nuns
repetition 140–141; and doctrine 148–153; and ritual 141–143; and textual composition 143–148; threefold 142–143
Rhys Davids, Caroline A. F. 151
Rhys Davids, T. W. 143–144, 177, 221
ritual(s): for benefit of ancestors 157; of exchange 117; funerary 161, 165, 194–204; of giving 117, 124; and governmentality 79–80; merit-making 117–119, 161; and Pāli language 52–53; and repetition 141–143
robe/robes: allusions to 258, 334; of the Buddha 328; dustheap 334, 338; offering of 59; styles of wearing 90, 183, 190
Royal Asiatic Society 264
Saffron Revolution 121
saṅgha (monastic community) 3; centralization of 88, 90, 191, 194, 201; criticisms of 179, 184; donations to 117, 124, 172, 252; and king 72–73; and masculinity 189; protests by 96, 121; purification of 48, 84, 245, 251; split in 23; veneration of 52, 141, 263
Saṅgha Act (1902) 194, 195, 201
Saṅghamittā 99, 245
Sanskrit: Abhidharma 228; bilingualism 271–272, 280–281; Buddhism 289; canons 2, 4, 210; cosmopolis 71–73; and cultic activity 346; grammar 49; inscriptions 160; knowledge systems 60, 73; and Pāli language 45–46, 50–51, 73, 178, 210; poetry 148; textuality 59, 67; works in 48, 50, 279, 290, 299, 329; writing on sects 15, 22
Sāriputta 48–49
Sarnath 103–104, 160
Sarnatha Trust 134–135
Sarvāstivāda: Abhidharma 228–229, 240; canon 212, 214, 221; dedicating merit in 166; *dharmas* in 232, 236–237; material world in 235; as *nikāya* 18, 27; treatises of 231
Sarvōdaya 92
sāsana (dispensation/tradition) 3–4; preservation 28; purification 33; *see also* tradition
schools 94, 120, 177, 186–187; eighteen 16, 210, 220–221, 228
Scott, James 71, 77
scripturalism, in Siam 89–91
sculpture: animal 333; of *bodhisattva* 344; colossal Buddha 293; Hindu 345; of *jātakas* 5; presence of Buddha in 306, 312; *see also statue*
sect/sectarianism, as terms 16, 35n1; *see also nikāya*
sermons 217; on radio 266
service of others *see parahita*
Shan 195, 199, 218
Shwedagon Pagoda 173, 222
Shwezigon Pagoda 280, 351
Si Sattha/Śrī Śraddhā 60, 61, 63–65, 316–319, 321–322, 324
Sīhaḷa order (*nikāya*) 287–288, 296–297, 302
sīla (morality) 5, 179, 257, 258, 260, 262
sīmā (boundary markers) 6
Sipsongpannā 10, 186–188; *see also* Yunnan
Sisowath Monireth 87
Sitagu Sayadaw 121
Skilling, Peter 245, 308–309, 314
slaves 74, 118; *see also* labor
Soma Mahā Thera, Kotahene 87
Somdet Phra Vanarat 211
Sophy, Him 337
spirit 77, 348, 350; *see also* ghost; *phi*

Spiro, Melford E. 171, 173
Srivichai, Khruba 79, 195, 201
state, the 70; and monastics 99–100, 107–109, 185
statecraft, Buddhist: modern 78–81; notion of 70–71; in Pāli-Sanskrit cosmopolis 71–74; in premodern Lao and Tai kingdoms 75–77
statue(s): of Aśoka 72; of Buddha 5, 322; donation of 160, 163; as a god 321; iconization of Dharmma in 307, 309; and kings 79; objectification of Dhamma in 6; as receptacle for ashes 163; as receptacle for relics 306; *see also* image and sculpture
stele(s) 75, 160, 215, 319
Stone, Jacqueline 194
Strong, John 328–329
stūpa (funerary monument) 6, 116–117, 306, 311, 315–316, 322, 327
Subhūti, Vaskaḍuvē 46
subjects/subjectivity/subjecthood: of the British 355; Buddhist 94–95; colonial 94, 358; ethical 329; of kings 60–61, 66, 118, 251; of monks 182, 186; and races 363–364; sources of 65, 89; of the state 119–120, 362
Sudharmachari 100–103
Sukhothai 58–62, 65, 67, 297, 313, 316
Sumangala, Inamaluwe 103–104, 106–109
Sumaṅgalavilāsinī 148, 258–259, 261
Sūryavarman II, King 319, 320
Suttanipāta 145–146, 153, 171
Swearer, Donald 72

Tambiah, Stanley 72, 84, 89, 329, 350
teachings *see dhamma* (teachings)
Teh, David 330
temple wives 186
textual composition, and repetition 143–148
Thai forest tradition 135, 136
Thammayut 89
Than Tun 301
Thanlyin Thabawa Meditation Centre, Yangon 123
That Luang 79, 80
Theravāda: and authority 251–253; as Buddhist sect 19–20; canon *see* Pāli canon; civilizations 7–8; expansion of 245–248; as habitus 6, 8; idea of 2–7; and materiality 248–251; as term 1–3, 19–20, 23, 33
Theriya (Nikāya) 19–21
Thittila, Sayadaw U 87
Thūpavaṃsa 51, 244, 247, 253
Tipiṭaka ("Three Baskets") 1, 4, 5, 44, 210, 212–213; inclusive 215
tradition 101–103, 109–110; *see also sāsana*
Tripiṭaka see Tipiṭaka
Turnour, George 43

universal decay, idea of 28
U Nu 91, 92, 96, 119, 121, 211, 222
Upagupta 213
Upāsakajanālaṅkāra 257, 261, 267
upasampadā (higher ordination), of Theravāda Buddhist nuns 99–101, 103–109; recitation in 142; on behalf of one's father 166
Upulvan (*deity*) 346–347

Vajirañāṇavarorasa, Prince 86, 183
Vajrayāna: artistic developments of 312; in Sri Lanka 32, 34; texts of 29; in Thailand and Laos 313
vaṃsa(s) (chronicles/genealogical literature): emotive force of 329; as genre 243; history in 245, 247, 251; and images 249–250; and kings 72, 250–253; narrative in 243; *nikāya* identity in 21–23, 33–34; other names for 244; Pāli 51; predictions in 247–248; and relics 245–249; religious diversity in 15, 26; spread of 60, 244, 254; themes in 244, 245; Theravāda lineage 214, 219, 251, 253; *see also* Dharmakīrti, Jayabāhu; *Nikāyasaṅgraha*
Vasubandhu 237
Vasumitra 24, 26
vernacular: bitexts 271–272; canons in 213, 218; differences in styles 5–6; elaborations in 48, 51–52, 244, 276, 281; obligations to parents in 164; practice 332, 338; reworked in Pāli 49, 51; texts in 46, 51, 73, 91, 131–132, 244; transcended by *nikāya* 18
Vessantara Jātaka 60, 115, 116, 222, 317–318
Vimuttimagga 230
Vinaya (monastic disciplinary code) 2, 3, 16, 84, 90, 182–183
Vinaya Vardhana movement 175, 179
violence: in death 199, 336; experience of 336; and Khmer Rouge 93; of *nats* 351; of nation-state 79, 85; against monastic protestors 122; against non-Buddhists 95; political 330, 339; *sāsana* purifications as 33; witness to 333; *see also* war
Vipassana: as contemplation 258; lay practice of 131, 174, 176, 179; as merit practice 122; and mindfulness 133; purpose of 127, 130
Viṣṇu (*deva*) 64, 319, 321, 346–348
Visuddhimagga (Path of Purification) 5, 131–133, 229–230

Wales, H. G. Quaritch 195, 196, 357
war: affective histories of 333; Buddhism and Cold War 87, 91, 330–332; captives of 199; effects on Theravāda of 95–96, 296; freedom from 119; in historiography 360–364; and reconciliation 91, 334; remains of 339
Wat Si Chum 311–319, *315*, 321, 322
Weber, Max 170
Weerasethakul, Apichatpong 328, 330–333, 339; *Fireworks (Archives)* 332–333, *334*; *Phantoms of Nabua* 331–332, *331*
weikza (wizard) 119, 130, 137n5
Western 133, 209, 221, 335, 350; *see also* Eurocentrism
Wichasin, Renoo 77
women: advocating for 123; in encounters with monks 189–190; higher ordination of 109; among laity 178–179; mastery of Dhamma by 171; support of monks by 177
Woodward, Hiram W. 61, 301–302
World Fellowship of Buddhists (WFB) 87, 91–92, 95; inaugural conference in 1950, 100, 108–109

Yangon 121, 122, 173
ye dhamma stanza 219, 221, 323n5
Young, Ernest 196–197
Young Men's Buddhist Association 177
Yunnan 2; *see also* Sipsongpannā